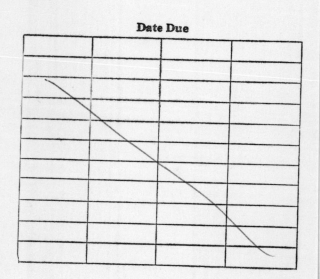

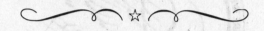

THE BEST FROM

YANK

THE ARMY WEEKLY

A WARTIME BOOK

THIS COMPLETE EDITION IS PRODUCED IN FULL COMPLIANCE WITH THE GOVERNMENT'S REGULATIONS FOR CONSERVING PAPER AND OTHER ESSENTIAL MATERIALS.

Published in co-operation with the Council on Books in Wartime

Produced by Robert T. Weaver Associates, Columbia Lithographic Co., Inc. and American Book-Stratford Press, Inc.

The Best from YANK the Army Weekly

D811
Y3

★ *Selected by the Editors of Yank* ★

CLEVELAND · THE WORLD PUBLISHING COMPANY · NEW YORK

PUBLISHED BY *The World Publishing Company*

2231 West 110th Street · Cleveland · Ohio

By arrangement with E. P. Dutton & Co., Inc.

First Published April 1945

Second Printing August 1945

A B

The material and format of this edition are the same as
of that originally published by E. P. Dutton & Co., Inc.

INTRODUCTION

By THE EDITORS OF YANK

IF A BOOK has to be designed deliberately to please the taste of the general reading public in order to become popular, this one is doomed right now to spend its old age gathering dust on the cut-rate bargain counters.

Although General Hershey and his draft boards have tried hard to scrape the bottom of the barrel these last few years, most of the general reading public is still composed of civilians. The writings, drawings, photographs and cartoons in this collection were never intended originally to please civilian tastes. They were made to order for the pages of YANK, The Army Weekly, by enlisted men on active duty in the armed forces who wanted to please other enlisted men and nobody else.

This may sound rather snobbish, as though we were attempting to discourage civilians—and commissioned officers—from looking into this book, but we don't mean it that way. We hope they do look into it and we hope they like what they find. The point we are laboring is that the average reader may find this anthology, written by soldiers who never expected their work to be read by anybody except other soldiers, quite different from the usual books about the Army and the war, written by soldiers or correspondents who were making a conscious effort to win the attention of a civilian audience. The difference between these two approaches, like the difference, say, between reviews of the same play in the *New York Times* and *Variety,* is wide and distinctly marked. A good example of an Army book written for civilians is *See Here, Private Hargrove.* Hargrove, now a sergeant on YANK's editorial staff, wrote the sketches in the book during his training days at Fort Bragg, N. C., for his old newspaper, the *Charlotte News,* with the idea of letting people in his home town know what he was going through in the Army. But nothing that Hargrove has written for YANK is like his book. He knows that you cannot speak to soldiers in the same tone of voice that you use in addressing the fathers, mothers, sisters and younger brothers back home. Even the most firmly stylized professional writers, finding themselves suddenly in the Army and writing for an exclusively military audience, instinctively realize the necessity for making this change in technique. For some of them, it does not come easily. When Pfc. Irwin Shaw began to write for YANK, he said, "It's like starting in all over again."

Because it is written by and for enlisted men, the material in this book is nothing more or less than soldier shop talk. Shop talk, when it is overheard by somebody who doesn't work in the shop, may sound at times unintelligible since it is filled with trade terms and special within-the-family humor whose full significance is often lost on an outsider. The civilian reader will find in YANK's combat stories casual reference to such things as "the line of departure" and "BAR men" which may seem somewhat obscure. (Before we go any further, a BAR man is not a vendor of alcoholic drinks; he is a soldier who carries and fires a Browning Automatic Rifle.) And the GI jokes in this book often vary from the accepted movie and radio formula for Army gags. Unlike the Hollywood comedians, the soldier of today sees nothing particularly funny about K.P. or second lieutenants. There is absolutely nothing humorous about K.P. after you have been subjected to it a few times. And the present crop of second lieutenants are former enlisted men who came up the hard way and whose job in the combat zone is too dangerous to be laughed at. The average soldier prefers to joke about things that civilians may not quite appreciate, such as K rations, the table of organization (the standard Army excuse for its lack of higher ratings), Off Limits areas, the rotation plan, Good Conduct ribbons, USO Commandos, the classification system or T-5s who wear a whistle and a brass chain draped over their shoulder.

But if the exact meaning and significance of shop talk is sometimes elusive, an outsider can often find in it a certain compensating flavor of authenticity and intimacy. We feel that this anthology will give the civilian a clearer and more penetrating picture of life in the United States Army during this war than he could get from most of the books that have been written to date on the subject. Certainly nobody is better qualified to describe life in the United States Army than the American soldiers who are living it.

The Army life described in these stories, photographs and drawings covers the period of the war between the summer of 1942, when YANK began publication, and the fall of 1944, when American troops were closing in on the border of Germany and preparing to return to the Philippines. Geographically they cover almost every part of the world where U. S. soldiers have been stationed; both combat and non-combat areas. The material in the book comes from two sources: from YANK's own soldier staff correspondents, photographers and artists, and from enlisted men in line outfits all over the world, who spent their valuable and limited free time writing or making sketches for their Army weekly, and received no reward for their efforts except the dubious pleasure of seeing their stuff in print. Like YANK itself, this anthology has no contributions from commissioned and warrant officers, except for a few letters in the Mail Call section, the only part of the magazine that is open to their opinion. YANK has nothing against officers. It simply feels that they have no place in an enlisted man's publication.

The YANK editorial staff, therefore, consists entirely of enlisted men. Many of them have turned down the opportunity to get a commission because it meant leaving YANK. Some of them in civilian life were experienced writers and editors on big metropolitan dailies and slick paper magazines; others were mere copy boys or reporters from small newspapers in towns like Paducah, Kentucky, and Long Beach, California. They live under military discipline and work for army pay (and not high pay, at that; most of them are corporals and buck sergeants and staff sergeants). YANK's main editorial office is in New York, where it publishes a U. S. edition for the camps in this country and prepares rotogravure, offset and letterpress pages for its overseas editions, printed weekly in London, Sydney, Honolulu, Rome, Paris, Cairo, Teheran, Calcutta, Puerto Rico and Panama. The Paris edition of YANK, incidentally, made its first appearance early in September, 1944, rolling off a rotogravure press that only a few weeks before had been printing the Paris edition of *Wehrmacht,* the German Army's equivalent of YANK. The New York office also puts out weekly an Alaska edition, shipped from Seattle to Alaska and the Aleutians, and a general overseas edition for overseas bases not covered by the foreign printing operations. In addition to its regular Pacific edition, the Honolulu bureau of YANK also publishes a South Pacific edition and a pony-sized Pacific Air Mail edition for troops on the lonely islands of Admiral Nimitz's far-flung ocean command.

With such a worldwide territory to cover, YANK's editorial staff naturally sees plenty of overseas duty. The editors, writers and photographers are rotated constantly from desk jobs to combat assignments, from the main office to the overseas bureaus and from one theater of operations to another. For in-

stance, Sgt. Joe McCarthy, YANK's managing editor, who received the Legion of Merit for helping to establish the Army weekly as a worldwide magazine, is now in France, has reported the war in Italy and was the first American GI to enter Athens when it was liberated.

Then there is Sgt. Merle Miller, who after he had established the Pacific edition in Honolulu and landed in the Marshalls as a combat correspondent, returned to the U. S. to work for four months as an editor in the New York office and as a YANK correspondent in Washington. Then he went overseas again to France, where he became editor of YANK's Paris edition. Sgt. Dave Richardson won the Legion of Merit for his front line coverage of the New Guinea campaign for YANK. Then he went to Burma and completed one of the toughest assignments undertaken by a correspondent in this war—a 500-mile march through the jungles with Merrill's Marauders that took him behind the Jap lines for three months. When he returned to civilization, Sgt. Richardson wrote to the office:

"Besides the regular 60-pound horseshoe-type pack which every Marauder carried (containing a blanket, poncho, *kukri* knife, three to five days' rations, entrenching shovel, water wings for swimming rivers and an extra pair of shoes) I lugged two cameras, film, notebooks, maps, pencils and my carbine. And I brought along a typewriter. But the only chance I had to use it was during a two-day rest period after our first battle. I spent the first day repairing the damage that had been done to it by the incessant rain and by its being carried on a mule over bumpy ground. The second day I managed to bat out some picture captions. The rest of the time my stories had to languish in my notebooks because we usually walked from dawn to dusk, spending the rest of our time before dark cooking supper (no fires were allowed after dark in this Jap territory) and after dark sleeping in our ponchos and blankets on the ground, often in pools of water from the heavy rains."

Miller and Richardson are not the only YANK men who have seen more than one side of the global war. Sgt. George Aarons and Sgt. Burgess Scott, after a tour of duty in Britain in 1942, went all the way from El Alamein to Tunis with the British Eighth Army. A few months later they established what they considered a record for long-distance jeep travel, starting from Cairo, driving to Aleppo in Syria to make a memorable picture story of the execution of two Nazi spies, and then turning around and going all the way across Africa to Algiers. There they managed to load their jeep on a transport plane and take it to Italy, where it accompanied them on several trips to the Cassino front, landed with them at Anzio and chugged into Rome with the advance tanks of the 1st Armored Division. Scott has returned to the States for a tour of duty in YANK's main editorial office, but Aarons and the jeep are somewhere in France. Aarons says he won't be satisfied until he drives the jeep in triumph up to the front door of YANK's Berlin bureau.

Then there is Sgt. Walter Peters, a veteran of many air missions over Europe (he was the only American correspondent on the murderous Schweinfurt raid), later cited for bravery under fire with the Infantry at St. Lo and now on his way to China to write about our Chinese allies and the men who are flying the B-29s. And Sgt. Georg Meyers, decorated for his conduct in the invasion of Attu. And Sgt. Walter Bernstein, who probably beats every YANK correspondent when it comes to globe trotting. Bernstein left the U. S. in the early spring of 1943, traveled by ship across the South Pacific to Australia and then across the Indian Ocean to the Persian Gulf. He spent some time in Iran and then moved to Cairo and to Algiers, just in time for the invasion of Sicily, where he saw action with the 45th and 3d divisions. When Sicily fell, he returned to Cairo and traveled in Palestine and Syria. He then went to the Italian front when it was near Naples and left it to return to Cairo again to cover the conference between Churchill, Roosevelt and Chiang Kai-shek. In the spring of 1944, Bernstein managed to make arrangements with Yugoslav Partisan representatives in the Middle East and Italy for a personal interview with Marshal Tito, who had not yet been visited by a correspondent from an English-speaking country. The Partisans took Bernstein from Italy to an island in the Adriatic and then landed him on the Yugoslavian mainland, where he walked for a week across German occupied territory and over the mountains to Tito's headquarters.

"That walk was a nightmare," Bernstein wrote afterward. "We only had actual trouble once when we had to cross a main road at three in the morning between two German garrisons about a kilometer apart. We sent about ten men to each garrison to start a little disturbance and keep them busy and while they were doing that we double-timed across the road and into the woods on the other side. The bullets were flying around but nobody got hurt except a few Germans or Chetniks. That was the only real trouble we had, although we were near the Germans on several other occasions, but the walk itself was dreadful: over all the mountains in Yugoslavia. We would start in the morning and by three in the afternoon we would be up at the snow line and then we would go down the other side and start up again on the next mountain. We would walk sometimes all night and part of the next day and then sleep for a few hours and start again and I would lose all track of time and think that the dawn was sunset or vice versa. Anyway, I wouldn't want to do it again. I got sick when we finally arrived at headquarters, ran a fever for a few days and my eyes wouldn't focus, but I stayed in bed a while and ate and slept and got over it."

Then Bernstein got his interview with Tito. A few days later the Anglo-American mission in Yugoslavia discovered that he had entered the country without proper permission and hustled him back to Italy on the next available plane. "It had Pullman seats, no less," says Bernstein.

Thus far in the war, two YANK men have been killed in action. Sgt. John Bushemi was fatally wounded by Jap mortar fire during the invasion of Eniwetok in the Marshalls. Sgt. Peter Paris, the first enlisted man to cross the threshold of the New York office and report for duty when The Army Weekly was established in May, 1942, met his death on D Day in Normandy when he landed with the first wave of the 1st Division. Others have narrowly escaped with their lives. Sgt. Barrett McGurn was hit by mortar fire during the second battle of Bougainville. And during the fighting at Gloucester Bay, Sgt. Dick Hanley, a staff photographer, climbed out of a foxhole 15 yards from the enemy and turned his back on the Japs to make a picture of some Marine machine gunners. "Go ahead," the Marines told him when he deliberated the wisdom of such a risk. "If they get you, we'll get them." Hanley managed to return to cover still in one piece.

Besides the stories, photographs and sketches from its staff men, YANK depends heavily on the unsolicited contributions it receives from soldiers all over the world, the riflemen, mechanics, truck drivers, message center clerks, radio operators, supply sergeants, military policemen. Most of the cartoons and fiction and all the poetry in this book came from such contributors. The two stories by Sgt. Newton H. Fulbright were written during rest periods in the Italian campaign, where the author served in the same Infantry battalion of the 36th Division with the celebrated Sgt. Charles E. (Commando) Kelly, and escaped from the Germans after being captured near Altavilla. Pvt. Justin Gray, who fought in Sicily and Italy with the 3d Ranger Battalion, never attempted to write for publication until YANK encouraged him to put "Security Mission" on paper. Pvt. Asa Autry, a big raw-boned engineer, had no previous experience with journalism or any kind of creative literature when he composed "Setting Up a Base" during the dull, cold winter evenings in a Quonset hut at Adak in the Aleutians. His original manuscript was laboriously written with a stubby pencil on rough, mildewed sheets of paper.

There are also two departments in YANK that are only for outside GI contributors: Mail Call and What's Your Problem? Mail Call is probably the most important department in the magazine. It is, in a definite sense, the touchstone of YANK. The criterion of any soldier's magazine should be the extent of the participation in it of the soldiers themselves. In our Army, only a small proportion of the men get around to writing articles or sonnets, but a great many of them write letters. They write letters to YANK about everything; they gripe and they criticize and they suggest more or less politely how the war should be run and they ask questions. This question business became so intense that a new department finally had to be started, just to answer them. Now any soldier who is worried about how the new GI Bill of Rights applies to him or how he can get a better allotment for his dependents can write to YANK and get the official answer, with complete instructions on how to apply it. Some of the more interesting or typical letters are printed in the magazine, but all of them are answered.

This volume is therefore representative of YANK. It is not all of the magazine. A good deal has been left out because it was a little too Army. The extensive coverage of the home front was omitted because we felt that space in this book ought to be devoted to a picture of the Army in the war, rather than to a picture of the civilians in the war. Some of the material was too timely and, while still valid, seemed a little dated to include here. And much was left out simply because there was no room.

But what is left is still YANK. What you read in this book was dictated only by the conscience and ability of the enlisted man who wrote it, his knowledge that it would be judged by other enlisted men with whom he must live, his sense and understanding of the war, the natural restrictions of military security and the remote possibility that if he turned out a good story he might get another stripe.

There may be parts of this book that you will not understand and sections that you will not like. But the Army is frequently incomprehensible, and there is nothing likeable about war. Most YANK writers make little attempt to comment or editorialize in any way; they are simply representative soldiers trying to portray honestly and effectively the strange, uncertain, frequently dangerous world in which they live. You may not like what they say, but you could do worse than listen to them. They are not only the Army. They are a sizeable hunk of America.

"And just who the hell are you supposed to be—Lily Dash-ay?"
—*Pvt. Normon Shadley.*

CONTENTS

Introduction . . . . the Editors of YANK vii

War Reports

PAGE

Infantry Battle in New Georgia, *Sgt. Mack Morriss* 5

Jungle War . . . . *Anonymous* 9

The New York Subway System on the Italian Front . . . . . *Sgt. Newton H. Fulbright* 11

With Free China's Flag Upon His Back, He Died in a Great Sky Battle . *Sgt. Marion Hargrove* 13

Schweinfurt Raid . . . . . *Sgt. Walter Peters* 14

The Five-Day Attack on Hastings Ridge *Sgt. Mack Morriss* 17

Security Mission . . . . . *Pvt. Justin Gray* 20

Sgt. Kevin McCarthy . . . *Sgt. Merle Miller* 22

The Partisan from Brooklyn . *Sgt. Harry Sions* 25

The Sergeant and His Adam's Apple Start a Sensation in China . . . *Sgt. Marion Hargrove* 29

The First Yank Who Didn't Meet the British Eighth Army . . . . *Sgt. Milton Lehman* 30

The Gun . . . . . *Sgt. Walter Bernstein* 32

Duffie's: Where Iran's Elite Meet *Sgt. James P. O'Neill* 34

Jilted GIs in India Organize First Brush-Off Club *Sgt. Ed. Cunningham* 35

What Do We Think of the British? *Sgt. Burgess Scott* 36

Modern Living on a Beachhead in Bougainville *Sgt. Barrett McGurn* 39
Sketches by Sgt. Robert Greenhalgh

The Big Bastard . . *Robert L. Schwartz Y2c* 43

Infantry Battalion Sweats It Out in Italy *Sgt. Walter Bernstein* 48

The Second Battle of Bougainville *Sgt. Barrett McGurn* 51
Sketches by Sgt. Robert Greenhalgh

Cameraman in Cassino . . *Sgt. George Aarons* 57

Staging Area . . . . . *Pvt. Alan Surgal* 64
Sketches by Sgt. Howard J. Brodie

GI Report from Iran: It's Cold, Expensive and Strange . . . . *Sgt. Al Hine* 66

Yugoslav Diary . . . *Sgt. Walter Bernstein* 68
Sketches by Sgt. Howard J. Brodie

PAGE

Iran Cooties Share Top Billing with Marx Brothers at the Movies . . . . . *Sgt. Al Hine* 73

With the U S A F I S P A . *Sgt. Mack Morriss* 74
Sketches by Sgt. Howard J. Brodie

The Last Days at Guadalcanal *Sgt. Howard J. Brodie* 77

Rosie's Riveters . . . . *Sgt. Saul Levitt* 85
Sketches by Sgt. Howard J. Brodie

The Dead End Kids . *Sgt. Dave Richardson* 91
Sketch by Cpl. Jack Ruge

Capture of Cherbourg . . *Sgt. Walter Peters* 105
Sketches by Sgt. John Scott

Square-Cut Diamond . . *Allen Churchill Y3c* 110

Sketches of the Guam Campaign *Sgt. Robert Greenhalgh* 112

Palestine Express . . . . *Pvt. Irwin Shaw* 115

B-29 Raid on Japan . . . *Sgt. Lou Stoumen* 117

Rangers Come Home . . *Sgt. Mack Morriss* 122

Psychological Warfare . . *Sgt. Bill Davidson* 127

Stilwell: the GI's Favorite, *Sgt. Ed. Cunningham* 129

"Rommel—Count Your Men," *Sgt. Bill Davidson* 133

Negro GIs in the Fijis Prefer the Manual of Arms in Jazz Time. . . . *Cpl. George Norford* 135

Landing on Los Negros . . *Cpl. Bill Alcine* 144

Picnic at Sansapor . . *Sgt. Charles Pearson* 147

Why Old Soldiers Never Die, *Sgt. Burtt Evans* 148

Valiant Attempt of a Chicago Tovarich to Uphold the Tradition in Iran . *Cpl. James P. O'Neill* 165

The Colonel and the Rock . *Sgt. Burtt Evans* 167

Blown Off the Deck of an LST *Sgt. James P. O'Neill* 168

Notes from a Burma Diary, *Sgt. Dave Richardson* 176

Road to Tokyo . . . *Sgt. Ed Cunningham* 177

Blindman's Buff with Bullets *Sgt. Georg N. Meyers* 180

PAGE

Sports: Ex-Prisoner Tells of Sports in Jap Concentration Camp . . . *Sgt. Dan Polier* 185

Nudge in Rear Came too Soon, So He Bombed Wrong Target in China, *Sgt. Marion Hargrove* 186

The Alaska Scouts . . *Sgt. Georg N. Meyers* 190

The Assam Dragons . . *Sgt. Ed Cunningham* 194

Supplies Are Brought Up in Italy on the GI's Back . . . . *Sgt. Burgess Scott* 196

A GI View of the Teheran Conference
Sgt. Al Hine & Cpl. James P. O'Neill 199

MP's Know What's Good for You If You Tipple in British Guiana . . . *Sgt. Joe McCarthy* 201

Setting Up a Base . . . . *Pvt. Asa Autry* 202

The Birth of a Mission . . *Sgt. Walter Peters* 205

PAGE

Liberation of Athens . . *Sgt. Joe McCarthy* 218

GI Artist in Bethlehem . *Cpl. Richard T. Gaige* 222

Hospital Ship . . . . . *Sgt. Mack Morriss* 223

Guadalcanal Goes Garrison, *Sgt. Barrett McGurn* 231

After the Battle at Kwajalein, *Sgt. Merle Miller* 234

Houses of Italy . . *Sgt. Newton H. Fulbright* 239
Sketch by Cpl. Jack Ruge

My Old Outfit . . . . . *Sgt. Mack Morriss* 242

Interview with Tito of Yugoslavia
Sgt. Walter Bernstein 247

Surprise Party at Eniwetok . *Sgt. Merle Miller* 250

PT Boat Mission . . . *Sgt. Dave Richardson* 253

Fiction and Humor

PAGE

Secret Weapons for the Invasion of Germany
Sgt. Ralph Stein 62

A Sack of Mail . . *Cpl. Paul E. Deutschmann* 83
Sketch by Sgt. Frank Brandt

Chief Petty Officer . . *Bernard Dryer PhM3c* 89

Great Day . . . . . *Cpl. Len Zinberg* 95

How to Get Lost in a Jungle, *Sgt. Joe McCarthy* 96
Sketch by Sgt. Ralph Stein

The Sad Sack . . . *Sgt. George Baker* 98–102

Artie Greengroin, PFC . . *Sgt. Harry Brown* 98

First Epistle to the Selectees
PFC Harold Fleming 104

Nomenclature of Whistle, M1
Pvt. Raymond Zauber 121

Invasion of Mae West's Dressing Room
Sgt. Al Hine 132

The Sweetheart of Company D
Pvt. William Saroyan 136
Sketch by Cpl. Jack Ruge

Over the Hill . . . . . *Sgt. Ray Duncan* 138

The Hot Jeep Department . *Cpl. Tom Shehan* 139

Nomenclature of the Package, APO
Cpl. James P. O'Neill 140
Sketches by Sgt. Ralph Stein

PAGE

A Dogface Answers a Collection Agency
Pvt. Oris Turner 142

Soldier Meets Civilian . . *Sgt. Leonard Silk* 143

Little Red Riding Hood, a GI Bedtime Story
S/Sgt. Don Davis 155

Skyward a Sparrow . . . *PFC Knox Burger* 157

Guardhouse by Mistake, *T/Sgt. Edgar L. Acken* 158
Sketch by Cpl. Jack Ruge

Life Goes to a Party . . . *Sgt. Ray Duncan* 159

Furlough Greetings . . *T-5 James P. Charles* 160

Hopeless McGonigle's Brother Wins the DSC
S/Sgt. L. A. Brodsky 161
Sketch by Sgt. Ralph Stein

I Shoulda Ate Alone . . *Pvt. Seymour Blau* 163

Tell It to the Chaplain . *Cpl. Grant Robbins* 164

Superman and the Army
PFC Harold D. Schwartz 166

Fall Out for an Interview . *Sgt. Ray Duncan* 175

The Bulletin Board Mysteries, *Sgt. Ray Duncan* 181

Humphrey, Franchot and Victor
Cpl. C. G. DeVan 182

PFC Shea's Merriest Christmas,*Sgt. Joe McCarthy* 183
Sketch by Sgt. Ralph Stein

PAGE

How to Take Care of Your Replacement
                 Sgt. Ralph Stein   184

Fifty Missions   .   .   .   . *Pvt. Joseph Dever*   187

Line of Duty   .   .   .   . *PFC Raymond Boyle*   193

275,000 Ratings   .   .   .   . *Sgt. Ray Duncan*   204

"Five Minutes After I Left You . . ."
                 Cpl. Len Zinberg   209

The Colonel and the Paper Boy
                 Cpl. Richard Eells   224

PAGE

The Rotation of Sgt. Regan, *Sgt. Ray Duncan*   225

A GI Invades the Fashion Front
                 Cpl. Hyman Goldberg   227

Mess Hall in Alaska   .   .   . *Sgt. A. N. Maloff*   229

Why I Left Grand Central Palace
                 Pvt. Knox Burger   236

When We Get Our New T.O. . . . .
                 Sgt. Ray Duncan   236

What's Your Problem?

PAGES 170-174

Mail Call

PAGES 210-218

Poems

PAGE

Cpl. Doyle Is to Africa Come!, *Cpl. John J. Doyle*   35

Sunday at Sanananda   .   . *T-5 Don E. Rohrig*   37
     Sketch by Cpl. Jack Ruge

The Legion of the Uncouth
                 S/Sgt. Thomas P. Ashlock   84

A Plea to the Post-War Planners
            T/Sgt. Philip Reisman, Jr., USMC   97

A Soldier's Dream   . *Sgt. Bob Stuart McKnight*   142

THE POET'S CORNERED
   Litany for Homesick Men
                 Cpl. Hargis Westerfield   151

   Army Chapel   .   .   .   . *Pvt. Darrell Bartie*   151

   Buna Beach   .   .   . *PFC Keith B. Campbell*   151

   Obituary   .   . *S/Sgt. Franklin M. Willment*   152

   Travel Note   .   .   .   . *Sgt. Jack N. Carl*   152

   On the March   .   .   . *Pvt. Edmund Zaslow*   152

   In Memoriam   .   .   . *Pvt. John E. Brown*   152

PAGE

Night March   .   .   .   .   . *Pvt. John Rolfe*   152

Quatrains on Brass   .   . *Sgt. A. L. Crouch*   153

The Mourners' Bench, *Pvt. Raymond E. Lee*   153

The Heroes   .   .   .   .   . *Pvt. Rudy Bass*   153

The Death of Pvt. Jones
                 Sgt. Harold Applebaum   154

The Reconversion, *PFC Edward Blumenthal*   154

France, 1944   .   .   .   . *PFC John M. Behm*   154

The Beautiful Ruins, *S/Sgt. Charles E. Butler*   154

Twenty-One Dash One Hundred
                 T-4 John W. Greenleaf   155

The Poems of an Army Nurse
              2nd Lt. Elizabeth Itzen   156–157

A Stranger and Alone   .   . *PFC John Behm*   189

Aleutian Joy   .   . *S/Sgt. LeRoy A. Metcalf, Jr.*   198

The Love of Islands, *Sgt. Harold Applebaum*   198

Lullaby   .   .   .   .   . *Sgt. Charles E. Butler*   246

Cartoons

PAGE

Aldo, PFC 172

Baker, Sgt. George 98, 99, 100, 101, 102

Borgstedt, Sgt. Douglas 67, 131, 238

Brandt, Sgt. Frank 30, 60, 147, 150, 235

Breger, Sgt. Dave 129, 195

Caplan, Sgt. Irwin 24, 123, 225, 255

Carlson, PFC H. N. 146

Chamberlain, Cpl. Jerry 165

Cowan, Sgt. Roger 238

Flannery, Pvt. Thomas . . 61, 67, 166, 179, 228, 238

Frazer, Cpl. William 60

Gallivan, Sgt. Bob 203

Gates, Cpl. Art 255

Hartwell, Sgt. Basil 221

Jaffee, Sgt. Al 167

Jamme, Cpl. Louis 67

Kaelin, Sgt. Al 143, 256

Keane, PFC Bill 73

PAGE

Kennedy, Cpl. Hugh 72

Kramer, PFC Joseph 67, 164, 238

Locke, Cpl. LaFayette 50

Mansfield, Pvt. Walter 137

Maxwell, Cpl. Ernest (Cpl. Emax)
    12, 169, 175, 228, 238

Miller, M/Sgt. Ted 132

Newcombe, Sgt. Bill 162

Pearson, Sgt. Charles 238

Ruge, Cpl. Jack 16, 126

St. George, Cpl. Ozzie . . . . . . (2) 163

Salkin, Leo-Pho M3c 225

Schwab, Cpl. Fred 104

Shadley, Pvt. Norman x

Stein, Sgt. Ralph 62, 63, 72, 184

Torbert, Cpl. F. J. 208

Turner, A/S Gerry 209

W., Cpl. S. Q. 128

Zibelli, Pvt. Tom 28, 73

Photographs

PAGE

Yanks wade ashore on Makin Atoll
    Sgt. John Bushemi 258

A soldier of the Shamrock Battalion moves up on
    Makin . . . . *Sgt. John Bushemi* 260

Feeding ammunition to a P-40 in North Africa
    Sgt. George Aarons 261

Gun captain of an LST in the Pacific
    Sgt. John Bushemi 261

GI with a Bar moves over a ridge on Attu
    Sgt. Georg Meyers 262

A soldier of the emperor lies dead on Attu
    Sgt. Georg Meyers 262

In liberated Rome a Yank holds an Italian baby
    Sgt. George Aarons 263

U. S. cruiser framed in a U. S. gunsight off Buka
    Sgt. Dillon Ferris 264

PAGE

Marines wade through surf to strike Cape
    Gloucester . . . . . *Sgt. Richard Hanley* 265

Yanks and a Sherman tank in France
    Sgt. Reginald Kenny 266

Building an airfield in China, *Sgt. Lou Stoumen* 267

Bathing time for Burmese nurses
    Sgt. Robert Ghio 267

Nazi prisoners at Anzio observe an LST
    Sgt. George Aarons 268

A fresh-caught Jap is interviewed at Hollandia
    Sgt. Richard Hanley 269

In Syria, Free French execute convicted Nazi
    spies . . . . *Sgt. George Aarons* 270

The Army unloads supplies as it moves into New
    Guinea . . . . . . *Sgt. Richard Hanley* 272

B-25s on a raid in Africa . *Sgt. George Aarons* 273

PAGE

U. S. flyers in Africa relax . *Sgt. George Aarons* 273

Jap power plant at Kwajalein blasted by naval shelling . . . . . . *Sgt. John Bushemi* 274

Bugle lesson in the Fijis . *Sgt. John Bushemi* 275

A mule train winds along the hills below Rome *Sgt. George Aarons* 276

A GI baker in Africa carries his wares messward *Sgt. George Aarons* 277

A Yank in Italy piles up a load of dead Nazi mines . . . . *Sgt. John Frano* 277

American troops and half-tracks move into a Tunisian town . . . . *Sgt. Pete Paris* 278

Outside Cerami, Sicily, camouflaged howitzers fire at Germans . . . . *Sgt. Pete Paris* 279

From the bow of an LST, Yanks wave a greeting to France . . . . *Sgt. Reginald Kenny* 280

A light machine gunner peers through the New Guinea jungle . . . . *Sgt. John Bushemi* 281

Infantrymen in New Georgia wait for action at their post . . . . . *Sgt. John Bushemi* 281

Pass at the pyramids . *Sgt. George Aarons* 282

Desert dust in Africa . . *Sgt. Steven Derry* 282

Tight fit in a Pacific transport *Sgt. Richard Hanley* 283

Approaching Japanese positions in New Georgia *Sgt. John Bushemi* 284

This wave has just hit the beach at Eniwetok in the Marshalls . . . *Sgt. John Bushemi* 286

"The Hump," air supply line to China, from 16,000 feet . . . . *Sgt. Robert Ghio* 287

Italian kids play with a captured Nazi self-propelled howitzer . *Sgt. George Aarons* 287

Mountain climbing lesson in Italy *Sgt. George Aarons* 288

An artillery observation post in Sicily attracts a fan . . . . *Sgt. Pete Paris* 289

A GI mule skinner in Hawaii with one of his big-eared charges . . . *Sgt. John Bushemi* 290

Italian partisans take cover with a Yank patrol in the Nemi valley . . . *Sgt. George Aarons* 291

An American MP stands guard in Algiers' Casbah *Sgt. John Frano* 292

GIs, silhouetted on a ridge, pass ammunition on Attu . . . . *Sgt. Georg Meyers* 293

On Adreanof Island in the Aleutians, the wind made tent life tough . *Sgt. Georg Meyers* 293

A soldier helps his wounded friend. Admiralty Islands . . . . *Sgt. Bill Alcine* 294

German prisoners in France await removal to prison camp . . . *Cpl. Joe Cunningham* 295

Civilians give Lt. Gen. Mark R. Clark a warm welcome to Rome . . *Sgt. George Aarons* 295

Yanks in Puerto Rico look seaward from ancient El Morro fortress . . . *Sgt. Ben Schnall* 296

Thirty yards from the Japs in New Guinea, these GIs hold fire . . . *Sgt. Dave Richardson* 297

Cassino's ruins are half obscured by battle smoke *Sgt. George Aarons* 298

Processing a Nazi prisoner in Sicily *Sgt. Pete Paris* 300

Eniwetok natives take cover from Jap fire *Sgt. John Bushemi* 301

Near an Anzio hospital tent a nurse digs in *Sgt. George Aarons* 301

Yanks stalk Jap snipers on Makin *Sgt. John Bushemi* 302

Fifth Army men wait for the ship that will take them to battle . . . *Sgt. George Aarons* 302

First aid near front lines in New Guinea *Sgt. Dave Richardson* 303

Six combat-wise sergeants stroll down an Italian street . . . . *Sgt. John Frano* 303

A tired mess sergeant in North Africa feeds himself for a change . . . *Sgt. George Aarons* 304

Frontispiece and Title Page sketch by
Sgt. Howard J. Brodie

THE BEST FROM

YANK

THE ARMY WEEKLY

STAFF MEMBERS

YANK'S SIXTEEN EDITIONS

AARONS, PVT. GEORGE A., *Editorial*
ABBOTT, SGT. KENNETH, *Editorial*
ABRAMSON, CPL. ROBERT J., *Business*
ALCINE, SGT. BILL, *Editorial*
ALEXANDER, SGT. ARTHUR H., *Business*
ALPERT, SGT. SOL I., *Business*
AMES, CAPT. KNOWLTON L., *Administrative*
ANDERSON, SGT. EARL H., *Editorial*
ANTROBUS, CPL. EDMUND, *Editorial*
ARMSTRONG, PVT. JOHN O., *Editorial*

BACHER, PVT. ROLLIN C., *Business*
BAILEY, CPL. GEORGE, *Business*
BAKER, SGT. GEORGE, *Editorial*
BANTON, PVT. HAROLD G., *Business*
BARRETT, CPL. GEORGE A., *Editorial*
BECK, CPL. FRANK J., *Business*
BERGER, PVT. DAVID, *Editorial*
BERNARD, SP(X)1C THOMAS, USNR, *Editorial*
BERNSTEIN, SGT. WALTER S., *Editorial*
BERTRAND, CPL. LOUIS C., *Business*
BIGBEE, CAPT. JESSE NORTH, *Administrative*
BODE, SGT. FRANK, *Editorial*
BORGSTEDT, SGT. DOUGLAS H., *Editorial*
BOYCE, SGT. RALPH L., *Editorial*
BRAND, SGT. CHARLES S., *Editorial*
BRANDT, SGT. FRANK M., *Editorial*
BREIMHURST, SGT. DONALD, *Editorial*
BREWER, SGT. DONALD E., *Business*
BRODIE, SGT. HOWARD J., *Editorial*
BUCKLEY, PVT. PAUL F., *Business*
BURCH, CPL. VERNON C., *Business*
BURKE, SGT. FRANCIS, *Editorial*
BURNS, PFC. GEORGE F., JR., *Editorial*
BURROUGHS, CAPT. HAROLD A., *Administrative*
BURROWS, CPL. TED, *Editorial*
BUSHEMI, SGT. JOHN L., *Photographer* (Killed in Action)

CANNIZZO, CPL. SALVATORE, *Business*
CARREGAL, CPL. JOSEPH A., *Business*
CARSWELL, CAPT. HOWARD J., *Administrative*
CLAY, LT. GRADY, *Administrative*
COFFEY, PVT. PATRICK V., *Editorial*
COGGIN, PVT. EMMETT R., *Business*
COGGINS, CPL. JACK B., *Editorial*
COOK, CPL. GEORGE J., *Editorial*
COOKE, SGT. DONALD E., *Business*
CORBELLINI, CPL. GEORGE J., *Editorial*
COWAN, SGT. ROGER W., *Editorial*

CRAEMER, MAJOR JUSTUS J., *Administrative*
CROCCA, PVT. WILLIAM, *Business*
CROWE, SGT. JACK F., *Editorial*
CUNNINGHAM, SGT. EDWARD J., *Editorial*
CUNNINGHAM, CPL. JOSEPH P., *Editorial*
CURCHIN, CPL. CLARK M., *Business*

DAVIDSON, SGT. WILLIAM J., *Editorial*
DAVIS, CPL. MARGARET B., *Editorial*
DERRY, SGT. STEVEN, *Editorial*
DOUGLASS, CPL. RICHARD W., *Editorial*
DuBOIS, CPL. WILLIAM PENE, *Editorial*
DUNCAN, SGT. RAYMOND E., *Editorial*

EATON, SGT. DOUGLAS W., *Business*
ECKER, SGT. ALLAN B., *Editorial*
EPPINGER, MAJOR JOSUA, JR., *Administrative*
EVANS, SGT. BURTT, *Editorial*

FAMIGLIETTI, PVT. CHARLES R., *Business*
FASIG, SGT. MARVIN, *Editorial*
FERRIS, SGT. DILLON J., *Editorial*
FLANNERY, PVT. THOMAS, *Editorial*
FLEMING, SGT. THOMAS E., *Business*
FORSBERG, COL. FRANKLIN S., *Administrative*
FRANK, SGT. JAMES V., *Editorial*
FRANO, SGT. JOHN J., JR., *Editorial*
FRAZER, SGT. WILLIAM L., *Editorial*
FREEMAN, PFC. IRA H., *Editorial*
FRIEDMAN, SGT. SEYMOUR T., *Editorial*
FRITSCH, PVT. HENRY E., *Business*

GAFILL, LT. DAVID L., *Administrative*
GAIGE, CPL. RICHARD T., *Editorial*
GALLAGHER, CAPT. BASIL, *Administrative* (Killed in
   Line of Duty)
GHIO, SGT. ROBERT A., *Editorial*
GILLENSON, CAPT. LEWIS W., *Administrative*
GLADSTONE, CAPT. FRANK L., *Administrative*
GOBLE, CPL. JAMES B., *Editorial*
GOLDBERG, CPL. HYMAN, *Editorial*
GORBULEW, CPL. MILTON, *Business*
GRAY, PFC. JUSTIN, *Editorial*
GRECO, CPL. EDWARD, *Business*
GREENHALGH, SGT. ROBERT F., *Editorial*
GRUPPO, SGT. NELSON, *Editorial*

HABER, SGT. STANLEY B., *Business*
HANLEY, SGT. RICHARD S., *Editorial*

HARGROVE, SGT. MARION L., JR., *Editorial*
HARRIS, CPhoM KENNETH, USCG, *Editorial*
HARRISON, SGT. JOHN D., *Business*
HARRITY, SGT. RICHARD, *Business*
HAVERSTICK, CPL. JOHN M., *Editorial*
HAWLEY, MAJOR HAROLD B., *Administrative*
HAY, SGT. JOHN, *Editorial*
HINE, SGT. ALFRED B., JR., *Editorial*
HOFELLER, SGT. LEO, *Editorial*
HOLT, MAJOR CHARLES L., *Administrative*
HORNER, SGT. DURBIN L., *Editorial*
HORTON, PVT. DONALD L., *Business*

IORIO, PVT. JAMES G., *Editorial*

JOHNSON, MAJOR HENRY E., *Administrative*
JOHNSTON, SGT. PAUL A., *Editorial*

KALLMAN, SGT. JOHN H., *Business*
KATZANDER, PVT. HOWARD, *Editorial*
KAUFMAN, CPL. BENJAMIN, *Business*
KEENEY, PVT. JAMES J., *Editorial*
KENNY, SGT. REGINALD D., *Editorial*
KRAMER, SGT. HENRY, *Business*
KYNCH, CPL. ALFRED J., *Editorial*

LANTZ, CPL. BERNARD D., *Business*
LAURITZEN, CPL. WILLIAM C., *Editorial*
LAWTON, CPL. AUGUSTINE D., *Business*
LEVIN, CPL. ARTHUR, *Business*
LEVITT, SGT. SAUL, *Editorial*
LOCKE, SGT. LaFAYETTE, *Editorial*
LOEB, SGT. AUGUST, *Editorial*
LOWE, PVT. BERTRAM, *Business*
LYONS, SGT. HILARY H., JR., *Editorial*

MACAULEY, CPL. ALEXANDER R., *Editorial*
MAGOON, PVT. LAWRENCE E., *Business*
MAXWELL, SGT. WALTER J., *Business*
McBRIDE, SGT. GEORGE S., *Business*
McBRINN, SGT. ROBERT J., *Editorial*
McCARTHY, SGT. JOSEPH W., *Editorial*
McFADDEN, SGT. LOUIS E., *Business*
McGOVERN, CPL. RAYMOND T., *Editorial*
McGURN, SGT. WILLIAM B., JR., *Editorial*
McLEOD, CPL. JOHN F., *Editorial*
McMANUS, SGT. JAMES L., *Editorial*
MEEK, CPL. PRICE, *Business*
MEYERS, SGT. GEORG N., *Editorial*
MICHAELS, SGT. JOSEPH H., *Business*
MILLER, SGT. MERLE D., *Editorial*
MORRISS, SGT. MARION M., *Editorial*
MOSLEY, CPL. CHARLES M., *Editorial*
MURPHY, PVT. RICHARD F., *Business*

MYERS, PVT. DEBS, *Editorial*

NIHILL, SGT. RICHARD J., *Business*
NOVACK, CPL. MAX D., *Editorial*
NUGENT, S1c DONALD, *Editorial*

O'BRIEN, CPL. THOMAS L., *Editorial*
OLIPHANT, SGT. HOMER N., *Editorial*
O'NEILL, PVT. JAMES P., *Editorial*

PARIS, SGT. PETER M., *Editorial* (Killed in Action)
PAUL, SGT. RICHARD H., *Editorial*
PAWLAK, PhoM1c MASON H., USNR, *Editorial*
PEARSON, SGT. CHARLES D., *Editorial*
PETERS, SGT. WALTER F., *Editorial*
PETZEL, SGT. HERBERT W., *Business*
POLIER, SGT. DAN A., *Editorial*
POTTER, SGT. WILLIAM T., *Business*
PRESTON, CPL. JOHN D., *Editorial*
PYLE, SGT. CARLOS, *Business*

RATHE, SGT. CHARLES, *Editorial*
REED, SGT. WILLIAM K., JR., *Editorial*
RICHARDSON, SGT. DAVID B., *Editorial*
RICHESON, PVT. MAURICE, *Business*
ROBERTS, CAPT. HARRY R., *Administrative*
ROCK, CAPT. GERALD J., *Administrative*
ROSEN, SGT. FRED, *Business*
ROY, PFC. ROLAND, *Business*
RUGE, SGT. JOHN A., *Editorial*
RYAN, SGT. ROBERT G., *Business*

SANFORD, SGT. RUDOLPH, *Editorial*
SAVAGE, CPL. DONALD E., *Business*
SCHLOTZHAUER, SGT. JUSTUS E., *Editorial*
SCHNALL, SGT. BEN., *Editorial*
SCHONBERG, CPL. LESTER, *Business*
SCHWIND, CPL. CARL L., *Editorial*
SCOTT, SGT. BURGESS H., *Editorial*
SCOTT, SGT. JACK DENTON, *Editorial*
SCOTT, SGT. JOHN, *Editorial*
SHAW, PVT. WILLIAM D., *Editorial*
SHEHAN, CPL. THOMAS F., *Editorial*
SHOWERS, SGT. PAUL C., *Editorial*
SIGAL, PVT. ABE, *Business*
SILVERSTEIN, PVT. WILLIAM H., *Business*
SIONS, SGT. HARRY A., *Editorial*
SLOAN, SGT. HENRY J., *Business*
SMITH, CPL. IRVIN, *Business*
STALEY, PVT. JOE E., *Business*
STEFANELLI, CPL. JOSEPH, *Editorial*
STEIN, SGT. RALPH, *Editorial*
ST. GEORGE, SGT. OZZIE, *Editorial*
STOUMEN, SGT. LOUIS C., *Editorial*

STRAUSS, PVT. ALEX, *Business*
STROTHER, MAJOR ROBERT S., *Administrative*
STUBBLEFIELD, LT. CHARLES H. E., *Administrative*

TEMPLETON, CPL. LELAND O., *Business*
THOMPSON, LT. H. STAHLEY, *Administrative*

VANDERBILT, SGT. SANDERSON, *Editorial*
VAN DE STEEG, SGT. HAROLD, *Business*

WALSH, CPL. THOMAS, *Business*
WATHALL, CPL. LIONEL, *Editorial*
WEEKS, MAJOR JACK W., *Administrative*
WEITHAS, SGT. ARTHUR G., *Editorial*
WHITCOMB, PVT. DAVID, *Editorial*
WILSON, CPL. LON H., *Editorial*
WOOD, CPL. CURTIS L., *Business*
WRENN, CPL. ROGER, *Editorial*
WRIGHT, SGT. JOSEPH G., *Business*

FORMER STAFF MEMBERS

AIKMAN, SGT. EVERETT R., USMC, *Editorial*
BALTHROPE, MAJOR CHARLES W., *Administrative*
BARNES, SGT. JOHN P., *Editorial*
BAYLESS, SGT. ARTHUR H., *Business*
BEACON, SGT. TONY, *Editorial*
BERRY, CPL. THOMAS E., *Business*
BICK, CPL. GEORGE A., *Editorial*
BIGGERSTAFF, SGT. CLYDE T., *Editorial*
BLACK, SGT. FRANK, *Business*
BREGER, LT. DAVE, *Editorial*
BROWN, SGT. HARRY, *Editorial*
BURCHARD, LT. JAMES A., *Editorial*
CHURCHILL, LT. (JG) ALLEN, *Editorial*
CONANT, SGT. PAUL E., *Editorial*
CRONYN, CPL. THEODORE 2D, *Editorial*
CUNEEN, CPL. CHARLES J., *Editorial*
DEBLOIS, SGT. FRANK, *Editorial*
FARLEY, SGT. WALTER L., *Editorial*
FLYNN, SGT. GEORGE M., *Editorial*
FRAZIER, PVT. BENJAMIN W., *Editorial*
FRYE, CPL. GORDON T., *Editorial*
GEISSLER, CPL. EVERETT, *Business*
HARRIS, PVT. MARTIN, *Editorial*
HAWORTH, SGT. WILLIAM, *Editorial*
HAYSTEAD, SGT. LADD, *Editorial*
HOLCOMBE, PVT. CHESTER E., *Editorial*
HUSSMAN, MAJOR WALTER E., *Administrative*

KELLY, PVT. ROBERT S., *Editorial*
LONG, SGT. TOM G., *Editorial*
LUSTIG, CPL. EDWARD S., *Business*
MADDEN, CAPT. CHARLES, *Administrative*
McGUIRE, SGT. DONALD A., *Editorial*
MONAGHAN, CPL. GEORGE W., *Business*
MOORA, LT. ROBERT L., *Editorial*
MORAN, SGT. JOHN, *Editorial*
NEVILLE, MAJOR ROBERT, *Editorial*
O'CONNELL, MAJOR DESMOND H., *Administrative*
REYNOLDS, MAJOR DONALD W., *Administrative*
RICHARDSON, SGT. WILLIAM H., *Editorial*
SCHWARTZ, Y2CL ROBERT L., *Editorial*
SHEARER, SGT. LLOYD, *Editorial*
SKILLMAN, PVT. THOMAS, *Business*
SNEIGR, PVT. DENNIS, *Editorial*
SPENCE, LT. COL. HARTZELL, *Administrative*
THURMAN, LT. COL. DONALD B., *Administrative*
WADE, SGT. JOHN W., *Editorial*
WALSH, LT. RALPH, *Administrative*
WARREN, SGT. PAUL C., *Editorial*
WEIGAND, CPL. DENNIS F., *Editorial*
WEISSMAN, CPL. SAM Q., *Editorial*
WHITE, COL. EGBERT, *Administrative*
WOODS, PVT. WARREN W., *Editorial*
WOOLLEY, SGT. PETER, *Editorial*
YOUNG, SGT. BILL, *Editorial*

INFANTRY BATTLE IN NEW GEORGIA

By Sgt. MACK MORRISS

WITH U. S. FORCES IN NEW GEORGIA—"When they got on the target, one Jap went 40 feet in the air, over the tops of the trees, just floated up lazy like, turned over one time and came back down.

"Then there was another that went up like a pinwheel, all arms and legs twisting in the air. He was an officer, I think, because I saw a saber go one way and a pistol the other. Next morning I stumbled over that saber and Howie got the pistol. There was one Jap blown plumb out of his pants. We found the breeches hanging way up the limb of a tree."

That was how 1st Sgt. Orville (Pappy) Cummins of Spokane, Wash., described the results of mortar fire on a Jap gun position during one of the 12 days that his infantry battalion drove a wedge from the jungleland behind Munda airfield to the sea.

They fought three separate actions, each as different from the other as night from day. The story of the battalion and particularly of 1st Sgt. Cummins' A Company is the story of jungle combat—of attack and counterattack and then attack again.

Their first engagement lasted seven days. It was fought on a hillside and in a gully that was the jungle at its worst, where visibility was normally 15 yards and the war between Jap and American was waged at a distance that was often not more than 15 feet.

The hill was named O'Brien Hill for 1st Lt. Robert M. O'Brien of Everett, Wash., who died there. A second hill, immediately to the front, was named for 2d Lt. Louis K. Christian of Pullman, Wash., who had received a field commission from the ranks on Guadalcanal and was killed at the beginning of the seven-day fight.

The battalion had shot its way from the line of departure to O'Brien Hill, and on the afternoon of the second day C Company attacked due west toward Christian Hill, followed by B Company. When they reached the foot of the slope and could go no farther, they pulled back to allow the artillery and mortars to give the place a thorough working over.

Then, with B Company in advance, they tried again next day. The battalion attack was again stopped cold. Insult was added to injury when the infantry found itself being shot at with our own weapons, our grenades, our BARs. Some of the Japs even wore our jungle "zoot suits." In some previous fight their take had been good, and they made the most of it.

With night coming on and the enemy still intact, the battalion pulled back to O'Brien Hill, and set up a perimeter defense of outposts pushed out ahead of a circular main line of resistance. They were there on the fourth day, throwing fire across the hill in front and directing fire at a strong point to their left, under assault by another unit.

On the fifth day occurred a series of events that were the beginning of a battle with all the trimmings.

The unit on the battalion's right had pushed ahead, had been badly hit and had been ordered back to reorganize. At chow time the unit, weary and somewhat bewildered, started back through the 1st Battalion lines. Behind it came the Jap, engaging its rear elements. In the jungle there was a confusion of friend and enemy, and for a while nobody knew exactly what was going on, least of all the Jap.

But he soon learned. He had been following a unit in withdrawal, and he ran flush into another unit of unknown strength, firmly emplaced on O'Brien Hill. The withdrawing unit moved through, its rear elements disengaging the enemy and leaving him to the men of the 1st who waited for the counterattack to reach them.

At 1430 the Jap hit and the fight was on. Twenty-six hours later it was over. An estimated enemy body of two reinforced companies, which just about matched the battalion's strength, had been so completely wrecked that in the days to follow there was no evidence of it again.

The first contact, when the advancing enemy ran head-on into light machine guns, rocked him back on his heels. For two hours, in the light of the afternoon, the attack came in squad groups as the Jap sought to probe the defensive lines, to see what this was he had smacked into. He stabbed inquisitively here and there, testing the front, testing the flanks, with six men, then a dozen, rushing forward. He got nowhere. When darkness came the battalion heard him digging in.

On the battalion's right flank was a saddle that led from O'Brien Hill to another rise to the right front. To the immediate front, stretching from right front to left, was the gully that was dense with jungle. The forward slope of O'Brien Hill was fairly open. The outposts were at the edge of the jungle and the main line of resistance not more than 15 or 20 yards behind them, with the CP a little higher and to the rear.

That night the Jap, more sure of himself, came in. He came across the saddle and up from the gully. It was obvious that he was trying his old trick of attempting demoralization because he yelled like a Comanche when he rushed, and when he was preparing to rush he yelled threats:

"American soldier will die tonight. Prepare to die, Yank-eee!"

He worked by familiar formula, throwing in his little grenades which exploded with much noise and little effect, tossing in his knee-mortar shells, pouring in his fast-firing, brittle-sounding automatic fire. His yelling, which was mostly inarticulate, was constant, and the men of the battalion yelled back insult for insult.

"Americans cowards!" yelled the Nips.

"Tojo eats ——!" yelled the infantry.

Three times during the night the Jap attacked in what would amount to platoon strength, and each time the attack was cut to pieces. That night the .30-caliber light machine guns did the work of the defensive design heavies. In the morning the air-cooled lights looked as if they'd been in a fire, with their barrels burnt orange and flaking. But they kept on firing.

In the jungle the first light of dawn always brings heavy fire, and this time it was heavy. But the Jap tried no further attack. He was saving himself for something else, perhaps waiting for a better time.

At 0800 the battalion, commanded by Lt. Col. Joe Katsarsky of Battle Creek, Mich., sent out a combat patrol to the extreme right flank. They cracked a body of Japs who were attempting to cut the line of supply and then work into the flank and rear.

By pulling out the officers and men for the patrol, the battalion weakened the perimeter, but it had to be done. The Jap had machine-gun fire on the supply trail, cutting it off, and men died as they started back with casualties or came forward with supplies. Drivers were shot at the wheels of their jeeps. Before it was over four jeeps blocked the trail.

The patrol went out, fought sharply and within two hours was back again, just in time. The Jap apparently was aware of the move, and even before everyone was back in position the grand assault got under way. Nothing could be more typical of the vaunted Japanese do-or-die technique than the 45 minutes in which they stormed the battalion's defense.

Everything in front of the battalion came forward, screaming. Jap bullets raked the hillside in a grazing fire that ranged from 6 inches above the ground to 3 feet. Shelter halves that had been stretched above foxholes were cut to ribbons and the sticks that held them up were splintered. The men tore them down to avoid getting entangled in the canvas.

The Japs used tracers and explosive bullets that trailed a brief string of fire and cracked sharply when they hit twigs. The Jap soldiers came forward in bunches, leaping and running like maniacs and yelling at the tops of their voices. Their bayonets were fixed and they might have tried to use them, but they never got that close. Two of them tumbled into outpost foxholes, dead before they hit the emplacements themselves.

The outposts withdrew to the main line of resistance as the battalion tightened against the strain. The aid station, which had been on the forward slope, moved to the other side of the hill because the fire was so thick that the medics could not get off the ground to attend the wounded. During the melee, when there was no work for them, the message-center people kept low and played Battleship. Finally, their shelter shot to ribbons, they moved.

The CP and the MLR stayed put. Men were hit. Once a man was gutshot and two medics picked him up and walked him, one on either side, through the fire to safety. Another man was shot and as he raised up he said, "I'm hit." As he fell forward he said, "I'm dead." He was.

Capt. Ralph Phelps of Spokane, Wash., the battalion exec, was in a foxhole conference with the CO of A Company. As they talked, a stream of machine-gun bullets went between their bodies, less than 6 inches apart. They scooted down further, looked at each other, and went on talking. In the v of a tree was a Jap with a BAR which he let fly at intervals as he ducked up and down. They called him "Jack-in-the-box." A grenade got him.

Because there were no men to be spared for ammo carriers, the noncoms divided their time between controlling their men and supplying them, which in either case meant exposure to murderous fire. A corporal was killed as he crept forward with ammunition for his men. A buck sergeant, Hubert Santo of Medford, Oreg., held his part of the line together by galloping over the hillside in the dual role of ammo carrier and platoon leader. His outfit had no lieutenant.

In the heat of the fight, men were too busy to think of anything but the business at hand. A lieutenant, wounded on the patrol action when a bullet hit his helmet and cut through the back of his neck, found time to have it dressed 2 hours later. Men said strange things, like the soldier whose shelter had been riddled with bullets. A flare dropped on the already-demolished canvas and he yipped in anguish, "There goes my tent!"

The fight centered on the right flank. In some positions there were mortar men armed only with pistols, put there to fill in while the patrol was gone.

On the right-flank center was a light machine gun with both gunners gone, one sick and the other momentarily absent at the start of the attack. Manning the gun was the ammunition carrier, a sandy-haired, drawling buck private named James Newbrough of Monument, Colo.

When the attack started Newbrough was on the gun. A Jap in front of him yelled, "Americans cowards!"

"The hell you say," Newbrough snorted.

"Come on out and fight," yelled the Jap, tossing a rock.

"Come on in and get me," said Newbrough.

The Jap and his comrades thought that over, threw a few more rocks and then screamed, "Here we come!"

Three of them sprang out with .25-caliber light machine guns, which they fired as they rushed. Two of them died in their tracks. The third ran.

As the fight progressed Newbrough, alone on the gun, kept it going constantly. Nobody, not even he, knows how many belts of ammunition he expended. As the gun continued to fire, it attracted more and more attention until it seemed that Newbrough was the only target. Bullets splattered into everything, cutting down the shelter half on top of him and clearing the underbrush from around him.

Newbrough unfastened the traversing mechanism and, crouching low, sighted along the under side of the barrel so that no part of him was above the level of the gun itself. With his hand over his head he hung onto the trigger and raked the ground before him.

His gun corporal, Dick Barrett of Rosburg, Wash., managed to get through to him with ammunition when the supply was almost exhausted, and Pfc. Hollis S. Johnson of McKenzie, Ala., came up to cover him with a BAR. Newbrough, a shy kid with a country brogue and the faintest show of a beard, probably saved the battalion that day.

The attack, once stopped, was not repeated. The battalion smashed it, but not until other units approached from two sides did the Jap see proof that his case was hopeless and withdraw in the late aft-

ernoon. With its ordeal over, the battalion took Christian Hill against little opposition and advanced 800 yards through the jungle before darkness halted it.

On the ninth day A Company was in front of the battalion advance, which skirted northward of Biblio Hill overlooking Munda airfield, moving across country that itself was hilly though less densely jungled as it ran westward to the sea.

The battalion chose a bivouac area for the night and A pushed out in advance, taking up positions and setting up an OP on the forward slope of a hill in front of the bivouac. On the left, on Biblio itself, another unit was engaged with the enemy.

From the company OP on the morning of the tenth day the company commander, Capt. Donald Downen of Pullman, Wash., saw an amazing sight —probably one of the few such scenes any American has witnessed in the war in the Pacific.

Immediately before him in a slight draw less than 100 yards away were Jap shacks, their tin roofs bright and a searchlight position in the midst of them. He saw Japs moving leisurely across the terrain, going in and out of the huts, puttering around as if there were no war within a thousand miles. Aware that his company's presence was completely undetected, he watched the Japs and studied the terrain ahead.

Then he reported back to Battalion, which moved up to direct an artillery concentration that shortly went plowing into the peaceful scene. When the guns had done their work, A Company threaded its way down across the draw and up the gentle rise immediately ahead.

Capt. Downen set up his CP in a 1,000-pound bomb crater. Almost abreast of it and perhaps 50 yards away, Cpl. Garrit Hulstein of Hospers, Iowa, established an OP in a similar crater. Although there was a little fire from the front, the terrain ahead looked comparatively harmless.

Then a heavy-caliber gun blazed, and Hulstein reported what he took to be a 77-mm mountain gun almost directly ahead and 50 yards away. As the barrel moved slightly, the corporal shoved the man beside him downward just as the gun blasted again. This time a foot and a half of the rim of the bomb crater was shot away, leaving men dazed and one man buried beneath clay dirt and coral. He was pulled out, unhurt.

Of the gun the men could see only the mouth of the barrel and two upright objects on either side, which they thought were wheels.

Battalion was contacted, not without trouble, because the gun was firing into the CP. A mortar treatment was started on the way. Hulstein went back to bring up the weapons company commander and while the mortars tossed in 81-mm shells, A Company began to move, not yet aware of what it was up against. It was entering one of the most unusual fights of two campaigns.

One platoon moved to the left and the other moved to the right to flank the piece. A machine gun in the OP crater covered their advance, peppering the top of the emplacement. As they moved, six Japs started across in front of them heading toward the gun. The left platoon, under Lt. Bob Brown of Bellingham, Wash., blazed away. Sgt. Elmer McGlynn of Seattle grabbed a BAR and turned it loose on automatic: the Japs never got where they were going. The platoons moved on, waiting for the mortar barrage to lift.

Company Headquarters, composed of the captain, his runner, the first sergeant and the mail orderly, went forward to coordinate the flanking attack. They were looking straight into the bore of the gun and knew only that, whatever it was, it was beautifully camouflaged.

When they were close enough the mortars quit, and Downen and his three men realized that they were nearer than either of the two platoons. There was no time to waste so they rushed the gun. Not until they were upon it did they realize that, instead of a field piece, it was a dual-purpose anti-aircraft gun—and not one but two and perhaps more.

The captain got one Jap outside the emplacement. His mail orderly, T-5 David Lloyd George of Kalispell, Mont., got another. Then Pfc. Wiley Howington of Asheville, N. C., the company runner, went into action.

He leaped into the gun emplacement and found the Jap gun crew still huddled in the dugout, which was tunneled into the side of the emplacement itself. The mortars had driven them inside, and they never had time to get out. Howie fired a clip of M1 slugs into them, then leaped across to the other side of the entrance, fumbling first for another clip and then for a grenade.

George followed him in and opened up with a tommy gun.

"By Gawd," drawled Howie with an accent that was straight from the North Carolina hills, "I tell you there wuz some scramblin' down in there."

Five Japs were dead and a sixth was at the far entrance, trying desperately to get out. 1st Sgt. Cummins, who is built like a pint-sized quarterback, got him by degrees.

"I could see just about six inches of his rump sticking out and I bored him," Cummins said. "He'd keep sliding back—never could get that part of himself out of the way—and every time he'd slide back I'd bore him again. Finally he slid back too far."

Now one gun was out. But there was another, some 35 yards away. In the first gun pit the four men could see the 75-mm rifle turn toward them, the elongated barrel moving fast. Cummins had one of the two grenades in the group and he heaved it —a perfect throw into the emplacement. The barrel stopped.

He grabbed Howington's grenade, which Howie hadn't been able to unhook when he wanted it, and it burst at the mouth of the dugout. Next day when the mop-up came, there was nothing left there to bother them.

When the excitement momentarily died, Capt. Downen saw men of his right platoon motioning to him frantically, pointing somewhere beyond the second gun at a place almost directly in front of them. At that instant the third gun roared, firing directly into the face of the platoon but just over their heads.

Downen yelled at them to get out, but the muzzle blast of the piece, not more than 20 yards away, had deafened them. Finally he waved them back, and they crawled to the rear, dazed by the terrific shock of the explosion. A Company with two guns down and a third discovered, withdrew to the bomb craters and called for mortar fire. That's when Cummins saw the Japs flying through the air.

"But the prettiest thing was when the mortars hit the ammunition," he added. "It looked like a million tracers going off at the same time."

No. 3 gun was gone. By that time the fourth and last was discovered and a direct hit by the 81s put it out of action. Actually there were five of the dual-purpose pieces, which the outfit thinks was a Jap Marine AA installation, but the fifth gun was never fired. The six Japs who started across in front of the left platoon were the crew, caught out of position.

On the eleventh day the battalion was on the move again, cleaning out the bivouac area behind the guns and capturing two other AA positions without opposition. They moved through a hospital area, rich in booty which they had no time to collect.

As they passed through, there was scattered firing. In a bombproof dugout there were several Japs and one of them held up his hands crying, "Me surrender! Me surrender!"

Defense of the beach was set up facing the sea and when the battalion hit them the Japs tried to turn around and fight with their backs to the water. There were not many of them but they were trapped and desperate. The beach wire, meant to stop a seaborne invasion, was cut through from behind.

The battalion hit the beach defense at 1530 on the eleventh day. They received fire from pillboxes and pulled back to let the mortars in. But as they did, the Japs moved in toward them, letting go with a Lewis gun and machine guns and rifles in grazing fire 2 feet off the ground.

The terrain was of bomb-chewed coral, underbrush and water holes. A Company found itself in a position where practically the whole outfit was pinned down without a field of fire, only a few feet from the sea.

Behind a log was Pfc. Charles Boughner of Seattle with an M1. He alone was able to get in effective shots and soon it was apparent to everyone that Boughner in his position could do more than a platoon, or even the company.

He fired the M1 until there were no more clips. Someone tossed him a tommy gun and he emptied it. Another M1 was passed to him. S/Sgt. Bob Isa-man of Chewelah, Wash., was at his feet and loaded clips as fast as Boughner could fire them. In the heat of the fight Isaman noticed what Boughner did not—that Jap bullets were smashing faster and closer to the log. He made the rifleman get underneath it instead of over it. The firing position was just as good; he could still see the enemy.

A BAR was passed to him. Boughner emptied clip after clip and the men around him threw every available cartridge toward his position. Isaman loaded them and passed them on. A belt of machine-gun bullets was tossed over, and they were reloaded and expended. Finally the Jap positions were quiet.

"That," said Sgt. Cummins, "was one time when a man was in attack supported by a company."

It was too dark to do more. That night the infantrymen heard the splash of wading feet and they fired when they caught sight of dark shapes against the water. Some of the Japs may have made it to a tiny island near by, but whether they did or not, their fight for New Georgia was over.

Next morning the battalion stood on the beach and looked out to sea.

JUNGLE WAR

YANK reprinted this anonymous report on combat conditions in New Guinea by a wounded noncom from the Intelligence Bulletin *with permission of the War Department's Military Intelligence Service.*

WE WERE flown over the Owen Stanley range to relieve an Australian combat unit, which was keeping open a trail over which natives were bringing up supplies.

The first day we had snipers firing into our perimeter (an area with all-around defense) with explosive bullets, which were very irritating and nerve-racking. The next morning the same thing started. I got permission from my lieutenant to go out and see if I could find the sniper. I walked about 40 yards out of the perimeter, and I saw him in a large tree about 300 yards away. Since this was the first Jap I had seen, I was quite nervous. I took my time and fired five shots. The Jap fell only partly out of the tree; he was tied in by his legs, and his rifle was strapped to a limb.

Our first general activity was to send out patrols under company noncoms, to be sure there were no Japs digging in.

One day about noon, our commander asked for volunteers to go into an area believed to be occupied by the Japs. I asked for two men to go with me into the area. We had gone about 300 yards when we thought we heard something moving in the undergrowth. I left the two men behind and crawled up to a place where the growth had been cut down to about knee height. There I could see fresh dirt, so I lay still and listened for about 30 minutes. Then I brought the other two men up with me and I left them in my position while I crawled forward to investigate. I found a freshly dug hole, with a banana-tree trunk forming a wall about waist high on two sides of it.

I called the other men up, and we decided to go back and report what we had seen; however, just then a .25-caliber machine gun opened up, and we immediately dived into the hole. We thought that the enemy was covering the hole with this one gun, but another .25 caliber opened up from another direction. All during the afternoon we exchanged fire with them, using our Thompson submachine guns and the one Browning automatic rifle we had with us. At about 2000, after dark, we went back into the jungle and got away without a shot being fired at us. We stayed in the jungle that night because it is absolute suicide to go into your own perimeter after dark.

Next morning we reported what we had seen.

At night you're not permitted to fire your rifle because it would reveal to the Japs exactly where you are—you use only hand grenades and the bayonet.

The Japs will go from tree to tree during the hours of darkness and make noises, or call familiar names of people, or call your medical personnel. When they have located your perimeter, they fire their machine guns about waist high over your position; then they send a group of men crawling in under their own fire. They crawl very slowly until they feel the edge of your foxhole; then they will back away a bit and throw in hand grenades.

Another favorite Japanese trick is to capture a wounded man and place him near a trail or perimeter and then cover him with machine-gun fire. They will torture him until he screams and yells for help, but it is absolutely suicide to send him help.

One morning at 0845 we were told we were going to attack the Jap perimeter at 0900. The lieutenant in charge took with him two runners, who carried a telephone and the necessary wire. When we were at the right position, our artillery and machine guns laid down a barrage until the lieutenant telephoned back for them to stop. We moved on, on our bellies. The Japs were out of their pillboxes and seemed to be doing some sort of fatigue work. There were six of us who got within 20 yards of them without being seen. We had three Tommy guns, a Browning automatic rifle, a Springfield rifle, and a Garand rifle. The lieutenant motioned for us to start firing. One sergeant threw a grenade, and, as it hit, we opened up with all our guns. There wasn't a single Jap who escaped, but there were some left in pillboxes, and they pinned us down with fire from one .50-caliber machine gun and from several .30-caliber machine guns. One of our six men got hit near the hip with a .50-caliber bullet, which lodged in his left shoulder. The Japs also wounded three more of our men who were behind us. The lieutenant telephoned the commanding officer and told him our situation, and we were ordered to retire. Later we made another attack on this perimeter and took it.

There was a lieutenant who had been shot down near a pillbox, and our commanding officer asked for volunteers to go in and get him. When he was last seen he was still alive, but when we got to him, after wading through swamp water waist deep, he was lying on his stomach—dead. While we were going toward him, the Japanese had killed the lieutenant by slashing his stomach, and had placed him on an "island." We put him on a litter and started back into our own perimeter, but the Japs opened fire on us, and we had to leave him and take cover in the trees. I thought the fire was coming from only one pillbox, so we all started firing in the direction from which the fire was coming. We soon learned, however, that there were two more pillboxes from which we also were receiving machine-gun fire. When they stopped firing, another boy and myself went out and got the lieutenant and took him into the perimeter. Later he was taken to battalion headquarters (command post) where he was buried in the regimental burial ground.

A few weeks later our battalion moved into a position to make an attack on a large Japanese perimeter. All artillery and machine-gun fire was concentrated on this perimeter before the infantry started pushing forward. The heat was terrific. We moved in about 100 yards under Japanese fire, with two platoons forward and one in reserve (the squads also were two forward and one in reserve). My squad was in reserve when we started forward.

The lieutenant sent back for me to bring my squad forward and relieve the right squad. Because so many of this squad had been killed and wounded or had passed out from heat exhaustion, I thought I might find a better place to put my men. So I crawled forward to find positions for them. I had found a few good shell holes, some logs, and depressions in the ground, when a .30-caliber machine gun opened fire on me. The first burst hit the front handle grip of my Tommy gun, and, of course, I got as low as possible; but the second burst hit my Tommy gun drum, and two bullets hit me in the arm. Also, fragments of the drum hit me hard—on the hand and shoulder. These .30's were explosive bullets which broke up my arm and tore a great deal of flesh away from it. It felt as if an ax blade were shearing through the flesh of my arm.

I rolled over into a small depression of the ground, and took my knife out and tried to cut off the sleeve of my coveralls. While I was cutting, I saw the barrel of the .30 caliber sticking out of a small pillbox, so I rolled back and got my Tommy gun, thinking there might be a chance of knocking out this one machine gun, which was about 20 yards away.

Just as I was getting in the right position to shoot, a .25-caliber machine gun opened up from the left. One bullet hit me in the elbow and one in the ribs—the latter went through my pipe and a can of tobacco and only broke my rib. I pulled out this bullet myself, burning my index finger on the hot lead. Another bullet went through my helmet and just grazed my scalp.

I lay there for about 3 hours in the hot sun, bleeding profusely. Figuring that I would bleed to death if I remained there, I began to crawl back to my own men—only hoping and trusting to God that He would give me strength and protection to get back. I got back to my men, and the platoon medical personnel made a hasty cross splint and sling for my mangled left arm.

One of my men helped me back to the command post where litter bearers took me back to a dispensary. Attendants gave me morphine and put me on a jeep, which carried me back—with several other casualties—to a portable hospital. There medical officers removed two bullets. Next day I was sent to a landing field where a plane was waiting to take casualties to Port Moresby.

THE NEW YORK SUBWAY SYSTEM ON THE
ITALIAN FRONT By Sgt. NEWTON H. FULBRIGHT

WITH THE FIFTH ARMY IN ITALY—Perhaps some busy somebody has taken care of the matter—I haven't been able to read anything much lately—but in case it hasn't been done, I think the New York subway system should receive proper credit for its part in the war here in Italy.

I first came across this curious connection of the venerable and undramatic subway with the war here in Italy one morning shortly after daylight on the beaches of Paestum. I was standing behind an Italian farmhouse a little undecided about things. A German M34 machine gun had been chattering a little while before across a corn patch, and I was supposed to go in that direction. I was sitting there thinking about things when a little Italian farmer came up and started speaking English.

The Germans had gone, he said, up the road they had gone.

"Thanks," I said. "Where did you learn to speak English?"

"I work for the New York subway system five years," he said.

Later in the afternoon a few of us from L Company and M Company plodded up the 3,500-foot slope of Mount Soprano, overlooking the beach. A battery of 88s had rained concentrated hell on us from the mountain since daylight.

Nearing the town of Capaccio, we slowed up a little. Red communication wire, Jerry's sure trail, led around the mountain, where the forward observer had been, and along the rugged winding road to Capaccio, where the 88s were supposed to be. We didn't know what was in front of us, so we moved along cautiously.

Then an Italian came out of a farmhouse and told us all about it.

"They've gone—all gone! Run away to the east. They all been drunk all afternoon. They get all *vino* in the town, then they run away."

He had worked for the New York subway system five years.

I met a Boston subway worker a night or two later.

Some of us had taken a patrol into Trentinara just to see if there were any Germans in the place. I found myself walking up a main street as dark as deep-land sorghum syrup and as crooked as the stick held by the crooked man who walked a crooked mile in the nursery rhyme; and the place was not only dark, it seemed completely deserted. Our artillery had been shelling the town and the natives had mostly taken to the hills.

I nosed along, followed by a few GIs who didn't like the situation and plainly said so. Suddenly an Italian stepped out of a dark alley with outstretched hand and said "Hello."

We had quite a conversation there in the dark street. Other Italians crept out of hiding timidly, and presently there was a small crowd of us talking and laughing.

The Germans had all gone. They had left the day before, 18 of them, dressed in civilian clothes.

"They throw away their guns, they go northeast," one man said, pointing to a mountain. Tall and wistful and white in the daytime, it reminded me somehow of the Chrysler Building in New York. "No more Germans left in this whole country. The shepherds come in from the hills and report all Germans fleeing," he said.

He wanted to talk more about Boston (he had helped build the Boston subway) and Brookline and all those Back Bay places.

Some days later when I managed to escape from the Germans about 100 miles behind their lines, I had the courage to stop at an Italian farmhouse largely because I remembered these incidents and the New York subway system.

I had been captured with five of my men while on reconnaissance behind enemy lines on Sept. 14 at the bloody battle of Altavilla. Five days later I made my escape and started back in the night toward our lines, far to the south.

Jerry was all over the country but principally on the highways, trying to withdraw his tremendous, ponderous equipment to new positions north of the Volturno River. I stumbled across country, dodging villages and dogs. Dogs sailed out every so often, yelping and howling. The moon was down; I was glad for that, and yet it was a hindrance. I was always bumping into things. Once I suddenly discovered I was walking down the principal street of a village, but I was able to back out of the place without being discovered.

After a few of these mishaps, I decided to travel by day.

I picked out a nice-looking farmhouse, a couple of miles west of a village, and crawled into a strawstack to wait for morning.

The old lady who saw me first was scared out of her wits. She dashed for the doorway while I stood in the yard trying to smile and wiping wheat-straw out of my beard.

In the farmhouse I discovered that no one could speak English. The farmer couldn't, his wife couldn't, his mother couldn't, his sister couldn't, and neither could his three little daughters or a boy whose mother was dead.

I'd say something in Spanish or English or a mixture of both, and they'd just shake their heads and laugh. I would shake hands with every one again, point at myself and say like a bright Fuller brush man: "*Americano!* Me *Americano! Americano* and *Italiano* (stepping hard on the *ano*) friends! Good! *Bueno!*"

Suddenly someone entered the door.

I turned and faced a bulky, heavy-set Italian with a red important-looking face, who held a pistol within a few inches of my stomach.

This should have been serious. Yet I wanted to laugh. The pistol was so small it looked like a cap pistol, and it was so completely covered with rust that I doubted whether it would fire at all. I stood there while the heavy fellow went through my trouser pockets. He hauled out the few items I possessed: a broken pencil, a fountain pen, a notebook, a billfold containing three genuine American gold-seal 10-dollar bills, and a picture of my girl.

After that he sat down on a little stool and put the pistol in his hip pocket. He didn't seem to know just what else to do.

Then an old Italian with proud, graying mustache entered the door.

"Gooda de mornin'!"

"Good morning!" I shouted. I jumped up and grabbed him by the arm and started shaking hands as though I were an Elk meeting a fellow Elk in Amarillo. "But where in hell did you learn to speak English?"

"I work 17 years for the New York subway system," he said. And from that moment on I was a firm believer in the New York subway.

We sat down and talked a long time. I got rid of my GI clothes and got into a ragged civilian shirt and trousers. I felt like going out and grabbing a hoe and going to work on the farm right away.

That night the mayor of the town and other influential Italians called on me.

One of them, a miller, pulled a yellowed sheet of paper out of his pocket and showed me an honorable discharge from the United States Army, dated 1918.

"I lived in New York before the war," he said. "I was a doorman for the New York subway system."

He opened his mouth and started shouting the names of the stations—Spring, Canal, 14th, 34th, 42d. After that he sang songs that had been popular during the last war: "Oh, How I Hate to Get Up in the Morning" and "Are You from Dixie?" I remembered my aunt singing that one years ago.

I hid in the farmhouse for five days. Meanwhile the British Eighth Army was driving up rapidly from the south. When the flash of artillery could be seen plainly in the mountains and when the rumble sounded loud like spring thunder in Texas, I headed out for the wars again.

It was tough going; I was 16 days getting inside our lines. And—well, there were other former employees of the New York and Boston subway systems along the road, or I probably wouldn't have made it.

So my hat is off to the New York subway system. *Viva* the New York subway system, a great institution!

"You men with the National Geographic Society?"
—*Cpl. Ernest Maxwell.*

WITH FREE CHINA'S FLAG UPON HIS BACK, HE DIED IN A GREAT SKY BATTLE   By Sgt. MARION HARGROVE

SOMEWHERE IN CHINA—There was a great battle in the sky and the people stopped their work to look at it. And then the battle moved away until there was nothing left of it but one plane of the *Mei-Kua fi chi* (the American flyers), with its large white star with the red border around it, and two planes of the Japanese devils, the *Yi Bin Kwe-Tse*. There was much shooting and then the first and then the second of the Japanese planes fell to the earth with much smoke and great noise.

And after this had happened the people saw that the little plane of the *Mei-Kua* was also greatly harmed. There was much noise such as one hears from trucks on the great road when they are using gasoline of pine roots and there are too many yellowfish riding on the top of the load. And finally the *Mei-Kua* came down to the earth, not smoothly but with a heavy crash, so that the great body of the plane was crumpled and the wide wings were twisted and bent.

And the people found in the wreckage of the plane the *fi chi* who had driven it in the air and beaten the *Yi Bin Kwe-Tse*. He was tall and large, as are all the *Mei-Kua,* and on the shoulders of his jacket were two narrow strips of white embroidery and on his back was sewn the flag of China, with the white sun of *Kuo Min Tang* in the corner, and the chop of the Gissimo himself was stamped below the writing that said this was one of the men who had come from across the wide waters to help drive the *Yi Bin Kwe-Tse* from the soil of China.

The people took him up gently and carried him to a house and attended to his wounds, although they knew he could not live for long. For his arm and his leg were broken and there were many wounds made by the bullets of the *Yi Bin Kwe-Tse* and his stomach was torn so that the guts of the man could be seen within it. But they did what they could to make him comfortable, although the *Mei-Kua fi chi* knew as well as they that he could not live for long.

And while they did the little that they could for him, he laughed with them and made jests in a poor and awkward Chinese that they could not understand, for it was not the Chinese spoken in that village. But they could understand his labored laugh and they could see the greatness and the goodness and the strength and the dignity of the dying man.

And when he was dead, this man with the flag of Free China upon his back, they wrapped his body in white, for white is the color of the honored dead, and they laid it in the finest coffin in the village and they placed the coffin upon a barge in the river to take it to the people who would return it to the great general of the *Mei-Kua fi chi, Ch'e Ne T'e,* and the others of the *Mei-Kua.*

And in a box beside the coffin they put the clothing they had removed from him when he was in pain, and with the clothing they put the things that had been in his pockets. They put the little leather case with his money, and the pieces of heavy paper with his picture and the other pictures of the woman and the two children, the *Mei-Kua* cigarettes and the little silver box of self-arriving fire, the two small metal plates on a little chain, the knife that folded within itself and the small brown *Mei-Kua* coin with the picture of a bearded man upon it.

And when this had been done four of the young men of the village took poles and poled the barge up the river to return the *Mei-Kua fi chi* to his own people.

And the news ran quickly all along the river that the dead hero was returning to his people. And all of the villagers along the river and all of the people who lived in the sampans tied along the banks of the river waited to see the barge go slowly by. And wherever it passed, the people lit long strings of firecrackers and honored the *Mei-Kua fi chi* who had fought for China and laughed and jested and died as a hero should.

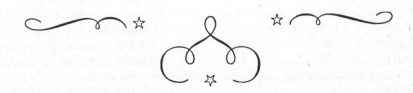

SCHWEINFURT RAID

By Sgt. WALTER PETERS

IT COST PLENTY BUT IT WAS WORTH IT

The Eighth Air Force raid on Schweinfurt in southern Germany was probably the most devastating single air battle ever fought. We shot down 99 Nazi planes, scored 26 probables and damaged 17 others. It cost us 60 Flying Fortresses and two P-47 fighters (about $20,000,000 worth of equipment) and 593 men. But the raid crippled a vital German ball-bearing plant and, according to Gen. H. H. Arnold, chief of the U..S. Army Air Forces, it would help save thousands of lives when Allied ground forces moved farther into Europe against the Nazis.

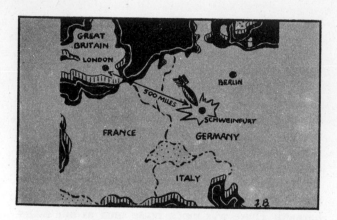

A BOMBER BASE IN BRITAIN [By Cable]—It was still dark when they woke the crews. The fog lay thick and cold over the countryside that morning, and inside the barracks all was pitch black and silent except for the deep, steady breathing of the sleeping Fortress gunners.

I had been awake for some time and I heard the door of the next hut slam shut, and then the sound of footsteps outside. Someone struck a match and announced that it was 6 o'clock. Then the door opened and the lights went on, cold and glaring when viewed from a warm bed.

The squadron operations officer, bundled up warmly against the morning's cold in a sheepskin jacket and flying boots, walked toward the center of the room. He started to read the list of names from a slip of paper, quietly so as not to wake up those who weren't flying that day.

"Baxter, Blansit, Cavanaugh, Hill, Sweeney," he read. The men whose names were called sat up sleepily, slid their feet a little wearily to the cold floor and stayed there on the bunks, most of them, for a few seconds before getting dressed. They shivered in the damp and cold.

"Briefing's at 0730," the officer said. Then he went on to another hut.

The men dressed quietly, trying not to disturb those who could sleep a little later and secretly envying them. Next to me bunked Sgt. Bill Sweeney, a former tire salesman and now a gunner. He lit a cigarette and came over to my bunk and said he thought this would be a fine day to christen his Fortress, which had made a dozen missions but until now was without a name. This was the first mission since the crew had decided a few days ago to name the ship *YANK*.

I drew back the blackout curtain carefully and looked out at the gray morning. "It looks pretty foggy to me," I said. "You never can tell about English weather," said Sweeney. "You're very goddam right you can't," said a sergeant gunner sitting on the next bunk. "You never can tell."

We headed for the combat mess. There, in the noise of conversation and the clatter of dishes, we had a big breakfast and polished it off with a cigarette before walking on to the briefing.

It was beginning to get light now. The briefing room, like the mess hall, was bright and noisy, until a mild-mannered Intelligence captain rose to speak. He had a long ruler in his hand and he kept toying with it as if it were a swagger stick.

Nobody knew where we were going, and there was a dead silence as he raised his ruler to the map. He pointed first to our base in Britain, then moved the ruler slowly over the North Sea into Belgium, as though he himself were exerting a tremendous effort to get us over the target.

The ruler moved through Belgium slowly and ate deeper and deeper into Germany until I thought for a moment we were being briefed for Austria. Way down in the southern reaches of Germany near Frankfort the ruler stopped. "This, gentlemen, is your target for today—Schweinfurt."

The men listened intently, leaning forward from the long rows of benches and chairs. The air was clouded now with cigarette smoke. "Schweinfurt," the captain continued, "is the most important target in all of Germany. We cannot go ahead with other targets until it is seriously crippled."

The gunner ahead of us strained forward to get a better view of the map. "Half of Germany's ball bearings," the captain went on, "are produced at

Schweinfurt, and ball bearings are important to Hitler. If we destroy these factories, we will have crippled the enemy's production of tanks and planes and submarines to a very great degree." Then the captain gave technical information about the target, the wind and the weather, and the briefing was over.

"I think this Schweinfurt is named after a very special kind of pig," said one of the radio operators as we headed toward the truck. We rode up the taxi strips to our head stand, where the crew stood around the ship. Station time was 30 minutes ahead, and the guns, ammunition, radio and bomb bays had been checked.

The skipper of YANK was a 21-year-old giant from Monterey, Calif., Capt. Ivan Klohe. While we waited for the take-off he wrestled with the two waist gunners, Sgts. Charlie Hill and Edward Cavanaugh. Though Cavanaugh was only a little over 5 feet tall, he succeeded in pinning the captain's shoulder to the ground, and Hill put a deadly lock on the captain's legs. The rest of the crew stood by and cheered for the gunners.

Then station time was announced. The men, suddenly serious, took their positions in the ship. I climbed into the nose with Lt. Howard J. Zorn, the navigator, and Lt. Richard J. Roth, the bombardier. "The right gun's yours," Roth said. YANK took its place on the runway.

Lt. Herbert Heuser, the co-pilot, announced over the interphone: "There goes *Piccadilly Queen*." We watched as she sped down the black runway, at 50, 60, and then 90 miles an hour. It was a beautiful take-off. So was ours.

About 11,000 feet the pilot told us to check our oxygen masks. We put them on. Heuser imitated a fireside chat over the interphone. "My friends," he began, and the crew ate it up. Then he sang, and Cavanaugh and Zorn chimed in occasionally with a razzberry, a hard sound to produce over the interphone. There were more songs from Hill, from Sweeney and from Sgt. Roy (Tex) Blansit, the top-turret gunner. The war seemed beautiful at that point.

Our formation across the North Sea was perfect. We led the "Purple Heart" element, and in front of us the sky was literally clouded by B-17s. We counted as many as 190 and then quit counting. Zorn told us to look toward the long file of P-47 Thunderbolts on our right. They left a beautiful silver vapor trail behind them.

At 1302 the captain warned that we were approaching enemy territory. We were above 20,000 feet and suddenly over the interphone somebody shouted: "Unidentified vessels down below." A couple of seconds later he said: "They're shooting." "Why, the silly bastards," somebody else remarked.

By 1330 we were over Luxembourg. The sun was still with us, and the nose was so hot we didn't even bother using our electric suits. A pair of white silk gloves was enough to keep our hands warm. Enemy fighters were getting hot about that time, too.

Heuser did most of the calling, singing out the fighters' positions in a cool and undisturbed voice. From his place he could see all of the planes, and he didn't miss a German. "Fighter at 5 o'clock high . . . fighter at 10 o'clock . . . fighter at 8 o'clock low . . . fighter at 3 o'clock . . . fighter at 12 o'clock. . . ."

There were fighters everywhere, but mostly on our tail. "The whole goddam *Luftwaffe* is out today," somebody said over the interphone. There were even Dornier bombers. There were single-engined ME-109s and twin-engined 110s. There were JU-88s and a few 190s. There were ME-210s and heaven only knows what else.

"This is nothing," Zorn said, evidently trying to calm me down. "We've seen worse on other raids. In about 25 more minutes we'll come to the target."

The captain put the Fort into a little evasive action, banking to the left and then to the right. On our right we sighted a huge column of smoke, like a great black cloud. That was the target. Liberators and Fortresses had passed the ballbearing works already, scoring hits on the plant.

The navigator told me to look out on the left side. A couple of planes were burning there, a Fort and an enemy fighter. Three white chutes and one brown were floating in the sky near by. The whites belonged to our boys. Under the brown chute was a German flyer.

"When the hell are we getting over the target?" Time had crawled by in the last 15 minutes. In 10 more we'd be there. Heuser was still calling the fighters off. They were coming in from all sides now, but not too close.

Looking back through the fuselage, we could see Tex's legs, his left one planted on a box of caliber-50s, the right one lazily dangling into space. From the interphone we knew that Tex was very busy in his top turret. His gun was tracking fighters all around the clock. Occasionally he concentrated his fire toward the tail, where his friend Sweeney was busy shooting at the enemy as they queued up from the rear.

A JU-88 and a 190 attacked Sweeney's position from 4 and 9 o'clock high. Tex's guns worked fast. Both planes peeled off. The 190 shied off but the

88 returned from about 500 yards to the rear, flying smack at Sweeney.

Tex called out directions to Sweeney. "You're shooting at him just a little high. Get him lower. A little lower." The 88 came closer and lobbed two of the rockets the Germans are using now—deadly looking affairs shooting out like huge red flames.

Tex kept on guiding Sweeney over the interphone. "A little lower, Bill." Bill fired a little lower. The 88 wavered, flipped over, and Sweeney and Tex saw the German catch fire and trail smoke. Then there was one JU-88 less, and one less JU-88 crew; they didn't get out.

Klohe headed the Fort northeast, hitting a straight course for the tall column of smoke 6,000 feet high that marked the target. At our level and even higher flak blackened the sky. Roth was ready. It was only a matter of 20 seconds before he released the bombs.

Then came a hell—great black balls of flak all around us. It seemed impossible to escape the barrage. We weren't having fighter trouble now; our enemy was flak and there was nothing we could do about it except to take evasive action. Klohe did just that, and he did it beautifully. It seemed a miracle that we ever escaped.

Suddenly we heard a loud, jangling noise, even above the roar of the four engines. I looked toward the navigator. A fragment of flak had broken through the plate glass at his side. Zorn lifted his head quickly, took off his gloves and fur cap, and felt around the part of his face not covered by the oxygen mask. He winked when he found that he was okay.

The flak had stopped now but enemy fighters and fighter-bombers were back again. Heuser, too, was back on the job. "Fighter at 11 o'clock," Heuser announced. Zorn tracked the German with his 50s until the plane was out of sight. "Fighter at 12 o'clock," Heuser reported, and Roth followed him. "Fighter at 5 o'clock," and Sweeney was back at his guns. "Fighter at 2 o'clock," and I grabbed my gun and tracked the German until Heuser bawled me out for using too much ammunition. I stopped fast.

Now Heuser's voice again: "Fighter at 3 o'clock." Tex saw the fighter, recognized it as a 190 and waited until it came closer before letting loose a barrage. Sweeney congratulated him. From where Sweeney was, he could see the 190 spiral down and the pilot bail out. That was Jerry No. 2 for the boys of YANK.

A third fighter was claimed by Cavanaugh, the left-waist gunner, who bagged an 88. The plane went spinning toward the ground in flames but the crew of two bailed out.

All this time Sgt. Ralph Baxter, the ball-turret gunner, and Hill in the right-waist position were engaging two 88s. Baxter had spotted the Germans diving after a lone B-17, forced out of formation with a feathered engine, and he called to Hill for a hand. Between them they saved the crippled Fort from destruction.

It was about 1650 now, as we were heading home, but the watch on the panel wasn't running any more. We cussed, and when some more fighters came at us, we cussed some more. A half hour later flak started bursting again, but it wasn't as heavy as the stuff at Schweinfurt. Zorn said he thought we were near Amiens, France.

Just then I heard another loud jangle of broken glass as flak hit the left front plate. Roth ducked, but Zorn went calmly about the business of navigating. I put on a helmet and then took it off a few seconds later; it interfered with my vision and I wanted to see. Roth picked up a piece of flak and handed it to me. "Maybe you'll want this for a souvenir," he said.

We tried guessing the time. I figured it was about 1730. We were well across the English channel and in a few minutes the English coast would be in sight. Klohe began losing altitude. At 17,000 feet Roth and Zorn took off their masks, and I did, too. Zorn smiled.

Tired but happy voices began coming over the interphone. They were kidding again. Heuser sang. Zorn told us how sharpshooter Sweeney hadn't been able to hit a single skeet out of 15 a year ago. Somebody else kidded Tex because he was once rejected by the Army for flat feet. Cavanaugh gave the captain a riding over the interphone, and Klohe dished it right back at him. Personally, I just sat back, relaxed with a cigarette. The mission was over.

"Does this entitle us to wear the American Defense Ribbon?"—Cpl. Ruge.

THE FIVE-DAY ATTACK ON HASTINGS RIDGE

By Sgt. MACK MORRISS

WITH U. S. OCCUPATIONAL FORCES ON NEW GEORGIA —Hastings Ridge is just a little place, a sort of quiver in the convulsions of New Georgia's terrain.

If the rough coral slopes were leveled and the steel-scarred trees were cleared away, there might be room for a football field, certainly nothing larger.

Yet the Ridge was literally crawling with Japs— one machine-gun company and one rifle company at least. For five days the Infantry attacked it and when they gained a foothold, they fought all day and all night and then the next day to hold it.

In the jungle, war is always a personal sort of thing, one man against another. On Hastings Ridge it reached a point where individual action and individual courage were knitted together in two- and three-man units of assault, pitted against similar little units of Japs crouched in pillboxes. And the best fighters won because they cooperated with each other best.

On the first day S/Sgt. Clarence Terry of Arco, Idaho, worked his platoon up the Ridge. Two of his sergeants were ahead of him, almost on top of a Jap pillbox, working together as a team. They were using grenades and rifles, and when Sgt. Robert Chambers of Bend, Oreg., ran out of grenades, he called for his buddy to throw him more. The other sergeant tossed them forward and as he did a Jap rifleman in the pillbox shot him through the chest. The sergeant was on his feet, and when the bullet bit into him he wheeled to face the Jap and yelled like a man fouled in a fist fight: "Why, you dirty little bastard!" He raised his rifle, started forward and fell dead.

Chambers, a few feet away, went blind mad. He hurled two grenades into the Jap position as though he were stoning a snake, then leaped into the pillbox with his trench knife. When he came out, he crouched over his teammate but there was no heartbeat; he had done all he could.

Terry, in the meantime, was kept busy by a machine-gun pillbox that had pinned him down behind a tree. As he fired with a tommy gun he saw Chambers start down toward him and yelled a warning. Chambers hit the ground—a shallow fold in the coral—as the Jap gun swung toward him. Terry breathed easier. Then, seconds later, Pfc. Bob Russell, also of Bend, followed Chambers. Terry yelled again and Bob hit the fold.

With two men almost in the open before them,

the Japs abandoned Terry. The cover was too slight to offer real protection and Terry saw Jap .31-caliber bullets rip into the ground and come lower and lower across the two backs until they actually were brushing the clothes of the men as they tried desperately to dig deeper.

Terry saw that the men were directly in front of a low brush pile and that just behind it was an empty foxhole. He yelled to them to edge backward and try to get to the hole. Chambers tried it but the brush stopped him. Jap bullets sprayed around his feet and he could only lie and hope with Russell.

As soon as Terry saw it was impossible for the men to slide backward, he found another solution. He called instructions to them, telling exactly how far they could move their legs and explaining his plan.

Then Terry leaped from behind the tree and let go a burst of .45 slugs at the pillbox. The Japs swung their gun toward him, and in the instant that the fire shifted, Chambers sprang backward across the brush pile and into the foxhole behind it. The Japs swung back on Russell, but half the plan had succeeded.

In a few minutes Terry leaped out again and fired, and Russell performed the back flip to safety. The platoon's teamwork was still clicking.

However, the initial American assault on Hastings Ridge had been stopped. The Infantry pulled back to gather itself for another try.

On the second day the Yanks sought to feel out the hill and spot each individual hole from which the Japs poured fire. In the dense undergrowth it was impossible to locate the Japs unless you got up within a few feet of them. A lieutenant and a sergeant pushing forward were nailed by a pillbox and probably never knew what hit them, or from where.

A scout named Herbert Hanson of Lincoln, Ark., stepped out from behind a tree and as he did a grenade exploded in his face. He dropped his rifle and without a word started back to the rear. The fragments had marked his face but had done nothing more.

Flame throwers were brought up in an effort to heat the Japs out of the ground, but without success; the flames couldn't get close enough.

So the Infantry butted and rammed and then retired.

For the next two days the Japs sat on Hastings

Ridge and the Infantry sat on a hill opposite, not more than 100 yards away, and the two shot across at each other. Mortars and machine guns blasted into the Ridge until the trees broke out in thousands of brown spots and the limbs crashed down or teetered dangerously and became a menace themselves.

Then on the fifth day the stymied Infantry sent out patrols. The static war on the two hillsides, and in the draw between them, exploded with a suddenness that caught the Japs with their guard down. The attack on Hastings Ridge began to move.

The patrols were combat-reconnaissance. On such patrols, as the Infantry says, "you either do it or you don't," which means you strike if you think you can win, and if you don't think so, you report back with information and let it go at that.

Patrols went to right and left of the Ridge, and one patrol went straight up the hill. This patrol of 10 men, including a lieutenant known as the Mad Russian, was the one that cracked the thing wide open. Ten men alone didn't take the Ridge, but they gained the crest of it and held until the rest could get up there, take over and go on with them.

The Mad Russian was the patrol leader. Called Tym by his men, his full name is Walter Tymniak, and he is a graduate of the College of the City of New York, where he captained the water polo team. In the summer he was a lifeguard and after college he became an accountant in Manhattan, working nights.

Tym's right hand was a staff sergeant named LeRoy Norton, an ex-lumberjack from Bend, Oreg., who was awarded the Distinguished Service Cross for heroism on Guadalcanal. His left hand was Pfc. John Cashman of Brooklyn, who used to be a press foreman on the New York *Herald Tribune*.

The patrol moved up the face of the slope in the early morning. Tym and Nort and Cash were together, and the rest went up as skirmishers, three on the right and four on the left. Their strongest weapon was the element of surprise and they guarded it well while they could.

They hit and destroyed three pillboxes before the Japs knew what it was all about. Altogether they knocked out nine pillboxes in six minutes, and Hastings Ridge was theirs.

Norton hit a machine-gun emplacement in which there were three Japs goggle-eyed and half asleep. He shot one of the three inside the foxhole and a fourth who came stumbling up the hillside from the rear, then swung back and killed the remaining two at the gun before they could collect themselves to fire a round.

Pfc. Joe Shupe of Ogden, Utah, coming over from the left, joined him and together they moved on to the right to a .31-caliber machine-gun emplacement. Nort yelled to Tym that Japs were manning the gun, then with two bullets he put it out of action. Someone tossed him grenades and he threw them into the face of three Japs who were on the gun. Then he and Shupe moved on.

In the meantime Tym had grenaded out one position; to his right Pfc. Jose Cervantez of Solomonsville, Ariz., had shot out another with a BAR; to his right and in front of him the team of Pvt. Anton Dolecheck of Dickinson, N. Dak., and Ervin A. Bonow of Altura, Minn., had cleaned up two more. Tym, crouched near the mouth of a blasted-out pillbox, heard a rustling in the hole and looked in to see a Jap scampering for the opposite exit. The Mad Russian flipped in a grenade, almost indifferently, and then moved on to direct the fight.

Cashman had borrowed a clip of ammunition for his BAR from Shupe and as he saw a Jap raise his head, he fired a burst. The Jap was killed, but a ruptured cartridge jammed the gun. Cash burned his fingers pulling it out, then went on into the fight. As he and Tym worked together, they sent in a volley of grenades. Seconds later the Japs countered with a grenade barrage of their own. When the explosions ceased, Cash stuck his head around a tree and grinned at Tym: "We musta peeved 'em off."

All this happened in six minutes, and the patrol of 10 had not been hurt. The crest of the hill itself was neutralized, but now came the problem of holding it. Cash went back to bring up the battalion commander, Lt. Col. David H. Buchanan of Bluefield, W. Va. Other fights raged on either side of Hastings Ridge, and "Col. Buch" got the lay of the land and went back to coordinate the action.

More men had to be brought up quickly, but the others in the company were on patrol to the right and left flanks, in the draws that led round Hastings Ridge, and they were having troubles of their own. So Cash went back to the company bivouac to find anybody who could handle a gun.

He came back with cooks and the permanent KPs, a machine-gun section from the weapons company, 1st Sgt. Armond Pearson of Spokane, Wash., and S/Sgt. Arthur Toothman of Kirkland, Wash., the mess sergeant. These men were committed to the line.

By this time pillboxes over the crest of the ridge were causing trouble. Nort formed a patrol to wipe them out, with Cash and Shupe in it. The patrol worked to a point within a few yards of the Jap guns. Then Shupe and another man were hit almost simultaneously. Cash got Shupe out and back to the aid station. The patrol withdrew, taking its other wounded with it, and the situation on Hastings Ridge settled down to a period of consolidating, digging in and blasting with the mortars.

During this action Terry was with the patrol on the right, stabbing at the flank of the Ridge. In the denseness of the jungle it was almost impossible for them to accomplish even a reconnaissance mission without moving blindly into the path of enemy fire. The Japs had the Ridge defended in concentric circles, roughly three deep stretching around the entire perimeter, and they could and did fire from anywhere.

Terry decided that burning the brush would help. Since flame throwers had been unsuccessful three days before, he sought another method.

He left the patrol, went back to the medics and gathered all the empty plasma bottles he could find. From Transportation he got gasoline to fill them. Then he took caps and fuses from hand grenades and fitted them into the tops of the bottles. Now he had Molotoff cocktails, made from the materials at hand.

There was one particular Jap in a pillbox who had caused too much trouble. The men called him "Button" because of his unusual accuracy with a rifle. Terry decided to work on Button. With S/Sgt. Eugene Pray of Moab, Utah, he moved up to a position behind a two-foot-thick banyan tree about 25 yards from the pillbox.

Feeling safe behind the tree, he and Pray, who was spotting for mortar fire, stood up and huddled close to each other. Button almost surprised them to death, literally, by firing a .25-caliber bullet through the tree, putting it between them and filling their necks with harmless splinters of wood and lead. Terry and Pray crouched down. Button's next shot, also through the tree, skinned across Pray's leg.

If Button hadn't been expert enough to hit the soft-wood banyan dead center, Terry figures he might have added two more men to his score for the day.

Thoroughly aroused, Terry brought his cocktails into action. Stepping from behind the tree he hurled first one and then a second gasoline-filled plasma bottle at the foxhole, then swore powerfully when both of them hit trees in front of their target.

He went back, got two more bottles and approached from another angle. Same thing—trees in the way. Button remained untouched but around him on two sides his precious camouflage blazed

and melted away. Eventually that was his undoing.

Cashman, after rescuing Shupe from underneath the Jap machine guns, spent the rest of the day carting up ammunition to the men on the line. He helped bring up chow to the line, then sometime around dusk—he doesn't know exactly when—he collapsed from exhaustion. He woke up at the aid station and the medics evacuated him to a hospital.

Arriving there, Cash talked for a few minutes with some of the wounded men from the outfit, who wanted to know how things were going. Then he pulled the casualty tag off his jacket, hitched a ride on a passing jeep and went back to the fight.

During the night the Japs, perhaps 15 of them, tried infiltration.

The American outfit, wise in jungle combat, makes a habit of remaining silent and stationary at night; then, if anything moves or makes a noise, it must be the enemy. This is a measure taken in self-defense, but apparently one man forgot it.

Lying in his foxhole, he looked up to see a dark figure approaching, walking straight upright. The infantryman, curious, demanded: "Who the hell are you?" The figure moved boldly up to him, dropped a grenade and moved on.

But in other foxholes on Hastings Ridge the men remembered the policy and adhered to it: absolute silence and immobility.

Sgt. George Ray of Walla Walla, Wash., occupied a hole with Bonow and Dolecheck. Three Japs moved toward them. When the first Jap reached the hole Ray quietly spitted him on a bayonet. The second went down under a hand grenade. The third came on. Ray picked up his helmet and hurled it into the Jap's face. For a while no more Japs appeared. Then a grenade landed in the hole. Bonow was lying with his helmet between his legs and the grenade hit in the helmet, tearing his calf muscles almost completely away. Bonow kept silent. Dolecheck, next to him, knew he was hit but it was not until two hours later that Ray was aware of it. Bonow made no sound until he was evacuated next morning. Even a whispered word might have meant the death of all three.

In another foxhole a mortar shell tore off a man's arm below the elbow. His buddies were all around him, silent in the dark. Next morning they found he had bled to death, in silence.

The Japs were firing their knee mortars on a flat trajectory by placing the curved bases against the trunks of trees. One mortar shell hit a tree, took a freak hop and landed in the company CP. Art Toothman, the mess sergeant, was mortally wounded. Pearson, his closest friend, was badly wounded beside him. The company commander, 1st Lt. Charles J. Hastings of Walla Walla, for whom the Ridge was named, was hit.

Two men with them were unhurt. One was Pfc. Earl Addington of Maupin, Oreg. They say of Addington that he has a one-track mind—communications—and it must be true because his first act when the shell hit was to check the phone. The wire was dead. He crawled from the foxhole, traced the wire to the break, repaired it, returned and reported the line in.

All night long the outfit remained silent and stable, picking off the Japs as they crept forward. The Japs were trying to confuse the Americans and to break up their defense by provoking them into revealing their positions. Next morning one man found that he and a Jap had spent the night in adjoining foxholes, so close together that either could have raised his head and spit in the other's face.

And next morning the positions on Hastings Ridge were still intact. From there the American attack moved forward until eventually all of New Georgia was cleared of Japs.

SECURITY MISSION

By Pvt. JUSTIN GRAY

*Pvt. Gray's story is a true report on one of his combat experiences.
He fought with the 3d Ranger Battalion in Sicily and Italy.*

ITALY—There were 12 of us. We were called by the colonel and told that we were to go on a security mission to guard a 4.2-mortar OP a half-mile in front of the lines. There was no tenseness—rather a certain sense of relaxation. It looked routine. We had been afraid that we would have to go on combat patrol.

We went back to our equipment, chattering. We were to meet the mortarmen—three observers—in half an hour. I drew two K rations, a dinner and a supper unit. Bills, our section leader, said: "Take *beaucoup* grenades." I took eight of them and made sure my bandolier was full of ammo. To make room for the grenades in my meat-can pouch, I put aside assorted Life Savers and dextrose tablets, keeping only a few peppermint drops. I started to pack.

Enemy artillery fire started laying in on us. Somebody said: "Those bastards down by Vesuvius. What the hell can we do with mortars? We can't even reach the Germans." I packed my field jacket, tooth brush and shaving equipment. I considered leaving my training gas mask behind but decided to take it. Stancil asked: "What are you going to do with a sharpshooter rifle, Gray? Shoot leaves?" I traded it in for an M1 with a boy who wasn't going on patrol. I filled my canteen with water and put leaves on my helmet.

We were on a little wooded knoll with short shrubby trees and shallow slit trenches. I leaned back in a trench, using my helmet as a headrest. I tried to kid with the boys. The tenseness mounted. Gerhardt, a Dutchman from Pennsylvania, made believe he was going to sleep. "Make me vake in 15 minutes." He always pretended to sleep but was more nervous than the rest of us.

Rona said: "Gray, don't you wish you were back in the noncombatant Engineers?" I snorted: "That redhead wouldn't love me so much if I were." My captain came along and suggested that I change my red-top socks so only the gray showed. "Sonuvabitch, these damned leggin' laces always break. Wish we had those new combat infantry boots." Sgt. Bills took over and told us the order we were to march in. Bills was to lead off. "Nemo next with his tommy, supported by Nickson. Ford follows with his BAR. High-Gear Hodal next with extra ammo. Rona will lead the riflemen. Gray, you bring up the rear."

Then silence. We continued to wait. It was about noon. Complete quiet on the entire sector. It was warm for September. There were no combat patrols hitting us. Then machine-gun fire started above us. We heard German machine pistols. Some *Tedeschi* had infiltrated behind our lines. We wondered if there were more where we were going. "Damn, there are only 12 of us."

I wondered how long the colonel wanted us to hold that OP if the Germans hit us. He never did tell us. "Why doesn't Bills go and find out?" "Gee, maybe a combat patrol would be better than this— at least you're moving." High-Gear Hodal started singing: "There's a Star-Spangled Banner waving somewhere, over a distant land so very far away. Only Uncle Sam's brave heroes get to go there; O how I wish I could go there, too . . ." Nickson swore: "I'll kill the bastard that wrote that song." But the tenseness relaxed. We were brave heroes far from home. Hodal was a cool character.

The three mortarmen came up and we moved out. We had a job to do; we were moving. I forgot my tension. I began to think of what I had to do and of the redhead back home.

Our lines were thinly stretched across the mountain. We had to go up through A Company, which was holding the line. It was surprising to see Rangers dug in like Infantry. The Army wasn't moving as fast as expected. I saw Stovell, my buddy in A Company. He yelled: "Bring back some souvenirs, Gray."

Our position was about a half-mile down the mountain in front of the lines. There were no Jerries in sight, and we reached it without incident. I could see Vesuvius and Naples in the distance. The valley stretched below us, green and clean. Overhead flew some P-38s on patrol. Everything looked easy. The mortarmen indicated the positions they wanted. We fanned out, knowing exactly what to do without orders. I took a position ahead of a little waddy. I threw off my pack and sat down. "Kay" Kyser called: "This is going to be a cinch." I thought so, too. I thought we'd be able to rest all afternoon. We deserved an easy job after the past few days.

I opened up my dinner unit and began to eat. Everybody was just as relaxed. We called back and forth to each other. We might as well have been out of combat. It was a beautiful clear day. Bills asked: "How about trading your cheese unit for my ham and eggs? I've got the GIs." I laughed at him. "The hell with you. I've got the GIs, too." I started munching away. There was so much undergrowth I couldn't see more than 15 yards ahead. One of the boys said: "It looks as though Italy couldn't grow a man-sized tree." Fleas started to itch in the seams of my pants. I scratched and swore.

Suddenly I saw something moving in the brush about 12 yards away. My jaw froze. I felt like vomiting. It was a Jerry. Only one, I hoped. He was coming right up the waddy. He came out in the open, looked around and turned to signal the others to come through. Another came in sight. I don't know what the hell I did. Instinctively I must have dropped my food and picked up my rifle. I was glad I'd traded my sharpshooter rifle for an M1; I could fire from the hip.

Without looking around I knew that Gerhardt had seen them, too. I knew I should have held my fire, but my finger squeezed the trigger. Almost immediately Gerhardt fired at the second one. Both of the Jerries went down. And then we knew there were many more Germans behind them. You could hear them moving in the bushes maybe 20 yards away, fanning out to see if we were an isolated unit or the main line.

It was only a matter of minutes before they would envelop us. Bills told us to cover our flanks. I moved way off to the right. I wondered whether Bills had asked the colonel if we had to hold this damned position. I was ready to leave. Some cinch! I got a pretty good position in a little defilade. I was still scared as a bastard. I wondered if the rest were as well located. At least the bullets couldn't reach me. I rose up to take a look. From my right flank a machine pistol sputtered. I smacked my face down on the ground. That was close. I took another look. Another machine pistol sputtered in front of me. A third one started on my left. I fired a couple of rounds at the man in front of me. Then I knew what was happening. One machine-pistolman was firing while the other two crawled closer to me. I could hear them. Then another fired and the other two crawled. I couldn't rise up any more to fire back.

I heard a scream on my left. Nemo was standing up, his tommy gun in his hands. He was hit in the chest. He ran at the Germans. A machine pistol opened up and tore the top of his head off. The rim of his helmet dropped down around his neck. I turned away and saw one of the mortarmen firing futilely with a .45 automatic.

My three Jerries were about six yards away. I could hear them. I couldn't do a thing. Suddenly I heard myself screaming: "Bills, Bills, get me the hell out of here." And there was Bills at my side. He had rushed down and surprised the Jerries. He killed two. I got the other.

It was time to leave the position. More Jerries were coming up. We all knew now that it was a full-fledged German assault on the main American lines. We could do no more good there. Bills gave the order and we started to retreat in pairs. Gerhardt covered me. I covered Gerhardt. We had to leave Nemo behind.

It was hard going up the steep mountain. It hadn't been so steep when we came down. I thought about throwing away my rifle so I could scramble more quickly. The rifle was in my way, and I couldn't use my hands. "If we can only get up to A Company," I thought. "We have to warn them. What if they don't recognize us? What if they fire on us?"

We reached the top. We made it. The Germans hadn't been aggressive enough. A Company recognized us and held their fire.

I saw Stovell and dropped into his ditch. I just looked up and said: "Sorry, Stovell. No souvenirs."

SGT. KEVIN McCARTHY

The Personal History of an Infantryman in the South Pacific

By Sgt. MERLE MILLER

SOMEWHERE IN THE SOUTH PACIFIC—In an obscure corner of his foot locker Sgt. Kevin A. McCarthy keeps a small tin box containing the souvenirs he has collected since April 1942 when he first arrived in the South Pacific.

He has Australian shillings, New Caledonian francs, a sou from the Hebrides and a few Japanese invasion coins he picked up during some 50 days under fire on Guadalcanal.

"They'll make a nice necklace for Lorraine," he explains. Lorraine is Miss Lorraine Meilke, who is head waitress in a cafe in his home town, Jamestown, N. Dak.

In addition, Mac—as he is known to privates and lieutenant colonels in the 164th Infantry Regiment—has a Jap soldier's pay book, some Nipponese machine-gun shells and citations, and his superior officers have recommended him for a Distinguished Service Cross.

But Mac, a blue-eyed, 21-year-old section leader of two machine-gun squads of Company H in the 164th, would gladly swap his citations for a chance to return to his home at 302 Third Avenue, S. E., in Jamestown. There was a time, during the peak of the Battle of Guadalcanal, when he hoped he would be home in a few weeks. In his less optimistic moments he repeats the slogan that is chanted everywhere in this area, "Golden Gate in '48."

Except for one 15-day furlough in June 1941, he has not been home since he was inducted into Federal service with the North Dakota National Guard on Feb. 10, 1941. Since he sailed from the mainland early last year bound for an unknown Pacific destination, his 19-year-old brother William has been drafted and is now a member of a Tank Destroyer outfit at Camp Hood, Tex. Another brother, Robert, 17, has enrolled in the Navy V program for college and pre-flight training at the Valley State Teachers College.

John, 15; Donald, 13; Tommy, 11, and two sisters, Margaret, who is 8, and Mary, 6, are still at home with Mac's father and mother, Mr. and Mrs. William S. McCarthy.

A cousin on his mother's side, Pvt. Don Tracy of Jamestown, is a Japanese prisoner of war; he was a medic on Bataan. Two other cousins, Pvt. Francis Tracy of Hettinger, N. Dak., a field artilleryman, and Pvt. James Tracy of Jamestown, member of a searchlight outfit, have been under fire in North Africa.

Mac gets a letter from Lorraine at least once, sometimes twice a week, and his mother writes every Sunday. Occasionally he hears from Father Gerrity, who is still at St. James', and from some of the nuns who were his teachers at St. John's Academy. He was graduated in June 1939, one of a class of 36.

Like most Americans in the Army, Mac had not planned to be a soldier. At St. John's he took a business course, typing and shorthand. For several summers he worked on Dakota wheat farms. One summer he was a laborer in Yellowstone Park, and another he worked with his father, a section boss for the Northern Pacific Railroad.

Ever since he can remember, Mac has gone rabbit hunting in the winter. He was a Boy Scout, a member of the Catholic Youth Organization, and played football and basketball in high school.

After his graduation he took a job as a short-order cook working nights in a small cafe. That was only temporary. Two evenings a week, from 7:30 to 9 P.M., he drilled in the local armory. He had enlisted in Company H of the 164th in the summer of 1938 mainly "because almost all the fellows I knew were joining the National Guard."

When Company H and the rest of the North Dakota National Guard were inducted into Federal service, he was a private first class, the No. 2 gunner on a Browning heavy .30 machine gun. He was working in a garage then, towing used cars from Milwaukee to Jamestown.

Nobody thought much about it when he and 64 other Jamestown boys left for Camp Claiborne, La. They were going away for a year; that was all.

"It'll do you good," said his father, who had been a private in a Quartermaster outfit on the high seas when the 1918 Armistice came.

Mac thought Claiborne was tough. The 164th was temporarily attached to the 34th Division, which later took part in the first landing in North Africa and fought the famous battle of Hill 609 in Tunisia. Like the others, the men of Company H drilled with wooden rifles and broomsticks. They went on a few night maneuvers, sleeping in shelter halves and bitching, and in August and September took part in the Louisiana maneuvers.

Someone occasionally chalked OHIO signs on the barracks. That meant "Over the Hill in October," and there was a lot of beefing when Congress passed the bill extending service to 18 months.

Late in November a corporal from New York City was making bets that the United States would be at war with Japan by Dec. 12. Everybody laughed at him—until he collected $500 the morning of Dec. 8. That morning the 164th was alerted and on Dec. 12 started for the West Coast.

They were in San Francisco a few days, attached to the San Francisco Bay Defense and sleeping in the stalls of a livestock pavilion. On Christmas Day they were on their way to Oregon, and Chaplain Thomas J. Tracy of Bismarck, N. Dak., said mass in the snow beside the train.

In a few more weeks they were on their way to California again, this time to prepare for shipment overseas. Latrine rumor said their destination was Australia, and Mac bought a map of the Pacific to see how far he'd be from North Dakota. They sailed on Mar. 18.

In Australia he had two dates with a girl whose name he can't remember, but "she was lots of fun, and she thought all Americans, including me, were wonderful. We had a swell time."

A few days later the 164th sailed from Australia for a place Mac had never heard about. It was New Caledonia.

There he walked seven miles to see 2-year-old movies and learned a few words of French, like saying *bon jour* or *tres jolie* to the girls. He learned to drink hot chocolate instead of coffee and fought mosquitoes that made the memories of Camp Claiborne seem like kindergarten stuff.

The training program was tougher, too. Ten days in the field was not unusual, and Mac and his crew took turns carrying their Browning automatic and its tripod. The gun with water weighed 40 pounds, the tripod 54, and the ammunition 21 pounds per box. There were times both in New Cal and later when he and the crew swore the whole shebang weighed a ton. In the crew were Pfcs. Alvin Knapp of Groton, S. Dak., second in command; James Johnson of Jamestown, No. 1 gunner; Carl Bowlin of Duluth, Minn., No. 2 gunner; and Emory Mercer of Kankakee, Ill., and David Smercansky of Glen Robbins, Ohio, ammunition carriers.

About the time they'd decided they'd be in New Cal for the duration, secret orders came through. Sergeants from headquarters said it was Guadalcanal. On the evening of Oct. 12, 1942, they saw the dim, shadowy outline of the Solomon Islands. It was Mac's twenty-first birthday.

The first scouts left the ship in Higgins landing boats at a spot near Lunga Point on the north central shore of the 'Canal. At 5 A.M. Mac's party landed, and an hour later they were bombed for the first time by two-motored Mitsubishi bombers.

"Sure we were scared," Mac will tell you. "Show me a man who says he isn't scared when he's under fire, and I'll show you a liar."

It took several hours to unload the transports, and Mac piled ammunition on the beach. There were two other raids during the day, and at dusk Jap artillery near Point Cruz fired on them intermittently. That night everyone dug foxholes, deep but not as deep as they were to dig later. About midnight a Jap naval force began firing toward the shore. Fourteen-inchers and star shells zoomed over their heads, but there were no hits.

"It was the noise that got you," Mac recalls. "You thought it would never stop. You thought every shell had your number on it. That night was the worst for most of us, I guess. Probably because it was the first."

The shelling stopped at daylight, and there was another bombing attack at 5 A.M. That made the fourth. There were 30 during the first 10 days.

The 164th moved into the perimeter of defense about a quarter of a mile north of Henderson Field, relieving the Marines. "They were so glad to see us, some of them lay right down on the ground and cried," Mac says.

On Oct. 26, the second day of what has since become known as the Battle of Henderson Field, Mac performed what Col. Bryant E. Moore, then commanding the 164th, said was "commendable service in keeping with the traditions and past performances of our regiment."

What he did seemed ordinary enough to Mac. "Anybody would have acted the same way."

He and his crew were manning the last gun on the Second Battalion flank, about half a mile northeast of Henderson on the perimeter of defense. Japs were moving up with infantry supported by machine-gun and mortar fire. The orders were to hold.

About 50 yards to the left was the Lunga River; to the right was a thick jungle in which a detachment of Japs was firing light machine guns. About 200 yards straight ahead the Japs had established a CP, and in front of the CP and directly in the Jap line of fire was a Marine outpost. There had been heavy fire for about 15 hours, and the Japs were advancing.

That was when Mac got his idea. It was easy to see the marines couldn't last long under the heavy

Nip barrage, so he shouted to Pvt. Thomas Campbell of Minneapolis, Minn., who was driving up a Bren-gun carrier filled with ammunition.

"We can save those marines. Want to help?"

"Okay," said Campbell. Cpl. Floyd Springer of Jamestown, who was in charge of a nearby gun squad, also agreed. So did Knapp. The four of them mounted a light machine gun on the rear of the carrier. There was already one on the front, and they were ready.

Cpl. Bob Havelick and Pfc. Leroy Chilson, both of Jamestown, opened the barbed-wire gate in front of the gun position, and with Campbell driving and Mac, Knapp and Springer keeping up a heavy barrage of fire, they moved to the spot where they thought the marines were.

Although it was only mid-afternoon it was dark as night, and they missed the marines. Then they drove back to their gun, and Mac shouted to the marines. One of them stood up, and Mac shot an azimuth with his compass. They started a second time and brought back seven marines in the carrier. On the third trip they brought back two who were wounded and three others, and on the fourth they rescued the last eight. In all, 20 were saved.

The Battle for Henderson Field lasted until dawn on Oct. 27, when the Jap offensive was repulsed and Mac and his crew, who had been three days and three nights without sleep, were relieved.

They rested for two days and on the morning of Nov. 2 began moving with the rest of the Second Battalion toward Koli Point, where a reported Jap force of 3,000 had been landed. They marched almost 170 miles in nine days, fighting every inch of the way after the second day, taking turns carrying their gun, tripod and ammunition and sleeping on the ground. They had one hot meal in nine days.

They would shout at the Japs "Surrender, you bastards!" and the Japs would holler back "Hell with you" or something less printable. When they charged, the Japs would shout in English, "Blood for the Emperor."

On the evening of Nov. 12, Mac and his squad watched the biggest naval battle of the Solomons, only 20 miles off shore, between the islands of Savo and Tulagi. "It was a pretty big thing, I guess; I mean it was exciting and all, but it just reminded me of the fireworks at the Stutsman County Fair back home," Mac says.

The next day the Japs were driven from Koli Point, and Mac had two days of rest. Then the regiment was sent to Point Cruz to relieve another outfit. Of that engagement, he says: "We didn't get into much of the heavy fighting. We dug in for 28 days; we didn't have one hot meal in all that time, and there were so many air raids I forgot to count them. It was mostly a holding action."

When they were relieved, the battle was nearly over. Company H moved behind the lines and was placed on guard duty. On Dec. 22 Mac came down with malaria, and he spent Christmas in the hospital. After five days he was back on guard duty, but on Jan. 28 the medics ordered his evacuation to this quiet South Pacific island. He had been made a sergeant on Jan. 13.

Mac is no story-book soldier. He does not pretend he enjoys war. He's been in the South Pacific for almost a year and a half now, and he wants to hear American spoken again. First, however, he recognizes that a war must be won.

He is proud of the Infantry, prouder than he was when he became a soldier in February 1941. "They said airplanes would win the war," he says. "Well, they help, sure. They're necessary. But over the 'Canal and in North Africa and every place else they find out that in the clinches it's not the planes or the tanks, it's the Infantry that wins wars."

Sometimes he worries about what will happen after the war, worries about a job and whether he wants to spend the rest of his life in Jamestown or whether he'll stay in the Army. He worries mainly about the fact that in the Infantry he hasn't learned a trade, and he thinks the Army ought to give all infantrymen a chance to learn one after the war.

Meantime, he's anxious only to finish the hard fighting that he knows lies ahead. "It's like going to the dentist; you don't like it, but it has to be done."

Down on the 'Canal he got acquainted with Capt. (now Maj.) Joe Foss of Sioux Falls, S. Dak.

What did they talk about?

"We talked about home, of course," says Mac, "and wondered how the crops had been and if things would be changed when we get back. What else is there to talk about?"

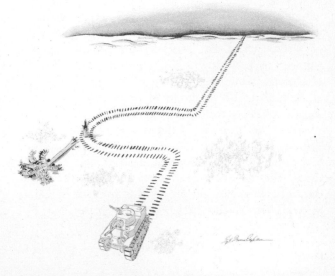

THE PARTISAN FROM BROOKLYN

BY SGT. HARRY SIONS

SOMEWHERE IN ITALY—About the middle of the afternoon of July 14, 1944, a rough-looking, oddly dressed character walked up to the entrance gate of a parachute battalion's encampment here and said he wanted to go inside. The stranger wore British Army shoes, mustard-colored cotton pants, a torn GI paratrooper's jacket and an Italian straw hat with an orange band. Cpl. Milo Peck of Barre, Mass., who was standing guard at the gate, was not impressed.

"And what do you want inside?" asked Peck.

"I want to report to my outfit," the stranger said. "I'm Manuel Serrano. Don't you remember me?"

"Serrano!" said Peck. "I thought you were dead a long time ago, back in Tunisia. Where the hell have you been all this time?"

"Well," said Serrano, "I've been to a lot of places, but for the last 10 months I've been fighting with the Eyetie Partisans up in the hills."

"Well, I'll be damned," said Peck. "Come on in."

And that was how Sgt. Manuel Serrano, the first American soldier known to have fought with the Italian Partisans, returned to his outfit after an absence of 20 months.

Serrano is a six-footer, deeply sunburned and husky. He has a small black mustache and thick black hair streaked with gray. Born in Puerto Rico 24 years ago, he had lived in Brooklyn, N. Y., since he was 5, and before the war played the maraccas and drums in a rumba band in a Greenwich Village hot spot. In February 1942 he volunteered for the Paratroops, trained at Fort Benning, Ga., and found himself in rapid succession at a POE, in England and on the North Africa invasion.

A month after the November 1942 landing in Tunisia, Serrano—then a buck sergeant acting as first sergeant—was on a mission to blow up a bridge near El Djem. His patrol was surprised by the Jerries, a few of the 38 GIs were killed and several, including Serrano, were captured.

Four days later Serrano was put on an Italian destroyer with a batch of other Allied prisoners and shipped to an Italian prison camp at Palermo, Sicily. When Serrano arrived at Palermo, he weighed 190 pounds. When he was transferred to the Italian mainland one month later, he weighed 145 pounds.

His first stop in Italy was a concentration camp called No. 59, at Servigliano on the Adriatic coast.

He stayed there nine months. No. 59 had an assortment of American and British prisoners, Yugoslav Partisans, Albanians and Jews of various nationalities. When they heard via the grapevine of the Italian surrender in September 1943, they made a general break.

The day after the break, Serrano met three of the Yugoslavs in the hills. They were on their way to an Italian Partisan camp in the mountains near Sarnano, about 60 miles to the south. Serrano asked the Yugoslavs what the Italians did and was told they killed Germans and Fascists. That was good enough for him, so he went along.

It took Serrano and the Yugoslavs three days to make the Partisan camp. The hide-out was buried so deeply in the mountain underbrush that they would never have found it except for the help of a friendly farmer. At the hide-out they met 50 Italians and a few more Yugoslavs. The Partisans weren't too happy about their new recruits. They had scarcely enough food or weapons for themselves, and they wanted to know why Serrano had come without a good rifle and something to eat. They tried to prevent him, but he stayed.

Two weeks later Serrano was picked to go on his first raid. Like all Partisan raids, it would be made at night. The objective was Penna, about 15 miles to the east, where the raiders were to pick up several of the town's leading Fascists and bring them back to camp for trial.

Early in the afternoon a couple of Partisans dressed in civvies circulated through the town to check on the number of Jerries there. If the place was heavy with Jerries, the raid would have to be postponed. There were only a few Jerries around. The raid was on.

Serrano and 19 other Partisans made their way down the mountain paths to the outskirts of the town where they waited for complete darkness. Then they sneaked in, one by one.

"I was pretty nervous," says Serrano. "They taught me a lot of tricks at Benning and in England, but Fascist-hunting wasn't one of them. Those Eyetie towns close up early at night, and of course there weren't any street lights. I couldn't hear a sound except maybe a dog howling far off or the footsteps of a Jerry or a Fascist *carabiniere* patrolling the street. I'd duck down until he passed, praying he wouldn't see me."

Serrano headed for the house of a Partisan sympathizer, first making sure that a red light was showing in the window; this meant the coast was clear. Inside he found the other Partisans. The sympathizer led them to the houses of the five Fascists on the night's calling list. Four or five Partisans worked each house, quietly and smoothly. They bound and gagged the Fascists and carried them swiftly out of town and up to the Partisan camp in the hills.

"They hanged those five Fascists," says Serrano. "They gave them a trial and then they hanged them. But the Partisans didn't always hang the Fascists they caught. It depended on what they were accused of. If they worked with the Jerries, or if they were black-market operators, then they were sure to get strung up. Some of them helped Jerry fight us, especially if we were caught in a tough spot and it wasn't too dangerous for them. Or they'd denounce us to Jerry if they knew where we were hanging out. Or they'd pick up escaped Allied prisoners for the Germans; they got 3,000 *lire* for every prisoner they captured, dead or alive.

"In a way, those black-market operators were the meanest of all the Eyetie Fascists. That La Marche region is a very poor country, and by the time the Germans got through stealing everything worth while, it was poorer still. The people have just enough to keep themselves and their kids alive. Well, these black-market operators were all big-shot Fascists. They'd corner the market on shoes, or *pasta*, or clothes, and then they'd sell them at terrific prices. They'd been doing it for 22 years, but they really went to town when the Germans came in. There was one town where the shoemaker —he was a Fascist—was charging such wild prices that an ordinary Eyetie couldn't buy shoes. We finally got that guy, along with all his shoes. We hanged him and handed out his shoes to the poor people of the town.

"Some of the Fascists we let go—if they weren't active in the party but just paid their dues or turned on the radio to listen to Il Duce when they were ordered to. We scared the sugar out of them first before we let them go. Some of them even wanted to join up with us, but the Partisans wouldn't have them.

"And then there were some in-between Fascists we let go, but we gave them the castor-oil treatment first—just so they'd have a taste of what they used to hand out. We'd raid the Fascist headquarters and grab their stocks of bottled castor oil. Then we'd dose it out. If a Fascist was in the party 10 years, then we'd give him 10 doses, a dose a

year. I know; it doesn't sound pretty. But if you expect a pretty story, I might as well stop now."

When the going was tough, the Partisans hid out for weeks in the mountain recesses, in caves or in forest groves on the hillsides. They wore nondescript uniforms—part British, part German, part American, part civilian clothes. Their only weapons were a few old Italian Army rifles and *ballila* (hand grenades) and some captured German pistols. They carried sharpened Italian bayonets and used them as knives. Six months after Serrano joined the Partisans, British planes dropped machine guns and rifles to them.

The band of Partisans to which Serrano belonged was evidently only one of many bands operating all over Italy, wherever the Germans were. The units were organized and controlled through a radio station known as *Italia Combatte* (Italy Fights).

"Every night," Serrano says, "we'd turn on the radio to listen to our code signal, '*Sole tra monte* (the sun is between the mountains).' When we heard that, we'd take down the instructions for our next raid.

"These orders came in code, too. 'Pietro's beard is white' might mean to blow up a railroad bridge. 'The snow in Russia is getting cold' might mean to tear down telephone wires along a certain road. The Jerries kept putting the wires up and we kept tearing them down. It got the Jerries so sore they'd shoot anybody they caught standing near a telephone pole."

Some of the instructions were repeated every night, such as the order to shoot individual Jerry motorcyclists or to help escaped Allied prisoners. Other instructions were longer and more involved. Serrano recalls one order about catching a big-shot Fascist in the town of Ascoli. The radio listed the homes the Fascist lived in at different times, his favorite coffee shops and the hours he visited them, his latest mistress and the color of her hair, and the address of their love nest. We located that Fascist late at night in the love nest, where he was waiting for his girl friend to show up. We didn't bother taking him back to the mountains. We let him have it right there."

The band was organized on a semimilitary basis. "There was a captain in the Italian Regular Army," says Serrano. "He was our CO. He gave the orders, and I mean orders. He was tough. Then there were a couple of lieutenants, I guess you'd call them. They were in charge of the units when we went out on a job. And about a half-dozen sergeants. The rest of us, including me, were privates. Of course, rank didn't make much difference in where we slept or what we ate. There weren't any special officers' quarters in our caves, and we all ate the same food when we got it."

The Partisans had no special insignia but they always wore something red. "Didn't make any difference what it was," Serrano says. "A red scarf, or a red handkerchief, or a red arm band. At first I thought it meant they were all communists, but they hardly ever talked politics. So one day I asked one of the lieutenants, and he explained that they wore these red things, first because the Yugoslav Partisans wore red, but mostly because it was the color the Jerries and the Fascists hated most."

The Partisans in Serrano's band came from all classes. There were workers and a couple of businessmen. There were Italian sailors, and officers and men of the Italian Army. And for a few months there were a couple of GIs from the 1st Division who had been captured and then escaped.

One of the most important Partisan jobs was to help escaped American and British prisoners. Serrano estimates that his band helped more than 100 prisoners back to Allied lines. Three girls worked with the Partisans on these deals, getting the names, ranks and serial numbers of escaped prisoners who had taken refuge in farmhouses in the area. The Partisans radioed this information to Allied headquarters at Bari.

But not all the escaped prisoners were able to make the Allied lines. Many of them were caught. If the Germans got them, the prisoners were usually just taken back to their prison camps. But they weren't always that lucky if the Fascists caught them first.

One morning in March, while the Partisans were camping in the hills near Comunanza in the La Marche region, a farmer reported that the Fascists had captured and killed six escaped Allied prisoners. They had stripped the prisoners of their identifications and clothes, he said, and had taken them to a field near by. Then they had forced the prisoners to dig a long shallow ditch. When the ditch was dug, the Fascists machine-gunned the prisoners, threw their bodies into the ditch and covered them with a few shovelfuls of dirt.

"That night," Serrano says, "three of us made for the field. We saw the ditch but the bodies had disappeared. We checked around and learned that nuns had taken the bodies to the convent in Comunanza after the Fascists left. We went to the convent and there were the six bodies, wrapped in white sheets and lying on slabs of wood. The nuns had cleaned the bodies and wrapped them in the sheets. I lifted up the covers from the faces and

recognized them all. Four were GIs from the 1st Division, the other two were British. The nuns said they would give them a decent burial. Then we left.

"I walked out of that convent and back up the hills to camp. When I got to the top of the first hill I turned around toward the convent and those six dead soldiers, and I swore that for each one of those soldiers I would kill a Fascist with my bare hands. I think for the first time I really knew what it meant to be a Partisan."

Even the Jerries didn't like the Italian Fascists, Serrano says. "Once when I was walking down the main street in Porto San Giorgio, dressed in civvies, I saw a Jerry soldier walk past an Italian Fascist officer without saluting him. The officer stopped the Jerry and said: 'Why didn't you salute me?' The Jerry took his pistol out of its holster, bashed the Fascist on the head and killed him. 'That's my salute to you,' he said and walked away.

"The Jerries stopped me three times, but only to ask directions. They thought I was an Eyetie—I was dark and spoke the language with the accent of the La Marche people. Once in Servigliano a Jerry stopped me on the street and asked the way to a certain road. While we were talking he pulled out a pack of Chesterfields and offered me one. I asked him where he got American cigarettes and he laughed. He told me they came from Red Cross parcels for the prisoners of No. 59. Later I learned that the Fascists had kept the parcels for themselves, but when the Germans came in they took the parcels away from them."

From April to June the Germans started going after the Partisans in earnest. Jerry planes tried to bomb them out of the hills and mortars tried to blast them out. In the last week of April a mixed unit of Fascists and Jerries had the band surrounded for three days.

"Most of us got away," says Serrano, "but five were caught. The Fascists hanged them. Not a quick hanging, like we gave them, but the slow Fascist hanging. They pulled the bodies up above the ground, then let them down slowly till the toes touched the ground, then up again after a while. That way the hangings could last a couple of days. I tell you, those Fascists were no good. The Yugoslavs were right. When we had that first trial, they said: 'What are you wasting time with trials for? Hang the swine.'"

The Partisans did not let the enemy hold the offensive against them but struck back. "One day about the end of June," says Serrano, "we did a job on a Jerry convoy that was moving north up a mountain road near Sarnano. A guy named Giulio was in charge of a forward patrol of eight men. This Giulio was about 21 years old and a little guy, but he had a pair of shoulders as broad as this. He ran away from Rome when the Jerries started sending the young Eyeties to work up north.

"Each man in Giulio's patrol had a Bren machine gun, part of a supply the British had dropped down to us. The patrol was waiting on a rise just overlooking a bend in the road when the convoy showed up ahead of time. There were five trucks, loaded with supplies, and about 200 Germans.

"Giulio let go at the first truck and put it out of commission. Then the other Partisans fired their Brens at the rest of the trucks. The Jerries scrambled out and took cover behind their trucks. For five minutes there was a hot little battle. Then the Jerries ran, with the eight Partisans chasing after them. Giulio caught two Jerries and was disarming them when one Jerry pulled a pistol on him. That got Giulio mad. He lined them up against a tree and machine-gunned them."

When the rest of the Partisan band arrived, they burned the Jerry trucks, first removing all the supplies of food, clothing, pictures and silverware stolen from Italian homes. The Partisans counted 20 Jerry dead and picked up seven wounded, whom they took to the British hospital at Ascoli.

The next day the Germans came back in force, blowing up seven houses in the vicinity with mines. "They blamed the people for not warning them," Serrano says. "The people knew, all right. They always knew."

But the Partisans had their revenge, too. As the Germans retreated by night over the back roads before the advancing British, the Partisans struck and ran and struck again. For three straight nights they raided all the neighboring towns, seizing and shooting all the Fascists they could find. They used up all the ammunition from the Brens and all the fire they had taken from the Germans.

"I told the Partisans," Serrano says. "I told them: 'Get all the Fascists now, before the Allies get here. They might be too easy on them.'"

On the fourth day the captain called the Partisan band together and told them their work in La Marche was done. Those who wished could go up north to continue the fight behind the enemy lines.

Serrano made his way back up to Servigliano and rested for a few days in the home of an Italian friend. Those were happy, confused days for the people of Servigliano. The Germans had gone and so had most of the town Fascists, but the British had not yet arrived. The people dug up all the *vino* they had hidden from the Nazis and they danced in the streets. At night they gathered in their homes and drank and sang the half-forgotten songs of a free Italy, songs they had not dared to sing in the open for 22 years. Partisans who hadn't seen their families for months came back, hailed as heroes.

On the day Serrano left, he made a speech in the town *piazza*. "I told them I'd be back some day," he says, "and that I would tell the American soldiers what I had learned from the Partisans. They begged me to stay. They even wanted to make me mayor of the town. In fact, they wanted to give me the town's prettiest girl for a wife. But I guess I'll wait till I get back to Brooklyn and find a nice Italian girl there. I like these Eyeties. Maybe it's because I'm a Latin, too, and understand them a little better than some other American soldiers."

Forty miles from Servigliano, Serrano met an American Paratroop major, who told him where Serrano's old outfit was stationed. It wasn't very far away. A truck gave Serrano a lift and dropped him about eight miles from his unit camp.

"I walked those last eight miles," says Serrano. "But it felt like floating on air."

Back in camp Serrano met his old buddies. There were 75 left out of the original outfit as it was activated at Benning more than two years ago. After Tunisia, where Serrano was captured, the battalion had gone on to fight in Sicily and in Italy.

"I don't know what the outfit's going to have me do," says Serrano, whose first sergeant's rating came through a couple of weeks after he was captured in Tunisia. Whatever happens to him, he won't be short of folding money. He has 20 months' pay as a top kick coming, plus $50 a month jump pay, plus 20 percent overseas pay.

"I don't know what I'll do, but I know what I'd like to do. I'd like to drop back behind the Jerry lines again with an M1 and take 20 of these fellows with me."

"This is Sgt. Hunter. L-o-o-k o-u-t h-e i-s p-l-e-n-t-y t-o-u-g-h."—*Pvt. Tom Zibelli, Camp Davis, N. C.*

THE SERGEANT AND HIS ADAM'S APPLE START A SENSATION IN CHINA

By Sgt. MARION HARGROVE

SOMEWHERE IN CHINA—Their post is hundreds of miles off any beaten track, and they don't see even an American plane more than once a month or so. There's only a handful of them, with three or four officers. Neither the town nor the hostel offers anything in the way of amusement. There's no radio, no newspapers, not even an occasional GI movie.

"What do you do for entertainment around here, besides wearing out that checkerboard over there?" I asked.

A corporal replied: "We get along. We go shopping in the evenings."

"And we 'make face' with the Chinese," said a sergeant.

This sounding intriguing in a dull sort of way, and since the corporal intended to go to town that night in search of a package of envelopes he had no hope of finding, I decided to tag along.

We passed a couple of Chinese theaters and stopped to see what pictures were showing. There was a double feature at one house—an ancient film starring Jessie Matthews, the British actress, and "The Return of the Cisco Kid." All three of us had seen both of them in better days. The other theater advertised a gripping Chinese drama with some appetizing stills.

"We might see the Jessie Matthews picture and the 'Cisco Kid,'" I suggested, but the corporal and sergeant both turned thumbs down. "You wouldn't hear the thing," they explained. "The pictures probably have Chinese subtitles, and when you get a whole house full of the townspeople reading the subtitles aloud to each other, you wouldn't be able to hear even the fire siren."

The only thing left was to go in search of the nonexistent envelopes and attend to the little matter of "face making."

The corporal explained that his command of the Mandarin language was extensive, so he did all the talking. At the first shop we entered there were a number of Chinese envelopes, the kind with the bright red rectangle for the address. After the usual greeting—"Hao pu hao," which literally means "good not good" and passes for "How are you?"—the corporal started his palaver by pointing to the envelopes.

"En lai kan kan," he said. This is very good Mandarin and means "Pick up bring see see." The shopkeeper picked up brought see see. The corporal looked sadly at the envelopes and shook his head. "Ni yu mei yu mei-kua—?" he said. This was all right as far as it went; it meant "Haven't you got any American—?" but he got stuck when he came to the word for envelopes.

"That," said the corporal, "is a helluva note."

While all this was going on, accompanied by urgent gestures by the corporal, the sergeant was busy outside "making face" with the Chinese. By this time there were about 50 village children staring and giggling at him.

"Ni kan ni kan," said the sergeant, expressing in beautiful Mandarin the command, "You see, you see." The sergeant pointed to his throat, from which protruded a large but decorous Adam's apple. The children gawked attentively and the sergeant swallowed hard, with a loud and musical gulp. His Adam's apple slid down his throat and rose majestically again, to await a repeat performance.

The children gasped and burst into roars of wonderment and joy. The performing larynx moved beautifully up and down, making a tuneful gulp with each downward glide, and the children grew tense with excitement. Several of them tried to do the trick themselves but, not having Adam's apples, were unsuccessful.

Now the corporal emerged from the shop, looked with solemn severity over the crowd, and began to wave his finger at child after child as he chanted the mystic phrase: "Meeny, meeny, tipsy teeny." Then, with great dignity, "Applejack and Johnny Sweeney. Have a peach, have a plum, have a stick of chewing gum!" The corporal's finger flew at a frightened little Chinese face and the other children shrieked with relief and enjoyment. The corporal swung toward them once more. "O-U-T spells out and out you go, you dirty old dishrag, you!"

The sergeant opened his umbrella and pushed it gently through the crowd, which now numbered at least 150 children and a few scattered adults. We headed down the street and the crowd fell in behind us like a parade. The sergeant began to swing the umbrella the way a drum major twirls his baton, to the immense delight of the children, their parents and a couple of white foreigners who applauded loudly. Away we went.

At the next shop, the sergeant inquired for envelopes, while the corporal "made face" with the townspeople. This time he changed his routine by hotly winking one eye, which is apparently impossible for the Chinese to do, and by wiggling his eyebrows rather furiously.

The crowd had swelled to 225 as we headed for the river. They left us at the bridge, and we entered a tea boat for refreshments. "I've heard a lot about 'making face,'" I said over our third cup of tea. "Is that what it is?"

"That's all there is to it," said the corporal. This was a crock of extremely erroneous information.

"You know," said the sergeant, "I've been out here only three months, but they say after you've been here a year or so, you start turning a little whacky." The corporal answered, "That's all imagination. Like as not, China won't have any effect one way or another on either of us."

"No," I said rather weakly, "not a chance." I got the hell out of there the next day.

"Ya sure there's no liquor in there, Mac?"—Sgt. Frank Brandt.

THE FIRST YANK WHO DIDN'T MEET THE BRITISH EIGHTH ARMY

By Sgt. MILTON LEHMAN

SOMEWHERE IN TUNISIA [By Radio]—If the trip hadn't gone sour and if I had been able to find the right road, I might have been the first American to meet the British Eighth Army.

That day when all those Yanks were shaking hands, laughing and passing around flasks of Scotch and cigarettes with the Eighth Army Tommies somewhere on the road between Gabes and Gafsa, I was one of the few Joes who had absolutely nothing to do with the historic meeting. In fact, I am a little bit disgusted with the whole business.

Now don't get me wrong. It's not that the meeting of the Americans and the British Eighth Army wasn't a fine thing and a good meeting, as good

meetings go. Military historians will write in their books that Sgt. Joe Randall of State Center, Iowa, greeted Sgt. A. W. Acland of Maida Vale, London, with the words, "Hello, you bloody limey," and Acland replied, "Very glad to see you."

The historians may also note that T/5 Ed Berg of Albany, N. Y., had the accelerator of his jeep down to the floor but couldn't quite pass Sgt. Randall in the photo-finish of the American race to Acland's outstretched hand. T/5 Berg's classic remark for the history books might have been quite different if Sgt. Randall's armored car hadn't gotten there first. As it turned out, T/5 Berg merely snorted:

"The bastard beat me."

While all this excitement was transpiring at the famous spot on the Gabes road, I was back in Gafsa, studying a map of the Southern Tunisian terrain, trying to figure out what happened to me during my trip to Mdilla.

I got mixed up in that trip to Mdilla because I was just as willing as the next fellow to be the first American soldier to meet the British Eighth Army. I had an inside tip that Australian armored cars were going to break through and shake hands with the Americans somewhere near that town.

So I jumped into my jeep and headed for Mdilla. I thought of several historic statements to make when I welcomed Gen. Montgomery's boys and finally decided to say, "Franklin Delano Roosevelt, Dwight D. Eisenhower and George A. Patton asked me to send their greetings, and I also bring tidings from the American enlisted men. We will fight a good fight together."

That would have made much better copy for the historians than "Hello, you bloody limey."

However, I never found Mdilla. Furthermore, the Australian armored cars were not able to get through the German mine field in the neighborhood of Kebili that day. It was a bad break for both of us.

I did everything I could. I found a sign on the outskirts of Gafsa which read "MDILLA—14 KM" and pointed to the right, down a dirt road. I turned right and the road wasn't so bad—for the first 200 yards. Then it became very bad in a big way. The small ruts in the road turned into great chasms which lifted the rear end of my jeep high into the air and pointed the front end down into the ground every 20 seconds or so.

It was a nice warm day with a brisk African wind that started to whip up a sandstorm and threatened to lift me out of my jeep every time we went around a curve. There was no shrubbery in sight with the possible exception of a few clumps of cactus and a bushy and lonesome burro whose master had probably forgotten to beat him for the last few days and who had come out there to get away from it all.

Every time the road met a clump of cactus it divided and became three other roads. When you are out in the middle of a desert, no road makes sense unless it goes matter-of-factly in one direction. This one went in a dozen directions, branching all over the place like a pear tree.

I took the road with the most shallow ruts and followed it until I got so hungry that I had to stop and open my C rations. I had lunch there in the middle of the desert with gusts of sand blowing into the can to season my vegetable hash. A few planes circled overhead, which I hoped were friendly.

After lunch, I kept on moving, making decisions every 10 minutes about which road to take. There was no sign anywhere of the British Eighth Army. In fact there was no sign of anything except one young camel, sitting and sunning himself by the side of the road.

About 3 o'clock in the afternoon, I began to think less of the British Eighth Army and more about getting back to my bivouac. For the next hour, I let the jeep make the decisions for itself and it did a good job, bringing me with great relief to an American command car which I followed to an area near Djebel where Lt. Robert Porter of Warren, Pa., was bivouacked with his artillery battery from the Ninth Division.

Lt. Porter, whose words I took as authority, said he hadn't seen the British Eighth Army either. Then T/Sgt. Perry Maki of South Swansea, Mass., who used to run the 100-yard dash for Boston College, pointed out the direction to Gafsa and I started away from the battery. Being something of a pioneer by nature, I headed the jeep across country. I came out on a road 10 yards from a familiar-looking sign which pointed toward the right and read: "MDILLA—14 KM."

I never found the British Eighth Army. I haven't even seen it yet. But if Gen. Montgomery is reading this, I would advise him to do something about those roads in Southern Tunisia. Whenever I think about it, I am astonished that the good general ever managed to find his way here from the Middle East in the first place. I am sure that I never would have been able to find the way myself.

THE GUN

By Sgt. WALTER BERNSTEIN

WITH THE 45TH DIVISION IN SICILY—They were given the Gun in Texas. It was delivered right to C Battery of this 45th Division Field Artillery battalion with the compliments of the Erie Ordnance Depot. With the Gun came a field manual and a log book. The manual said it was a caliber 105-mm howitzer, Model M2A1, Serial No. 1008; the log book for recording the number of rounds fired was empty.

Today the log book is full. They took the Gun from Texas to a tomato patch in a valley on the north coast of Sicily, firing as they went. They fired for record in the dust of Camp Barkeley in Texas and in the snow of Pine Camp, N. Y., and now they are firing for keeps. For three weeks the Gun was not silent for more than six hours at a time. The crew is proud of the Gun. The enemy is afraid of it.

The history of the Gun is not like the story of a Flying Fortress or a British destroyer that battles overwhelming odds, staggers through action after harrowing action and finally goes down in a literal blaze of glory. The Gun has been under fire, but only for a short time, and never dangerously. This does not mean that it was not up there; it means simply that the battery commander knew his stuff. The better the Gun does its work the more chance it has of coming through the war without ever being under any more fire. Its crew has never seen the enemy in action and probably never will. No one immediately connected with the Gun has ever seen the effect of its fire.

The Gun, just a typical Field Artillery piece, is completely unheroic and absolutely necessary. So is the crew.

There are nine in the crew, headed by Sgt. Elden W. Yoder of Chandler, Okla. The gunner is Cpl. Virgil Irwin of Aline, Okla. The cannoneers are Pvt. Emmitt Osborn of Davenport, Okla.; Pfc. Paul J. Hemmelgarn of St. Cloud, Minn.; Pvt. Leonard Jacona of Philadelphia, Pa.; Pvt. Sigmond Biernacki of Baltimore, Md.; Pfc. Rudolph Bistany of Yonkers, N. Y.; Pfc. Walter Flanagan of Williamsport, Pa., and Pvt. Forest Saunders of Ringos Mills, Ky.

There is also a truck driver, T-5 Olen Beasley of Chandler, Okla., who operates the six-by-six that hauls the Gun from position to position.

The crew has been together for more than a year now, operating as a team, and each one knows the other guy's job. They are completely unsentimental about the Gun; they have never given it a name other than the Gun, and if it should be destroyed they would not weep over it but simply cuss out the days they would have to wait for another. But they like it. They think it's a hell of a piece, easy to work and terrible in its effect. They wouldn't trade it for any gun in the Artillery, even if they could get another.

The crew is Section 4 of the battery. Its members were first introduced to the Gun at Camp Barkeley. They spent the next three days trying to separate it from several coatings of cosmoline. This did not exactly endear them to the piece, and it was probably fortunate that they did not get a lecture immediately afterward on how the artilleryman's best friend is his howitzer.

They spent the next three months making dry runs. Then they fired on the range. Then there were more dry runs and maneuvers and night problems and amphibious problems, and just enough real firing to make the men think maybe they would get to use the Gun some day. The outfit traveled from camp to camp. Then all of a sudden they found themselves on a transport, with the Gun in the hold.

The Gun was unloaded in Sicily on a morning that the crew will never forget. Before the landing Pvt. Osborn tied a horseshoe on the Gun for luck, and two bombs missed it by 20 feet. The crew preceded the Gun ashore, leaving Cpl. Irwin on the landing boat. The boat couldn't land where the crew landed, so it went about 10 miles farther down the coast and put Irwin and the Gun off there.

By that time all hell was breaking loose. The initial enemy resistance had been pushed back by the combined naval, air and ground forces, but there was still plenty of counteraction. The air was full of whizzing objects, and no one had a very clear idea of what was going on.

In the midst of all this bloody confusion Irwin found himself with one gun, no ammunition and no means of transportation. Beasley and the truck were with the battery, 10 miles up the beach. Irwin finally managed to borrow a jeep that was standing around, hitched the Gun to that with the aid of some sailors and a couple of stray infantrymen, and started up the beach.

Meanwhile the rest of the crew had landed under heavy enemy fire and made their way inland about two miles, until they found high enough ground for artillery operation. They dug in and Irwin finally found them there.

The rest of C Battery had already assembled and was firing, and Sgt. Yoder soon had the Gun in action. It was their first real action. They were too excited to be nervous. The battery had put an observer up with the infantry, and he was calling shots at 1,600 yards with a charge five, and the Gun was really popping them out. The observer kept yelling, "More! More!" and no one in the crew actually remembers what went on that day more than five yards from the Gun.

The men didn't sleep that night, and the next night they began to move forward. They worked like a good body puncher, moving in all the time, throwing short, hard punches; and the infantry was the final right hand. For three nights, the crew didn't sleep and the Gun didn't stop firing. There wasn't even a chance to clean it during that time.

After the third night, progress was routine. The men kept moving forward behind the infantry, but they were no longer fired upon. They kept the Gun camouflaged and in defilade. Several times enemy guns sought it out; many times there were Stukas overhead. When the planes came the Gun shut up, so as not to give away its position. After they left, the Gun started again. Hour after hour, day after day, the Gun kept throwing its 33-pound projectiles.

And nothing went wrong with it. On that first landing the battery's gun mechanic was killed, and from then on the crew had to look after the Gun's care. Once it fired 236 rounds in 12 hours, getting so hot the paint burned off the tube. That was the time Yoder had to get a jeep driver to take his place at the earphones. He couldn't hear anything because of the constant explosion, and had to go back hauling ammunition. He couldn't hear anything for two days afterward. That was also the time everyone pitched in to haul ammunition, from the mess sergeant to the first sergeant.

Once the recoil mechanism had to be filled with oil because the barrel wouldn't go far enough forward into battery. Once the Gun threw Pvt. Flanagan while he was standing on one of the trails, digging it into the ground with the recoil. Once while the Gun was being pulled to another position, it broke loose from the truck, and Yoder and Bis-

tany chased it half a mile. But the Gun fired every time they wanted it to fire, and that was practically all the time. And it fired rapidly; hundreds of the German prisoners here in Sicily keep asking to see those "automatic" howitzers the Americans have.

The push from the south to the north coast of Sicily was interesting for the crew but not highly exciting. Most of the time they were too busy doing their routine job to realize they were making history. They worked hard and steadily, with a minimum of snafu, and while they were rarely in positions of great danger they were never entirely out of danger. In the little spare time they had, riding to a new position or sitting by the Gun, they looked at this strange country and collected souvenirs and tried to talk to the people. Pvt. Jacona spoke Italian, and that helped to get fruit and an occasional spaghetti dinner.

And all the time they were doing a job. The Gun and its crew made infantry advances possible and beat back counterattacks. Their observers crept forward ahead of the infantry and spotted targets for them. If there was anything at all romantic about the operation of Model M2A1, it was in the work of the three-man observation crew, who ducked rifle and machine-gun fire to spot enemy positions and spent long nights in caves and foxholes. The observers were Lt. Neil McPhail, a former salesman for Firestone in Cincinnati, Ohio; Pfc. Frank Baker, who used to drive busses in Elida, Ohio, and Pfc. Jesse Ferrell, fresh out of business college in Bristow, Okla.

The Gun itself does essentially uninteresting work, and it is dependent on a number of equally prosaic little jobs: the men who string wire from section to battery, the men who run the supply truck up with the ammunition, the officers who do the thankless mathematics that makes the Gun hit where it's supposed to hit, the instrument corporal with his aiming circle, the cook with the chow. All these serve the Gun; and the Gun serves them.

Now that the Sicily campaign is over, Section 4 is waiting to push into the continent and keep on terrorizing the enemy. The Gun is still working and will continue to work until it is put out of action or retired after the war in front of an armory or in a public square.

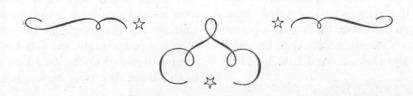

DUFFIE'S: WHERE IRAN'S ELITE MEET

By Sgt. JAMES P. O'NEILL

NORTHERN IRAN—To most GIs, ration day is just the day when the mess sergeant gathers up another 10-day supply of luncheon meat, spinach, carrots 'n' peas and sundry other unpalatable items which he and the QM laughingly call food. But to dogfaces in a camp here, ration day has a much more pleasant meaning: it's beer time at "Duffie's Tavern."

Sgt. Francis H. McDuffie of Seneca Falls, N. Y., was running a PX when beer hit Iran after a long dry spell. One night a few weeks later, he noticed four dogfaces sitting outside one of the PX windows and drinking their beer. It was windy; the air was so thick with the dust of Iran that Mac could hardly see their faces.

"What are you doing, drinking that beer out there?" he asked the GIs. "Why don't you guys swill it in your barracks where it's comfortable?"

"We're not looking for comfort," one of the boys answered. "We're looking for a place to have a beer bull session. How can you enjoy your beer with half the barracks snoring and the other half yelling at you to keep quiet?"

That reminded Mac of a lonely night in Albany seven years before, and he invited the GIs inside and took them to the dinky storeroom next to the PX. Turning on the light, he put four big cartons on their ends. "Have your bull session in here," he said, "but don't let any of this PX stuff fall into your pockets. There's an AR against it."

What McDuffie had remembered was the night he went into the bar at Menand's Bowling Alley in Albany seven years before and had a beer. Mac was new in Albany then—he'd just started working for Western Union—and he was very lonely. The bartender, a wise old man, spotted the loneliness in the small-town kid before the beer was half finished. He treated Mac to the next round and introduced him to some of the steady customers. Before the night was over, the lad from Seneca Falls was feeling right at home.

In a way, what Mac did in Iran was in repayment for what the bartender had done in Albany. By the next ration night, Mac had moved all the PX supplies out of the storeroom and piled them behind the PX counter. And then he dug up a piano somewhere and found a sergeant named Al Delong, who used to play in the clubs around Los Angeles, Calif.

When the four GI lovers of beer and small talk made their appearance, Mac ushered them into the storeroom. Delong started rambling on the piano, and in a half hour the room was filled with smoke, beer, conversation and GIs. One of the boys who worked in the PX with Mac tacked up a sign over the storeroom doorway: "DUFFIE'S TAVERN."

After a few more ration nights, you could scarcely recognize the place. Delong brought along a few hep artists from the Special Service band and the Tavern really began to jump. Cpl. Billy MacIntyre, professional comic from Washington, D. C., came over to tell a few jokes, and before he was through, he had organized a few amateur talent acts and put on a floor show. There wasn't room to hold all the GIs who crowded the Tavern after that. McDuffie's boss, 1st Lt. F. J. Riel, had to have the place enlarged three times; it takes up two-thirds of the PX building now, and there are three assistant bartenders.

As much as Iranian fixtures and the Army will allow, Duffie's Tavern resembles a saloon. There are plenty of chairs and tables, a bandstand and a long bar that stretches from one end of the Tavern to the other. Scattered around the walls you'll see some signs put up by one of Mac's friends: "DON'T TRY TO CON ME; I'VE BEEN CONNED BY EXPERTS. 8 CANS PER RATION." "NO WOMEN ALLOWED BUT WE CAN'T STOP YOU FROM DREAMING." "DON'T THROW BEER CANS. THIS AIN'T A BALL PARK."

McDuffie himself is more than a PX manager; he is a cross between Mr. Anthony and King Solomon, the friend of every GI in camp, and better informed about what's going on than G-2.

MacIntyre, now "first assistant in charge of entertainment," dishes up a different floor show every ration night. Generally he leads a community sing and invites ambitious members of the audience up to do their stuff, too. One night a truck driver from a GI convoy came up and said he was a magician. He made cigarette lighters, coins and handkerchiefs disappear. Then he asked McDuffie for a 100-rial note, which the proprietor quickly produced. The truck driver said he'd make it disappear as soon as he came back from the latrine. Mac is still waiting for the magician to return.

Every ration night the GIs begin festivities with a song dreamed up by Bob Lewis, one of the boys in the band. It's sung to what is roughly the tune of "There Is a Tavern in the Town." The chorus goes this way:

> Fare thee well, for I must leave thee
> To go drink my cheery beery,
> Watch the foam and think of home the way things
> used to be.

> Adieu, adieu, kind friends, adieu (yes adieu)
> Where is a better place to have a brew?
> It is clean and neat, a perfect place to meet;
> You leave no tips, just smack your lips,
> And no one's blue.

JILTED GIs IN INDIA ORGANIZE FIRST BRUSH-OFF CLUB

By Sgt. ED CUNNINGHAM

AT A U. S. BOMBER BASE, INDIA—For the first time in military history, the mournful hearts have organized. The Brush-Off Club is the result, in this land of sahibs and saris; as usual, it is strictly GI.

Composed of the guys whose gals back home have decided "a few years is too long to wait," the club has only one purpose—to band together for mutual sympathy. They meet weekly to exchange condolences and cry in their beer while telling each other the mournful story of how "she wouldn't wait."

The club has a "chief crier," a "chief sweater" and a "chief consoler." Initiation fee is one broken heart or a reasonable facsimile thereof.

Applicants must be able to answer appropriately the following questions:

1. Has she written lately?
2. Do her letters say she misses you, and is willing to wait no matter how long?
3. Does she reminisce about the "grand times we had together, and the fun we'll have when you . come back"?
4. Does she mention casually the fellows she is dating now?

Membership in the club is divided between "active members" and "just sweating members"—the latter being guys who can't believe that no news is good news.

Members are required to give each other the needle; i.e., full sympathy for all active members, encourage "hopeful waiting" in the just sweating members. By-laws state: "As we are all in the 'same transport,' we must provide willing shoulders to cry upon, and join fervently in all wailing and weeping."

One of the newest members of the club was unanimously voted to charter membership because of the particular circumstances of his case. He recently got a six page letter from his fiancée back in Texas. In the last paragraph she casually mentioned, "I was married last week but my husband won't mind you writing to me occasionally. He's a sailor and very broadminded."

This GI, so magnanimously scorned, is now regarded as fine presidential timber.

Present officers of the club, all of whom are active torch-carriers, are: Cpl. Henry W. Asher, Jr., New Orleans, La., president; Pvt. Francis M. McCreery, Marshall, Mo., vice president; Cpl. John McConnell, Garden Grove, Calif., chief crier; S/Sgt. George M. Lehman, Bozeman, Mont., assistant chief crier; Sgt. John Crow, San Jose, Calif., chief sweater; and Lt. Richard L. Weiss, Milwaukee, Wis., chief consoler.

Cpl. DOYLE IS TO AFRICA COME!

By Cpl. JOHN J. DOYLE

North Africa

Oh, sound the trumpet and beat the drum!
Cpl. Doyle is to Africa come!
To Africa come in enormous force
To alter the global battle's course.
Already the dastard foemen fly;
We'll all be home the Fourth of July.

Oh, clash the cymbals, sound the tabor!
For Cpl. Doyle, his gun and saber,
His tanks and artillery (self-propelled),
With which the enemy shall be quelled.
Already in dread the Nazi blenches;
By Christmas we'll be out of the trenches.

Oh, smite the zither, rattle the goard!
Cpl. Doyle's in *Afrique du Nord!*
Now for a speedy end to the war;
Summon a hearse for the Afrika Korps,
For here comes the guy the enemy fears—
The paragon of the Engineers.
So smite the zither, rattle the goard!
Cpl. Doyle's in *Afrique du Nord!*

WHAT DO WE THINK OF THE BRITISH?

By Sgt. BURGESS SCOTT

Cairo—The medium-sized figure of this story is the average buck private I've met in the British Desert Army—British in this case meaning the United Kingdom and Northern Ireland. He's got a sun-browned face and hands, and he comes from England, Scotland, Ireland or Wales.

His speech is naturally the first thing that strikes you, but after a few weeks or a month you're able to place him, like you'd place a man from Georgia or Maine. You can walk up and say, "You're from the Midlands" or "from Scotland." You can't guarantee to be 100 percent right, but it gives you a kick when you are.

You're just about used to his speech when you realize that he doesn't speak much. He's a quiet man. When he says, "I'll lay on a lorry," he doesn't mean he's going for a nap. That's his way of saying, "I'll go rustle up a truck." He's pretty good at verbal short cuts.

After you talk a while you find that, although he's pretty well up on his British Isles and has a speaking acquaintance with the rest of the Empire, he knows less than a Brooklynite about the outside world. He's not quite certain whether Alaska is one of the 48 states of the Union or whether the Grand Canyon is the title of a Hollywood film. And he wants to know if all our girls are like movie stars.

You try to learn something about his country and soon find he hasn't the average American's yen for politics. He's just not interested in the doings of his or anybody else's statesmen.

He wants to get on with his job. But he'll open up on the subject of football or his home town or his neighborhood beer joint.

He's a good cook. He can take some tin cans, a pile of sand and a pint of gas, and do swell things to a can of bully or M & V. And he is a wow at brewing tea, which he can prepare and drink while you think that there isn't time.

He's kind-hearted. He shows that in his dealings with the inhabitants of any country in which war places him. In the desert he'll take time to give biscuits and bully to a needy Arab, and he'll take in any pie-dog that hangs around his bivvy.

He won't take "bastard" from you, not even if you smile. It's just not done in his Army. But you can call him a "bugger" and he'll give you no more than a chuck in the ribs or an American "goose" he's learned to administer.

He's not worried about sex to the extent of letting it get him down. He hasn't the Ities' mobile passion; rather, he's marking time for better days. Given the chance, he's handy with his nights off.

For a man who hails from a verdant land, he takes to the desert uncommonly well. A quart of water will if necessary, last him for two days. But even when water is plentiful you never see him take a drink of it straight, no matter how much you watch him. His tea and his beer—when he can get them—evidently provide enough liquid for his system. He can go for hours without sleep and not show it. When he does get a chance for some shuteye, he doesn't appear really to relish it. He just disappears into his bivvy and emerges several hours later looking no better—or worse—for his rest.

Watching him soak up his arid hardship, you get an impression that nothing ruffles his military calm.

Which is correct so long as you don't try to chisel him out of his rights. But try to put anything over on him, and you have a righteous uproar on your hands. In the desert, for example, a man's bivvy is his castle and shall not be invaded. You can't turn him out of it, but he'll step outside any night of the week and give you his bed if you're in a jam.

He writes reams of bad poetry on two subjects, home and the desert, which he promptly mails to his service paper.

The poems about Britain are noble and nostalgic; the poems about the desert are not usually complimentary to that section of the earth. Both types carry on in a rather bumpy meter guaranteed to leave his editor with a headache. When not writing a poem, he's writing a letter to find out why his last one wasn't used.

He's brave under fire. He doesn't dash to the top of the rise among the bullets to wave a Union Jack in Jerry's face. His is a calm valor, as displayed by the member of the Durham Light Infantry who stayed by his gun with one arm blown off and fired on till he fell dead.

He's brave with a bullet in his guts or a leg left behind. If the pain gets too great, he breaks down like any man will, but you have to lean close to hear it. Recently a hospital orderly picked up a letter to mail for a wounded man. It read: "Dear Dad: I'm knocked about a bit, but I'll be all right. Don't worry." That guy had an arm off and an eye out. Tommy's like that.

SUNDAY AT SANANANDA

By T-5 DON E. ROHRIG
New Guinea

This is the Huggins perimeter.

As you are standing, Gona's ahead of you,
The green desert of Papua and Dutch New Guinea
Beyond it; beyond the Halmahera Sea, the islands of Molucca
And the far-off places of the Moros and the temple wor-
   shipers.

To your left are the Owen Stanleys—
The spinal column of the Papuan tortoise;
And behind you the mightiest of the oceans,
Though from here it is only a breath and a sigh.

To your right, a scant mile up this devious, bucolic trail,
Around many a bend, through the haunted, primordial
   tangle,
Past dugout and slit trench, by ford across tropical rivers,
Through mud to your thighs, and the murmuring clouds of
   mosquitoes,
Through *kunai* and sun . . . oh, when you get there
You'll know . . . you'll not mistake it, this hell hole:
The bloody black sands, the brown tainted sea water—
This Point Sanananda . . .

Don't mind the skeletons. We haven't had time to remove
   them;
And while we sit here with hands limply folded,
We haven't the heart.

No, it isn't the heat or the dampness;
And it certainly isn't sickness, at least not physical sickness—
Though they may come later, the retching, the spewing.
They had it, these grandsons of Heaven,
These stench-making ex-patriots lately of Honshu:
From the slums of Kyoto, from gay Nagasaki,
These pallid-complexioned mother's sons from the rice pad-
   dies,
From fermenting Formosa and the smokes of Fujisan . . .
They had the sickness, and not wholly the fevers,
Though the swamp miasmata weren't the least of it.

And so here's what is left of them . . . hell, I don't wonder
Your face grows a bit green . . . it's not a sweet atmosphere
Here with the cadavers.

But after you've slept with them—
There's Charlie the brainless one; and Henry the Horror.
He was clever at sniping, but my cobber resented him,
And even the tree-boys are shy at machine guns!

That beautiful specimen under the quarter-ton
Will have to grow features or else his ancestors
Might fail to remember him among the chrysanthemums
In the honorable Heaven of Japanese heroes . . .
But these are the harmless ones. If you wait until nightfall
You won't be misled by the quiet out yonder;
They're clever, resourceful, and they're not the half of it . . .

The jungle draws in on you, the sound of the wild things
Keeps your heart in your gullet, and I'd not advise you
To sleep with both eyes closed, for fear you might yield
   to it—
To sleep—for above all, give the go-by to nightmares.
You see, there's the nightmares, and the start-up in cold
   sweat,
The scream that you can't suppress though the darkness is
   listening;
And the terror remembered, of the sudden reversal
When these foul, bloody messes that lie here so motionless
Became boys from Brooklyn or Terre Haute or Omaha,
And you recognize all of them and hear the low crying
Just before the death rattle, since none of them wants to die.

And the shadowy shapes glide around in the midst of them,
And the glinting of bayonets and the steaming red rivers
Of warm blood gushing soundlessly . . .

You're pale . . . you're pulling out . . . back to the cities?
Glamorous cities up and down the land.

Well, don't let me detain you
With ranting and preaching. That's just our habit here.
Your blood turns to wormwood.

Though here it is Sunday
We forget the days. Just tell your newspaper
That the boys are still pushing, the Japs still pocketed.

You'd better tone down a bit—don't tell them too much of
   it—
Of the corpses and skeletons, the stink and the filthiness
On Point Sanananda.

This is the Bougainville home of S/Sgt. William Orick, Cincinnati, Ohio; Sgt. Francis Johnson, Ashtabula, Ohio, and Pvt. Frank Pistacchia, the Bronx, N. Y.

MODERN LIVING ON A BEACHHEAD IN BOUGAINVILLE

By Sgt. BARRETT McGURN

Sketches by Sgt. Robert Greenhalgh. (South Pacific)

BOUGAINVILLE, THE SOLOMONS—When the communique mentions a "beachhead," a GI fresh from the States is likely to picture a strip of sand, with grim fighters struggling desperately to keep their flimsy foothold a few feet inside the jungle wall where the sand ends.

But at this beachhead, just a month or so after the initial attacking wave, here is what we find:

Instead of hand-to-hand struggle with the wily Japs, there are movies being shown 300 yards behind the front lines.

Instead of bearded figures, caked with mud, there is a colonel out of *Esquire* going by, smoking a cigarette in a six-inch holder.

Instead of tired runners and battle-scarred pigeons carrying messages, there are French telephones in the machine-gun nests to keep the gunners in touch with every other part of the beachhead and to summon artillery to their assistance in a matter of seconds.

Instead of notches in the trees as guide marks for the pathfinders, there are wooden signs right out of your home town: "Speed Limit: Recons, Jeeps, 20 mph; Trucks, 15 mph." "No Parking." "Have You Had Your Atabrine Today?" "Reserved for CG." There are gag signs over the mess sheds, such as those lettered in Gothic print and elegant Spencerian script at the 37th Division headquarters company: "Bougainville Grill." "Empress Augusta Tea Room." "Ye Old Bake Shoppe." "Torokina Trocadero."

Instead of reading "Superman" and the "Green Hornet," T-5 Donald N. Roberts, a machine gunner from Coshocton, Ohio, who used to be a Pennsylvania Railroad trackworker, is busy on his correspondence course in automobile mechanics. T-4 John Alcorn, of San Francisco, Calif., is conducting free nightly classes in Spanish, and studying Japanese on the side.

Finally, instead of a blackout, there are lights sparkling gaily over bridge games until sirens give air-raid warnings.

The beachhead has a depth of four miles rather than four feet as one might be apt to think. Going ashore with a .45 ready, a GI is astonished to find hundreds of jeeps and 2½-ton trucks rumbling placidly up and down sands where scores died four weeks before. Thumbing a ride, you are driven down along the beach a couple of miles, asked for "any new rumors," and then motored inland along a four-lane all-weather highway that would rate a blue line on a gasoline map back home.

The story of the road is the story of the beachhead itself.

Marines made the initial landing and there was bloody fighting for several days. A week after the Marines landed, the first echelon of the Army came in and took over half the front. No sooner did the first wave hit the beach than Army specialists of every variety began installing the things of civilization. They were obeying the unwritten Army rule, not found in any manual but practiced faithfully at the front, that "war is bad enough without being any more uncomfortable than necessary."

One of the few signs of civilization up to that time was the Marine brig, complete to stockade and padlock, whose first customers included two fellows who went AWOL from a supply detail to do some fighting on the front.

Ashore with the Infantry in the first Army wave came Engineers, Signalmen, doctors, dentists, chaplains, supply experts—and the Special Service officer. In two weeks the latter was having movies flown in by officer courier. By the fifth week 3,500 soldiers were seeing movies at least once a week, and most of them three times a week. By the sixth week after invasion the SSO had movies running in a hospital ward tent 50 feet behind the front line, between two machine-gun nests. Japs could hear the swing music of Hollywood from an eighth of a mile outside the barbed wire.

Five weeks after the Army landed, the SSO had phonograph records for the boys, including a set that Hildegarde made in San Francisco at the same time the first troops came ashore.

The Engineers, from their experience on New Georgia, believed that the greatest immediate need was an excellent States-type road to permit rapid dispersal of the thousands of troops and hundreds of tons of supplies being brought ashore. With bulldozers and a wonderful "tree-dozer," which knocks over 100-foot trees like bowling pins, the Engineers smashed into the gnarled tangle of the jungle. Within five weeks they had 10 miles of the

"The Thick and Thin Lumber Company." A busy sawmill in the combat area at Empress Augusta Bay turns mahogany and teakwood into building material.

type of highway known in the States as "improved," and 130 miles of jeep trails. Every outfit in the wilderness was thus within 15 yards of a road.

Almost incidentally, the Engineers built five bridges with 15-ton capacity and 10 five-ton jeep spans. Before the Engineers had left Guadalcanal, G-4 told them there was no space in the ships for lumber or such things as bridge nails, so they had to find these materials on the beachhead.

For bridge nails, the Engineers sharpened the ends of bolts out of artillery-shell cases. The bolts, two feet long and three-quarters of an inch thick, proved quite serviceable when thus adapted.

A sawmill, nicknamed the "Thick and Thin Lumber Company," was started, and was soon producing as much as a mile of lumber a day. Scientists in Engineer clothes began making stress and strain tests on every local wood, much of it strange stuff none had seen before. One tree, called "Benus" by the natives, proved to be as strong and straight-grained as many of the world's finest known woods. After the bridges were done, the sawmill was kept going at top speed, and next priority was given to latrines and mess halls, because insect pests can be as dangerous an enemy as the Jap.

When the Signalmen hit the shore in the first wave, they had radio communication established with the rear in a matter of minutes, using portable equipment. In another day or two, they had strung 50 miles of telephone wire, and in six weeks they had 5,000 miles of it in place. The result was that S/Sgt. Jim Smith of Cleveland Heights, Ohio, divisional public-relations noncom, could sit in his pyramidal tent at division CP and egg on his regimental reporters by phone—French phone, of course.

Not even such things as a toothache or, for that matter, an embarrassing missing incisor in front that would spoil the good looks of the junior warrior, were neglected for long. Two weeks after the Army touched shore, dentists were calmly making false teeth at an average of one set a day.

Even loneliness came under prompt attack. Postal Service had regular mail flowing in within two weeks, and many of the letters received had been written in the States only 14 days before. GIs like Alcorn found they could even get some non-GI companionship by catching wombats for pets. The wombat is a peculiar local animal, the size of a dog, with the fur of a bear and the pouch of a kangaroo. The wombat's charming but popeyed offspring peer out from this pouch.

Wherever the Army left off in providing comfort, the boys took over themselves.

There is no GI equipment for warding off direct hits by big bombs, so each GI set about making his own arrangements. S/Sgt. William A. Orick of Cincinnati, Ohio, found a banyan tree with 2,000 pole-like roots. Banyans are queer trees whose roots start before the trunk reaches the ground, and this one, granddaddy of them all, had roots 40 feet up. At ground level Orick found a space inside big enough for three to live in comfort. Most GIs pass the frequent air raids underground, but Orick figures no bomb fragment made could pick its way through all those roots, so he slumbers peacefully in his cot above ground as the Mitsubishis do their worst.

Another eminent root dweller in a different part of the beachhead is 1st Sgt. Melvin E. (Speed) Spiedel of Headquarters Company, 37th Division, a former guitarist, amateur poet and ball player of Cleveland, Ohio. Spiedel took a tree which comes out of the ground in one piece in the conventional way and gouged out a hole under it big enough to accommodate a table and seven guests. It is always full house at Spiedel's when a raid is under way. Usually the sergeant leads in singing, but sometimes when the bombs are close, more sober thoughts are entertained. "Speed's Sanctuary— Where Men Learn to Pray," says the sign over the hole.

Boys of Co. C of one outfit found the ground water level in their area of the front line was 20 feet down, but by salvaging the bilge pumps from wrecked barges, they got all the water they wanted. The same company literally bayoneted the jungle clear. The machine gunners wanted a wide open space in front of the lines so that they would have an unobstructed view of attacking Japs. With 14 machetes and 180 bayonets, the company cleared out 25 acres in three weeks.

GI ingenuity was also brought to bear on the laundry problem. At one spot a coconut palm was felled across a brook, and the trunk, notched at the midstream point, made a perfect washboard.

All this does not mean that there has been any lack of discomfort and suffering and fighting and dying here. There has been lots of it.

The Marines suffered the worst casualties in the initial close-quarter struggling, but when the artillery set up positions, the Japs never were able to come close again in large numbers. In a single day 5,000 rounds of artillery fire were laid down on one advancing Jap unit and next day 1,100 dead were counted in half of the shelled area.

The chief mission of the Bougainville beachhead has been to provide a location for a fighter strip from which to attack such points as the strong Jap base at Rabaul, New Britain. To do this meant capturing 20 miles of jungle and then digging in behind a barbed-wired perimeter with antitank guns mounted for antipersonnel use, a defensive arrangement making our beachhead a bush Gibraltar. This done, the secondary troubles of life on an equatorial island showed up.

Centipedes in foxholes and hammocks proved about the worst. One bite, and the blitzed spot aches for a week.

Then there are the snapping ants, one of which

The sand along this beach is always torn with truck and jeep ruts. Even though the Japs are only a few miles away, soldiers go swimming here regularly.

got me. Although they are only twice the size of black ants back in the States, they are ferocious creatures, always on the warpath, and they snap their jaws so hard you can hear them 15 feet away—by actual test. Their bite feels like a stab from a hot needle.

Along the same line are the vicious local cousins of poison oak and sumac. No one is quite sure what plants or trees are responsible for the itchy, quickly spreading rash that is common hereabouts. As a matter of fact, I have that, too, and am writing this story in a bed at the clearing station.

Rain is another minor woe. When the Marines landed, all they had time to do at night was dig a hole, drop a poncho in the bottom and let it rain in. It did, every night. Bougainville is one of the wettest places on earth. More than 11 feet of rain come down each year. The Army has managed shelter of sorts from the first, but the rain sometimes makes sleeping in soaked clothes necessary. It takes three days to dry a pair of coveralls and a week for some kinds of wash.

The mile-high Bougainville mountains scoop cool air down onto the beachhead so that you need a blanket at night, but there is wilting heat at midday. You perspire freely, and the medics say this weakens you. Vitamin pills and an easy work schedule help you over this hurdle.

As for chow, even the officers admit it leaves something to be desired. There are no fresh vegetables, fresh meat, eggs in the shell or milk the way it came from the cow. Even bread is scarce; at 37th Division headquarters, one slice per man per meal is issued, and GIs have been known to run to get seconds. However, medics say the rations give a balanced diet, and the tropics take the edge off your appetite anyway.

Not all the primitive features of beachhead life are unpleasant to the boys. Although fatigues are the general uniform for all occasions, from combat to the occasional three-can-a-man beer parties, men are allowed to wear anything or nothing. A surprising number choose the latter. Many make it a practice to walk stark naked from their outfits to the bathing stream, often a stroll of a third of a mile down busy roads. You feel you have seen everything when one of the martial nudists goes by in his birthday suit, riding on the running board of a truck.

One reason for the fearless lack of attire is that no one has any worries about coming across any women. The men of the 37th Division headquarters detachment, for instance, have seen only one white woman in nine months, and that is Lois, the nude

on the chest of Pvt. Albert Herron, an MP who used to drive cabs in Toledo, Ohio.

It's not true that the war has passed this place by, however. There are still as many Japs on Bougainville as there are GIs. The cemetery keeps growing slowly, as men get killed on patrols outside the lines or bombs fall unluckily. And even after 40 air raids you still get a physicky feeling in the stomach when the bombers drone overhead in the light of a lover's moon.

"z-z-z-z-Z-Z," the plane will whine as it approaches, then "a-a-a-A-A-Ahh" as it dives. "wah-wah-Wah-Wah-WAH," whoosh the bombs as they fall and then "bawmph" as they hit. You crouch in your foxhole as low as you can get, say your final prayers as fast as you can for fear you won't get them done in time, and then over again slowly to be sure you have them right. Then you wait, your mind a little dull but not very troubled, content in the thought that you have done everything you could and it is now out of your hands.

Even GIs who claim they have been through 500 bombings admit raids are still no fun. There is many a ripped jungle hammock netting on this beachhead to testify that the owner left in such a hurry that he had no time to unzip it.

Even your own artillery can be wearying as its "barum, barum, barum-barum," day and night for weeks on end, sends shells overhead with a sound like the last car on a fast train, or like the rumbling of thunder through a long cloud.

Perhaps the worst part of the almost nightly air raids is getting out of the warm hammock and into the damp foxhole, something that has happened as often as six times in one night. After a while it gets almost mechanical, however, and even the sleepiest GI is glad he is not in the Jap bomber's place as it catches the thunderous attack of the ack-ack or the even deadlier assault of the night fighters. Occasionally the pearly moonlit sky will flush into rose color as a Jap bomber plunges in flames.

THE BIG BASTARD

By ROBERT L. SCHWARTZ Y2c

THE BIG BASTARD, *a U. S. battleship, got her nickname when she first arrived in the South Pacific to protect American carriers from aerial attack.*

She did her job so well that a carrier admiral radioed his planes, "Stay away from that big bastard. When she gets through shooting down Japs, she'll use you for target practice." Now, throughout the Pacific, she's known as the Big Bastard and her men wouldn't swap her nickname for a general citation.

This is the story of the Big Bastard's first surface action, pieced together from the accounts of the men of her complement. The action—the Battle of Savo Island—began at dusk, 24 hours after the Boise and the San Francisco steamed between two columns of Jap ships and smashed them apart. It formed a part of what's known in naval annals as the Fifth Battle of the Solomons.

On the afternoon of Nov. 14, 1942, a task force of the Big Bastard and several other battleships and destroyers cut away from its carrier for a little show of its own. And at Savo Island, just north of Guadalcanal, it found a nest of hiding Jap ships and got mixed up in one of the roughest night surface engagements ever fought anywhere.

When general quarters sounded at 9:30, no one aboard the Big Bastard knew the size or strength of the enemy. But at midnight someone on the bridge sighted three enemy ships in the channel ahead and reported the formation to the Admiral's flagship nearby. Fifteen minutes later the Admiral's ship fired a nine-gun salvo that set afire the leading Jap battleship. From that moment on, the Big Bastard and the rest of the U. S. task force saw plenty of action.

Her range finders set on the enemy fire, Big B swung her heavies into play, sunk her first target and blew up her second. Meanwhile Jap guns exploded three U. S. destroyers.

Big B's third target was a Kongo class battleship that passed her starboard beam and was cut in half by a salvo from her No. 3 turret aft. Her secondary batteries continued to pour fire into eight Jap destroyers hiding in a cove.

There was a lull then. Big B steamed alone in a circle of burning ships. The Admiral's battleship had disappeared in the darkness. Into the narrowest part of the cove came four more enemy ships. The second one threw searchlights on Big B and she opened fire. From her rear came supporting salvos, indicating that the Admiral's ship was still in the fight.

The assistance was welcome for Big B was being pounded heavily by the guns of three hard-punching Jap warships. Six- and 8-inch shells ripped through the top of her superstructure, then cut into her secondaries. Her deck was riddled with shrapnel. Fire broke out in the tattered superstructure. Her own wreckage lay everywhere.

But Big B kept right on rolling. She opened her main battery on the enemy line. Her secondaries chattered continuously and soon a tongue of fire poked up at the sky from each of the enemy ships. Then the Big Bastard knew she had won.

During the night, the Big Bastard and the other U. S. ships ran completely around the island and wiped out an enemy fleet in less than 50 minutes. Most of the men said later that they thought they had been running the channel at least half the night.

The story of that 50 minutes, as told by some of the men of the Big Bastard's crew, appears below.

SOMEWHERE IN THE SOUTH PACIFIC [Passed by Navy Censor]—Hodgen Othello Patrick Y1c, talker on the *Big Bastard's* sky patrol, highest lookout post where the ship took its first hit during the Battle of Savo Island, came as reasonably close to being killed as can be expected of any man.

Patrick remembers squaring for battle and from his high perch seeing the Jap ships come up. He saw the first salvo leave the flagship up ahead. His next recollection is of being thrown against a bulkhead and finding somebody's arm, without a body, across his face. A dead weight lay across his chest, pinning him.

"I'm dead," he thought, and the remembrance of it is still clear in his mind. "Here I am dead. This is what it's like to be dead." But the earthly touch of shrapnel in his knee and his hip convinced him that he was still alive. He looked around. The two officers lay dead. Seven enlisted men were still. Four

wounded looked at Patrick, not knowing what to do next.

Patrick pressed the button on his headset. "Sick bay," he called, "send help." He doesn't know why he took command. There was another petty officer who not only rated him but was able to struggle to his feet and walk around. The sound of firing roared up from his own ship. He heard hits coming aboard. But no help came.

Patrick ordered the two least wounded to go below and then put tourniquets on the other two, using their own belts. He applied the same treatment to his own leg above the bleeding knee, then remembered to loosen all three every 15 minutes throughout the night. He hunted a long time for morphine before he found it and divided it with the others. As he was about to take his share of the sedative he noticed that several of the men he had thought dead were stirring. Without a moment's hesitation he divided his share among them. He didn't feel heroic about it. He didn't even think about it.

Despite his injuries, Patrick found that he could get to his feet. He saw that he could report better while standing and remained that way until the end of the battle. Afterward, he fell again to the deck but never stopped his regular reports until he was relieved the next morning.

Patrick was the only enlisted man of the crew who was recommended for the Navy Cross.

When general quarters sounded on the *Big Bastard,* Rufus Mathewson Y2c took his post as a talker in the conning tower.

"It'll be a push-over," he heard someone say. "Just a bunch of armed transports. We'll knock 'em off like sitting ducks."

Mathewson said to himself, "I wish I was home." The thought kept running through his head as he watched the captain and the navigator walk calmly back and forth in the narrow steel-walled compartment.

Hours ticked by. Shortly after midnight the loudspeaker carried a cold steady voice from plot room. "Target 20,000 yards, bearing 240° . . . target 19,800 yards, bearing 241° . . ." Slowly the target drew closer.

There was a terrific explosion up ahead. Mathewson dashed to one of the slits and felt his stomach drop as he saw a battleship ahead silhouetted by flame. "Lord, let me out and I'll change my ways," he said aloud. A direct hit had dissolved one of the destroyers.

The captain called for a stadimeter reading to determine the distance to the battleship ahead. A lieutenant on the bridge tried unsuccessfully to take a reading through the narrow slot in the armor. It would have been difficult in the daytime and it was virtually impossible at night.

"What kind of a crew have I got when I can't get a stadimeter reading?" the captain asked.

Mathewson felt sorry for the lieutenant. Over the lookout's phone came a voice, "Destroyer sinking on our starboard bow." The captain ordered left rudder, and the helmsman swung the wheel. They skirted the destroyer, then came back on their course. From over the phone came the Admiral's voice: "Fire when ready."

The men on the bridge looked at each other. For a full minute no word came over the amplifier from plot room, then a voice giving the range and bearing. The captain looked at Mathewson. "Tell them they can fire now." Mathewson relayed the command. He could hear compressed air being blown through the 16-inch barrels as the gun crews cleared them before loading. Thirty seconds later shells screamed out. The captain and the navigator were jarred away from their positions at the 'scopes, but voices came in over the phone.

"Right on!"

"The damn thing has dissolved!"

"Looked like a cruiser."

"That was a battleship!"

In rapid succession Mathewson heard a loud crash, a rolling explosion, and then the searing rattle of metal fragments as they crashed into cables, guns and superstructure. The ship shrugged, leaned back into a volley of 6- and 8-inch shells that raked through the sky control tower, topmost position on the ship.

Quickly Mathewson called sky control on the battle phone. "Patrick, you there?"

"Here, but our officers are dead, and all of us are wounded."

Mathewson asked for permission to go relieve Patrick but his request was denied. Mathewson and Patrick were close friends, and now the thought of Patrick lying wounded on sky control beyond the help of anyone because of fires burning below him almost brought tears to his eyes.

Methodically *Big B* went on firing.

"Torpedo off the port bow."

"Hard starboard rudder."

The tremendous craft swung over. Everyone strained, bracing for another explosion above the crashing shells and shrapnel. The torpedo missed, but in the confusion following the battleship's evasion tactics she became separated from the other ships and lost her own course.

"If you swing to port you can go back out the way you came in," chart house advised, "but the water's shallow off that way. If you turn to starboard you have to go around the island."

"Starboard," said the captain. And then, as a pleasant afterthought, "Full speed ahead."

Six- and 8-inch shell fire peppered the bridge with steel fragments. It was almost impossible for shrapnel to penetrate the armor of the bridge but the men inside heard one shell smack through the gun director just aft the bridge and then explode against the chart house. Directions for course and bearing stopped coming in.

Over the amplifier from chart house came a voice, "My God, this man's bleeding to death. Send help. Hurry. Please hurry."

Melvin McSpadden, the engine control talker, was first to answer. "Sick bay is on this circuit and they'll send a doctor. Give us some bearings."

"This poor guy's bleeding to death. Have you got any bandages? I can't leave him like this."

McSpadden tore down a blackout curtain hanging over one of the slots, stuffed it through the aperture and shouted to a seaman on the catwalk outside, "Take this to the chart house quick."

Another torpedo was sighted and the ship swung sharply to starboard. From all over the ship came the excited voices of talkers, "We're heading for the beach!"

"Why did we make that turn to starboard?" The query came in over McSpadden's phone and he recognized it as that of Batt II, which he had thought abandoned.

He quickly reassured them: "The captain is conning the ship!" That stopped the queries, the torpedo failed to materialize, and the captain swung again to port. The huge ship churned up a massive letter "S" in white-topped water. Some of the waves in the wake astern were 20 feet high.

Batt II, which is the auxiliary control room situated inside the superstructure below the sky control tower, was the hardest hit portion of the ship. One of the talkers in Batt II was Tom Page S1c of Greensburg, Pa.

Page remembers it was a beautiful night. There was a big moon and it was very warm and quiet. The smell of gardenias was strong from off Florida Island. The association of the gardenias with the action that followed caused Page to lose all desire to smell a gardenia again.

Over the amplifier came a voice, "Guadalcanal on our starboard hand." Big vivid flashes lit the sky —some of it gunfire in the distance, some of it lightning. Everybody in Batt II was tense. Not until the *Big Bastard's* guns went off did everyone's confidence return. Page went to one of the slots and watched the shells fly through the air like three red dots slowly converging into one, then landing off in the distance. He saw Japs running back and forth on the beach with flashlights.

Page sat in a corner on an overturned bucket, feeling comfortable now that the big guns were booming. He noticed that the commander, usually a very nervous man, was very calm. Then he was knocked off his bucket by a shell hit. The molten metal from the shell ran across the floor like lava and he stepped out of the way. Steam pipes were broken, electrical fires sputtered. Noise and heat from the steam were unbearable. He screamed over the phone to engine control to shut off the auxiliary steam line that went through the compartment to the whistle. Somebody on the bridge answered, "They heard you, Page," and in a moment added,

"Secure and get out if there's nothing else you can do."

Several men who had walked out on the catwalk reported that flames were climbing up the tower. Robertson, a quartermaster third class, came through the opening from the catwalk and said, "I've lost my shoe, help me find my shoe." He stood there holding one bare foot off the hot deck, groping in the dark. Everyone helped him, even two commanders. The shoe was not found until next morning—under a body on the catwalk.

No direct hits had been scored on Batt II but flames, explosions and escaping steam threw the place into disorder. Bernard Wenke S1c, the auxiliary helmsman, had been thrown from behind the wheel and lodged in between the bulkhead and the deck. He stayed there, keeping one hand stretched out to hold the bottom of the wheel. Not until flames from below made the deck almost red hot and set his pants afire did he move.

The executive officer pushed aside one of the men to look out the slot and drew back his hand covered with blood. For the first time he realized that men had been wounded. He called for a talker to relay the information to the bridge but got no answer. He felt in the darkness until he found a talker with phones on and dragged him to a standing position. Shaking him vigorously, he gave him the message to relay. The talker repeated the message over the phone, and the commander walked away. The talker slumped back to the deck.

Another officer came into the compartment. He walked to the quartermaster and said in a strained voice, "Feel my arm. It's been hit and I can't tell if it's still there. Go ahead, tell me." The quartermaster, still standing without his shoe, timidly reached for the officer's shoulder but then decided to find out the other way. He groped his way up the officer's leg until he came to his hip, then reached out for his hand. Finding it still there, he ran his hand up the officer's arm until he came to a gaping shrapnel wound in his shoulder. He reported what he had found and the officer said "Thanks" and walked out.

During the entire action one of the lookouts standing by a slot kept repeating in a low voice: "Lord, I'm scared. Nobody has any idea how scared I am. How could anyone be this scared? My God, I'm scared." He said that over and over for about 10 minutes. Nobody thought it strange.

Men began crawling to their feet. Above the noise of the steam and the fire there rose excited voices. Men asked each other who was hurt, where was the ship damaged, how high were the flames.

They speculated on their own chances of getting out. Occasionally they shot glances at the executive officer looking for help. He noticed but didn't know what to say. Finally he blurted out, "Shut up! I'll do all the talking in here!"

The talking stopped. Only the noise of the steam escaping could be heard above the gunfire below. Then the gunfire ceased and within a minute the steam went off. A new noise could be heard now—the moans of the injured and the dying. Pharmacist's mates went among them, injecting shots of morphine. From below came the noise of damage control parties, fighting their way through with hoses and extinguishers. Page grabbed the end of a hose that was passed up to him and pulled on it but it was too heavy. As someone walked past him into Batt II he called out, "Lend a hand, you fool!"

"Shut up, Page," said a voice. "That's Commander Gorton!"

"That's all right," said the commander, "I'm just one of the boys."

Working with the hose they extinguished the flames, then settled back in the darkness to await further action. The steel under their feet was still so hot that they were compelled to keep moving. Outside on the catwalk Page noticed a life jacket on one of the bodies periodically smoulder and burst into flame. Using steel helmets, the men scooped water from the compartment deck and poured it on the life jacket.

Damage control parties are formed when general quarters sounds. They go to their posts and wait for calls. When there is damage in their area they run to the spot with equipment that includes everything from fire extinguishers to monkey wrenches.

John Hagenbuch was a nozzle man on a hose party. While he was directing the stream on a fire in the shadow of the No. 3 turret, Chief Turret Capt. Bowman came out from inside and passed the word for the group to move along. He was ready to fire a salvo and the concussion would be tremendous.

Everybody evacuated the area but Hagenbuch. Standing at the head of the line, he had been forgotten when the word was passed. The guns lowered directly over his head and went off with a blinding flash.

Hagenbuch was thrown to the deck so hard he almost bounced. Slowly he staggered to his feet, temporarily blinded and deafened by the explosion. It had been so powerful that two planes were blown out of their catapults and into the sea.

As Hagenbuch groped his way back and forth, the guns went off with another mighty roar and

again he was thrown to the deck. One of Hagenbuch's hose men saw the whole action and rushed out, lifted him to his feet and dragged him away from the turret as a third salvo thundered.

Thirty minutes later he was back on his feet, volunteering to climb to the top of a smoke stack to put out a fire there.

When John P. Buck left Athens, Ohio, and enlisted in the Navy he went in as an apprentice seaman. Several months later, while cruising the Pacific, the chaplain found that Buck could type. He got him a rating and had him placed on the muster roll as chaplain's yeoman.

Buck's duty at general quarters was after-battery lookout. Technically speaking, his post was in the surface, horizon and lower sky lookout station, situated just below the after main battery direction finder.

Buck leaned against the open door to the compartment and felt the warmth and silence of the night. Early in the channel run he had noticed the smell of the gardenias and had started to put on his gas mask before a talker on the bridge told him the smell was really just gardenias. About 65 feet aft from where he stood, Buck could see the big 16-inch barrels poked out over the starboard rail. He was lazily watching them when they suddenly fired a salvo with a deafening roar. Buck was picked up bodily and thrown inside the compartment. He heard his helmet fly off and strike a bulkhead 30 feet away, then roll around the floor. The explosion blinded him for about 15 minutes, during which time he groped on the floor and found his helmet. When he took it off the next morning he found it wasn't his. Whose it was and where it came from, he never learned.

Regaining his sight and finding that there was a lull in the battle, Buck offered to aid the pharmacist's mates in caring for the wounded. Before he could leave, however, the after battery once again opened fire, so Buck stayed where he was.

Over five miles away a 14-inch shell came screaming out the muzzle of a gun on a Jap battleship. Buck first saw it when it was about two miles away from him, looming larger and larger as a red dot in the sky. He knew it was going to hit and knelt down in the compartment.

The shell came through at exactly deck level. It tore through a slight coaming where the deck joins the hull, made two neat holes through a rim around a hatch leading below, and then crashed against the barbette of the after turret. There was a blinding flash and roar, and shrapnel rained down like cinders. Buck mentally marked turret No. 3 off his list. But when he went out to look he found that the turret was still there but beside it was a yawning hole in the deck.

Looking over the starboard rail he saw a Jap ship racing up. He reported it but worriedly wondered how they were ever going to hit it with the after turret almost certainly out of action. Then he heard the secondaries open fire with a staccato bang-bang-bang, finally reaching the ear-splitting regularity of machine-gun firing, though in each of the little turrets men were flinging in shells by hand.

The after turret, meanwhile, turned slowly toward the approaching ship, now so close that the elevation on the barrels was almost nil.

Nobody was more amazed than Buck when the after turret fired. He had no idea it was still in action. Then he saw that the Jap ship had been hit almost point-blank by all three shells. There was a big flash where the ship had been and then smoking, bubbling water. In the few seconds before the Jap went under, Buck had seen one of its turrets fly high into the air and the ship start to split in the middle. But it sank before it had chance to fall apart.

The firing stopped and Buck left to help in the care of the wounded. At sick bay he found men stretched out on every available table with doctors and pharmacist's mates working over them while standing in 4 inches of blood and water on the deck.

He was sent with a doctor to the top of the superstructure to help the wounded men who had been cut off there. Only Patrick was still there. The doctor stayed with Patrick, giving Buck syrettes of morphine to administer inside the superstructure on the way down.

Descending on the inside of the tower, Buck found a man lying on one of the upper levels with one leg shot off. He took out his knife and walked over to a dangling electrical wire, cut it loose and wrapped it around the injured man's leg. He wrenched loose the shattered rung of a ladder and used it to twist through the wire, making a tourniquet.

On the next level down he felt his feet get tangled in something in the water on the deck. An officer came along with a flashlight and they discovered that his legs were entwined by someone's insides floating on the water.

- He kicked himself loose and went down to the main deck where he saw a man sitting wearily against a bulkhead.

"Hey, Mac, are you okay?" asked Buck.

No answer came so Buck asked him again. When he got no answer this time, Buck reached down to feel his pulse. The man was already cold. Buck left and went back to his post.

Up above decks the wounded Patrick was giving out morphine. Page was trying hard to keep breathing above the escaping steam, and Buck was trying to recover his sight after being dazed by shell fire. Below decks, in engine control room, was Chief Yeoman Cheek reading an old issue of the *Reader's Digest*.

The huge panel of gauges in front of him was functioning perfectly. The engine was at top speed, the boilers were maintaining a magnificent head of steam, and the blowers were keeping the room quite cool and comfortable. When a command came through, Cheek carried it out, then returned to his reading.

There was nothing else to do.

The noise of the battle was distant and removed. Around him the men stood talking quietly or merely looking at the gauges. In a vague sort of a way they all worried about the 600 pounds of steam coursing through the pipes all around them. Engineers always worry about steam. But they had faith in the armor, faith in the engine, faith in each other.

So Cheek kept on reading the *Reader's Digest*.

Some reports of injuries could be heard over the phone but not much. The men down in engine control couldn't tell the difference between hits and the noise of their own guns.

It was morning when Cheek walked up onto the deck and saw the destruction. Then he realized, for the first time, how many shells had ripped into the ship during the night.

After he saw the damage, he couldn't sleep for three days.

INFANTRY BATTALION SWEATS IT OUT IN ITALY

By Sgt. WALTER BERNSTEIN

WITH THE FIFTH ARMY IN ITALY—It is strange the way some people still think of war as all shooting and Commando raids, when as a matter of fact it is nine-tenths ordinary grind with no excitement and a great deal of unpleasantness. Sometimes there is excitement, but it is mostly the loose-boweled kind that you would just as soon be without. Sometimes, of course, there is more than excitement; there is the good feeling that comes from being with men you trust and doing a job you believe in.

But most of the time, for the men who are really up there, the war is a tough and dirty life, without immediate compensation. It is cold nights and no sleep, the beard matted on your face and the sores coming out on your feet, the clothes stiffening and the dirt caking on your body. It is digging and crawling and sweating out the 88s, inching forward over rocks and through rivers to mountains that no one in his right mind would ever want. It is doing the same filthy job day after day with a kind of purposeless insanity; and dreaming all the time of warm beds with clean sheets and a steak the size of your arm; and pushing, always pushing. Maybe to some people it also means being able to eat again and live without fear, but to the American infantryman in this campaign it is primarily one large lump of Sugar Howl Item Tear.

At least that's the way it was with one battalion of Infantry when it pushed ahead of the rest of the Fifth Army and then had to wait until everyone else arrived. Maybe if this were a Hollywood war the battalion would have wheeled to the flank and cut off the Germans from their main route of escape. It had the position, all right. It was on top of a mountain almost overlooking the main road that the Jerries were using.

Other American elements were fighting for a town some four miles to the flank and five miles behind the battalion. All it had to do was march the four miles across to this road, cut it, and there would have been a good solid minor victory. All the battalion needed to do this was a supply line, communications, artillery, reinforcements and guts. All the battalion had was the guts.

The battalion arrived on the mountain at night, the way it had been arriving at each of its objectives for the past week. The rest of the regiment was some six or seven miles behind. The battalion arrived about midnight, having climbed since dark,

and the first thing it did was set up security. The CO figured that with enemy on three sides a little security might come in handy.

The second thing the battalion did was try to sleep. This wasn't so easy, and not because the men weren't tired enough. It was cold on the mountain. It was cold enough, as one of the men said, to freeze the ears off a brass monkey, and he didn't say ears. Most of the men had only one blanket; they had forded a river on their way up and their feet were freezing. So they wrapped themselves in the one blanket and searched for hollows where the wind wasn't so much like a knife. Some of them slept two together for warmth, and they got through the night that way.

The next morning the colonel moved the battalion CP into town. The town was just off the crest of the mountain: an old town with a castle and narrow cobblestoned streets. The colonel was invited into the mayor's house. There were already three families living there, but the dining room was free and so was the mayor's study, and there was a kitchen with running water and a fireplace. The colonel moved his staff and their blankets onto the floor of the study and the enlisted staff section took the floor of the dining room. The rest of the battalion stayed on the mountain.

That first morning they also discovered what a position they held. They heard the shell fire behind them where the Americans were still storming the other town and knew that if they could reach the road in force they could cut the retreat of several hundred Germans.

They also knew that in their present condition there was absolutely nothing they could do about it. They were out too far as it was, thrust forward in one of those positions that look so dramatic on a situation map and usually end with a hurried retreat. The colonel decided to sit tight and send out patrols. When you got right down to it there was nothing much else he could do.

The patrols went out and the battalion settled down to wait. It was warm in the mayor's house. The colonel was out around the mountain somewhere, seeing what he could see, and the major was out trying to arrange a mule train to go down and get some rations. The rest of the section sat before the fire and listened to the mayor's family. One of the staff section was a T-4 from New York who spoke Italian. His name was D'Crenzo and he had been a golf pro and artist in civilian life; now he was the battalion draftsman. The family thought D'Crenzo's dialect very funny and laughed whenever he spoke, but they brought out wine for him and even potatoes, which they baked in the fire.

The mayor's family all wore black because the mayor had been hanged by the Germans before they left. He had been hanged together with five other citizens of the town as reprisal for the killing of a German soldier by one of the townspeople. The soldier had been stealing the Italian's pigs and chickens, and finally the Italian had taken a gun and shot him. The Germans took the mayor and 10 other hostages, held them overnight in one of the buildings and hanged six of them the next morning in the town square. The corpses were kept hanging there for two weeks until the stink was so bad that they had to be cut down and buried. The Germans said the bodies hanging there would teach the Italians a lesson.

The story was told to the Americans by the mayor's daughter, a black-haired girl named Ines. She told the story in French, so that her mother wouldn't understand. The mother had been away when the incident occurred and believed her husband had died of a heart attack. She sat there while the daughter told the story, smiling and nodding and not understanding a word.

Later that morning one of the patrols returned with news that there were Germans evacuating north along the road. About two hours later shots were heard on the other side of the mountain and another patrol returned, marching a group of Germans before them. They were the remnants of a patrol the Americans had accidentally run into. Two other Jerries had been killed.

The Germans were taken into one of the other buildings where they talked with an American boy of German descent. All the Germans except their sergeant talked. They were all 20 years old, except one who was 19, and all had fought in Russia. They were very anxious about what was going to happen to them, but they all thought that Germany would win the war. They also thought the German Army was still advancing on the Russian front. The German sergeant was stubborn, though, and refused to talk. He was a real *Hitlerjugend* and declared passionately that a sergeant had his honor and had no right to talk. The assembled Americans admired his stand on the matter. They also said he was a real soldier, and, out of respect for the sergeant's honor, did not question him. The Germans were locked up and a guard placed outside their building while

the Italians stood around and shouted curses.

That afternoon it started to rain. More patrols returned with news of the German retreat to the north. They reported to the colonel in the kitchen of the mayor's house, standing wet in the doorway, eyeing the fire. Then they returned to their positions on the mountain.

The rain made any sort of observation impossible, which did not displease the artillery liaison officer at all. He had no communication with his artillery anyway, but he had felt obliged to go out and observe as a matter of form. Now he didn't even have to do that.

He just sat with his sergeant in front of the fire and talked of the German soldier they had killed two days ago. They had gone out to observe the effects of their fire at close range and had strayed into an Italian house for a glass of wine. There they had been surprised by a German private, who stepped into the doorway with a machine pistol. He caught them both flat-footed; the only mistake he made was reaching for the grenade that was tied to the sergeant's jacket. When he reached to take the grenade the captain said "Now," knocked the machine pistol aside and hit the German with a left hook. The sergeant did the same thing, and they knocked the German through the door, pulled their 45s and didn't stop firing until they ran out of cartridges. They stood by and watched while the Italians from the house grabbed the German's boots off his feet and then slammed him over the head a couple of times with a fence post to make sure he was dead.

The captain now had the machine pistol slung over his shoulder. The only thing he regretted was that his shots had ruined a pair of Zeiss glasses the German had around his neck. The only thing the sergeant regretted was that now he had to clean the machine pistol as well as the captain's .45.

It rained all through that day and into the night, a cold driving rain that went through you and out the other side. Patrols came and went. The colonel sent one platoon five miles north to a town believed occupied by the Germans. The platoon found the town empty but met a Jerry patrol coming in as they went out. There was a brief skirmish, with no casualties, and after a while both patrols withdrew gracefully.

Back at the CP the colonel and his staff sat before the fire, cursing the weather and the impotence of their situation. The mayor's family sat all around them, the old people mute in a corner, the children hovering on the fringe of the gathering, waiting for the candy and sugar from the C-ration cans. Also with the family this night was a cousin, an artillery officer recently escaped from German territory. He told with flourishes how badly the Germans treated the Italians and how he and his comrades had spiked their guns before they left. He was dressed now in army boots, sport jacket and knickers, and was on his way to Naples where he lived.

The next morning was still full of rain, but it cleared by noon and the colonel and the artillery captain went out to find an artillery OP. The mule train returned from the valley with boxes of ammunition and K ration, and the men even ate the biscuits and the dextrose tablets.

At exactly 1 o'clock in the afternoon someone wondered out loud why the Jerries hadn't shelled the town, and 15 minutes later they did. Only one shell fell in the town, however, and no one was hurt. The shelling lasted about 20 minutes, and the mayor's family huddled in the kitchen, badly frightened. Later that afternoon the battalion medics set up an aid station across the street from the CP and began handling the sick cases. Many of the men were suffering from some sort of overexposure, but only those hot with fever reported to the station. The battalion sergeant major sweated over his status report, trying on paper to make the battalion come somewhere near battalion strength. "If the Jerries only knew what we had here," he kept saying. "If they only knew."

The patrols reported a slackening of the German retreat along the road, and the colonel realized that, if he ever had a theoretical opportunity of attacking, it was gone now. Toward evening a regimental wire crew arrived with communication and the colonel discovered that the Americans had finally taken the town to the battalion's flank. The colonel beat his head, thinking about what he could have done, and sent out more patrols.

The men on the mountain squeezed the water out of their clothes and wondered why they didn't move. At this point they didn't care much what was in front of them or whom they had behind; there was nothing they wouldn't do to get the war over sooner and go home.

The regimental executive officer hiked up from the valley, wearing a trench coat, his feet wet. He was a tall, soft-spoken man and he told the colonel that Corps and even Army were well pleased with the job the battalion was doing: even if they didn't fire a shot, they were exerting pressure on the German flank, making their position untenable, forcing them to retreat. The colonel shook his head and agreed.

That evening the mayor's daughter turned in the name of a local Fascist, a man in town who had been head of the Blackshirt organization and also helped the Germans when they were here. The S-2 went to the man's house; he was out; the house was searched and the S-2 returned with the report that evidence of Fascist activity had been found, but there wasn't anything he could do about it. It would be a different story if the man were helping the Germans now, but being just a Fascist was in itself no crime. He told D'Crenzo to tell the girl to get in touch with the civil authorities about the matter.

It rained again that night, and the patrols reported the town to the north was clear. During the night the regimental CP moved into town, taking the old castle, and one other battalion moved up to secure the first battalion's flank. The rain stopped in the morning, and the colonel had a conference with the regimental CO. There was a little shelling in the morning, but not much. It was answered immediately by the 75s, which had moved into the valley at night. The artillery captain directed their fire from the mountain top.

When the colonel returned from his conference he called a meeting of all his company commanders and told them to be ready to move out as soon as it got dark. They were moving to the high ground overlooking the town five miles to the north. Then the colonel dispatched a platoon to survey the route and act as guides.

In the afternoon, as the enlisted staff section sat before the fire, the mayor's daughter baked them a *pizza*, which they ate while it was still hot. The men on the mountain had been told they were moving again and some of them were trying to sleep, stretched out on wet shelter halves.

Just before dark the colonel assembled the battalion, keeping them under cover. The rain had stopped and the sun was suddenly out, sinking over the edge of a mountain. The air was cold and crisp, mixed with the heavy rain smell from the earth. As the men began their march they could see the mountains ahead of them, covered with snow.

此の頃は何か良い風聞
を聞いたが

Cpl. LaFayette Locke.

Eyewitness drawing showing action against the Japanese
by the 37th (Ohio) Div. on Bougainville.

THE SECOND BATTLE OF BOUGAINVILLE

By Sgt. BARRETT McGURN

Sketches by Sgt. Robert Greenhalgh. (South Pacific)

Empress Augusta Bay, Bougainville, the Solomons—Battles are not like the ones they show in the movies; at any rate the Second Battle of Bougainville was not. Most American soldiers, after all, are just civilians in uniform, who carry over to the battlefield many of their peacetime habits and points of view. The result is a strange melee of the grim and the unconsciously comic.

Like thousands of other Jap soldiers on the bypassed Shortlands, Choiseul, Buka, New Britain and New Ireland, the Japs on Bougainville were faced with the choice of starving because their supply lines had been cut or of making suicidal attacks against the American military machine. Four months after our seizure of the Empress Augusta

Bay beachhead, the Japs on Bougainville chose to fight. They were composed of the picked Jap Imperial Marines and one of Japan's most celebrated army outfits, the 6th Division, veterans of six years' fighting in China and of the rape of Nanking. The U. S. forces on the beachhead were the Americal Division, veterans of Guadalcanal, and the 37th Division, veterans of New Georgia and Vella Lavella. Both outfits have spent more than two years in the Pacific.

In the Second Battle of Bougainville, there were great numbers of maimed and dead on both sides. Some 7,000 Japs were believed killed in their assault on the prepared U. S. positions, and our forces counted 20 Jap dead to one American.

As I rode up to the battlefront, just past Coffin Corners on Major Fissell Highway, I was confronted by a bold sign: "ALL SIGHTSEERS FORWARD OF THIS AREA WILL BE ARRESTED." Up at the front somebody explained that kibitzers from corps headquarters, service-command and combat outfits not currently in the line had been scooping up all the best souvenirs and even getting in the way of the shooting. The fighting infantrymen were pretty bitter about it.

The matter came to head during the battle when a Marine darted forward under fire to relieve a fresh-killed Jap officer of his saber and pistol. A rifle poked out of a foxhole at the officer's feet and covered the Marine. "I killed that Jap to get those souvenirs," said the soldier in the hole, "and I'll kill you, if I have to, to keep them." The marine retreated.

While the infantrymen were still too busy to hunt souvenirs, one fearless GI businessman trotted back and forth, bringing out fallen Jap rifles and selling them at $30 apiece. Another souvenir hunter refused $150 for a Jap light machine gun with bayonet attachment.

Eventually order was established. Some one called in the MPs. Since then the fighters have been left more to themselves.

This bizarre souvenir hunting during battle had a variety of explanations. For one thing, the Japs' tactics were to concentrate all their force at one point, throwing as much as a regiment against a 100-yard-wide stretch of wire. Consequently battlefields were often only the size of a football field or even of a couple of tennis courts. This meant that sightseers could walk up almost to the scene of the fighting itself in comparative safety.

For another thing, the Bougainville beachhead in four months of occupation had become so American that it was sometimes easy to think of it as a secure corner of the States. A couple of hundred yards from the Americal Division front, for instance, ambulances and trucks rolling forward came upon a warning in red: "DANGER. STEEP HILL. LOW GEAR."

But the principal explanation lay in the character of the enemy himself. In front-line pillboxes a popular subject for debate was whether the Japs were (a) crazy, (b) dumb or (c) literally dopey. Many thought (c) was the correct answer; a lot of Japs carried a soft brown pill, believed to be a narcotic.

One Jap, not yet classified, walked down a trail outside our lines carrying an American helmet and (upon the word of the GI who shot him) whistling "Yankee Doodle." Another Jap, in a foxhole a few yards from American positions, raised his head to yell: "What's the score, Joe?" Before any unsuspecting Yank could put up his own head to reply, a GI off on a flank answered the Jap with an accurate shot.

During the fighting I visited Bloody Hill (Hill 260) outside the Americal front. An acting MP came up, and I thought for a minute that I was back in basic training. A group of us had gathered around to hear about a Jap trick that cost us four dead and 22 wounded the day before, a couple of hundred yards down the east slope.

"Spread out, fellows," the MP interrupted us. "The colonel will get sore if he sees a lot of guys together. Too many get killed at one time."

We spread. We didn't want the colonel sore.

Then, at longer range, we heard the rest of the story: A patrol had succeeded in pinning down the Japs occupying several pillboxes. When five Japs raised their hands and stood up in full view, the Americans ceased firing and came out in the open, too. An interpreter told the Japs to throw down their weapons and promised them that they would not be harmed. Suddenly a wounded Jap in shorts, apparently an officer, screamed something, and the Japs dived back into their holes. Instantly mortar fire lobbed out at the exposed Americans, hitting 26. The patrol had to withdraw.

The hilltop where we were chatting was jointly occupied by Americans and Japs at that very moment. The Japs were dug in 75 yards from us, beneath the roots of a banyan tree.

Down the hill below us resounded the "dat-da dat-da dat-da dat-da" of a machine gun, the "pow-pow" of M1s, the "pha-lot" of 4.2-inch mortars and the hammering "baa-da-da-banh" of 90-mm guns. The Japs on the hill with us were quiet for a change, although two-inch slugs of shrapnel occasionally struck in our area.

A group of Americans off to one side had a burner going under coffee, and medics in an aid station in a log-covered pillbox were busy sprinkling sulfanilamide into the fresh wounds of soldiers who drifted in periodically. Getting hit was regarded as an occupational hazard, and nobody seemed to worry about it.

The colonel was not sore about anything when we met him. He volunteered to put a barrage of 4.2-inch mortar shells on the Jap positions just to show that the U. S. marksmen on Bougainville, shooting 1400 yards from far below us on the flat beachhead, could lay shells 25 yards from our own men.

But before the colonel could put on his mortar

show, the telephones from the beachhead reported that our 155-mm guns were going to maul the Japs a little. Everyone on the hilltop got into holes to escape the 155 shrapnel. "On the way," shouted a fellow at the phones, and then the shells came over, crackling like ripped newspaper. The ground shivered as they hit.

Then the colonel called for his mortars. The shell bursts walked across the Jap holes, planting bushes of black smoke with brilliant blossoms of red-orange flame.

Another colonel, inventor of a Rube Goldberg flame thrower, agreed to demonstrate it. We scooted through shallow trenches to a spot 25 yards from the Japs. The colonel's invention consisted of cans of gasoline fastened to rods that fit into the mouth of a mortar. In quick succession he lobbed six cans into the Jap holes, but the mortar got so hot that the next can burst into flame and spilled only a few feet in front of the barrel. The colonel apologized; the device was not perfected yet, he said.

All of this finally succeeded in waking up the Japs or getting them sore. A Jap knee-mortar shell suddenly exploded 15 feet from us and sent me to the hospital along with two other GIs. The shell blast felt like a board slamming flat against my chest, but I didn't notice the small wounds from the fragments until moments later.

The shell served at least two purposes. It demonstrated to my satisfaction that you never know about the one that gets you until most of the damage has been done. And it labored the point that, for all the sporting flavor, this pocket-sized war was the real game and for keeps.

Among the GIs who thought the Japs were dopey was Pfc. John W. Colvard of Tallahassee, Fla., assistant BAR gunner in an American unit. He and Pfc. John C. Buntain of Paris, Ill., were credited with killing 20 or 30 Japs with BARs, while mortars directed from the same pillbox took care of 50 more.

"You'd shoot one," Colvard said, "and he'd never look at you—he'd just keep on walking. Some were armed; some weren't. Most of them were just carrying sacks. We shot the Japs till they lay still. Then we shot them some more sometimes. I figured they were just doped up or dazed or something from so much shelling."

The two men did their firing from a pillbox alongside a Jap supply trail. Jap mortar shells finally drove them out after three days.

T/Sgt. Denis J. Fullerton of Lexington, Mass., an American platoon sergeant who was converted into a stretcher case by the mortar shell that broke up the demonstration of the home-made flame thrower, leaned to the theory that the Japs were bomb-happy. "We were picking them off all morning," Fullerton said. "The Japs would stand up there on the hilltop, shell-shocked, I suppose. My men got seven who did that today."

According to Pfc. Sebastian B. Porretto of New York, N. Y., the Japs acted "sort of happy-go-lucky, as if they didn't give a damn." Porretto set an ambush for the Japs 3,500 yards beyond our lines. With 12 bullets he killed nine and got one possible, although in training back in the States he had failed to win an expert rifleman's medal. "I didn't give a damn in the camp," Porretto explained. "But here I just shot when it counted. Just took my time, kept cool and, damn, I got them."

"I'd say they're a poor class of fighter the way they go at it," commented Pfc. Harold R. Mueller of Jamestown, N. Dak., who refused corporal's stripes to keep his BAR. "In a set-up like this, they could never whip us. That's for sure." Mueller was credited with 35 Japs but insisted he and the two others in his hole got at least half the 158 Japs whose bodies littered their positions after an attack on that part of the line.

"It seems to me they don't give a damn whether they live or die so long as they get in," said Mueller. He spotted one Jap officer trying to get into a pillbox and shot him. Instantly there was a terrible bawling, and Japs spilled wildly out of a banyan tree near the fallen officer. "It seemed they all wanted to get out at the same time," Mueller said. "I just mowed them down. I figured I got 25 or 30."

Some Japs came down a gully below Mueller's pillbox one night. "They were all columned up," said Sgt. Dominic Verde, a BAR man from Brooklyn. "They seemed to come in close-order drill." Maybe the Japs liked each other's company. Anyway, their close formation also pleased Mueller, Verde and the third man in the box with them— Pvt. Jim Holtz. Mueller and Verde opened fire with BARs, and Holtz rolled grenades down the slope. Hearing the grenades, the Japs prodded for mines. Next morning 54 Jap corpses lay there.

"The Japs are dumber'n hell," insisted S/Sgt. Delfred G. Sadler of Neponset, Ill. "Either they've got lots of guts or they're dopey. I think they're dopey." One Jap officer tossed his pack over a fence and then climbed over the top after it. Sadler got him against the skyline.

Throughout the battle, the Japs seesawed between shrewd know-how and striking ignorance.

When the Jap artillery opened up, it directed some embarrassingly accurate fire on a number of key objectives. Several times each of the three airfields had to shut down for a few hours, and when 50 shells landed on it, an Americal regiment's rest area suddenly became an unhealthy place to rest.

The Japs also displayed an amazing ability to infiltrate. At one point they tunneled under the barbed wire and kept on crawling deeper into our area all night long, creeping from bush to tree, through our communication trenches and even from one heap of dead to the next. One group of Japs opened a grave we had dug for others killed two days earlier and huddled among the corpses. Still another Jap used a latrine hole as a pillbox; Sgt. Charles F. Kandl of Easton, Pa., got him with a rifle grenade.

Sadler told how the Japs sneaked through our wire with incredible stealth and silence. "But once they're inside," he said, "they stand up and give orders. One Jap shouted: 'All carbines, cease firing.' Unfortunately for him and his men, we didn't. Another Jap called out: 'Where are you, F Company?' They knew who we were, all right."

In contrast to this cunning, there were instances of stupidity. After penetrating 300 yards behind our lines and reaching a battalion CP, 50 Japs were dumb enough to sit down placidly for breakfast at dawn, the very moment our tanks rolled in for the counterattack. A pointblank hit with a 75 HE shell made one Jap vanish like a stooge in a magic show, and soon all the rest were dead. One of our major casualties was the battalion victory garden where the encounter took place.

The Japs broke most of the rules in the book. On Hill 600 they attacked frontally in waves, just what our machine-gunners would have ordered. The overwhelming automatic firepower facing the Japs proved too much for them, and 700 were slaughtered in one day. Every time they pierced our lines they seemed to march into one of our 37-mm antitank guns, mounted for antipersonnel use. They could hardly be blamed for that, however, because those guns were everywhere.

Pfc. Larry Haselhuhn of Rogers City, Mich., said the Japs were afraid only of flame throwers. "They're not scared of our bullets," he said. "Throw thermite bombs, and they'll throw them right back at you." All in all, he thought the Japs were "pretty slick" fighters, but that didn't keep him from getting seven verified plus "a lot banged up" with his light machine gun at the foot of Hill 260. Haselhuhn had plenty of respect for the Jap knee mortars. "They can lay them in on you," he said; "don't let anyone kid you about that. They can drop a

shell in your hip pocket." I had good reason to agree with him.

Our tanks brought a varied reaction from the Japs. In the Americal sector, the big Jap Imperial Marines, ranging from 5 feet 6 to more than 6 feet, "laughed at the tanks, ran up to them and threw grenades and Molotov cocktails on the backs to set them afire," according to Cpl. Fred Angelo of Schenectady, N. Y., commander of a light tank. "They couldn't harm the tanks, not with the bean shooters they had," he said. "We mowed them down with the bow gun."

In another sector, the 37th Division was facing Jap soldiers of the 6th Division, some of them so small they looked like dolls. When the tanks struck, a few of the Japs jumped from their foxholes and ran, a maneuver that proved as fatal as the marines' daring.

What caused the most comment among the Americans was the Jap knack of digging in anywhere, any time. "They dig in while you're shooting at them," said Haselhuhn. "I was firing with a machine gun at one fellow, and dirt was coming out all the time."

Sgt. Sadler agreed. "If they get three shovelfuls out," he said, "you can't hit them."

A few Japs tried to tunnel into tenanted American foxholes but without success. The foxholes the Japs dug inside our lines after breakthroughs were not much wider at ground level than a man's torso, but at the bottom they were burrowed forward. Practically the only way for a GI to kill the Jap occupant with a rifle was to get behind the hole and shoot in at an angle.

Advance American patrols often heard the pounding of axes as Japs chopped logs for their dugouts. 2d Lt. Carl D. Johnson of San Francisco, an Americal platoon leader, was 4,500 yards outside our lines when he heard a wood-chopper, and presently he found himself in one of the battle's most remarkable hand-to-hand duels—a slugfest with rifle butts.

The lieutenant's carbine misfired as he leveled it at a little moon-faced Jap only an arm's length away. In too-cramped a position to return fire, the Jap swung his long Arisaka rifle as a club, slamming the flat side of the stock across the lieutenant's head. The last thing the lieutenant remembered doing before he passed out was pulling the butt of his own rifle out of the Jap's forehead. Mechanically he had dashed it in up to the oiler. He was out for 20 minutes but got back to the lines all right.

"The Jap officers may be brilliant," said Lt. Raymond H. Ross of Medford, Oreg., "but the men are sure dodos." Lt. Ross is head of the Dime-a-Dozen Club, a 10-man group of volunteer Americal snipers. The lieutenant has agreed to pay 10 cents out of his own pocket to each member of the club who kills 12 Japs, each kill to be witnessed by at least one other club member. So far the club has 21 victims, but no member has an individual total of 12. Two of the club members have been killed, and two are MIA.

"The Japs have always been so damned ignorant," Lt. Ross said. "We'll go behind their lines and kill three or four, and next day we'll go back and do it all over again. Out in the rear of Hill 260 on the fork of the Torokina River, four Japs came down the trail in their pajamas. It looked as if they had just had breakfast. They evidently didn't expect us until 0800 or 0900. We blew them all to hell with M1s. Not that they're not brave fighters. They fight like wildcats. But they're so easy to catch."

Some of the Jap officers also are far from model warriors, Lt. Ross said. On one patrol the Dime-a-Dozen Club, plus a large party that had gone out with them on the job, spotted a Jap officer and managed to surround him with 69 men before he suspected anything. Lt. Ross whistled because he felt guilty about shooting him in the back. Then, as the officer turned, the lieutenant shot him through the buttocks. He wanted to take him prisoner. The Jap officer played dead until Lt. Ross approached and then leaped at him bare-handed. A BAR man sliced the Jap officer in two, from the belly through the head.

S/Sgt. Ralph E. Brodin of Spooner, Minn., who said he joined the Dime-a-Dozen Club to earn the down payment on a ring for his girl, a WAC corporal, was the leading enlisted man in the group, with three Japs to his credit. Lt. Ross was showing the way with eight, plus another five for which he couldn't get club credit because there were no club witnesses.

One Dime-a-Dozener, S/Sgt. Harry E. Schulte of Gary, S. Dak., was not a rifleman but a mortarman. "I joined the club," he said, "with the idea of getting a few Japs with the old rifle, I guess, instead of indirectly." He had two so far. Schulte was also doing OK at his platoon job. On top of Hill 608 he had a home of canvas, bamboo and sandbags, labeled "Sky Room."

Across a 700-foot-deep ravine from Schulte was Hill 11-11, from which the Japs were firing 77s and 47s for a while, taking advantage of the jungle cover that prevented the Americans from locating

them. But Schulte figured out a system. For hours he stared at the green slope, waiting for a gun flash. When it came, he fired instantly with his 50-caliber machine gun and kept up tracer bursts until our heavy artillery could come in on the target pointed by Schulte's fingers of flame. A Jap 47 objected one day and threw several rounds at Schulte, but the gangling farmer boy said: "I got in the last shot. I don't know whether he ran out of ammunition or got tired or what."

Like everybody else on the beachhead who didn't want to go nuts, the Dime-a-Dozen Club looked for laughs even on patrol. Once they heard a noise in the jungle dark and stealthily surrounded the spot from which the noise had come. As guns pointed, they flashed on a jungle light. A slimy-tailed, terrier-sized ball of fur blinked in the glare. It was a "banana bear."

Another time Pfc. Richard Kowitz of St. Paul, Minn., had to lie still while a big green jungle spider with inch-long legs built its web under the peak of his helmet. A Jap was combing the area, and the slightest move would have spoiled Kowitz's camouflage. So he had to lie there and watch the spider spin. The club members thought the whole episode very funny.

The Dime-a-Dozeners worked out several new wrinkles in jungle fighting. In addition to blacking their faces and pulling their hats low over their eyes, the members painted their weapons OD. On large patrols, the men slept in groups, with a sturdy vine reaching under their arms so that a single jerk would awaken the whole party. That way, only three men needed to stay awake in a patrol of 40 or more.

Not the least odd feature of the battle scene was the behavior of Jap prisoners in the stockade. Our men preferred killing Japs to capturing them, until a case of beer was offered for each captive. Most of the Jap prisoners were deep brown and quite

From a jeep, an American watches curiously as a big MP takes a little Jap prisoner to the rear.

pleased with life as they washed their laundry or did other personal chores inside the wire. One Jap with a splitting grin offered sun glasses to a group of GIs who were squinting into the sun to stare at him. Another prisoner cut out the characters in an American comic strip and decorated his tent with them. When Sgt. Robert Greenhalgh, YANK staff artist, sketched the stockade, one Jap asked to see the drawing. "Very good," he chuckled.

Two other Japs threw the Bougainville panorama into what was probably the correct focus. The first Jap clutched his army's favorite weapon, the bayonet, and charged a tank with it. The tank ran over

him. The second Jap, a prisoner, asked permission to broadcast a message to his comrades over a front-line public-address system. "With our ancient ideas," he said to the other Japs, "how can we expect to win over the arms possessed by the civilized and world-prominent country of America?"

That seems to be just about the score. The Samurai swords, cruel weapons used for generations to lop off the heads of the Emperor's powerless enemies, are now mostly souvenirs for American curio collectors. Our automatic and heavy weapons are seeing to that.

When Sgt. Greenhalgh sketched the stockade, one Jap inspected his drawing and chuckled, "Very good."

CAMERAMAN IN CASSINO

By Sgt. GEORGE AARONS

WITH THE FIFTH ARMY IN ITALY—They gave me a Tommy bowler and a leather jerkin and made me take off my combat suit. Otherwise, they said, the British snipers might shoot at my American helmet because it looked like the German one. The captain briefed us, explaining that our load would be rations and barbed wire. He gave us the password and checked to see if everyone knew the rendezvous at the edge of town.

There were 11 in our party: eight of the men carrying rations; the captain, another man and myself carrying wire. The moon had come up by this time, bringing the slopes of Montecassino out of the darkness.

The captain, the wireman and I started off in a jeep, sitting all three in the front; the back was loaded with the five reels of barbed wire. The windshield was down, so I got the full benefit of the cold night air. It seemed as if we were the only mechanized travel. Soon we began to pass long, slow lines of mules, heavily laden and led by soldiers. The mule lines turned and wound with the road into the valley.

The soldiers leading them were evidently of several nationalities, because whenever our jeep turned a corner and came up unexpectedly on the rear of a column, we heard voices cry out warnings in French and English and sometimes in Italian.

When the mule trains became scarcer, we caught up with jeeps pulling loaded trailers. Occasionally we passed companies of Infantry replacements moving up.

The driver was familiar with the road and he began to speed up, never lingering long on the high points or crossroads because, he said, "they have those spots zeroed in." Although the flats in front of the town were occasionally shelled, nothing fell near us.

I noticed that smoke shells were being put down in front of the town, blocking out the lower slopes but leaving the monastery clearly visible above.

We passed a few dead mules by the side of the road and then a Bren-gun carrier lying in a ditch. There was a heavy smell in the air, a mixture of dead mules and the bright yellow flowers patching the flats in the valley.

Then we came to the flats flooded by the Germans. We made the turn at Hell's Fire Corner, clearly marked by strips of mine tape strung on two shot-up six-by-sixes and two wrecked ambulances.

The driver stepped on the gas, and we raced across the Rapido, bounced past a couple of knocked-out tanks and came to an intersection. The inevitable MP stood there, directing traffic. We turned left at a barracks, and it was then that we began to see the first effects of the terrific shelling and bombardment the town had received. Only a few pillars remained standing above the debris of the barracks on the outskirts. Here and there were dead Shermans, which had thrown their treads as a snake sheds its skin.

Pulling up in front of our meeting place, we quickly unloaded the wire. Before we could acknowledge the hurried "Bye, Yank, see you tomorrow night," the driver raced away, leaving the captain and me alone with our reels of barbed wire.

I'd expected the worst during the ride but nothing had happened, and now I remarked to the captain: "It's pretty quiet tonight." He turned and said quietly that there was an understanding among the men never to mention things like that on these trips. He told me he made a trip like this one every night.

While we waited for the truck to arrive, he demonstrated how to carry a coil of barbed wire. You stand inside the coil and then grab hold of the looped pieces of insulated wire on each side.

Soon there was a terrific clanking down the road, and I was sure every German in Cassino could hear the truck coming. The noise was made by chains carried over the truck's bumper.

The men scrambled out and the captain checked to see that each man had his proper load. The rations were carried in pairs of sandbags tied together at the mouth and then slung over the men's shoulders. Each man also carried a small bag in each hand.

While the captain was attending to the final details, the Germans started. There's a funny thing about mortars: when they're going to miss you they can be heard, but the closer they get the quieter they sound.

There would be a swish-swish, a burst of flame and then a loud explosion. I felt very uneasy. The shells were exploding in the very path we were traveling, and I whispered to the New Zealander behind me: "It's getting kind of noisy." He whispered back: "Jerry's having his bit of hate."

When we moved off, the captain placed me behind him and explained that we must keep five yards between us. He picked up his coil and started off, hugging the bank alongside the road. Picking up my coil, I noticed that it was off balance but decided there was no time to do anything about it now and took up the trail right behind the captain. I heard the man behind me do the same.

Everything was still all around us. Suddenly a burst of machine-gun fire shattered the silence, synchronized with a single tracer that lazily arched its way across us toward our lines. This was followed by a couple of mortars, and then all was quiet again.

It was a beautiful night, filled with all the signs of an awakening spring. A lonely night bird was sounding off over in Purple Heart Valley, and the sting had gone out of the breeze coming down off the mountain.

When we got to the edge of the town, the captain set his coil down near an overturned Sherman and stopped. I was puffing hard and was grateful for this chance to rest. In the distance we could hear the sound of long-range shelling. Occasionally the tanks bedded down in the flats would fire a mission, and then all would be quiet again.

The captain asked me how I was doing and then said that we didn't have much farther to go, but that it would be rougher now; we were coming to the rubble. "I hope Spandau Alley is quiet tonight," a Kiwi whispered in my ear, explaining that it was a spot along our route that the Kraut sprayed every so often in the hope of catching just such a party as ours. "We've been pretty lucky so far," he said. "He's just missed every time."

As we started off again, I hoped silently that he would continue to miss. In a few minutes we were in the rubble, and when someone stepped on a tin can my heart seemed to stop. As it resumed its normal beat, I could see that we were walking on what had once been a street; we were trying to hug the stumps of walls of houses. It was so quiet that I could hear a cat crying.

There was actually no shape to the road as we climbed over heaps of rubble covering the first floor of what had once been a house, down the other side into a bomb crater and then around a tank that lay on its side. I had no idea at times whether we were going up or down a slope and just followed the man in front of me.

Suddenly the near quiet was broken by a very sharp swish, then by the crash of a mortar. The captain shouted: "Take cover, blokes." Everybody dropped what he was carrying, stretched out flat and tried to crawl to some hole or to get behind a heavy wall that was still standing.

I could hear the captain moving about to make sure that everyone was safe. I found myself sprawled out behind a two-foot-thick wall, in the company of a Kiwi who wasn't wearing a helmet. Shivering and sweating at the same time, I whispered to him: "Isn't this a helluva place?" He whispered back: "I wish I was in the desert again." So did I.

There was another crash and a burst of flames, and the ground shook under us. The falling plaster dust tickled my nose, and I tried to get closer to the ground and curl my long legs in under me. Pieces of rubble pelted us, and a pebble hit me in the back of the neck, making me wish I was wearing my deep American helmet.

After a few seconds I raised my head. There was a lot of dust, and the smell of the shell was still hanging in the air. But I could see the captain going from man to man to check whether they were all okay. He had plenty of guts.

I heard a lot of swishing in the air over our heads. Some of it was our stuff, and I remembered someone saying that we give the Kraut about seven for every one he sends over. Any other time I would have been comforted by the thought, but at the moment it wasn't very reassuring because a lot of his stuff was coming at us. We all stayed where we were, but finally no more came, and then our guns stopped firing, too. All was quiet again, but we didn't move until the captain said: "Let's get cracking, blokes."

I went back to where I had dropped the wire. "Quite close, eh, Slim?" the captain said. "Too bloody close," I mumbled.

The dust had cleared away but it was quite dark now; some clouds had blown in front of the moon. Stumbling over huge blocks of masonry, girders and bomb craters large enough to hide a six-by-six, we made our way along.

Every so often we'd pass some Infantry replacements going in, others on their way out. I could understand now why I'd had to change uniforms. Someone seeing my different rig might have thought I was a German who'd infiltrated.

Coming out of a crater behind a tank, I saw the captain step out of his coil. "We're here," he said as I came up to him. All I could see was a ruin similar to those we had passed.

The Kiwis filed in with the rations while we left the barbed wire outside. Squeezing into the entrance, I heard a voice in the dark say: "Give me your hand, Yank." I stuck my hand out, groping, and the owner of the voice grabbed it. I followed him in the dark, turned right and went down some steps into a room. It was dimly lit by a shielded candle in a box.

Coming out of the dark, I found even this light seemed bright. There were many coats and blankets lying on the floor, some American and some British. I plopped down and wiped some of the sweat off my face.

There was a double-decker bunk in one corner of the room. The Germans had built it, but none of our men was sleeping in it because it was too hard. This was company headquarters, and the bunk was serving as a set of shelves.

From here men went to various other houses to deliver the loads. I was introduced to the major in charge and to the rest of the men in the house.

A walkie-talkie was going in the corner of the house and the radioman was trying to contact a forward platoon in another house. The telephone lines were out, and headquarters was using the radio to maintain contact with this platoon.

When the men of the carrying party got back, they threw themselves down and started to light up. The major cautioned them against smoking in the outer room. One fellow lit his cigarette with a match and then passed the cigarette around so the others could light up.

The soldiers occupying the house gathered around the carrying party to get all the latest news and rumors from camp. Loud talking interfered with the radioman's reception and he shouted: "Shut up, back there!"

The captain asked if there was anything else the men wanted, but there was no answer. He picked up their letters and waited for a barrage of shelling to stop before he left. He shook hands and said that he would see me tomorrow. Then he gathered his men together and left. On the return trip they carried back salvage—broken rifles, clothing and even the dead.

The major went out to make the rounds of his forward platoons. After every barrage, the man on the phones checked to see if the wires were still in. If the platoons could not be contacted, headquarters would try to reach them by radio until a man could be sent to repair the break.

When the major came back, he said I could take any place on the floor and handed me two blankets. I picked out an empty spot and spread them out. There was a layer of debris dust insulating the blankets from the bare floor.

The radioman left word with the sentry to call him every hour, the major snuffed out the candle and I crawled in between the blankets with all my clothes and shoes on. All through the night many shells hit near the building; occasionally one would hit the house, but this house had withstood many previous hits. Often I could hear short bursts of machine-gun fire. They say you can tell a German Spandau from our guns because it fires more rounds per minute, but to me they all sound the same.

Early next morning we were awakened by the sound of machine-gun fire coming from every direction. The major leaped up and called out: "Take position, men." It was just beginning to get light, and someone said it was 5 o'clock.

The major called his forward platoons by radio to find out what had caused all the noise. He was told that the Germans had attacked earlier in the night with a strong patrol but had been detected. Flares were sent up, and our artillery had shelled them. The patrol had hunted around most of the night and at first light had attacked again. They had been beaten off and three prisoners taken. The major told me the Germans were just testing our strength.

I didn't feel like going back to bed and decided to look around the place. As I came up the stairs out of the cellar, I saw two Kiwis on guard at the window of a room right across the way. There were two guards at the lookout window at the opposite end of the room and two guards at the only entrance to the house. They all had tommy guns.

The walls of the house were at least a foot and a half thick, and there were two floors of fallen rubble over our heads. The only thing that could knock us out was a direct bomb hit. I could understand now how Stalingrad had held out. We and the enemy were so close that neither side could effectively use heavy artillery or bombs for fear of hitting its own men.

I peered out the lookout window but couldn't see much because of the early morning haze. The guard was reduced to one man at the lookout and one at the entrance, while the others set about preparing breakfast. The room used for a kitchen was also a combined dining room and latrine, and the odor left you in no doubt as to the latter function.

After breakfast two of the men stepped cautiously out of the house and crept to a nearby well to get water. Just as the men reached the well a barrage of mortars let go, and some of the shells hit the house, shaking up the rubble. The men at the well got back safely, though I never thought they would. It was my first lesson in the unwisdom of walking outside in daylight.

Though I spent most of the morning looking out the window with binoculars, I couldn't pick out a living thing. There must have been at least 60 houses occupied by our troops, besides those held by the Germans—more than a thousand men concealed before me. Yet I never saw a soul or heard a human sound. Nothing ever happens in Cassino in the daytime.

The day passed quickly. The men who were not on guard sat around talking sex and politics, except for the night guards who were sleeping. The telephone man was checking up to find out which wires he'd have to repair that night. He said that no repairs are ever made by day and that never a day goes by that wires aren't torn up by shell fire.

From my post at the lookout window I could see smoke shells landing on the flats. Each side uses smoke shells to hinder observation. As I looked out, Cassino reminded me of a ghost town wearing down with the years.

Above the house on a ridge sits the castle—or what's left of it—which we now occupy; and on the ridge right behind is Hangman's Hill, so called because a piece of framework that looks like a gallows stands there. The Germans, who hold Hangman's Hill, look down our backs as we use the outdoor latrine.

Later that afternoon the major asked if I'd like to go visiting. We started off for our next-door neighbor's. Although the distance between the houses was only about 25 yards, it looked like an obstacle course. As the major led the way, I side-stepped our barbed wire, jumped over a block of masonry and leaped in and out of a crater, never daring to look back. We rounded a chunk of wall, wiggled through an entrance that was nothing more than a shell hole in the wall, then slid down a pile of rubble to the main floor, where we ran smack into a Kiwi with a tommy gun. The Kiwi seemed to have heard all about the Yank with a camera, so I figured the communications system was still functioning.

We were barely inside when we heard the crash of mortar shells dropping on our recent route, as if to say: "You're not putting anything over on us."

This house was about the same as the other except that it had more armament. There were Bren guns, and the Kiwis were setting up an antitank gun, carried up during the night. I took a few pictures and then decided to go back. We made the same quick scramble between houses, and a few minutes after we got inside, the Germans loosed a burst of machine-gun fire that hit the outside of the house. "It's not good to run around like we did," the major said; "it angers the Kraut and he wakes up the men who are trying to sleep."

There was little doing the rest of the day, and life in a Cassino fortress seemed pretty dull. The boys had a pin-up of Marguerite Chapman, salvaged from a beat-up British magazine. They also

"Going ashore early tonight, eh, Wilcoxen?"—Sgt. Frank Brandt.

had a bottle of Scotch, donated by some correspondents. They'd had the bottle for a week but there was still some Scotch left. "We're saving it for a tough spot," they said. These boys have been fighting the war for three years now, so I reckon it's going to be a pretty tough spot.

While we were eating supper the Kraut threw over some stuff. "Here comes his iron rations," one soldier said to me, looking up from his stew. "He puts over a stonk every day at this time."

By this time mortar fire sounded as commonplace to me as an auto horn on a street back home. I felt perfectly safe in this temporary home.

Time wore on after supper and there was nothing to do except wait for the ration party. I sat at the entrance and made conversation with the guard. "The ration party is our only link with the outside world," he said. "They bring us our letters every day and anything we want. They had a tough job getting some rat poison we asked for."

Since the bombing of Cassino, the rats have increased in number and boldness. They feed on the dead and run all over the place at night.

I looked out the entrance and couldn't see a hundred yards in front of me. We seemed to be an island in a sea of smoke. The guard was increased; this was the time of day when most of the attacks came. Soon it was dark. There was nothing to do, so I went back in to catch a nap.

I was awakened by the noise of the entrance of the ration party. Now that the time had come, I was afraid to leave this safe house. I could under-stand now why the men never liked to go outside. We said the usual "good lucks," shook hands all around and stepped out into the darkness. The Germans had just finished a barrage, so this was the best time to leave.

Most of the men had loads of salvage on the return trip, but there was nothing for me to carry. As we were leaving the town, we heard some machine-gun fire. Looking back, I could see the faces of the men behind me reflecting the light of flares. There was mortar fire, but none came near us. I was glad I had changed my helmet; we were certainly visible to British snipers.

It had rained during the day but the sky was clear now. We kept moving, hugging the walls. In the distance the flashes of our big guns lit the sky at intervals. When we passed the spot where we had hit the dirt the previous night, the captain dropped back and showed me where a shell had landed right in the path. "It came only a few yards from the last man," he said.

The captain walked quietly beside me. Then he asked: "Do you get this kind of training in America?" The big guns were splashing the sky with angry dabs of flame. I looked back at the town, still lit by the flares, listened to the mortar shells exploding and the machine guns playing, studied the valley that the Americans had so appropriately named the Valley of the Purple Heart, and turned back to the captain.

"They didn't when I was there," I said, shaking my head, "but I sure hope they do now."

"I hate this apologizing Business."—*Pvt. Thomas Flannery.*

SECRET WEAPONS FOR THE INVASION OF GERMANY

By Sgt. RALPH STEIN

OLD TOWN INVASION BARGE, SUBMERSIBLE, MARK VII, SECTION 8 (WITH PARASOL AND BANJO)

OUR simple-hearted Nazi coast sentry thinks that he sees only romantic couples, spending Sunday afternoon in canoes. But beneath the surface our invading troops are lurking, well supplied with Spam for the fight that looms ahead and studying their comic books as the Zero Hour draws near. TECHNICAL DATA: Notice the young lady, or frail, in the stern of the canoe. She steers the barge with that innocent hand which she trails so languidly in the water and conceals with her distracting legs, or hockeys, the trap door in the floor of the canoe which serves the attacking force as an exit from the barge.

TRACTION REDUCER, BOOT M13, OR PRATT-FALL INDUCER

THIS two-man motorized dignity destroyer features a pair of automatic hands which pick bananas very rapidly, dropping the peels in the path of advancing enemy infantry. Rest of the banana goes into GI pudding which is used as a devastating booby trap. Automatic hands can also be used to snap fingers under the noses of enemy officers and make other insulting gestures.

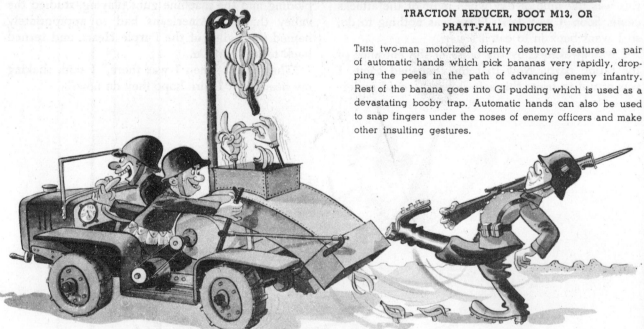

HERE is our secret bottle weapon which is used to float troops in battle equipment to Germany by the Gulf Stream, if it happens to be going that way.

KNACKWURST AND SAUERKRAUT PROJECTOR, OLFACTORY

TRACTOR at left carries an engine-driven fan which forces the odor of knackwurst and sauerkraut, cooking on gas range, through the projector tube. Drool sergeant at projector controls can elevate or depress tube through an arc of 70 degrees. Drool meter under Nazi's chin registers excitation of salivary gland. If victim doesn't drool enough, put some more kraut in the pot. METHOD OF USE: The enemy follows the smell of the knackwurst and kraut and he is yours. Then you don't let him eat it.

WENCH MORTAR

THESE weapons create confusion by dropping tasty babes or reasonably exact facsimiles upon installations. SERVICE OF THE PIECE: Tube should be swabbed often with perfume, preferably Chanel No. 5.

INCENDIARY, PEDAL M1922 OR HOT FOOT

THIS is a light, mobile, single-seat infantry co-operation weapon, which can also be used to illuminate GI crap games at night when the invasion is over. METHOD OF OPERATION: The bewildered Nazi is chased until exhaustion. Then the embracing ring, or hugger, clamps over his head, pinning his arms to his side while the automatic hand appears with a lighted match, applying a hot foot in the customary manner. When a storm trooper or OBERFELDWEBEL is bagged, the weapon applies the blowtorch with satisfactory results. How do the matches get stuck in the boots of the Nazis? They are placed there weeks before the invasion by fifth-columnists disguised as poor but honest shoe-shine boys.

PARACOOK, PTOMAINE

THIS cruel weapon of invasion is used only under extreme provocation. Cooks and accomplices armed with copies of the "Army Cook's Field Manual" are dropped behind the enemy's line to cook for him. No special training necessary. Supplies of dried eggs and creamed beef on toast may also be dropped but only as a desperate last resort.

STAGING AREA

By Pvt. ALAN SURGAL

Sketches by Sgt. Howard J. Brodie

At a Port of Embarkation Staging Camp—It is 0700. You hitch your field bag forward where it cuts into your shoulders and stumble stiffly out of the curtained coach, still wiping the hot dusty sleep from your eyes.

You stare at the vast cindered expanse, and a squadron of butterflies spills into a soft-shoe power dive in your stomach.

You stand nervously waiting for directions, and they're not long in coming.

"Troops will form at the rear of the train in a column of threes," booms a bodyless voice through an invisible amplifier.

You scramble to obey, and the butterflies level off a little.

You look at your buddy, Florida, and he grins back at you. You start to say something, but the voice without a body breaks in again.

"You are now at a classified address," it explains. "You will send no letters or telegrams, and you will not be permitted to telephone until you have specific instructions."

Censorship! You've heard about it, and now it's here. You feel a momentary exhilaration and then a sudden isolation. You think of a dozen messages that suddenly seem desperately urgent, but you can't send them. Not for the duration and six you can't.

Even Florida is quiet.

Then for the first time you notice your officers, especially your platoon commander. Dressed in regulation GIs, scuffing his unpolished combat shoes on the cindered siding, he looks inches smaller than in his tailored pinks. And a lot more nervous. You're suddenly liking him better than you ever have before.

He steps back, bawls "Battery atten-tion!" and you stiffen into position.

"Forward march!"

The morning echoes abruptly with the cadenced crunch of GI shoes on cinder. Somewhere in the rear a band strikes up, and you're off to your last camp in the States.

It is 0900.

You're in your barracks now, and you're snatching a little bunk fatigue. You've captured yourself a lower and Florida is on top.

At first you both waited uneasily for someone to bark you out into some detail or formation, but no one has and it doesn't look as if anybody intends to. So you've settled yourself comfortably, and you're quietly thinking.

"Wonder where we're going from here, Florida?" you ask idly.

"Wonder if they give any passes?" he says, completely ignoring your question.

You notice a name carved on the board above your head.

"Pfc. C. E. Hollis," you read aloud.

"I wonder what Pfc. Hollis is doing right now," you add meditatively.

"Don't get corny," Florida replies.

You settle back again with your thoughts, but after a moment they're sharply interrupted by the staccato bark of your platoon sergeant.

"Okay, boys! Off and on! Hit the deck!"

"What is it this time?" you ask, propping yourself on your elbow.

"Show-down inspection."

"*Show-down* inspection?" you repeat incredulously. "Why, we had 12 of those at the other camp!"

"See the chaplain," snaps the sergeant.

You pause, transfixed, staring vacantly past him.

"Funny," you think to yourself. "That's not a bad idea—now."

It is 1300.

You've had your clothing inspection, and you're on your way back from chow.

By now you've looked over the camp, and you're impressed most by its impermanence. Not the buildings so much, though even they seem less stable than the ones at the other camps. Mostly it's the people.

Ever since you knew for certain that you were

"The Boat!" It's been only a stabbing little flanking thought until now, but now it's ripped through to the front-center of your consciousness.

The MI officer is a breezy, good-humored fellow with a slight Bronx inflection, and you like him immediately. He starts out by telling a few GI yarns right out of "Private Hargrove," but you don't mind because he tells them well.

And when he begins to talk in earnest about the boat, you get the secure feeling that he's not reading from any prepared script. You listen closely, and you learn plenty.

You learn, for example, that you will mess only twice a day aboard ship; that water is scarce; that fire and panic are more dangerous than submarines. And, above all, you learn that the greatest menace to your safety is *you*. You and your big fat mouth.

You can see everybody's impressed.

You turn to Florida, who's looking unnaturally solemn.

"What's on your mind?" you ask sympathetically.

"Chow," he snaps without hesitation. "I'm hungry."

You can see everybody's impressed.

It is 2300.

"Lights out," and you're lying quietly in bed, thinking.

It's been a full evening, and you've written your first censored letter and made your first restricted telephone call. You've sneaked off for a lonesome walk in the nearby fields, drinking in your last few glimpses of American landscape, your last few draughts of American air. You've idled back to the barracks and continued guessing with the boys, trying to decide on your overseas destination. You've dropped a fast deuce in a friendly crap game, and before you know it, the evening's spent.

Now it's "lights out," and you're lying quietly in bed, thinking.

going overseas, you've somehow resented the cadre at the other processing camps. Jaunty noncoms with colorful shoulder insignia preparing you for something they may never undergo themselves.

But here it's different. Here everybody seems to be going. Everybody's a transient. Here, literally, everybody is in the same boat. And somehow it makes you feel a lot better.

It is 1500.

"Christ, Florida, did you ever see so many GIs in one place before?"

You're gathered in a huge commons for what they call a general orientation meeting. A saltwater bull session. All the GIs in the world seem to be here.

You listen politely through the speeches of the Army Emergency Relief officer and the Red Cross man, and you're impressed when the chaplain tells you to buddy up with God now and not to wait until you get foxhole religion.

But you're eagerly attentive when the Military Intelligence officer steps forward and starts to talk about "The Boat."

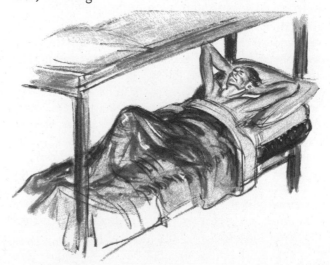

GI REPORT FROM IRAN: IT'S COLD, EXPENSIVE AND STRANGE

By Sgt. AL HINE

SOMEWHERE IN IRAN—If there's any truth to the old proverb, "Early to bed, early to rise," GIs in Iran (Persia to you) are going to be mighty healthy, wealthy and wise. Reason: there's an 8 o'clock curfew that sends the sidewalks scurrying out of sight, closes the bistros and cabarets, and drives the dogfaces to bed.

Only catch in the formula is that one about getting wealthy. Prices here are high, and wealthy is one thing you're not likely to be after even a short spell in this self-styled "Little Paris of the East." Food is high, board is high, cigarettes are high, feminine companionship is high; and drinks are so high that the average U. S. soldier below the rank of a brigadier general has a hell of a job getting high himself.

A pack of any one of the leading U. S. brands of cigarettes costs 80 cents on the black market. And the black market is about the only place where American cigarettes may be bought.

Customs and living conditions, trying to approximate the European or American, are strange. The curfew is only one example. Language is another. Iranian is the local lingo. French and, in some instances, Polish and Russian are spoken. English is rarely used except by GIs and graduates of the Presbyterian American University.

Currency is in Iranian *rials* and is complicated by a division into technically nonexistent units known as *toumains*. A *rial* is roughly 3 cents and a *toumain* is 10 *rials*. Most Yanks master the system after a few days of costly experimentation. The trouble with the *rial* as a unit is that the GI is used to thinking in terms of 1 cent. Suddenly faced with a 3-cent basis for his folding money, extravagance becomes rife. By the time he wises up nothing is rife.

Folding money is the proper term here, for all values except the half *rial* are issued in banknotes scaling from 5 to 10 to 20 to 50 to 100 and so on up. The half *rials* are coins and are used mostly for change-making or tipping. If a GI produces a 1000-*rial* note in public he is in danger of being swamped by solicitous citizens anxious to advise him how best to get rid of it.

There is no girl shortage, and the girls like the GIs. The language difficulty is a slight barrier but love laughs at linguists as well as locksmiths.

Transportation is by *droshky* and the *droshky* driver is far and away the least cooperative citizen. He seldom attempts to understand the GI. To "how much?" he responds with an agonizingly sad roll of his eyes. And whatever note is given him in payment, he reacts in the same sad way. A guy susceptible to this dramatic acting would part with the greater portion of his base pay.

Streets are wide and traffic menaces include American cars as well as *droshkies* and goats and camels. Parking is in the center of the street, leaving plenty of room on either side for the Iranian Army which is strong on marching.

The Iranian soldier wears a very classy yellow uniform; the higher the rank the classier the duds. Officers carry swords. Iranians are good horsemen and a body of Iranian cavalry passing by is quite a sight. They've got swords *and* rifles. The infantry marches to the tune of a flute.

Billets for Americans range from Army barracks to hotels. Most of them have taught the GIs that the old familiar straddle-trench was a luxury. A simple hole punched in the floor is considered ample here. The latrine rumor is dying out as a result. No one wants to hang around long enough to start one.

There is skiing available less than an hour away from the city—but there's a catch to it. They don't rent skis and what skis there are for sale are prohibitive.

Entertainment isn't too bad in spite of the early curfew. The cabarets simply run their dancing and floor shows earlier to conform. There are five-year-old American movies, and softball and basketball. There are occasional soccer matches between British and Iranian teams. These are well attended by Iranian, British and U. S. soldiers ranging in rank from buck private to the Iranian King of Kings. Feeling runs high and all that is needed to create a reasonable facsimile of an American football game is a sextette of co-ed cheerleaders.

Iran is cold and expensive and strange. But at that it's far from being the worst place in the world to soldier.

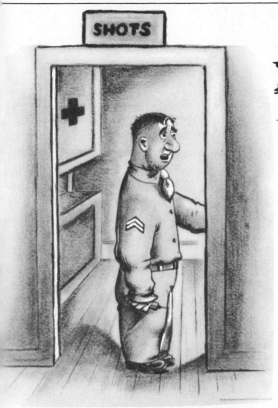

"Quick! A tourniquet!"—*Pvt. Thomas Flannery.*

"Oh, some slip-up somewhere. I imagine we'll be back on regular rations in a day or two."
—*Sgt. Douglas Borgstedt.*

"Just carry the messages we give you. Never mind the peace propaganda."—*Cpl. Louis Jamme.*

"Now, before we go any further, is there anyone who doesn't understand what we're doing?"—*Pfc. Joseph Kramer.*

YUGOSLAV DIARY

By Sgt. WALTER BERNSTEIN

Sketches by Sgt. Howard J. Brodie

TUESDAY

SOMEWHERE IN YUGOSLAVIA—The route into the interior is closed, so I must remain here for a while. The Yugoslav front is composed of patches rather than any sort of line. The Partisans have freed large chunks of territory and these are usually connected by narrow strips, along which couriers can be sent. A year ago the liberated territory consisted of little islands in a German sea; now the situation is being reversed. But sometimes the Germans close the corridors between the masses of liberated territory. That is the case now, and it is necessary to wait until a new route is found.

I am staying at the headquarters of the newspaper, *Free Dalmatia,* in an old stone house on the edge of an old stone village halfway up a mountain. The mountain itself is stone, or seems to be. The trees grow fugitively between the rocks and there are stones everywhere. From the village you can look across a valley to another mountain, and over the top of that you can see another and another. Beyond the first mountain are the Germans.

The paper is a hand-set, six-page weekly, distributed throughout Dalmatia (the section of Yugoslavia along the Adriatic coast) by a committee of AVNOJ, the congress of the new Yugoslavia.

Since the Germans at present occupy most of Dalmatia, the paper has to be circulated secretly. It is an indication of Partisan unity and organization that there is probably less warfare incident to the weekly distribution of their several thousand papers in occupied territory than there is every day with the *Chicago Tribune.*

The paper is run by an organization of some 15 people: intellectuals, printers, stenographers, a cook, a handyman. They live, eat and work together, and most of them have seen action as fighters at one time or another. There are five women: the cook and her assistant, two girls who do stenography and technical work, and an elderly woman who works in the printing department with her son. The editorial staff is composed of an ex-lawyer, a young architect, a couple of students, an ex-professor, a white-collar worker and a poet. Their press is an ancient foot-pumped affair that used to print prayer books somewhere in Dalmatia. It can turn out only one page a day, and by now the letters are so worn that sometimes it is hard to make them out. Despite this, the staff manages to print other pamphlets

when necessary, turn out a mimeographed new bulletin every other day and monitor radio news f the provincial committee, the staff of the near division and other interested parties.

The only one who speaks English on the new paper is the lawyer, a thin, sunburned man wi glasses. He speaks quite well, although bookish "Our paper is small," he says, "but it is much rused." His lungs are not good and he must re every day after lunch. Before joining the staff was military judge for Southern Dalmatia, a sometimes he talks about the trials he conducte "We were very lenient with the traitors," he say "Only those who pillaged with the fascists we shot." He tells of two Ustachi (Croatian fascist who were captured by the Partisans. They ha been Ustachi for only a short time and had n taken part in the usual looting and torturing, they were freed and told to return home. "The wept when we allowed them free," the lawyer sai "Everyone wept, I also."

Each morning they gather around the public address system and listen intently to the news broadcast.

WEDNESDAY

Today there is ice by the well where everyor washes in the morning. It is technically spring, b you would never know it here. The wind whi around the mountain and it is very cold. There is radio news broadcast in Croatian from Londo every morning at 0700, and by 0630 the peop have gathered around the public address syste which the staff has rigged up outside the hous They come from the village and the units aroun e village, and they wait patiently in the cold. hey are mostly fighters from the division: tough, apable men, women with grenades hanging from eir belts, even little boys who act as ammunition arriers. This morning there are also two old men n donkeys and an old woman seated on the steps, ewing a patch on a pair of pants. One of the old en wears a felt hat with a red star on it. They sten intently to the news, occasionally making omments. When it is over, they drift quietly away.

The staff of *Free Dalmatia* takes its meals in the ttic of the stone house, where there is a long bare ble and a small stove. The food is simple and adequate. There is usually only one dish to a eal, but the staff is used to that. Some of the food American, since the village is close enough to the ea to receive a tiny part of the scanty supplies the llies are sending to the Partisans. They are very rateful for what help they do get.

For breakfast there is bread and tea. The bread hot from the oven, with a heavy, sweet-smelling vetness. The tea is eaten with a spoon, like soup. After breakfast everyone goes to his job, and I vander through the village. It is a poor little village, very old and built on a slant, with the houses umbled together and narrow dirt paths winding rookedly about. There are a few skinny chickens crabbling in the dirt and three lean dogs that stare vith mad eyes. On the walls of all the houses are logans: "Long Live the Army of Liberation," "Long Live Free Yugoslavia," "Long Live Marshal Tito."

Supper consists of a plateful of string beans with pieces of Vienna sausage. There is also a large can f chowchow (mixed pickles in mustard sauce). The Partisans need chowchow like they need a hole n the head, but they regard it as simply some peculiar American dish and eat it. After supper everyone sits around and sings. The songs come naturally; they are beautiful songs, simple and immediate. There is one song about their rifles, and a song about one of their national heroes killed n battle, and one addressed to Marshal Tito by the girls in which they ask "When will you send the boys home?" and Tito answers "It is not yet time, it is not yet time."

In the evening the staff also listens to the radio. There are Croatian broadcasts from London and Moscow every night and occasionally one from New York. American broadcasts seem to be the least popular, because the broadcasters do not seem to have much of an idea of what is really happening in Yugoslavia. Everyone here is very interested in America, although many of the people's ideas about the States come from the movies.

They are extremely interested in the present status of gangsters and Indians. One of the students on the staff of the paper wants to know if it is true about the installment plan. The others are also interested in more basic matters, such as the attitude of our people toward the war, our political situation, our educational system and what has happened to Laurel and Hardy.

THURSDAY

This morning, right after breakfast, there was the drone of planes, and then a whole group of Liberators came over. There must have been 70 of them, heading north. They were very high, flying a beautiful, tight, precise formation, not fast but with a heavy deliberate purposefulness. Everyone in the village ran out to watch, running around and pointing up at the planes and cheering them on. That name "Liberator" really means something here.

In the afternoon one of Yugoslavia's champion soccer players came over to give the staff some material on the relation between sport and the present struggle. His name is Matosic. Big and athletic-looking, he played on the all-Yugoslav team against England before the war.

All day there has been the muffled sound of gunfire from beyond the mountain. The division is in contact with the Germans. The poet went to headquarters early in the day and everyone wonders if he has managed to get in the fight.

There was much excitement at dinner. Two friends whom the staff had thought were dead showed up. They had been in a concentration camp for three years, and finally escaped and made their way to the Partisans. One of them is a man of 27 and the other is 35, but they look much older. The younger man did most of the talking; the other was quiet and seemed almost a little punchy. He kept touching the younger man, putting his head on his shoulder as if for support. The younger man talked

The younger man talked between mouthfuls. The other one kept leaning on his shoulder as if for support.

between mouthfuls of food. He ate delicately, almost shyly, arranging the food carefully with his fork before lifting it to his mouth, then chewing it with great thoroughness. The others opened a can of peaches especially for the two: peaches are like ammunition, and the whole room seemed to eat the fruit with the two men, slowly and with a quiet, enormous enjoyment.

The two of them had been put to work by the Germans in a factory at Wiener Neustadt, the big industrial center near Vienna. The younger man spoke of the conditions there, the lack of food and the great devastation caused by American bombers. But he said there were no signs of an internal crack-up, and little organized sabotage in the factories. The German plan is to fill the plants with different nationalities and keep them suspicious of each other, so that no one ever feels he can trust anyone else. The younger man had also been in the notorious Ustachi camp at Jasenovac in Croatia. This is the camp that is known for burning men alive; its record is 1,500 in one night. While he was talking, the handyman came over and sat down. He had been sent to Jasenovac but escaped. He was a Sephardic Jew from Bosnia, and he still spoke a kind of bastard Spanish. The Germans murdered his father, mother, wife and three-year-old child.

The route is still closed.

FRIDAY

There was a little snow this morning, but it melted when the sun came out. The countryside looks as though a glacier had just retreated. The mountains are thrown up in spasms and the rocks seem torn apart. The people are as hard as the country, but very impressive. They have an immense dignity; they have transformed their fight against the Germans into a struggle to build a new country, and they have a deep pride in what they are building. There seems to be a complete democracy in their army. It is not merely that the officer sits down with his men; it is that they each have an equal share in the present and the future, and they recognize this equality. There seems to be a complete understanding that each is serving according to his capacity. There is practically no one in the army who has not seen action, either at the front or in the underground. There are no soft jobs and no privileges except those that have been earned. The discipline is very high. It is not parade-ground discipline but comes from a knowledge and belief in what they are fighting for. There is also much saluting. Everyone salutes everyone else, regardless of his rank. And all the Partisans have a simple,

understandable attitude toward the future: only those who have fought deserve to share in it.

There was a show of photographs at dinner; the two girls passed around pictures of themselves before the war. They became very coy at this point. The pictures were conventional poses taken at the seashore and in the park. The girls looked modern and pretty in their dresses, and very feminine. One of them is divorced; she has a three-year-old daughter whom she hasn't seen in a year and a half. The other has been married for six months to the secretary of the provincial committee. She gets to see him once in a while. She shows his picture in civilian clothes—a young, good-looking boy who looks as though he were just out of college.

The poet returned tonight. He was in the battle. Only three Partisans had been killed and thirty Germans taken prisoner. The Partisan method of dealing with prisoners is simple enough. If there is proof that they have been pillaging and torturing they are shot. The rest are offered the opportunity of joining the Partisans. If they refuse they are put to work and held for exchange. In this batch, the poet said, there was only one who wanted to join. The rest wished to be exchanged and fight again except three Austrians who wanted to be sent to Africa. The Partisans know who has been looting. The intelligence of a people's army is usually good since its forces are everywhere.

The poet is a tall young man with a mop of black hair. The others always refer to him as "our poet." He had a book of poetry published before the war and everyone says he is a good poet. The only thing they regret is that he is not much interested in world affairs. "He lives in the realm of the esthetic," the lawyer says. The poet is an old Partisan, however, having joined more than two years ago, and he has fought through several offensives.

Everyone listens closely while he tells about the battle. One of the Partisan dead is a woman fighter who had also been in the movement for a long time. They shake their heads when the poet tells about her, and say she will be missed. They are hardened to violent death but will never be used to it. Afterward they kid the poet about his lack of interest in what has been happening in the world while he has been away. "You are only interested in poetry," the lawyer says. "I am for a free federal Yugoslavia," the poet answers. There is no argument after that.

SATURDAY

Talked this afternoon with the girl secretary of the Anti-Fascist Youth Congress, to be held somewhere in liberated territory later this month. The Partisans expect delegates from all the Balkan countries and even the Soviet Union. This will be their second congress; the first was held two years ago. The secretary explains that many of the delegates who were at the first congress will not be at this one; they have been killed fighting. The secretary is young and pleasantly attractive. She is small, has long brown hair and looks like one of the more intelligent co-eds at a state university. She is also something of a hero, the lawyer says. During one of the offensives she held a hill alone with a machine gun against repeated German counterattacks.

At dinner there are three Slovenian performers, who have been going from brigade to brigade, giving shows. One used to be an actor, the second a theater director and the third was director of the opera in the city of Ljublana. They all fought through the early German offensives, but now they are doing cultural work. The opera director is remaining here for a few days to mimeograph a book of Partisan songs.

For dessert tonight there was an air raid. About 30 German planes came over, looking for a village on the other side of the mountain, where there is some important stuff. They dropped flares and lit up the whole sky. Everyone came pouring out of the village to watch. There are some fighter detachments in the village and they came out on the double, fanning into position on the mountain. One of their officers is a woman and she kept yelling orders in a high firm voice. There was some ack-ack, but not much. The tracers shot into the sky like fireworks and you could hear the dull boom of the bombs as they dropped on the other side. The raid lasted about 20 minutes. Then the planes went away and the firing stopped and the flares died out slowly, returning the sky to the night.

SUNDAY

The poet went across the mountain today and came back with the information that the planes had hit only a few houses and the left wing of a hospital. Only a few people were killed and no damage done to the important matériel. One of the dead was a friend of several of the staff here and they are going to her funeral today.

All day listening to the radio. There is a piano recital from Moscow, opera from Italy, a talk from Berlin on the senselessness of aerial warfare, an RAF dance band from London, and a talk from America addressed to the people of Europe. Everyone thought the American talk a little out of the world, because it seriously discussed the question of bombing Rome and the Montecassino Abbey as if there were two sides to the question. To the people who are doing the fighting, there is no debate on whether or not to bomb places where there are German soldiers.

There is much admiration and friendship for America among these people, and they still visualize us as the great, young, uncorrupted nation. Most of them would like to visit the States after the war, and they ask many questions. They are amazed that there are houses in America as poor as the one they are in now and want to know if there are beggars on the streets.

The old woman covered the mine and sat down to wait.

The poet also returned with a story that gives some indication of part of a people's war. One of the old women from a nearby village was walking along a road when she saw a Partisan mine that had been planted but insufficiently camouflaged. She covered it up herself and then sat down at a safe distance to watch. After a while a German scout car came along, passed over the mine and blew up. The old woman got up, walked back to Partisan headquarters, told them what had happened and then gave them a good bawling out for permitting such sloppy work.

Tonight the staff had the weekly political meeting. Everyone was present, including the cooks, and they all discussed world events and the present necessities of their new Yugoslav state. Afterward they sat around and sang and there was some spontaneous dancing, much like our square dances.

No news about the route being open.

Need a bath.

MONDAY

The paper came out today. It contains articles about the coming Youth Congress, the Russian offensive, the air war on Germany, the decisions of AVNOJ, developments in the Partisan campaign and accounts of new German atrocities. There are also articles on what is happening politically outside of Yugoslavia.

There are reports that the Germans are increasing their terror in occupied regions, before the Red Army arrives. It is impossible for Americans to realize the extent of this calculated, sub-human slaughter. The stories make you sick when you hear them. The amount of suffering is beyond belief, and this is one reason why these people have no respect for those who ran to safety. You can only understand the people who have been under the Germans if you realize what they have suffered. That suffering has made the people of Yugoslavia, at least, bitterly definite that only those who have suffered and fought will share the victory.

At dinner there is a hot scientific discussion about when light becomes heat. There is also a discussion about modern art and an argument between the poet and the architect on the relative merits of liberal and classical education. They are all extremely well-informed and highly intelligent. They kid the printer about the fact that he was so well-paid before the war; they accuse him of having eight pairs of pajamas and feeding white bread to his dog. He protests. The lawyer quotes the Gettysburg address and the Declaration of Independence; he is

very happy when I tell him I was born in the States. "Now you can be president!" he says. "Otherwise you can only be vice president." There is excitement over the report that the British have closed their eastern coast. The second front here is more than a problem in logistics.

There is much static over the radio tonight, and then suddenly there is a blast of music and the unctuous voice of a real American announcer introducing the Original Dixieland Band. Then the music comes, blatant and foolish, the corn blaring without shame. Everyone smiles politely, but it is wonderful, heavy with rhythm and nostalgia. It is a program for the troops overseas and there is the announcer again, patronizing the soldiers, talking to them man to man. He is on a different planet, a million miles away; he has no relation to this room, these people, this war. But the music is friendly; after a while the others like the music, humming the trite tune, tapping out the rhythm with their feet. And then it is over and there is the announcer, and the coaxed, artificial applause, and the new wartime commercial to sell you-fellows-overseas. And the studio orchestra fading softly out; and the room back to normal, the people concerned, interested, turning the dial for news; and the poster on the wall saying boldly in a flash of red: "Together in the Fight Against Fascism."

Tomorrow they think there may be a route open. The Germans have begun a new local offensive, but there is a way through the mountains.

It looks like rain.

"You're sure you are not just trying to get out of a detail?"—*Sgt. Ralph Stein.*

"Frankly, fellows, I need the extra dough."
—*Cpl. Hugh Kennedy.*

IRAN COOTIES SHARE TOP BILLING WITH MARX BROTHERS AT THE MOVIES

By Sgt. AL HINE

TEHERAN, IRAN—If you're smart, you go to the GI movie in camp. But you're not smart—yet. So you try your luck at one of the half-dozen cinemas in town. Cinema comes from a Greek word meaning move, which is what you do before the feature is half over.

You begin quite undramatically by paying for your ticket—10 *rials* to the wall-eyed girl in the ticket cage. Your ticket is a flimsy bit of colored paper something like the revenue stamp on a whisky bottle. After it has been torn in half by the 3-year-old ticket taker, it is like nothing.

The evening's entertainment opens with news reels in French, Russian and Persian. Very interesting for Frenchmen, Russians and Persians. The news reels are followed by colored lantern slides advertising cafés, hair lotions and the *Agence de Publicité* which prepares them. Then the feature.

"The Big Store" with the Marx Brothers (you saw it in Topeka, back when you got in for half price as a minor) boasts some scratchy English dialogue. It takes a minute or so before you notice that a running commentary in French is being flashed on the bottom of the screen. It doesn't matter whether you understand French or not; you still keep glancing down curiously at this phenomenon, missing a good part of the action and the English dialogue as well.

After a little concentration, you master the technique. You ignore the French and apply your talents exclusively ·to the mangled English. You are going along swimmingly when the film flickers to a stop. The Brothers Marx are replaced by a blank white space, which is soon covered with black Per-

sian script explaining the action so far. Persian is a tedious tongue and it takes a full 10 minutes to tell what happened in five minutes of screen action.

The Marx Brothers take over once more. You have lost track of the continuity but fortunately, with the Marx Brothers, that doesn't matter much. Back in the swing, you are just trying to remember what it was you laughed at so hard in Topeka when the film stops again.

This time it's an intermission of sorts. A corporal's guard of white-coated urchins pads along the rows, selling chocolate, coffee, gum drops and, for all you know, opium. You buy some sweet Palestinian chocolate and munch hopefully.

When the lights go off again, it's a snafu for the operator. He runs four Technicolor minutes of "Gone With the Wind" before he realizes his mistake. Lights on again. More chocolate and then back to the Marx Brothers.

By this time you are beginning to wonder whether a beer wouldn't have been better. You have been invaded by a number of small animals left on the seat by some earlier visitor. As they deploy unerringly for the more vital parts of your anatomy, you wonder whether you need a shot for typhus.

Scratching with one hand, clinging to the now-dissolving chocolate bar with the other, and totally confused between French captions, Irani cut-ins and English dialogue, you may as well give up. It's a nice cool ride back to camp in the truck, long enough for sober thought. You resolve to stick to beer and leave the movies to Special Service.

"So what do you propose to do—rotate me or bust me?"
—*Pfc. Bill Keane.*

"Look, fellas, I'm a civilian!"—*Sgt. Tom Zibelli.*

WITH THE USAFISPA

UNITED STATES ARMED FORCES IN SOUTH PACIFIC AREA

By Sgt. MACK MORRISS

Sketches by Sgt. Howard J. Brodie

A U. S. Base in the South Pacific—This is one of those places in the South Seas you've read about but, brother, smile when you use the word "paradise" down here. The U. S. Army isn't on location for a sarong opera.

If the average GI stops long enough to take in the natural beauty of the place, he may set it down as "picturesque," but he'll have neither the time nor the inclination to say more.

However, if operations have stemmed desires to wax wacky and make with the soft lights and sweet music, it certainly doesn't make this spot any less interesting—especially if you're a new Joe and still aren't used to American-made cars with the steering wheels on the wrong side.

In some places farther south you could spot a newly-minted overseas man because he invariably walked on the wrong side of the sidewalk and looked the wrong direction when he crossed a street; but here that doesn't make any difference. If you're walking you look both ways, and if you're driving you head for the side of the street that happens to be vacant for the moment.

Everything about the island is foreign to a newly-arrived

GI. You're apt to speak to somebody in American and be met with a blank look or a bewildering line of something that might be either native, Javanese, French—or a mixture. In town you may pass a row of run-down buildings, private and public, then run smack into some modernistic structure that looks like an architect's pipe dream. You step high off the curbs; the drainage system is strictly public.

In the shops—such as are still able to be open—you can get sandwiches of a kind, delicious chocolate, tea, cake, fruit drinks—and at some places, the worst coffee under the sun. Two sandwiches, cake and a beverage cost about 70 cents American.

Liquor for sun-helmeted soldiers? Oh, no. Dates with the local belles? Not today, Junior—this ain't Main Street back home, you know. Music? Well, yes—in the local version of a drug store there is a juke box like none other you've ever heard. A big sign says: "Latest American hits—'Jingle, Jangle, Jingle'; 'Boogie-Woogie'; 'Praise the Lord and Pass the Ammunition.'" You pass a nickel over the counter, indicate your selection, and the girl puts the record on a phonograph.

You'd be surprised how good home-grown jive sounds.

But even if this so-called "Paris of the Pacific" offered Coney Island's amusements, U. S. soldiers here wouldn't have time to enjoy them. There's too much going on. Men who have been away six weeks have trouble in finding their way around when they get back. You can't escape the atmosphere of hurry up, hurry up—get it done, get it done. Sheet-metal quarters glisten in the sun today where yesterday there was nothing. Rows of pyramidal tents line a field that this morning was bare.

Prefabricated offices are pounded together in almost nothing flat by sweating engineers.

Strange as the bustle of army life must be to the resident population, the population itself is even stranger to the Army. You walk down the street past tiny Javanese women, barefooted and with the long folds of their skirts hobbling them at the ankles. They carry their children in sashlike cloth contraptions which only a slant-eyed little Javanese could appreciate.

The native men—nicknamed "Charleys" and black as the deuce of clubs—are beautifully built guys who in some cases treat their hair so that it turns out like a sienna nightmare. Fierce-looking fellows, they're perfect physical specimens. Their women are just specimens.

Even so, civilians of any race are the exception. Flags of three nations fly here, and the mixture of arms and services is staggering. Most colorful are the Fighting French; native troops with their gaudy headgear and even gaudier green-striped khaki shorts pace back and forth on post before military installations. French officers manage to look dignified and comfortable at the same time in khaki shorts and shirts, with knee-length cotton socks.

For all the bizarre picture-book strangeness of the place, the nearness of war is ever present. Men who have seen action walk the streets, and convalescent cases test their legs while perhaps a nurse in khaki lends moral support. A sailor with a green fatigue jacket or GI shoes walks by with a red arm band, and you know why he's in mixed uniform. Marine buddies meet on the street and their faces light up and they start off by saying, "Whatever happened to Joe at . . ."

You pick up odds and ends of information that are worth remembering. Things like doing push-ups in fox holes during shellings, instead of lying flat on the ground; like leaving Jap dead alone because sometimes their own guys have taken the firing pins out of grenades and laid the grenades under the bodies; like leaving your chin strap loose so that the concussion of a close one won't get under your helmet and snap your neck.

And the stories those Marine kids can tell you. About the time they cornered some Japs who had the habit of pitching back grenades, and how the Marines threw coconuts at them just for fun and the Japs were so excited they threw the nuts back. But that's just mild. Some of the other things aren't funny—the way they fought and how they went in after the Japs and got 'em.

This is a South Sea island at war. Save the "paradise" stuff for Hollywood.

Pfc. Frank R. Boddy of Chicago covers a draw below "Bullet Junction," a slope on Mount Austin.

THE LAST DAYS AT GUADALCANAL

By Sgt. HOWARD J. BRODIE

YANK's *staff combat artist, Sgt. Howard Brodie, completed these sketches at Guadalcanal on February 9, 1943, the day the last Jap resistance on the island ended. By that time, Brodie was as tired as a jungle fighter. He had been working for weeks at the front under difficulties that would have forced most artists to throw away their pencils and pads in despair.*

Brodie sketched most of his pictures in foxholes, CPs, dressing stations and artillery positions. He was never able to complete a drawing without being interrupted by air raids, mortar bursts and Jap snipers who seemed to delight in taking pot shots at him just when he was beginning to concentrate on his model. "I don't know which was worse—the snipers or the bugs," he says. "I think I was bitten by every insect on the island."

After he did his original sketch on the front lines, Brodie would take it back to the tent he shared with Sgt. Mack Morriss, the YANK staff correspondent who works with him in the South Pacific area. There he would darken and finish the drawing. Brodie did all his sketches in pencil on thin paper and, by the time the fighting ended, most of his pencils were short, one-inch stubs.

Soldiers from California are probably familiar with Brodie's drawings. He was a staff artist on the San Francisco Chronicle for seven years before enlisting in the Army last August. He was training to be message-center clerk with the Signal Corps at Camp Crowder when he was transferred to YANK.

Two days after the fighting on Guadalcanal stopped, Morriss and Brodie left the island to try to gain back some of their recently lost weight before proceeding to their next assignment.

"I wouldn't have missed Guadalcanal for anything," Brodie said. "But I was damned glad to leave the place."

"Road to Kokumbona," Guadalcanal.

Cannoneer. This artilleryman with two bluebirds tattooed on his chest is Pvt. Steven Kitt of Wilmington, Del., who won the Purple Heart at Pearl Harbor before he went to the Solomons.

Pvt. Melvin "Mike" Levine, Mass. I sketched this tired infantryman on a trail coming from a patrol.

Litter bearers at work on a jungle trail near the Guadalcanal front.

"This is the way you can light a cigarette in a front line foxhole at night. Bend over and stick your head inside a sack or a fatigue jacket."

This infantryman came in from a patrol and dropped down to show me how he had just fired his Reising gun at Jap snipers.

Along the Kokumbona Road Inf. pull a 50 cal. machine gun cart.

"I drew this one at the infantry platoon command post
on 'Bloody Knoll' where things were plenty hot."

Natives bring up supplies to U. S. Army troops
during the Mount Austin offensive.

This marine officer, Lt. Col. M. L. Curry, was sketched
as he came up to confer with Army infantry officers.

Infantrymen lugging Jap prisoner back on shelter-half who wouldn't walk and wanted to die—On the "Horse's Neck" front.—*Sketched between daytime air-raid alarms.*

I sketched this battalion commander, Lt. Col. Earl J. Ripstra of Nashville, Tenn., in his foxhole at the front.

Pvt. Merlin Murray sits on a ridge, guarding native supply bearers from Jap snipers. Notice the matches stuck in his helmet.

Burial on the spot—

"I believe I was bitten by every bug in the jungle while I was sketching this advance base bivouac area."

"Here are the engineers and the medics bringing the wounded down the Matanakau River after one of the battles."

A SACK OF MAIL

By Cpl. PAUL E. DEUTSCHMANN

Sketch by Sgt. Frank Brandt

SOMEWHERE IN SARDINIA—Mail call is one of the most important things in a GI's life, I was reading the other day. It's good for that ethereal something that USO hostesses, advertising copywriters and sundry other civilians back home call morale. With the correspondents some GIs have, though, no mail is good mail. Leave us look at some of these morale-boosters.

FIDGETY-FILLY TYPE

"Snookie, dear—I drove out to Petter's Perch the other night, along the Old Mill Road. You remember, don't you, dear? The moon was bright and the stars twinkled just like when you were there with me, and it made me feel so-o-o romantic!

"Some girls complain about the man shortage. But not me! Last night three fellows took me to the movies, and afterwards they took turns with me out on the back porch—dancing. But don't worry, dear, they were all servicemen. I won't go out with a man except in uniform. One of them, Casper Clutchem, who is sorta blond and cute and a Marine sergeant, says for me to tell you 'the situation is under control.' He is *awful* strong.

"Guess what we were drinking? Those potent daiquiris. They really make me forget myself—almost.

"And, did I tell you? Casper is stationed just outside of town and has promised to come see me real often. I couldn't very well refuse him because he said he was leaving for overseas almost any month now. I believe in doing my bit to help the servicemen because, after all, some of them are so far from home and don't know a soul in town."

HOME-GUARD TYPE

"Dear Corp—I am back in Dayton for another furlough and I am looking after Lulu, just like you asked me to. She's really a wonderful gal and a smooth dancer. And if she weren't your wife I could really go for her myself. Do you realize, I've gotten to know Lulu better than you do—almost! And boy, can she hold her likker!

"We had dinner at the Cove tonight and are now back at your apartment. It is just midnight, and while Lulu is slipping into something more *comfortable*, I thought I'd drop you a line. Ha ha, old man, I'm only kidding."

MAN-OF-AFFAIRS TYPE

"I've been doing swell at the office. Just got the Whatsis Soap and Whoozis Hosiery account. That's $4,000,000 billing besides the pleasure I get from interviewing models for the 'leg art' pictures. But it's nothing like the swell job you boys are doing over there. I wish I were in there with you, but——

"Give 'em hell for me, old fellow! They asked for it—and we're just the guys to give it to them. I'm buying War Bonds like an insane stamp collector. I really wish I were out in the foxholes with you, but——"

CIVILIAN BRASS-HAT TYPE

"Dear Bill—All of us here at the Old Company, from the office staff up to me, are thinking of you boys in the service and doing our part to help you fellas. We're all buying War Bonds and cutting down on meat and butter—and some of the girls in the office are even rolling bandages on Saturday afternoons, when they aren't working.

"Rationing is pretty grim now. Steaks only twice a week and no more cherries in cherry cokes. But we don't mind because the papers say that you fellows overseas are getting all the good things—and you certainly deserve them.

"Yes sir, no one can say that the Old Company is not well represented in the foxholes and trenches of our fighting fronts all over the globe. Rollie is a warrant officer at Camp Dix, N. J., and Jim is at the Brooklyn Navy Yard, and Harry is a chauffeur to a Marine colonel in Philadelphia. Van is way down in Texas and Charlie is a quartermaster clerk in Georgia and you're in the Infantry in Italy. Give 'em hell, boy."

OH-YOU-DEVIL TYPE

"You guys over there in Italy must be having a big time with all those little dark-eyed signorinas. Do they wear those grass skirts like Dorothy Lamour?"

LOCAL-BOY-MAKES-GOOD TYPE

"Your cousin Herman is now a technical sergeant and he has only been in the Army five months. I can't understand why you're still a corporal. Are your officers mad at you?"

ALL-IN-THIS-TOGETHER TYPE

"Dear Pal—Things are really getting rugged now at good old Camp Kilmer. I can only get off every other week end. We went out on bivouac last week and, boy, was it rough! We slept in pup tents for three nights—right on the ground.

"Last week I was awarded the Good Conduct Ribbon at a special ceremony. You might not hear from me for a while, as I am expecting to be shipped out any day now—to North Carolina.

"By the way—what is this Spam we hear so much about?"

THE LEGION OF THE UNCOUTH

BY S/SGT. THOMAS P. ASHLOCK

Australia

The pages of the magazines back home
That feature stuff of war—the march of men,
The awesome crawl of tanks, the flight of planes—
Have shown a tiresome lot of "glamor Yanks,"
With trousers razor-creased and shirts that still
Retain the sheen of new-spun factory cloth;
With ties adjusted right, and shoes, the gleam
Of which will blind. Too much of new-blown rank,
With chevrons bright and neatly sewn on sleeves
Of sarge or corp; and when I view those lads,
So sartorially complete and nice, I think
Of Hollywood, with extras dressed to fit
A part in some stage scene, instead of soldiers
Girt for deadly, bloody, filthy war.

From the Stevens in Chicago town,
To our sun-blistered, bug-infested post,
Is a far, unholy cry—and the difference
Much the same as that which lies between
My lady's boudoir and a stable stall:
For here we boys are not—oh, really not
The photogenic type! Our hair grows long,
We seldom shave; Svengali would be proud

To flaunt the beards that some of us have grown.
Our pants are frayed and bleached and baggy-kneed;
We wear no shirts—and as for ties,—say, tell
Us, please—what is a tie?
And it's a certain sign
You're "tropo," if you start to shine your shoes!

We're a motley, rugged, crumby lot,
No subjects for a Sunday supplement:
But somehow, I don't think a man of us,
Deep down within his heart, would trade his place
With fortune's darlings in the Stevens lounge.
We're "in" the thing, you see—not quite as much
But something like—our buddies at Bataan,
Corregidor, the Solomons, and Wake;
And because we walk in shabbiness—unkempt,
Ungroomed—and live with pests, and breathe red dust
And thirst and bake in searing heat, and drown
In tropic rains,—like them—we're fiercely proud.
Let others have the dress parade, the show,
The full-page spread in magazines. We like
Our role—the real, the earnest, cussin' sweatin'
Dirty, ugly role of men *at* war!

ROSIE'S RIVETERS

By Sgt. SAUL LEVITT

Rosie poses for a picture at his home base in England with some of the men who have sweated out many missions over Europe in his veteran Fortress.

Front (l. to r.): Lt. R. C. Bailey, Capt. R. Rosenthal, Lt. C. J. Milburn and Lt. W. T. Lewis. Back row (l. to r.): S/Sgt. L. F. Darling, T/Sgt. M. V. Bocuzzi, S/Sgt. J. F. Mack, T/Sgt. C. C. Hall, S/Sgt. W. J. DeBlasio and S/Sgt. R. H. Robinson.

ENGLAND—For newspapers, bigger victories in this war are a simple problem—you just use bigger type on page one. Like the American daylights raids on Berlin. In somebody's 20-volume history of the second World War, to be written in 1955, an aging crew chief like J. E. Woodard and a tail-gunner like Bill DeBlasio will find the Berlin raids rating a paragraph or two on page 963. For the men concerned with them only yesterday, they meant another evening return of tired, living men—or another ship sloping down to the limbo of "missing in action."

Sometimes even a working airfield gets a sense of something special and enormous. On one field the crews had this feeling about the Berlin raids, when a certain plane came swinging low over the tower, home from Berlin, one late afternoon.

The plane was Capt. Robert Rosenthal's—*Rosie's Riveters*. Her crew came home to a sudden, unrestrained, crazy holiday greeting. It was a private party; nobody else was invited. It was their own hunk of bitter victory—for many were lost over Berlin, taking part of the *Luftwaffe* with them.

But Rosie, the pilot, had completed his tour of duty. The sky was filled with flares—the armament men had given them two extra boxes before take-off that morning. They threw the Fourth of July up at the cold gray sky; and the control tower, which is a grave and dignified institution at an airfield—something like the Supreme Court—came back with more flares.

The crew's request to the pilot that morning, when they learned it was to be Berlin, had been for a "beautiful buzz job" coming in. The pilot gave it to them with his low swoop over the tower. It is said—though J. E. Woodard, the husky crew chief denies it—that big tears rolled down his face when *Rosie's Riveters* showed at last over the tower.

Then the crew rode off in great style to the interrogation, each man on a jeep. All except T/Sgt. Michael V. Bocuzzi, the radio operator; he rode on the rear of a proud MP's motorcycle.

Capt. (then Lt.) Rosenthal and his crew came overseas quietly enough last September. They brought with them their own crew name, to be duly inscribed on the nose of a Fort by some weary Joe who has seen all kinds of names tagged on to B-17s that can't answer back.

The pilot was a quiet, inconspicuous young man of 26, who wore his visor cap clamped down on his head and walked with the shambling gait of a countryman, although he hailed from the Flatbush farmlands of Brooklyn, N. Y. With him was one of those typical American "mongrel" crews that the Army arranges so well—as if in conscious answer to the "racial unity" armies of Nazi Germany. Their backgrounds were German, Irish, Scotch, Italian and others, and their home places were scattered from the Eastern seaboard to the Far West.

In Dyersburg, Tenn., Rosie had quietly canvassed his crew to find out how they felt about combat. No one backed out. Yet no one could possibly have wanted the combat they got in their first three days of flying in this theater. As S/Sgt. Ray H. Robinson, the ball-turret gunner from Arkansas City, Kans., put it, "the first night after Bremen we were too scared to sleep, the second night after Marienburg we were too tired. The third night after Munster we were bushed—finished."

Bremen was bad. On that one, the squadron lead crew, piloted by Capt. (now Maj.) Everett E. Blakely, had hell smashed out of it. On the Operations blackboard Sgt. Jennings wrote after all the plane numbers "severe battle damage." Marienburg, with only a few hours' sleep intervening, was one of the longest flights ever undertaken in this theater. And then came Munster, the very next morning.

The haggard, griping crew of *Rosie's Riveters* went down to the Munster briefing that morning in the company of experienced crews—men who had been on the first Regensburg shuttle raid to Africa and on the "longest flight in the ETO," to Trondheim.

Late that afternoon, as fog settled over East Anglia, *Rosie's Riveters* came back alone—the drone of its two engines a mournful elegy for those men who had been to Regensburg and Trondheim. Careful landing procedure for formation was unnecessary. There was only the one plane coming in—actually half a plane—with two of its engines out. Thirteen planes had failed to return. The interrogation was very exclusive, like a consultation with a private physician. There was only the evidence of the dazed, battered men of *Rosie's Riveters*.

It had been a ferocious and concentrated attack.

One by one the planes of the group had gone down. Left alone, Lt. Rosenthal had decided to go on with the bombing run.

"Shall I drop them now, Rosie?" the bombardier kept asking.

"Not yet."

"Now?"

"No."

"We're over Munster," Lt. C. J. Milburn, the bombardier, finally said.

"Now," said Lt. Rosenthal.

Then they fought their way back from Munster to the French coast, enemy fighters queueing up on them. S/Sgt. L. F. Darling of Sioux City, Iowa, crept up to the nose to help Lt. Ronald C. Bailey, the navigator, spot the landing field. At last came the landing.

Rosie came down through the bomb bay to look over his crew. Darling was wounded and so was the other waist-gunner, S/Sgt. J. H. Shaffer. As Rosie stepped out and went along in the ambulance with his wounded, he got a glimpse of something new—the torn-down skin of the right wing where a rocket shell looping from above had plowed between empty gas tanks, cutting a hole a foot across.

Mike Bocuzzi, tumbling out white-faced, yelled: "I'm through flying these things. That's enough."

"C.J.," the bombardier, round-faced and amiable, a little quieter than Mike, didn't say anything but he thought: "Well, if this is the way it is, they must get you sooner or later, but I'll go along until it catches up with me."

Young Bill DeBlasio, the tail-gunner, wrote in his battle diary: "By the grace of God we were the only ship to come back. Our pilot brought us home safely."

That was Munster, and it was five months more until Berlin.

Mike Bocuzzi, who had yelled that he was going to quit, griped that way many more times—and never quit. T/Sgt. C. C. Hall of Perry, Fla., a pleasant guy with a sour puss, went on shooting down fighters that he was reluctant to claim. And Rosie, the pilot, went on making his laconic reports to interrogation officers when they tried to pump him.

"The flak was meager," he would say. "We landed with our flaps out."

"Flaps out? Were you hit?"

"A little bit. But if you get back it's a milk run."

They flew to Bremen, Rostock, Brunswick. On the second Regensburg, the target area was snow-covered. Lt. Bailey, the navigator, gave the crew a little running lecture on European history and geography. Here were the Alps. Over that way was

Switzerland. Those long, wide lanes below were the "six-laned highways built by the Germans for this war." And here was where the Germans had broken through in an earlier war with France, in 1870.

Before Rostock, Bocuzzi was tired and jumpy. Rosie came down to the line, put his arms around Mike's shoulders and said: "What's the matter, Mike? We're all nervous. I'm always scared myself. What's the matter?"

"Nothing," said Mike.

In his battle diary, DeBlasio wrote darkly: "They better give us a rest and a few short raids. I am very tired now."

The pep talks had mounted. "By this time we'd had 102 since Dyersburg," says Ray Robinson. "I counted them. Rosie always gave us a pep talk before a mission. After that he never spoke on a raid, except when he had to."

For Berlin, the briefing was like all the others. But it was for Berlin, the "Big B," to be hit in daylight. Last August, as a gag, someone had put up the red ribbon across to Berlin, and no return route was indicated. Now it was no gag, and there was a return route. Through the briefing room came the shuffle of heavy boots. Cigarettes were lighted. As the pointer touched Berlin, Bocuzzi said to somebody: "Who got drunk last night and dreamed this one up?"

They went down to the line. Behind them were more than 20 raids. They dived into the ground crew's kitty of cigarettes in the tent. Bocuzzi borrowed a pencil from the ground crew. "No. 12, this is. I owe you 12 pencils," Mike said.

It was a cloudy day. Berlin could always be postponed, couldn't it? Couldn't it wait for tomorrow? They looked toward the tower where the flare might go up announcing "mission scrubbed." There was no flare, only the dull gray sky.

A new navigator was along. Instead of Lt. Bailey, riding the bike and looking like a professor with his navigator's brief case under his arm, there was a new man who had to be put at ease by Rosie.

The co-pilot, Lt. Winfrey (Pappy) Lewis of Houston, Tex., came down and did his pre-mission job of checking equipment. Then he dived for the cot in the tent—a regular thing with him, this sack time before a mission. S/Sgt. Marion J. (Junior) Sheldon of Arkansas, who had replaced Darling, carefully hung his two rag dolls, "Blood" and "Guts," to the receiver of his gun. All the little things had been done, and pep talk No. 103 took place—with Rosie's usual delivery: "You worry about your guns and let me worry about the plane."

The only changes this time were that they got into the plane a little earlier than usual and the silence over the interphone after the take-off was greater than usual. Interphone discipline had always been strict, but this was quieter than it had ever been. "We were a shipload of nerves," says Ray Robinson.

As they came over the German coast the clouds began to lighten. Moving into Germany, things were getting clearer. Pappy Lewis, the "bald eagle," looked over toward Rosie, beginning to sweat.

"It was only 30 below," says Mike. "Not too cold."

They got over the "Big B." It was clear below them, although smoke was already billowing high in the air. Flak was thick about them—"but not worse than Bremen," says DeBlasio. Nervousness disappeared with the first fighters.

"On this one," says Mike, "we didn't want them to get in close."

The bombardier got one and so did the top turret. Rosie's Riveters made their turn past the target.

Now the enemy coast was behind them. Over the interphone Rosie said: "Interphone discipline is now a sack of something." Voices broke in a frenzy of babbling, laughing noises. There was a hell of a squabble in the waist, and DeBlasio was refereeing between S/Sgt. Jimmy Mack and Junior Sheldon.

England again, after Munster, Bremen, Brunswick, Rostock, Stettin—and Berlin. After unloading bombs on the map of Germany. After 103 pep talks by Capt. Robert Rosenthal of Brooklyn and Brooklyn College.

They buzzed the field. Down below were friends. Maj. Blakely, the CO, was waving. The flares went up. It was private victory, but in this roaring excitement there was the knowledge of men who had not come back. In four raids on the "Big B," American bombers had dished it out, but they had taken it, too.

At the interrogation Capt. F. E. Callahan asked his questions, and the answers were, as usual, laconic. "We never get anything out of you," said Capt. Callahan gloomily. The new navigator told most of the story. Somebody was always pushing over to shake Rosie's hand, and the navigator said complainingly: "I wish this guy weren't so popular, so we could get through."

Lt. Col. Kidd and Col. Harding pulled Rosie aside to find out things. They found out little, and after he had downed a Scotch, Rosie asked politely: "Would it be all right if we had a couple of bottles of Scotch tonight at the barracks?"

It seemed very much OK.

One evening, a week later, they went to get decorations at the Officers' Club. There were Capt. Rosenthal, Bill DeBlasio, Ray Robinson and Mike Bocuzzi. They sat quietly shoulder to shoulder dressed in Class A's. Lt. Gen. Spaatz and Maj. Gen. Doolittle spoke. It was brief and to the point about the war. Jimmy Doolittle, answering a question, said in his resonant voice: "After all, it's not a matter of you and me going out, it's a question of winning the war."

Rosie went out and walked down toward his hut in the dark. Capt. Putnam, a close and good friend, had gone down a few weeks before. This Berlin raid was a thing of the past; let its history be written elsewhere. And tomorrow was another day, another raid.

At the Aero Club some mechanic got to the piano and played boogie woogie, and boys with "Berlin" inscribed on their jackets tapped their feet to the music, standing around the piano.

Over in the BOQ Ray Robinson found Rosie in the midst of a lot of clothes, with his B-4 bag open. Robinson shook his head and said pityingly: "Someone always has to pack your stuff. How on earth do you ever expect to get off on that leave tomorrow?"

He packed Rosie's stuff carefully into the bag.

"You won't need that," he said, throwing an extra suit of underwear to one side, after counting out the number he thought Rosie would need for the leave. And then he zipped the bag shut.

"Thanks, Ray," said Rosie.

"What train are you taking?"

"Early one, I guess."

"It's at 8 o'clock, so you better get out of the sack early—or do I have to come over and get you up? Good-night, Rosie."

"Good-night, Ray," said Capt. Rosenthal, settling into his sack.

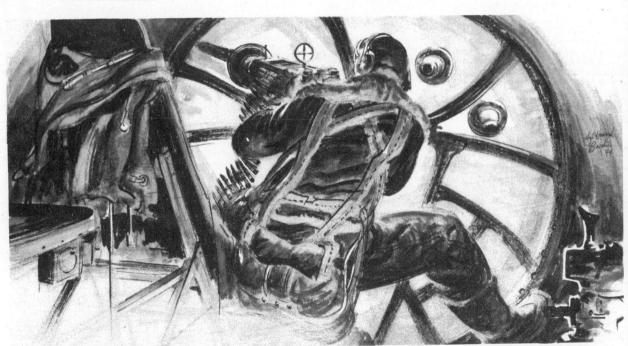

The bombardier got one and so did the top turret. Rosie's Riveters made their turn past the target.

Sketches by Sgt. Howard J. Brodie

CHIEF PETTY OFFICER

By BERNARD DRYER PhM3c

"I DON'T object as much to what you're doing, Church," Chief Williams said. "It's who you're doing it to." He rubbed his cigarette out and looked through the shifting planes of smoke at the younger chief across the desk. "Hell, I'm not trying to mess with your job—you can have the lousy personnel office. But this don't go so good."

Chief Church tilted slowly back in his chair and ran one thin hand back over his hair. He had admired this gesture of calm controlled power when he had been a first mate under Lt. (jg) Bronson; now that he had the rocker under the eagle on his arm, and the all-metal swivel chair with it, he had adopted the movement without recalling its source. He was fond of telling his roommate that even though he had never been to college no one would guess the fact just by watching him. Not that he wanted stuff on his shoulders—hell, he had enough responsibility now for two men—but it was kind of good to know he could keep up a smooth front like any junior gold braid.

"What do you want me to do, Williams," he said quietly, "cry over this guy Harvey?"

"Don't cry," said Williams. "Just give him a break."

"My God, he's due for night duty, isn't he?"

"Sure he is. But you don't give a guy 30 nights in a row and no leave. Not when he goes overseas the thirty-first day."

"The hell you say. To me the guy is a brick labeled third mate. He can replace any brick with the same label. That's policy and it's plain common sense." Church liked his last statement. I can use good English with the best of them, he thought.

"For Chrisakes, Church. I don't know whether to be sorry for you or sore."

"Sorry I annoy you, sir."

"Bricks, labels—where did you pick up that kind of talk?"

"Relax, admiral, relax."

"How can I, with you rocking back and forth stroking your hair?"

"All right, go ahead, get personal. I had to make the decision, so I made it."

Chief Williams blew the air out of his lungs in one long blubber sound and dropped his hands on his knees. "Church, listen. The guy is married. Him and his wife, they're just like that together."

"When you guys with hash marks up to the el-bow get sentimental, you're the worst of all. Are you a wet nurse or a chief petty officer?"

"I go for the word chief. You sort of lean toward petty."

"Christ almighty, Williams! I never seen you like this before! What's Harvey's wife got to do with it?" Church had a picture of Harvey's wife in his mind: she was probably pretty in a sort of high-tone way, and very respectable under the blankets. But on the other hand, maybe not. You could never feel sure of where you stood with that kind.

"The Old Man likes to see people get a couple days off before going overseas," Williams was saying. "You're getting 10 days off yourself. Give the boy at least a week end."

Church spread one hand out on the desk before him, slowly opening his fingers, admiring the long slender fingers and the clean short nails. "It's a rule," he said, "and you know it. If you go on nights, you stay on 30 days. And don't call him a boy, Williams. He's as old as I am."

Mr. Coggeshall, the warrant officer, came out of the head buttoning his trousers. "Jesus, if you two knew what you sound like through a door. Nyah, nyah, nyah. Why don't you knock it off?"

Church smiled and rocked a little in his chair. "I've always tried to be fair, and I'm kind of proud of it. But this is tough stuff for Harvey."

Harvey came striding into the office. Church noted with satisfaction the brittle little smile on his face. So many of them came in with armor on, but boy, oh boy, how fast they cracked. That's why it was better to call them up to the office instead of telling them by phone. He leaned back in his chair, feeling Mr. Coggeshall and Chief Williams watching him. He lit a cigarette with the cool competent carelessness of a woman putting on lipstick before going downstairs to a tiresome party.

"How goes the battle, Chief?" Harvey said as he came up to the desk.

That was one thing Church frankly disliked about these guys who had been to college. They always had something to say. Always an answer or a bright remark. He rocked in his chair a little and stroked his hair with his free hand, thoughtfully contracting his brows into a serious mask of dutiful concentration.

"How do you like your job down there, Harvey?" he asked. This was the regular opening. If they said they liked it, they were vulnerable to a change. If they said they didn't, they invited a change. In either case they risked getting something worse.

"Oh, so-so," answered Harvey. "Why?"

"What college did you go to, Harvey?" It always threw a smart bird off his stride when you kept changing the tack of your questions.

Harvey looked at him, then at Mr. Coggeshall and Chief Williams. Slowly he broke into a grin. "What is this," he asked, "a gag? What do I do now, write some memos for the skipper?"

Chief Williams took out a pack of cigarettes and thrust it at Harvey. "Grab one and take a load off your feet, Harvey," he said. "God's right hand is playing chess with you."

"What am I," Harvey asked, "a knight or a pawn?"

Mr. Coggeshall smiled. "Knight," he said. "That's a good one. Night. That's good."

Church didn't like Harvey's kind of talk because you were never too sure what it meant, so he interrupted with: "Maybe you'll say no if I ask you to write some memos, huh? You turned me down on a little job last week."

"Why hell, Church, you wanted me to work as plumber's helper. I'm busy as six people in that lab. I thought the Navy wanted to use men at their top skill unquote."

"No kidding, Harvey," Mr. Coggeshall said suddenly, "what college did you go to?"

"Harvard," Harvey answered and then added with a sidelong smile: "But don't hold that against me." A few small beads of perspiration had formed just below his hairline, and he wiped these off with one fingertip. He leaned over to light his cigarette from the match Williams held out between cupped palms. "Thanks," he said to Williams, exhaling the smoke in a great cloud. "Well, Church, I smell the dirty end of a stick."

Church's face fell into its frown of official concentration. He told Harvey about going overseas and the 30 days of night duty and ended with: "I'm sorry, but that's how it is."

Harvey was looking straight at him when he said slowly: "You're sorry, but that's how it is."

"Take it easy, Harvey," Church said.

"And you don't have 200 men in those barracks to replace me, do you?"

"If you were a second mate, Harvey, you couldn't be moved except on Bureau orders. But you're not, so you're on the draft."

"To hell with the draft, Church! I don't mind going so much. It's going without seeing my wife."

"You're in the Navy, mate."

"But it's so damned unnecessary to do it this particular way!"

"It's TS, mate. See the chaplain if you want."

Harvey got up. Mr. Coggeshall said: "Jesus, I forgot to wash my hands!" and went into the head, closing the door behind him. There was a moment of silence. Church opened his Clear-Vu personnel index file with a slight rattle to indicate the interview was finished.

Harvey leaned across the desk and said in a husky low voice: "If we ever meet in civilian clothes, Church, I'll beat your face in."

"What'll you do, chum?" Church snarled. "Hit me with one of them volumes of Shakespeare?"

Chief Williams took Harvey's elbow and said: "What do you say to a beer? Broke as I am, I'll let you buy me one."

Harvey continued staring at Church. "Church," he said, "I'd see a psychiatrist if I were you."

Church jumped to his feet. "Get out of here!" he shouted. "Get your goddam smart talk the hell away from my office!"

Harvey shook his elbow free of Chief Williams' grip, then he turned and walked out. Chief Williams looked at Church once and followed him.

For a moment Church stood there feeling a little fire dance in his chest. Then he pulled out the comb that clipped on the lining of his breast pocket and went over to the small steel mirror on the wall. He noticed with surprise that his hand was shaking a little as he combed his hair.

"Well, Church," he said, "I smell the dirty end of a stick, but what's the stick this time?"

THE DEAD END KIDS

By Sgt. DAVE RICHARDSON

BEHIND JAPANESE LINES IN NORTHERN BURMA—
Things were a little too quiet, even for a Sunday.
After all, there should have been some fireworks by
now, considering that part of the Jap 18th Division
was dug in on one side of the muddy 40-foot-wide
Nambyu River and our unit of Merrill's Marauders
was on the other.

"Looks to me," observed a BAR man as he
stripped his gun for cleaning, "like the lull before
the storm. The Japs won't take this lying down." He
didn't know how right he was.

The Marauders had just completed a 75-mile end
run around enemy positions in the Hukawng Valley and now our unit was only 200 yards from
Walawbum. We had met only small resistance from
Jap patrols during our march. But surely the Japs
would stand and fight us here. The native village
of Walawbum was the bottleneck through which
all supplies had to flow to their front-line troops,
15 miles to the north.

Across the river from us was a pretty tough bunch
of Japs. We could hear their trucks pulling up, and
every once in a while we could spot a few of them
for a fleeting instant as we moved through the
dense jungle. These were the Japs who had smashed
their way into Singapore two years before and now
had succeeded in slowing the Chinese drive down
this valley to a measly 10-mile gain in the last
month. They were fighting a stubborn delaying action from well-chosen positions, falling back from
foxhole to foxhole, pillbox to pillbox.

On our side of the river were some Marauders
known as the Dead End Kids. This was an appro-
priate nickname for this unit of Brig. Gen. Frank D.
Merrill's volunteer American raiders. They had already fought the Japs in the jungles of Guadalcanal, New Guinea and New Georgia. They had
joined the Marauders after President Roosevelt had
issued a call to their outfits for volunteers for an
"extremely hazardous" jungle-fighting mission in
another theater.

"Most of us guys volunteered," one of them explained, "because we figured we might get back to
the States for training first. We had all been overseas 18 to 24 months at that time and we wanted
to get home. Don't get the idea that we volunteered just because we were itching to fight the
Japs again."

I would have believed that statement if I hadn't
heard Brig. Gen. Merrill say, a few hours earlier,
that the Dead End Kids had been begging all day
for permission to attack Walawbum. And if I hadn't
come to know them in training camp.

The Dead End Kids wound up in India for training instead of in the States. At Christmastime they
went AWOL in droves, popping up in several Indian cities to spend wads of dough that had been
useless during their months in the Pacific jungles.
When they returned to camp, broke but happy,
they were reduced to privates. But they didn't give
a damn.

They hated the GI routine of garrison life—standing formations and inspections, shooting on the
ranges and going on field problems. They broke the
monotony by disappearing alone into the woods
and shooting deer, then bringing back the venison
for a change of chow.

On training problems with other Marauder units,
most of whom were proud of their preparation for
combat in the jungles of Panama, Trinidad or
Puerto Rico, the Dead End Kids confused and harassed their make-believe enemy with screwball tactics they had picked up while fighting the Japs. At
night they would sit around their tents and bitch
about "parade-ground soldiering" or reminisce about
their fighting exploits.

"Combat," as one of them put it, "seems to se-
duce a guy. He's scared as hell while he's in it, but
get him back in garrison and he'll start longing for
those foxholes and shellings and bombings."

This Sunday afternoon the Dead End Kids had
patrols out across the river to the north and south
of Walawbum. As the patrols returned, they reported that the Japs were digging artillery and
mortars into position and bringing up truckloads
of men and ammunition from the south.

But the night was just as peaceful as the day had
been. Next morning at 0930 hours, Sgt. Andrew B.
Pung of Malden, Mass., a mortar observer, shinnied
up a tree to a perch 40 feet above the river from
which he could look down across a grassy clearing
on the other bank.

Pung had a walkie-talkie radio with him. Soon
he reported seeing some telephone wires and several emplacements at the edge of the grassy clearing. Then his routine report changed to an excited
one. He forgot all about radio etiquette.

"Listen," he blurted into the microphone, "there's

a bunch of Japs coming out of the jungle and into this grass across the river. A big bunch. Get ready for an attack. I'll tell you when they're near enough to open fire."

The Dead End Kids jumped into their holes all along the riverbank. Bullets were clicked into chambers and machine-gun bolts pulled back twice to cock them. Pung sent firing data to the mortars as crews ripped open shell cases. Minutes ticked by. There was a tense silence.

"Give it to 'em," yelled Pung from his perch. The Japs had crossed the clearing to within 35 yards of the opposite riverbank. They were now in plain sight. Machine guns, BARs, mortars and rifles opened up in a deafening deluge of fire. Shrieks and yells came back from the field. Then the Japs began returning the fire. Their 90-mm mortar shells soared over the river and burst in trees behind the Dead End Kids. Shrapnel and bullets hummed through the brush.

Up in the tree some of the lead knocked off Pung's canteen and splattered all around him. He dropped the walkie-talkie and shinnied down.

The Dead End Kids were dug in on a bluff along the riverbank, a couple of dozen feet higher than the grassy clearing on the opposite bank where the Japs were advancing in spread-out skirmisher formation. This high ground was natural cover; the Japs were firing into the bluff or high over the Marauders' heads. The Americans just lay in their holes and blasted away.

Wave after wave of Japs poured out of the jungle and into the clearing, running and diving and creeping and crawling. Many of them carried machine guns and ammunition boxes. Some, probably the officers and noncoms, yelled "*Susume! Susume!*" which means "advance." Others shrieked "*Banzai*," the familiar battle cry.

In a few minutes Jap bodies lay sprawled on the field in little bunches. The Dead End Kids could hear the wounded crying and moaning. But the Japs kept coming—at least a company of them.

The Dead End Kids were happy. They yelled at their machine gunners and BAR men to "Mow down that bunch over there, boy!" and then shouted "Atta boy," as they concentrated their rifle fire on single targets. Pfc. George Fisher Jr. of Napoleon, Ohio, spit a gob of tobacco juice every time his M1 got a Jap.

"Those little bastards must think we're amateurs at this jungle-fighting stuff," grinned 1st Lt. Victor J. (Abie) Weingartner of St. Albans, N. Y., commanding the platoon in the center of the American positions along the riverbank. "*Banzai* charges might have terrified the civilians in Singapore, but they're nothing but good, moving target practice for us."

Lt. Weingartner was considered one of the most daring leaders of Dead End Kid patrols. Characteristically, he insisted on wearing into action the same dirty mechanic's cap that brought him through New Georgia unscathed; he willingly paid a $100 fine for not wearing a helmet at the last showdown inspection before the Marauders started their 200-mile march into battle.

Half an hour after the Jap attack began, it halted abruptly. But the Dead End Kids knew that the Japs would try again. Almost as soon as the attack ended, Jap artillery boomed several hundred yards back in the jungle. The shells whistled overhead and landed a half-mile behind the Americans, near a rice paddy. This field had been used in the previous two days as a landing area for Piper Cubs evacuating a few wounded, and as a dropping area for transport planes supplying the Marauders with rations and ammunition. Jap mortars threw a few shells into our positions the rest of the morning.

In the afternoon the good news came that another unit of Marauders had thrown a road block on the main enemy supply route from Walawbum to the front. With Walawbum threatened by the Dead End Kids' position and with the supply route blocked, the stubborn Jap defenses 15 miles northward had collapsed. As the Japs streamed back to reinforce the Walawbum garrison, the Chinese began driving through to relieve the Marauders and make a large-scale attack. As a hit-and-run raider outfit, the Marauders were supposed to keep their positions only until relieved by Chinese divisions with the men and large weapons needed to do the main attacking. The Chinese were expected within 24 hours.

But a lot could happen in 24 hours. The Dead End Kids cleaned their guns, opened more ammunition and placed men every three or four feet along the riverbank. While they worked they could hear the Japs digging, driving up more trucks full of men and ammunition and wheeling in their artillery closer.

At 1645 hours the broiling Burma sun had sunk low in the sky. It glared into the faces of the Dead End Kids as they kept their eyes focused on the field across the river. The attack would have to come from the field again because the terrain was unsuitable at other places along the river, where the banks were too high or the jungle too dense for a field of fire. And it came. Two Jap heavy machine guns hammered away like woodpeckers from the flanks of the field. Artillery and mortar fire increased. Knee mortars started clicking out grenades at close range.

The Japs really attacked this time. They came in waves that were wider and more frequent than in the first attack. And they had better support from weapons of all kinds, placed nearer the river. In each wave were several two-man teams lugging heavy machine guns. As soon as one team was hit, another ran out and grabbed its gun, only to die within a few steps. Then another.

Again the machine gunners and BAR men did most of the killing for the Marauders. They raked each wave with fire. But the Japs surged on across the field until they fell. A few of them even reached the river before they were hit, but nobody crossed. This time there was at least a battalion of Japs attacking the Dead End Kids.

And this time the Japs were more accurate with their fire. Bullets sped only a few feet over the Americans' heads. Practically every leaf and every tree were marked by the fire. Some of the stuff barely cleared the bank and did some damage. Bullets smashed two BAR magazines on the bank of the foxhole where T-5 Bernard Strasbaugh of Lewisburg, Kans., was stretched. Another bullet nicked his helmet. Strasbaugh was in the center of the attack, firing as fast as he could shove magazines into his weapon. When he spotted five Japs in a group running toward a dropped machine gun, he stood up, riddled them with fire and flopped down again. He hit the ground just soon enough to escape a burst of fire.

"All a guy has to do to get a Purple Heart here is stand up for 10 seconds," he muttered.

Pfc. Clayton E. Hall of Strawn, Tex., had a close call at his machine gun on the right flank. A knee-mortar shell burst only three yards in front of him. Then two bullets pierced the water jacket on his gun. With his machine-gun corporal, Joseph Diorio of Cleveland, Ohio, Hall managed to keep the gun going by pouring water into the jacket from every available canteen. He burned his hands on the red-hot jacket doing it, but the gun fired 4,000 rounds in 45 minutes.

Back at the Dead End Kids' CP, Maj. L. L. Lew of Baker, Oreg., the unit commander, received a message saying that the Chinese would relieve his unit around midnight. It was then 1730 hours.

The Dead End Kids were running low on ammunition. Men started shouting back and forth above the din: "Hey, you got a spare clip of M1?" From the left flank came a request for every available hand grenade. A unit there, commanded by Maj. Edwin J. Briggs of La Grande, Oreg., was being attacked by Japs who had infiltrated through the jungles from the south.

As ammunition ran out, the tension increased. Dusk turned to darkness, but the Japs still fired furiously and attacked fanatically. Their bullet-riddled bodies littered the field from the edge of the jungle to the river. The wounded screamed.

Then, as suddenly as the morning attack had ceased, the dusk battle halted. Both sides stopped firing. The silence was broken by a Dead End Kid who rose to his feet on the river bank, cupped his hands to his mouth and yelled:

"Come on, you little bastards. Come and get your lead!"

A Jap yelled back. The tension was broken. To a man, the Dead End Kids scrambled to their feet, stood along the riverbank and shouted cuss words at the Japs. From the other bank came only a few bursts of light machine-gun fire. The Japs, too, must have run out of ammunition.

Now they removed their wounded from the field in the dark. The Americans could hear the wooden sound of litters being carried through the brush and the terrifying cries of the wounded as they disappeared in the jungle.

Among the Dead End Kids, thanks to the natural protection of the high riverbank and to the dug-in emplacements, there had been only three casualties all day. But several pack mules, which carried mortars, radios and ammunition, had been wounded or killed by mortar shells.

The little remaining ammunition was doled out equally. A patrol from Maj. Briggs' outfit south of the Dead End Kids brought up some more BAR and machine-gun ammunition.

At 2000 hours T/Sgt. Jim Ballard of Spokane, Wash., chief of the unit radio section, entered the perimeter, leading a mule pack train loaded with all kinds of ammunition. He had tried to contact Brig. Gen. Merrill's CP early in the attack, but couldn't get it on the radio. So he had taken Maj. Lew's message requesting more ammunition and run back four miles to another Marauder unit, over a dark trail flanked by Jap patrols and through Jap shelling part of the way. He brought back the ammunition mule train through an even more severe shelling.

The hours dragged on and a heavy fog set in. A few Japs had sneaked across the river and were booby-trapping trails in the vicinity. Across the river the Japs seemed to be getting reinforcements and ammunition again for another attack.

While some of the men peered through the mist at the field across the river, others dozed off in their foxholes, with their heads propped on horseshoe-type packs. The Dead End Kids weren't cocky or swaggering tonight; they were exhausted from the tension of the two attacks.

Finally the expected message came: "Withdraw at 0200 hours to join Marauder CP. Chinese are taking over your position."

The weary Dead End Kids put on their packs and moved silently Indian-file out of their perimeter with their pack mules.

A little way down the trail another column passed the Americans, going in the opposite direction. It was the Chinese.

"*Megwaw, ting hao!*" they grinned as they plodded past the Dead End Kids. They meant: "Americans are okay." A Chinese divisional commander later put it another way: "Your unit," he said, "made it possible for us to gain more ground in one week than we covered all last month."

One of the Dead End Kids, after returning the Chinese greeting, turned and said to the man behind him: "You know, I could almost kiss those guys, they look so good to me now." He wasn't the only one who felt that way.

Next morning an official report reached Merrill's Marauders that one of their units, as the first American infantrymen to fight a battle on the continent of Asia, had left 800 Japanese dead on the field near Walawbum.

Hearing this, a cocky, swaggering bunch of Americans swung along the jungle trail toward an area where they could rest for two days before going on another mission behind Jap lines. The Dead End Kids were back in their element.

The Dead End Kids scrambled to their feet and cursed the Japs. From across the river came only a few bursts of fire. The Japs, too, had run out of ammunition.

Sketch by Cpl. Ruge

GREAT DAY

By Cpl. LEN ZINBERG

Italy—Cpl. Robert Stenker was a quiet, mild-mannered man, about 34, with thin blond hair and soft brown eyes. He was just beginning to get a little stomach. On the morning of June 6 he came into the S-2 tent and sat down behind his typewriter, humming to himself. The invasion had started; it was a very fine morning.

At exactly 0845, 2d Lt. Joseph NMI Hillard stepped into the tent. Cpl. Stenker jumped to his feet and saluted. Lt. Hillard gave him a very snappy salute in return. In all Italy, this was probably the only tent in which an officer was saluted at the start of the day, but as the lieutenant often said: "I'm not a stickler for rules and regulations nor do I believe in being too GI. However, some Army traditions must be upheld. So you salute me once every morning, and we'll let it go at that."

Lt. Hillard was neat and trim, as lean and hard as any 21-year-old boy should be. He had clean-cut features, a small fierce dark mustache and a crisp elocution-class way of speaking. He sat down behind his field desk and asked: "Anything new this morning, corporal?"

Cpl. Stenker said: "Of course, sir, you heard the invasion had started?"

Lt. Hillard jumped up in his chair and banged the desk with his fist. "By God, no?" For a moment he stared at the corporal in thoughtful silence. "So they've done it! Of course you know what this means?"

"Why, it means the end of the war is in sight," Cpl. Stenker said happily. "I've been overseas 23 months. I'll be glad to get home, see my wife and get a job."

"A job?" Lt. Hillard repeated slowly. "Corporal, have you had many jobs?"

"Quite a few," Cpl. Stenker said, filing his reports. "Of course I had the usual run of small jobs. But I was sales manager for an electrical concern for several years. Got married then. I was 24."

"I suppose marriage is quite a responsibility?"

"Yes and no. If you make decent dough, you don't have much trouble. I was getting 75 a week then. I worked as an office manager for about a year; that only paid 60 a week. I've worked as a salesman and once I wrote copy for ads. Just before the war, I managed a direct-mail advertising concern. Going rather well. I'll probably return to it."

"Sound like decent jobs," the lieutenant said, lighting a cigarette. He always lit his cigarettes with a neat brisk movement. "I suppose most jobs pay around 50 a week?"

"Maybe in boom times. About 30 is the average."

"Thirty isn't much, when you have to consider rent and food," Lt. Hillard said.

"You certainly have to take those items into account. Clothes, too."

"I suppose this sounds strange," Lt. Hillard said, "but I've never had a job. I was in my second year at college, taking a BA, when I came into the Army and went to OCS. Civilian life will be quite a change. Don't think I'll go back to college. Too old. Have to look for a job."

Cpl. Stenker lit a cigar and went on with his filing. Lt. Hillard smoked his cigarette and read a bulletin. Then he put that down and said: "So the invasion's started. I guess it's about time." He suddenly blew out a big cloud of smoke and killed his cigarette. "Bob," he said, "working in civilian life— I mean, getting a good job—it's about the same as the Army, isn't it? I mean, if a man could advance in the Army, he ought to—you know."

Cpl. Stenker was about to say it was pretty much the same, especially if you worked for a big concern. But he looked over at Lt. Hillard, noticed the tenseness in the lieutenant's face, and said casually: "No, I'm afraid it isn't, sir. I should say it was very much different. The Army is one thing, a civilian job another."

"I suppose so," Lt. Hillard said weakly.

"Yes, it's quite different," the corporal said.

Lt. Hillard opened a War Department letter and read it absently. Cpl. Stenker went on filing reports. He puffed on his cigar slowly, blowing out thin smoke rings. It's a fine day, he thought—first the invasion and now Lt. Hillard.

HOW TO GET LOST IN A JUNGLE

By Sgt. JOE McCARTHY

Find some monkey who knows the neighborhood. Watch what he eats. Then follow his example.

EVERYBODY in the Army seems to be writing handy pocket guides these days telling you How to Keep from Getting Lost in a Jungle. These books are all right but a lot of my friends are not reading them. In the first place, my friends never read anything, anyway, except beer bottle labels and the *Daily Racing Form*. In the second place, my friends are all goldbrickers and they don't want handy pocket guides that tell them how to keep from getting lost. All they want is to *get* lost, as soon as possible.

"The thicker the jungle the better," one of them remarked the other day, squeezing himself into the barrel of his M1 when the first sergeant approached to select a detail.

So my friends have requested, through channels, that I write a piece about How to Get Lost in a Jungle. They couldn't have picked a better man.

I happen to be an expert on getting lost. I spent most of the Carolina Maneuvers in 1941 at the top of the center pole in my pyramidal tent, where nobody could find me when there was a truck to be unloaded. As a matter of fact, I would have beaten Shipwreck Kelly's old record one week but a cer-

tain corporal, who shall be nameless, set the tent on fire and smoked me out.

I also happen to be an expert on jungles. I spent most of my summers as a youngster in a jungle near the Gillette razor blade factory in South Boston, Mass.

The first thing to remember if you want to get lost in a jungle is not to lose your head. There are a lot of head hunters in the jungles. If you put your head down somewhere for a minute while you are washing your feet or pressing your pants, a head hunter is liable to pick it up and walk off with it.

And don't be afraid of a jungle. A lot of soldiers get nervous when they find themselves in a jungle and notice that it has no traffic lights or sewers. But the jungle is really your friend. It provides heaps and heaps of food which can be found in the form of animals and plants. It also provides malaria mosquitoes, leeches, snakes, crocodiles and nettles but there is no need to go into that now. However, you will be glad to learn that you have much less chance of catching poison ivy in the average jungle than you have around Lake Winnepesaukee, New Hampshire. Here is another bit of good news about jungles: it hardly ever snows there, so the chances are you won't be liable to slip on an icy sidewalk and hurt yourself.

I see that the T-5 down there in the fifth row with the Good Conduct ribbon and the whistle has a question. Would you mind speaking a little louder, bully? You say you want to know what kinds of food in the jungle are safe to eat?

Well, my fine chowhound, my advice to you is to make the acquaintanceship of some young monkey about your own age who knows the neighborhood. Just watch what he eats. Then follow his example and you'll make out okay. But be careful about the kind of monkey he is before you start associating with him. Be sure he doesn't drink too much or run around with loose women. Many a careless GI in the jungle has been led to rack and ruin by hanging out with the wrong type of monkey.

Now let me see, where was I?

Oh, yes. The best way to get lost in a jungle is to get rid of your compass. I wouldn't recommend this, however, because the supply sergeant may get nasty and swear out a statement of charges to be deducted from your next month's pay. Pawning the compass wouldn't do either. You might get grabbed for hocking government property and sent to Leavenworth to cool off for a few years. But then again, if you want to look at the bright side of it, Leavenworth is an excellent place to get lost in, too. Even better than a jungle because it has no malaria mosquitoes.

I find the best way to get lost is to ask directions from an MP. Simply go where he tells you to go and, in no time at all, you won't have the slightest idea of where you are.

But be careful about crossing state lines. Even though we are at war, don't forget that they are still able to get you for violations of the Mann Act.

That covers about everything except malaria mosquitoes and the natives. The best remedy for mosquitoes is to burn punks. This is getting rather difficult to do now because most of the punks in the Army have either gone to OCS or have been released under the 38-year-old law.

There is no need to try to cover the natives. They have been walking around without clothes all their lives so you can't expect them to do anything different.

In closing, I suggest that you bring this page with you next time you feel like getting lost in a jungle. It might come in handy to light a fire with.

A PLEA TO THE POST-WAR PLANNERS

OR, PLEASE DON'T STREAMLINE MOTHER WHILE I'M GONE

By T/Sgt. PHILIP REISMAN JR., USMC.

Marine Barracks, Quantico, Va.

Sitting here, in my foxhole muddy,
please don't think me fuddy-duddy
if I say that I'm not fighting
for plywood pants and Neon lighting;
and if I seem to doubt the worth of
some things *you* seem to think the earth of.
Oh, hear, far seers: permit a Pharisee
to sing his sour song of heresy.
Your *post*-war world is strictly "pheasant";
today is "Spam"—my needs are *present*.
I've little need for breakfast toasters,
built like shiny roller coasters.
Cummerbund of soy-bean sacking
from my wardrobe's plainly lacking.
I need no girdle wove of plastic
nor baseball bat of glass elastic
nor yet a plane that's minus torque,
or even razor blades of cork.
I've little use for synthesized
soup, or operas (soapy) televised,
or trips to Mars in Roman candles,
or caskets trimmed with lucite handles,
or wireless ballots for brainless voters,
or Buicks with transparent motors,
or movies shown in four dimensions,
or breakfast foods of fringed gentians.
Give Gernsback back his grim inventions!
My love for them is sub-platonic.
I can do without your supersonic,

combination, candy-coated,
radium-dialed and ruby-throated,
chromium-plated,
numbered, dated,
ultra-hyper generated,
electro-magno-gyro steered,
acorn-fueled, six-speed geared,
strato-turbine,
intra-urban,
rotor, rocket,
plug-in socket,
superdooper-dyne devices,
born of copywriter's vices—
too much gin and orange ices,
(plus Pernod, Sterno, benzedrine)—
portrayed in poster-magazine,
the livid-vivid world they mean
for us to want, when on returning,
we resume our pre-war yearning
for spending more than we are earning.

Oh, post-war planners, men of science,
though I applaud your each appliance,
permit this note of loud defiance.
Your genius I will gladly bow to,
even curtsy and kowtow to—
but not until you've figured how to
send a female
via V-Mail.

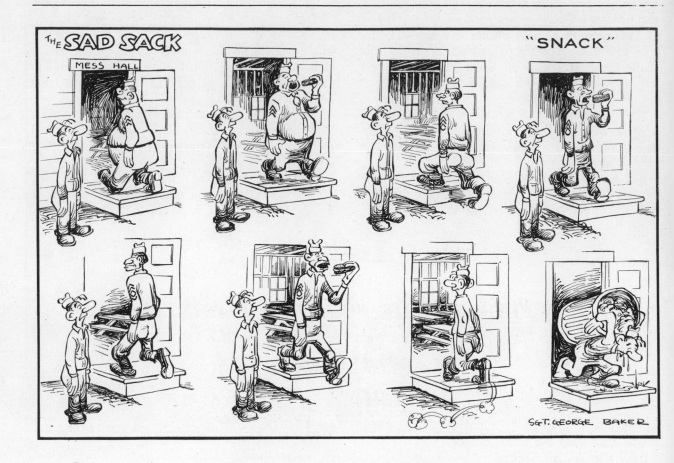

ARTIE GREENGROIN, PFC.

By Sgt. HARRY BROWN

GREENGROIN ON THE TELEPHONE

"Srr right here," Artie Greengroin said to us. "This is where it's going to happen."

"Here in the orderly room?" we asked.

"Yeah, sure," Artie said. "This is the oney telephone in the whole joint. This is where it's going to happen, awright."

He sat down behind the first sergeant's desk and began to bite his nails, starting with the third finger, left hand.

"I've jess had me a change of life," Artie said. "Did you ever think a ole bassar like me could have a change of life?"

We remained noncommittal.

"I am a new man," Artie said. "A new Greengroin. The old Artie is dead. And you know who done it to me?"

"No," we said. "Who done it to you?"

"Her," Artie said, gesturing at the telephone.

"My dream goil. She's like a sunset over Flatbush. She's like the third beer at Tim's Grill."

"Is she like the first sergeant when he comes in and sees you sitting at his desk?" we asked.

"I ignore that rummy," Artie said. "I ain't on speaking toims with him. What's he got that I ain't got?"

"Five stripes and a good left hook," we said.

"Thass beside the point," Artie said. "I mean man to man. But I got no reason to complain on a day like this. The boids is singing, the grass is growing, and the captain's dorg is making love up in the village. I got one thing to say for spring. I like it."

"What's this new doll of yours like?" we asked.

"Aw, she's wunnerful," Artie said. "Mine you, jess met her lass night, but I'm completely gone. I'm a loss soul. You ought to see them eyes she's got. They're blinding."

"Is she a darb?" we wanted to know.

"Aw, sure," Artie said. "Mine you, I ain't saying she's perfeck or nothing like that. She don't speak English too good. But her face and form are unconstitutional, honest to gaw. In exactly six minutes

she's going to give me a phone on this phone here and tell me where we're going to meet tonight."

"And in about one minute," we said, "the top is coming in here and kick you out of his chair."

"Don't talk to me about that top," Artie said. "He's beneath me contempt."

"For how long, Greengroin, for how long?" came the booming voice of the top from the door.

"Hello, there, ole boy," Artie said.

"Get yer crummy feet offen my desk," the top said. "Get yer crummy tail offen my chair. Get yer whole crummy carcass out of this orfice."

"Thass a hell of a way to talk to one of your own noncoms," Artie said. "I jess come in here to ast a favor, thass all."

"I ain't doing no favors terday," the top said, "and I ain't giving out no passes. If the favor you want is a pass fer ternight, ferget it. Ternight everybody's got to stay in and shine their buttons. Coinel's orders."

Artie's face dropped as though Lefty Gomez had thrown it when he was in his prime. "Aw, wait a minute, ole man," he said.

"I ain't a ole man, and I ain't waiting," the top said.

"Look," Artie said, "they's a goil going to call me. On that telephone."

For the first time the top became civil. "Oh, a doll, huh?" he said.

"Yeah," Artie said, "a real darb of a doll."

"Oh," said the top, "thass different. Wass she like, Greengroin, ole man?"

Artie told him. We blushed, ever so slightly.

"I tell you what, Greengroin, ole man," the top said after Artie had finished, "I got me orders not to issue no passes ternight because everybody's got to shine his buttons. But being as I never stood in the way of true love, I got an idea as far as you're concerned. Now, you run over to yer hut and polish yer buttons like a little man, and I'll give yer a pass for ternight."

"But what about the phone call?" Artie said.

"I'll take care of it for yer," the top said. "I'll find out the time and the place for yer."

"Sergeant," Artie said, really moved, "I never really unnerstood you until now. I'm very proud to be one of your noncoms."

"Greengroin, ole man, it's nothing," the top said. "Go and polish yer buttons."

With a whoop, Artie lit out of the orderly room

in the direction of his barracks. With a saintly smile, the top sat down at his desk.

We were about to take our leave when the telephone rang. The top picked up the receiver. "Sgt. Flump," he roared. Then his voice suddenly went gentle. "Who?" he whispered. "Pfc. Greengroin? Oh, he ain't here. He's in the guardhouse. Huh? . . . What for? Oh, drunk and disorderly. The usual thing with Greengroin. Tonight? Well, I ain't doing nothing. . . ."

We got out of there. It might be a good idea, we thought, to go up and speak to Artie. Something told us he was going to be awfully mad about the sergeant.

ARTIE THE BIRD FANCIER

"They been giving us drills," Artie Greengroin said.

"That's nice," we said. "What kind?"

"It ain't nice and they's all kines," Artie said. He sighed. Artie was in a very melancholy mood that afternoon. We were lying on our backs on the side of a green hill, looking up at the sky and watching a couple of birds circle overhead.

"Look at them gawdam boids," Artie said. "Happy as clams, they are. And why are they happy as clams? Because they don't have to do no drilling. They jess float along up in the air and spit in everybody's eye. I wisht I was a gawdam boid."

"The drills getting you down?" we asked.

"That ole bassar of a extended order is getting me down," Artie said.

"Are you in fighting trim these days, old boy?" we wanted to know.

"I'm awways in fighting trim, ole boy," Artie said. "Thass what I come in the Army for. Then they stick me in a truck and say to me, 'Greengroin, all

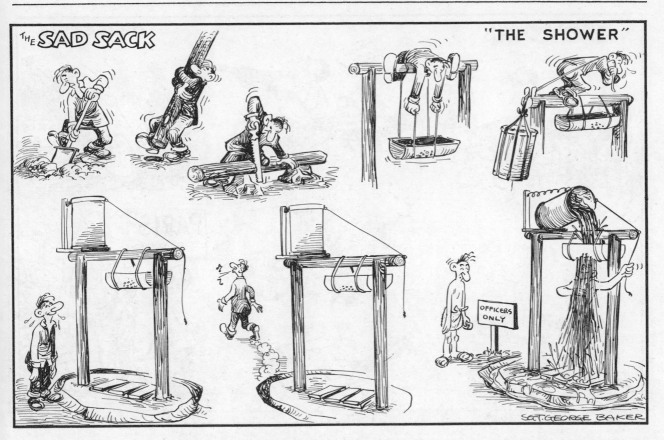

the fighting you're going to do is with shell holes in the road, maybe,' so I say 'OK,' and now they slap this close order on me neck. Maybe in a battle or something I can do close order in the blassid cabin of me truck. I'm fed up with the Army."

"You shouldn't take things so hard," we said.

Artie sat up and turned steely, or at least glassy, eyes on us. "Thass a hell of a thing to say," he said. "Yer ignorant of the facks, thass the trouble with you. Here, give a feel of me stummick."

We gave a feel of his stummick. "A little soft," we said.

"Yeah, it's soft, all right," Artie said. "And you know how it got soft? Naw, of course you don't. When it comes to drilling yer a voigin. You ain't even had yer surface scratched. Look, tell me something. What happens when you keep dropping a orange on the floor? It gets all softed up, don't it?"

"Guess it does," we said.

"Well, thass what happened to me stummick," Artie said. "I been truning meself down on me stummick in a extended order so much that it's got all softed up. It ain't doing me no good, believe me."

"It sounds to us as if they had you, old boy," we said.

Artie spat on a buttercup. "Naw, they ain't," he said. "I'm a natural born rebel. I'm going to thwart

right back at 'em. When I get this private army of mine going they ain't going to be no close order dri!l. But until I get this private army of mine I'm going into a seclusion unner me truck. Let that ole bassar of a top trot around the area yelling, 'Greengroin, where are yer?' Jess let him, thass all I got to say. I'll be unner a truck with a piece of literature in me hooks, boning up on Shakespeare or something."

"Do you read Shakespeare?" we asked.

"Aw, all the time, all the time," Artie said. "Now that Hamlet, he was a character. A smart apple, that Hamlet. He was a lot like me."

"That's what we've always thought," we said.

"Look at them gawdam boids," Artie said. "All they got to do in the woild is whiz around the air, eating woims. Some set-up."

"Cats get them," we said.

"Thass a chance anybody's got to take," Artie said. "Remember me and that Wren?"

"We'll never forget it," we said.

"Compared to my troubles, boids has it easy," Artie said. "Of course, I ain't got too much to complain about. I'm a pfc. I got rank. I eat well. I oney owe about 10 quid around the joint. I been keeping out of the clink. I'm laying off the dames. All in all, I should be a happy guy. But I am not a happy guy. And why? Because some ole bassar has trun

me out in the cold every morning to do a extended order, to be polished off with some close order. Some war, thass all I got to say."

"You've got more to say than that," we said.

"Them boids," Artie said, "have been buzzing around the English Isle since gaw knows when. Nothing bothers them. They get tired, they sleep. They get hungry, they knock off a couple of woims. They get the old vernal urge, they meet up with some woman boid. They got no troubles at all. Honest to gaw, I want to be a boid."

Artie suddenly jerked himself to a sitting position. "Jess a minute," he said. "Jess a minute. A idea jess give me a clip on the clipper. They ain't going to drill ole Artie termorrer."

"How so?" we asked.

"Hamlet," Artie said.

"Hamlet?" we said.

"He went nuts," Artie said.

"So he did," we said.

"So am I," Artie said. "Termorrer morning."

"It's a hanging matter," we said.

"A Greengroin was never a man to dodge risks," Artie said. "And besides, if it woiks I might sweat meself into a Section 8 and be discharged from the Army. And anyways, I'm out of a morning's doity woik. What've I got to lose?"

We didn't know and we said so.

"Jess you come around termorrer morning and watch old Hamlet Greengroin," Artie said. He got to his feet. "Well," he said, "I got to hop along now. I'm a blassid table waiter."

ARTIE BEHIND THE SECTION 8 BALL

"Awright," we could hear the sergeant shouting, "come out wit' yer light combat packs fer light combat."

"This is it," Artie Greengroin said. "This is where I do me ack. He says light combat but he means a extended order. Me gut can't take it no more."

Artie was sitting on his bed, smoking a weary old fag. "I ain't the kine of man that likes light combat," he said. "I'm strickly a heavy combateer."

"You're going to wind up in the bastille as sure as you're born," we said, "if you try to play looney with that sergeant." We knew that sergeant.

"Poop on it," Artie said. "I knowed that sergeant ever since they trun me in khaki. He's a rummy. I repeat, Sgt. Crud is a rummy. Poop on him."

The platoon, wearing light packs, dutifully filed out of the hut. Outside, Sgt. Crud called the roll. Finally the ominous word "Greengroin" rang out in the misty air.

"Lazy ole bassar's in the hut, sarnt," someone said.

"Dirty ole bassar's making faces at everybody, dirty ole bassar," said someone else.

The roll call went on. "He'll be in in a minute," Artie said.

"That he will, Artie," we said. "That he will."

"I better start losing some of me poise," Artie said. "I better begin looking disheveled like."

"You'd better," we said.

Artie ruffled his hair and drooled a bit. While he was indulging in this bit of beautification, the sergeant came into the hut.

"Greengroin," the sergeant said, "I want yer."

Artie looked at him blandly. "Nobody can have me," he said. "I'm me mother's."

"In this Army," Sgt. Crud roared, "I'm yer mother and yer father and yer sister and yer brother and yer gawdam ole Aunt Agnes. Why ain't you out wit' yer pack on yer back?"

"The trouble with you is you want to hurt me," Artie said. "Everybody wants to hurt me. I'm a sensitive plant. I bruise."

"I'll bruise yer blasted ole brains with the butt of a bazooka," the sergeant said.

"Thass it," Artie cried. "You want to get me out of the area so's you can moider me. Yer a moiderer."

"I am not a moiderer," the sergeant said. He was beginning to look a little worried. "I jess want yer to come out an do a extended order with the boys."

"Moiderer!" Artie screamed.

"Wass the matter with him, anyways?" the sergeant asked us.

We shrugged, implying that God alone knew.

"I think maybe I better go see Sgt. Flump," the sergeant said.

"Moiderer!" Artie shrieked.

The sergeant went out. Curious men of the platoon were peering enthusiastically in the door of the hut.

"Wait'll he comes back with that ole bassar, Flump," Artie said. "Thass where I'm really going to look good. I got faith in meself, ole boy."

There was a commotion and a shoving away of privates before the door. Sgts. Crud and Flump entered, Crud worried, Flump fierce.

"Greengroin," Sgt. Flump said, "I got me eye on you. Yer a devil, Greengroin, but I got me eye on you. Yer a disgrace to the Army."

"I'm a moiderer," Artie said, his eyes flaming. "A moiderer."

"He said I was a moiderer when I was in before," Sgt. Crud said.

"Thass confusing, ain't it?" Sgt. Flump said. "You done somebody in, Greengroin?"

"I'm a moiderer," Artie shouted. "I'm a sergeant-killer."

"He's nuts," Sgt. Crud said glumly.

"I'm going to kill every sergeant in the blassid Army in little pieces," Artie said.

"I better get a doctor," said Sgt. Crud. "Two doctors."

"Not so fass," Sgt. Flump said. "Not so fass. They's nothing the matter with this man."

"I'm a moiderer," shrieked Artie.

Sgt. Flump waved a magnanimous hand at Artie. "I come in here unner a mistapprehendsion," he said. "They's nothing the matter with this man except esprit de corpse."

"Wass that?" Sgt. Crud wanted to know. "Thass some kind of a disease, ain't it?"

"Ah, nah," said Sgt. Flump, "thass a state of mine. If yer a good fighting man you got esprit de corpse. If you ain't a good fighting man you ain't got nothing. Now Greengroin here is a good fighting man."

"I'm a moiderer," Artie said, much fainter.

"Sure, yer a moiderer," Sgt. Flump said. "All good fighting men is moiderers. I'm a moiderer. Greengroin, I'm proud of yer. I didn't know you had it in yer."

Artie stopped drooling. "Honess, sergeant?"

"Yerse," said Sgt. Flump. "You keep on this way yer gonna make corporal, sure as hell."

"Is thass so?" said Artie. He ran his hands through his hair.

"Yerse," said Sgt. Flump. "I'm proud to have yer in me company."

"Well, well," said Artie. He got to his feet.

"And now if you will jess join the boys for a little outing." said Sgt. Flump, "I will report me finding to the capting. He will be pleased."

"Thass a good idea, sergeant, ole boy," Artie said. He started to put on his combat pack.

Sgts. Flump and Crud went out of the hut.

"You see how it is?" Artie said. "You jess use a little brains and you make corporal."

"You've still got to do extended order," we said.

"They's nothing to it," Artie said. "To a man who's got the ole esprit and who's about to be permoted a little extended order is nothing. Well, ole boy, I got to go fall down on me gut for a while. Keep the home fires boining."

FIRST EPISTLE TO THE SELECTEES

According to Pfc. HAROLD FLEMING

Lo, ALL ye miserable sinners, entering through the Gate of Induction *into* the Land of Khaki, hearken unto my words; for I *have* dwelt in this land for many months and mine eyes have witnessed all manner of folly and *woe*.

2 Verily have I tasted of the bitter Fruit of TS *and* drained the dregs of the Cup of Snafu:

3 Gird up thy loins, my son, and take *up* the olive drab; but act slowly and with exceeding care and hearken first to the counsel of a wiser and sadder man than thou:

4 Beware thou the Sergeant *who* is called First; he hath a pleased and foolish look but he concealeth a serpent in his heart.

5 Avoid *him* when he speaketh low and his lips smileth; he smileth not for thee; his heart rejoiceth at *the* sight of thy youth and thine ignorance.

6 He will smile and smile and work all manner of evil against thee. A wise man shuns the orderly room, but the fool *shall* dwell in the kitchen forever.

7 Unto all things there is a time: there is a time to speak and a time to be silent: be thou like unto stone in the *presence* of thy superiors, and keep thy tongue still when they shall call for volunteers.

8 The wise man searcheth out the easy details, but only a fool sticketh out *his* neck.

9 Look thou with disfavor upon the newly made corporal; he prizeth *much* his stripes and is proud and foolish; he laugheth and joketh much with the older noncoms and looketh *upon* the private with a frown.

10 He would fain go to OCS, but he is not qualified.

11 Know thou that the Sergeant of the Mess is a man of many moods: when *he* looketh pleased and his words are like honey, the wise KP seeketh him out and praiseth his chow and laugheth much at his jests:

12 But when he moveth with great haste and the sweat standeth *on* his brow *and* he *curseth* under his breath, make thyself scarce; for he will fall like a whirlwind upon the idle and the goldbrick shall know his wrath.

13 The Supply Sergeant is a lazy man *and* worketh not; but he is the keeper of many good things: if thou wouldst wear well-fitting raiment and avoid the statement of charges, *make* him thy friend.

14 He prizeth drunkenness *above* all things.

15 He careth not for praise or flattery, but lend him *thy* lucre and thy liquor and he will love thee.

16 Hell hath no fury like a Shavetail scorned: he walketh with a swagger and regardeth the enlisted man with a raised eyebrow; he looketh upon his bars with exceeding pleasure *and* loveth a salute mightily.

17 Act thou lowly unto him and call him sir and he will love thee.

18 Damned *be* he who standeth first in the line of chow and shortstoppeth the dessert and cincheth the coffee.

19 He taketh from the meat dish with a heavy hand and leaveth thee the bony *part*.

20 He is thrice cursed, and all *people*, even unto the pfcs, will revile him and spit upon him: *for* his name is called Chow Hound, and he is an abomination.

21 Know thou the Big Operator, but trust him not: he *worketh* always upon a deal and he speaketh confidentially.

22 He knoweth many women and goeth into town every night; he borroweth all thy money; yea, even *unto* thy ration check.

23 He promiseth to fix thee up, but doth *it* not.

24 Beware thou the Old Man, for he will make *thee* sweat; when he approacheth, look thou on the ball; he loveth to chew upon thy posterior.

25 Keep thou out of his sight and let him not *know* thee by name: for he who arouseth the wrath of the Old Man shall *go* many times unto the chaplain. *Selah*.

"It's from the old man. He says we're due for typhoid booster shots."—Cpl. Fred Schwab.

We were ready for the repair job on the Transatlantique dock at Cherbourg. Army reconstruction plans were drawn up over a year before the invasion.

CAPTURE OF CHERBOURG

By Sgt. WALTER PETERS

Sketches by Sgt. John Scott

WITH U. S. FORCES IN CHERBOURG, FRANCE [By Cable]—On our way to the front lines in the battle for Cherbourg, we stopped at a town not far away, where a large crowd of natives was gathered on the highest point facing the great harbor city. The artillery fire had stopped, and there was silence everywhere except for the barking of dogs. It was Thursday, four days before Cherbourg fell.

A gray-haired woman who spoke perfect English said we shouldn't go any farther without investigating a certain young woman whom she suspected of being a German spy. "I saw her with my own eyes," said the woman, "giving signals through the window last night. I warned one of your officers about her, but she's still free. I think something should be done about her pretty quick before she does serious harm."

A jeep came by with three MPs and stopped. "What house is she in?" asked one MP. The woman gave them the address and the MPs drove off. We followed them. They stopped in front of the local hotel and asked the café proprietor downstairs where they could find the suspected spy. The proprietor led the way upstairs to a room on the top floor and knocked on the door.

A brunette, about 25 years old, answered the knock, and we followed the MPs into the room. Three other women were sitting on the bed. The girl in the center was still very much undressed and screamed when she saw the MPs.

"Okay," said the shortest MP. "Which one speaks English?" One of the girls, another brunette who wore dark-rimmed glasses, asked the MPs in a mixture of French and English what they wanted. "We want the girl who flashes a signal light at night," said the MP. "Where's the light?"

The brunette with the glasses insisted they had no flashlight and never had any relations with the Germans except "business relations."

"We hate the Germans," she said. "They take what they want from us and never pay for it."

After 15 minutes of questioning, the MPs began to search the room. "What's this?" asked one MP as he lifted a German signal flashlight from a suitcase.

The girl who'd been doing all the talking began to do plenty more. She had never seen the light before, she said; she didn't know how it got into the room, and if she did, she didn't know how to use it.

"Okay, girls," said the short MP. "Get yourselves decent and let's get moving to somebody who can speak French better than me."

"I think three of these girls are honest whores," he said to me, "probably brought here by the Germans. But the one doing all the talking is a German, okay. I'll stake anything she's done more than just entertain the Jerries."

A group of natives in front of the hotel smiled their approval as the girls were led out. One man grabbed an MP's arm and said: *"Merci, merci."*

There was a loud roar coming from the skies in the direction of Cherbourg, and people came from all over town to join those already on the hill. Word

The Cherbourg beachhead. A burned-out LCI, hit by an 88-mm shell, rests in the foreground.

had gotten around that the Infantry was having trouble driving the Germans from their positions in the area of Mont du Roc, so the Air Force was coming in to bomb them out.

I stood on the roof of a chicken coop to get a better view of the bombing. The distance was too great and the planes were flying too high for us to see them clearly, but smoke columns caused by their bombs rose high over the hills and into the blue of the sky.

Later we learned that some of our more advanced troops were in the bombed area, but they had retreated several hundred yards so the bombs wouldn't hit them.

After we had watched the bombers for 30 minutes, an elderly Frenchman with a long white mustache invited me to his house. As I entered, he kissed my hand and offered me a drink of cognac. In sign language he explained that his daughter lived in Cherbourg and he was very happy the Americans were closing in on that city. He filled the glass again.

"Vive l'Amerique," he said.

"Vive la France," I said.

Fighter-bombers of the Ninth Air Force were still attacking the German stronghold at Mont du

Roc when we arrived at the regimental CP. Enemy flak was bursting all around the planes, and the infantrymen sweated out the flyers at every burst.

"The forward battalion's going in now," said the commanding general of the division after the last plane had dropped its bombs.

"If you're going down to the forward battalion," a young lieutenant warned me, "you'd better be on your guard for snipers. They got a couple of our men around here this morning. There are still a number in the area."

I piled into a jeep with three other correspondents—Bruce Grant of the Chicago Times, Tom Henry of the Washington Star and Cpl. Joe Cunningham, a YANK photographer—and we drove off. About 200 yards from the CP, there was the soft crack of a rifle.

We turned off at a junction into a road. Artillery fire had resumed soon after the Air Force completed its job, and the closer we approached the front lines, the louder the burst of the guns became. None of us had ever been over this road before, but it was evident that we were traveling in friendly territory. Here and there on either side of the road were the bodies of dead Germans, their equipment scattered around.

Barrage balloons, tied to ships and shore, dot the sky.

There was another rifle crack that seemed to come from the hill on our right. "Yep," said the driver, "that's a sniper. You can always tell the difference between a sniper's fire and our own carbines by the flat sound, like the sound of your knuckles beating against marble."

When we caught up with the tail end of the forward battalion, our driver parked the jeep under a tree and we proceeded on foot alongside the infantrymen. Our first stop was in an orchard where a heavy-weapons company was firing.

Cpl. Howard Hodgson of Calumet, Mich., the No. 1 man, was kneeling by a mortal while Sgt. Kongslie of Upham, N. Dak., relayed information he was receiving from the OP by walkie-talkie: "1,200, fire for effect, six rounds." As he shouted, Pfc. Eugene Rossman of Ellwood City, Pa., assistant third gunner, pulled the pins out and took off increments from the shells. He and Pfc. George Evanoff of Hammond, Ind., the second gunner, loaded the mortar. Then Hodgson yelled back to Kongslie: "Six rounds ready."

"Okay," Kongslie replied. "On the way," Hodgson yelled again. Right after Hodgson fired the six rounds, there was a whining sound overhead. "Incoming mail," Rossman shouted. Everybody took cover in a foxhole. Jerry was hitting back hard.

Company A's OP was about 500 yards in front of the mortars. I found my way by following our communication wires. The OP was in a large hayfield, surrounded by trees and hedges. In the center of the field were wooden dummy guns, made by the Germans to fool our reconnaissance crews. Our men were dug in around the edges.

As I walked toward the advance section of the OP, a sergeant behind a machine gun told me to keep well under cover "or get your goddam head blown off." There were Jerry machine-gun nests and snipers in front and at the sides of the OP, and the Germans tried to pick off our men as they passed through open sections.

When I reached the advance section, I found Sgt. Frank Brusic of Passaic, N. J., a platoon leader, giving orders to cease firing. "Look out there on the hill," Brusic said. Through his binoculars I saw a Jerry waving a white flag. "That sonuvabitch has waved that flag for a half hour and he still isn't coming in," Brusic said.

Some of the men in the platoon started to yell. One yelled in Polish, another in German and a third in Russian. "Come here," they yelled, "come here." But the German just kept waving.

Engineers clearing away the wreckage of a Nazi-destroyed bridge in Cherbourg. They cleared the whole mess in less than a day.

"We've stopped firing," Brusic said, "but they haven't. I'd send a man after him but it looks like the old Jerry trick. They shot my best friend in Italy by pulling that stunt." The next man asked Brusic whether his friend had died. "Hell, no," said Brusic. "He's an Irishman."

Right about then a shell whizzed by us, followed quickly by more. "Screaming Mimis," Brusic said. He picked up the phone and said: "Let's give them some incoming mail." When Brusic got the heavy-weapons company on the phone, he gave them fire directions. Then he corrected the fire as the first mortar shells hit.

On Friday morning, two rifle platoons advanced to the foot of the enemy hill. I went forward with a group of medics. The road from the OP advance section was wide open for snipers. We ran and ducked at 50-foot intervals. When we reached the forward medics, a private warned us to hug the roadside. Snipers were shooting at everybody in the center.

A couple of medics brought in a wounded man on a litter and laid him carefully on the ground. Then Capt. Edmund Torkelson of Seattle, Wash., came up and began cutting the wounded man's pants so he could administer first aid. "How do you feel?" the captain asked. "All right, I guess, sir," said the soldier. "What got you," asked the captain, "a machine gun?" "No, sir," said the soldier, "a sniper." The soldier had scarcely said that when a sniper's bullet passed over us. The captain ordered the litter to be moved back.

When the wounded man had been carried off, the captain looked at his hands. "I've washed them a dozen times today," he said. He looked at his hands again. They were stained with blood.

Another wounded man was brought in. "My God," said one of the medics. The man's face was half blown off, his chin hanging by a few threads of skin, his nose not visible. A 20-mm shell had hit him in the face, an infantryman said.

By the time the captain was ready to leave with the medics, Pvt. Frank Volpa of Fresno, Calif., came running up. "They got my lieutenant, sir," he said. "They got him with a machine gun right in the arm, and the bone is sticking out. We dragged him from the hills but we've got to get help to him in a hurry."

"What was it like on the way over?" the captain asked. "Many snipers?"

"Yes, sir," Volpa answered, "there are quite a few of them, but I think we can do it all right."

"Okay," said the captain, "let's go."

By Saturday night there were reports all over the lines that a U. S. division had entered the eastern section of Cherbourg. Rumors can be wilder on the battle front than in any barracks latrine back in the States, but anyway I joined a well-known regiment moving up.

"There goes the Old Man," said Cpl. Thomas Donnelly Jr. of Jersey City, N. J., as the colonel passed by in a jeep. "He's the fightingest guy I've ever seen."

S/Sgt. Marvin Bogart of Lima, Ohio, commander of a half-track, told me he thought we might march into Cherbourg that night. "You can ride in my half-track," Bogart said. "I think all they're waiting for is to get rid of some more pillboxes and that 88 over there. Then in we go."

As if in answer to Bogart's crack, the 88 began to belch fire. Everybody took cover. A couple of shells hit across the road from us, and one of them split a tree. Another shell hit Bogart's half-track.

"Don't worry," Bogart said. "We'll have it ready so that we can ride into Cherbourg in the morning."

On Sunday night I was with the same regiment in a town called Octeville, about two miles from Cherbourg. The colonel was standing in the church cemetery and around him were all his battalion liaison officers. He pointed a pencil at a map of the Cherbourg sector.

"If we get that far," he said, "there may be street

fighting from then on. That's why I'm putting Tucker here." The colonel looked at one of his lieutenants. "Tucker's had special training in that."

"Yes, sir," Lt. Tucker said.

When the briefing was over, a soldier brought the colonel a canteen full of black coffee. Then another soldier poured in some sugar. "Who's going to split this coffee with me?" asked the colonel. He looked at a pfc, whose face was unshaven and whose eyes were tired from lack of sleep and from lying in foxholes.

"You'll split this coffee with me, won't you, son?" asked the Old Man.

"Yes, sir," said the pfc.

The colonel lifted the cup to his lips. "To tomorrow," he said.

"Yes, sir," said the pfc. "To tomorrow."

The next day they both marched into Cherbourg.

A guard stands by as engineers remove an 88-mm gun from an enemy flak ship sunk in the harbor of Isigny.

SQUARE-CUT DIAMOND

BY ALLEN CHURCHILL Y3c

THE United States Marine Corps is celebrating its 168th anniversary this month, so that makes Lou Diamond, the most famous marine in this or any other war, 200 years old.

Any leatherneck will tell you that Lou has been the best mortarman in the Corps since it was founded by the Continental Congress, Nov. 10, 1775. They claim he was rather old when he enlisted—32; so by now he must be rounding out his second century.

Nobody is exactly sure about this, however, because Master Gunnery Sgt. Leland Diamond is not a man who likes publicity and he flatly refuses to divulge his correct age to anybody. It is on his service record, of course, but Lou takes great care to make sure this record is kept secret. According to strict Marine standards, Lou was even rather old for combat service in the last war, but his boundless energy and tremendous vocal powers were well known all over France.

Last year, just before his outfit was to embark for Guadalcanal, there was scuttlebutt that the tough old sarge might be left behind because the South Pacific was no place for such a venerable and ancient man, even though he was twice as strong and three times as nasty as the youngest boot in the Corps.

When Diamond heard these rumors, as he hears everything, he acted upon them as he always acts—energetically and in full voice. All the ground he had to cover he covered at a fast trot. All the orders he had to give—and he gives more orders than five generals—he gave in a raucous bellow. The trotting and bellowing began every morning at 5 A.M. and in three days Lou had everybody in the camp worn to a frazzle. But when the transport moved away from the dock, Lou was aboard.

The Diamond legend grew considerably in the South Pacific where Lou roared his way through the battles of Guadalcanal and Tulagi and did much to back up the Marine Corps contention that he is far and away the most expert mortar sergeant in any branch of the service.

At Tulagi he demolished 14 Jap buildings with his trusty 81-mm. Then he turned to the colonel and bet him $50 that he could put a shot down the chimney of the 15th. He won.

The story was a bit different one morning when a Jap destroyer tried to creep around the island.

Diamond's first shell fell in the water a few feet behind the tin can.

The sergeant's bull voice arose in anguished thunder that shook the tropical foliage. From the deluge of profanity, only the last sentence was distinguishable:

"Forgot to allow for the —— forward movement!"

John Hersey, the war correspondent, saw Diamond in action at Guadalcanal and described him as "a giant with a full gray beard, an admirable paunch and the bearing of a man daring you to insult him. As we went by, he was, as usual, out of patience. He wanted to keep on firing and he had been told to hold back. 'Wait and wait and wait!' he roared. 'God, some people around here'll fall on their a—— from waiting!'"

Writing in the Marine magazine, *The Leatherneck*, Frank X. Talbot describes Diamond as an inch or so under 6 feet, pushing the scales to the vicinity of 200 pounds. Most of the time he is talking or roaring, and when he isn't roaring, his tongue hangs out of the corner of his mouth, relaxed and ready for the next outburst. When he can get it, he drinks beer by the case. He always drinks standing at the bar, with his hat on.

In mid-November last year the tension of the Guadalcanal campaign showed signs of wearing on Lou. He was ordered to New Zealand for hospital care. Protesting with wolf-like howls, he was dragged into a plane and later deposited in a clean hospital bed where he immediately got into trouble because he refused to permit his beard to be shaved off and because he patted a pretty nurse in the right place. Lou had been there only two days when the hospital superintendent said: "I thought I was head of this hospital until Diamond got here. Now I'm not so sure."

When the sergeant was released from the hospital he promptly made tracks for Guadalcanal. When he got there he found the Army in charge, his unit gone and himself farther than ever from joining them. His curses of rage and frustration tore the air and made the soldiers cringe. Anger spent, Lou then efficiently began thumbing a ride across the Coral Sea to Australia.

Some weeks later his burly figure appeared on the remote Australian field where his company was drilling. It was 50 miles from the nearest port to that field. It was hot and there were no transportation facilities, but Lou had covered the distance on foot. Walking smartly up to the major, he snapped to attention, saluted and said: "Sir, I'm here."

Diamond gives his mortars more affection than anything in this world. At the Marine base in New River, N. C., he spent many nights sleeping with a ring of 81-mm mortars around his bunk. He called them his sweethearts, and nobody dared approach them.

The only other things for which the sergeant shows affection are his pets, of which there has been an endless chain. They include Bozo, the ugly bulldog described by Master Gunnery Sgt. Mickey Finn as much prettier than Lou, and a disagreeable goat named Rufus and a couple of trained chickens whose names are unprintable. This select menagerie is now waiting patiently at New River for the momentous day when the rough Diamond returns from the wars.

Lou rules his men with an iron hand. They fear him at first, get to like him when they know him and end by loving him as much as a marine can love anything. Lou treats anyone who has less than 10 years of service like the meanest boot. This gripes some of the men who serve with him, but they end by taking it philosophically. "After all," one of them said, "if you can get used to that old bastard's voice, you can get used to anything."

DEAR YANK:

In reference to an article in your YANK magazine [in a November issue], I wish to state that I have been insulted by the article on "Square-Cut Diamond," written by Allen Churchill Y3c, and I have written to my lawyer in Toledo, Ohio, to take action on the article. 1) I am not an old bastard. 2) I am not 200 years old. 3) My tongue does not hang out and I did not hike 50 miles to get back to my outfit. 4) And those chickens I had was named "Bud." 5) I had orders to report to the 1st Marine Division on Guadalcanal, which was on the same place and I did leave with a part of the 1st Marine Division. 6) Who gave your outfit permission to use my name? 7) Also I am figuring on a nuisance charge against you. I served in the last war and am trying to do my bit in this one, and I do not like the way your outfit is trying to do.
Parris Island, S. C.
—MASTER GUNNERY SGT. LOU DIAMOND

DEAR YANK:

The article on Lou Diamond was splendid and everyone in our office enjoyed reading it. It was called to the commandant's attention. We thought it an especial tribute, on our anniversary, to have a meeting of the services in your article: a Marine subject in an Army publication, written by a Navy man. Let those who are captious on the cooperation of the services be silent.
Hq. USMC, —BRIG. GEN. ROBERT L. DENIG
Washington, D.C. Director, Division of Public Relations

Bringing supplies up the Matanakau River in captured Jap boats—"We went up that way and the lizard was on the log just where he is."

Getting ready for the Guam show: A Liberty ship is loaded with supplies for the assault on the island.

SKETCHES OF THE GUAM CAMPAIGN

BY

SGT Robert Greenhalgh

Pennant flying from radio mast, an amphibious tank moves into position. Men look out from open hatches.

Marines, relieved from one sector of the front, move on to another combat zone through Agat.

Robert Greenhalgh made
set of drawings after
ering a Marine brigade's
erations from its landing
D Day to the capture of
uam airstrip. "Slogging
round in the rain and mud,"
ne wrote, "I got my notes
soaking wet and now they
are almost obliterated. Then
the transport with my art
equipment pulled out. But I
found some materials on a
flagship, so I was in business
again."

A Pack Howitzer
Message Center is
housed in a Guam man-
sion. The runner has
just arrived from the
front.

Wounded ride back from the front on a tank.

Four Marine riflemen search out a Japanese sniper's nest.

Marine with automatic in shoulder holster.

SKETCHES OF THE GUAM CAMPAIGN

Weary Marines rest in the rain and mud of Agat town on the fourth day. The men flop anywhere in the ruins as their lieutenant talks to the MP at the far left.

PALESTINE EXPRESS

By Pvt. IRWIN SHAW

Tel Aviv, Palestine—The train for Palestine pulled out of Cairo station slowly, to the accompaniment of wailing shrieks from the platform peddlers selling lemonade, cold coffee, pornographic literature, grapes, old copies of *Life* and flat Arab bread.

The train was long and crowded, and it had seen better days. It had been standing in the wild Egyptian sun all morning and part of the afternoon, and it had a very interesting smell.

It carried Englishmen, Scots, Welshmen, Palestinians, Indians, New Zealanders, South Africans, Australians, Americans, French, Senussi, Bantus, Senegalese; it carried Egyptian civilians, Arab civilians, Palestinian civilians; it carried generals, colonels, lieutenants, sergeants and privates—and it carried bugs. The generals and lieutenants it carried first class. The sergeants it carried second class. The privates it carried third class. The bugs it carried all classes.

It didn't travel fast. A good, strong man in the prime of life, who did not smoke too much, could have jumped out and trotted beside it without too much trouble from Cairo to Lydda. It stopped as often as a woman in a bargain basement. It stopped for coal, it stopped for water, it stopped every time a barge appeared somewhere on one of the hundreds of canals we crossed, it stopped every time the tracks ran near two palm trees growing within 50 yards of each other, for that constitutes a settlement in this part of the world.

When it stopped, hundreds of Egyptians of all ages would spring up, selling pale round watermelons, dirty bunches of grapes, hard-boiled eggs, tomatoes and warm lemon soda right out of the Nile. The merchandising was carried on in hurried shrill yells, like a girls' dormitory after lights out, and your salesman was likely to disappear suddenly in mid-purchase as the local policeman came into view, snapping a long bullwhip over slow calves and buttocks.

The third-class cars were built by firm believers in the Spartan life for the common man. They spurned straw, spurned springs, spurned leather. Everything was made out of good solid wood, at stern right angles with more good solid wood. Every seat was taken and there were packs, rifles, musette bags and piles of canned apricots all over the aisles.

Native women squatted alongside the tracks doing their washing in canal water that had been there since St. Paul; brown boys splashed and waved at us; water buffaloes, blinded by straw hats tied over their eyes, went round and round endlessly, drawing water up to the field.

In my end of the car there was a general confusion of British Tank Corps men, returning to their units from the hospital in Cairo, and six Indians who made themselves very much at home, setting up camp in all available space and preparing and eating their native dishes from 3 P.M. until bedtime. Across the aisle were two very tanned South Africans in shorts, who looked disapprovingly on the whole thing and conversed coldly in Afrikaans as we chugged past Suez.

By nightfall, despite the immense quantities of watermelon and lemon soda that had been consumed, there was an air of deep hunger hanging over the car, and when the word was passed around that at the next station there was a NAAFI (British Post Exchange) where we would be fed, there was a determined rush to get out Dixies and tin cups. The British soldier would no more think of going any place without his Dixie and tin cup than he would think of appearing without pants in Piccadilly Circus.

I had neither mess tin nor cup and was mournfully admiring British foresight when a little middle-aged Tommy on my right, who had spent the whole afternoon silently and religiously reading a magazine called *Gen*, perusing advertisements and fiction page by page without partiality, quietly offered me a mess tin.

There was a great combing of hair in the tradition that the Briton dresses for dinner no matter where the meal finds him, and thousands of us started leaping off the train before it had fully stopped. We lined up and were served sandwiches, cakes and good hot strong tea by Egyptians in elegant white cotton gloves.

"There's beer at the other end of the station," reported a British sailor. "Ruppert's. Half a crown a can." There was no movement toward the other end of the station.

On the train was a party of sailors who had just come back from Sicily and were feeling good about it. They had manned the landing barges in the invasion and said it hadn't been bad. "We only had two boat rides," they said. "Boat rides" meant bringing in troops under fire. "It was just like the movies," one of them said. "They kept firing at us and the water kept shooting up all around, but they never hit us."

One of them had been at the Brooklyn Navy Yard for six months during the war while the ship he was on was being repaired. "Oh, it's a lovely city, Brooklyn," he sighed. "And I had a lovely girl in Jamaica. It took me an hour in the subway each way, but it was worth it. A lovely city, but I couldn't live there. The pace is too fast for me. I'd be worn out in a year."

While everybody settled down for the night, I foolishly sat on the open platform, smoking and watching the desert roll by in the starlight. When I went in to go to sleep, I discovered that the Indians had spread a little more, and there was no place to sit, stand or lie inside. Everyone else seemed to be asleep and the car was full of snores and the rich smell of many soldiers who had traveled far in a hot climate with no water available. Only the two South Africans remained awake, staring coldly out through the closed windows at the desert.

I went into the next car. Luckily one of the sailors had rolled off the bench on a turn and remained where he was on the floor, too lazy to move. So I curled myself among the arms, legs, snores and sleepy cries of love and battle in the crowded car and tried to sleep.

When I awoke at 4 A.M. we were in Palestine. As I sat there watching the first orange streaks over the little dark tree-crested hills, the two South Africans came out. We began to talk. They had just come from near Tripoli after 2½ years in the desert, fighting most of the time. This was their first leave, 21 days, and they had flown down to Cairo and were on their way to Tel Aviv.

One of them had suggested getting a truck ride up to Tel Aviv, but the other had said: "No. We are on a holiday. Let's spend some money and be comfortable. Let's take the train." They chuckled sourly as they told me.

"Third class," one of them said. "Why, in South Africa we wouldn't send cows to market in these trains. How about in America?"

I told him that I guessed we wouldn't send cows to market in America in these trains, either.

"Third class," the other said. "Why, before the war, any place I went I would only stay in the best hotel in town."

"And in Cairo," the first one said, "any restaurant with a tablecloth is out of bounds to other ranks. I've had it. I've had this war. I volunteered and I fought for 2½ years and we were among the first to get into Tripoli. I've heard a lot of bullets go by. I've been dive-bombed and I've gone without water and I was perfectly satisfied. But this train ride finishes me. I've had this war, and they can have it back any time they want."

And he went inside to think about the pretty girls on the beach at Tel Aviv.

I sat on the platform and watched the morning sun break over the hills and light the orange groves and vineyards.

A little later the train stopped and we got off to take the bus to Tel Aviv. On the bus I met a lieutenant, a friend of mine, who had also come down by train. He looked very tired.

"What's the matter?" I asked

"That damned first class," he said. "No room to lie down. You sit up all night. Next time I take this blasted ride, I'm taking my bars off and traveling third."

Behind me I heard a wild, snorting sound. It was the South Africans, laughing.

B-29 RAID ON JAPAN

By Sgt. LOU STOUMEN

A FORWARD AIR BASE IN CHINA [By Radio]—For three weeks I had sweated out a ride on one of the B-29 Superfortresses that were going to bomb Japan. Luck finally came my way just two hours before take-off. I was given the chance to flip a coin with a British civilian correspondent for the last seat. "Tails," I called, as he tossed an Indian coin in the air. Tails it was. He tossed the coin again. Tails a second time. I grabbed a parachute and rushed to the field.

Brig. Gen. Kenneth B. Wolfe, the homely, smiling commanding general of the XX Bomber Command, was sitting in a jeep in front of Operations and looking unusually glum. He had just received orders from Washington not to fly with the mission he had planned for so long. Brig. Gen. La Verne G. Saunders, wing commander of the XX, who has a lot of South Pacific B-17 combat flying time under his belt, was going to fly this mission to represent the higher brass.

Soon I was drawing my equipment. I replaced my parachute with another, because mine had no jungle kit attached. I also drew a helmet with earphones and an oxygen mask, a rubber Mae West life jacket, a plastic-boxed survival kit (fishhooks, dextrose tablets, first-aid materials and other stuff), a pointie-talkie book of Chinese and English phrases in parallel columns, a heavy steel-filled flak suit and certain confidential material.

They told me that, except in an emergency, there was no need to take oxygen; one of the secrets of the B-29 is its sealed pressure cabin, which makes possible normal breathing and movement without oxygen at any altitude. I was also told the target: Yawata, the juiciest industrial center in all Japan, home of the Imperial Iron and Steel Works.

"Crew inspection! Let's go!" Capt. R. A. Harte of Lafayette, Ind., plane commander and pilot of our B-29, was speaking. The enlisted crewmen lined up in front of the silver Superfortress and alongside the big black letters K-26 on her nose. Each man showed his dogtags to Capt. Harte; each said yes, he carried an extra pair of socks. Then the captain, unsmiling, made a brief speech.

"We have," he said, "a pretty fair ship and a pretty good chance of coming back without a scratch. We are going to take as much cover as possible from the clouds. We won't take cover at the expense of hitting the target. If any plane pokes her nose near us, you know what to do. We take off in about 10 minutes. Man your stations!"

The B-29 needs a longer runway for take-off than any other plane. I stood on my knees during the take-off and looked out of a side blister as the ship, the world's heaviest aircraft, pounded and blasted her way down the runway. The strip unfolded like a never-ending drive belt of a factory motor, going by in slow motion until it semed we had been roaring along for a full 10 minutes and were still not airborne. Then there was the green end of the runway, and we were skimming a few feet above trees and rice paddies.

During the take-off I also watched Sgt. D. L. Johnson of Rio, Ill., the right gunner; Sgt. R. G. Hurlburt of Gaines, Pa., the left gunner; S/Sgt. A (for Algernon) Matulis, the chief gunner, and 2d Lt. Tash of New York, N. Y., the bombardier. They held on tight. When we were airborne, their faces cracked in smiles and their bodies eased. "She's a good ship," said Johnson, as he wiped a wet hand across his face. "But some good guys get killed in take-offs."

That was the first of several sweating outs. A few miles out and a few hundred feet up, someone noticed the No. 2 engine smoking and reported it over the interphone to Capt. Harte. "Probably the fuel mixture's too rich," said Lt. Tash. And that's what it turned out to be; the smoking soon stopped. But the men sweated it out anyway. They were afraid the ship might have to turn back. As anxious as they were to return home safely, the dangers of the mission evidently meant much less to them than the danger of missing out on bombing Japan.

One ship did have to turn back, we learned later. The men returned only four hours after take-off, both GIs and officers with tears in their eyes, some of them openly crying and all of them cursing. The pilot kept repeating, over and over: "God damn the engines! God damn the engines! God damn the engines!"

After getting the plane commander's okay over the interphone, I followed Lt. Tash forward on hands and knees through the long padded tunnel over the bomb bay. Lt. Tash took his position in the greenhouse nose, and I kneeled over the hatch cover behind the pilot and next to the engineer, 2d Lt. G. I. Appognani of New York, N. Y. The engineer sits before a four-foot panel of dials, flashing lights, switches and control levers. He handles the main throttles for the four engines, controls the fuel supply and mixture, regulates the ship's electrical system and operates the pressure cabin's mechanism.

There was still light in the sky as we crossed the border of Free China into Occupied China, flying higher now, and began our next sweating out—waiting for interception by enemy fighters. There was a large force of B-29s on the mission, but we saw only an occasional plane ahead of us through the clouds or above and to the left of us. A B-29 needs elbow room to fly, to shoot and to bomb. This was not a formation flight.

Still no Jap fighters. It was dark now, and we were approaching the coast of China. Each man was wearing a Mae West over his parachute. The plane groaned on at terrific speed. There was practically no vibration inside and very little noise. In the cabin, the ride was as comfortable as a Pullman—a design for the airliners of the future. But the Jap fighters—where were they?

"We are four and a half hours from Japan," said 2d Lt. E. K. Johnson of Portland, Oreg., over the interphone. Then came the voice of Matulis: "No. 3 engine throwing a lot of sparks." The engineer, Lt. Appognani, looked out his window and confirmed this. No. 3 engine kept throwing sparks most of the way out and back. That was something else to sweat out.

The radio operator, Sgt. E. A. Gisburne of Norway, Maine, broke open a carton of rations and handed a candy bar to each man in the forward compartment. We were one short, and the engineer shared his bar with me. Candy never tasted so good. We downed it with long swigs of water from canteens. The engineer and the navigator also took benzedrine tablets, the same drug I remembered using back in school to keep awake for my final exams. By this time I was comfortably stretched out on the hatch cover in back of the pilot's, using my parachute and jungle kit as a bed. We were flying over the Yellow Sea toward Japan, but the sea was not visible; the weather was too dark and too cloudy.

At last a voice came over the interphone: "We are approaching the target." Everyone began to struggle into his heavy flak suit, putting it on over the parachute, strapping it securely at the sides and pulling the bottom flap down over the thighs like a baseball catcher's chest protector. Only Capt. Harte and the co-pilot, Lt. Haddow, busy at the controls, didn't put on their flak suits.

We were over Japan now. Through breaks in the clouds I could see the ground below. The Japanese blackout was perfect. Then dead ahead, a faint white globe—Jap searchlights over Yawata, the target city.

The sharp voice of Matulis, the chief gunner, came over the interphone: "Tracers. They are coming right past the ship." There was a pause, then someone said: "Tracers, hell. It's only No. 3 engine throwing sparks again." He was right. Over the interphone came a chorus of wry laughs.

The searchlights were brighter now, but their dangerous pointing fingers were diffused through the undercast of clouds. The tail gunner, S/Sgt. F. G. Hodgen, said our tail was caught several times by lights. Apparently we were not seen through the clouds, and the lights moved on. Still no Jap fighters.

The target was just ahead. There was no fiery glow through the clouds to show it had already been hit. We had been the fourth plane to take off from the field and were evidently one of the first over the target.

Flak! The gunners said the sky was full of exploding ack-ack shells, some close, most of them beneath us. Intelligence reports confirmed this later, calling the ack-ack "moderate to intense." But I saw no flak.

Later we learned that searchlights caught one of the last planes over the target, the one on which Bill Shenkel, *Newsweek's* correspondent, was a passenger, and held it in a firm bracket of light until gunners shot it down with all four motors streaming fire.

Our bomb-bay doors were swinging open now, without noise and without making the rest of the ship vibrate. The bombs dropped, one by one, one by one. . . . Then, over the interphone: "Bombs away!" The doors closed.

The K-26 seemed to sprout an extra set of engines and props. At a terrifically increased speed, she made a sharp left turn and headed back toward the Yellow Sea. Over the interphone, tail gunner Hodgen yelled: "I can't see very much through the clouds, but there's a big glow over the target."

The clouds were still below us. B-29s that came in later could see, from 50 miles away, columns of smoke and fire rising 5,000 feet into the air. Yawata, the Pittsburgh of Japan, had been hit hard. This was no token raid but, as Brig. Gen. Wolfe put it, "the beginning of the organized destruction of the Japanese industrial empire."

We were still tense after the bomb run. The Jap fighters had not come up to meet us yet, and the sweating out continued. We left Japan without interception and flew out over the Yellow Sea.

An hour out and radio operator Gisburne broke into the ration box. For each man there was a large can of grapefruit juice, which we opened with jungle knives, and chicken sandwiches, not too expertly made. The bread was too thick. Good, though. We chewed gum and smoked.

Over the China coast—Occupied China—not a single fighter came up. 2d Lt. E. M. Greenberg of Brooklyn, N. Y., combat observer, had by this time crawled forward to his station amidships and was helping the engineer make fuel-tank adjustments. "You know," said Lt. Greenberg, "the Fourteenth Air Force must have done a hell of a good job with their B-24s over the Jap fighter fields in China." Being a last-minute passenger, I had missed the briefing, so he explained: "The Fourteenth went out yesterday and bombed the Jap fighter strips we're flying over now."

But still, the raids could not have knocked out every Jap plane in the area, and even if they had, that wouldn't explain why there were no fighters over Japan. Either we really caught them flat-footed or they were plenty scared of B-29 firepower. Probably both.

Time marched on like a crippled snail. We had been flying almost half a day. With the flak suits off again, we were more comfortable. The No. 3 engine was behaving well enough. My parachute-bed was soft. I slept.

Dawn over Free China: a wild, gray sky of tumultuous clouds, empty of aircraft. I crawled back through the tunnel and batted the breeze with the gunners for a while. Then I returned to the forward compartment. Capt. Harte and Lt. Haddow looked plenty different from the eager beavers who had coaxed the K-26 off the ground so many hours ago. Now their bloodshot eyes hung heavily over pouches that looked like squashed prunes. You'd have thought that someone had been beating them about the head with a rubber hose, judging by their appearance toward the end of this longest bombing mission in history.

"Fighters!" exclaimed Lt. Tash. He put his binoculars on them. They were ours—fast, high-altitude American fighters flying top cover over the B-29 fields. At last, at the dead center of our course, the home field came into sight. It looked miles long, even from our altitude. Loud flopping, banging noises came from the No. 3 engine. "Engineer to pilot," said a voice over the interphone, "don't count on No. 3 engine for landing." "Maybe," said Sgt. Gisburne, "we got hit by ack-ack after all. It sounds like No. 3 was hit." There was a burst of sparks from No. 3's exhaust, and the engineer said he was afraid the engine would catch fire.

We made a long, sharp bank and approached for the landing. No. 3 continued to bang and throw sparks, but it didn't get any worse. We came in fast, about 20 feet above the end of the runway. Gently Capt. Harte set her down, like a mother placing a child in a crib. We rolled a great distance, about the speed of a fast car on a U. S. highway. Then slower, without stopping, we turned and taxied to a parking strip. The crew piled out through the bottom hatches, limp and happy. Ground crewmen and intelligence officers were there to greet them.

While the handshaking and congratulations were still going on, M/Sgt. Herb Coggins of Nashville, Tenn., chief of the K-26's ground crew, was already walking around the ship with Lt. Appognani, the engineer, looking for flak holes.

Later, in the interrogation room, A-2 officers gave each man some egg sandwiches, coffee and suitable refreshments. Then the questioning began. When the intelligence reports were finally tallied up, it turned out that four B-29s had been lost—one shot down over the target, one unreported and two lost in accidents. The entire crew of one of these planes, which made a forced landing just this side of Occupied China after completing the bombing mission, came back two days later. The pilot was wounded in the eye when Japs strafed and bombed his grounded plane.

Back in the barracks, still sweating out their unreported buddies, the weary flight crews turned to their sacks. From beneath the mosquito-net cover on a bed came a last crack: "Somebody tell me a spooky story. I love to hear a spooky story before I go to sleep."

A SUPERFORTRESS BASE, WESTERN CHINA—Half a million Chinese laborers, working from dawn till dusk and getting about 10 cents and a bowl of rice a day, built the vast system of forward airfields in China that made possible the first B-29 raid on the industrial heart of Japan.

Lt. Col. Waldo L. Kenerson of the U. S. Army Engineers, a native of Marblehead, Mass., supervised the construction of the air-base system, together with officials of the Chinese Ministry of Communications. The bases form a great Chinese fan covering many square miles of former riceland. Several of the fields are oversized and extra hard, so they can take the B-29s. Others are fighter fields, housing new high-altitude pursuit planes. Still others are outer-ring emergency fields.

Army engineers here compared the job with the

building of the Burma Road and the Great Wall of China. But they said this project was so vast and so quickly accomplished that it has no parallel in history. Construction of the airbase system cost 6 billion inflated Chinese dollars (about 150 million dollars in U. S. currency).

On Apr. 24, 1944, just 90 days after the first dike was broken to drain the water from the rice paddies, the first B-29 landed on one of the airfields. It was piloted by Brig. Gen. Kenneth B. Wolfe, commanding general of the XX Bomber Command, and co-piloted by Brig. Gen. La Verne B. Saunders, a wing commander of the XX.

Exactly 26 American officers and enlisted men, plus a large corps of Chinese engineers and government officials, supervised the half-million Chinese coolies. Individual U. S. GIs, such as T/Sgt. Aaron Jones of Shelton, Conn., Sgt. Henry B. Dresen of Seattle, Wash., and T-5 B. W. Harwood of Laredo, Tex., had as many as 23,000 men working under them at one time.

Behind the building of the superbases was the epic building and proving of the B-29 Superfortress. Behind it was much sweat and long-range global planning by the General Staff in Washington—for the XX Bomber Command is accountable not to the local China-Burma-India command but directly to Gen. H. H. Arnold, CG of the AAF, and to the Joint Chiefs of Staff.

Target dates for completion of the bases were set by President Roosevelt and Generalissimo Chiang Kai-shek at the Cairo Conference in 1943. These dates were met and in some cases bettered.

Lt. Col. Kenerson, his small American staff and Chinese engineers began paper work in January 1944. Working 18 hours a day, they finished this part of the project in 20 days.

While the plans were still on the drawing boards, the preliminary draining and clearing of the land was already in progress, and the governor of "Air Base Province," under orders from Chungking, was already conscripting Chinese farmers for the heavy labor ahead. About 360,000 laborers were drafted.

The other 140,000 were employed as workers by private Chinese construction firms which had contracted to do various specific jobs, and as rice carriers, pay clerks, Red Cross workers and administrators servicing the armies of laborers.

Only in patient, hard-working China, with its manpower reservoir of 400 millions, could this job have been done in such jig time. "I doubt very much," said Lt. Col. Kenerson, "if we could require a job of similar magnitude in the States to be completed within the time allowed, even with the skilled labor and mechanical equipment available."

The air-base labor draft hit the Chinese farmers hard. Already millions of China's fittest young men were in the Army, and many were dead. Old men, young boys, heads of families, women and young girls had to leave their homes and their growing crops in the hands of neighbors while they went to do unaccustomed manual labor on the airfields. These people were farmers, and they had to be taught the construction trade.

Families were broken up, crops were lost, the work was harder than any they had done before, and incomes dropped almost to the vanishing point in China's spiraling inflation. But the farmers of Air Base Province responded to the need with patience and good humor.

They moved out to the field sites in armies, as many as 110,000 on a single field. They smiled smiles of curiosity and genuine good-fellowship at the few Americans they met there, and exchanged thumbs-up signs and the words *"Ding Hao!* (Everything's okay!)" with them. And, best of all, the Chinese understood why they were working so hard—working all the time they were not eating or sleeping. Chinese propaganda units from Chungking explained to them why the Americans had come to China.

Specifications for the China air-base system were exceptionally rigid, for these fields were designed for the world's heaviest military planes. Slight dips and ridges that were okay on a B-24 or a B-17 field could not be tolerated here. And the high landing speed and long take-off run of the B-29 meant that the fields had to be longer than any forward combat fields ever built, so long that a man at one end could scarcely distinguish a man at the other.

The rice paddies were drained. The soft century-old mud, sometimes six to nine feet deep, was carried away in the picturesque shoulder-borne tandem baskets so common throughout Asia. Tons of stones, worn round by the water, were carried from river beds to the strips in the same useful baskets. Larger boulders were patiently crushed with small sledges, the fragments were crushed again into gravel, the gravel was carried in the baskets to the strips. Acres of dirt were dug up with iron Chinese tools, a cross between a pick and a shovel. The dirt was carried to the strips in the baskets by never-ending queues of workers—men, women and children doing the job entirely by hand.

And then 10-ton rollers, some carved by hand from sandstone and others made of iron, were pulled on ropes by many hundreds of workers the wearying length and breadth of the strips. No bulldozers or other mechanical equipment had been flown across the Hump to do the job, although there were a very few trucks with very little gas on hand.

When the strips had been rolled, black tung oil—a tarlike substance that comes from a Chinese tree—was spread out to bind the dirt and gravel and help keep down the dust.

More than 80 Chinese workers lost their lives in construction accidents. The most terrible of these deaths were caused by the 10-ton rollers, which could not be stopped quickly. If an unlucky worker stumbled and fell in the path of one of these rollers, he was squashed into a bloody pancake—and the roller went on, for the work could not stop. Some 25 men died this way.

As barracks, built for the Americans at the expense of the Chinese government, went up, and as more U. S. administrative, ground and maintenance

men flew in over the Hump to prepare for the coming operation, a new level of Chinese-American friendship was established. The Army and the U. S. Office of War Information brought American movies with Chinese titles to the laborers and townspeople. As many as 30,000 Chinese, few of whom had ever seen a movie before, craned their necks at one time on one flight strip to see an American film.

The Chinese reciprocated. Those who could afford to do so invited Americans to their homes, making no distinction between officers and GIs.

And when the B-29s roared back from Yawata, word of where they had been and what they had done spread quickly. Shouts of *"Ding Hao!"* were almost as loud as the motors of the B-29s, and Chinese grins of welcome to the flyers were almost as broad as the landing strips the Chinese had built with their own sweat and blood.

NOMENCLATURE OF WHISTLE, M1

By Pvt. RAYMOND ZAUBER

(Description of the simple air-cooled whistle, as done in GI handbook terms)

THE U. S. whistle, model M1, is a self-repeating, shoulder-strap model. It is lung-operated, air-cooled, reverberating-blast type. The whistle weighs an ounce and a half, and the chain another half ounce.

The whistle is divided into two parts—the whistle-cylinder blowing assembly, and the whistle-retaining chain assembly. At the blowing aperture there are two raised sections, one on each side, called the upper-teeth guard lug and the lower-teeth guard lug, respectively. The opening from the blowing end into the cylinder is known as the compressing-blow channel. The remainder of the whistle apparatus is known as the chamber-cylinder operating assembly. This consists of the opening-sound emission slot, the cylinder-butt lock onto which the whistle-retaining chain assembly is attached, and the cylinder-reverberating operating cork.

The whistle-retaining chain consists of the shoulder-strap button-hook catch which secures the whistle for carrying and operation. The shoulder-strap button-hook catch is locked by the upper-chain re-

taining ring. The chain is also fastened to the lower-chain retaining ring which is looped through the cylinder-butt lock of the whistle cylinder-blowing assembly.

The whistle is carried in the upper left pocket of the blouse or jacket. To use, unbutton or unsnap pocket with fingers of the right hand, remove whistle by raising directly up on retaining chain. When the whistle swings free of the pocket grasp the sides of the whistle-blowing assembly with the thumb and forefinger of the left hand and with the upper-teeth lug facing up and to the rear. Then place between the center of lips and clamp lips firmly so that no air can escape.

The sound is produced by taking a deep breath through the nostrils and exhaling it through the mouth into the air-compressing blow channel. After the blast return the whistle to the pocket by the reverse of the steps used for removal.

Disassembling of all parts, other than the shoulder-strap button-hook catch and the lower-chain retaining ring, is for ordnance only.

RANGERS COME HOME

By Sgt. MACK MORRISS

CAMP BUTNER, N. C.—Frankie was reclining on his bunk.

Another Ranger drifted over rather aimlessly, observed that liquor and women are fine American institutions and then corked Frankie smartly on the arm. The smack of fist against shoulder was sharp in the still barracks.

Frankie lay there and swore long enough to give the guy a head start. Then he casually rolled off his sack, picked up a GI shoe and hurled it the length of the room at the retreating Ranger. The shoe hit a fire extinguisher and dented it.

Frankie settled back on the bunk, grunted, smacked lazily at a fly and went to sleep. His target went down the stairs without looking back. The other Rangers in the squad room, resting or writing, didn't look up. The shoe lay where it fell and the fire extinguisher ceased reverberating.

The Rangers, those few who were left of the old 1st and 3d and 4th Battalions, were back in the States.

Most of them had been overseas two years and more, and all of them saw action enough to add up to eight solid months of continuous fighting. They went home on furlough and talked about the war, then reported in to Camp Butner and talked about it some more. Pretty soon they were weary of hacking their gums. So they answered the questions they were asked in public, and then in the barracks they swore rippling oaths at each other and wrestled and spoke gently to the dice and made themselves at home.

The Rangers are an independent bunch, and it was that yearning for freedom of action that appealed to most of the men who volunteered in June, 1942 in North Ireland. The Rangers offered them a rugged future, but at least a man could call his soul his own. "I joined this outfit," said T-5 Clyde Thompson of Ashland, Ky., "because they sent out a letter saying they wanted men to work in little groups that would hit and run. Well, we hit more'n we run, but I'm satisfied they kept most of their promises, and we were on our own most of the time."

The Rangers spearheaded every Allied invasion in the Mediterranean. Being shock troops got in their blood. One of them, who will remain anonymous here so that his rough-riding outfit won't ride him for it, let himself go: "There was just one thing about that kind of fighting—by damn, it gave you a thrill. We never had to ask no questions about who was out front; we just started shooting. Hell, nobody wants to get killed and I was plenty scared sometimes—but it gave you a thrill, the way we fought."

Perhaps it was because they found a certain fascination in combat that the Rangers had remarkably few cases of psychoneurosis, although, as an Irish first sergeant put it: "Sometimes, when you were under it, that Jerry artillery made you want to cry."

The original outfit, the 1st Ranger Battalion, was activated in North Ireland on June 19, 1942, with 600 men selected from more than 2,000 soldiers who had volunteered. Their training was in Scotland, and they had more casualties there than they had on their first African landing. The British Commandos were their instructors.

"Those bastards tried to kill us, or we thought they did," said Thompson. "We maneuvered with live ammunition. There were accidents, too, that sort of went with it. They had us out in a place one time that still wasn't entirely cleared of old land mines they'd put there when invasion was expected. Two of our boys jumped a barbed-wire fence and landed right on top of a mine. We were picking them up two days later. Another guy fell off a cliff and broke practically every bone in his body."

Then, on Aug. 18, came Dieppe. While it was predominantly a Canadian show, a small party of Rangers were in on the deal. A few of them got into the fight. Others were intercepted by German E-boats and never got ashore.

But less than three months later the long series of combat operations began in which the Rangers as a whole spearheaded drive after drive across Africa through Sicily to Italy. On Nov. 8, 1942, the Rangers landed at Arzew, 30 miles east of Oran. Their mission was to seize four coastal guns overlooking the town and two others guarding the approaches to the harbor.

The attack began at 0130 when four companies landed three miles above the town and came in from the rear to take the French defenders by surprise. Two other companies came through the jetties, where they were met by machine-gun fire, but their element of surprise was so great that a small fort and the two remaining coastal guns were taken with a minimum of casualties.

Three hours after the initial landing, the CO—Col. William O. Darby of Fort Smith, Ark.—fired success flares and the central task force of the African invasion came ashore.

"We went into a garrison and got them Frenchmen out of bed," grinned one Ranger reflectively. D-plus-two saw a Ranger company lend a hand to the 1st Division at St. Cloud; after eight hours the break-through came, paving the way to Oran.

The Rangers, no longer needed, resumed combat training for three months. Then, on Feb. 7, 1943, they were suddenly ordered into transport planes and flown to the Tunisian front, mission unknown. They were landed at a front-line airport and three days later moved into Gafsa, which already had changed hands several times.

Sgt. Sherman Legg of Handley, W. Va., was on the point approximately 1,000 yards ahead of the Ranger advance party. He was riding a motorcycle and was armed with a tommy gun.

"It was my job to find out who was out there and where they were. It could have been Germans in front of us and it could have been Frenchies. I didn't know what to expect. Anyway, I was moving along and I saw this figure, dark like, over in the ditch, so I jumped over on him and threw my tommy gun into his back. He let out a yell and turned around. You know the first thing he said when he saw I was an American? He said: 'Cigarette, comrade?' So I knew it was all right. I knew he was a Frenchman."

Two days after entering Gafsa, the Rangers pulled what will always be their favorite action. Back in the States now they talk about it fondly, the way advertising men might discuss a beautiful sales-promotion job. This was the Sened Station raid or the "AEF raid"—so-called because those three companies were in on it. It was the kind of thing they were most schooled in.

Their mission was to destroy a fortified position. They entrucked at night and rode 18 miles to a French outpost and then marched cross country for 12 more miles. By dawn they were holed up in the saddle of a mountain overlooking an enemy position five miles northwest of Sened. All day, covered by shelter halves and natural camouflage, they watched proceedings at the outpost four miles away.

When darkness came, they moved forward. Around midnight, 600 yards away from their objective, they went into a skirmish line on a battalion front. When they were 200 yards away, the outposted enemy, sensing that something was out in front of them, opened fire. The Rangers continued forward without firing a shot. Then, within 50 yards of their objective, they assaulted. For 20 minutes they worked with bayonet and tommy gun and rifle and grenade, and then it was over. By dawn they were back at the French outpost, their starting point.

Almost every Ranger who was there has a favorite tale about the 20 minutes at Sened:

"This was the kind of stuff we loved to do—coming in under their fire which sometimes wasn't a foot and a half over our heads but knowing damn well those Ities didn't know where we were. We could watch their gun flashes when we got close enough." . . . "The Ities called us 'Black Death' after that, on account of our work was at night." . . . "I remember watching a motor pool, and this Itie ran out and tried to get away on a motorcycle. We were laying down a mortar concentration on the motor pool and this guy got the cycle started all right and was about to get out, and just then a 60-mm hit right on top of him and he just disappeared." . . . "There was some pretty rough infighting there."

When the Germans attacked at Kasserine Pass, threatening Gafsa from the east, U. S. forces with-

"When I think of all the time I spent in basic training creeping and crawling it makes me sick."

drew to Feriana and from there to Dernia Pass, which was threatened by a German push aimed at Tebessa, the main Allied base. For three weeks the Rangers sat at Dernia waiting for the big drive that never came.

"Our work," said one Ranger, "was mostly knocking off stray German vehicles that either blundered into the Pass by mistake or were nosing around to find out if we were still there. There wasn't any real rough stuff. Funny thing about how those people would roam around. We hit a car one day and captured an Italian officer. He was a pilot, and said he was just out sightseeing."

After Dernia the outfit drew back for a rest and then went back into action by leading the American drive back through Feriana and into Gafsa again. There wasn't too much trouble that time either, but then came El Guettar. There they had another job they liked. Beyond El Guettar was a pass leading to Sfax that the Germans and Italians had defended. It was the Rangers' mission to clean up the defended ridges, which commanded a dominating position over the surrounding terrain.

Cpl. Robert M. Bevan of Estherville, Iowa, a sniper throughout the African campaigns, scored his longest accurate shooting there when he silenced a machine-gun nest at 1,350 yards.

"We came up on them by a circular route of about 10 miles and hit them from behind and above, working our way down to where we could use a bayonet. This set-up was Italian EM with German officers. There was some bayonet fighting.

"As a sniper I picked targets that were out of range for the riflemen, so I started working on this machine-gun nest. I was using our sniper rifle—a plain old '03 with telescopic sights. I ranged in with tracers and then put two shots right into the position. The gun was quiet for a couple of minutes, and then a crazy thing happened. Somebody threw a dirty towel over the gun, and then the crew came out and sat down."

After El Guettar the Rangers pulled back to Nemours, on the coast of Algeria. The 1st Battalion was split into three groups to cadre a reorganized 1st Battalion and the new 3d and 4th Battalions, which were formed there.

Then, on July 9, 1943, the 1st and 4th landed at Gela and the 3d at Licata in Sicily. From then on, the war got progressively tougher for the Rangers.

The Gela landings were made at night, and searchlights picked up the incoming landing craft when they were still a mile out. There were pillboxes and land mines ashore, but by 1000 the town was in Ranger hands. At 1100 the fun began.

It was then that "we thought we'd have to grab the lifeboats." With only the two battalions of Rangers in Gela, Italian tanks came barreling into town, blasting. "We fought them from the rooftops by dropping TNT and sticky bombs on them. We had a 37-mm that shuttled to its targets, going from one corner to another, taking potshots at them as they came in from different directions. Our bazookas were firing point-blank."

1st Sgt. David (Soupy) Campbell of Medford, Mass., and 1st Sgt. Vincent Egan of Staten Island, N. Y., both had some hard fighting and some laughs to remember. "We were using bazookas then, and I'll never forget the trouble one guy had with one," grinned Soupy. "He was firing from inside a house, and this tank was right up on him; so he hauled down on the thing point-blank—and missed. I don't see how he did. And the backfire off the thing! The guy did more damage to the wall behind him than he did to the tank in front.

"I remember another thing there. We had this young kid with us who hadn't been in the outfit so long, and he was really dying to get into a fight. So he was coming along a wall and when he turned a corner he ran smack into a Jerry. The kid was so shocked he didn't know what to do. So the Jerry shot him, right through the chest. One of our guys across the street got the Jerry, but it was too late to help the kid."

"We finally got rid of the Ities," said Egan, "but the next day came worse trouble—or it might have been. We looked out and saw 18 big Tigers (PzKW VIs) coming in. Between fire from our cruisers offshore and fire from a chemical outfit's new 4.2 mortars, 12 of the Jerry tanks were knocked out and the others quit. It was the first time those 4.2 mortars were in action, and they did damn well."

It was on that first day at Gela that Sherman Legg had his troubles, too. He had parked his motorcycle in an alleyway and was leaning against the opposite wall, just waiting for developments. Developments arrived in the form of a shell that blew his motor upside down and blew Legg back through the alley, through an open door and into a building. He was knocked out. After a while he came to, went back to his motor and found it would still run.

"I got on the thing, and this guy across the street stuck his head out. I thought he looked sort of funny. 'Hey, Legg,' he yelled, 'ain't you hurt?' I asked him what did he think. He said he didn't think I was hurt, he thought I was dead. He'd seen me standing there, and then the shell hit and he didn't see me any more."

Earlier that same morning Legg accomplished in actual fact what has been done very rarely anywhere except in the movies. He shot down a Messerschmitt-110 with a BAR.

"I was on the beach right near a wall when this bastard came over, strafing. He scared me silly. I ducked behind the wall, and he came back. I let fly at him and missed, but I found out why I missed. So the next time he came in, I put the gun on the wall and held it there and he flew right into my fire. I could see the bullets rake him. He went along a little farther, and then I saw flames coming out around the gas tanks where I'd hit. He crashed into the sea."

The Rangers spearheaded the way across the Plain of Gela toward Butera, a 4,000-foot citadel "that looked like a castle sitting up there." One Ranger company cleared it.

T/Sgt. Francis P. Padrucco of Miami, Fla., then a buck sergeant acting as platoon sergeant, had 20 men who were part of the outfit that went straight up the long road leading to the citadel itself. It was a brash maneuver, coming flush up the obvious approach, at 2300 hours.

"We got to a bend in the road and a machine gunner opened up on us at a range of about 20 feet. He wounded my lieutenant and the radio operator. But our scout, with a tommy gun, let go with a whole drum of ammo; he got seven.

"The platoon killed about 15 and took 60 or 70 prisoners. We got a bunch of A-T guns by surprise, and some flame-thrower people. The whole thing took about 20 minutes.

"Here again it was German officers and Italian personnel. This time some German, farther back, was giving orders to two Italian officers, a colonel and a lieutenant. The Italians wanted to surrender, and the German told them to keep fighting. We told them to give up or we'd kill them. The German told them if they made a move to surrender, *he'd* kill them.

"Poor devils. They got killed. We chased the Jerry, but he got away."

Paddy, for his work that night after his officer was out of action, got the Silver Star. The Rangers moved by different routes to the northeast side of Sicily. When the campaign ended, they pulled back for training and replacements.

On Sept. 9, they landed in Italy. The landings were above Salerno, and the 4th fanned out in opposite directions toward Salerno to the east and Sorrento to the west. The 1st followed and drove to the high ground overlooking the Plain of Naples. The 3d fought at Chiunzi Pass. The Rangers held

the left hinge of the beachhead against every German attempt to close in and knock U. S. forces back into the sea. For 22 days they had nothing but counterattacks. It was rough work, but the Salerno sector was rough work for everybody.

T-4 Frankie Ziola of South Amboy, N. J.—the man who throws shoes—was one of four cooks in his outfit at Chiunzi Pass who volunteered for duty as litter-bearers. He spent 18 days bringing out the wounded and was awarded the Silver Star when the fight was over.

"They asked for volunteers for that detail, so we volunteered. I got me an Italian as a helper, and the two of us would go up and pull the guys out when they got hit and take them back to Battalion Aid. I didn't know anything about medicine or first aid or anything, but I damn sure learned. Funny thing about those Rangers when they were wounded. Almost every time the first thing they wanted was a cigarette."

Finally, with enemy counterattacks broken, the Rangers spearheaded the way into the Valley of Naples and relieving forces went on into Naples itself. The Rangers pulled back again to train. Their hardest fighting was still ahead.

On Nov. 1, the Fifth Army encountered strong opposition at Venafro, about 40 miles above Naples. On Nov. 3 the Rangers began a 35-day fight that was to open the way to the valley leading to Cassino. That day they crossed the winding Volturno River with the mission of infiltrating six miles behind enemy lines and taking the heights commanding the road to San Pietro.

They marched all night, passing enemy outposts, and at dawn were still undetected. They attacked, seized the enemy positions and held them for two days. Then, with their supplies gone, they came back through the enemy again to Sesto Campano. Then they moved toward Venafro. When they were through, the Rangers had advanced the lines by 12 miles.

T/Sgt. Robert O. Johnson of Shinnston, W. Va., a battalion communications sergeant, was wounded at Venafro when a shell blasted him down as he and his lieutenant were carrying a wounded man to shelter. It was in that sector that communication maintenance became a matter of survival.

"I had 22 men in my section," said Johnson, "and before we were through there, the battalion communications was being handled by only the lieutenant, a maintenance man and myself. The other 19 were knocked out by either mortar or artillery fire. I almost got it good there. I had to go two miles up Venafro Mountain checking telephones, and the whole way I had mortar fire right in my hip pocket."

After Venafro the Rangers were pulled out for a little more than a month and on Jan. 22 they went into Anzio.

"We were 66 days on the beach at Anzio," said Egan. "It was rough. We attacked a red farm on the left flank at Carroceto. Finally there were only four men left, and they took the place."

Sherman Legg, still on his motor, had another close one there: "I was going along without paying much attention where I was, and I came over the brow of this hill and a machine gun let loose on me. I guess the Jerries were excited because I don't see how they missed. Anyway, I threw the motor over on the ground, spun it and started the hell out of there. I was afraid even to duck, because I might duck right into a bullet. I'm glad they were lousy gunners, or I wouldn't be here. I made sure not to take any more wrong roads around there."

Soupy Campbell likes to talk about the Ranger mortar concentrations at Anzio. "There was one time we saw this German come out of his foxhole for a minute, so we gave him concentration No. 3 (we had everything zeroed in). He must have had some ammo in that hole because the next thing we saw of that Jerry he was about 20 feet in the air, turning end over end."

Soupy grinned. "We had things to laugh at even at Anzio. There was that machine gunner on our flank who'd clear his gun every morning just about

dawn. He always did it to start the day off right. 'Shave 'n' a haircut—two bits,' he'd play on that thing."

Then, on Jan. 29, disaster struck. The 1st and 3d Battalions were to attack and take the town of Cisterna, while the 4th was to support their assault. But something went wrong: the Germans had reinforced their positions and when the Rangers struck at dawn, they hit a force that overwhelmed them. Two battalions went into Cisterna; 26 Rangers came out.

Sgt. Milton Lehman, *Stars and Stripes* correspondent, wrote the story as it was reconstructed for him by survivors:

"When the sun came up, the Rangers were surrounded. Between sunrise and 0700 hours when radio silence was broken, the Rangers knew that the battle was lost. Sunrise doomed them and marked the beginning of the hopeless, heroic fight. . . . The sand was running out in the hour glass. The Rangers knew it and the Germans knew it. Slowly and bitterly the last orders were given by the company commanders . . . the tall, bespectacled, thin-faced West Pointer telling his men to go. 'I hate to do this,' the captain said, 'but it's too late now. That direction is south. Take out, and God bless you.'"

The 4th Battalion, also stopped but not decimated, fought on after Cisterna and, with the few survivors of the 1st and 3d, came back to the States as a unit. They have friends among the newer Ranger outfits now in France.

But the Old Rangers are out of action.

"Vot does der 'T' stand for?"—Cpl. Ruge.

PSYCHOLOGICAL WARFARE

By Sgt. BILL DAVIDSON

ENGLAND—The Fortresses were taking off for one of the first big daylight raids over Berlin. Most of them lumbered down the runway for a long take-off and climbed slowly into formation with their heavy bomb loads. But once in a while a Fort would go down the runway swiftly and become airborne sooner than the others. It would climb faster and take a key defensive position in the formation.

Inside, this Fort was different from the others. Instead of bombs, it carried tight, heavy packages, designed to open when they were released through the bomb-bay doors. This was a leaflet plane, one of the newsboys of the Air Forces.

The leaflet planes went in over Berlin with the bombers, released their hundreds of thousands of paper bullets, shot down a respectable number of enemy fighters in the bargain and came back. The special Forts were heavily armed and gave good accounts of themselves in battle, but more than one leaflet pilot must have sighed during the long trip and wished that his plane were carrying a little HE.

From the yelp of pain the German press and radio let out the next day, you would have thought the leaflets were even more damaging than high explosives.

One leaflet entitled "Stalingrad No. 2" told Berliners that 55,000 German troops had been killed and 18,200 imprisoned at Cherkasy on the Russian front. The pamphlet, beautifully illustrated with maps and charts, gave complete data on the lost divisions and the parts of Germany from which they came.

The second leaflet told the Germans that peace would be much more pleasant than bombings and that President Roosevelt guaranteed the natural development of the German people as a member of the European family of nations.

The third pamphlet was the regular edition of *Sternenbanner (Star-Spangled Banner)*, a miniature four-page, four-column newspaper printed in German.

Soon after the bombs were dropped, an official Nazi commentator went on the German radio in a hurried attempt to answer the news stories in the three pamphlets. The Nazi radio program, *Mirror of the Times*, broadcast a play attempting to show that the "Stalingrad No. 2" leaflet was Jewish propaganda and that the divisions had never been lost at all. Another commentator, known as OK—his real name is Dr. Otto Koischwitz and he was formerly a professor at New York City's Hunter College—attacked the second leaflet, the one that urged peace. He said that President Roosevelt promised an honorable peace but that "Roosevelt is known as a man who makes promises and then doesn't keep them." There were a half dozen other broadcasts on the same lines.

In previous raids we had dropped leaflets, but the German air-raid wardens always swept them up before sounding the "all clear," and the Nazis even boasted how few of the leaflets were read. But the day after the Berlin raids, Heinrich Himmler, chief of the Gestapo, issued a decree imposing prison sentences and more serious penalties on anyone caught reading a leaflet.

Seven days later, however, a traveler from Berlin reported in the Swedish newspaper *Dagens Nyheter* that "Germans now read leaflets openly in the Berlin streets."

This was strategic psychological warfare.

Shortly before the leaflets were dropped on Berlin, Allied bombers in Italy were preparing the intensive aerial blitz that was to reduce Cassino to rubble. But first, leaflets were dropped by long-range artillery and planes, telling the people in Cassino about the terrible destruction that lay ahead, explaining why it had to be done and warning everyone to get out. In one sector, German units that had been hemmed in were pelted with safe-conduct passes urging them to surrender. In other sectors, leaflets told the Nazis about the bombings of their home cities and the disastrous defeats of the *Wehrmacht* in Russia.

This was tactical psychological warfare.

Tactical psychological warfare, like tactical bombing, has short-range, immediate objectives. It is used on the battlefronts, and its only purpose is to cause or hasten the surrender of specific units of enemy troops already in a tough spot. When the Russians dropped leaflets urging the surrender of the German Sixth Army, hopelessly encircled before Stalingrad, they gave a perfect example of tactical psychological warfare.

Strategic psychological warfare, like strategic bombing, strikes at German cities far behind the lines and has strictly long-range objectives. A man can't surrender to a leaflet or a radio. But by pounding away at home-front morale and raising doubts in the German mind, psychological warfare may create a sense of defeat that eventually will seep through to the fighting zones. It's like destroying a Messerschmitt plant; it doesn't affect the fighting front immediately, but some day in the future there will be a shortage of fighter replacements when the enemy needs them badly.

Psychological warfare, both tactical and strategic, works more effectively when your side is winning. Leaflets and broadcasts by themselves can't accomplish much. As a member of the joint British-American Psychological Warfare Branch said: "You can't do much against a stone wall with a nail file. But when a stone is loosened by hammer blows, you can chip around it with the nail file and finally pry it out."

Tunisia was the first big triumph for psychological warfare since the first World War; then Gen. Erich von Ludendorff, chief of the German general staff, wrote: "We could not prevent the leaflets from poisoning the hearts of our soldiers." At first the leaflets didn't work at all in the Tunisian campaign, because Field Marshal Erwin Rommel and his Axis troops were on the offensive. Besides, we made several blunders, such as promising the Italians a nice comfortable prison camp in the States; this petrified them, because German psychological warfare had already convinced them that every ship crossing the Atlantic would be sunk.

But then the Allied power was unleashed, and Rommel's troops were hit by everything we had. Right at that moment we threw a verbal punch to the solar plexus of the Italians. We simply told them in leaflets that Tripoli had fallen. They didn't know this. They thought their flank, hundreds of miles away in Libya, was still secure. We knew they'd doubt us, so we mentioned streets, cafes and places that only somebody who had been there would know about. Our leaflets were dropped by plane and fired into the enemy lines by 25-pounders and 155-mm guns. Within three days thousands of Italians had surrendered, and Mussolini announced in Rome: "Whoever believes the enemy's

messages is a criminal, a traitor and a bastard, too."

As the Germans and Italians retreated northward from Sfax, Gen. Sir Harold Alexander called for a five-day leaflet barrage. In the closing stages of the campaign, the Arab population around Tunis, Bizerte and Cape Bon made a fortune by collecting British-American surrender leaflets at night and selling them to the Germans and Italians by day.

The day before Lt. Gen. George S. Patton Jr. sent his Seventh Army into Sicily, he called in his psychological-warfare men and told them he wanted a million leaflets dropped before the offensive began. In record time the general and one of the PWB officers wrote a leaflet entitled "Capitulation With Honor." Then a pilot grabbed the copy and flew it to Tunis. All night the printing plants hummed. The next day planes of the Tactical Air Force dropped a million leaflets from Palermo to Marsala. Thousands of prisoners came in as a result of this leaflet barrage, which softened up the enemy just as surely as an artillery barrage.

But in Italy the situation was different. Although Adm. Sir Andrew Browne Cunningham credited psychological warfare with causing almost unaided the surrender of the Italian fleet, our propaganda was not as successful against the German armies. As their military situation improved, their resistance to psychological warfare stiffened.

Our best efforts in Italy so far have been the leaflets dropped on Rome explaining why we were bombing the city, and a brilliant series of humorous and inspirational posters tacked up by special squads of GIs all over liberated territory. Those posters gave a tremendous lift to the Italian national spirit.

The Psychological Warfare Branch works with all the armed forces. It is a joint British-American undertaking, staffed by British and American officers, enlisted men and civilians, working side by side. Most of the American GIs are former newspapermen or radio-newsmen; others were selected because of their knowledge of foreign languages and countries.

One of the Psychological Warfare Branch's major functions is publishing one of the world's biggest newspaper chains—weekly, pint-sized sheets turned out in German, French, Dutch and Flemish, and dropped by the millions over Germany and the occupied countries. The Germans get bombs with their morning papers; the occupied countries don't.

Straight news is stressed; there is no attempt to propagandize or even to answer German propaganda. "You don't have to do that when you're winning," says the head of the Publications Section. "Straight news, when it's favorable, is the most potent weapon we have. It puts the enemy on the defensive. Soon you find him trying to answer your truths and getting caught up in his own lies."

These little newspapers are doing their job. One of the best indications of that came from the French underground recently, which passed along a fake edition of *L'Amerique en Guerre,* the newspaper put out by PWB for the French. The Germans had imitated the format but had cleverly sandwiched in their own propaganda into the news accounts. When they go to all that trouble, they're stung.

In spite of the importance of the work they are doing, the American leaflet crews gripe because they can't carry a few bombs in their specially equipped Fortresses. The psychological-warfare boys let them gripe for a while. Then they send some agents of the European underground to talk to the crews for a few hours about what is going on in their target areas. This is psychological warfare in reverse. It works.

"That's my sergeant friend from the Searchlight Squad— he's crazy jealous!"—*Sgt. Dave Breger.*

STILWELL: THE GIs' FAVORITE

By Sgt. ED CUNNINGHAM

GEN. JOSEPH W. STILWELL, the U. S. Army's newest four-star general, is as regular and down-to-earth as the scuffed GI shoes he wears when tramping through the Burma jungles.

Known among his men as Vinegar Joe or Uncle Joe, he is no glamor-boy general. He's a tough, rank Old Army man who hates Japs with unwavering intensity. One day during the Hukawng Valley campaign a frightened Jap prisoner tried to shake hands with him. Scorning the outstretched hand, Gen. Stilwell snapped: "Not with you, you dirty bastard!"

In the field, where he prefers to be, Stilwell is no collar-ad for what the well-dressed West Point man will wear this season. His usual uniform is a mud-stained field jacket with no rank insignia, ordinary GI pants and leggings, topped off with either a battered felt Infantry campaign hat or a Chinese Army cap.

What goes for Gen. Stilwell goes for his men. They wear clothes best adapted for jungle fighting, without fear of being eaten out by some very GI superior. Uncle Joe justified such departures from military custom with a typical Stilwell explanation: "We're out to win battles, not dress parades."

More than once Gen. Stilwell has been hailed as "Hey, Mac!" by a private who failed to recognize him without his stars. The general recalls with relish the time he was returning from Brig. Gen. Frank D. Merrill's bivouac four miles off the Ledo Road. A pack-mule company of Merrill's Marauders, moving up, forced Gen. Stilwell's jeep to the side of the narrow jungle trail. The general, inelegantly garbed in a Chinese cap without insignia and with a carbine between his knees, was spotted by a GI, who turned around and shouted back to his companions: "Hey, look! Duck hunters!"

Another Marauder approached Stilwell's jeep, rested his carbine on the fender and asked: "How far is it to the bivouac area?"

"About four miles," Stilwell replied.

"Holy hell!" the GI hollered. "Couldn't they build the damn thing a little closer to the road? What's the use of having a road if we can't use it?"

Stilwell smiled and, turning to his aide, observed with obvious pride: "These guys are really tough."

Despite his 61 years, Gen. Stilwell is the walkingest general in the United States Army. Ever since he arrived in Burma to direct the Chinese troops there, he has made almost daily trips to forward positions. Most of those trips are on foot because the narrow jungle trails stymie even jeeps. Uncle Joe sets the pace on all hikes. He keeps to a steady 105-steps-a-minute stride with a 10-minute break each hour.

On many of his trips to the front, Gen. Stilwell spends the night with U. S. liaison troops who work with the Chinese. He stretches his jungle hammock between two trees and sleeps there with his clothes on, just as his soldiers must do to ward off the clammy moisture of the Burma night. He often joins in the bull sessions of the corporals and privates as they brew a nightcap of GI coffee over a bamboo-kindled fire. If his men have any complaints, they lay them directly before Uncle Joe.

One night up front, a corporal with blunt GI vigor assailed censorship of mail. "Why is it, general," he asked, "that we can't mention we're in Burma when we write letters home? Guys can say they're in India or China but we can't say we're in Burma."

"We'll see what we can do about it," the general promised.

The next day he radioed the chief censor's office in New Delhi inquiring why letters could not be marked "somewhere in Burma." When no plausible objection was offered, Stilwell ordered that the Burma dateline could be used from then on. However, one mail censor—a scissors-happy second louey—arbitrarily decided that "Burma" must still not be used in letters. The GIs kicked again. Stilwell sent another radio to New Delhi. Two days later the shavetail was relieved of his censoring duties.

Another time Stilwell visited a U. S. base in India where one of the men complained about the ban on pets at the post.

"Let them have pets if they want 'em," ruled Uncle Joe.

Now some U. S. bases in the CBI have virtual menageries of bear cubs, wildcats, dogs, jackals, monkeys, parrots, mongooses and snakes.

Although he is a strict disciplinarian when occasion demands, Stilwell is no stickler for the more rigid military courtesies. At a staff conference shortly after Pearl Harbor, all his officers jumped to attention when he walked in the room.

"Sit down, for God's sake!" he snapped. "We're fighting a war now and we'll dispense with all this jumping-up-and-down business."

Gen. Stilwell side-steps formalities even when presenting decorations. Entering a hospital to award the Silver Star to a wounded American soldier, the general found the GI in bed naked except for bandages and a sheet that covered him to the hips.

Gen. Stilwell introduced himself to the surprised soldier, smiled and said:

"I'm going to have to embarrass you a little."

Then, after his aide had read the citation, the general pulled the sheet over the soldier's chest and pinned the Silver Star on the sheet.

Uncle Joe takes a dim view of decorations for staff men, or even for himself. Returning to headquarters one day after a long trip in the field, he was informed that he had been awarded the DSC.

"Who thought up all this?" he groused. "I'm not so sure about this business of decorating staff men when there are so many men in the front line fighting. I was a lieutenant once and I used to wonder why desk men got so much glory."

Stilwell's understanding treatment of his enlisted men is responsible for his most popular nickname, Uncle Joe. Thanks to his rulings, a GI is not a social outcast in the CBI and "officers only" restrictions are at a minimum. Any enlisted man may visit the best restaurants, night clubs and theaters.

Another popular Stilwell ruling was the one he handed down soon after the first American Wacs arrived in the CBI. The enlisted Wacs were scarcely off their plane when lieutenants, captains and even some of the higher brass were pressing them for dates. The GIs (some had spent two years in the CBI without meeting an American girl whom they could date) figured they were outranked on this deal.

Then came an order from Gen. Stilwell's headquarters forbidding officers to date enlisted Wacs and enlisted men to date WAC officers. The second part of the order was the sheerest of formalities. GIs weren't getting to first base with the WAC officers, anyway. Gen. Stilwell's ruling simply rendered unto Caesar the things that were Caesar's, to GI the things that were GI.

Lean and wiry, without an ounce of excess weight, Gen. Stilwell has the energy and endurance of a man half his age. His perfect conditioning dates back to West Point, where he was a track star and a 140-pound quarterback on the Army eleven when vest-pocket gridmen were all but unknown. He wears glasses, smokes cigarettes in a long holder, chews gum frequently and has his iron-gray hair cropped in GI style.

Uncle Joe can usually be found where the firing is heaviest. He scorns the comfortable rear-echelon headquarters in New Delhi, preferring to stay up with his men. His combat headquarters is usually within artillery range of the enemy's lines.

Recently a Jap artillery shell landed less than 10 yards from Gen. Stilwell during a heavy shelling of the position he was visiting. Only the soft, muddy jungle earth, which buried the shell before it burst, saved the general and his aide from injury.

Gen. Stilwell was born on Mar. 19, 1883, at Palatka, Fla., where his parents were vacationing from the family home in Yonkers, N. Y. After graduating from Yonkers High School, where he played football and basketball, he entered West Point in 1900. He graduated with top honors in languages—he now speaks six fluently, including Japanese—and was commissioned June 15, 1904. In the first World War, Gen. Stilwell, then a captain, served as a liaison officer with the French and British.

Fortunately for American-Chinese relations, Gen. Stilwell understands the Chinese soldier as completely as he understands the American GIs. In 1920 he went to China as one of the first two U. S. Army officers ever assigned to that country. He studied at the North China Language School in Peiping for three years, making frequent trips into the interior to learn the varied dialects and customs of the Chinese people. One summer he worked as an ordinary day laborer with a coolie gang building roads in Shansi Province.

After six years back in the States, Gen. Stilwell returned to China in 1929 as executive officer to Gen. George C. Marshall, who was then commanding the 15th Infantry at Tientsin. Later, in 1935, he was appointed U. S. military attache at Peiping.

Despite the administrative nature of his work, Gen. Stilwell was no armchair officer even then. He seldom missed a major military operation in China. Occasionally he was on the Japanese side of the battlefront but he spent most of his time with his old love, the Chinese fighting man. He marched with Chinese troops. He ate Chinese chow with chopsticks. He carried his own bedroll and slept in Chinese bivouacs. He talked with Chinese soldiers in their own language. Gradually he even reached the point where he could think in Chinese.

Returning to the States for retirement in 1939, Gen. Stilwell was kept on the active list and ordered to take command of a 2d Division brigade when war threatened. He went to Fort Ord, Calif., in July 1940 as CG of the newly activated 7th Division, which later invaded Attu and the Marshall Islands. The 7th was 85 percent selectees but it ran rings around its "enemies" in the 1941 California maneuvers under Gen. Stilwell's expert leadership. On one occasion during the maneuvers, the gen-

eral was absent from his headquarters for two days. His adjutant finally found him sleeping on the floor of a high-school cloakroom in the maneuver area. It was the first sleep he had had in 48 hours.

The 7th Division's showing in the maneuvers resulted in Gen. Stilwell's appointment as CG of the III Army Corps, a post he held until February 1942, when Generalissimo Chiang Kai-shek asked for a U. S. general to direct American military activities in China. Gen. Stilwell, the U. S. Army's foremost authority on China, was the logical selection. He and his staff arrived at Chungking in late February. Two weeks later he was on the Burma battlefront directing the Chinese forces in his dual capacity as chief of staff to Chiang Kai-shek and CG of Chinese troops in Burma.

Gen. Stilwell took a licking in Burma but he candidly admitted it. Grimly confident, even in 1942's dark days, he said he would go back to retake the ground he had lost. He's making good on that promise now, having recaptured Northern Burma in the only really successful Allied offensive yet staged in the Far East.

Uncle Joe's one ambition is to win the war and get the hell home as quickly as possible. He has no personal post-war political or business aspirations. When peace comes, he plans to retire from the Army and settle down with his family in Carmel, Calif. There on the beach he will be able to don his old corduroy trousers and spend his days slogging through the sands with his favorite dog, a soft-eyed giant Schnauzer named Gareth. The little things in life are what Uncle Joe enjoys most.

'See here, Harvey, you are not going to wear those bars on your pajamas!"—*Sgt. Douglas Borgstedt.*

INVASION OF MAE WEST'S DRESSING ROOM

By Sgt. AL HINE

BOB SCHWARTZ Y2c, YANK's sailor, and I arrived a little early at the theater for our date with Mae West. We had to wait 10 minutes in a backstage passage before the great lady, who is playing the Empress of All the Russias in a tailored turkey called "Catherine Was Great," could see us.

Mr. Rosen, Miss West's manager, came out to tell us she would be ready in a minute. A little blond girl who had already changed her costume hit Mr. Rosen for five dollars. "This is a very expensive place for me to stand," said Mr. Rosen.

Everyone stared at Schwartz's uniform and at my uniform; they were both so drab next to those of the stage Russians who were passing by.

After we'd waited some more, Mr. Rosen finally showed us into her dressing room. Directly in front of the door was a washstand with a friendly but empty Piel's beer bottle under it. To the right was Miss West in a flowing robe and a headdress trimmed with gold sequins, with red-rimmed spectacles in her left hand and a diamond ring on her right-hand third finger. The ring was composed of six or four ice cubes. It was large and heavy enough to fell a kulak or a prime minister at one blow. We could see that "Catherine Was Great" indeed.

"It never ceases to amaze me, Colonel, the way these little girlies always steal the show."—M/Sgt. Ted Miller.

Unhappily to report, we couldn't see much more. Miss West's famous frontpiece was in evidence but chastely shielded. She kept switching the skirts of her dressing table over her lap as if she were ashamed of her legs. The sailor and I asked her odds and ends of questions, and she answered them in a very good humor.

"I created this Di'mond Lil character so well," she said, chewing vigorously on her gum and slurring her speech in the manner that has made her famous, "that I was gettin' so I was typed. That's why I figgered on doin' somethin' in a little different line. I bet you boys really thought I was that kinda woman—Di'mond Lil like—di'n't you? Bet you thought when you came in I'd just throw it at you?" She laughed a little, and then we laughed a little at the very thought of anyone having such a ridiculous impression.

"First idea I had, a long time back, before I went to Hollywood, was doin' a play on the Queena Sheba. When I got around to it, I figgered that it was maybe too Biblical—might make trouble. So I took a look at history just to see what other queens there was around. That's how I found Catherine.

"Wunnerful character, Catherine. Great woman. She had a real bad streak in her a little like my Di'mond Lil. But mighty smart.

"Know why she was so smart?" Miss West snapped this one out like a school teacher. We stammered "No."

"Smart because she had so many lovers," Miss West said triumphantly. "Mostly a woman just has one man. She gets to know everything he knows, but that's not much. Now my Catherine, she had 300 lovers. Started out when she was 11 years old. That's a lotta men, and she got inside their minds, too.

"These pillow conversations," Miss West purred. "You learn a lotta stuff that way."

The sailor asked her how she felt about the criticisms of her show; it had been panned unanimously by the first-night wolf pack, but it was still playing to full houses with standees.

"I never read 'em," said Miss West. "I'm constructive kinda person. Don't believe in readin' destructive kinda trash. The way I figger is those critics came up against a play that was so fine, so sincere, so puhfick they knew there wasn't anything they could write in praise would add to it. So they went off and panned it. See what I mean? That's kinda people critics are."

Mr. Rosen popped his head in the door and reminded her that there was a rehearsal of a tricky part of the last act coming up. Mae shooed him away. "They still got all that stuff before I come on to rehearse," she said. "After I come on it goes smooth anyway."

"Do you have many servicemen in your audiences, Miss West?" I asked. "Do GIs write you fan letters? What do they write about?"

"Always servicemen," Miss West said, "and thousands of letters from servicemen. You know what they write about? You know what they want to know?"

As I shook my head she removed the gum she had been working on throughout the interview.

"They wanta know if I wear padding," said Miss West. "Hah!" and she patted herself delicately about the prow.

Mr. Rosen popped his head in again, more urgent. Yeoman Schwartz and I rose to leave.

"Come back any time," Miss West said. "Here, I'll give you a pitcha. When they took this we di'n't have a throne or anything on the stage so the bottom part isn't so hot. I'll give you this half." She tore the lower section off a large glossy print and gave it to us. "That's what I look like," she said.

We went out into the alley past the autograph seekers clutching our scrap reverently.

"ROMMEL—COUNT YOUR MEN"

By Sgt. BILL DAVIDSON

OUTSIDE ST. MALO—The heavy artillery siege of St. Malo on the Brittany coast already had begun when a crack 155-mm howitzer battalion of the 333d Field Artillery, with which I am traveling, received orders to move up. Negro GIs make up this battalion, commanded by white officers.

I took off in a radio command car with the CO, Lt. Col. Harmon Kelsey of Livermore, Calif. At the wheel was T-5 Martin Simmons of Williamstown, N. J., described by the colonel as "the best damned driver I have ever seen and not scared of a damned thing."

We drove slowly up a broad asphalt highway past long rows of doughboys in trucks parked along the road. The battalion's new area was on the fringe of the town less than 10,000 yards from the besieged concrete citadel of St. Malo. The day before, an Infantry battalion had fought a bitter action here and had suffered heavy casualties when the enemy's coastal guns had been turned around to fire inland. We knew those guns were still zeroed in on the area.

The orchards and wheatfields stank with the dead and into many of the caved-in slit trenches had been swept the debris of war—torn GI raincoats, V-mail forms, bloody helmets, riddled rifle stocks and canteens. Three men had died beside the wall of a farmhouse when a tank shell bored a clean, small hole through the stone walls of the house and exploded where they stood talking on the other side.

The artillerymen prodded unconcernedly about the area, which had not yet been cleared of mines.

Passing signalmen gingerly stringing their first lines stared at them incredulously. "Fee fie fo fum, I smell the blood of a Boche," said Cpl. David Smith of New York City. Sgt. Gibson Sapp, also of New York City, was looking at the debris-filled slit trenches and composing poetry. "They died under an apple tree," he wrote; "the apples were not yet ripe."

The officers were busy laying out battery areas and gloating about the lack of traffic on the roads this far forward. Some of the men discovered a system of underground fortifications built by the Germans and went foraging for bedroom slippers, shaving mirrors and stationery.

One by one the batteries of the battalion rolled in and began to dig emplacements for SPs and howitzers. By evening they were set up and ready to fire. The big guns pointed short, ugly snouts seaward under camouflage nets. In the battalion fire-direction center men kidded and dug a little deeper while they waited. In the next field a cannoneer sang a song called "Low-down Babe" in a high minor key. At 2035 orders to fire came through and Lt. A. J. Howell of Altus, Okla., left to take off in a Piper Cub. At 2101 Lt. Howell radioed that he could now observe the concrete fortress target. T/Sgt. Henry Washington of New York City and Sgt. Sapp worked furiously over computing charts in the fire-direction center. At 2104 Sgt. Washington picked up the telephone. At 2105 gun No. 2 of Battery B opened fire to register a target for the other 11 guns.

The gun crew went about firing the round quietly

and methodically. There was no time for kidding and singing now. No one even muttered the battalion's now-famous battle-cry which goes "Rommel —count your men" before firing and then "Rommel —how many men you got now?" after firing. The projectile slammed into the breech. The crew whirled about rhythmically and the bagged propelling charge flew through the air from man to man. It looked like a well-drilled college backfield handling a tricky lateral-pass play. The breech swung closed. Then No. 1 man, Pfc. Arthur Broadnax of Autaugaville, Ala., pulled the lanyard. There was a blinding flash, a roar and a whistle. Seconds later we heard the 95-pound projectile crash into the crumbling Nazi citadel.

This was the 10,000th round the battalion had fired into the myth of the Aryan superman.

The battalion fired its first round a few hours after debarking on Cherbourg Peninsula June 30. On that occasion the men had barely water-proofed their vehicles and set up for what they thought was a waiting period outside Pont L'Abbe when a strange Piper Cub circling upstairs radioed a code word. The Cub simply said: "The coordinates of the target are such-and-such. Will adjust." That was all.

Col. Kelsey rushed to the map and looked at the target. It was a towering church steeple in the town, which the Germans were using both as a sniper's nest and an OP. "Fire mission," the colonel said into the phone. "Battery adjust shell HE, fuse quick, compass 5,000, elevation 300." Four rounds and 90 seconds later three heavy shells crashed into the invisible steeple, completely knocking it out— and the infantry advanced through the town.

That's the kind of shooting the battalion has done ever since. It was the first Negro combat outfit to face the enemy in France. Today it is greatly respected. It is rated by the corps to which it is attached as one of the best artillery units under the corps' control. And I've heard doughboys of five divisions watch men of the battalion rumble past in four-ton prime movers and say: "Thank God those guys are behind us."

The battalion once fired 1,500 rounds in 24 hours, which didn't leave any time for sleeping. I watched the men set a new unofficial record by firing three rounds in a little over 40 seconds. They've developed the reputation of throwing high explosive for anyone who asks for it, regardless of affiliation, and in the Mortain sector they calmly swung their guns over the corps boundary line to help out the 4th Division when it needed some heavy slugging.

The battalion fired steadily for two weeks after it arrived in France and helped pound two vital hills

into submission. After that it moved into the fight for La Haye du Puits and on to the bloody Moncastre Forest battle, where C Battery got out in front of the infantry and was so close to the enemy that it was pinned down by machine guns and mortars and couldn't fire. The battalion poured shells across the Periers-St. Lo road the day of the big July 25 attack and swept on through Normandy and Brittany with the big offensive. It was strafed and bombed and it absorbed occasional counterbattery fire from enemy artillery. It got shelled in foxholes and lost valuable men on OP hills. After La Haye du Puits it was issued mine detectors but it has not had time to use them. Its .50-caliber machine guns accounted for one strafing ME-109 and drove away 19 others.

The outfit captured seven prisoners on reconnaissance near Avranches. At Coutances it got out ahead of the infantry and captured a town.

Once when some ME-109s came strafing, the battalion was in a truck column on the road. Cpl. Pink Thomas of Batesville, Miss., stuck at the .50-caliber machine gun atop his truck and traded round for round with a Messerschmitt until it was the Nazi who gave ground and crashed in flames on the next hill. Lt. Joe King's 21-man wire crew was shelled off a hill three times and lost two men to machine-gun fire and shell bursts, but it managed to keep the lines open to OPs. That day the infantry moved ahead to La Haye du Puits under the battalion's protective barrage. Just before the big breakthrough along the Periers-St. Lo road the Germans tried to delay us with concentrations of 88s. Five of the 88s were firing on the battery at one time against our 155s. S/Sgt. Frank Crum of the Bronx, N. Y., crawled forward then up Hill 92 and in five minutes he'd spotted the gun flashes. Two volleys from the battalion silenced the 88s.

One of the things the battalion is most proud of is the time it scored a direct hit on the turret of a Tiger tank from 16,000 yards. When you consider that 16,000 yards is over nine miles, that the 155 howitzer fires a very heavy projectile at a very high arc, that the target was completely out of sight and that even if it were visible a Tiger tank at that distance would have looked about as big as a Maryland chigger—you realize that was some shooting.

The incident took place at Hill 95 north of La Haye du Puits. The position was still obscure on the hill but a three-man reconnaissance patrol took off anyway to look over the site as a forward OP. The patrol consisted of Lt. Edward Claussen of Bridgeport, Conn.; Pfc. Johnny Choice of Milledgeville, Ga., and Cpl. Howard Nesbitt of New York City. As this three-man patrol advanced they strung a telephone line all the way back to the battalion.

At the foot of the hill they ran into a paratrooper. "Who's up there?" asked Claussen. "Some of us and some of them," said the paratrooper. Whereupon Claussen swapped his pistol for the paratrooper's tommy gun and they proceeded up the hill. On reaching the top they started digging. They stayed there for eight days, observing the fire while an infantry battle surged back and forth around them.

On the ninth day some 88s got zeroed on the top of the hill and shelled it spasmodically day and night. This kept up for three days while Choice and Claussen spotted flashes and the battalion engaged the slippery self-propelled 88s with counterbattery fire. The telephone lines were cut and repaired and cut again.

Suddenly on the thirteenth day Claussen and Choice spotted the turret and apron of a single desert-camouflaged tank just barely showing above a hedgerow on the road alongside a house. Just as they were phoning the information back, the 88s opened up again. One shell burst five feet behind them and cut the telephone wire. Then another burst three feet in front of them and covered them with dirt in their foxholes.

"Let's get the hell out of here," said Claussen. They left with the phone and nothing else. A platoon of paratroopers just in front of them on the slope was falling back at the same time. One paratrooper came bounding over a hedgerow. "This is the first foxhole I've left since I landed 34 days ago," he said, "but, brother, this sure is one I'm saying good-bye to now."

Claussen and Choice moved down the hill 100 yards. Then they plugged into the telephone wire again. They phoned the coordinates of the tank back to the battalion and took chances dashing up to the top of the hill to observe results.

C Battery did the firing. The men used delayed-fuse shells timed to burst after the projectile had penetrated. The first round fell short. The second round dropped right down through the turret. The third smashed through the rear end of the tank. The fourth fell long. The second shell exploded inside the tank. The tank flew in half like a walnut smashed by a hammer.

They told me at gun No. 2 of C Battery that someone had reverted to the old GI custom and had scribbled some words in chalk on that shell. The words were: "From Harlem to Hitler."

NEGRO GIs IN THE FIJIS PREFER THE MANUAL OF ARMS IN JAZZ TIME By CPL. GEORGE NORFORD

FIJI ISLANDS—Down the company street swings a squad of Negro GIs, stomping their feet as a private first class sounds off in the cadence of Duke Ellington:

PFC. [*his voice like a trumpet hitting a high note*]: Cadence count!

SQUAD [*counting as their left feet strike the ground*]: One—two—three—four.

PFC. [*rhythmically*]: You shoulda stayed home but . . .

SQUAD: You left—you left.

PFC.: You hada good gal but you left . . .

SQUAD [*now on the right foot*]: Right.

PFC.: You left . . .

SQUAD: Right.

It's time for evening chow but these 12 soldiers look as though they could go marching forever and be happy about it. They're working harder for the pfc. than they've ever worked for a sergeant, and they carry their rifles smartly. Everything, indeed, is very military about this remarkable squad, though you fear, as the pfc. sings the cadence, that the No. 2 man is about to swing out in a furious Lindy Hop.

Then the pfc. yells out:

"Squad halt! Slide it!" [*In four movements, distinct yet somehow miraculously merged into one, the M1903s come down to Order Arms.*]

"Cross yer right eye!" [*Up go the rifles to Right Shoulder Arms.*]

"Cross yer left eye!" [*The pieces move to Left Shoulder Arms.*]

"Cross yer chest!" [*Port Arms.*]

"Peep in it!" [*They snap to Inspection Arms.*]

"Big Man coming!" [*They close their bolts and Present Arms.*]

"Big Man gone!" [*They return to Order Arms.*]

"Get off it!" [*They stand at ease.*]

This new nomenclature is said to have won many adherents, even in the ranks of sergeants, when the CO is not around. There are some who see the day when the War Department will have to scrap FM 22-5, Infantry Drill Regulations, and FM 23-10, U. S. Rifle, Caliber .30, M1903. For the seed has taken root.

There they go again:

"Get on it!" snaps the Pfc. [*His squad is stiff at attention.*] "Kick off!" [*They swing down the company street to the rhythm of his cadence.*]

"You hada good gal but you left . . ."

THE SWEETHEART OF COMPANY D

BY PVT. WILLIAM SAROYAN

THERE is something in the heart of street dogs which draws them close to men, and there is probably no camp or post of the Army which does not have at least one dog, whether the post is in a Far Western desolation or in a suburb of New York, as my post is.

Our Company D has one of these dogs. He is called Shorty by some of the men, Short End by others and Short Arm by still others. Shorty is small, lazy and given to a bitter attitude toward civilians, including children. Somewhere in Shorty's family is a dachshund, as Shorty has the lines of such a dog, but not the hair.

The theory of the men of Company D is that Shorty spends the greater part of his time dreaming of women—or at any rate women dogs. He doesn't come across such creatures very often; he doesn't come across any kind of dog very often. Whenever he does, male or female, Shorty goes to work and gives the matter a stab, so to speak. It is a half-hearted stab, with Shorty more bored than fascinated and not the least bit sure of what he is trying to do, or whether or not he isn't making a fool of himself.

Now and then Shorty will be discovered in the middle of the street, dreaming of love or whatever it is, while two or three trucks stand by discreetly waiting for him to make up his mind. Shorty may have come into the world thoughtlessly, but it is not likely that he will leave any children standing around. He is either too tired, too troubled or too old, even though he is probably not more than 2.

I have observed that Shorty makes himself available to any man in uniform, bar none, and while our post is made up mostly of men of talent, Shorty is not above giving himself over to the affections of a man of practically no talent at all, such as our top sergeant, who was not in civilian life the famous man he is now. Our top sergeant may be a genius, the same as all the rest of us: Two-Teeth Gonzalez, Bicycle Wilkinson, Henry the One Hundred and Fifty-first Million and all the others. He probably deserves a story all to himself, but somebody else will have to write that story, as I want to write sonnets. (That is, if I ever learn to spell.)

My hero is Shorty, not our first sergeant. The sergeant is his mother's hero, I suppose, and I wish to God she'd never let him out of the house. If he thinks getting me to do KP is the way we are going to bring the war to a satisfactory conclusion, I believe his education has been neglected. That is not the way to do it. Give me a map of the world, a pointer and a good-sized audience and I believe I can figure the whole thing out in not more than an afternoon. The idea that generals are the only kind of Army personnel capable of figuring out ways and means and all that stuff is unsound. For every general there ought to be one private on the ground floor. As it is, half the time I don't know what is being done, what the idea is, or anything else. The result is that I must go out into the yard and whistle for Shorty, who instead of leaping to his feet and running to me opens his eyes and waits for me to run to him.

Shorty knows me all right, but what kind of planning can you do with a dog, and a sleepy one at that—a day-dreamer, an escapist, a lover of peace, an enemy of children in sailor suits? I don't know who the chaplain of Company D is, but for my money he can pack up and go to some other post, because Shorty is doing the same work and sending in no reports to anybody. He is a quiet creature, he is patient, he will listen to reason or anything else, and he will get up after a half hour of heart-to-heart talk and slowly wag his tail. He will wag thoughtfully, with effort, and unless you are blind, you will know what advice he is giving you after carefully considering your case.

Now, there was the celebrated case of Warty Walter, the Genius from Jersey, who had a secret weapon all worked out in his head which he believed could finish the war in two weeks. Warty mentioned this weapon to our top sergeant only to hear the man say, "You do what I say, Warty, or you're going to hear otherwise."

Warty went out into the yard to Shorty and unburdened his heart, whereupon Shorty got to his feet, stretched his body until it hurt, wagged his tail three times, kissed Warty on the hand, turned and began wending his way across the street where a girl of 6 in a sailor suit was looking at a movie billboard. That was the end of Warty's secret weapon. The following day he got his orders to go to Louisiana, took Shorty in his arms to say good-bye, and the war is still going on—a good three months after Warty got his idea for the secret weapon. Our top sergeant said, "If it's a secret, what the hell are you coming to me about it for? Keep it a secret."

Not every man at our post is as brilliant or as sincere as Warty, but I can think of no man who is not as devoted to Shorty. No girl of the USO has done Army morale as much good as Shorty. He may not be a dancing dog, but he's got eyes and many a man's seen a lot of understanding in those brooding eyes—many and many a man.

As for the little girl in the sailor suit, she turned

and ran, so that Shorty, not knowing what else to do, went up to a second lieutenant and bit him. The following day there was a notice on the bulletin board saying: "Yesterday an enlisted man was bitten by a dog who might or might not have had rabies. Therefore, in the future, any man caught without his dog tags will be given extra duty." This of course was a subtle way of saying that Shorty had rabies, a lie if I ever heard one.

The basic failing of Shorty, if he must be given a failing, is his love of comfort, his passion for food and his devotion to sleep or The Dream. Shorty probably does not know this is 1943. I doubt very much if he knows there is a war going on, and I am convinced he does not know that the men of Company D are soldiers. I believe he has some vague notion we are orphans.

Shorty eats too much and never does calisthenics. He has seen a lot of men come and go. He has loved them all, and they have all loved him. I have seen big men with barracks bags over their shoulders bend down to whisper good-bye to the sweetheart of Company D, get up with misty eyes, swing up into the truck and wave to the little fellow standing there in a stupor. And I have heard them, as the truck has bounced out of the yard on its way to the war, holler out—not to me or to our top sergeant, but to Shorty: "So long, pal! See you after the war!"

I don't think they will see Shorty after the war. I think he will lie down and die of a broken heart once the boys take off their uniforms. Shorty lives to watch them stand reveille and retreat. All that stuff will stop after the war and Shorty will be out in the cold, just another dog of the streets, without honor, without importance—lonely, unfed, despised and unwanted.

That is why I have written this tribute to him.

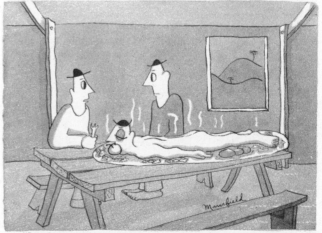

"I understand he and the mess Sergeant had a little spat."
—Pvt. Walter Mansfield.

OVER THE HILL

By Sgt. RAY DUNCAN

It was almost exactly 1530 hours when Walt Durkee went over the hill. The adjutant, in the orderly room, glanced up at the clock and noted the time.

"Looks like your new man is taking off," he observed to Snell. The duty sergeant glanced out the window. "Who, Durkee? No, he ain't takin' off. He's policin' up the area. Nobody ever goes over the hill from this camp."

Which was exactly what the sergeant had been telling Walt Durkee.

"Welcome to Desert Hole Army Air Base," Snell had said. "We hope you'll like it here." And he had waved his hand at the sage-dotted desert that stretched far away to the hills.

"No," Walt Durkee said, "I don't like it here. I've been in camps like this before. Don't be surprised if I go over the hill."

Sgt. Snell glanced sharply at the new man, an odd light in his eye. "Oh no, you won't go over the hill. Funny thing, nobody ever goes over the hill from this camp."

"No?"

"No. You will be assigned general duty. Your first duty will be to police up the area." Again the sergeant waved his arm at the desert around them, and handed Walt a little brown sack.

After two hours of policing up Walt found three small bones and a dried-up rattlesnake skin. "I sure would like a glass of beer," he thought. "I would like very much to sit under a tree somewhere." It was then 1100 and time for a break. He began to work away from the orderly room, so he could lie down for a while with his head in the shade of a sagebrush.

But as soon as he was settled and beginning to drowse in the desert silence, Walt heard a sharp click as the orderly-room door opened half a mile away.

"All right, all right," said the duty sergeant. "Let's get on the ball out there, Pvt. Durkee."

Durkee roused himself. "Yeah," he muttered, "okay, you loud-mouthed orderly-room jerk."

"I heard that!" rang Sgt. Snell's angry voice across the desert.

At noon chow Walt Durkee picked up extra sandwiches and fruit. "I sure would like to see a tree," he kept thinking as he resumed his policing-up duties. "See a tree, see a tree," something sang in his ear, "over the hill and see a tree."

He kept drifting farther from the orderly room,

pretending to pick up cigarette butts. After three or four miles he dropped pretense and strode boldly toward the hills in the east, toward his home in New Hampshire.

"Look," said the adjutant, "look at that man Durkee now. He's definitely taking off. Aren't you going to say anything to him?"

"No. Not yet." Snell came to the window. "But don't tell the Old Man about this. He promised me another stripe on the first of the month if none of my men went AWOL. He's proud of our record."

All that night Walt walked toward the east. He lay down by a big sagebrush just before dawn, but after a few hours he wakened suddenly. Someone was calling his name.

"Here!" cried Durkee instinctively, sitting up.

"Okay," came the voice of the duty sergeant across the wasteland. "Just taking roll call. Carry on!" Walt heard the faint far-off slam of the door.

"I'm afraid," said the adjutant three mornings later, "that we'll have to mark your man AWOL. He didn't answer roll call for today."

"But sir," argued Snell, "it's windy today. You can see him for yourself, heading for those mountains to the east. After all, you can't count a man AWOL when he's in plain sight. They'd laugh you out of courts martial!"

"We've argued this out a hundred times, Snell, every time one of your men takes off. But I'll check regulations again."

"Can't we put him on special-duty status for a while, till after the first of the month? Let's say he's a weather observer on special duty. It's not like we didn't know where he was."

Walt Durkee's food was beginning to run low, but he wouldn't give up. He could see the hill he was going over, looming closer and closer, as he plodded along a dimly marked trail leading east. The orderly room now was only a speck in the distance.

"No," said the adjutant firmly on the following Monday, "I certainly will not permit the use of binoculars. As soon as he can't be seen with the naked eye, he's AWOL."

"Everything's gotta be just *so* with you," muttered Snell. "Anyhow I think he'll be startin' back soon. I had the observation plane drop a little more food."

"Well, I took him off special duty this morning.

I had to. The Old Man was beginning to wonder, I think. Durkee's now carried as detached service."

Sgt. Snell grabbed the binoculars. "Look!" he cried, "I think he's turned around at last. We can put him back on squadron-area duty as of tomorrow's morning report!"

When Pvt. Walt Durkee staggered into the orderly room about eight days later, he kept trying to lick his swollen lips with a dry tongue. "I've come to give myself up," he gasped.

"Did you finish policin' up?" asked Snell, now a staff sergeant. He glanced out across the desert. "Looks pretty good. Now why don't you get back to the barracks before the Old Man catches you in that ragged uniform."

"I was AWOL," muttered Durkee, "I was over the hill—I mean——"

"You mean you got lost," said the staff sergeant, shoving him toward the barracks. "Nobody ever goes over the hill from this camp."

THE HOT JEEP DEPARTMENT

BY CPL. TOM SHEHAN

HIS name doesn't make much difference, because nobody called him anything except Hot Jeep. What's more, he's too good a guy to have land in Leavenworth just because I want to tell his story.

Braidwood McManus, our battery clerk, was responsible for his monicker. Some of the boys from the ack-ack outfit down the road were over one night, and they asked what this character did in our battery. Braidwood, who has a knack for names that fit, told them that he had charge of the "Hot Jeep Department." So they called him Hot Jeep, and it stuck.

That was back when we first landed in Africa. Everything was confused: police supervision hadn't been organized too well, and it was a rare occasion when an outfit had the same number of vehicles at reveille that it had at retreat. Not that they were stolen. Nothing of Uncle Sam's is ever stolen; somebody else just uses it. When our outfit found itself with fewer vehicles than was called for in the table of basic allowances, Hot Jeep would go out and pick up enough to make up the deficit, with maybe one or two extras thrown in.

This was known as "moonlight requisitioning." Hot Jeep became so proficient at it, particularly at picking up the vehicle from which he derived his name, that he was not bothered much even by the padlocks and chains the MPs ordered as required equipment for every vehicle.

At one time Hot Jeep had been Dutch Schultz's chauffeur, but he got mad when we introduced him to visitors as a gangster. "The only rap I ever had against me," he would scream, "was when I voted three times in Waterbury at two bucks a pop. I wouldna been caught then only I forgot how to spell McGillicuddy, the name I was votin' under."

Hot Jeep was a technical sergeant and maybe he deserved the rating. The top kick always gave us that old business about the T/O when any of the

rest of us asked about ratings. But Hot Jeep's work did not go unnoticed; we took inventory after we got to Italy and found we had 105 vehicles whereas our TBA called for only 25.

"The Old Man made me a tech the time I sneaked behind the Jerry lines at Gafsa and got him a *Volkswagen*," Hot Jeep would explain when anybody asked him about his five stripes.

More than commercial reward, Hot Jeep craved appreciation. It must have been the ham in him because he would talk as long as the boys would sit around and listen to his stories of how he "requisitioned" this or that item the battery had needed.

He got so good that the CO even loaned him out to his friends. All they had to do was let the Old Man know that red tape had them down and he would tell them to let Hot Jeep know what they wanted.

Hot Jeep probably reached his peak on a trip to Oran. It was a little out of his line, but he put it across. We hadn't had any PX rations for a month when the CO got word that a boat had docked at Oran with all kinds of supplies such as razor blades, candy, cigarettes and the like.

Hot Jeep was ordered to go to Oran with a weapons carrier and pick up our rations before the word got around to the other outfits and the stampede started. He asked to have another vehicle and another driver sent along with him, and the CO, probably guessing what he had in mind, told Sgt. Hardfeet, a dumb guy with no imagination whatsoever, to take a vehicle and follow Hot Jeep's instructions.

As we were able to reconstruct the story afterward, our friend Hot Jeep had Sgt. Hardfeet fill out the requisition slips for our outfit's PX supplies. Then when the major in charge turned to Hot Jeep and asked what he could do for him, Hot Jeep replied that he wanted to draw supplies for the Two-O-Sixth Field Artillery at Maison Carree, Col. Wilson in command. The major signed the requisition slips, and Hot Jeep drew the rations at the same dump where Hardfeet drew his.

They had been back from Oran for an hour or two and were sitting around with the boys when

Sgt. Hardfeet said: "Hey, ain't you gonna take those rations over to the Two-O-Sixth?"

"Ya blockhead," said Hot Jeep, the rage of an unappreciated artist written on his face, "there ain't no Two-O-Sixth!"

NOMENCLATURE OF THE PACKAGE, APO

By Cpl. JAMES O'NEILL

SOMEWHERE IN THE PERSIAN GULF—Now that the Army Postal Service has restored the soldier's privilege of getting packages from home, we would like to commend the APS for putting in the clause which says the soldier must ask for a package to get it.

This requirement that soldiers must ask for packages is not, as some believe, an effort to limit the number of packages. It springs from the demands of soldiers that they be protected against the parcel-post system. Reports might show that the first AEF in Ireland as long as a year ago was actually sabotaging incoming box-laden boats by purposely *not* claiming title to the merchandise at time of delivery.

This practice spread until thousands of boxes lay purposely unclaimed on wharves all over the combatant world, and the Army Postal Service probably conducted an investigation to discover why. The APS no doubt discovered the reason: no soldier would claim a package because (a) he knew what was in it, (b) he had had enough of what was in it or (c) even his worst enemy and first sergeant had had enough of what was in it.

From now on we get an even break with the people who make up packages. We get to tell them what to put in.

Up to this time there have been only four variations of the box-sending theme.

Let us discuss them, now that they are a thing of the past:

TYPE A—THE GOODIE BOX

Invariably consisted of one of two items—candy or home-made cookies. There were two choices open to the unfortunate recipient of home-made cookies. He could, if still in love and his sweetheart sent them, try to eat the cookies. This love-lorn type cabled home the next day for a new upper plate and a stomach pump. If the guy wasn't in love or just didn't give a damn, he took the sensible course of donating love's handiwork to the Engineers for road markers or dummy land mines.

TYPE B—GOOEY-YUM-YUM KANDY KIT

En route the kit was placed by considerate stevedores between the engine-room boilers and a shipment of Grant tanks. When the soldier received it, he could use the mashed-up goo for pasting French postcards or YANK pin-ups on his barracks wall. Or, if he had a little goat's blood in him, he might start right in eating Gooey-Yum-Yum's wrappings, partitions, string, APO number and all.

Suppose the sender was the thoughtful type and sent hard candy that stayed hard. Tell me who in hell is going to sacrifice his native-likker-weakened molars on a job a couple of Grant tanks couldn't do? The ingenious AAF is said to be using these dextrose blockbusters over Berlin, the only practical use so far discovered.

TYPE C—THE KNIT-ONE-AND-PURL-ONE BOX

The sort of box that caused the recent high female death rate by accidental self-stabbing. It contained The Knitted Glove or The Knitted Pullover Sweater. Already enough has been said on this gruesome subject in newspaper editorials, syndicated columns, joke books and returned packages marked "Wrong Address."

TYPE D—THE ODDS-AND-ENDS BOX

This always fell into one of the following subdivisions:

1. The Sewing Kit. This was the 1,442d one the helpless GI received. Despite all the Boy Scout and Sewing Kit Concession propaganda, the average GI doesn't know how to sew. Even if he did, Whistler's Mother couldn't darn the craters he plows through a sock. Upon receipt of the sewing kit, the soldier carefully took out the needles to pin up that picture of Jane Russell and threw the rest away.

2. The Compact Shaving Kit. This monster was delivered by a detail of 10 and, when opened, resembled a surgeon's operating room, complete with X-ray equipment. It so scared the dogface he refused to shave with anything for a month.

3. The Cigarette Lighter. It didn't work, but there was plenty of fluid at the PX. It did work, but there was not a drop of fluid at the PX. Or no PX.

4. The Photograph. Usually sent by that much-maligned creature, the Girl Back Home, who, unless she was straight out of *Vogue*, included an original little note, "Put this in the mess hall to scare the rats away." It could do the job very well.

If the girl was a looker, she had had the picture taken with one of the boys back home "just to make you feel a teeny-weeny bit jealous." The guy looked like Cary Grant and was either sporting a pair of oak leaves or clutching a $1,000 war-industry check in one hand.

5. The Canned Tidbit. Usually tied in a maze of fancy ribbon, this was something the dogface hopefully ripped open with anxious hands only to discover a can of Spam. (Last week the mess sergeant was clubbed to death with empty cans that had contained this ersatz chicken.)

Now that us soldiers overseas are allowed to select the contents of our packages from home, here are four types of gift boxes that we would like to receive:

A—One Lana Turner and one case of Scotch.
B—One Dinah Shore and one case of Scotch.
C—One Rita Hayworth and one case of Scotch.
D—One Scotch and one case of Jane Russells.

A DOGFACE ANSWERS A COLLECTION AGENCY

Pvt. Oris Turner, 39168771,
APO 000, c/o Postmaster,
San Francisco, Calif.

Dear sir:

Re: [Creditor's name]—$14.80

You have had an opportunity to settle this claim without trouble or expense, but it seems you will not settle until forced to do so. You failed even to reply to our recent letter.

Therefore, unless immediate arrangements are made for settlement, we will have no alternative but to instruct our attorneys to file a complaint against you and have you summoned to appear at the time of trial. An officer of the court will also be empowered to seize your goods, attach your earnings, automobile, bank account, or any other funds or property that may belong to you or be due you.

You would be wise to make settlement, etc., etc.

Yours,
[NAME OF COLLECTION AGENCY.]

New Guinea,
Jan. 26, 1943

Dear sirs:

Your letter of 11/19/'42 was duly rec'd today and after reading the contents therein I am pleased to note that I will be summoned to appear in court to make payment due you of $14.80 plus interest and costs.

Gentlemen, the opportunities your letter presents are beyond my wildest dreams.

I believe by law the court is required to send a process server to deliver the summons in person. In that case I will inform you of certain essentials he will require for jungle travel.

The first item advisable is a self-inflating life raft, as ships even in convoys are sometimes sunk. The raft will also be useful later in crossing rivers and swamps in New Guinea. He should also bring the following items: Mosquito bars, head net, pith helmet, quinine, salt tablets, vitamin pills, mosquito and sunburn lotions, medical supplies for tropical infections, poisonous snakes, spiders, steel helmet, gas mask, waterproof tent, heavy caliber rifle for shooting Japs, crocodiles and other game, machete, chlorine capsules, flashlight, and soap.

In choosing this process server make sure that he is not an alcoholic, as there isn't a drink to be found on the whole island. Furthermore, he must not be allergic to mosquitoes, heat rash, malaria, dengue fever, snakes, spiders, lizards, flies, crocodiles, and tall grass with a few head hunters in it. These are trivial matters and he may never come in contact with any of them, especially if his convoy is attacked by the enemy's battle fleet.

I am telling you all this as I am much concerned over his safe arrival. If he reaches this location our meeting will be much more impressive than Stanley and Livingstone's. I will see that the best possible care is taken of him on arrival. As soon as he has recovered from his jungle trip we will be on our way back to civilization and the law court. I trust he is already on his way, and I am packing my barracks bags to avoid any waste of time.

Here's hoping that this letter finds you in the best of health.

Respectfully yours,
—PVT. ORIS TURNER

A SOLDIER'S DREAM

BY SGT. BOB STUART MCKNIGHT

Scott Field, Ill.

A listless hag with a Lyster bag
    Came to me in a dream.
The listless hag rode a shiftless nag,
    The Lyster bag was green,
I don't know what was in that bag,
    What overflowed its brim;
But the listless hag had a merry jag
    And her breath was foul with gin.

The listless hag slunk off her nag
    And smiled a toothless grin.
The shiftless nag with a briskless lag
    Immersed his head in the gin.
Quite soon the shiftless nag did wag
    His tail in gruesome glee,
And the listless hag danced a teasing tag:
    Oh, what a sight to see!

The listless hag leaped on her nag
    And sailed away in the night.
The mistless moon sang a shiftless tune
    As I wept to see their flight.
I only pray some day I'll find,
    Amidst the battle's din,
A listless hag, a shiftless nag
    And a Lyster bag full of gin.

SOLDIER MEETS CIVILIAN

By Sgt. LEONARD SILK

"Why, hello there, civilian!"

"Huh? Oh, hello."

"Now you sit right down. Plenty of room on this train for both of us. Have a cigar?"

"Well, I don't usually smoke cigars, but——"

"That's it. Well, how do you like being a civilian?"

"Oh, it's all right, I guess. Some things about it I like, and some things I don't."

"What outfit you with?"

"Oh, I'm in insurance."

"No! What outfit?"

"Well, the Prudential."

"Whaddaya know! I've got an uncle who's a civilian in insurance. He's with the Metropolitan. He's a district manager. What're you?"

"Me? I'm just a kind of statistician."

"Hmm. Seems to me a man of your intelligence ought to be a manager. Tell me, how much do you make a month?"

"About $200, I guess, but——"

"Well, that's not so bad. Tell me, you statisticians still using Monroe calculators?"

"Oh, yes."

"What kind you got—the old model you have to crank by hand or the new electric kind?"

"Well, I have to crank mine, but I hear the company's getting some of the new kind."

"Well, they ought to! How long you been with Prudential?"

"About 18 months."

"And before that?"

"I was a file clerk."

"Where?"

"In Canton. With the electric company."

"And how do you like your office manager? Pretty tough baby, I guess?"

"Oh, he's all right. He doesn't bother me much."

"Doesn't, eh? Well, I guess there are all kinds. You know, I was once a civilian myself. I bet you civilians raise the Merry Old Ned once in a while."

"Yes, sometimes we have fun."

"Excuse me, but I've been wondering what that button in your lapel was for."

"Oh, that's just a Rotary Club button."

"I see. What'd you get it for—unearthing some subversive activity? Trapping some fifth columnists, eh?"

"Why, no. I got it for joining the Rotary Club."

"Oh. Just for joining the Rotary Club."

"Yes."

"I see. It does *something* for your suit, but not much. Frankly, don't you think your suit is kind of drab? I like these Harris tweeds some of the civilians are wearing. Much snappier."

"Yes, they are."

"Well, where are you going now?"

"To Columbus. To visit my mother."

"I bet she really thinks a lot of you! How long's it been since you saw her?"

"About five months."

"Well, she'll be glad to see *you*. Do you write often?"

"Pretty often, I guess."

"That isn't nice. You should write all the time. But tell me, what's the War Production Board planning for next year? I mean, being a civilian, you probably hear a lot about that."

"Gee, I don't know. I just work for an insurance company."

"Oh. Well, my goodness, this is where I get off. Say, if you're ever at Fort Snark, look me up. I'm in Barracks 3428, Street L. Just ask for Cpl. Snowbird. Everybody knows me there around Company D. Glad to see you any time. Been nice talking to you."

"Sure has. I mean, you, too."

"Well, so long. And don't forget what I said about writing to mother!"

"Thanks mister. I'm Pvt. Beegle. I've been at Camp Callan for 10 months. I like the Army okay. It looks like a long war. No, I don't think we'll get bombed. I'm in favor of cargo planes, and I'm going as far as Fourth and Western."—*Sgt. Al. Kaelin, Tobyanna (Pa.) Army Air Base.*

LANDING ON LOS NEGROS

By Cpl. BILL ALCINE

Los Negros, the Admiralty Islands [By Cable]— "I feel just like a June bride," said Pvt. Warren Planthaber of Sterling, Ill. "I know just what's going to happen but I don't know how it'll feel."

We were crouched low in a landing barge headed for the 50-yard-wide channel into Hyane Harbor. These GIs were men from the 2d Squadron, 5th Regiment, 1st Cavalry Division, who had left their horses back in the States. Planthaber, dripping like a gargoyle, shivered in the rain.

"Put a slug in that tommy chamber," he told another cavalryman. "You think we're going to a picnic?"

As we neared the channel, the Navy men in the bow hollered to us to keep our heads down or we'd get them blown off. We crouched lower, swearing, and waited.

It came with a crack: machine-gun fire over our heads. Our light landing craft shuddered as the Navy gunners hammered back an answer with the .30-calibers mounted on both sides of the barge.

As we made the turn for the beach, something solid plugged into us. "They got one of our guns or something," one GI said. There was a splinter the size of a half-dollar on the pack of the man in front of me.

Up front a hole gaped in the middle of the landing ramp and there were no men where there had been four. Our barge headed back toward the destroyer that had carried us to the Admiralties.

White splashes of water were plunging through the six-inch gap in the wooden gate. William Siebieda S1c of Wheeling, W. Va., ducked from his position at the starboard gun and slammed his hip against the hole to plug it. He was firing a tommy gun at the shore as fast as wounded soldiers could pass him loaded clips. The water sloshed around him, running down his legs and washing the blood of the wounded into a pink frappe.

When we reached the destroyer nearest us, the wounded men were handed up. Two soldiers and our cox'n died right away. One of the GIs was a private to whom I had handed a pack of Camels just before we went on board.

Pfc. Wayne A. Hutchinson of Goodland, Kans., the fourth man in the prow when the 40-mm shell came through, was untouched, but he was shaking slightly now as he lit a cigarette.

An undamaged barge came alongside. We reloaded silently. By this time the destroyers had worked over the point with their five-inch guns, and we had little trouble making the beach.

We piled out quickly at the beachhead. Three tiny Jap coconut-log jetties stuck out into the water from the strip of sand. GIs were hauling ammunition and rations up a low rise, then along muddy tracks parallel to the Momote airstrip, which lay straight in from the beach.

Fifty yards ahead we could hear sporadic gunfire: behind us the Navy had started to slug the shore again. The rain was heavier now.

An excited GI came up. "Gee," he said, "those Navy guys are nuts. They're up there with tommy guns and grenades, acting like commandos." Later a wounded soldier told me "the sailors just don't seem to care. They see a Jap, they have a grenade and they run after him like they were kids playing at war."

The first landing barge had hit the shore three-quarters of an hour before, and already the tracks were mucked up and field wire was tripping the feet of GIs digging in all around. I asked a soldier investigating a pillbox where the front was. "I don't know," he said, waving toward the strip. "There's some guys up there." A B-25 screamed over the coconut grove. On the other side of the airstrip guns were firing.

Lt. Decatur B. Walker of El Paso, Tex., slogged up and offered to show me the airstrip. "My men are on patrol on the other side," he said. The force had achieved its final objective just a half hour after the landing. The patrols had gone on ahead— too far, the lieutenant said, because if the Japs counterattacked he would be spread out too much. He said he was going up to bring them back.

Momote airstrip was a bombpocked mess of puddles, weeds, rusting fuselages, a truck and a sorry-looking Jap bulldozer. There were no troops in sight; only the crack of rifles off to the right reminded us that there was a war on.

Somebody whistled softly from the bushes. An M1 appeared, followed by Pfc. Juan Gonzales of Taylor, Tex. He had been on patrol and had seen only one Jap. "He's up there about 100 yards," said Gonzales. "Alive?" asked Lt. Walker. "Nope," said Gonzales, "he's my first one." The lieutenant told him to round up the men and withdraw to the edge of the strip.

On the right flank there was more action. The Japs had set up a dual-purpose antiaircraft gun that was giving us trouble. Then our planes bombed it. Cpl. Wilbur C. Beghtol of Eldon, Iowa, a member of F Troop, 2d Squadron, went out on patrol to see if the gun had been silenced. He found a deserted light machine gun and two 20-mms.

When he returned, he discovered that a Jap counterattack had forced F Troop back across the strip. The men were dug in alongside a clearing. A major was bedding down near a pillbox. He advised me to string a hammock between a couple of trees. "There's nothing like comfort," he smiled.

During that night 10 Japs crept into the pillbox nearby. The next morning they were sprawled lifeless around it and in the two holes that served as entrances. But retaking the pillbox was a chore. At about 0730 the divisional wire chief, a captain, passed the pillbox and a Jap shot at him, hitting him in the groin and chest. Lying in the mud six feet from the tip of the V-shaped dugout, the captain pointed to the pillbox.

Pfc. Allan M. Holliday of Miami, Fla., and Cpl. James E. Stumfoll of Pittsburg, Kans., who were coming up the track when the captain was shot, ducked behind palms and began firing at it.

When four Japs ran out of the other entrance, they were cut down by a squad on that side. Holliday and Stumfoll crept up, tossed grenades into the opening near them. The Japs threw back two of the grenades but the others exploded inside the hole.

There was no noise after that inside, so Holliday and Stumfoll—with Sgt. John T. Lee of Las Cruces, N. Mex., and Pfc. Tony C. Reyes of Corpus Christi, Tex., and a handful of other cavalrymen—circled to the other entrance and started to pull the palm fronds away from the hole.

A Jap was sitting up inside, drawing a bead with a rifle. About 20 carbines and tommy guns practically sawed him in half. He folded over like a man in prayer.

The GIs heard more noises inside the pillbox but didn't bother to find out who was causing it; they just blew the roof in with TNT and grenades, and the battle for this particular pillbox was over.

Meanwhile the wounded wire chief had been pulled out of reach of the Japs by the ranking Medical Corps officer in the force, a colonel, who himself was slightly wounded by a grenade. A Signal Corps photographer, who tried to get movies of the action, was shot through the stomach.

The major who had suggested sleeping in a hammock had done just that himself. During the night the men heard him call out: "Don't, boys, it's Maj.

—" Evidently the major thought the Japs who were hacking him to pieces were Yanks. His almost headless body was found tangled in the hammock in the morning.

H Troop had been guarding the left flank, where the Momote airstrip ran almost to the ocean. It was through and around this troop that the Japs came. "There's no way in the world," said Lt. Sam A. Durrance of Glennville, Ga., H Troop's CO, "of keeping the Japs from coming in at night, because you can't hear or see them."

Lt. Durrance had posted three squads to guard the perimeter. The Japs seemed to be coming from all sides, thrusting at one point after another with a soft pressure to determine their resistance, like a yegg prying open a window. The stealthy sound of bodies moving was all the cavalrymen could hear. If they threw a grenade or opened up with their weapons, the Japs would try another point.

"The only way we could see the Japs," said a GI in H Troop later, "was to let them get close enough so we could make them out against the sky over our holes. Then we'd cut loose."

H Troop did all right. One man was killed and four were wounded, but in the morning the others found 66 dead Japs lying in the area they had tried to take. One more GI was wounded by a Jap sniper while carrying wounded men to an aid station.

The dead Japs were big men, Imperial Marines—all evidently fresh troops, in good condition, very well equipped, cool, tough and smart. A large number evidently could speak English in the bargain.

Cpl. Joe Hodoski of Chicago, Ill., heard a noise outside his foxhole and stuck his head up. There was a Jap setting up a machine gun barely a yard away. "How you doin', Joe?" said the Jap. Joe was doing okay. He killed the Jap with his automatic.

Beghtol and some other GIs went on another patrol on the second day to check Jap strength on the portion of the island near an inland bay, with a native boy as guide. "I swear that little guy could smell Japs," Beghtol said.

"We were going down a track when we came to a road block. The little guy went on ahead. He saw a Jap and was drawing a bead on him when we spotted about 50 more Japs off a little way. We were afraid he'd fire but he didn't. He knew those Japs were there even though he couldn't see them. Our patrol reported to headquarters, and a bomber laid some eggs on the spot."

If the first night had been tough, the second night was tougher. The Jap attack started on the same left flank about dusk. Fortresses had dropped supplies and ammunition all day, and our men gave the enemy a hot welcome. One machine-gun crew in a rugged position fired 4,000 enfilading rounds by dawn. Tracers from both sides lighted the sky like neon lights. When the moon came up, we could see the Japs and pounded hell out of them.

One tough cavalryman from Philadelphia, Pa., Pvt. Andrew R. Barnabei, was guarding a pack 75 when two Japs crawled up. He threw a grenade that blew one of them apart but only wounded the other Jap, who tossed a grenade right back. "It missed me," Barnabei said, "but got the sergeant in the leg. Then two more Japs came up and I guess I forgot what I knew about fighting because I stood up and killed 'em both with my carbine. I might have been killed myself, I guess."

Cpl. John Dolejsi of Hallettsville, Tex., was in the same foxhole with Barnabei and threw a grenade that got two more. In the morning, after it had started to rain again, Barnabei saw one of them move. He took no chances and shot them both. "The second one jumped when I shot him in the belly," Barnabei said, "so I guess he was alive, too."

A little sandy-haired GI, who was badly wounded by a grenade in the left buttock early in the evening, bled all night but kept firing his tommy gun at anything that moved. He probably accounted for two of the four Jap marines found lying dead around the hole in the morning.

Three other GIs of a mortar crew were crouching by their weapon when a grenade bounced in. One man tried to toss it out but got tangled up in the mortar. He hollered "Jump" and got out. The second man rolled over the top of the hole but not before a fragment hit him in the foot. The corporal in the back of the emplacement was wounded.

Men had no chance to get medical aid when they were wounded at night. The air was full of grenade fragments, tracers and Japs, so the wounded lay in their dugouts and some of them bled to death. One man with a bullet through his arm couldn't stop bleeding. When morning came, he needed two transfusions to bring him back. "But that didn't worry me," he said. "A buddy of mine in the next foxhole had both legs blown off by a mortar burst, and I had to lie there listening to him call for help until he bled to death. I'll never forget that."

It started to rain again—that same chill heavy rain—toward dawn. Then the Japs made one last try, throwing everything they had to break the back of the Regular Army squadrons. It didn't work.

But with daybreak came a stream of wounded into the canvas-covered dugout that served as a field hospital. Major operations were performed 150 yards away from the Japs while medics steadied trays of instruments against bomb concussions. The operating table was moved each time the tent sprang a new leak. Utensils were sterilized in a bucket over a wood fire. Parachutes were used to augment the soggy blankets covering the wounded.

Doctors who had to work at top speed all day could get no rest at night while the ceaseless fighting went on around them. One doctor, just before the Japs started up the second night, wiped sweat from his face and said: "If those bastards get in here and ruin what equipment we have, I'm going to be really annoyed."

On the morning of the third day, a concerted sigh that should have been heard in Australia went up from Momote airstrip as the first LST stuck its ugly snout through the narrow passage into Hyane Harbor, deck guns blazing into Jap positions ashore.

Battle-weary GIs laughed and hammered each other on the shoulders as the LSTs grated into shore to the accompanying roar of B-25s flying in over the Jap-held coconut groves.

When the LSTs started to unload, a lone Zero flashed over and zoomed away again as everything aboard and ashore turned loose at him. It was the first Jap plane any of us had seen over here.

The Army had come to stay five hours after the first LST opened its cavernous mouth. Food, heavy guns, fresh troops and thousands of rounds of ammunition crowded the beach area, which had been cleared by bulldozers What had begun as a "reconnaissance in force" was now being developed into complete occupation. The beachhead no longer depended on the .50-caliber machine guns and K rations that had come ashore with the 5th Regiment, 1st Cavalry Division.

The outfit had learned quickly. As one muddy, exhausted GI said: "Well, we was rarin' to get in there, so I guess we got what we come for."

"The count is now 2 and 3 on Lombardi and the crowd is going wild."—Pfc. H. N. Carlson, Truax Field, Wis.

PICNIC AT SANSAPOR

By Sgt. CHARLES PEARSON

SANSAPOR, NETHERLANDS NEW GUINEA [By Cable]— If there had been some ice cream around, the invasion of Cape Sansapor would have been a picnic. It was a surprise landing. Instead of warships plastering the beach to clear the way for the invasion craft, LCVPs chugged in unescorted, hoping there would be no one ashore besides the usual hermit crabs.

The infantrymen poured out on the beach and nothing happened. No one shot at them and no one ran away from them. There just wasn't anyone there. Wave after wave came in and disappeared in the jungle. LCIs and troops proceeded up the beach. It was Sunday morning with the sun shining and no shot fired. A soldier wiped the sweat off his face and said: "Well, why don't we choose up sides?"

Two and a half miles offshore was Amsterdam Island and two miles farther out, Middleburg Island. A company in buffaloes went to Amsterdam and a platoon occupied Middleburg. There were no Japs on either island.

Back on the beach, GIs speculated on the whereabouts of the next landing, gambled with *guilders* and discussed women. A photographer walked by.

Up on the left flank, a machine gun opened fire suddenly, followed by a few bursts of rifles and tommy guns. There was no answering Jap fire at all. "Someone saw a rabbit," a soldier said by way of explanation.

Two young natives came up the beach and were chased into the water by a small barking puppy. Some ducks and trucks were using the beach for a highway. Five photographers strolled past.

A small force moving up the right flank to the river passed through a native village, and 10 minutes later all the natives were smoking American cigarettes.

Back at the landing point a whole platoon of photographers went by. There wasn't much of a battle but it was getting a lot of attention.

Cats and bulldozers were building roads and clearing the ground. Ack-ack guns were in position. A small fellow went past with a large white sign lettered in blue: TO LATRINE. The beachhead was civilized now.

Next morning a force left Sansapor beach in LCMs and headed up the coast to a small settlement, evidently used by the Japs as a barge-relay station. The landing was made a mile and a half to the left of the village. Like the first landing, there were no shots fired. Part of the infantry started for the jungle trail and the rest headed up the beach.

There's a peculiar thing about infantrymen. Whenever they march in, there's always some madman at the head of the column with a seven-foot stride, and everyone in the second half of the column puffs and sweats. It was like that here. As the force approached the village it slowed down and advanced cautiously. The precaution was unnecessary since a rooster, a hen and a pig in the village offered no resistance. The rooster was killed, the hen was captured, and the pig escaped.

We found the village clean and in good order. The Japs who had been living there had scrubbed out the place before leaving. They left practically nothing of value or interest behind. The huts were set in around coconut palms and some banana, breadfruit, kapok and lemon trees. Flowers, red hibiscus and frangipanni were everywhere, and it was the kind of place some bum who had never been there would describe as a tropical paradise. The heat was stifling.

There had been no air attacks thus far, and there was little likelihood that the Japs, who had been in the place and taken a powder, would return. All in all it was a cheap victory. No one was sorry about that.

This was not the first action for the troops who took Cape Sansapor. They had fought in earlier New Guinea battles where the going was really tough. The surprise landing probably was more of a surprise to these infantrymen than to anyone else.

The operation will never be made into a movie starring Dorothy Lamour. It undoubtedly will not make everyone forget about a second front. But it does bring us 200 miles closer to the Philippines and the Japanese jackpot. At the moment that's the general idea behind all our movements in this theater.

WHY OLD SOLDIERS NEVER DIE

By Sgt. BURTT EVANS

WITH THE FIFTH ARMY IN ITALY—The infantrymen of a rifle platoon crouch miserably behind an embankment, getting scant protection from the morning rain that beats down endlessly upon the bleak Italian countryside. The platoon sergeant, a stocky, weather-beaten young Texan with a handle-bar mustache and deep-set eyes, strides up purposefully.

"Well, we're attacking," he announces, in a tone that is not without challenge.

The new men, replacements, fumble as they fasten hand grenades to their ammunition belts, their eyes grown big and their helmets dripping.

The old men curse the rain.

The platoon moves out.

Nine hours later—one knoll, two pillboxes, five machine-gun nests and 30 dead Germans closer to Rome—the platoon sergeant crawls and slithers from cover to cover, checking his outposts and reorganizing his gun positions for the night.

Counting noses, he notes something that never fails to interest him, although it has long since ceased to surprise him: the old soldiers, with one wounded exception, are all present; the new replacements, on the other hand, have suffered nearly 50 percent casualties or missing.

"Old soldiers never die," the experienced infantrymen say. "The same old men always come back. Luck stays with them."

But is it luck? Or instinct? Or experience?

To get the answer, YANK went to the men of the 36th (Texas) Division, the tough Infantry outfit that has borne much of the bitter brunt of the Italian fight ever since it first waded in under withering fire at Salerno. As everyone from the company commander to the sorriest yardbird will admit, the platoon sergeant is usually the key man in any line action. So YANK had a get-together in a field tent one afternoon with six battle-tested platoon sergeants, two from each of the division's regiments.

Six more combat-wise soldiers could hardly have been chosen. Nearly every one had the Purple Heart; one had been wounded four times. Several had Silver Stars; one had the Distinguished Service Cross. None of the sergeants knew any of the others, but each had an instant respect for the others' experience and abilities. These were "whole" men, physically and mentally—men who had survived the most trying ordeals that war could offer and who had emerged with confidence in the ability of the intelligent foot soldier to take care of himself.

Priding themselves on being soldiers, in the finest sense of the word, they were natural, surprisingly articulate, unassuming leaders with the rough edges somehow worn off by what they had undergone. ("The loud, tough guys in the States turn out to be the weak sisters over here," one said.) Their impromptu discussion offers the American soldier some front-line pointers that may save his life.

"The first mistake recruits make under fire," began T/Sgt. Harry R. Moore, rifle platoon sergeant from Fort Worth, Tex., "is that they freeze and bunch up. They drop to the ground and just lie there; won't even fire back. I had one man just lie there while a German came right up and shot him. He still wouldn't fire back."

"That's right," said T/Sgt. William C. Weber of St. Marys, Pa., another rifle platoon sergeant. "When a machine gun opens up, the new men squat right where they are. The same way when flares drop and bombs 'baroom' down at night. The old man dives for cover. He doesn't stay out where he's exposed."

"They're scared of tracers, too," put in T/Sgt. David H. Haliburton of Ballinger, Tex., rifle platoon leader. "Me, I like to see tracers."

"Jerry fires lots of tracers," said Bill Weber. "He has a trick with tracers. Jerry has one gun shootin' tracers up high. Then he has other guns shootin' grazing fire."

"At the Rapido some replacements couldn't tell the difference between our fire and Jerry's," commented Moore. "And they were scared of Jerry's machine pistol. It's not accurate at all. If it doesn't get you in the first minute, don't worry about it. Its first four to six shots are the only ones that count."

"The Germans don't try for accuracy in small-arms fire," said Ed M. Taylor of El Paso, Tex., sergeant of an 81-mm mortar platoon. "They spray and try for a high concentration of fire."

"I got four machine-pistol shots placed an inch apart in my sleeve there," said Moore, holding out his right arm. "But that was an accident. I still don't think the machine pistol is accurate."

"The machine pistol goes 'bzt'—like ripping a piece of cloth fast," said Weber. "When you hear a sharp crack over your head like popcorn, or just like a bullet going through a target on the rifle range, that's the time to duck. Don't worry about the sniper who hits around your legs. The guy to fear is the one who puts a shot close to your ear—ping! He has telescopic sights."

"That's another thing," said Moore. "This Army doesn't use enough snipers. We need more Springfield-'03 men with telescopic sights. We could easily have killed six Germans on the Rotondo if we'd had a sniper. They walked right through our front lines."

"What do you think of the M1?" asked Taylor.

"It's wonderful," replied Moore. "It will take all kinds of dirty treatment and still fire when you need it. But I don't like the carbine. You can't trust it; three little grains of sand will stop one up."

"The Germans counterattacked early one morning, and my men came to me and said their M1 rifles were frozen tighter than a by-god," said Sgt. Haliburton. "They asked me what to do. 'Hell,' I said, 'urinate on the sonuvabitches.' It didn't smell so good after firing a couple of hours, but it saved our lives."

"If you could have only one weapon, what would you take?" asked Taylor.

"The BAR," three men answered simultaneously.

"But that bipod is useless," said Moore. "We've never yet had a chance to set it up. And it's heavy and catches on things on patrols. While I'm mentioning it, I wish they'd get rid of that stacking swivel on the rifle. It's always catching on something."

"That goes for the T on the shovel, too," said Taylor. "I've sawed mine off short. Of course, you don't need a shovel. The pick is the most valuable tool we've got."

Everyone agreed to that.

"There's a trick to this digging," said Haliburton. "None of the new men dig deep enough or quick enough. Incidentally, we don't have foxholes any more—we have fighting holes. They're six feet deep, and the step goes down to four feet."

"I've seen a lot of men die because they didn't dig their holes deep enough," said Taylor. "Most of them were crushed in tank attacks. Ninety-five percent of the men in my company are alive today because they dug down the full six feet."

For the first time S/Sgt. Manuel S. (Ugly) Gonzales of Fort Davis, Tex., spoke up. At Salerno Gonzales, the most popular and quietest man in his outfit, single-handedly knocked out four German machine guns, one mortar and one German 88-mm gun, going through machine-gun fire that came so close it set fire to his pack. He's been recommended for the Congressional Medal.

"Two of our men were killed in their foxholes,"
Ugly Gonzales said. "You know we usually have two men to a hole on an outpost, one on guard and one asleep. Well, for some reason I can't figure out, Americans like to sleep with a blanket or a pack *over* their heads. Why one was sleeping instead of being on guard I don't know, but when we checked up in the morning, we found their bodies bayoneted right through the blankets. They never knew what got them."

"Some of the boys just don't have common sense," said Weber. "They seem to expect the Army to think for them. When you're under fire, you've got to think six ways from Sunday."

"Why, the Germans were climbing out of their foxholes and retreating," said Haliburton, "and some of my new men didn't know what to do about it. They just lay there. They could have moved two feet, for a better range of fire, and knocked the whole outfit out."

"Sometimes they don't even know the man beside them or where he is," Taylor added angrily. "After we'd had one bunch of boys 12 days, they didn't even know their own squad leader. Now every man has his name taped on his helmet."

"It's important for men to train together and to know each other," said Haliburton. "If I want to take out a patrol and don't know who to take, I'd rather go alone. You've got to know your men. I don't eat first—I eat with them. There are two kinds of boys, I've found out—the ones you can pat on the back and those you have to keep after."

"I never like to take more than three men with me on reconnaissance patrol," said Gonzales. "One man can give you away if he doesn't know how to pick up his feet and walk on grass and rocks. First thing you know Jerry comes out of a ditch with that machine pistol ready to turn and shoot. He has that long baseball cap on. Man, that's when you'd better have your tommy gun on full automatic."

"That's another thing," Moore added. "Many of the new men we get have never had any night work. They're blind; a couple get lost every night. Why, I've seen boys fall off in a ditch in the dark and break their legs. They're used to flashlights. You couldn't give me a flashlight."

"They're too loose on the men in the States," T/Sgt. James H. Arnold of Killeen, Tex., said: "Ten-minute breaks, go to town every night—they'll never get in shape that way. And they never ought to have a dry run. They ought to fire every weapon, and there ought to be tin-can rifle ranges around every Army post where the men could practice in their spare time."

"They ought to learn to shoot from the hip in a

hurry," Taylor agreed. "And we get men who are supposed to be qualified with mortars who have never fired more than two rounds. You can't sense how to fire a mortar just by mounting it. At Salerno we had two boys who had fired their mortar often and had lived with it. They could put a mortar shell anywhere they wanted to, but they were the only ones who could."

"What kind of gun emplacements do you use for heavy weapons and machine guns?" asked Haliburton.

"We use a four-foot-deep emplacement for a mortar," Arnold replied. "We've never been where we could dig one, though. We pile up rocks."

"You can dig an emplacement by blasting during a barrage," said Taylor. "We've often done that. But men ought to be trained to set up guns on all kinds of terrain."

"You know what I think?" Haliburton asked. "I think we tend to keep our machine guns up too close. The weapons platoon tries to go right up with the rifle platoons. We've had machine guns knocked out by mortars, and sometimes our machine guns get pinned down when they stay up with us. The heavy weapons should be in support, in back of us shooting over our heads. You've got to guard against the tendency of the American heavy weapons to move right up."

"That's the American's worst fault," said Moore. "He's just like a turkey. He wants to see what's on the other side of the log."

"One thing I wish you heavy-weapons men would do," commented Haliburton, the rifle platoon sergeant. "When you fire, always judge over, never short." Haliburton was deadly serious, and nobody laughed at what might have seemed a dry joke in other circumstances.

"Our 60-mm mortars and even our 81s are usually stuck out singly," said Taylor. "They should be in a battery."

All agreed.

"One thing we haven't mentioned is the rifle grenade launcher," said Moore. "That's one of our best weapons. It will break up an attack every time."

"Hand grenades, too," put in Haliburton. "New men are always afraid of them. At Salerno some men had them taped up so tight they couldn't use them. One thing that's needed is a better place to carry grenades. If you hang them on your ammunition belt, they get in your way when you're crawling along the ground. What we do is to have pockets sewed in our combat suits for them."

"Fragmentation grenades, you mean, of course," said Weber, "or maybe white-phosphorous gre-

nades. Concussion grenades are handy only in street fighting."

"The most valuable thing I learned in training was how to lob a grenade," said Moore. "You have to lob them correctly. You can't get any distance if you throw them like baseballs. It takes experience to knock out a pillbox at 25 yards from a prone position."

"They taught us some useless things, though," said Arnold. "For instance, we never use a rifle sling, except maybe to carry it. And we don't fasten the chin straps under our helmets for fear of concussion. And we can't be bothered with packs. What do you usually carry into action?"

"All I ever take," said Weber, "is a raincoat, a rifle and rifle belt, all the ammunition and hand grenades I can carry, a pick, one K ration and a canteen. About that canteen, incidentally, water discipline has never been stressed enough. When our whole battalion was cut off for three days at Mount Maggiore, the new men almost died of thirst. We caught some water in C-ration cans and helmets. They tried to drop rations to us by plane, but most of them fell in enemy territory. The boys got tired of staying in their holes, but I threatened to shoot the first one who stuck his head out. When we were in the mountains you'd be surprised at how many men would beg me to let them make the long, dangerous haul down and back for rations at night, just for the exercise."

"There are three damned important points for replacements to remember," summed up Moore. "First, dig deep fighting holes. Second, learn how to take care of yourself, particularly how to be silent on patrols. Third, know your weapons. We've had BAR men who don't know how to fix stoppages. Some guys expect to pick up a new gun from a casualty whenever they need it. They must think it's a gold mine up front. When you need a gun, it's not there. You can count on that."

"Just one more thing," said Gonzales. "Keep out of draws. Jerry has his mortars zeroed in on them."

THE POET'S CORNERED

LITANY FOR HOMESICK MEN

BY CPL. HARGIS WESTERFIELD
New Guinea

A litany for all men homesick:
For all men crying sick
In all camps over all America
And too far away across the waters
For even the furloughs we yearn about,
In a circle under the one dim bulb
In the barracks.

A litany for all men:
Those who dream at night of home
Before battle-dawn and the bombers rising;
And those with too much time to think
Here in the humdrum barracks,
Training finished and waiting for shipment,
With MPs at the gates; and those
Behind electric wires with the jaded guards.
Japanese or German, hoping to shoot
When they cross the dead line.

A litany of all our longings,
Walled in overweight khaki
Or turreted in the nauseous tanks
Bolted down for the break-through.

A litany of yearnings:
For the town we came from, Joe's place on the corner
And beer and chili and Cincinnati Dutch accents;
For the sickish ozone of the 6 o'clock rush
In the subway; or the Polish cry
Of the El conductor in Chicago; for the thick steaks
Of a little restaurant in DuBois, Pennsylvania;
Or the sleepy streets of Georgetown, Kentucky,
Walking into stone-walled blue-grass meadows;
For Memphis and the great bluff on the Mississippi
And the high woods of the Arkansas shore
After sunset.

A litany for all homes we lived in:
For the tall apartments in Yonkers with zig-zagged
Fire escapes, and round and rich with the Yiddish voices;
For the cabin in a Kentucky cove, puncheon-floored
And with a Spanish rifle won from another war
Gracing the mantelpiece; for the tall-gabled
Brick villa in the wide-lawned suburb.
For my own home, small weathered white cottage
On a quiet street in Bloomington, Indiana,
And a robin nesting under the front-porch eaves,
And a rabbit in the garden thinking it his right
To lop my tomato plants, and a great black table
With a line of my books on it, and Peggy my wife
To walk with on the back lawn among limestone walls
With twilight coming on.

A litany for all of us;
O words that bring back our homes for a space
And give us a quiet place for worship,

And peace in our hearts, after the cursing camp.
Home will always be with us, whether or not
We ever see it again, a picture in our brain,
Colors and odors and sounds half remembered.

When hate of an unseen enemy cannot hold us,
This homesick litany will lead us into battle;
For the homes we lived in once long ago
Are strength on the march and a steady grip
On the killing tools and a tried hand
On the poised trench mortar.

ARMY CHAPEL

BY PVT. DARRELL BARTEE
Camp Crowder, Mo.

The doors stand open for the files of men
Whose step is lighter at the Sunday dawn.
These are the ones who yesterday had been
All fierce and heavy with their weapons on.
They are the grimmest worshippers of all
Who come to sing the quiet songs today,
Who have the strident marches to recall
And who have knelt to fire, but not to pray.
Just what the troubled heart will call its own
And will remember from this steeled place,
If fully felt, but not precisely known,
And written only on the soldier's face.
It is a search for rightness, little more—
The strangest, strongest weapon of the war.

BUNA BEACH

BY PFC. KEITH B. CAMPBELL
AAFTAC, Orlando, Fla.

(On seeing a picture of three dead American soldiers on Buna Beach, see page 246)

Perhaps they struggled with geography
When they were boys, lisping the sinewy names
Of far-off lands they never hoped to see,
With thoughts intent upon their outdoor games;
The wild halloos and shouts of after-school,
A rag-tailed kite against a gray March sky,
And boyish laughter ringing "April Fool!"
When someone took their bait.

    Well, here they lie,
Three lads on Buna Beach, grotesquely laid
In the informal pose of sudden death;
While we, who live secure because they paid
In currency compounded of their breath,
Would hesitate and ponder on a scheme
To bargain interest to preserve their dream.

OBITUARY

BY S/SGT. FRANKLIN M. WILLMENT

Camp Gordon Johnston, Fla.

Under a friendly tavern spigot
Lay out my grave and write my ticket.
My life was raw but always cricket
And Bacchus my partner and guide.

This be the verse that you grave for me:
"Here lies a GI where he longs to be
With a flask on his hip and a blonde on his knee
And a quart of shellac in his hide."

TRAVEL NOTE

BY SGT. JACK N. CARL

Southwest Pacific

From London to Tahiti,
From Attu to Port of Spain,
From Bougainville to Martinique,
You'll hear a new refrain;
From Frisco to Pearl Harbor
The legend will appear
That during World War No. 2
Mrs. Roosevelt slept here.

ON THE MARCH

BY PVT. EDMUND M. ZASLOW

San Angelo AAF, Tex.

After the seventh mile the men
    Prefer the chanting of the shoes
To singing thrice-sung songs again—
    Too little breath to lose.

A mental song does just as fine
    To add some voltage to the chaste
Cadence of our marching line,
    And gives each man his taste.

Pete in the second section, last
    Platoon, squad number five,
Is beating him a rhythmic feast
    Of Dixieland jive.

Out front the right guide steps alone,
    Pivot of the column's tread,
Drawing strains of Mendelssohn
    From fiddles in his head.

Old homely hymns, tart ballads, blues,
    Songs of all times and recent date
Sung to the chanting of our shoes—
    Silent conglomerate!

And there's a private music lingers
    In the helmet of many a rover,
Of houses to be built, and fingers
    Ringed, when this is over.

IN MEMORIAM

(Freeman Nimhauser, killed in action)

BY PVT. JOHN E. BROWN

ASTP, Atlanta, Ga.

From pen to rifle
It was a long way,
From Greenwich Village to New Guinea
Yet it was the same.

Mourn for the dead who died in vain,
But not for him.

When the poems gave out,
When it wasn't enough
To sing of freedom,
He fought for what he wrote for,
He died for what he lived for.

Mourn for the dead who died in vain,
But fight for him.

NIGHT MARCH

BY PVT. JOHN ROLFE

Buckley Field, Colo.

Light, through the open doorway, brushed a feeble
    gleam
Of yellow on the night, and the boy stood
Square in its beam, shock-haired, bowlegged, dirty fist
    in mouth—
A stout, small silhouette against the glow—
Staring upon the road.

Clearly he heard
Through the soft cushion of the star-hung dark
The swift unending whisper of their tread, the rush
And pad of hurried feet, a hushed unease
Much like the rumoring of hidden leaves
Portending storm.

Clearly he saw
Their blackened shape against the lighter night—
The lurching packs, the forward-pressing file
Flung like a rack of angry summer clouds
On the horizon. And the boy felt
Quicken within himself the smoky thrill,
The formless, fearful joy that always came
When the sky cracked and blazed and the maniac wind
Beat like a flail upon the stubborn trees.

Not a star blinked
In all that quiet night, yet the boy knew
That on the dusty red-clay road which ran
Before the farm a storm was being born.
How great a wind would rise, how many towers
Would topple, Caesar's thrones and fasces fall,
How many hollow eagles overturn,
No barefoot farmer's boy might even dream.
    Nor yet might they,
Whose silent, purposeful columns in the dark
Were shaping fury that would shake the world.

QUATRAINS ON BRASS

BY S/SGT. A. L. CROUCH

Camp Shelby, Miss.

Rank Among Lieutenants
Proclaim the truth with flying pennants
  And nail them to your mental storehouse:
This thing of rank among lieutenants
  Is rare as virtue in a whorehouse.

Missing Link
  If you ask what the officers think,
    They'll assure you first-hand
  That there's many a missing link
    In the chain of command.

The Colonel
  In the Army, as well
    As the *Nut Grower's Journal,*
  They say a hard shell
    Protects the colonel.

Puzzler
Of all Army enigmas, one of the worst
  Is how ratings and ranks will be reckoned:
For instance, the second lieutenants come first,
  And the first lieutenants come second.

THE MOURNERS' BENCH

BY PVT. RAYMOND E. LEE

Alaska

The mourners' bench is full, and still they come
From neighboring homes or from some foreign shore.
The mourners' bench is full, and still it seems
There's always room for more.

What matters now the language that they speak?
What shape of nose, what gods, what hue of skin?
For by the rule of Death's democracy
All dead are friends, all fallen kin.

Here weeps a Russian mother for her son
Who died upon the charge that made
A widow of the *hausfrau* next to her,
And who can say these debts are paid?

Now listen to a Shinto prayer that pleads
For one who sniped ere Buna's ring was breached;
The while in Brooklyn silent candles burn
For him whose heart that sniper's bullet reached.

While in Berlin a new small grave assures
A child's peace from a Fortress-haunted sky;
And back in London one more woman learns
To count no more the bombers as they fly.

So goes the tale; from every land they come,
For sorrow's congregation knows no ban.
The mourners' bench is full; its crowded ranks
Decry man's inhumanity to man.

THE HEROES

BY PVT. RUDY BASS

Camp Reynolds, Pa.

Upon reading "The Mourners' Bench"

A soldier said: There is a mourners' bench
Where our mothers sit and share their sorrow
For our dead with German mothers—
A wailing wall, with Death a bond—
And little does it matter on which side one fell.

It's true, there was a time for mourning.
The sky was red. They burned the books,
The temples fell. Old men in prayer shawls
Were dragged and hung with signs: *"I am a Jew!"*
But no one cried. They taught their sons
To spit into a gagged man's face
Because he knew such words as "Freedom"
Or "Christ" or "Labor Unity" or "Liberty."

But yet no tears. The guns that held Cassino
Were zeroed at Madrid. "Sieg Heil," "Heil Hitler"
(Read "Theft" and "Rape" and "Murder")
Drowned out the cries in Holland, Poland,
Czechoslovakia, France. The Zeros
That stunned Pearl Harbor took their test flights
At Kholchingol. The grinning death
That jumped ashore on Luzon was rehearsed
With putrid splendor at Shanghai and Nanking.
And still no tears. The loving *Hausfrau*
Received a bundle; there small shoes, a coat,
Blood-spattered, fur-lined, warm.
Dear wife: Here are some things for Fritzchen.
But pigs don't cry. They grunt and swallow children.

Now Hans is dead. And Franz and Fritz.
And wreaths are hung, and now the cries and tears
And wailing. But the tears are cold;
They will not make the grass grow, and the pain
Is hollow and a wasted seed.
Are dead men heroes just because they died?
Are rats like warriors if they bare their teeth?

Let them die quickly and be buried quickly,
Unwilling graves in a sickened earth. But we
Shall waste no breath, no pity on them. We shall finish
What they begot and save our love,
Our heart for all who help us drain
Our world-land from this stench and filth.
Let those who learn to follow them be welcome.

THE DEATH OF PVT. JONES

By Sgt. Harold Applebaum

Camp Butner, N. C.

Let's say that Pvt. Jones died quietly.
Let's say that when the first wave stormed the shore
A single shot went through his heart, and he
Slipped lifeless to the sand. Not one man saw
Him die, so busied they with lying hid
And crawling on, yet all men felt the breath
Of leaden wings come close, and when they did,
It made his passing seem a public death.
So much for Jones. He died as one of scores,
And on a distant beach. But when they bring
The news to those who count the cost of wars,
A private's death becomes a private thing.
How strange that war's arithmetic discounts
The spread of sorrow as the sorrow mounts!

THE RECONVERSION

By Pfc. Edward Blumenthal

Fort Knox, Ky.

The man you sent off to war may be a problem for a while when he gets home even if he never left the country. That's the opinion of Col. William C. Menninger, chief of the division of neuropsychiatry, Office of the Surgeon General, who believes that many veterans are going to have first-class problems in reconversion on their hands. Some of the worst sufferers, the Army psychiatrist predicted, will be the clerks who became colonels and the messenger boys who became majors.—Louisville (Ky.) Times.

When bugles sound their final notes
    And bombs explode no more
And we return to what we did
    Before we went to war,
The sudden shift of status
    On the ladder of success
Will make some worthy gentlemen
    Feel like an awful mess.

Just think of some poor captain
    Minus all his silver bars
Standing up behind some counter
    Selling peanuts and cigars;
And think of all the majors
    When their oak leaf's far behind
And the uniform they're wearing
    Is the Western Union kind.

Shed a tear for some poor colonel
    If he doesn't feel himself;
Jerking sodas isn't easy
    When your eagle's on the shelf.
'Tis a bitter pill to swallow,
    'Tis a matter for despair;
Being messengers and clerks again's
    A mighty cross to bear.

So be kind to working people
    That you meet where'er you go,
For the guy who's washing dishes
    May have been your old CO.

FRANCE, 1944

By Pfc. John M. Behm

Europe is a quiet land.
There is something dozing
In the soil here
That all the noise and rattle of war
Will never awaken.

It is the sound sleep of the old philosopher
Resting in the shade,
The weary nod of the scholar
With the dusty book and the half-closed eye.

He has been everywhere,
Has seen it all,
And his taste for battle
Has long been satisfied.
Now he will not even turn his head
To watch these new warriors
Crawl through the hedge and
Die on his trampled breast.
He is not moved.

Listen to the earth call to us:
"Come back to your mother's womb
And rest a while."

And the nervous poets look
At the tired dirt
While the jealous claw
That holds them fast to the great root
Of America
Slackens its grip,
As if the journey was over
And this at last
Was perhaps the spirit's final sanctuary.

THE BEAUTIFUL RUINS

By S/Sgt. Charles E. Butler

Do not be proud that you destroy the cities.
Remember gardens shimmering in the sun,
Doorways in shadow and the peaceful duties
Of women there. If this is to be done,
Let it be done without the shame of pride,
That in an hour to come our unbelieving
Sons, judging us, must say: "The cities died;
Our fathers did this; but they did it grieving."
For with the cities die the guiltless dreams
Of all the brave, the innocent unwary,
Who long ago, pausing by unnamed streams,
Began to build the tall and visionary
Cities that were to be their children's shroud.
Destroying them at last, do not be proud.

LITTLE RED RIDING HOOD
A GI Bedtime Story
By S/Sgt. DON DAVIS
Luke Field, Ariz.

ONCE upon a time there was a little girl who lived alone with her mother in a dismal 30-room mansion in the outskirts of Los Angeles. This young girl had a red raincoat with a hood to cover her head and, since the sunshine in California comes down by the bucketsful, she often wore her raincoat and they called her Little Red Riding Hood.

One morning while she and her mother were having a glass of tomato juice before going to bed (they had just come in from an all-night session at a neighboring honky-tonk), her mother said, "Red Riding Hood, today I want you to take this quart of bourbon and package of marijuana cigarettes to your grandmother."

So that afternoon Red Riding Hood set out to go to her grandmother's house. She had to walk, as the local ration board only gave them an A card for the limousine, and that was just enough to back the car out of the garage, wash it and put it back again. The route she had to take brought her past the famous intersection of Hollywood and Vine. On the corner stood a brainless individual of the male species with a 1-A suit on a 4-F figure. He twirled his lengthy key chain as his fangs drooled and his eyes became saucerlike at the approach of our heroine.

As she walked by bubbling from head to hips with sex appeal, his lips puckered into a low whistle and he gave out with the all too famous "Call of the Wolf." Being a very innocent young lady, Red Riding Hood raised her nose and walked briskly by, paying little if no attention to him, but being certain to drop on the pavement a map of the city of Los Angeles with the course she would take marked in red pencil and grandmother's house labeled with a huge cross. (After all, men are scarce and one has to make the best of an opportunity, for it may only knock once.)

The wolf hailed the nearest taxicab and hurried to Granny's joint so as to be there when Red Riding Hood arrived. Arriving there, he found grandma in her silk pajamas trying to get some sleep after working the swing shift as a riveter at Lockheed Aircraft. He promptly gave her a quart of Scotch, locked her in the closet and took her place in bed. Soon Red Riding Hood tapped lightly on the door and entered. She took one look at the occupant of the bed and said, "My God, Granny, you look like

hell. You'll have to stop drinking so much." Then, as she approached closer to the bed, she said: "My, what big eyes, nose and mouth you have, Grandma. Don't tell me you have gone in for plastic surgery." Just then the wolf jumped out of bed and chased Red Riding Hood through the house. He couldn't catch her, however, as her dress had fast colors in it.

Luckily for our little heroine, just then the air-raid siren sounded and, since the wolf was an air-raid warden in his local area, he had to leave. Red Riding Hood was a nervous wreck and after he had gone she released Granny from the closet and they each had a straight shot to calm their nerves.

When Red Riding Hood returned home and told her mother how the wolf had followed her and chased her through the house, the mater sat open-mouthed with amazement. She promised never to send Red Riding Hood on a journey like that again.

"Hell," she said, "if that's the kind of stuff you run into, I'll go myself."

TWENTY-ONE DASH ONE HUNDRED
By T-4 JOHN W. GREENLEAF
Camp San Luís Obispo, Calif.

The old familiar Basic Field Manual, *officially known as FM 21–100, is no more. A new pamphlet "Army Life," fills the orientation needs of basic-training recruits, and everything else in the* Basic Field Manual *is either duplicated in other training manuals or is obsolete.*

Aye, tear its tattered pages out;
　Declare it obsolete.
All for the scrap drive's open snout,
　Rescind, destroy, delete!

What matter that this midget tome
　Was blueprint to our life,
Adviser, counsel, bridge from home
　To Army? Whet the knife!

Yes, abrogate, annul, revoke;
　Proclaim afar the ban.
Replace the Handbook? Heartless joke!
　It fears no mortal man.

It lives, in spite of protocol,
　Ingrained in all our brains;
Shot though it was against the wall,
　Its spirit still remains.

THE POEMS OF AN ARMY NURSE

BY SECOND LIEUTENANT ELIZABETH ITZEN

One week in POET's CORNERED we gave one writer all our space. What's more, the writer was an officer and officers are not usually allowed to contribute to this paper. But this officer is a girl, an army nurse. We feel the exception is justified. Her name is 2nd Lt. Elizabeth Itzen, and she comes from Wyckoff, N. J.

A PRAYER

Dear God—Please give me peace of mind,
And in my work please let me find
  some kind of consolation.
I guess I've put up quite a bluff,
I really thought I had the stuff
  to help them save our nation.
But now I find that I was blind
To all those things I left behind;
  And fully understand
Without Your help I cannot do
The many things they want me to—
  I need Your helping hand.

THE WHOLE DARN INFANTRY

"Good bye," he said, "And thank you, nurse,
This has all been swell;
But now that I am well again
They'll send me back to hell."

He handed me an old grass skirt
That he had highly prized.
"I know you had your eye on this,
It's a gift from all us guys."

"We're going back to mud knee deep
And cooties in our hair,
And any souvenir like that
Would never help us there.

"I hope you'll say a prayer or two
Not for only me,
But ask the Lord to look out for
The whole darn Infantry."

He turned and swiftly strode away
To join the other guys,
But not before I saw the tears
That welled up in his eyes.

I held the skirt in one limp hand
And watched him out of sight,
And thought of what a kid he was
And how that kid would fight.

So now each night I kneel to pray
And say "God just for me,
Please look out for my patient
And the whole darn Infantry."

TO SOME OF THE BOYS I KNEW

To you who flew so gallantly
We bow our heads in memory
And know at last that you are free
  from earthly care.

And so we're copying your style,
Laughing at each weary mile
In hopes that you'll look down and smile
  from home up there.

OFFICER OF THE DAY

So I'm O. D.—Boy what a job,
  My duties are untold;
I shall relate my troubles now,
  my tale of woe unfold.

First nonchalant and quite blasé
  a flyer makes the gate,
"You see," says he, "I'm all alone
  and looking for a date;

Fix me up—a little girl
  with eyes of baby blue.
Sometime when you're not O. D.
  I'll do the same for you."

Another man with peppy steps
  approaches from afar
The coast artilleries hit the deck
  and says he's up to par.

"I like 'em tall and dark and slim
  with teeth of pearly white,
Heaven help the army nurse
  Artilleries out to-night."

I fix each one up as they come
  in person or by phone
And out they go to dance or show
  but I must stay at home.

At twelve o'clock with light in hand
  I check each girlie in;
I chase the boys and stop the noise;
  The O. D. just can't win.

PERSONAL REPORT

My life consists of bully beef,
  Soggy clothes and wiggly teeth,
Gun-shot wounds and jungle rot
  and days that are so bloomin' hot
That even hell compared to this
  would seem a simple life of bliss.

ONE DAY WITH A GOLD BRICK

I starch my cap and shine my shoes,
Then off to work I go,
Across the red dust cow lane
Where the hot winds always blow.

My tents are lined up in a row
With painted little signs
Telling what I'll find within
The heavy canvas blinds.

My patients lounge about the place
Cracking jokes and such,
And doing little odds and ends
But never very much.

The sun grows hotter than a fire,
We sweat and talk some more,
And cuss the guy right inside out
Who started up the war.

Five o'clock rolls slowly round
And so it's time for chow;
The chow hounds get their mess kits out,
And exit with a bow.

And now the sun sinks slowly
Like a ball of angry red;
A cool breeze springs from nowhere
And so it's time for bed.

I go around and check each bed
With only half a will
To see how many angels
Took off—over the hill.

And so my day's completed,
And I will stroll once more
Back across the cow lane
Into the hen house door.

JUST THINKING

Parked alone on my army trunk
  —the girls all have a date—
I shut my eyes and make believe
  I'm in New Jersey State.
My trunk becomes a rocking chair,
  the lights are soft and low;
There's a fire in the fireplace
  with ashes all aglow.
Mother's baking layer cake
  the fragrance fills the air,
And Dad is reading politics
  and of the county fair.
A roaring noise zooms overhead,
  I wake up with a start
And return to earth and war again
  with memories in my heart.

SKYWARD A SPARROW

By Pfc. KNOX BURGER

Pratt AAF, Kans.

"Do you often get letters from young girls?" she asked.

The soldier and the girl were sitting on a couch in the shoddy hotel lobby, with the sun streaming opulently through the windows behind them.

"I'm sorry," he said. "I don't suppose I'm being very polite." He looked up from the envelope—there was a postscript on the back—and over to the girl sitting beside him, her black dress shining in the sunlight.

"Your dress shines in the sunlight," he said.

"Yes, I know," she said.

He opened the letter and started reading the second paragraph:

I don't know what it is. It's something that makes leaves turn gold in autumn and green again in the spring. It makes the wind sweep skyward a sparrow to see what man may never see. It is time caught between tomorrow and today, the time that never comes and yet is always there just beyond your fingertips. . . .

"What seems to be on her mind?" the girl on the couch was saying.

"Oh, nothing much." He smiled to himself. "The weather, mostly."

"Isn't that nice."

He went on reading. *Maybe some day, if I reach high enough, long enough, hard enough, I'll know. . . .* He skipped down to the end . . . *and you shall tell me of all the wonders, just beyond the stars.*

"What's she like?" the girl asked.

"Like?" The boy stuffed the letter into his pocket. "She's only 15. Let's go eat."

GUARDHOUSE BY MISTAKE

By T/Sgt. EDGAR L. ACKEN

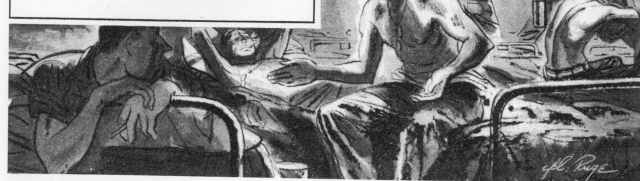

THE whole length of the one-story narrow stone barracks that served as guard-house dormitory hummed with conversation from the groups sitting on the steel cots, smoking and talking and occasionally horsing with one another. But Jake paid no attention to the others. He had a listener—bought and paid for with Bull Durham. The listener knew it. He was out of smokes and Jake had the makin's.

Jake waited until his victim had rolled a smoke and lighted it. Then he began:

"A frien'a mine come off a furlough an' tol' me. He says, 'Jake, I hear ya ol' man ain't feelin' so good.' So I says, 'What they do, catch him drunk and jug 'im again?'—jokin', see? An' this fella says, 'No, honest, I hear he's sick.' So when I hears that I goes outta the mess hall—I was doin' a week KP; that damn cap'n again, jus' 'cause I missed reveille. Anyhow, I goes to the orderly room an' sees the firs' sergeant.

"I tol' him how it was, how the ol' man was sick, had pneumonia or somethin'."

An accidental listener on the bunk behind Jake interrupted him: "Howja know he had pneumonia?"

"Oh, I dunno. Guess this guy tol' me or somethin'. Anyway, I tol' the first sergeant about it, and he tells me to see the comp'ny comman'er. So I do.

"Lotsa good 'at done me. The CD looks at me fishy like and asts me where the letter was. An' I says, 'what letter?' An' he says that letter that tells me that my ol' man's so sick. So I tells him how it was—I didn't get no letter, this guy tells me.

"He keeps lookin' at me funny, an' then he says, 'I tell yuh, yuh can't get no furlough unless yuh got

proof that ya ol' man's sick. Now if yuh wants yuh can go see the Red Cross an' get them to send a wire an' see if ya ol' man is sick. If they say so yuh can get a furlough.'

"So I went back to the mess hall madder'n hell. Here that cap'n wouldn't let me off jus' 'cause he hated me. My ol' man sick an' all didn' make no difference to him."

The second interrupter spoke up again: "Did you go ta the Red Cross?"

Jake turned. "Nah! Whatsa use? If he was sick the capn'd said he wasn't sick 'nough or som'thin'." Jake settled in a position where he could face both his listeners. The first one had finished the cigarette and had slumped on the bunk, now and then putting an interested look on his face. The second man seemed the more interested of the pair, and Jake concentrated on him.

"Anyways," he continued, "I got madder an' madder. There I was, peelin' them spuds an' scrubbin' floors an' washin' pots, an' my father ready to die. I didn' do nuthin' then, though—I couldn'. But that night I borrowed fi' bucks and got in a crap game and won 10, an' I took the 15 an' went to town.

"I had a few beers an' messed aroun' some, but all the time I was mad. Fin'ly I made up my mind. I says to myself, 'Maybe the ol' man's dyin' or som'-thin'. So I started out. I caught a freight up inta Kansas and was goin' on inta Colorado where the ol' man's at, an' then I happened to think maybe the MPs or cops might look for me there. So I gets off at Wichita an' gets a flop.

"Then I was broke. So I got me a job in a hamburger joint. I figgered on maybe writin' the ol' man an if he was all right, I'd come on back. So I work on there an' I had a little dough an' I was ready to come on back, an' I goes inta a beer joint an' I has a coupla beers an somebody clips me f reverthin'."

"Were you drunk?" his new listener asked.

"Nah! I had a few beers but I don't get drunk on beer. Why, I can drink a whole case of beer an' don' hardly feel it. I 'member——"

"What did you do then—after you got clipped?"

"Oh, I went back to the hamburger joint. I couldn't come back with no money, could I?"

"You coulda taken a freight back, couldn' you?"

Jake looked hard at his interlocutor. "You know how dirty yuh get on a freight," he said. "Yuh wouldn't expec' me to come back to the compn'y all dirty, would yuh?"

"Yeah," the other said, "I guess ya right. Got the makin's?"

Jake felt the wrong pockets first. "I guess I got a little som'eres." He found the sack and held it out.

The other rolled a smoke and handed the bag back. "Then what happened?"

"Oh, I was workin', and a guy gets flip in the joint. He claims I short-changed him. We has an agyment an' damn if he don't call a cop! The dirty louse!

"The cops take me in. Then they fine out where I'm from, an'—here I am. Jus' on account the cap'n hates me an' won't lemme see my sick ol' man, I'm in here."

"How is he?"

"Who?" asked Jake.

"Your father."

Jake got up. "I dunno, I ain't heard from him in a coupla years an' I never did get ta see him."

LIFE GOES TO A PARTY

By Sgt. RAY DUNCAN

THE ALEUTIANS—We seldom see *Life* up here. Mac got the June 5 issue after searching 30 miles on a dogsled, and he had to slip a native four Good Conduct ribbons for it.

Mac was lying on his bunk, reading his *Life*, while the rest of us stared at him in envy. Suddenly the magazine dropped from his grasp. He cupped one hand over his mouth and ran for the latrine.

I grabbed the open magazine to see what troubled Mac. It was a series of pictures called "Life Goes to a Bicycle Party for GIs." One page showed a movie actress welcoming five handsome soldiers to her house. She stood in the doorway, turned three-quarters from the camera, a position which accidentally showed her figure to advantage.

Then the soldiers and starlets went for a bike ride —and guess what happened? Ooops, they took a spill! Luckily the photographer was there with his camera when they fell. Things got even wilder back home later on, when everyone drank beer and cokes. "To make it a real Hollywood party," whispered *Life*, "they shot craps, played slot machines free."

That party happened some time ago, and maybe it's better that way. There are five men in our hut who hope to return to the States pretty soon, for the first time in 27 months. I hate to think what might happen if Mac, Slim, Vic, Fred and Tony were invited to a GI bicycle party.

"Say there, colonel," says this man in the check-ered sport coat, "how'd you and your buddies like to go on a party?" He steers the five soldiers out of the stream of Hollywood Boulevard traffic.

"I ain't no colonel," Mac begins.

"That's okay, colonel. Just hop in my car, all of you. My name's Flash Bennett. Have a cigar. We had five soldiers from the USO lined up for this thing, but at the last minute they had to go on a clambake with *Look*."

"Say, wot's the deal?" Mac asked. "Geez, wot house is this we're stoppin' at?"

"Just stand there in the doorway for a minute, all of you," says Flash Bennett. He takes a camera from the trunk of his car. "This is Beatrice Buxom, fellahs. She's giving you a bicycle party. Hey, close your mouths, fellahs! Now, smile."

Miss Buxom is wearing a very tight blouse, and her attractive midriff is bare. Behind her are four other starlets in sweaters. The five GIs fidget while the picture is snapped, then they crowd into the 20-room house.

"Say, nice of ya to have us over," grins Mac at Miss Buxom. "Got some music? Let's dance—just to get things started. Know wot I mean, babe?"

"Where's the liquid refreshments?" Slim asks after he and the others finish staring at the starlets. The girls retreat as the soldiers advance.

"Just a minute, fellahs," says Flash Bennett sharply. "We must get a picture of you boys dunk-ing doughnuts with the girls in the patio."

"Look, junior," says Mac. "Here's 20 bucks for ya. Go away with that camera, will ya? We're gonna be busy for a couple of days."

"Flash, who are these men?" cries Beatrice, retreating behind a sofa. "I thought you were bringing some nice boys over, like the ones we toasted marshmallows with for *Pic.*"

"Please, fellahs," says Flash. "I've got a cute idea for a picture. You're all playing Musical Chairs, see——"

"We just blew in from the islands, honey," says Mac, drawing closer to Beatrice. "We're lonesome, that's all. How's about you an' me takin' a stroll? You show me aroun' the place. Know wot I mean?"

One of the starlets, barricaded behind the grand piano, decides to try a different plan.

"So you boys are from overseas!" she says. "How nice. We think you boys are doing a grand job, and we folks here at home can't do too much for you."

"Well?" leers Slim.

"Are you interested in music?" she says hastily. "We're ever so glad that you're enlisted men, because we like enlisted men especially. So do the editors of the picture magazines. Officers are so stuffy, and besides it isn't the uniform, it's the man inside that counts."

"Come on, fellahs," pleads Flash Bennett. "We're all going bike riding, and I'll take lots of pictures."

"Look, junior," says Slim, "bike ridin' don't appeal to us. We came home for a rest."

"Hey, junior, take a picture of this," cries Mac, and he makes a dive for Beatrice. She screams. The other GIs all grab their squealing starlets and dance them violently around the room.

Flash Bennett grabs the ivory telephone to call the police. During the scuffle several GI shoes trample his camera underfoot.

"Stop!" A colonel steps into the room, hand upraised. "What is the meaning of this?" Reluctantly the five soldiers let go of their starlets.

"You men are a disgrace to your uniforms. Leave this house! I want your names, ranks and serial numbers!" But the five Aleutian GIs have already obeyed his first command, by diving out through the French windows.

"Beatrice," says the colonel, "aren't you through posing for those pictures yet? The four majors and I are tired of waiting outside for you girls."

FURLOUGH GREETINGS

By T-5 JAMES P. CHARLES

"My, how nice you look in your uniform. Stand over here in the light so I can see you better."

"So *you're* what's defending me!"

"You've certainly filled out since you got in the Army. You must get awfully good food."

"You may as well stay home nights while you're here. All the girls are either married or gone off to work in defense plants."

"How come you've been in nine months and only one stripe?"

"Gee, I wish I was in your shoes. They wouldn't take me on account of my eyes."

"You can be a lot of help to me while you're here. The cook just quit."

"I don't see why you don't write more often, with all the free time you boys have."

"You young fellows are lucky. If I wasn't an old man with a family, I'd volunteer in a minute."

"I don't see why you want to go out with that girl tonight. After all, we haven't seen you in six months."

"Why don't you and your wife spend your first night home with us? We can put you up in the living room on the day bed."

"I saw your old girl friend out dancing the other night. She was with a lieutenant."

"Why don't you wire your captain for an extension?"

"The Army will be a good thing for you. It'll teach you to obey orders."

"The trouble with this Army is, they're making it too easy on you men. Why, back in '17——"

"Would you like to ride out and take a look at the new Army camp?"

"There's a dance at the USO tonight. Why don't you and Sally go?"

"Did they issue you oars with those shoes?"

"How do you-all like it living down South?"

"Remember that fellow who was trying to cut you out with Mary Lou? He's got a job at the airplane factory."

"Aw, I'll bet one of those Southern belles has got you under her thumb."

"Charlie, dear, can I have your regimental insignia? I'm making a collection from all the boys I know in the Army."

"Gee, I think those fatigue hats are cute."

HOPELESS McGONIGLE'S BROTHER WINS THE DSC

By S/Sgt. L. A. BRODSKY

It is right after mail call, and me, Stripeless Murphy, and my main associate, Hopeless McGonigle, is reclining on our GI Beautyrests in Leaky Gables, which is the name what we give our home away from home for the duration.

I am just finishing reading a long explanation from a certain chick about how come she ain't home when I make a LD station-to-station call what sets me back a sawbuck to talk to her old lady, when Hopeless says to me, "Stripeless," he says to me, "I am puzzled."

This is a normal state of affairs, so I says, "What causes your puzzlement?"

"My brother," says Hopeless.

"I don't even know you got a brother," says I.

"I got a lotta brothers," says Hopeless, "because my old man is always unemployed and hanging around the house. But this ain't neither hither or thither, because this letter what I am in receipt of is from my brother what is known as One-and-One-Makes-Three McGonigle."

"So," says I, "what?"

"He is formerly in the Army," says Hopeless, "and he is now out."

"Why?" says I.

"I don't know," says Hopeless, "but in this letter he says something about street cleaning which he is getting for a reward."

"What you mean?" queries I.

"He got a DSC, what anybody knows stands for department of street cleaning."

"You," says I, "are a dope. Let me see the letter." This is what I read:

"Dear Bro. Hopeless," the letter starts out. "It is

a long time since I am having the opportunity to write to you a letter, because as you know, I am with a Infantry outfit on a certain island where we are very busy swatting mosquitoes and little guys what eight out of 10 wear glasses and got buck teeth which we kick out. The reason I got time to write is because I am now under the care of a bunch of pill rollers which is having a swell time putting me together like I used to be. I am all broken up following a certain thing for which I get a DSC and maybe even a Purple Heart."

Hopeless says to me, "Hey, Stripeless, see what my brother says about a Purple Heart? I am worried as I am thinking that my old grandmother, may she rest in peace, is dying of a purple heart and also diabetes."

"You are," says I, "a jerk. Let me continue this letter." I read on.

"So Bro.," continues the letter, "I shall tell you how I am getting busted up to pieces almost. It is like this.

"Last Wednesday I am sitting on a rock gnawing on my iron rations, when the lieut. comes up and says, 'McGonigle, I got a very important mission for you to execute.' To make a long story short I am getting a job as a advanced scout on the lookout for the enemy.

"So, I goes off into the jungle and locates a hollow tree what I climb into. I ain't in the tree no minute and a half when I hear two guys talking in a language what sounds like Donald Duck with static.

"Aha, says I to me, this must be the rats.

"I am correct.

"I peek out a knothole and I see two of these little guys talking and one of them finally goes away and the other climbs into the tree what I am inside of and he hangs from a branch and starts throwing lead in the immediate vicinity of the direction from what I am coming from.

"I don't like this situation on account of there is a couple of guys back in camp what owe me dough from last pay day and if they get themselves air conditioned by this son of Tojo I ain't never going to collect my investment, so One-and-One, says I to me, you gotta stop this guy from being a nuisance and perchance making null and void several just debts you got outstanding. OK, I answers me, and starts looking around.

"This tree what I am squirreled up in is very narrow and I ain't got no maneuverability with a gun, but the tree is empty all the way up to the branch on which the son of the rising sun is located on, so I crawls on up to the branch to investigate. When I get up there I find that I can reach out and touch the Nip on account of there is a hole in the tree.

"I start thinking. One-and-One says I to me, what are the brass hats always talking about. Firepower, I answers me in a flash. OK, One-and-One, I replies, you gotta use firepower. So I pull out a box of matches and go to work.

"Start at the bottom and work up is a good motto, I think, so I give this guy a hotfoot. I insert a match in the guy's shoe and light it. There is no response and the match goes out.

"You gotta increase the firepower, says I to me, so I inserts two matches and light them. There still

ain't no reaction. If I don't see it with my own eyes I would believe that I am dealing with a corpse as there ain't no guy what is still living that never jumped to a One-and-One-Makes-Three hotfoot. This situation is making me very angry. My professional pride is hurt. So I do something which ain't strictly ethical, but I am figuring that all is fair in love and war.

"I remember that the brass hats is always talking about strategy and attacking from the rear, so I take the packet of matches and stick them in the Jap's back pocket and light it. A merry blaze on the spot of the Jap's anatomy where the back goes off into the legs is the result. It blazes brightly.

"*Banzai*, yells the Jap and jumps off the tree.

"When I get down to the ground the Jap is got a broken neck and is dead besides.

　　　　　"Your Faithful Bro.

　　　　　　　"One-and-One-Makes-Three.

"P.S. When they hear about what I do to the Jap I get a DSC.

"P.S. Jr. The reason I am in the hospital is because I try to collect my just debts and the guys what owe me the money find out I am charging interest. The lieut. thinks I get these wounds in battle."

I hand the letter back to Hopeless. "Hopeless," says I, "a DSC is a medal and you should be proud of your brother.

"I am," says Hopeless, "except I am worried about that Purple Heart business on account of they put my uncle Joseph Aloysius McGonigle in the nut house when he said he had blue blood."

"Of course you realize you're out of uniform."—*Cpl. Bill Newcombe.*

I SHOULDA ATE ALONE

By Pvt. SEYMOUR BLAU

So you finally got here. Well, it's about time. Keeping me waiting in a restaurant since 6 o'clock. What's the excuse this time? You had to get a gun from ordnance? Well, Lucy's husband is a sergeant, too, and it's funny he comes home every night at half past 5.

Hungry? I'm starved. I shoulda ate alone but I always wait for you like a sap. What am I doing in this terrible town anyway if you can't even eat *one* meal with me?

What happened? Well, the place got kinda crowded, and a captain and his wife wanted to know could they sit here, so I said why of course sit right down. I figgered as long as his wife was along I wouldn't get into a funny situation with a soldier like you're always growling about.

Steak; I want a decent meal for a change. No, I don't care one hoot about the bank account. I always have to pinch pennies. You're 10 times smarter than Janie's boy friend. Why can't you be a lieutenant?

Shhh! Darling, please don't make a scene. This is the only decent place in town. Awright, awright; that's enough; I'm sorry. I think you're wonderful anyway. Love me?

Mmmm. This soup is good. The captain? Oh. Well, I know you never try to push yourself ahead, you dildock, so when we got to talking I tried to put in a good word for you. I figgered you never can tell who a captain is. I was only thinking about you, dear, and nothing woulda happened if you hadn't left me alone like that.

I told him what a good sergeant you was, always taking care of the men and lettin' 'em go to town all the time and everything. And how they like you, and——

Why are you stopping eating, darling? What else did I say? Well, I told him how you never made the men walk too fast on a hike and always gave them plenty of time to rest their feet an' all. Then the captain said sometimes the men have to walk fast, and I said my husband says the time to walk fast is to chow, and they laughed. His wife was the prettiest thing and so nice, asking me did I have trouble finding a room and all. They live at the Town Hotel and pay $25 a week and have to furnish their own sheets.

Huh? Oh, I said you were really the smartest man in your company and how mad you got when things went wrong at camp and if they'd only listen to you everything would be okay.

By now they were putting their coats on, and I thought maybe he could get you a good desk job on the post where you could come home every night like Sally's husband.

So I asked the captain couldn't he use a good sergeant like you in his company, because, I said, my husband says that if there ever was an awful jerk it's his company commander.

What's your husband's name, the captain asked me. Sgt. Willie O. Smithley, I said. Is that so? said he. Sometimes I find out interesting things about my men in restaurants. I'm his company commander. So right away I said——

Darling, what are you standing there like that for? What did I do?

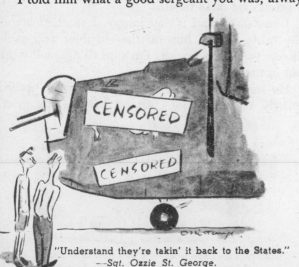

"Understand they're takin' it back to the States."
—*Sgt. Ozzie St. George.*

"Are you the athletic noncom?"—*Sgt. Ozzie St. George.*

TELL IT TO THE CHAPLAIN

By Cpl. GRANT ROBBINS

China

"Look," said the first sergeant. "Why don't you just tell it to the chaplain?"

I gave him the look I'd give to a two-headed thing pickled in a bottle, then I turned and walked out. When one has been in the Army for two years, at home and abroad, he becomes a little tired of the so-called GI slang, the oft-repeated phrase picked up in boot camp by a stunned civilian mind and dropped immediately thereafter—unless the mind remains stunned, as in the case of 1st Sgt. Stein.

I had gone into the orderly room because my name was not on a new rating list. My sad story has such a long background of pyramided woes that I shall not go into it more than to say that only a good heart-to-heart talk with someone would straighten me out.

All right, I decided, I *would* see the chaplain. Of course that interview required considerable preparation, like finding out which chaplain in camp had the highest rank, investigating the CO's religion and memorizing a few chosen texts from my Gideon Bible. It doesn't hurt to talk their language.

The following day I stood before the door of a chaplain dressed neatly in patched fatigues to give the impression of a poor but honest homespun GI.

"Hello," he said, eying me suspiciously as I closed in on his desk. "Have a cigarette." That wasn't on the schedule, but I sprung a text on him anyway.

"Chaplain," I began, "I was greatly inspired by the sermon you gave on the parable of the loaves and fishes at No. 4 mess hall last Sunday at 2 P.M. Right now I am badly in need of a rod and a staff to comfort me, and I hoped that you might show me how to find a place beside the still waters."

The chaplain winced. "What have they done to you now?" he asked. "And kindly make it short."

I sat down and let him have it straight. I went back to the very first—the double stretch of infantry training; the misassignment to mechanics school; the lost records and the three solid months of KP; the transfer to an outfit that didn't need men of any classification but guards; all ratings filled by men ahead of me; no furlough; one small stripe thrown to me like a bone to a starving dog, then held in that rank for eight long hideous months. When the torrent had subsided I sat back and searched the face of the chaplain for a reaction. He gazed at his feet and shook his head slowly.

"I just can't understand the Army," he said. "Now, take me for example. You may think that I am doing pretty well, but I'll tell you appearances are deceiving. After five country churches with an average salary of $10 a week, I finally get settled in a good town with a good congregation. And then, of course, I leave it to become a chaplain. Where do they put me first thing? Out on a sand-blown camp in the desert with a tent to preach in and a bunch of tank men who have no more inclination toward religion than an equal number of Hottentots. Then the wind blows the tent away."

I said that that was too bad.

"That was only the beginning," he continued. "Shortly after I experienced a slight success in bringing some of the boys into the fold, they put another chaplain over me."

He went on and on, from one misfortune to another, and as his story developed one could easily see that he and Fate were at odds, and that it was getting to be too much for him. Tears trickled down his cheeks and splashed off the bars on his collar.

Since passes were issued now only on Sundays his congregation had suffered a heart-breaking drop in attendance. And he had been ousted from his warm office to make room for the Red Cross. When he protested to the commanding general he was mistaken for a mess officer and installed in a cubbyhole, just off the mess kitchen, where from 0600 to 2100 came a heavy odor of frying Spam.

"And to top it all," he said, "I have not received a promotion in 18 months."

I couldn't stand it any longer. I reached across the table, patted him on the shoulder and said: "Keep your chin up, sir. I'm sure things will work out in the long run."

He smiled miserably and thanked me. I tiptoed quietly out the door, leaving him in his grief.

"Gorman would like to know if he can take his finger out of the leak now, Sir."—*Pfc. Joe Kramer.*

VALIANT ATTEMPT OF A CHICAGO TOVARICH TO UPHOLD THE TRADITION IN IRAN

By CPL. JAMES P. O'NEILL

TEHERAN, IRAN—When President Roosevelt, Prime Minister Churchill and Premier Stalin held their historic conference here, all the personnel at the camp were restricted. Cpl. Jimmy Martin, a sax player who used to give out with the dream stuff at the Sherman Hotel's Panther Room in Chicago and now plays with a Special Service band called the New Friends of Rhythm, celebrated his 38th birthday during this restriction.

Now, it has been Jimmy's custom to celebrate his birthday with two or three drinks and a nice dinner. "Never more than three drinks," explains Jimmy. "I'm not a drinking man."

Jimmy sweated out the conference and as soon as the provost marshal took the lid off, he begged a pass from his CO. The pass was only good for the afternoon, because Jimmy had to play a dance that night.

Cpl. Martin was the first GI in Teheran that afternoon; most of the lads were saving their passes for night work. In the first bar Jimmy hit, he saw three Russians sitting at a table and drinking vodka. They were two captains and a first louey.

Jimmy went up to the bar and ordered his usual light vermouth. "As I told you before," explains Jimmy, "I'm not a drinking man." Jimmy had the light vermouth somewhere between his epiglottis and esophagus when it came up suddenly and spread all over the bar. Someone had hit him on the back.

When Jimmy picked himself up off the floor, he was staring into the smiling face of the Russian louey. "Raasvelt—Stalin—good, yes?" the Red Army back-slapper asked. "Yes," answered Jimmy.

"Americans—Russians—good, yes?" the Russian louey said. "Yes," repeated Jimmy.

"You have drink with me and my friends to Tovarich Raasvelt, yes?" asked the louey. "Yes," said Cpl. Martin.

Jimmy went to the Russians' table feeling very fine. After all, it wasn't every day you had a snort with two captains and a louey; it wasn't every day the Big Three had a powwow in your back yard—and it wasn't every day you had a birthday.

The two captains were introduced to Jimmy. "A Tovarich from Chicago," was the way the lieutenant introduced Jimmy to them. The louey poured out four stiff glasses of vodka.

Jimmy tried to tell them he wasn't a drinking man, but by that time the Russians had arisen. "To Tovarich Raasvelt," one of the captains said. After downing the vodka, Jimmy tried once more to explain to the happy Russians that he wasn't a drinking man, but now the Russians were on their feet again. "To Tovarich Stalin," they said, and down went four more glasses of vodka.

From there on, they toasted all the Allied leaders, all the famous Russian battles, and then each of Jimmy's 38 years. "I wanted to quit but, being the only dogface in the joint, I figured I hadda uphold our tradition," Jimmy moans.

Late that night two Russian captains and a first louey carried a limp form in ODs to the camp gate.

"This is Tovarich from Chicago. He is tired. Treat him kindly," said the first louey to the MP at the gate. "He is good, Raasvelt's good, Stalin's good, everybody's good—good night."

Cpl. Jimmy Martin is out of the guardhouse now and back with the New Friends of Rhythm.

"I didn't mind the rap in the guardhouse," he says. "In fact, the shape I was in, I didn't want any of my pals to see me anyhow. But I feel bad about the Russians bringing me home; it sort of hurt our tradition. It's a shame I'm not a drinking man."

"He's been there ever since I ate them K rations."— Cpl. Jerry Chamberlain.

SUPERMAN AND THE ARMY

By Pfc. HAROLD D. SCHWARTZ

Britain

WITH bankers in banks, with children in the streets, with housewives, cops and undertakers, even with generals, the most vital question today is: "Where is Superman?" "If only Superman would come and end this war." "If only he would join the Army, the war would be over in no time."

Poor, dear, innocent people. They must never know. Never.

I was standing in line, the first line in my military career. It was at Fort Dix near New York City. I got to talking to this guy in front of me—a nice guy. He said his name was Clark Kent. He looked sort of fat, wore glasses and had nice curly hair. He had, to put it mildly, a strange taste in clothes. He wore a blue cape draped over his shoulders and under his clothes, as we later discovered when we stripped in the dressing room, he wore long red underwear. Some of the other guys slapped their wrists when they piped the red long Johns. In the raw he looked kind of big in the biceps. Glands most likely.

We got talking with Kent. You know how it is, sweating out a line; you talk to anyone who'll listen. He told me he was a newspaperman. Worked on a rag called the *Globe*. Told me all about his girl Lois. She sounded like a dope to me, but I didn't say anything. He had damn good eyesight. In fact, he could read even the watermark on the eye chart. He was put in 1-A. I didn't do so good, either. I was put in 1-A, too.

I don't have to tell you what the next few days were like. We learned to police grounds, tear cigarettes GI style and eat bologna.

When we filed in for our IQs, it was around midnight. Kent sat next to me. We got the signal to start, and I just about finished wetting the pencil with my tongue when this guy leaned back in his chair and said, "Finished."

They wanted to court-martial him right there for cheating, but they gave him the benefit of the doubt and marked him 110.

Next morning bright and early we marched in to be classified. Then it all came out: It seems this guy was *Superman.*

"Never mind your nicknames," said the interviewer. "What's your real name? Clark Kent, huh? Whatcha do as a civilian? Newspaper, huh? Can you type?"

"Listen," said Kent, "I volunteered for the Infantry. Look." And quick as a flash, in fact quicker, he was down to his red underwear. He picked up the building we were in and flew all over the state, pointing out all the spots of interest.

"Or maybe," panted Kent, "I could get in the Armored Command, as a tank. Look." And he went zooming down the road through woods, knocking down trees and plowing through barns and latrines. Then he stood in the middle of the rifle range, bullets bouncing off him like ping-pong balls.

The interviewer looked bored. "Got any hobbies?"

"I'm a crime buster."

"Reads *Detective Stories,*" wrote the interviewer.

"Listen," said Kent, a wild gleam in his eye, "maybe I could be a fighter plane. Think of the money you'd save. I'd be both plane and pilot." And up he went into the air. Looped, rolled, what have you. And fast. He grabbed a passing P-38 and pulled it backward, "Well, how's that?" asked Superman when he came back.

The interviewer took a drag on his cigarette and looked unhappy. "Listen, wise guy," he said. "We don't like rookies coming in here and telling us how to run things. We have plenty of good fighting men, our equipment is the best, but we don't have enough clerks. So that's what you're gonna be."

"Have a heart," pleaded Superman. "Make me an MP, anything, but gimme action."

"Next," yelled the interviewer.

That was a long time ago. The other day I got a letter from Kent. He's working at Camp Dix with a chaplain. He runs a mimeograph machine, turns out a daily sheet about the post chapels and he's sweating out pfc. Damn nice guy.

"He says for you to take the marbles out of your mouth."
—Pvt. Thomas Flannery.

THE COLONEL AND THE ROCK

By Sgt. BURTT EVANS

ITALY—Many Allied soldiers have reason to remember the huge Rock of Venafro, which was cursed from the Tyrrhenian Sea to the Adriatic and from Bastia to Cassino. It held up the advance of the Fifth Army for weeks and weeks.

To take the town of Venafro, you had to take the mountain overlooking it. There was only one narrow passageway up the steep mountain, and this big rock sat plump in the middle of the path. On one side of the rock was the mountain, on the other a yawning cliff. The rock was the stopper in the bottleneck. Any Allied soldier foolish enough to stick his head over the rock promptly got it shot off.

When the company commander first reported back to Regiment with his story of the rock that was holding up the advance of an entire army, no one would believe him. The whole thing sounded incredible: one rock causing so much trouble in these days of modern warfare, with its demolition experts, heavy artillery and bombers.

So the flustered captain went back to his company, his problem still unsolved, his ears burning from the derision at headquarters.

He called in his engineers. They studied the situation and inserted dynamite where they thought it would do the most good. The troops were drawn back out of harm's way.

It was a lovely explosion. Even in a land rocked day and night by the thunder of Long Toms, bombs and ack-ack, it was a pip.

There was just one thing wrong. It was such a lusty shock that it unsettled another rock up the mountain. This boulder came tumbling down and made the shelf more impassable than ever.

By this time more than a week had passed, and the best brains and highest brass of the regiment decided to see for themselves.

A major who climbed up to take a look got his helmet creased by a bullet. Still he ordered direct assault. It didn't work. Some Rangers were brought in. They didn't do any good either.

Meanwhile the Germans were getting more and more insolent. They were so close they could hear the Americans talking and they knew every man on our side by his first name. Frequently they'd taunt the GIs on the U. S. radio frequency.

Casualties increased. The Americans took to lobbing hand grenades over the rock, and the Germans replied with their own potato mashers.

And all the while higher headquarters was getting more and more impatient. It was bad enough for the captain to have Regiment and Division on his neck, but now Corps wanted to know what had stopped the advance. A colonel from Corps came up, huffing and puffing to blow the rock in.

He arrived in midmorning when everything was quiet. The sky was blue, the sun was shining, birds were chirping and all was peaceful.

This convinced the colonel that the whole story was a humbug, just as he had expected—and he didn't mince words saying so.

Then, heedless of warnings, he climbed up on the rock, farther than anyone had gotten before. Higher and higher he went, until he stood on the very top, erect and exposed.

"Why, you men must be crazy," he shouted at the officers who had followed reluctantly, a good 50 feet behind him. "There isn't a Jerry for miles."

In perfect English a voice at the colonel's feet said softly: "You must be new around here."

Smiling up at the colonel from little more than arm's length away was a German, pointing a machine pistol straight at him.

The colonel hadn't moved so fast since he had his pants shot off as a second lieutenant at Chateau-Thierry in the last war. The German soldier must have had a sense of humor, because he didn't pull the trigger.

Much later, after days had melted into weeks, the passage to Venafro was won at heavy cost by direct assault.

"You realize, Ludlow, this goes on your service record."
—Sgt. Al Jaffee.

BLOWN OFF THE DECK OF AN LST

By Sgt. JAMES P. O'NEILL

WITH THE SEVENTH ARMY IN SOUTHERN FRANCE— At H-Hour-plus-10, Green Beach was clogged with crawling trucks trying to get ammo and gas to the forward infantry elements before nightfall. When the first Dornier came over, a tired MP at a crossroad was helping to straighten out a Long Tom truck and two 40-mm ack-ack vehicles that were all jammed together in a lump.

The Dornier was very high and the ack-ack fell far short. The plane headed for four LSTs anchored in the bay. You couldn't see the bombs fall, but there was a moment of suspense and then flames started to spit from one of the LSTs. The ship wavered and moved away from the others and then it bounced against the rocky part of the beach and lay there. You could hear the explosions on board, ranging from deep heavy roars to shrill whining cracks and the crackle of small-arms fire.

At that time I was about 300 yards inland, going toward the front, but I headed back to the beach. It was good and dark, and I wasn't quite sure where I was. There was a voice yelling off to my right. The voice belonged to a man who was wet and naked except for his right shoe, which was torn to ribbons. He was Cpl. Roman Pietrazak of Chicago, Ill., and he had been blown off the LST.

Pietrazak was very jumpy, almost hysterical, but he said he knew where other men from the LST were lying on the beach. We decided to try to find a blanket for Pietrazak first and then go after the others. We walked along the beach in the darkness. After a while we made out the outlines of a wooden shack. I called out to ask if it was an aid station and a voice coming out of the darkness said yes. We headed for the voice and nearly fell over a stretcher. Now we could make out a lot of other stretchers lying on the ground. There was a GI wearing a medic's armband and we asked him for a blanket. We also told him about the other men on the beach, and he said they'd already been picked up. He gave us the blanket and Pietrazak wrapped it around him, and we went over and sat on a ration box. Pietrazak had calmed down somewhat, but he was still nervous. Finally he said: "Do you mind if I talk? I got to talk to someone. I'm too damned jumpy to keep quiet."

I said I didn't mind and Pietrazak started to talk in a rush:

"We were just getting ready to debark. All the drivers were in the trucks and half-tracks ready to push off. There were two outfits on the boat, a bunch of ack-ack guys from Anzio and my outfit of Long Tom artillery. I was on deck watching the landing, and a bunch of us were talking about how easy this show was compared with Anzio when the plane came over. At first we just looked up interested-like. Then someone yelled that the Jerry was headed for the LSTs.

"It still didn't seem much until he started coming right down our alley. Then a bomb hit and I was knocked under a jeep. Everybody was screaming and yelling and a lot of guys were jumping off the side of the boat.

"Then someone yelled that the guys on the tank deck below were trapped. The hatch doors wouldn't open and the elevator between decks had stopped. The bomb had knocked the power out. A little blond kid with blood on his chest and half-burned ODs started asking for volunteers to go down and help the poor bastards below deck. Fifteen of us volunteered. We had to slide down the elevator shaft. The tank deck was in a helluva shape. Already the ammo was on fire and there were many wounded. The explosions made an awful noise as they bounced off the side of the tank deck.

"A couple of Navy kids had set up a temporary aid station on the side of the deck. They had plasma, bandages and a few litters. We started pulling the wounded out of the vehicles and carrying them over there. It was pretty awful. The guys took it okay but they kept looking at the LST doors. A bunch of GIs and sailors were trying like hell to get them open. A wounded guy asked how they were doing with the doors and they said they'd have them open in a minute. We knew damned well they'd be lucky if they ever got them open, and all the while the explosions kept getting bigger and bigger.

"A Navy kid and I had pulled a wounded GI out of a truck and were starting to make for the aid station when the first big blast came. It knocked us clear across the tank deck and piled us against the wall. We could hear screams and now we felt sure this was the end. We picked up the kid and put him back on the stretcher and carried him to the aid station. There were a lot of wounded all over the place now and every explosion bounced them around.

"The Navy boys ran out of bandages and plasma. There was nothing to do with the plasma anyhow. Every time they would string up the hose an explosion would knock it down. The guys working on the tank door came back; they couldn't get it open. They said we might as well save ourselves.

"The blond kid gathered all the guys together and he talked quietly so the wounded wouldn't hear. I'll never forget their faces. They didn't hear but they knew what he'd said. They didn't squawk, just looked at us in a funny way.

"We started to climb the elevator shaft. Four of us were nearly to the top when a big explosion came. I had hold of the side of the shaft. I was afraid I was going to fall. A lot of men did and I looked down and there was nothing but flames below. The blond-haired kid was right behind me. He didn't make it. I finally got up to the deck and started for the rail and the most horrible noise I ever heard came over the ship.

"The next thing I remember, I was in the water swimming for shore. I could hear voices and moans all around me, and now and then shell fragments skipped across the water. Every big explosion would shake me up inside like I was made of jelly. I don't know how I got to the rocks. Three other men were there, all badly burned. When I got my breath I started for help and that was when you found me. It wasn't until I talked to you I realized I didn't have any clothes on. The last explosion on the ship must have blown them off.

"I'll never forget those guys down on that tank deck or that blond kid. Sometimes I wish I'd stayed with them."

I gave Pietrazak a cigarette and went over to the shack. While Pietrazak had been telling his story we heard someone calling for litter-bearers and it seemed he never would get enough of them. It was dark inside the shack except for the light of three candles on a battered table. Someone had strung pieces of cloth, OD shirts and blankets over the windows. A medical captain was working over a badly burned boy. I introduced myself and asked if I could help. "We sure could use another litter-bearer," the officer said. He was Capt. Bernard Cohen; he had been on the beach when the explosion happened and had started to take care of the casualties as soon as they came in. He had little medical equipment.

For the next three hours we brought cases into the shack and Capt. Cohen worked over them. Then we would take them out another door. Through it all the captain maintained a quiet, easy manner. The men grumbled whenever we stumbled in a shellhole in the darkness and dropped them.

Soon more morphine and plasma arrived and with the supplies came more medical officers who had heard of Capt. Cohen's situation. By dawn we had the casualties down on the beach and loaded on the LSTs.

Here the Navy took over. The last man I carried was Pfc. Harvey Low. The only thing Harvey worried about was his buddy. He gave me his name and told me what he looked like. "He was on the rail of the ship when I got blown off," he said. "I don't know what happened then. But if he's on here and hurt bad—maybe he'd feel better if he knew I was around."

I went looking for Harvey's friend but found out that he had not been reported. I decided it would be better not to tell Harvey about it.

Soon the Navy medics had the boys fixed on the deck of the LST. I saw one Navy man giving a transfusion to a GI. The GI had a cigarette in his mouth and was arguing with two other Navy guys about the superiority of the Army over the Navy. The Navy boys were giving him an argument. Then someone called, "All Army personnel ashore." The Army medics and Capt. Cohen made one last worried check of their patients and the doors of the LST closed. In another minute the Seabees dropped the pontons and the LST nudged out to sea.

"For mother's sake, Dad, try to behave ashore."
—Cpl. Ernest Maxwell.

WHAT'S YOUR PROBLEM?

NAVY NUMERALS

Dear YANK:

A lot of Navy men I see have little numerals, like "1" and "2," pinned on their campaign ribbons. I think they signify the number of engagements the wearer has participated in, but my buddies aren't so sure I know what I'm talking about. Am I right?

Hawaii —JOE CURTIS S1c

You're wrong. Those numerals refer to the kinds of service the wearer has performed. The Navy has four kinds of service: escort, submarine, amphibian and patrol. If a sailor served on an escorting destroyer during a specific campaign and his destroyer was also engaged in amphibian landings, the numeral "2" on his ribbon would show that he had performed two kinds of service. Incidentally, you won't be seeing them any more; the Navy has decided to eliminate their use.

MEDICAL OPERATIONS

Dear YANK:

Just before I got into the Army I thought I needed an operation, but my doctor told me not to have one because it would have after-effects worse than the ailment itself. Now the Army tells me I must have the operation, and when I protested, the Army doctor said I could be court-martialed for refusing. I don't think I should have any operation I don't need, and I want to know whether it is true that I can be court-martialed if I refuse?

Hawaii —PFC. FRANK G. PENDALL

Yes. AR 600-10 (2-e-9) states that refusal to submit to a dental or medical operation in time of war may result in court martial. If you really doubt the necessity of an operation, the matter will be referred to a three-man medical board, which decides whether the operation is necessary in order for you "to perform properly" your military duties. If they say operation, operation it is; and if you still say no, you may be tried by court martial.

REFUSING A DISCHARGE

Dear YANK:

What's my problem? Here it is. I was drafted in 1942 with a bad ankle. I was discharged with a CDD five months later. After being a civilian for only two months, I was drafted again. Now the Army wants to discharge me again; I have recently rejected two CDDs but I am up for a third, and this time the Army doctor tells me I won't be able to do anything about it and that I will have to accept the discharge. But that's pretty damned dumb. If I am released I will be drafted right away again, and I don't mind saying I'm pretty sick and tired of going through induction stations.

How can I stay in the Army, YANK, and save myself a lot of mess and bother?

Panama —CPL. ANTON LACHENBRUCH

If the Army doesn't want you, you're out. Your draft board might try to reinduct you into the Army, of course, but our guess is that it won't. Army physical standards today are probably at rock-bottom, and if Uncle Sam can't use you now, you almost certainly will be let alone from here on in. Incidentally, that must be one helluva bad ankle you've got.

FATHER AND SON

Dear YANK:

I've a problem that even Mr. Anthony couldn't solve. He wrote me and said to go and see my chaplain. Well, sir, it's this way. I met a girl in the States in 1939. She was living with a fellow, not legally married. In 1940 she gave birth to a baby boy, my son. But as I wasn't at her side, she gave the baby this fellow's name. Later he died. I was away at that time, too, and couldn't get back to her. Later she married, legally, another fellow. Then in 1942 this man committed an FBI crime. He's now serving his second year of a possible 10-year sentence. I've written to her, and she's willing to cooperate in any way to have my son's name changed to mine as I'm helping with his support. I'm still not married to my son's mother, and at this time she is living with yet another fellow and by September will give birth to his baby. Isn't there some way I can give my son my name without having to marry his mommy?

Britain —SGT. M. C. H.

In most states it is possible to change an official birth record to show the name of a child's real father. You did not mention the state in which your son was born, but if you tell your legal assistance officer he will be able to inform you just how to apply to the proper state authorities to get your son's record corrected.

RETURN TO OVERSEAS

Dear YANK:

I am 38 years old. They told me, when I was over in North Africa last summer, that I could get out of the Army if I applied for discharge before Aug. 1. I fulfilled all the requirements and eventually found myself hanging on the rail of a transport sailing for home. Well, YANK, when I saw Liberty's statue in New York Harbor—and I know this sounds corny—I got to regretting I was gonna be a civilian. And that's what I told my new CO; I told him I wanted to withdraw my application for discharge. He blew up like an ammunition dump. When the smoke cleared, I found out that he had orders fixed up for me to be shipped right back to the North African Theater—to my old command! At this very moment I'm looking at the transport that is probably going to take me back across the Atlantic. But what I'd like to know is, can this CO *legally* do this to me?

Port of Embarkation   —S/SGT. JOE MORTON

He sure can. Ours is the sad duty to refer you to Sec. IV, WD Cir. No. 10, 6 Jan. 1944. Subparagraph 2 says that any man 38 years old serving overseas who has asked for a withdrawal of his approved application for discharge after he has already been returned to the States will be packed off in the first shipment heading back to his old command. One of the reasons for this circular, the Army says, is that some GIs were using the over-38 discharge rule, not as a way to get out of the Army, but simply as a pretext to get back to the States.

LOST TEETH

Dear YANK:

Does a GI have to sign a statement of charges if he loses the set of false teeth issued to him by the Army? Some guys say you do, and I'm worried. While we were crossing on the ship I was put on a detail as a sort of "bucket brigade" member who passes cardboard cases down to the galley below. One wise guy threw a box at my chest and the jolt bounced my false teeth into the Pacific. It wasn't my fault, and I'll be one damned sore dogface if I am expected to pay for them.

Australia   —PVT. DOMINICK ATRELLIA

False teeth are not considered "property" in the usual sense of the word, and the Judge Advocate General has ruled that a GI who accidentally loses his dentures does not have to pay for them on a statement of charges.

ALLOTMENT MUDDLE

Dear YANK:

I have been overseas since June 1942. My pay was stopped in October 1942 because my mother was supposed to have been overpaid by the Office of Dependency Benefits. Since then I have had a few partial payments amounting to about $200.

Now the ODB has cut off my mother's allotment entirely. They have also cut off my 6-year-old son's allotment. My mother is 68 and in very poor health. I can't understand why I get no pay and why the allotments were cut off. I've tried writing to the ODB and seeing my first sergeant, but it doesn't do any good. What can I do to get some money?

Italy   —NAME WITHHELD

You'd better get used to living on partial payments, brother; you owe the ODB a wad of dough. ODB's records show that your mother has been overpaid to the tune of $1,292. Here are the facts:

In May 1942 you made a Class E (voluntary) allotment of $25 a month to your mother. Later that month you discontinued that allotment and set up one for $45. Your orderly room failed to notify ODB about your discontinuing the $25 allotment, so ODB paid both amounts through September 1943, at which time the $45 allotment was stopped. The $25 check kept on going to your mother until January 1944. A third Class E allotment, based on an incorrect serial number, was also paid to your mother from October 1942 to September 1943. Total overpayment: $1,760.

You made out still another Class E allotment in June 1942 for $18 a month. The ODB never paid this one, however, so in theory at least they owe you $468. After this is deducted from the overpayments, you still owe ODB $1,292.

In January 1943 you applied for a Class F (family) allotment for your mother and son, retroactive to June 1942. This allotment was granted, costing you $27 a month back to June 1942, so that for over a year your mother received almost $200 a month in allotments. The ODB says that your wife, who you say died in 1941, is very much alive and has applied for a family allowance, claiming that your son lives with her. Your mother contends that the boy is with her. Both claims are being investigated now.

Don't worry, though. Money isn't everything.

TIRE RETREADERS

Dear YANK:

I am going nuts retreading tires. I am getting stale and despondent. Only YANK can help me. You see, I have always wanted to get into the Infantry, and when I heard about that new *WD Cir. 132* making it practically mandatory for COs to approve any GI's request for transfer into the Infantry I rocketed over to the Old Man here. Smiling blissfully, I told him to get me outa this unit pronto. Shocked, I heard him say he wouldn't let me transfer, and yet with my own eyes I had read in that circular where only the War Department could say "no" on such a deal. YANK, it's up to you now.

Aberdeen Proving Grounds, Md.   —PVT. F. L. H.

Sorry, but we have to fail you. WD Memo. W615-44 (29 May 1944) lists tire rebuilders among the specialists who "are and have been for an extended period of time critically needed by the Army." The memorandum goes on to say that such critically needed specialists "may not volunteer for assignment and duty in the Infantry" under the provisions of Cir. 132.

CHANGING NAMES

Dear YANK:

The name. Just look at it! Can I change it, YANK? Can I?

Hawaii   —PVT. WOLWOFF ZYLBERCWEIGZ

Sure. But you'll have to see your Legal Assistance Officer, because authority to change your name is granted by the individual states and state laws vary. Generally the court requires a good reason—for example, "it is too long" or "people can't pronounce it" or "for business." To get your new name on the Army records, you must show your CO a certified copy of the court order. See WD Cir. 254 (1943), Sect. II.

GI "MINORS"

Dear YANK:

I enlisted in the Army while I was under age; I lied to the recruiting officer and served two years before I was discovered. The Army gave me an honorable discharge, however. Since then I have been drafted and am now nearing the end of my first "drafted" year. This, added to my earlier service, gives me three full years in the Army, but I have been told that I cannot wear a hash mark for that three-year hitch because I enlisted under false colors. I don't think that's fair. After all, I've done nothing I should be ashamed of.

Iran   —PFC. JAMES N. HELLER

According to regulations, service stripes can be worn by those "who have served honorably," whether continuously or not, and the fact that you were discharged because you were under age does not bar you from wearing a service stripe. Your discharge is an honorable one, and that's what counts. Refer doubters to AR 615-360 (39) and AR 600-40 (46-e).

SHAVE AND HAIRCUT

Dear YANK:

I have a very serious problem that I would like your advice on. We are allowed to go to town in fatigues, mixed uniforms and practically anything we want. But can we grow a beard? Hell, no. I have started one four different times. They vary in length from five to 15 days. About that time a shave tail that isn't old enough to grow a beard pipes up: "Soldier, I will give you 30 minutes to get that beard shaved off." What we would like to know is, do soldiers overseas have the right to grow beards?

India   —CPL. GLEN CARLSEN

That's a tough one. AR 40-205, Paragraph 7, says the soldier will keep ". . . the beard neatly trimmed." Looks to us as if you'll just have to hide in the jungle until your struggling whiskers get to where they can stand trimming. Even then it's our guess that most COs will insist that a "neatly trimmed" beard is simply a smooth shave.

Dear YANK:

. . . I prize my sideburns, but an officer just told me to get a GI haircut. Do I have to, YANK, when I see lots of guys with long hair?

Panama   —PVT. SIDNEY MILLER

That's a little easier. The same AR says ". . . hair will be kept short." No room for question there. Those sideburns must go.

DRILLING SQUARE HOLES

Dear YANK:

Ever since I came into the Army I've been plagued by doubting Thomases when I told them what I did in civilian life, and I know I've lost out on some good deals because resentful officers thought I was pulling their legs when they interviewed me for various jobs. So YANK, if you will please put into print that fellows *can* make a living out of drilling square holes (and that this has no connection with left-handed monkey wrenches or sky-hooks), I will carry your clipping around as official protection against Army wise guys.

Australia   —PVT. NICHOLAS KOMITO

Glad to help. As a matter of fact, there is a tool firm in Pennsylvania that drills square holes. A special drill has three lips, with the heel of each "land" rocking the drill so that it turns a corner as its lip finishes a side cut. The motion of the chuck enables the drill to move in alternate cycloid curves whose cords ——. But, say, this can go on for a long time. Suppose we just say you're right. Okay?

"I keep him here for slamming down the telephone."
Pfc. Aldo, Jefferson Barracks, Mo.

MEDAL FOR FROSTBITE

Dear YANK:

A guy up here, a private, was in on the landing at Attu and he wears a Purple Heart. Well, that's okay—or so I thought until I found out that he got that medal because he got frostbite during the invasion. YANK, I've heard lots of stories about GIs lining up to get medals from a barrel the way we sweat out servings of stew, but I always rejected those stories as some of Goebbels' wildest fancies. I'm still skeptical. Just what authority says that an American decoration like the Purple Heart, which is often given posthumously to men killed in action, can be handed out for—heaven help us—frostbite?

Alaska —PFC. J. L. HENDRICKS

AR 600-45, Changes 4 (3 May 1944) says that the Purple Heart may be awarded to personnel wounded in action, "provided such wound necessitates treatment by a medical officer," and defines a wound "as an injury to any part of the body from an outside force, element or agent." The word "element," according to the AR, refers to weather and permits award of the Purple Heart to personnel severely frostbitten while actually engaged in combat. Incidentally, severe frostbite is a pretty serious business and sometimes results in amputation.

CRAPS AND CONSCIENCE

Dear YANK:

I come from the backwoods of North Dakota. I had never seen a crap game until I entered the service. When I saw my first game back in the States I joined in, just for the fun of it. It came my turn to shoot the dice. I shot $5 and made an "11." One of the boys told me this was an easy point to make, so I rolled again. The boys all offered to bet me I wouldn't make "11" again. The sergeant bet me $10 I couldn't make "11" on the next roll. I accepted all bets on this "11" and made it—breaking all my buddies, including the sergeant. After reading the gambling articles in YANK, I now realize that "11" was no point to roll for and that I should have won my $5 on the first roll. I also realize that making an "11" on one roll is a 17-1 bet. So here is my problem. Shall I return the money to my buddies, who I now see were trying to take advantage of me, or shall I keep it? Oh yes, I forgot to mention that I can throw an "11" any time I desire. I learned to do it while playing parchesi back home in Ellenville, N. Dak.

Iran —PVT. J. H. R.

Why write to What's Your Problem? *Any guy who shoots an "11" anytime he wants to can't possibly have any problems.*

BENEFITS FOR GIRL FRIENDS?

Dear YANK:

I have a problem and any help you can give me in solving it will be plenty appreciated. But please don't use my name. Shortly after I was inducted, my wife and I agreed to separate, but we didn't get a divorce. Sometime later I started living with another woman. Of course, I'm not married to this woman, but not long ago she applied for and received, with my knowledge and approval, a family allowance as my wife. Now I've been worrying about this lately because I've got a good idea that my legal wife is going to apply for an allowance also. If that happens, what can they do to the girl friend?

India —CPL. O. T. R.

Brother, you'd better sit down in a hurry and write that girl friend a long letter. And the first thing you should tell her is to beg or borrow enough money pronto to pay back every cent that she has received in allowances from the Office of Dependency Benefits. Then she should send that dough together with a full and frank confession of her unenviable position to the Allowances Branch, ODB, 213 Washington Street, Newark, N. J.

What can they do to the girl friend? Mac, they can stuff the book right down her throat. What's more, if you helped her in the fraud, they can gag you with a couple of pages yourself. See Public Law 625—77th Congress; Bull. 29, W. D., 1942. Sec. 116: "Whoever shall obtain or receive any money, check, or family allowance . . . without being entitled thereto and with intent to defraud, shall be punished by a fine of not more than $2,000, or by imprisonment for not more than one year, or both." Sec. 117: "Whoever in any claim for family allowance or in any document required . . . makes any statement of a material fact knowing it to be false, shall be guilty of perjury and shall be punished by a fine of not more than $5,000, or by imprisonment for not more than two years, or both."

Come to think about it, mark that letter "Registered—Air Mail—Special Delivery."

FAITHLESS WIFE

Dear YANK:

I am enclosing the exact wording of a letter sent me by wife and will be ever grateful for any possible solution, for I have tried everything I know, even prayer. Still TS. Question: Can wife get allotment without consent of me when I have this letter of bad faith? Here are her words:

Dear Ahmed—The time has come to clear things between us. You will have realized, before now, that our marriage was a mistake. I beg of you to put an end to this mistake and get a divorce. I left your house this morning, because I didn't want to saddle you with the role of a betrayed husband. As a matter of fact, I have never been yours, but now I belong to someone else, and this finishes things between us.

I have grown distrustful of what is generally known as "love," for the feelings that have alienated me from you are drawn elsewhere, and I've got to obey the secret promptings of my nerves. I want to thank you and wish you well. I am going away. It makes me unhappy to hurt you, but you are so strong. I am still your friend, and perhaps the time will come when you can be my friend, too. I am taking everything except your clothes and the typewriter, and am having my friend type this for me, for you know I write poorly.—ELAINE.

Iran
                                        —PFC. AHMED S.

Yours is simply a classic version of a common problem. All the proof in the world that a soldier's wife is faithless does not change the fact that a family allowance is given to her regularly as long as she remains legally married to the soldier. If you are interested in initiating divorce proceedings you should consult your Legal Assistance Officer, who can give you information about the divorce laws in your state.

MAXIMUM FINES

Dear YANK:

I have been court-martialed three times in special court, twice for AWOL and once for assault. The assault was merely a tussle with another soldier. In June 1943 I was fined $30 a month for six months. On July 22 I was tried for the second offense and was fined $33 for six months. Two days later I was fined $33 for another six months. The court fined me two-thirds of my pay, but they have been taking all of it. Since June 1943, I have only received $10. This was when I was at the POE. What I would like to know is this: Is it lawful for the Army to take all of your money, allowing you nothing for cigarettes, etc.?

Guadalcanal
                                     —PVT. RICHARD MACK

The Manual for Courts Martial [par. 104 (b), page 96] protects a man from having more than two-thirds of his pay taken away at any one time. Moreover a Judge Advocate ruling on that question makes it very clear that a GI may have no more than two-thirds of his pay taken away through action of a court martial unless the sentence of the court martial also orders a dishonorable discharge, and you have not been dishonorably discharged. Refer your Finance Officer to AR 35-2460 [par. 5(b)], and he will see to it that you get the money that is legally yours.

MEXICAN MUDDLE

Dear YANK:

I'll start from the very beginning. I'm 27 years old and I entered the Army in '41. While I was at Fort Sam Houston, Tex., I became infatuated with a girl and went to Mexico and was told by a priest (or monk) there that we were married by him. I lived with her only one night. There were no papers of the marriage, and I did not sign any such papers in Mexico. I paid her no allotment till June 1942 when, unknown to me, she applied for allotment. OK. In June 1943 I again went to Mexico and got a divorce (so I was told), but not one paper was signed by me or anyone else, for it was granted by this monk (or priest, or whatever he was) in Mexico.

I went to my first sergeant in my last camp to find out about getting the allotment to stop but failed. You see, this 70- or 80-year-old monk (or whatever he was) told me I'd have to pay her alimony. But me going to all the trouble I did, and with no one who could (or would) tell me anything, I went ahead and got married to another girl. Now I can't get an allotment for my second wife because of this other mess. I was told the first girl was married again and living in Mexico—where I do not know. I don't even know what happened to her, but they have been taking pay out of my $50 every month. Now, if my divorce was not legal how can the marriage be legal? Also where and how and when did she get papers asking for the allotment? Please can you help me as I'm in enough trouble as it is and do not want to lose the one girl I will really ever love. Several people here are calling me a bigamist, and I don't think I am.

Panama
                                       —PVT. J. C. H.

Wow! Well, here goes. In the first place, as far as the allowance is concerned, that first girl was pretty smart, because she obviously submitted a marriage certificate of some kind to prove that she was your wife; otherwise the Office of Dependency Benefits would not have approved her application for a family allowance. In the second place, many foreign divorces are looked upon with deep suspicion by the ODB, and where there is not even documentary proof of the divorce (as in your case) the ODB would probably have to continue payments to the girl in Mexico. The ODB suggests you send full details of your case to its office at 213 Washington Street, Newark, N. J. Don't forget to include your ASN. As for the legal, social and moral aspects of your problem, see your Legal Assistance Officer. See your CO. See your personal affairs officer. See your chaplain. Quick.

FALL OUT FOR AN INTERVIEW

By Sgt. RAY DUNCAN

I'M KEEPING a scrapbook of newspaper stories about movie stars in the service. I suppose the rest of you soldiers are doing the same thing. If you can bear to part with any of your clippings about Hollywood men in uniform, I certainly would like to buy them from you. Or maybe we could trade duplicates.

The newspapers are doing an excellent job of covering film actor-soldiers. Only trouble with this kind of reporting is that there's not enough of it. It would be nice if similar stories could be done about all of our servicemen.

Surely there are enough good writers in this country to cover the activities of every GI in full glamorous detail.

Take for instance Floyd Pringle. He used to be pin boy at the Sportland Bowling Alley in Little Ditch, Ohio. When Floyd was drafted there should have been a story like this in all the papers:

LITTLE DITCH, OHIO, Feb. 21—He used to set 'em up for the Sportland bowlers—now he'll mow 'em down for the United Nations!

Into the greatest match of his career today went pale, slender Floyd Pringle. The idol of thousands of Little Ditch bowlers joined the United States Army!

Grinning happily as he reported for induction, Pringle appeared pleased when informed that he had been selected for 13 weeks of basic training.

The famed pin boy did not apply for a commission. He stated simply that he wished to serve in the ranks with the ordinary soldiers.

Flashing the famous Pringle grin that thrilled thousands in Little Ditch, he said: "Anybody who can dodge bowling balls can dodge Nazi bullets!"

Floyd Pringle awaited his turn in line at the induction station, just like everyone else. Everybody said he was a "regular guy" and a "swell fellow," and the examining doctor declared he was a "splendid physical specimen."

Think of the boost to Army morale if every GI hit the metropolitan press with a story like that!

Now suppose that our hero comes home on furlough from foreign service. Still following the model of the write-ups about the movie stars, the press would flash a story like this over the wires:

LITTLE DITCH, OHIO, Dec. 19—Back from the battle front today came Pvt. Floyd Pringle, his face drawn and a little haggard beneath its rich overseas tan.

The celebrated pin boy from this tiny Ohio town has been on a dangerous ammunition-supply mission in a combat zone, the nature of which cannot be disclosed.

(This is an example of tactful handling of mate-

rial by a skillful newspaper writer. What Floyd actually told reporters was this: "I am a basic in a gun crew and I have to carry the shells from the truck and make a pile on the ground. We never saw no action. We had a dry run every day, and the rest of the time we set on our dead hams." . . . Now go on with the news story.)

Pvt. Pringle received an ovation when he arrived at the Little Ditch station. Women on the street stared at him in frank admiration, and several girls made low whistling noises.

The Pringle charm, which brightened Sportland alleys for so long, has not been dimmed by the strenuous army training which Pringle endured without complaint.

Pringle has been on a dangerous combat mission in a war zone. He goes on all the marches with the men in his crew and insists on sharing every hardship equally with the others.

Reports from the fighting front are that Pvt. Floyd Pringle is a "swell fellow" and a "regular guy," just as common and unaffected as any man in the dangerous combat war zone.

Remember, a glamorous soldier is a good soldier. Why be content with your name on a billboard honor roll in a vacant lot? Why not sit down right now and cut a stencil, to be run off and mailed to every editor in the land, urging the full glamor treatment for all of our boys in the service?

"I'd like a little fatherly advice, Sir."—Cpl. Ernest Maxwell.

NOTES FROM A BURMA DIARY

By Sgt. DAVE RICHARDSON

BEHIND JAPANESE LINES IN NORTHERN BURMA—Odds and ends from the battered diary of a foot-sore YANK correspondent after his first 500 miles of marching and Jap-hunting with Merrill's Marauders:

Volunteer. One of the Marauder mules balked at the bottom of every rugged Burma hill. The driver had to coax, cajole, cuss and tug at his animal constantly. Finally on one hill the mule stopped dead and lay down. That was the last straw.

"Get up, you sonuvabitch," cracked the driver, who had answered President Roosevelt's call to join the volunteer Marauders. "You volunteered for this mission, too."

Unwelcome Visitor. When the Marauders reached the rugged hill country of the Mogaung Valley, their columns started to string out as pack mules tumbled off ridges and bogged down in muddy ravines. Frequent messages were passed verbally from man to man up the column to keep the point platoon posted on the progress of the rear.

Usually these messages were "The column is broken behind the —th platoon" or "Lost contact with the pack train." Occasionally, however, the wording was varied, with confusion the usual result.

One rainy night, on a forced march through enemy-infested jungles, a message was passed up the line. "There's a gap in the column" was the way it started. But when it reached the front, it had changed to "There's a Jap in the column."

The front, unperturbed, sent back word to throw him out.

They Satisfy. In an enemy supply dump we found packs of Silver City cigarettes that showed the Jap flair for imitation. The packs were similar in size and design to those of popular U. S. brands. According to the English wording on each pack, they were manufactured by the "Eastern Virginia Tobacco Company." And there was a familiar ring to the blurb: "Silver City cigarettes are a blend of the finest Turkish, American and domestic tobaccos, manufactured by expert craftsmen and guaranteed to satisfy the most exquisite of smokers."

Books of the Month. For weeks the Marauders hadn't seen a piece of mail or a scrap of reading matter. Every time transport planes roared over to drop rations and ammunition by parachute, the men sweated out a few books or magazines. Then one wonderful day after an attack on the main Jap supply route near Laban, the unit I was with finally received manna from the sky—an airdrop of books. Not many—just one book to a platoon. Eagerly we scanned the titles.

They were a "Pocket Book of Etiquette," "Children's Book of Wild Animals," "Boy Scout Handbook" and—last but not least—a "Rhyming Dictionary of Poetic Words and Phrases."

Poets: 1 Quick, 1 Dead. Speaking of poetry, they say that when a GI starts composing verses he's been in the jungle too long. The Marauders and the Japs they fought each had at least one jungle-happy poet laureate among them.

Representing the Marauders was T-5 Stanley L. Benson, a gun-repair man. Here's his first effort as a poet:

> Four thousand dead Japs behind us—
> A hell of a stinking mess.
> The live ones now around us
> Soon will join the rest.
>
> When Tojo gave his orders
> To kill us one by one,
> He didn't know Merrill's Marauders
> Would sink the Rising Sun.

(Benson took a slight poetic license in his first line. The Marauders were credited with killing 2,000 Japs in six weeks.)

The Japs' weapon in this battle of poets was a hymn of conquest found on the bullet-riddled body of a dead Son of Heaven. It doesn't rhyme in English, but it still possesses undoubted literary merit:

> With the blood-stained flag of the Rising Sun,
> I'd like to conquer the world.
> As I spit on the Great Wall of China,
> A multi-hued rainbow rises above the Gobi Desert.
>
> On the Ganges River at the foot of majestic
>   Himalaya Mountains,
> Sons of Nippon look for some crocodiles.
>
> Today we're in Berlin,
> Tomorrow in Moscow,
> Home of snowbound Siberia.
>
> As the fog lifts we see the City of London,
> Rising high, as the ceremonial fish of Boys' Day does.
>
> Now we're in Chicago, once terrorized by gangsters,
> Where our grandchildren pay homage to our memorial
>   monument.

Oh, governor general of Australia and South America,
Only in Japan sweet odor of fragrant blossoms per-
meates.

When I die I'll call together all the devils
And wrestle them in a three-inch rivulet.

I've set my mind on making my home in Singapore,
For there my darling awaits my return.

Mail Call. For security reasons the Marauders could neither write nor receive mail while behind enemy lines. After two months of marching and fighting, however, they were pulled back for a rest and got that long-awaited mail drop and a chance to write V-mail replies.

In a stack of letters from the gal back home, S/Sgt. Luther S. Player of Darlington, S. C., came across this remark: "I'll bet you're seeing plenty of action." Player's unit had been cut off for 10 days while the Japs shelled and counterattacked constantly. He answered his gal's letter as fully as censorship would permit. "Baby," he wrote, "you ain't kiddin'."

T/Sgt. Joe Diskin of Hoboken, N. J., received a letter from a pal who didn't know Diskin was overseas. Joe is a veteran of the first World War who's been in the Regular Army for 27 years and was sent back to the States from Pearl Harbor as "unfit for foreign service" because of 1918 wounds and age. His pal's letter read: "I am in Italy and have been in action. Believe me, this war is too tough for you old guys. No wonder you're back in the States." Diskin had just led his platoon against a fierce Jap counterattack. His reply is not for publication in YANK's sacred pages.

ROAD TO TOKYO

By Sgt. ED CUNNINGHAM

ON THE ROAD TO TOKYO—All that separated the bulldozer from Burma soil was a red-white-and-blue ribbon. Over on the Burma side, a company of U. S. Negro engineers stood in formation in the deepening twilight. A cold rain spattered the American flag planted on the dividing line between India and Burma.

When the 12-foot blade of the big D-7 sheared the tri-colored ribbon, Lt. Col. Ferdinand J. Tate's .45 blasted out a salute. The bugler sounded off with "To the Colors" and officers and men saluted their flag—on Burma soil 3,800 feet above sea level. "The Road to Tokyo" had passed its first international boundary.

That brief military ceremony marked the completion of the first phase of an engineering feat that rivals the Alaska Military Highway as the war's outstanding construction job. Carved out of the mountainous jungles of India and Burma, "The Road to Tokyo" may become the new supply line to China. Along the road may travel the weapons, materials and men for the coming United Nations' all-out offensive in Burma and China.

Starting in the Assam jungles in northeastern India, "The Road to Tokyo" twists up and over the foothills of the Himalaya Mountains to its first international boundary on the Burma border. Plans call for it to continue on across many more miles of mountains and jungles to meet the old Burma Road, still in Japanese possession. Much of the area

between the Burma border and the Burma Road is also in enemy hands. Chinese, British and American troops must drive back the Japs before a junction of "The Road to Tokyo" with the old Burma Road can be effected.

Officially, the new military highway from India to China is not known as "The Road to Tokyo." That's just what it was christened by the hard-working Negro engineer regiments that hewed it out of solid rock-masses 100 yards long and carried it up over mountain ranges that rise as much as 1,000 feet in two miles. But the soldiers who built the road figured they had the right to name it. So it's "The Road to Tokyo" and they've posted signs bearing the name.

Unlike the Alaska Military Highway, which was worked by crews operating from both ends, "The Road to Tokyo" is moving in only one direction. The operator on the lead bulldozer thrashes his way through the forest wilderness knowing that nobody is coming from the other end to meet him. At least, nobody friendly. Maybe someday he will uproot a few trees and uncover a Japanese patrol party. Advance surveying parties have met Jap patrols deep in the Burma jungles and a stray enemy group may at any time swoop down on the American engineers working "The Point," or roadhead.

An enemy force of 200 was beaten off recently by Chinese troops attempting a reconnaissance in the muddy, jungle country through which the new road runs. The Chinese soldiers, veterans of the 1942 Burma campaign, had been rehabilitated and trained at a Chinese-American center in India. They had been guarding the approaches to the new road for several months and had engaged in a half-dozen minor patrol skirmishes, but this was their heaviest action to date. Led by Lt. L. J. Ten Sun, a graduate of Virginia Military Institute, the Chinese fought back the attacking force and hammered its communication lines during the withdrawal.

Because of the ever-present threat of enemy attack, all U. S. troops working on the new road keep their guns within reach at all times. Jap air raids are another constant possibility.

Maj. Gen. Raymond Wheeler, commanding officer of the Tokyo highway project, tells an amusing story of the danger of his men meeting Jap patrols.

Two jack-hammer operators were working all alone up near "The Point." One mentioned the latest latrine rumor on how close the Japs were and asked what two lone American soldiers could do if they were suddenly jumped by an enemy patrol party. He wanted to know what his buddy would do against such odds.

"Well," the second soldier replied calmly, "I'd keep shootin' until all my bullets was used up. Then I'd pull out my razor and cut my way out."

Oddly enough, a battalion of aviation engineers cut the original track through the dense mountainous jungles of this part of India and Burma. Brought in to construct U. S. airfields in Assam, the Air Corps engineers were pressed into service as road builders after they had finished their original assignment of building runways and dispersal areas.

Under the direction of Col. Tate, a 28-year-old officer from Eunice, La., the aviation engineers undertook their new duties on Dec. 12, 1942. The road had just been started by the British Army with Indian labor when the Yanks took over. A few months later it was cut through to the Burma border.

Orders from Gen. Wheeler called for the road to cross the India-Burma border not later than March 1, 1943. A lot of experts said it could never be done in that time. They pointed out that the crossing would have to be made at a point 3,800 feet up in the mountains, with a rise of 1,000 feet in the last two miles. The entire route was blocked by trees 150 feet high and 45 feet in diameter, and by huge boulders that had to be blasted by dynamite before the bulldozers could go into action.

But Gen. Wheeler had said that "in time of war, there is no such thing as a difficult job." The Negro soldiers in the aviation engineers battalion proved his point. When the lead bulldozer sheared the red-white-and-blue ribbon stretched across the borderline, it was exactly 5:06 P.M. on Feb. 28, 1943.

Three companies of the battalion spearheaded the drive that carried the road into Burma. A Company cleared the "Point," cutting a road wide enough for heavy Army vehicles. Soldiers of B Company did the drainage work, installing pipes up to six feet in diameter to carry off the monsoon rains into the huge ravines that line the winding mountain road. C Company widened, backfilled and graded the road.

It was a round-the-clock job, seven days a week, up on "The Point." At night drivers pushed their bulldozers into rock and dirt, always in danger of rolling too close to the edge of cliffs that dropped off into 500 feet of nothingness. In the weird glow of light cast by smudge pots, torches made from gasoline-saturated bamboo or flaming 5-gallon fuel-oil cans, soldiers from Pennsylvania and North Carolina, Ohio and Texas kept the road rolling on to Tokyo.

They encountered one of the toughest spots just west of the India-Burma borderline. A 100-yard formation of solid rock along an almost vertical cliff stopped the lead bulldozer cold. The 16-ton D-7 couldn't even get a bite in the cliff. So the air-line hose and jack hammers were put on the job, cutting eight-foot holes in the rock for charges of dynamite that would blast man-made ledges for the bulldozer to follow through. When the D-7 swept the huge boulders over the side, the men waited to hear them crash in the valley below. But no sound came back. They were too high up to hear it.

One portion of the new road into Burma follows the same tortuous mountain trail that British, Indian and Burmese refugees trekked across in the spring of 1942 to escape from the Japanese. Many of the refugees were too weak to continue on to India and at several points along that stretch of road the U. S. engineers found human skeletons. Beside one crudely made *basha*, or native hut, were the remains of a man, woman and two children. Apparently an entire family had stopped to rest and had never moved on again.

"The Road to Tokyo" is probably the most extensive road-building project that the U. S. Army Engineers have tackled under constant danger of enemy attack. But man-made opposition has not been their only problem here. Almost equally dangerous foes have been natural ones—monsoon rains, tropical temperatures that rise to 140 degrees, malarial mosquitoes, blood-sucking leeches and *dim-dam* flies.

As was expected, the 4-month monsoon rains

slowed up construction work. Slides and cave-ins kept the road maintenance crews on 24-hour duty. But the supplies to the boys up on "The Point" still went through every day, thanks to a fleet of jeep trailers which had been assembled for these emergencies. The jeeps, hauling small trailers filled with supplies, navigated stretches of road that stymied larger vehicles.

During the rush to reach the India-Burma border by March 1, Col. Tate issued an order forbidding vehicles not needed for work from going up to "The Point." Recon cars and even jeeps often got stuck in the mud and had to be hauled out with tractors and graders. So Pvt. Norris Humphrey of East Point, Ga., was posted to enforce the "Off Limits" edict.

Lt. Millard O. Peirce Jr. of Burlington, N. J., relayed Tate's order to Pvt. Humphrey, emphasizing that "nobody, not even a general, is to get through." As luck would have it, Gen. Wheeler—who hadn't been up to "The Point" for several days—chose that day to make an inspection.

When the general's jeep approached the forbidden strip of road, it was promptly haulted by Humphrey. With a loaded Garand to back his story, Humphrey courteously informed the general that his jeep could go no farther. Somewhat startled by Humphrey's curt pronouncement, the CG of "The Road to Tokyo" project asked the soldier if he knew whom he was talking to.

"Yessir, General, sir," the out-ranked but determined Humphrey replied. "You're Gen. Wheeler but my orders says nobody's car, not even a general's, gets by here today. And nobody's does."

Nobody's car—not even a somebody's with two stars on his shoulder—did. The general got out of the jeep, told his driver to wait, commended Pvt. Humphrey for carrying out his orders, and started walking through ankle-deep mud to "The Point" two miles ahead.

That determination of Pvt. Humphrey to carry out his orders is typical of the Negro soldiers who are building "The Road to Tokyo." They're doing a tough job with a maximum of effort and a minimum of complaints. They don't begrudge the toil and sweat they're putting into it: they know that some day they will get a return on their investment.

What that return will be was aptly expressed by T-5 Peter C. Clark of St. Louis, Mo., assistant to Chaplain Robert F. Harrington, 30-year-old Negro Methodist minister from Aiken, S. C. Clark drives the GI weapons-carrier which Chaplain Harrington uses to visit the various Negro units along the road for Sunday services. He puts it this way:

"This here road reminds me of that Road to Hell that Chaplain Harrington's always talking about. Only thing is the Chaplain says the Road to Hell is paved with good intentions. But this here Road to Tokyo ain't paved with good intentions. This here road is paved with our bad intentions. Millions of 'em. And every one stands for one dead Jap."

"All right! Let's dress up this damn line."
—Pvt. Thomas Flannery.

BLINDMAN'S BUFF WITH BULLETS

By Sgt. GEORG N. MEYERS

ATTU ISLAND, ALEUTIAN ARCHIPELAGO [Via Courier from Massacre Bay]—We are hunched around a small warm fire, a bunch of us, killing our last liter of captured *sake* and second-guessing the invasion of Attu.

On one point we are all agreed. War here is blindman's buff with bullets. Plus a single sinister, incombatable weapon by which a crafty, vicious swarm of Japs has been prodding off several times its number in battle-eager Yanks.

The weapon: fog.

"What kind of a goddam war is this! You can't see 'em!" swore a sergeant from his litter, while four medics, knee-deep in custard mud, lugged his tough, stringy body from where he lay on a muskeg slope with 11 machine-gun and rifle bullets in his arms and legs. The sergeant, an Alaska Combat Intelligence Platoon scout, had been assigned as bodyguard to Col. Edward Palmer Earle, regimental commander, on a recon foray in advance of the American lines. The sergeant was not told that the colonel was dead of mortar shrapnel, possibly the first American victim of the assault.

"Where the hell are they?" cried the sergeant. "You can't see the bastriches!"

Of course, you can't. All day and all night they crouch in their cliffside caves towering over both the east and west passes of Massacre Valley. From their invisible emplacements they command an uninterrupted view of our entire operations. Shielded by fog, on stubby skis and flypaper feet, they inch their way down the sherbet-snow ravines. When the fog rolls up, like a window curtain, for perhaps a quarter hour at a stretch a half-dozen times a day, they pepper away with their chattery machine guns and moaning, thudding mortars. Before our artillery can spot the range, down rolls the fog. When it goes up again, they are the little men who are not there.

"It's eerie," says M/Sgt. Charles Burgmann, who formerly handled chores for NBC in Hollywood. "It's a script by Ernest Hemingway, direction by Alfred Hitchcock."

It was there, the fog, when our formidably escorted convoy pushed its way blindly into the rock-fanged maw of Massacre Bay. It chased us down the Aleutian Chain. It forced the assault troops into the most bizarre invasion of enemy shore line in the second World War.

Even the cunning Jap gunner in his steep gopher hole must have doubted his senses when a U. S. Navy destroyer, with foghorn sounding full blast, nosed through the low-hanging mist at the head of an armada of amphibious assault barges.

But on the beach, no Japs.

Riflemen slogged up the central ridge forming the backbone of Massacre Valley. No Japs.

Machine gunners sweated their weapons up the hill, and the mud grew deeper. No Japs.

At the crest of the ridge, Massacre Creek, West Fork, trickled a thin line 1,000 feet below on the left. East Fork meandered deep down on the right. On three sides loomed the sheer, smooth shoulders of mountains whose snow patches were already bruised black by naval bombardment preceding the attack. For more than an hour the guns of warships offshore had hurled their high explosives to blast the Japs off the face of these cliffs. There could be no Japs here.

The fog lifted and the medics went to work. The line of unarmed litter bearers across the slippery snow patches, over the unjeepworthy swamp glades, has been steady ever since.

"We had a close go last night," drawls Pvt. Frederick Dulaney of Houston, Tex. "We'd picked up our patient and were starting back over the ridge when some machine gunner on the other side of the valley opened up. We had to hit the muskeg, and little divots of moss were flicking up all around us. We'd have got it for sure if some infantryman in his trench hadn't held up a lighted match. That drew the fire away from us right away."

Howitzers on the hummocky shelf above the beach have picked up where the heavy barrage from seaward left off. More snow is turning black on the mountains. When the fog lifts, there is a chatter of machine-gun fire. Tracers from our batteries lace the far face of the valley like sparks from a chimney in the wind. A few mortar shells crash up front where our emplacements are thickest.

In the CP a corporal moves toward the field phone in the soggy foxhole which is his sleeping quarters and the regimental message center. Zing! He goes down, clutching his shoulder. A private runs to pick him up, then stops short and looks bewildered as his own arm hangs limply, blood gushing from his wrist.

Snipers, too, play hide and seek in the fog.

Spiderlike, they cling to the crags overlooking our

camp areas and bide their time. Most of their hits are sheer luck. They're potshotting from 1,000 yards.

"Some of 'em work closer than that," says Pvt. Randolph Duboise of Phil Campbell, Ala. "The one who tried his luck on me was only about 15 yards away.

"I was slicing across a gulley over on the West Fork. I thought I caught sight of somebody skulking along behind me, but I reckoned it was one of the other boys. I stopped and turned around to wait for him to catch up with me, and there he was, lying on the top of a little mound, just drawing a bead on me. I plunked to the ground and scurried behind a little knoll. In a minute I was higher than he was. He was down on his hands and knees, still watching the spot where I had dived out of sight. He didn't even know I was watching him. He should have known better than to mess with an Alabama boy like that."

"If those snipers would only go to bed nights, everybody would have a cheerier disposition," says Cpl. Harold Peterson of Hampton, Nebr. "But they get the idea they can prowl around in the dark and sneak through our sentry lines. I guess they figure they'll get through somehow, then pick us off one by one in the cold light of dawn. Just this morning

we were all jerked out of our sleeping holes at 3 o'clock because some Jap patrols were working in close to the CP. Worst part of being pulled out when it's dark like that and you're sleepy is that everybody sounds like he's speaking with a Japanese accent."

The only time American planes have been able to try to give us a hand on the Massacre Bay side, four fighters went roaring up the valley into the gray veil. Only one came out. The same day, a transport plane trying to parachute food and supplies to an advanced position on the other side nosed low into the soup. We never saw it again. Fog.

The most amazing feature of this operation is the fact that every soldier here thinks the other fellow's job is tougher. The heavy-laboring shore-party crews wipe the sweat from their eyes and vow they wouldn't swap their 16-hour shifts for the midnight jaunts of the medics. The litter bearers regard their neck-exposing task as a soft touch stacked against the infantrymen's lot, firing away from their shallow mudslots. And the gunners themselves yell over their shoulders, "You just carry us some hot grub and dry sleeping bags, and we'll fight the goddam war!"

THE BULLETIN BOARD MYSTERIES

OR THE TRAPPING OF MAD MORGAN

By Sgt. RAY DUNCAN

THE way we caught S/Sgt. Morgan, or "Mad Morgan" as he came to be called, was by posting a guard around the bulletin board at night.

Very strange bulletins had been appearing on the board in front of the orderly room. They would be posted sometime in the night and read by everyone first thing in the morning. Eventually someone in authority would find them and tear them down, but by then it was usually too late.

"There will be underwear inspection for the entire unit at 8:45 this morning," said one of his earliest efforts. "Each man will be standing beside his bunk, at attention, in his underwear and stocking feet." Morgan, of course, was there in his underwear, beaming, and as puzzled as anyone when nobody showed up to inspect.

This was only a slight annoyance. Fake promotions were very embarrassing. A list of promotions would appear on the bulletin board, always including the eager boys who were sweating hardest for

stripes. By noon at least half a dozen men would be ripping new stripes off their sleeves and cursing the unknown practical joker.

Occasionally his bulletins were so wild that we should have spotted them. "There will be a special physical inspection at 9 this morning. All personnel will fall out wearing only shoes, raincoat and gas mask." Yet when we did disregard a bulletin we got into trouble. The one about "outdoor airing of all bunks in front of the barracks" sounded like one of the fakeroos to us, but it turned out to be straight, and 19 of us got gigged for ignoring it. You never know in the Army.

"The unit will assemble at 7:30 this morning," said the most embarrassing of all Morgan's bulletins. "The commanding officer has received word that a member of this unit has been having improper relations with a local girl. The man's name is not known, but his appearance is familiar to her parents, who will be here to review the men and pick the guilty one out of the line-up. Punishment will be much less severe if the guilty party will give himself up, by reporting to Capt. Jones in his office."

Several men, some of them with considerable rank, quietly requested an interview with the captain on the strength of this bulletin.

We posted a guard around the bulletin board, and a corporal caught Morgan in the act of pinning up a piece of paper which read, "The latrine in Barracks 3 has been contaminated. All men who have used the latrine during the past 36 hours will report at once to the hospital." Morgan giggled when he was captured. "Never did want to work in no orderly room anyhow," he gloated. Two days later he had his medical discharge. "Mental instability."

HUMPHREY, FRANCHOT AND VICTOR

By CPL. C. G. DeVAN
Camp Pickett, Va.

AFTER five straight days Kelly, Goldstein and Stetson began to get tired of practicing beach landings. So they welcomed the chance to help the engineers lay a wire road over the sand. They were even happier when they were told to go and gather stakes.

They wandered off behind the sand dunes, picking up stakes. In a short time they got tired of that, too. They were just knocking around, throwing stakes at each other, when Kelly started it.

"Hey, look at me," he hollered, "I'm Humphrey Bogart in 'Sahara.'"

With that he staggered up the dune. When he reached the top he shaded his eyes with his hand and looked out at the ocean. He turned slowly.

"Men, there's nothing. Nothing but sand."

"Hell," broke in Stetson, "I can do better than that. Look at me. I'm Franchot Tone in 'Five Graves to Cairo.'"

He took a couple of steps, then fell flat on his face at the bottom of the dune. After a moment he raised his head, wiped the sand out of his eyes and peered at the nothingness of it all.

"Not bad," commented Goldstein, "but what about Victor McLaglen in 'The Lost Patrol'? That really was acting."

He picked up a stake, cradled it like a heavy machine gun and charged up the dune. When he got to the top he shouted: "All right, you bastards, come and get me!"

Then he started spraying his stake machine gun, making noises with his mouth.

After he finished they changed characters. Goldstein was playing Franchot when they were interrupted; he was raising his head to wipe the sand out of his eyes when he saw two legs. The legs, much to their surprise, belonged to a major.

The major called the three over and asked them what they were doing. They told him they were gathering stakes. The major took their names and company and told them to tell their first sergeant that they were on KP the next day. Then he told them to get busy and gather some stakes.

In the afternoon they were still gathering stakes. Stetson was on top of a dune.

"Hey," he called out, "look at me. I'm Franchot." Goldstein was Humphrey peering into the distance and Kelly became Victor, blazing the machine gun. Then Goldstein turned around to find himself peering into the eyes of a colonel who had been watching the entire act.

The colonel wanted to know what they were supposed to be doing. They told him they were supposed to gather stakes. The colonel took their names and told them to tell their first sergeant to put them on KP the next day. As he walked away he said: "Now pretend you're soldiers gathering stakes."

After the colonel had gone the three discussed the situation.

"Well," said Stetson, "it looks like we're on KP tomorrow."

"I guess we are," said Goldstein.

"Yes, I guess we are," said Kelly.

They thought about this for a while. Then Goldstein broke out.

"Hey, look at me. I'm Victor."

He picked up a stake, cradled it like a heavy machine gun and charged up the dune. When he got to the top he shouted: "All right, you bastards, come and get me!"

Then he started spraying his stake machine gun, making noises with his mouth.

PFC. SHEA'S MERRIEST CHRISTMAS

By Sgt. JOE McCARTHY

Sketch by Sgt. Ralph Stein

'Twas the night before Christmas and all through the barracks not a creature was stirring, not even the CQ. He had tried to make his usual trip through the squad rooms around 11 to open the windows and now he was at the dispensary getting treated on the places where he had been hit by shoes, tent pegs, canteens and helmets.

In the downstairs room only six men were asleep. One of them was a cook named Anna May Wong. Don't ask me where he got that name, because he is not a la-de-dah and he is not Chinese either. As a matter of fact, he is as Irish as Paddy's Pig.

There is no need of listing the names of all the other men in the room because this is supposed to be a Christmas story, not a pay roll, but in the corner bed, next to the drinking fountain, was Pfc. Crusher Shea. This was the first time Pfc. Shea ever spent Christmas Eve with strangers.

Like everybody else in the barracks, Pfc. Shea always said he had given up a $150-a-week job as a big executive when the draft board caught up with him, but he had really been employed for the last seven years as the No. 2 man in his neighborhood A & P store. Christmas Eve was always a busy night for the Crusher, as he was known among his friends, but he usually cleaned up the last order around half past 10 and he used to get out of the store around 10 minutes of 11.

Then, after a fast one with the boys at the corner tavern, Pfc. Shea would hurry home to celebrate Christmas Eve at his mother's house. He was 36 years old but he never married because he didn't know any girls.

And, oh, what good times they had in the Shea family Christmas Eve and Christmas Day, too, when Crusher's sister Bertha came over from Jersey with her husband Frank, a plumber, and her six rosy-cheeked, good-natured little children. And then there was Aunt Minnie, who wore a red wig, and Cousin Adelaide. On Christmas afternoon the doorbell would ring and there would be Uncle Harry. He worked in a garage in Yonkers and the family never saw him the rest of the year. He usually showed up on Christmas with a load on. Last year, in fact, he showed up paralyzed and when Aunt Minnie opened the door he almost fell in on top of her.

But nobody had the heart to be cross with Uncle Harry on such a happy day as Christmas in the Shea house.

Now Pfc. Shea was spending Christmas all alone in camp, missing the familiar scenes of the holiday in his cozy little home, because he had a furlough Labor Day and would not get another one until God knows when.

His friends had been sympathetic when they packed up and went home for the holidays, borrowing his garrison belt and his civilian shoes.

"Poor Crusher," they murmured. "Imagine spending Christmas in this fire trap."

Strangely enough, Pfc. Shea did not cry himself to sleep Christmas Eve.

"Glad I'm not working in the store tonight," he said, taking off his fatigues. "Must be 10 times tougher than usual figuring out ration points for all them Christmas orders."

Christmas morning he awoke feeling fresh and rested. He couldn't believe this. Then he remembered that he had been enjoying a good night's sleep on Christmas Eve instead of working late, drinking a few shots with the boys, arguing with his mother and father about where to put the Christmas tree, staying up until all hours trying to find the bulbs and trimmings for the tree in the attic and then discovering that most of the lights were smashed during the summer and the rest did not work as the wires had been short-circuited.

He had a nice leisurely breakfast in the mess hall. The cooks let him fry his own bacon and eggs because there were only a few guys around, and he enjoyed it. Not much like Christmas morning at home when his mother used to chase him out of the kitchen because he was in her way while she was fixing the turkey.

There was no work Christmas Day because it was raining. Pfc. Shea passed a pleasant morning in the barracks playing blackjack and won eight bucks.

He had a fine big turkey dinner in the mess hall with beer out of the company fund and cigars afterward. He didn't have to worry about saying something that would make Aunt Minnie leave the table in tears, as she did practically every Christmas. And there was none of Bertha's kids sitting on each side of him knocking glasses of milk into his lap.

After dinner he enjoyed a two-hour nap on his bunk. Bertha's youngest boy, the one with the harelip, was not around to run his toy fire engine into his shins, and he didn't have to listen to Cousin Adelaide put on her regular crying act about how Christmas reminded her of her poor dead mother.

All in all, it was one of the most merry Christmases Pfc. Shea ever experienced, if not *the* merriest.

When the other guys came back from their Christmas furloughs they were all broke and had to borrow money from him. A couple of them wouldn't even talk because they had arguments with their girls.

"How was Christmas here, Crusher?" one of them asked. "I'll bet you wished you was home."

"Oh, I don't know," muttered Pfc. Shea. "It wasn't so bad."

HOW TO TAKE CARE OF YOUR REPLACEMENT

By Sgt. RALPH STEIN

Greet him with gusto. (This is easy.)

Screen him from reality.

Feed him well and regularly.

Protect him from heat . . .

. . . and from cold.

And don't let him get away!

SPORTS: EX-PRISONER TELLS OF SPORTS IN JAP CONCENTRATION CAMP

By Sgt. DAN POLIER

LATE one afternoon in 1942 at the Japanese concentration camp at Santo Tomas University, Manila, the imprisoned Americans gathered around the playing field to watch a soccer game between the American and British men. Suddenly there was a big commotion at the gate. The Jap guards, who had been leaning on their rifles watching the game, popped to attention and presented arms. A whole company of Jap soldiers marched onto the field and proceeded to drill alongside the soccer players.

"We were so stunned at first we didn't know what to do," said Royal Arch Gunnison of the Mutual Broadcasting System, who returned on the *Gripsholm* after spending almost two years behind barbed wire at Manila and Shanghai. "But we decided we had to save face. You know how important that is out there. So we continued to play. The Jap officer deliberately marched his company as close to us as he could. In fact, he got so close that the soccer ball got tangled up in the feet of his men. You never saw such confusion. The Japs were stumbling and falling over each other. Then to make things worse, this officer gave the command: to the rear march. Honestly, it was just like a Bob Hope comedy, only funnier.

"You know how the Jap carries his helmet on his back. Well, when these guys started bumping into each other their helmets fell off, and every time one tried to pick up his helmet he would pick up the soccer ball instead. Finally the officer saw he was losing more face than we were, so he marched his men off the field. We were afraid of how the Japs might take that embarrassment, so we quit playing. When we stopped the Americans were leading. It was the first time we had beaten the British. But they kept insisting we had to bring in Jap ringers to do it.

"That incident might sound funny to you, but actually it was serious business. If we had laughed, as most of us wanted to, they would have punished us severely. The Jap humiliates easily.

"They were always doing things like that if they thought we were enjoying ourselves too much. Sometimes they would come out to a softball game and pick four or five men from each team and cart them off somewhere to dig ditches until the game was over."

Gunnison continued:

"Sports were practically our only form of entertainment at Santo Tomas. Everybody from the little children to the women played some sort of game. We even built special fields for them. We held our own Golden Gloves boxing tournament and one for the children, too. The Japs let us organize softball leagues, and we had 30 teams playing. Each community in the camp had its own team. Some of the names were funny, like East Shanty Town, Frog Bottom, Room 13 (that room had about 30 fellows crammed into it), the Manila Polo Club and the Pan-American Airways. They were divided into the American and National League and, of course, we had our own World Series. As I remember it, the Pan-Americans won the series.

"Speaking of the World Series, we got full reports on the 1942 series through our underground system in Manila. The people on the outside would pick up the game on the short wave and slip us the batteries and inning-by-inning scores through the fence. Somebody put up a blackboard behind the lost-and-found department and kept it up to date. The Japs never did catch on. They thought it was the score of one of the games we were playing.

"As far as I know we played the Japanese in the first softball game between enemy teams in this war. The captain of the guard at the Shanghai camp was nuts about softball, and he watched us play every time he had the opportunity. One day he came over to me and said: 'Hey, *Gun San*, someday we play softball?'

"We stalled and tried to prevent the game, because we knew so many things could go wrong. But he kept insisting, so the game was scheduled. Everybody turned out including all the big shots from the Embassy and the Army.

"Before the game started we noticed that the Jap pitcher was warming up with an overhand delivery. Since I was one of the prison committeemen, the fellows said it was my duty to go over and tell him this was a softball game not baseball. I got the interpreter and we both tried to show the pitcher how to throw the ball with an underhand motion. He tried it once or twice and then said in Japanese: 'The hell with it.'

"As it turned out it didn't make any difference whether this Jap threw overhanded or not. We walloped the daylights out of him and scored 27 runs in the first inning. After the inning was over I got the team together and told them we had better throw the game and let the Japs save face.

"Well, it got so funny that everybody on the side lines, except the Japs of course, nearly choked while trying to keep from laughing. We dropped balls, muffed easy grounders and stumbled all over ourselves. But they still couldn't make it an even ball game. We even tried applauding every time one of them hit the ball or scored a run. We only applauded twice, though, because after the seventh inning the score was 28 to 2.

"Then the captain of the guard called time. He came over to me and said: 'Hey, *Gun San*, I think more better we do not keep score. I think more better we play for sportsmanship.' That saved face for everybody including the umpire who was a Dutchman. This Dutchman was sweating plenty. He knew if he called a close one wrong, the Japs would ask his name, number and nationality, and when they discovered he was Dutch they would give him hell. The Japs really hate the Dutch.

"That softball game was practically the only contact in sports we had with the Japanese except for a wrestling match. We had a big fellow with us, a guy named Chris Bell, who was 6 feet 2 and the rocky sort. He used to be a lumberman in Shanghai. The Jap guards were having a wrestling tournament at the guardhouse and they wanted Bell to come down and wrestle one of those huge *sumo* men. These *sumos* weigh about 300 pounds and are very agile. We tried to duck the challenge, but it was no use. They insisted. Anyway, Bell said he would like to take them on. We went to the guardhouse with him fully prepared to bring away the little pieces. But darned if they could pin him. He threw the *sumos* all over the mat. In fact, it became so one-sided that Bell had to make it look good and let them save face.

"After that the Japs always treated Bell with respect. Every time they saw him they would pat him on the back and say: 'Bell, you plenty big man.' "

NUDGE IN REAR CAME TOO SOON, SO HE BOMBED WRONG TARGET IN CHINA By Sgt. MARION HARGROVE

SOMEWHERE IN CHINA—This story has been held back for a while because the fellow was mighty sensitive about it, and he happens to be a tech sergeant, 6 feet 2 and weighing 200 pounds. He's cooled off a little, so now it can be told.

The tech sergeant is Karl May of Yakima, Wash., an aerial engineer and gunner in one of the local Mitchell B-25 bombers. The tale goes back to the time when he was still a buck private, working as an armorer in his squadron and bucking like hell for a job on a combat crew.

They finally let him go on a few missions to try him out. He got along fine until his third trip. That was the raid on the big Jap base at Hankow, former Chinese capital, on the Yangtze.

There were two minor defects that day in the bomber to which May was assigned: there were no racks in the ship for fragmentation bombs and the interphones were temporarily out of commission.

Well, they were working the thing out all right without fragracks or interphones. They had Pvt. May squatting by the photo hole with a stack of frag bombs and the understanding that when the turret gunner nudged him in the behind he was to cut loose with all he had.

It happened that the bomber had a passenger that day—maybe an observer from Washington, maybe a newspaperman, maybe just a sightseer.

This worthy person grew unaccustomedly chilly, saw that the draft came from the open photo hole and decided to ask the private beside it to close it. The private—yep, it was May—had his back turned, so the passenger sought to attract his attention with a gentle nudge in the rear.

Pvt. May reacted like the eager beaver he was. He held one frag bomb over the hole and let it drop. Then he turned another loose into thin air. He was preparing to drop every bomb in the ship—until he was rudely and violently stopped. To May's dismay he learned 1) that the ship was nowhere near Hankow, 2) that he had been given no signal and 3) that he had just wasted a couple of hundred dollars' worth of U. S. high explosives.

The mission proceeded to Hankow, where May dropped the rest of his bombs through the photo hole, an armful at a time. But his heart was heavy at the thought of having goofed off.

When the plane returned to its base, there was an intelligence report from the Chinese Army waiting for it. According to this report, two bombs dropped on a Japanese barge on the Yangtze had scored direct hits, sinking the barge and drowning 160 Japanese soldiers.

T/Sgt. May never tells the story himself and he gets mad when he hears anyone else tell it. Only those who've seen the records will believe it.

FIFTY MISSIONS

By Pvt. JOSEPH DEVER

YANK *Short-Story Contest Winner*

I AM on my way to see my girl in Boston, and it has been a long time. It has been 26 months since I said good-bye to her in Boston.

Fifty missions always seemed incredible to me. How could anyone ever come back to the States after 50 missions? How could anyone step off a DC-4 in East Boston and quietly take a taxicab to the Hotel Statler after having been over Europe 50 times?

I'm doing it, though; I'm home in Boston. And I'm not being sentimental when I say that it's damned good to be here.

I'm just like them now; I mean the gunners I knew at armament school—the exotic GIs with 50 missions, with their wings, their rainbow service ribbons, their medals and the quiet, easy way they had about them. They'd say: "You'll get your chance, kid." "Yeah, it's kinda rough up there." I wanted some day to be wordless, humble and friendly with other eager kids the way the gunners were with me. How far away it all seemed then: 50 missions, the ribbons and the quiet, easy manner.

And now I'm riding through East Boston; I'm just like they were. I know a hell of a lot of things, but I would rather turn my face away and ask about your brother John who is in the ASTP. I know what flak is now. I know how a gunner can make a chapel out of the Sperry lower ball; I know that he can pray with rich eloquence. I know what the enemy looks like. There is also, of course, the blood fleck, the mother-mercy-calling and the blubbering, steel-given death of the nice guys who were hilariously drunk with you just a few nights before.

And now I'm looking at Boston. My taxi driver is a maniac at the wheel, as all taxi drivers are. He is doing 47 miles an hour through this big-city street. On a street in Berlin he would listen for the menacing wail of the air-raid sirens.

"This is it," the Boston taxi driver says.

I get out, I pay him, I walk into a beautiful, thick-rugged Boston hotel, and I get a room.

It is a room on the seventh floor. My stuff is all unpacked, and I stand by a window looking out. I stand looking out at downtown Boston, and I see only the white face of a nun.

My girl Jane is a nun now. We were going to be married, but something struck her, some kind of

spiritual ack-ack, I guess. And now she's gone off and become a nun.

She's here in Boston now, in some kind of a cloister, and I'm on my way to see her. I figured the 50 missions wouldn't let me see her again, I was almost sure of it, but here I am in Boston looking out a window.

The Copley Plaza is over that way. And on the other side of it, about four stories high and facing Copley Square and the Boston Public Library, there is a little marble balcony. The night of my college senior prom I threw highball glasses into the square. I liked to hear the tinkling clatter of the glass against the cobbles, and I wanted to do it again and again.

"Jay, come inside," was all Jane had said.

I went inside; I loved her greatly, more than even the sound of breaking glass, and I always did what she said.

And over there to the right is Beacon Hill. We liked that place very much. When I was a feather merchant, Jane and I used to walk all over it in the blackout. We knew all the places—the quaint, cobbled, snaky alleys, the huddled coffee nooks, the little barny theaters where you could see Philip Barry's plays for 20 cents, the H. M. Pulham doorways with the white marble steps and the shiny brass door plates. We used to sit in those doorways at midnight, on our way home; I used to kiss her there a lot. We'd pretend we were locked out, and sometimes we'd yell loudly for Nana or Jeeves. If anybody came to the door we'd jump to our feet and run like scared rabbits all the way down the hill to the Charles Street elevated station.

And there, across the Charles River, is Cambridge. That's where I used to live; that's where Jane lived. Our playground's there, too.

In the summertime Jane and I worked on the playground. She was my boss, and Christ, did we have a time. There was a big brick schoolhouse called the Peary. There was a playground in back of it, a sun-baked macadam rectangle, and there were kids from the stinking Cambridge tenements.

She wouldn't say a thing when I'd come in, maybe an hour and a half late. Sometimes she'd pretend she was peeved and go on with her jigsaw project. She'd sit there in the sun wearing a colossal straw bonnet, and she'd prattle merrily but exclusively to the little girls who were gathered busily about her feet.

I'd keep teasing her. I'd hit a softball out to my outfielders from a place right near her; I'd make the ball roll right over to her sometimes and in retrieving it I'd get myself all tangled up in her and the jigsaw plywood animals she and the girls were making. After a while she would burst out laughing and come after me with a bat, a shrill chorus of girl voices urging her on.

It was on the playground that I really became infected with the planes. The P-38s would go over at about 8,000, and I'd stand down there by shortstop and crane my neck until the planes were little silver winks way out to the west.

I never knew about Jane leaving me then, but I did know that someday I was going to be up there in a plane.

About 4:30 in the afternoon we'd quit for the day and lock up. That was when Jane and I played our own little game. I'd go in the front door of the school and she'd go in the back. We'd both slam the doors and run quickly towards each other.

I'd take her in my arms, then I'd kiss her hair, her eyes, her lips and the very tip of her nose. I'd hold her close in my arms and we'd talk about being married and having a place of our own; we'd wonder what our children would look like and if they'd be scampering off to a playground like the Peary every day.

Then the kids would start banging on the door and hollering for us to come out. We'd kiss a few times more and walk innocently out to them. They used to escort us part of the way home, and they never said a thing about the kissing, even though they knew, as all kids know.

That was the way it was. It was a good way to be living and loving. Now it is all changed.

Well, anyway, I am going out to the convent to see her. It is a place called Mission Hill, which is in Roxbury. Roxbury's a part of Boston and only a short ride from the hotel.

A girl who used to double-date with Jane and me wrote to me when I was in England. She said she'd seen Jane and that Jane told her to tell me that if I ever got back to the States I was to be sure and make a visit to the convent. I wrote to the girl and said I would.

I am in a taxi again, riding very fast along Huntington Avenue. The Museum of Fine Arts is on the right. I used to look at the statues of naked women in there when I was a kid.

The taxi climbs up Mission Hill, and the convent is at the top. It is red brick with a red-brick wall around it. It is low and quadrangular, and there are those cylindrical clay shingles all over its roof and on the top of the brick wall.

I ring the front-door bell. You only ring once in a convent because that ring, however slight, is amplified by the silence and the distance that fills the inside of a cloister until the ring becomes something like an echoing clap of thunder.

A little nun lets me in. I ask for Jane. Jane's nun name is Sister Felicitas. I pretend I don't notice, but I see the little nun who let me in eat up the gunner's wings and the service ribbons. I go into the parlor and wait. There is always a large wall clock in this kind of parlor, and it always says: "Wait, wait, wait." It says this over and over again. You hear a door softly open and softly close way off in a cool interminable distance. You know then someone is coming.

Jane comes into the parlor.

She is just as I pictured she'd be. Her face is white, her eyes are sparkling blue pools of goodness and mischief, the backs of her hands have little red and creamy blotches as though she does a lot of dishes and scrubs a lot of floors.

She is all swaddled up as I was afraid she'd be, wound in endless and oppressive reams of black cloth; she wears a tremendous white starched collar and a black veil over her head. But she is my Jane all right, she is my Jane.

She stands in the middle of the room and looks right at me for about a minute.

"Hello, Jane," I say.

She doesn't say a thing. She walks over to me and takes hold of both my hands; she comes up as close to me as a nun ever can and squeezes both my hands until they sting.

She stays close to me that way for what seems a long time; she eases the pressure on my hands and looks strongly at me so I can see that everything is there just as it had always been: all the love and the light and the music are there for me in just the way they used to be, and even though these things are God's now, I can somehow see and know they are still mine, too.

"Oh, Jay," she says, and her eyes are a little wet, "I'm so very, very glad to see you. Let me look at you."

She steps away from me, and I notice that her step, although as light and graceful as ever, is now a swish instead of the swirl that it had once been. A girl has become a nun; an elfin skirt has become a ponderous petticoat.

"My, what a handsome soldier you are! You know, I've never seen you in your uniform before.

And the wings, and the ribbons. Jay, you're really a man now, aren't you!"

"Am I, Jane?" I gulp, fumbling desperately for words. "Wasn't I one before?" I finally ask.

"Of course you were," she says, "but you were a boy's man then, Jay. You're a man's man now. The kind I always knew you'd be. But come, let's sit down."

We sit down in separate, straight-backed wooden chairs. The chairs are cold, unyielding symbols of poverty, chastity and obedience. We sit in them a while and, although she does not come right out and say it, I think she wants me to talk.

But I don't want to talk. I want to be with her, to be near her, to hear her voice and watch her eyes. I want to sit with Sister Felicitas and think about my Jane.

She kind of guesses that I don't want to talk.

She says she likes it here; she has prayed for me night and day; she is happy teaching fourth grade to the little Roxbury urchins; she is proud of me and tells the little kids in her class stories about me all the time; she has read everything in the Cambridge *Clarion* which someone sent her, and she doesn't care if I never utter so much as a syllable about airplanes.

I have not changed greatly, she says; the wonder and the impudence are still in my face; my eyes have a distance in them that wasn't there before; I'm not as loquacious but—"Glory," she says, "things have happened!"

I have had enough of looking at her. I begin to ache for her like when I was across. I begin to want her in my arms, and I know that it is time for me to go.

I say I have to be going. We stand up. She looks at me a while and takes both my hands; she makes them sting again.

"What happens now, Jay?" she asks.

"They're sending me out to Denver as an armament instructor. I don't want to go, but you just go, that's all.

"Well, I guess this is good-bye, Jane," I stammer. "I hope you'll be very happy, kid." She hasn't heard me call her "kid" for a long time.

I turn to go.

"Wait," she says quickly. "Come in the chapel with me, Jay, and we'll say a prayer together. It's down here."

We walk down the hall toward the chapel.

"You can leave me inside," she whispers when we are about to enter the chapel. "You can go out the front door of the chapel and into the street."

She hesitates a little, then she says quietly: "I love you, Jay; I'll always love you and I'll pray for you constantly, all the days of my life."

She turns away swiftly and moves into a pew about three yards from me. She begins to pray.

I kneel down and I pray, too. I tell God I am sorry for not wanting to come back from 50 missions; I thank Him for bringing me back even though I had not wanted to come. I say three Hail Marys. I take a long look at Jane. I genuflect and walk out of the chapel and into the street.

A STRANGER AND ALONE

By Pfc. John Behm

We are the insolent invaders with many uniforms
Who have come to England from far away
Bringing gifts of chewing gum and Chesterfields.

We are the harsh strangers—the vain, hearty foreigners,
The aliens thoughtlessly trampling your calm vineyards.

The slim colored boys send our heavy trucks
Screaming along your narrow roads.
The big tanks rip up the pavings
Of your ancient towns.
The jeeps and weapons carriers
Do fifty-five around your Z-shaped curves.
The half-tracks hold your traffic up for hours.

The countryside rings
With the blare and whirl of our machines.

We are loud and fast and wild and lusty.
We are drunken, proud, hard and potent.
We could drink your island dry if you would let us.
We are the terrible, mischievous warriors
From far away.

We are, I'm afraid,
Just a trifle bestial
For your highly tempered tastes.

But, England,
Understand us!
Though we sneer and boast in the pubs,
Consuming your beer and belittling your glory,
We tremble and are afraid in the streets
Before the blind audience of closed doors.
We are young men whose roots
Have been left far behind
In strange places called Brooklyn and Sacramento and
    Tucson and Thief River Falls and Council Bluffs and
    Cincinnati and Coon Hollow.
We have been torn from the soil where we grew
And flung like exiles across an ocean
To a land we never dreamed of.

We are bewildered and weary,
Lonely to the point of madness,
And if we shout and curse
Through our quiet dreams,
Forgive us.

We are merely looking for a way to go home.

THE ALASKA SCOUTS

By Sgt. GEORG N. MEYERS

HEADQUARTERS, ALASKAN DEPARTMENT—You can't bring the war in the Aleutians into a bull session up here without someone mentioning the Alaska Scouts. But that's not hard to explain. They led the way.

Any yardbird in the Aleutian Chain will tell you that on the four biggest amphibious operations of the North Pacific campaign—Adak, Amchitka, Attu and Kiska—it was the Scouts who, in darkness, first paddled ashore from submarines or destroyers or troop transports to stake out landing beaches and locate the enemy.

The Scouts are not supermen and they're not a band of bloodthirsty thugs who eat raw meat. They're especially adapted to their assignment, sure. But that's because most of them are sour-dough trappers and miners and fishermen who know how to get around in Alaska and on the Aleutian Chain. Several of them are Eskimos, Indians and Aleuts. A few more are old-line dogfaces with years of service at the Territory's old Chilkoot Barracks. Until shortly before the U. S. went to war, Chilkoot was the only permanent garrison in Alaska. It was really there that the idea for the Alaska Scouts was born.

But the real organization didn't come into existence until Nov. 19, 1941, a few weeks before Pearl Harbor, at the headquarters of what was then the Alaska Defense Command. That morning Col. Lawrence Vincent Castner, ADC intelligence chief, called a corporal and three privates into his office. Norton M. Olshausen of San Francisco, Calif., was the corporal. The privates were James H. Radford, a stringy hillbilly from Tennessee; Donald O. Spaulding of Rexburg, Idaho, and William B. (Sam) Bates of Ogden, Utah, two of them pre-war veterans of Corregidor. Everybody knew everybody else, because when Col. Castner had been a captain several years before, he was their CO down at Chilkoot.

The colonel told them he'd gotten authorization from Lt. Gen. Simon Bolivar Buckner Jr., head man of ADC, to form an Alaska Combat Intelligence Detachment. "I've picked out you four for a starter," he said.

The colonel had also picked out the officer who was to teach the men the meaning of combat intelligence. This was a long-legged major—now lieutenant colonel—with a jaw like an anvil and a mili-

tary career probably almost as spectacular as he himself made it out in tongue-in-cheek bull sessions. His name was William J. Verbeck.

"I really gave those boys hell," Lt. Col. Verbeck recalls. "Fifteen hours a day. Hardening marches through the snow out in the woods. Sketching and map making. Day after day of shooting every weapon a man can carry over his shoulder or on his back."

When war came, Col. Castner got the nod to expand his Scouts to a platoon of 24 men and one officer. That original platoon was hand-picked from a collection of ruggedly independent characters who probably would have been a pain in the chair-knuckle to the commander of any ordinary outfit. Most of them wanted no part of Army routine. But Col. Castner knew a way to put their woodsmen's wiles and hardy attachment to the outdoors to vital military purpose.

Finding the right officer was not so easy. He finally settled on Lt.—now Capt.—Robert H. Thompson of Moccasin, Mont. In brute strength Thompson was as rough a customer as the men he was to lead, and the colonel was certain he could work with the platoon without snowing under the basic individualism which made them valuable. Today there isn't a man among the Scouts who wouldn't crawl on his stomach to hell with a sack of hand grenades if Capt. Thompson or Lt. Earl C. Acuff suggested it. Lt. Acuff, who hails from Moscow, Idaho, was assigned to the platoon when it was expanded later to 66 men.

By the time the Japs tried their sneak into Dutch Harbor, the Scouts had been split into small detachments and sent out as intelligence reporters to Kodiak, the Pribilofs, the secret bases at Cold Bay and Umnak, and Dutch Harbor itself. From the brow of Ballyhoo Mountain at Dutch Harbor, Spaulding—now a staff sergeant—and his detachment observed the Jap attack on Dutch Harbor. Their reports on the raiding flights and the Japs' tactical maneuvers were called by Col. Castner "cool, impartial, correct and the best" received by ADC Intelligence.

The Japs' feint at Dutch Harbor was their last advance toward North America. From then on the Yanks were headed west—with the Scouts leading the way. When we made one of the most important decisions of the Aleutian campaign, the decision to take Adak and fortify it as a main base, two Scout detachments, one under Col. Castner and the other under T/Sgt. Woodrow W. (Hank) Farrington, landed on the island from submarines on the nights of Aug. 27 and 28, 1942. Several days later they directed the occupation of Adak by blinker lights from shore with the help of two Navy signalmen and a radioman who volunteered to go with them.

Before the public back home even knew of the Adak occupation, Lt. Col. Verbeck, Capt. Thompson, S/Sgt. Edgar M. Walker of Merced, Calif., and Sgt. Joe Kelly, an ex-miner and trucker from Fairbanks, Alaska, were already scouting the next stepping stone, Amchitka, a 15-minute flight by Zero from Kiska.

Nine Scouts and 30 volunteers from the Infantry went ahead of the main landing forces at Amchitka on Jan. 12, 1943. Under the very nose of the Japs, and in the face of a rising storm that made the undertaking hazardous, the advance party sought out the safest beachhead. Then, as soon as landing operations of the main force were in progress, the Scouts struck out for the northern tip of Amchitka and established an OP from which they could see the shores of Kiska through breaks in the fog. A few days later, when the Japs began daily attacks on Amchitka, Scouts spotted the enemy seaplanes almost as soon as they left their Kiska anchorage.

Seven months later four Scouts, all Alaskans, were the first Yanks to set foot on Kiska. They were Sgt. Clyde Peterson, a Sitka fisherman, and Pvts. Stanley Dayo of Livengood, Chuck O'Leary of Nome, and Billy Buck, a half-Eskimo from the fishing village of King Cove.

But in the months between, the Scouts had their toughest assignment. It began in a veil of fog that made Holtz Bay on Attu a blind passage the morning of May 11. A special reconnaissance group with commando training had been picked to lead the 7th Division onto Attu. The Scouts were picked to lead the recon group.

Capt. Thompson, then still a lieutenant, commanded the biggest detachment of 25, which loaded into two Higgins boats with 10 days' rations, radio equipment, hand grenades, full ammunition belts and extra bandoleers. Each Higgins towed a string of smaller boats, called "plastic whaleboats." A thousand yards from shore the Scouts transferred into these noiseless boats and rowed through the fog toward Red Beach.

At the same time two other Scouts, Cpl. George Bishop of Fairbanks and Cpl. Raymond F. Conrad of Dubois, Wyo., were guiding another patrol ashore at Scarlet Beach. Conrad had transferred into the Alaska Scouts only two weeks before and said: "I'm only along for the experience." He got his experience; later he also got a Silver Star.

On the southern shelf of Attu at Massacre Bay still other patrols of Scouts were stealing onto the narrow strip of beach. One of the first casualties of the battle was Sgt. Clyde Peters of Anchorage, Alaska. Peters was accompanying Col. Edward P. Earle, regimental commander, on a reconnaissance foray high on a ridge when the first shots fired by the Jap defense entrapped them. Col. Earle was killed by mortar fragments. Peters, with 11 bullet wounds, was lugged to the beach by sweating medics, and the Scouts never saw him again. For months Pete was carried on their books as "killed in action" until finally one of the boys got a letter from him, mailed from a hospital in California.

Over on the Holtz Bay side the day after Peters was wounded, the only Scout killed in the Aleutian campaign was shot down. He was Cpl. Willis (Red) Cruden of Talkeetna, Alaska, an old seaman who had been trapping in the interior for several years. "He always said," Cpl. Philip N. Kendrick of Nome recalls, "that if he had his way about it, he'd never venture more than a half-mile from the sea again." He never did. He was cut down on a mossy Attu slope by a sniper's bullet through the heart.

Two more Scouts, Cpl. Albert L. Levorson from the Badlands of South Dakota and Pfc. Theron G. Anderson, once a ranger at Mount Rainier National Park, were given the sweet task of guiding 50 infantrymen over saw-toothed Sarana Ridge to wipe out a strong Jap machine-gun emplacement, spotted from aerial photos. They discovered that the Japs were also well fixed with mortars capable of outdistancing anything the Yanks had on hand. The patrol's radio equipment went sour, and the only way they could get word back to the CP was by sending the two Scouts.

By this time the Japs had closed in behind them on the crest of the range. Together Anderson and Levorson skulked their way through snow, down deep ravines slippery with moss and over rocks wet by waterfalls. When the Scouts were within sight of the American lines, the Japs spotted them and opened fire.

The shots roused the Yanks in the valley, and they cut loose at the jagged sky line. Anderson and Levorson were sewed up in the cross-fire for several hours. They finally made the valley in darkness. The next morning artillery and machine-gun bursts kept the Japs above the fog line busy, while Levorson scaled the sheer cheek of the mountain again to tell the infantrymen to hold on and that help was coming.

On the last day of the battle Cpl. Conrad and Cpl. Edward R. Bagby of Medfra, Alaska, were pacing a patrol of Infantry down the rocky slant of Chichagof Ridge toward the beach. They were spread wide, gunning for Jap stragglers not already killed by their own grenades.

"Our job was really finished," Conrad says. "We had already located the enemy's general whereabouts for the Infantry, but Bagby and I went along for the hell of it."

It turned out to be a small-scale massacre.

"We almost stumbled over the first Jap we saw. He was wrapped up in a blanket. When he heard us, he peeked at us from under the blanket, then covered up his head. He wouldn't surrender and he wouldn't fight. We shot at him a couple of times, and after he was mortally wounded he pulled out a grenade and blew himself to pieces. A fragment of the grenade hit one of the infantrymen in the finger.

"A little farther down we dumped some grenades into a stovepipe that was smoking over one of those half-burned huts. Ammunition was stored there. After the explosion it looked like a bomb had hit the place. We didn't stop to count how many Japs had been hiding in there.

"On a low mound within 100 yards of the beach we caught sight of three more Japs and two others diving into a cave. The infantrymen went to work on this bunch. By this time Bagby and I were getting interested, so we pulled ahead to see what next. Through his glasses Bagby spotted a Jap crawling toward a big boulder with a hollow behind it. Bagby pegged away at him five or six times, and we saw the Jap struggle over the ground and finally kill himself with a grenade. I saw one stand up and start running toward the rock, and I shot him.

"Bagby and I held a little conference. We'd been pretty lucky in some tight spots up to then, and we didn't want to stretch our luck too thin. We measured our chances. We didn't figure there could be more than four or five Japs behind that rock, and it would be a hell of a lot of fun to smoke 'em out."

So, yard by yard, Conrad and Bagby began their advance, one sliding forward on his stomach while the other lay in a position to cover him. On the way down the slope they killed four Japs who peeked out to try to take a shot at them.

"We guessed then there must be at least one more," says Conrad, "but it was getting risky. Bagby decided to crawl back and bring up some grenades. I played possum until he got back."

For an hour and a half they waited for the Infantry patrol to catch up with them. They covered the rock, and every time they decided it was safe to advance, another bullet came zinging past them. When they heard the patrol coming behind them, they prepared to close in.

"I had never thrown a grenade in my life," Conrad admits. "Personally, they scare the wadding out of me, but I hated to admit to Bagby I was a coward. So I let one go. I even held it a few seconds after pulling the pin so it would explode just right. It cleared the rock by six inches."

In a few seconds a Jap came running out with his clothes on fire. He had been lying in plain sight near the end of the rock and Conrad and Bagby thought he was dead, but the grenade set dry grass afire around him and finally set his clothes ablaze. At that moment the first man in the Infantry patrol crawled into sight. He drew a bead and shot down the burning Jap. Then he made the mistake the two Scouts had been making. He thought that was the last of the Japs. He crept to the mouth of the hollow behind the rock and looked in. A Jap bullet killed him.

Conrad and Bagby continued to inch forward, and Jap rifles kept poking up over the edge to fire on them. By the time the patrol finally arrived in force, they were close enough to see into the hollow. There were still four live Japs, but Conrad and Bagby left them for the patrol to exterminate. The two Scouts had disposed of eight Japs in the 90-minute point-blank duel. They were awarded the Silver Star.

Between missions the Scouts as an organization like nothing better than hitting the sack, except hiking off into the hills for some fishing or shooting. It took a year before they moved into a barracks building at their home station, and then it was only because their winterized tents had been dismantled during their absence.

On the march they eat better than anyone in the Aleutians. They lug along their own side meat for frying-grease and use a hip-pocket stove to cook up sourdough flapjacks and hamburgers from dehydrated beef. They carry all this in addition to ordered field equipment.

On Attu they advanced unerringly on a warehouse containing a hundred cases of *sake*, the potent Jap rice wine. At Kiska they unearthed a cache of *Suntory* whisky, and when that was gone, they brought out a supply of Jap bamboo gin from somewhere.

The biggest difference between the Scouts and other dogfaces is their sacktime conversation. Once in a while they work around to women, but only when they weary of their favorite topic—winding snares to trap blue fox.

The ranking NCO of the outfit, T/Sgt. Farrington, probably has more military service in Alaska than any enlisted man in the Territory except veteran members of the Alaska Communications System, who are practically Alaska pioneers. Farrington has 13 years in the Army, 10 of them in Alaska.

All the Scouts resent the nickname "Castner's Cutthroats," which someone pinned on them more than a year ago. They insist they're just a bunch of peaceable guys who like to be left alone and that not one of them, probably not even Lt. Col. Verbeck, has ever cut anybody's throat. But if they happen to bump into the prune-picker who first dreamed up that colorful catch-phrase, it might be another story.

LINE OF DUTY

By Pfc. RAYMOND BOYLE

THEY brought in this tech, a kid of 20, with a penetrating wound—a bayonet thrust in the right upper quadrant of the abdomen. The wound itself wasn't much to see as wounds go. It was a little ugly, though—bluish and all chewed up where some field medic tried out his book learning with a little *debridement*—that's a French word meaning to cut away the surrounding dirty skin from a wound. I leave that kind of stuff for the medical officers.

Well, anyway, this tech was really a very nice guy, and he tried to be stoical about the whole thing. But the tip of that bayonet penetrated the diaphragm and the pleura and nicked his right lung. A pneumothora it is called. Every time he exhaled he made a gasping snoring sound. He heard it, too, and I saw in his eyes that he thought he was going to die.

Then when we brought in an oxygen tent to ease his breathing, he seemed convinced. He was very frightened. Later, of course, he would casually show the scar and speak disparagingly of it, but when we placed that tent over his head, his eyes were filled with an anxious, despairing fear. He lay there with a dogged, shocked expression on his face and sibilant, jerky little flutings coming from his chest.

His captain, in dirty fatigues, came in after a while and said they had been on a problem during the divisional bivouac in the woods behind the camp, and this tech, in jumping a wall, had fallen on the bayonet fixed to his rifle and spitted himself. The captain, who is also a very young guy, acted the part of the grim field soldier. When he was questioned by the medical officers, his answers were very clipped and terse. Maj. Jennings, chief of surgery, looked at him mildly.

"What I don't understand, captain," Maj. Jennings said, "is how that boy stuck himself that way. If I remember correctly there is nothing in the bayonet drill that could possibly wound a man in just that way. The bayonet entered the right rib cage at the twelfth rib and traveled upward, nicking the hepatic flexure of the colon and penetrating the diaphragm, the pleura and the lung. He'll be all right, of course, but another inch over or so would make it a different story."

The captain smiled. "Sir, our patrol was on a tactical problem, and we weren't using the bayonet drill. We were simulating actual conditions. The sergeant fell on his bayonet when he leaped a stone wall. I didn't see it myself, but as a line man I can tell you those things happen when a bayonet is carelessly handled."

Maj. Jennings nodded. "I see, captain. Well, thanks a lot."

After the captain had left, the major went into the tech's room. "Come on in," he said to me, "and close the door."

I shut the door, and the major pulled open a zipper on the corner of the oxygen tent and said: "Sergeant, I want you to tell me like a good fellow just how you came to fall on your bayonet."

The tech hesitated for a moment; then, I suppose, a look at the major's face reassured him. He said: "I guess I should have told you before, sir. I was in a farmer's pear orchard, and when I jumped for a pear I accidentally came down on my bayonet."

The major smiled, zipped up the opening and went outside. In the hall he held me by the arm as we walked toward the door of the ward.

"Line soldier, my foot," he said.

THE ASSAM DRAGONS

By Sgt. ED CUNNINGHAM

Assam, India—Lt. Ira M. Sussky, the 23-year-old operations officer from Little Rock, Ark., leaned against the porch of the tea-plantation bungalow with the other fighter-pilots grouped around him. Over under the trees, the ground crew was warming up a grotesquely painted P-40 and Sussky had to raise his voice to be heard above the roar.

"There's a concentration of Jap troops in the jungle 500 yards north of the most northerly bungalow at Suprabum," he shouted. "We'll hit 10 minutes south of Suprabum, then strike out due north and come up the valley. Get in string, peel off and bomb from east to west. Drop your demolition bomb on the first run and your frags on the next one. Then strafe them twice and head for home."

Moving down the steps of the stilted bungalow which serves as their operations office, these American pilots of the Assam Dragon Fighter Squadron trotted toward their bomb-loaded P-40s, dispersed around the field that had once been a polo grounds for British tea planters. Lt. Ben McQuillen pronounced the customary pre-flight benediction in his deep Texas drawl:

"The Assam Dragon prowls again."

Within 10 minutes, a flight of eight fighter-bombers raced down the asphalt runway and took off toward the mountain range in the east that separates India from Burma, the white painted dragon mouths on their noses glistening in the sun.

We went back to the operations office to await their return and talked with Sgt. Manuel Valerio of Newell, S. Dak., about this bunch of Yank fighter-pilots who have raised so much hell with the Japs in Burma.

Hanging on the wall over Sgt. Valerio's head was the Assam Dragon Squadron's battle insignia, designed by Lt. Robert McClung, who was a commercial artist in Denver before the war. It shows a dragon with an ear-to-ear smile. The boys in the squadron say he grins like that only when they feed him generous helpings of his favorite dish—dead Japs.

"These guys are driving the Japs nuts," Valerio said. "They run almost daily bombing and strafing missions against the Jap bases and supply routes in northern Burma. Then when the Japs come over here to hit back at them, the Dragons are already up there waiting for them."

The last time the Japs came to retaliate, the Dragons did an awful job on them. Forty-six enemy bombers, fighters and observation planes swooped out of the mountains in daylight to hit the U. S. base and only nine were seen returning to Burma. The exact number of enemy losses was hard to determine because the dog fights covered a 3,000-square-mile area, and our searching parties are still hunting for crashed Jap ships in the mountainous jungle land. So far, eight bombers and six fighters have been confirmed and 14 others listed as probables.

The total American damage was one bullet hole in the wing of a Dragon ship. After the Japs were beaten off, the Dragons landed for refueling and bombs and took off immediately on a scheduled offensive mission in Burma.

The Dragons are always getting mixed up in incredible stunts. Like the time Lt. Melvin Kimball of Durham, N. H., from Chennault's 14th Air Force, made a belly landing in Burma after his engine conked off during a flight from China to India. Kimball thought he was in India. He walked innocently into the nearest town and right up to the military headquarters. But nobody happened to be around at the moment, not even the CQ.

So Kimball headed back to his plane and, as he reached it, soldiers hidden in the surrounding woods opened fire on him. He grabbed his .45 and fired back at them, still thinking he was in India and wondering what the hell all the shooting was about. Just then he noticed bomb craters around him and realized where he was—in the middle of a well-populated Japanese advance base.

While Kimball emptied his automatic, an Assam Dragon P-40 appeared overhead. It was Capt. Charles H. Colwell of Park River, N. Dak., coming home from a strafing mission with five bullets in his plane. Colwell dropped down and looking the situation over, immediately radioed headquarters.

"Keep Japs away from grounded plane and pilot until reinforcements arrive," headquarters told him.

Four Dragons rushed to the spot and relieved Colwell, who was running out of gas. Then four more came up and joined the party. They took turns diving down on the Jap troops and beating them away from Kimball, who was helpless now with all his ammunition gone. The Japs poured 30 bullets into his plane but luckily they didn't hit him.

Meanwhile, back at the Assam Dragon base, Lt. Sussky volunteered to attempt a rescue in a PT-17 trainer. When he arrived at the scene, the other Dragons were still strafing the Japs and keeping them from closing in on Kimball. In the midst of this battle, which looked like Custer's Last Stand, Sussky brought his training ship down safely in a small clearing in the thick jungle, pitted with the mud holes of water buffalo and rutted with elephant tracks.

While the Japs still fired on them from ambush, Sussky and Kimball worked frantically to get the PT-17 off the ground. Eight times they tried a take-off and eight times they failed. After every attempt, they ran across the clearing, dodging bullets, and chopped down trees and stumps to make the runway longer.

By this time it was beginning to get dark. They knew that if they didn't hoist the ship into the air before dusk they were lost. The P-40s overhead were already having a hard job trying to see the Jap soldiers in the gathering shadows and, when darkness came, it would be easy for the enemy to close in and take them.

Finally, on the ninth attempt, the PT-17 arose clumsily into the air and soared away to safety across the tops of the jungle trees. The P-40s escorted her home and then returned and blasted Kimball's plane to bits so the Japs couldn't use it.

"Our group A-2 officer here is Lt. Col. Harold Buckley, who used to be a Hollywood script writer," Valerio said. "Somebody asked him if Sussky's rescue stunt wouldn't make a good movie story. The colonel said the public would not believe it. He said they'd say Hollywood was picturing the impossible again."

The squadron commander, Maj. Paul C. Droz of Salt Lake City, Utah, has also rescued three U. S. flyers from the Burma jungles. Using a PT-17, he dropped into a box-like canyon and picked up Lt. Cecil Williams and Cpl. Matthew Campanella who had been lost 23 days after parachuting from a plane flying "The Hump." Two weeks later, Maj. Droz did a repeat performance for the benefit of Lt. William A. Wendt who had bailed out near Jap territory en route home from a strafing mission.

After lunch, the Dragons flew in from the morning Jap hunt in Burma and Lt. Jack Irwin of Phoenix, Ariz., gave us the score—three direct hits on Jap barracks, which were burning fiercely when the Dragons left, and probably heavy Jap casualties from fragmentary bombs and strafings.

"We really gave them a work-out," Irwin said. "Almost as good as when we caught that truck con-

voy flat-footed near Myitkyina last week. They say that the Japs had to bring up eight additional trucks to carry away the casualties when the smoke cleared."

Sussky, a beetle-browed youngster who joined the Air Force after his graduation from Arkansas Tech in 1940, hung up the phone and turned to the other Dragons.

"We got some more work this afternoon, fellows," he said. "A patrol mission over near Taungzup to look for troop movements and truck convoys. Carry the same load as this morning." He pointed to Lt. Bob Bixby of Helena, Mont., and Lt. Don P. Taylor of Los Angeles, Calif. "Everybody goes but you two," he added. "You fly cover for the transport that drops foods for those Kachin troops in the hills."

"Will we get back in time to see 'Wake Island' over at headquarters tonight?" Irwin asked.

"Think so," Sussky said. "Just to make sure, phone and ask them to hold it up until we get back. I want to see that picture myself."

A few minutes later the dragon-nosed planes lifted their tails and headed again toward the mountains on the Burma border. The Yanks were off with their Assam Dragon.

There is no connection between the reading and the sound of that last sentence. If you don't believe it, ask the Japs.

"Beg pardon, sir, I'm starting to wonder about the number four censor!"—Sgt. Dave Breger.

SUPPLIES ARE BROUGHT UP IN ITALY ON THE GI's BACK

By Sgt. BURGESS SCOTT

With the Fifth Army in Italy—We came up here for blood and thunder, for grenades and glinting bayonets and moaning mortar shells. We didn't get them because it was a quiet day as the Infantry business goes.

What we got, though, was better because we and few others had ever bothered to see it before. We followed a can of C rations into a foxhole, a .30-caliber cartridge into an M1 and a quart of precious water into an empty canteen.

We had bumped into the bitter tail end of the Army's supply web where the fancy term, logistics, becomes merely a weary private's aching back and the slimy path up a front-line peak. We were up in the country where shipping and trucking are un-heard-of words, where the only way to handle sup-plies is to manhandle them.

The location was a sector, half valley, half moun-tains, occupied by an American Infantry regiment. Regimental headquarters was in a row of damp caves at the base of a mountain which we had reached only after a half-mile slosh through a grove of sawed-off trees. The ankle-deep mud had worked crotch high by the time we reached the head-quarters.

The regiment had captured this position several weeks previously. Then it had been relieved for a rest. Now some of the headquarters men were dig-ging back into caves they'd lived in before. That's how slow the war moves on some sectors of this mountainous front.

Nevertheless, it was a good position, as positions go here. The headquarters caves were at the base of a steep peak. An enemy shell would have to have a pilot and a navigator with it to find this kind of a spot. The front line was around the peak and several miles up the valley to the north.

We saw that the men working around headquar-ters had their mud troubles, too. The mud was caked up to their belts and would have gone higher, but the rain water running off their backs and shoulders kept washing it off. We sat down by a pri-vate who was prying the caked mud from his instep with a trench knife. He was a supply man who had just come in across the stump flat with a 40-pound case of C rations for the headquarters cook cave.

"This ain't tough at all here," he told us. "This is just flat and muddy. You oughta see up front when it gets hilly and muddy at the same time."

He pointed to a distant embankment that inter-sected the stump flat. "That used to be an Itie rail-road but the Engineers have fixed it up into a road that gets the trucks this far. The trucks get mired up there a piece, and they have to switch the stuff onto mules. Then a piece farther the mules mire down, and they switch the stuff onto my back. I ain't had a chance to bog down yet. Been too busy."

Most of the men in the regiment had drawn the new combat suits, and the owners of these were faring as well as possible in the steady downpour. One of them said that the new suits turned water better than any clothing the Army ever issued. Most of the men had also received galoshes, and the net result of this issue was that the medics were treating far fewer cases of feet, trench and frozen.

A man went into the headquarters cave with our request to stick around for a few days to pick up a load of pictures and stories. The executive officer, a lieutenant colonel, came out to see us and his first question was: "How brave are you?" We told him we didn't want to stick our necks too far out, but that we felt brave enough to get a story and some pictures. He smiled and said he was leaving inside an hour on his daily trip to check on supplies and tour the line CPs, and we could go with him.

While we were waiting a fellow on guard told us why this was a dull day compared with most the regiment had seen. We could hardly hear him for the racket being made by a battalion of 105s on the far side of the flat. They were whanging a steady stream of HE (high explosive) over the peak at our back and into the Jerry lines ahead. We could hear the shells hiss as they went over.

Then we heard a different kind of hiss—more of a whine—and there was no explosion preceding it, so we knew it was an incoming one and ducked accordingly. We saw it burst with a flash and a spurt of smoke near where we'd parked our jeep in a wooded lot on the far side of the flat. We began to worry about our transportation.

Later we learned that our jeep was untouched but that the burst had killed two of the fellows who had offered to keep an eye on the jeep while it was parked there. A fragment of the shell had set off an ammo trailer and the resulting explosions had done the dirty work. Another GI lost a leg, but the medics grabbed him in time to save the rest of him.

An officer stopped to talk and explained the why of all the sawed-off trees in the flat at the base of the peak. He said the Krauts had sawed the trees down while they held the flat, for two good reasons. If the trees had been left standing, the shells our artillery was pouring in there would have hit the limbs and burst before they struck the ground, nullifying the protection of any foxhole the Germans could dig. And now that the trees were cut down, our advancing troops were left uncovered.

The colonel came out of the headquarters cave wearing his helmet and raincoat, and said we'd better be moving because there was a long tough walk ahead. A second lieutenant with a carbine was our guide. We slushed behind him across the stump flat and up onto the fill of the Itie railroad on which the truck road was being built.

When we reached the top of the railroad bed, we could see how our Engineers were able to convert it into a motor road. On each side of the roadbed lay pieces of track and ties, the remains of the railroad after the Germans had run their railroad wrecker over it. The wrecker is a railroad car with a 10-ton pointed hook hanging over the rear and a chute built on each side over the rails.

When Jerry retires he couples a locomotive to the wrecker and opens the throttle. The 10-ton hook drops down between the rails and drags along, snapping the ties like toothpicks. Explosive charges slide down the chutes at intervals, attaching themselves to the rails. After the wrecker has moved ahead, the charges explode, cutting the rails into short lengths.

As we struggled to keep up with our guide's pace, the colonel told us about his riflemen and his supply men.

"In the Infantry," he said, "we learn to depend on manpower. Trucks get stuck, mules get mired, but we can always count on a man getting through. The men up in the lines are our big shots. We've taught them to do only one thing up there, and they concentrate on only one thing: how to kill Krauts. That's all they have to think about, and the rest of the regiment will break its back to see that they don't have anything else to think about.

"Except for killing Krauts, the supply men take care of all the infantryman's needs. Those needs boil down to three things: food, ammunition and water. As long as the supply men have an ounce of strength left, the man up on the line won't have to take his eye off his sights."

Soon the road-crew units thinned out to a mere sprinkling of men and then disappeared. We knew by the stillness and the tenseness that we had reached the outer fringe of the front. The lieutenant led us down the railroad embankment and into a knee-deep donkey path along which we splashed until we came to a battered farmhouse. This was the CP of a rear battalion.

Aid-station medics sitting on the back steps told us it was an unusually lean day. Two litter bearers had just come in to report nothing doing, and a couple of fresh ones were buttoning up to go into the lines and keep up the vigil.

Inside the farmhouse the lieutenant colonel commanding the battalion and his staff were eating a meal of bacon, crackers and coffee. The battalion CO cautioned us about the last leg of our trip. "You'll probably be okay until you come to the creek about a mile and a half up," he said. "It's swollen and you may have to wade it. It may get tough between the creek and the forward CP because Jerry has been shelling that sector with something big. He's been hitting it for about 15 minutes out of every hour, but lately he's been slackening up. Just be careful."

There were three big open fields to cross before reaching the creek, and at each one the colonel made us keep a 60-yard interval between men in single file because a group crossing the clearing might attract the attention of an enemy observer and draw shell fire. Crossing those fields felt like walking naked across a stage before a big audience. A few hundreds yards to the left was the rolling, wooded valley floor where our patrols were out, and just beyond that were the German lines. Once, while we were strung out across the open space, we saw the guide fall flat and we fell, too, but nothing happened, and we continued on to the next field.

In this manner we crossed the three fields and came to the swollen creek. Some supply men had already started a timber bridge across it. The bank on our side was the mulehead, and the animals were nibbling grass as the men unloaded their precious cargoes of C and K rations, water and ammunition. This was as far as the mules could carry the load they'd taken from the trucks. Now the stuff had to be manhandled.

On the other side of the creek a thin line of mud-caked men was toiling up the slippery path of a 60-foot bluff, each with a 40- or 50-pound case or can on his shoulder. This was the only way forward from there. We saw a fagged-out soldier tug a case of rations to his shoulder and start for the creek, but as he reached the edge he leaned too far forward and the case tumbled into the stream. He splashed in after it, got it back on his shoulder and then made it across the creek. We watched him start up the bluff, his soggy clothes adding to the burden, and saw him lug the load over the rim and out of sight.

A rain-soaked lieutenant in charge of the detail was working on the bridge. Up to then, he said, the men had been wading waist deep with their loads across the creek, but the bridge would soon fix that. He said that his men had been working more than 12 hours a day keeping the line companies supplied. All but six of his original crew were out from pure exhaustion; they were no longer able to put one foot in front of the other. Lately he'd had to draw on reserves from the antitank company.

He said they had tried to get their mules beyond that point, but the first one had mired into mud over his back. "We almost had to shoot him," the lieutenant said, "but mules are too valuable. We managed to get a jeep near enough to tie a line on him, and two of the fellows waded out and held his head up while we pulled him out."

We teetered across the half-finished bridge and started up the bluff, remembering the battalion CO's warning about Jerry's habit of shelling this last portion of the route. We took our place in the line of carriers who were lugging the food, water and ammunition over the bluff.

It was tough going. You stepped one foot forward and slid back two. Tufts of strong grass should have been good handholds, but the grass was slippery with mud from the hands of other supply men. A man above us lost his balance and swayed a moment, his case of rations tilting backwards. We couldn't help him by pushing because the motion would have slid us down on the ones behind, so we clung on and waited. The carrier righted himself on a piece of brush and went on up. It was a hellish job for us to get up there, just carrying nothing. What an extra 40 pounds would have done to us!

We finally climbed to the top of the bluff, crossed a small shell-pocked flat and came onto the railway we'd left several miles back. Instead of climbing over its embankment, we walked through a gap blasted out of it and started up the rocky slope of a peak on the other side. After about 200 yards of straight-up climbing, we reached the CP we were looking for—that of the farthest advanced battalion in the Fifth Army.

The CP was in a fairly secure gully that none of the German shells had found up until then. The men had dug caves deep into the gully banks, with the floors several inches above the bed of the crevice. These, lined with dried grasses, made relatively comfortable homes.

While we were there, things perked up in the valley below. There was a moaning, banshee wail, and we saw smoke trails of the six projectiles of a Screaming Mimi (rocket projector) arch over the valley. Then we saw the six bursts in our lines.

A line of supply men arose from the cover they had taken and continued up the hill. The nearness of the burst worried a captain in the CP and he came over to the men. "The Kraut observer might see you with those square boxes," he said. "Better take the back trail."

After the captain went away, the man he'd addressed lowered his case to the mud and sat on it. "That screws up the short cut," he said. "Now we gotta go over the rocks." He passed the word down to the fork of the path. The rest of the supply men hiked their loads up on their shoulders and took the back trail—up the rocks.

ALEUTIAN JOY

BY S/SGT. LEROY A. METCALF JR.

Aleutians

Nothing daunted by perpetual chill
In his avid search for some tasty swill,
The raven dives at a moment's detection
Of a suitable dump of tainted perfection.

Shrilling, cawing, loud and brash,
On spotting a juicy pile of trash,
Down he swoops with corvine greed,
Soon joined by friends in noisy feed.

The extermination of this ravished ruck
Is soon announced by contented cluck,
As he homeward wheels from his diurnal glut,
Serenely happy with a bulging gut.

THE LOVE OF ISLANDS

BY SGT. HAROLD APPLEBAUM

Camp Shanks, N. Y.

The love of islands is a recent one.
When spreading seas across the globe revealed
Their dots of land beneath the foreign suns,
The hearts turned seaward from the battlefields
And longed for haven shores and peaceful planes,
For homes protected by an ocean's breadth,
For solitude and shelter from war's rain,
For winds untainted by the smell of death.
But overhead are wings and motors' roar,
And nowhere are there peaceful fields to name
As safe from war, or any bloodless shore
Untouched by death, and from the tide of flame
Across the world, the retrogressing waves
Force back on Man his ancient love of caves.

A GI VIEW OF THE TEHERAN CONFERENCE

By Sgt. AL HINE and Cpl. JAMES P. O'NEILL

TEHERAN, IRAN [By Radio]—GIs in Persia, long accustomed to considering their command the most humdrum place this side of a Cooks and Bakers School, were slightly dumbfounded when President Roosevelt, Premier Stalin and Prime Minister Churchill blew into town recently for the most historic conference of the war.

The railroad men, longshoremen and truck drivers who make up the bulk of this important supply depot's Army population couldn't believe their eyes when they saw the crowd of celebrities who followed the three United Nations leaders here for the big international surprise party—Gen. George C. Marshall, Adm. William Leahy, Anthony Eden, V. M. Molotov, W. Averell Harriman, Adm. Ernest King, Gen. H. H. Arnold, Lt. Gen. Brehon B. Somervell, Marshal Klementi Voroshilov, John G. Winant and Harry Hopkins, to name only a few.

One GI who had a ringside seat at the conference from start to finish was Cpl. Matt Volenski, a railroad man from Pittsburgh, Pa., who was in charge of the billets for the entire American party.

"There was never a dull moment," Matt says. "A couple of other noncoms and I got our first hint that someone big was coming when they told us to move all our colonels from their regular billets into the wing of the hospital. But they didn't tell us then what it was all about."

Needless to say, it was a rare pleasure for these corporals and T-5s to be able to tell the silver eagles to pack up and get out.

"We were hearing plenty of rumors about the reasons for the moving," Matt added, "and, of course, the Cairo Conference gave us something to base our rumors on. Sure enough, they told us one morning that the President was coming, so we finished moving the colonels, but fast, and brought in cots, soap, towels, sheets, food, envelopes, toilet paper and everything else we could think of.

"We had a hell of a time getting around, too, because we had no special passes and the whole town was being guarded as tight as a drum. We had to buck Russian guards, argue with our own MPs and run our old beat-up trucks like they were never run before. When the conference got into full swing it was even giddier. I had our minister to Iran, Louis G. Dreyfus Jr., guiding me on one trip from the Russian Embassy where the President stayed for two nights. He hopped on the truck and directed me through the jumble of guards and shrubbery. At one point, I ran up against a Russki secret-service man who gave me a puzzled look from head to foot and then, still puzzled, saluted me. I saluted him back and kept on going."

Since Matt was on duty all the time bringing in food and supplies, he had a good backstage view of the conference. What he didn't see himself, he picked up from the cooks who prepared the meals for the President's party.

They reported that FDR especially liked the gazelle that had been shot here by GI hunters for one of his dinners. His other favorite dishes were odd snacks and fish. The cooks said he made a crack about fish being brain food. The President eats plenty of spinach and likes a little garlic flavoring in his meals.

"That Soviet marshal, Voroshilov, was the biggest man I've ever seen in this command," Matt said. "And Gen. Marshall certainly looked like a general ought to look. He made a great hit with the Polish waitresses when he gave them mementos of the visit—wrist bands that he bought here in the GI PX. One waitress said to me: 'Oh, Gen. Marshall is such a clean-cut and good-looking man. He's got such good eyes you can see that he's foresighted.' She said she was so nervous she almost went to pieces every time she waited on him."

THEY SHOT THE WORKS

The official pictures of the conference were taken by six GIs in the 846th Signal Photo Bn.—T/Sgt. Arthur Daniels, S/Sgt. Robert Davis, Sgt. Robert Murray, Pfc. Munroe Oettinger, Pfc. William Coggswell and Pfc. Grant Nelrad, all former cameramen at top Hollywood studios.

Their photo section works with a 35-mm Mitchell movie-camera machine propelled by a gasoline engine that makes a hell of a racket. When they were suddenly called to the Russian legation to shoot conference pictures, they draped camera hoods over the machines to try to cut down on the noise. "The damn thing sounded like a B-24," Sgt. Daniels said afterward.

While these boys, who had taken pictures at El Alamein, Tripoli, Algiers and Malta, were "shooting" Stalin, Roosevelt and Churchill on the legation porch, a secret-service man came up and told them one of the hoods was on fire.

"To hell with the hood," Pfc. Oettinger told him. "We're busy. Put it out yourself."

Later the pfc. apologized. "I guess I sort of lost my head," he says. "Just think when this is all over and the cameramen back on the lot in Hollywood start bragging about the big stars they've shot, I'll step in with a story about this job and top them all."

The six GI photographers never expect to focus on anything more important for the rest of their lives. "Even the occupation of Tokyo will be an anticlimax after this assignment," says Sgt. Davis.

LONG WAY FROM HOME

The 19th Station Hospital is located on the road that leads to the field where the President reviewed the U. S. Army troops from Camp Amirabaq. All the convalescent patients were allowed to go outside to watch the President pass by. Pvt. William Wiley of Tacoma, Wash., confined to the hospital with a fractured leg, wangled the only wheel chair in his ward and maneuvered it to the side of the road.

When the President came along and saw the patients, he stopped his jeep in front of Wiley's wheel chair. "We're both a long way from home, aren't we, son?" he said.

"Yes, Mr. President, we sure are," Wiley replied. He has been overseas for a year with the 186th Quartermasters.

THE GENERALS EAT SPAM

T/Sgt. George McClusik, an ex-coal miner from Clarence, Pa., walked into his barracks after a hard day on a bulldozer and bumped into his first sergeant. The first sergeant was carrying McClusik's ODs in his hands. "Here," he said, handing over the clothes. "You're going on guard."

George tried to give the top kick an argument, but before he knew it he was posted outside the door of a small room off the officers' mess where the generals ate their meals. A louey told George not to let anyone through the door unless he gave an okay.

"What will I do if you are not around, sir?" asked George.

"Don't let anybody in except generals," said the shavetail.

George obeyed the rule, with two exceptions—Adm. King and Adm. Leahy. "The louey didn't tell me anything about admirals," he said, "but I figured they rated."

When the generals sat down for their first dinner in Iran the mess officer told Gen. Marshall that he was going to serve them the first fresh meat ever received by the command. It had arrived the night before by boat at a Persian Gulf port and the officials had flown the precious stuff to Teheran for the conference.

But Gen. Marshall refused the meat, graciously but very firmly. "If this is the first meat to arrive here," he said, "I think the men who have been stationed here should have the privilege of eating it. We'll take Spam and bread." And they got Spam and bread.

"This isn't hooey, either," says George. "I heard Gen. Marshall say it. And for my dough, he's a regular guy."

THE INTREPID IRISHMAN

Cpl. John Kennedy was the guard stationed outside the conference room. He had to check another door to the room. The only way to reach it was to walk right through the conference where the American, British and Russian officials were discussing confidential matters of world-wide significance.

Kennedy, an intrepid Irishman from Philadelphia, Pa., swallowed a couple of times nervously. Then he threw back his shoulders and marched straight into the room past the table where the astonished dignitaries were turning to stare at him. He tried the unchecked door. Then he about-faced and marched smartly out again.

"I sort of had a lump in my throat," Kennedy said. "But I guess those big shots understood that duty is duty. But I could see that they were wondering at first just what the hell I was doing in that room."

WHEN YOU GOTTA GO, YOU CAN'T

The assignment of guarding the President and his party was given to Co. H, 727 Military Police Bn., and this was a great honor for these MPs who, in a noncombatant zone like Iran, usually have nothing to do except boring town-cop duty.

The entire company was placed in strategic spots all over the grounds of the American Legation. They guarded the President so well that first day and night that they were also selected to watch over all three of the conference leaders throughout the historic two-day meeting that followed at the Russian Embassy.

The noncoms and men took their jobs calmly and refused to get excited about the importance of their assignment. They wouldn't let anyone go anywhere without proper authorization. One high-ranking British official, who attempted unsuccessfully to get past them and into the embassy without a pass, shook his head and muttered: "This is the most bloody guarded place I've ever seen."

Pvt. W. G. Atkinson of Scranton, Pa., was the guard on the back door of the embassy when a colonel came up and asked if he could go in to use the latrine. Atkinson refused to allow him near the door.

"Don't you know who I am?" demanded the colonel. He merely happened to be the commanding officer of Atkinson's own MP outfit.

"Sir," replied Atkinson coldly, "until this thing is over, I don't recognize nothing or nobody unless he's got a pass."

The colonel went out into the garden where there were plenty of trees.

PRESIDENTIAL REVIEWS

Reviewing the troops here before boarding his plane for home, President Roosevelt drove through the camp to the baseball diamond where he talked to the soldiers from his jeep.

The President took a microphone in his hand. It didn't work. Then he tried another that did not work at first, either. He smiled and said: "And these are supposed to be the most powerful weapons of the war."

His speech was short, lasting only about four minutes. He wore his familiar brown felt hat, a dark coat, a gray flannel suit, a white shirt and black tie. He looked rather tired after the long days of the conference.

He told the gathered troops how he had looked out the window the first morning he woke in Iran and thought at first that he was somewhere in Arizona. The terrain here does resemble that part of America. And he went on to tell them about his meeting with Churchill and Stalin.

"We discussed not only plans for getting the war over," he said, "but also more important plans for peace."

He told the soldiers that the people back home were aware of the fine job they were doing here. He said he wished those people could see the job with their own eyes.

"I am going home now," he concluded. "And I wish I could take all of you with me."

There were no cheers after he finished speaking. Instead there was a hushed silence that seemed to last for a full minute until the troops were called to order arms. The metallic clatter of the pieces rang out over the baseball field. Then the men shouldered arms and began to march away. Many of their faces were bright and many of them had strange marks around their eyes. For most of them, it was the first time they had ever seen a President of the United States.

MPs KNOW WHAT'S GOOD FOR YOU IF YOU TIPPLE IN BRITISH GUIANA

By SGT. JOE McCARTHY

GEORGETOWN, BRITISH GUIANA—U. S. Army MPs in this British colonial town take good care of G.I.s who go out in search of quiet relaxation. They have the habit of stopping soldiers who have had a few drinks and inviting them up to MP headquarters for a friendly prophylactic.

A private from the Air Force at Waller Field came down here as a roller-skating specialist to entertain the men at Atkinson Field. During his stay he visited Georgetown for a few British rum punches. After the third one he decided to get some air.

He hadn't gone half a block when an MP stopped him and whipped him off to the station for a pro before he could say, "Antilles Air Task Force."

The private walked out mopping his brow and walked around the corner into the arms of another MP, who looked him over suspiciously and said, "You better come with me, Bud."

"No, thanks," the private protested. "I just had one."

But the MP wouldn't take no for an answer. The visitor had to return to the station for a repeat performance. Then he took to the side streets to get back to his hotel but, sure enough, he was grabbed again under the first street light and hustled back to the prophylactic room for the third time.

"You musta been out in the jungles a long time," remarked the medical department attendant who was beginning to get tired of the whole thing.

"I tried to tell them I was innocent and a family man who wouldn't think of such a thing," the private explained. "But they wouldn't listen to me."

Finally he had to request an MP escort to protect him from other MPs. Once inside his hotel room, he locked the door, pulled the covers over his head and waited breathlessly for the first morning boat back to Atkinson Field.

SETTING UP A BASE

By Pvt. ASA AUTRY

AMCHITKA, THE ALEUTIANS—On Aug. 14, 1942, a small group of men sailed from a West Coast port. All the men knew they were going to Adak in the Aleutians, about 260 miles from Japanese-occupied Kiska.

We were lucky to have good sailing weather. It was foggy, and that meant we wouldn't be spotted by the Japs. And the water was calm, so very few men got seasick. On shipboard there were frequent drills in landing tactics. Wearing full field equipment, the men climbed up and down a rope net from one deck to another. They said they liked it.

At last the day drew near that all the men had been waiting for. Most of them were getting tired of the ship life. Then at 0030 on Aug. 31 we were told to rise and shine, eat breakfast and wait for landing orders. We anchored in the bay at Adak about 0430 and were in the landing boats by 0530.

The men had nothing to worry about; our scouts had landed 48 hours before to see whether the Japs had beaten us to it, and they had radioed back the "all clear" signal. In two hours 20 landing boats were beached, some with their bottoms knocked out on the rocky coast, which was unfamiliar to the men who brought the boats in.

It was a nasty day, raining and foggy, but that was the kind of weather we needed. It meant that no Jap scout plane could spot us. The water of the North Pacific was icy to the men, who had to wade several yards up to the beach.

There was no dock for the power barges, and the only way to get the supplies ashore was to carry them in from the barges through the water. The soldiers formed a chain between barges and shore, passing the crates from one man to the next. They worked two hours on and four off, but there was very little chance to sleep. They spent the off-hours trying to dry themselves at little fires kindled with wet driftwood. But on the third day a big barge was pulled up onto the beach to act as a dock. Then the power barges drew up to it and the supplies were unloaded on trucks. That was easier and faster for the men.

By this time the engineers had started bringing off heavy equipment and steel matting for an airplane runway. They worked day and night, changing the course of a stream so they could use the valley for the strip. When the area was leveled, they began to lay steel.

Nine days after troops came ashore at Adak, the first plane landed on the strip, carrying our first mail since we'd left the States. The next day B-24s, B-26s, P-40s, P-39s and P-38s came in, and by nightfall the field was full.

On the first clear day the planes took off for their initial bombing mission against Kiska, then in enemy hands. All the men turned out to watch them take off. We counted them, and were happy when they all came back.

During the first week we ate C rations, until the Quartermaster boys could get rations off the ships and break them down for each organization. A lot of fellows were too hungry to wait, and so some of the rations were filched. The first time I saw Maj. Gen. Eugene M. Landrum, who later commanded the Attu invasion forces, I was carrying away a case of Carnation milk on my shoulder. He just smiled; I don't think he blamed us.

Every organization furnished a man for a ration guard, and the result was that the guard just finishing his shift didn't know his relief man by sight. One soldier put on all his equipment, pretended to be on guard and went down to relieve the man at the ration pile. As soon as the real guard was out of sight, some men from the fake guard's outfit came and helped themselves to rations.

Our first raid by Jap planes came one morning about 0515. Two Jap float planes came over and dropped some bombs, but missed their target by a helluva long way. The only thing that bothered us about the raid was getting up so early in the cold.

The next night the Japs came again, but we knew when they were coming and we were all out to watch the show. In about 15 minutes we heard planes in the distance. We knew they were there, but all we saw was an explosion from one little bomb in the distance. The Japs never returned again.

By this time the men had fairly comfortable quarters, including steel huts for mess halls. Christmas was near, but letters were few and far between. A few Christmas packages were coming in. Every time a ship arrived, all the men turned out, hoping for a letter from mother, wife or sweetheart. The Red Cross sent Christmas trees. Each battery got one, and the men decorated the trees as best they could with the few materials at hand: some used colored paper and empty cartridge cases.

At last Christmas Day dawned. It was a white Christmas but not the kind you sing about. I went to wonderful church services conducted by Chaplain Jack Hergenston of Alabama. That was the first time I had ever seen him cry, but he wasn't the only one. It was the second Christmas he had spent away from home.

For Christmas dinner some of the organizations had turkey and chicken, but others had only canned hash, stew and Vienna sausages. The garrison had increased so rapidly since the order for food was placed that there wasn't enough of the fancier kind to go around. But we made the best of it.

Not long after, we learned that some of us were going to Amchitka, 68 miles from Kiska. We were all anxious to make the move. A small body of men landed on the cold, stormy night of Jan. 11, 1943. We had to wade ashore to the soft, muddy island. There was no wood for fire, and even if there had been we couldn't have used it. We were afraid of being spotted by a Jap sub, for the weather was too bad for us to send up a scout plane.

The only way to unload supplies was to come in as close as possible with a power barge, and then go the rest of the way through the water in a caterpillar and trailer. It was slow going.

The men slept in pup tents several nights, and some mornings they found themselves lying in a puddle of water when they woke up. But the sleeping bags kept them dry and warm. The weather was cold, but there was no snow the first few days —just lots of rain.

Chow was fine. We drew meats of all kinds from the ship, but we had no bread or sugar except what was in the C ration cans. But we all made out okay.

There were no roads. The ground was so soft that a tractor couldn't run over it. The only way to move supplies was to carry them on your back, and some units had as much as five miles to cover. We were lucky; our unit was less than a mile from the supply center.

About Jan. 23 a Jap scout plane came over Amchitka. The sky was almost clear, but there were a few scattered clouds, and the Jap came out of one of them at about 15,000 feet but never much closer. We knew that we were spotted and could expect a raid at any time.

On the beach next morning at 1030, I heard the same kind of motor above the clouds. The ceiling wasn't much over 600 feet. I looked up toward the sound and saw two Jap float planes diving through the clouds. We all fell down on the ground. The air filled with tracer bullets from our ack-ack. Three guns were shooting directly over me, and one of

the Jap planes dropped a bomb about 50 yards from me in the water.

The Japs came over the next morning about the same time, but their aim was still very poor. Then in the evening from 1800 to 1830 they returned with between three to nine planes, but they never made a hit.

Patrols of P-38s operating from Adak gave our Amchitka garrison fighter cover when weather permitted, but the Japs stayed away when the Lightnings were up. At last our own airstrip on Amchitka was completed, and on a clear evening P-40s landed on the strip. Later on they went up and played around at 10,000 feet, but no Japs came to challenge them. We were all disappointed; we wanted to see a dog fight.

The next evening they went up again, this time with better luck. Two Jap float planes were coming in at 3,000 feet. I was watching our P-40s; I thought at first they did not see the Japs, but they did. Four of our planes peeled off from the formation and opened up on the Japs. One Jap plane came down in flames. The other crashed in the water. That was the last time the enemy tried to bomb Amchitka.

With no more Japs to worry about, we settled down to work.

"Thanks for the promotion, Sir, but don't **expect** miracles."—Sgt. Bob Gallivan.

275,000 RATINGS

By Sgt. RAY DUNCAN

MY CONTACT with the Infantry has not been very great. An infantryman and I, in a Los Angeles barroom, once took two girls away from a couple of lieutenants. They were only medical lieutenants, but even so there was a gratifying sense of triumph. And I've liked the Infantry ever since.

That's why I'm interested in the War Department's move to give 275,000 ratings to the Infantry. This is a radical change of policy. I hope it works out as well as everyone expects.

All the infantrymen I ever talked to were privates, and they all seemed to like it that way. The idea of promotion seemed to puzzle and bore them.

Of course I'm judging only from those barroom conversations, and I've no way of knowing how the Infantry took its 275,000 ratings. But I imagine it might have been something like this:

"I've just wangled some ratings for you guys," says the first sergeant. He surveys the grimy faces of the men he has assembled in a little canyon 15 yards behind the lines.

"Now, can anyone tell me what a rating is?"

The men finger their rifles uneasily, looking around at each other. Finally Blakely, who was 29 years in the Army, speaks up:

"A rating," he says, "is a form of promotion, or whatever you call it. They have it in the Air Corps. I saw something about it in a training film."

"Very good. And just what is a promotion?"

No one volunteers to answer. "Oh," says the first sergeant, "here comes the lieutenant! I think he wants to say something to you men."

"I've managed to arrange some ratings for you men," smiles the lieutenant. "I went to bat and I stuck my neck out for you men. We're going to make seven of you pfcs!"

He pauses to let the dramatic effect of these words sink in. The men look at each other uneasily out of the corners of their eyes.

"Sir," says Wilton, sounding off, although he's a newcomer of only six years' service. "Sir, I don't want to be this pfc or whatever you said. I want to stay in the Infantry!"

"It isn't what *you* want," snaps the lieutenant.

"It's what the Army wants that counts. If we need a detail of men for pfc we'll get a detail of men for pfc, and no griping from you dogfaces."

At this moment the enemy attacks. The infantrymen go into action in a wild melee of rifle fire, machine gunning and bayonet charges. They leap on two advancing tanks and set them afire. A strafing plane is brought down by their angry rifles.

"We're going to have seven pfcs," continues the lieutenant when things begin to quiet down.

"Just a minute there," interrupts the major, who has dropped over to see what the shooting was about. "Just a minute. We're going to have two corporals, too. I succeeded in getting two corporals, besides the seven pfcs that I got for you men."

The apprehensive Infantry begins to melt away, the far ones disappearing into the underbrush, those up close milling around and maneuvering for the back of the formation.

"You and you and you!" yells the first sergeant, grabbing nine men and herding them forward. The major hands out the single and double stripes.

"Sir, what do I do with this?" asks Nolan, holding his stripe delicately between his thumb and first finger.

"Put it on your sleeve!" bellows the major. "You ought to know that much! Haven't you read your *Soldier's Handbook?* You men with stripes, you're supposed to be better soldiers than the men in the ranks. You're supposed to be an example for the other men! You've got to learn to accept a little responsibility. If you can't we'll take those stripes off you and give them to men who can! You men can be busted! We'll start a noncom school tomorrow."

The unhappy nine stare at the ground and make little marks with the butts of their rifles.

"Here, you noncommissioned officers and privates first class!" explodes the major. "Don't you know you're supposed to be at attention? You men ought to be ashamed to be wearing those stripes! You're busted, every one of you!"

He snatches back the stripes. "Go back to your duties, privates!" With a happy shout the nine men rush to rejoin their comrades.

THE BIRTH OF A MISSION

By Sgt. WALTER PETERS

A HEAVY BOMBER STATION, BRITAIN—Two second lieutenants, recent arrivals from the States, walked to the Officers' Club bar and ordered whiskies.

"Make it a double," said one of them.

"Sorry, sir, no whisky is sold during alerts," said the bartender, Cpl. James Mohafdahl of Dayton, Ohio.

"Oh, I see," the other lieutenant mused. "When'd the alert come through?"

"About 15 minutes ago, sir. Right, Dan?" The corporal turned to the other bartender, Pvt. Daniel Costanzo, an ex-cowboy and saloon owner from San Antonio, Tex.

"Yeah, about that long," Costanzo agreed.

The lieutenants smiled. "Well, we may as well get some sleep then," one said. They walked out.

"It's funny," the corporal said, "but I can practically always tell when there's going to be an alert and, better yet, whether the raid'll go through. It's just instinct. That's all. Just instinct. Ask Tiny. He'll tell you."

Tiny was a 6-foot, 260-pound former foundry worker, Pvt. Frederick Tard of Everett, Wash. He was also assigned to the club staff, but that night he was on pass.

"They're a swell lot of boys here," the corporal said. "There's no rank pulling. I've seen lots of them come in fresh from the States, and I've seen lots of them go on their first mission and never come back. There used to be one fellow, a lieutenant. He always used to come in and order a drink and never talk to anybody but me. He'd rather talk to me than to a lot of majors around. He went down on a raid. He always said: 'Corporal, you take care of me. And believe me, I always did."

Another lieutenant walked in and asked for a whisky. Costanzo explained again that no hard liquor was sold during alerts. Beer was okay, though. The lieutenant bought a beer.

The corporal took up where he'd left off. "I don't know whether the lieutenant is a prisoner of war or not. But I'd sure like to meet him again. He was a nice guy. One thing, all these fellows know where to come when they want something. They see me, Jimmy. If it can be gotten, I get it."

A sign on the wall behind the bar read: "MEMBERS OF THE WORLD'S BEST AIR FORCE ARE SERVED AT THIS BAR."

Costanzo looked our way, paused for a moment and said: "We don't sell whisky the night before a raid."

OFFICERS AND THE FO

Beyond a one-lane winding road from the Officers' Club, deep inside a single-story building, was the intelligence room. Large maps of the fighting fronts adorned the walls, and colored markings indicated important enemy targets and other information about them.

Except for the maps, the intelligence room might have passed for a board of directors' office. In the center was a long, well-polished table, surrounded by eight comfortable leather chairs. In the corner was a radio playing soft, slow music transmitted by a British Broadcasting Corporation station. An S-2 first lieutenant relaxed in one of the chairs, his legs slung over its arm. A staff sergeant walked in and out of the room incessantly, always looking very serious, always carrying what appeared to be important documents.

The sergeant walked out of the room, then returned. "The FO is in, sir," he said.

"Okay," replied the lieutenant, "call the colonel."

Three other members of the S-2 staff walked in— Maj. F. J. Donohue, chief of the group's intelligence section, a former Washington (D. C.) lawyer; Capt. Wayne Fitzgerald of Kalamazoo, Mich., the group bombardier, and Capt. Ellis B. Scripture of Greensburg, Ind., the group navigator.

The three men sat down and watched as the sergeant tracked a narrow red tape from the spot on the map that represented the base in Britain to the enemy target that was to be bombed the next morning. The tape followed the exact course as directed by the field order.

Presently a tall, middle-aged man walked in. He was a good-looking guy with a friendly smile. This was Col. John Gerhardt of Chicago, commander of the group. With him was Lt. Col. David T. McKnight of New York, the air executive officer of the group. McKnight was short and had a personality that makes friends quickly.

Each colonel was eating a bar of candy and they offered a bite to everyone in the room. Col. Gerhardt stood before the map and studied it. Then he asked for a copy of the field order. A cat strolled by lazily. Lt. Col. McKnight stroked her back until she lifted her tail and purred. When the field order was brought in, the officers began to study it.

SUPERSTITION AND FATE

The base theater, which also houses the chaplain's office and serves as a church on Sundays, was filled to capacity that night, as it usually is. The sergeant gunners and officers apparently liked the film, because they laughed a lot and occasionally somebody whistled. The picture was "Duke of West Point," featuring Louis Hayward and Joan Fontaine.

Inside the Aero Club, run by the Red Cross, enlisted men were reading home-town newspapers, playing billiards or standing in line by a long counter for an evening snack. A round-faced sergeant with a neat black mustache, Vincent Barbella of Brooklyn, N. Y., was drinking a Coca-Cola and doing a lot of talking. With him was T/Sgt. Harry D. Cooper, a radio gunner from Dayton, Ohio, and T/Sgt. Robert E. Bellora, a top turret gunner from Ellwood City, Pa.

"Tomorrow's my 12-B," Barbella said, then laughed. "To hell with it. I won't call it 12-B. I'm not superstitious. I'll call it straight number 13. I certainly hope we go tomorrow, though," Barbella said. "That will make it about the sixth time I've been trying to make my thirteenth."

Cooper smiled. "You'll make it tomorrow. I'll bet anything on that. The night is clear and the odds are that it'll stay that way until morning."

"It's not the raids that bother me," Barbella said. "It's these damned abortions. People don't realize how much there is to making a raid. They figure all you do is jump in a Fort and up you go. They don't figure that weather out here can change within a half-hour, or that after a guy is up there for a couple of hours, something can go shebang with an engine or the oxygen system, and then you have to turn back."

At an adjoining table a sergeant was reading a newspaper. Barbella turned and read the headlines. "Berlin," he said. "Boy, is the RAF giving them the works now. Boy, would I like to go there. It'd be nice to say I'd been over Berlin."

Bellora spoke up. "For all you know, you may get the chance. You never can tell. That's where they may send us tomorrow, but I doubt it. Tomorrow will make me 21 missions. Hell, it doesn't matter where you go. If it's going to get you, it'll get you over Bremen or over Emden or over Kiel or anywhere. It's all up to fate, I think. But I'm not taking any chances. I think my two .50s have a helluva lot to do with this fate racket."

Enlisted men from the theater filed into the Aero Club when the movie was over. A short, frail sergeant stopped and whispered something in Barbella's ear. Apparently it was some sort of a private joke. Barbella laughed so enthusiastically that he had to stand up.

"What the hell's eating you, man?" Cooper asked in a friendly tone.

"Oh, nothing. Nothing," Barbella replied. "But I'm going to eat somebody's stuff out if we don't go out tomorrow." He laughed again.

DISAPPOINTMENT AND HUNGER

Tall, bespectacled 1st Lt. David B. Henderson, in charge of the base photographic section, walked into the laboratory looking very sad.

"He wouldn't let me go. Said maybe it'd be okay next mission," Henderson said. He had just returned from the S-2 room where he'd asked Maj. Donohue if he could go on the next morning's mission. In civilian life Henderson worked for the Ashland Refining Company in Ashland, Ky. His job on the base was an important one, but you got the impression that he'd be happier as a sergeant gunner.

There was an aroma of fried onions in the laboratory. It came from a room where a couple of staff sergeants were packing film into the combat cameras.

Sgt. David B. Wells of Trona, Calif., walked into the room with a loaf of bread.

"No, sir. It's nothing like this back in the States. If we're hungry, we just scrounge some grub and prepare it right in here. Wish I had a nice piece of steak to go with those onions. A guy gets hungry at this time of night. I always get hungry before missions."

"You ain't kidding, bub," said T/Sgt. Berton Briley of Wilson, Okla. Briley was a musician in civilian life. Now he is a combat photographer.

Lt. Henderson walked into the room and poured some coffee into a large tin cup. "There's nothing like a good hot cup of coffee at night. Too bad I can't go out in the morning."

COMBAT AND COMRADESHIP

There was no electric power that night in one of the squadron areas, so a group of lieutenants sat around inside their flat-roofed quarters and chatted by candlelight.

Four of them—Lt. Robert Sheets of Tacoma, Wash.; Lt. Jack Watson of Indianapolis, Ind.; Lt. Elmer W. Yong of Roachdale, Ind., and Lt. Joseph C. Wheeler of Fresno, Calif.—had joined the squadron only that week. They had been in the Fortress that buzzed the Yankee Stadium in New York during a World Series game in September. Mayor La

Guardia raised an awful stink when that happened. The boys were hauled over the coals for it by their CO when they reported to their field in Maine.

"All of that looks funny now that we're going into actual combat," said one. "It's the first mission that counts. Once I get over the hump on that one I'll gain my bearings. I'm just itching to get that first one in."

A first lieutenant called Hapner, who kept talking about his home town, Hamilton, Ohio, stopped cleaning a carbine.

"I know just how you feel," Hapner said. "You change a lot after about the first five missions. I don't know how to put my finger on it, but you sort of become more human. You become more appreciative of the men you fight with and the men you live with. It's particularly bad when you lose some of the men on your crew, or if one guy finishes his ops ahead of you and then leaves the crew.

"My pilot just finished his ops and he's off combat now. He was a swell guy. He always said that as long as I was doing the navigating and he was holding the stick, we had nothing to worry about. That guy should have gotten the Congressional Medal if anyone ever should.

"Kit Carson went through more hell than anyone I know of, but he never complained. He was a very religious guy and talked about his mother an awful lot. He never talked about himself, though. Except for the way he talked, you'd never get it from him that he was from Texas.

"Kit lost his original crew. They went off without him once and never returned. He was really shook up by it. But would he complain?" Hapner turned as if expecting somebody to say something, then answered his own question. "No, Kit never complained."

"They assigned him as co-pilot on the *Brass Rail*. That's how we got on the same crew. The pilot at that time was Lt. John Johnson. Johnson was married and had a helluva pretty wife in East St. Louis, Ill. On a raid over Kiel, a 20-mm exploded against Johnson's side and killed him. The *Brass Rail* nose-dived about 4,000 feet and everybody in it thought sure they were goners. Ammo boxes and everything else were flying all over the plane. By some miracle, Kit was able to level the ship off. Except for Kit the whole crew would have been goners. He got the DFC for that. I really miss that guy."

The new lieutenants listened carefully. They had met Kit just before he left the squadron, but up to now they hadn't realized what he'd been through. One of the lieutenants said: "He certainly didn't toot his own horn, did he?"

"Well, neither will you after a while," Hapner said. "Combat does something to a man. You'll see."

Hapner began to undress. "Well, guess I'll turn in. It may be a long one tomorrow."

ARMAMENT AND THE MEN

It was 2230, and the weather was still holding up. A long single file of men, almost all of them with torches in their hands, walked out of a Nissen hut. They were the armament men. They talked, but in low tones. Most of the officers and gunners had turned in, and armament men respect sleeping men of the combat crews.

An armament man said: "Maybe we won't have to unload again for a change. It looks too good out tonight, even for English weather."

Two sergeants stopped playing blackjack for a minute and talked about the armament men. Almost everybody else in the hut was in his bunk. The two sergeants were sitting on the lower section of a double bunk. A spotlight hung from the spring of the upper bunk, throwing just enough light on the cards.

"I suppose we ought to turn in," said one. "It may be a tough one tomorrow. When it comes right down to it, these armament guys really have the toughest racket. It must be hell on them to load up and then have to go out and unload when a mission is scrubbed. I hope it isn't scrubbed tomorrow."

From the corner of the room came a loud protesting voice. It was a Southern voice. "Damn that fire. Who the hell wants a fire on at night? It only goes out before you get up, and then we're cold as hell."

"Aw, shut up, you rebel," another voice answered.

The Southern boy complained again. "Well, I don't want to be going on any missions with a cold. Somebody ought to throw water on the fire."

The sergeants who were playing cards stopped the game. One of them spoke up. "You're liable to blow the place up if you throw water into that stove now, boy."

"I don't give a damn," said the Southerner.

DOGS AND THE AAF

It was 0400 and all the combat men were sound asleep. An excited voice bellowed out of the PA system.

"*Attention all combat crews! Attention all combat crews! Breakfast until 0445. Breakfast until 0445. Briefing at 0500. Briefing at 0500.*"

In the kitchen of the combat mess, two cooks were standing by a stove with pans in their hands. They were frying eggs for the men scheduled to fly that morning.

"I don't know why it is," the short cook said, "but about every dog in England seems to have found a home on this base."

"You'll find the same thing on all the bases," the other cook said. "Even the RAF has its share of dogs. Some of them have seen more combat than a lot of guys."

"You know, I was thinking," said the short one, "almost every new crew brings in a dog from the States. Now, if some smart apple of a German spy wanted to figure the Air Force strength in Britain, all he'd have to do is figure how many dogs there are on the bases and then multiply it by 10."

The other cook gave the short one a disgusted look.

"You're as crazy a guy as I've ever met. Who the hell's going to chase all over Britain counting dogs? Besides, you've got to figure how many of these dogs get in the family way as soon as they land here. Trouble with you is, you read too many detective stories."

The short cook grinned. "Aw, I was only thinking," he said and went on frying eggs.

No. 25 and Herky Jerky

Briefing was over. A half-ton truck was rolling along the runway. It was about 0600, but still very dark. The truck turned into a narrow road and stopped at a small shed. Then about six men jumped out and went inside.

About 25 sergeants were cleaning caliber .50s on long benches. Above them were signs reading:

WITHOUT ARMAMENT THERE IS NO NEED
FOR AN AIR FORCE
Lord Trenchard, Marshal of the RAF

Sgt. Barbella was cleaning his guns alongside the top turret gunner on his crew, Dean Hall, a tall, slim boy from New Jersey. Hall and three others from the crew of the *Herky Jerky* were making their 25th mission that morning.

The sergeants carefully enclosed their guns in burlap bags and headed for the hardstand.

A Baby and a Mission

It was five minutes before stations. Capt. Rodney E. Snow Jr. of High Point, N. C., walked over by the tail of the plane and stood there for a moment. It was a ritual with him, just as it is with a lot of other men who are flying in this war.

Snow's bombardier, Lt. George Lindley of Seattle, Wash., was smoking a cigarette and telling the left waist gunner about his baby son. The baby was born on Oct. 16 and Lindley was sweating out a picture that was supposed to be on the way over. The mission didn't seem to bother him, but the absence of the baby's picture did.

In the ground crew's tent, a little off the hardstand, two other men from the *Herky Jerky* were debating whether they'd even get off the ground that morning.

"No. 7 was always my lucky number, and I think this is the seventh time we're trying for this mission. So I guess we'll make it," said the co-pilot. He was a big strapping fellow, Lt. John Merriman of Spokane, Wash. Everybody on the crew razzed him about his large belly and somebody kidded him about being pregnant.

"No, that's what I got for being a chow hound, I guess," Merriman answered, taking it seriously.

Snow called on all the men to get into the plane. Then No. 1 engine was started. No. 2 followed and 3 and 4 began to roar next. The plane taxied up to the edge of the runway and in a few minutes it was airborne. And that was the beginning of the mission.

"No Ma'am, it was neither Bizerte or Attu. It was an upper bunk at Fort Brookings, S. Dak."—*Cpl. F. J. Torbert.*

"FIVE MINUTES AFTER I LEFT YOU..."

BY CPL. LEN ZINBERG

WE HAD been on the road a long time and when we finally hit this camp and found it was near a big city, the three of us skipped chow and lit out for town. "This is supposed to be a soldier's town," Red Ducharme said.

" 'Soldier's town'—meaning they rook you with a smile," Razz, the old soldier, said.

"Aw, stop beefing," Red said, straightening his tie and brushing up his pfc. stripe as we stepped off the bus. "There's plenty of gals here, and I understand they're willing and anxious to be patriotic."

"Another latrine rumor," Razz told him. "One thing, no matter what happens, we skip the USO. I'm in no mood to play ping-pong tonight. Hey, you notice there aren't many soldiers here."

It was true; you didn't see many soldiers on the streets. In fact you hardly saw anybody. The streets were pretty well empty and dead. We cased the town. We saw lots of girls, all under 12. We got tired of walking and went into a crummy-looking beer joint and had a few. Some girls were dancing with their 4-F boy friends. A couple of middle-aged women were sitting by themselves.

Ducharme gave them the eye and fixed his hat at the proper cockeyed angle. "What the hell, they're not too bad looking," he said and strutted over.

"Are you in the Air Corp?" one of them asked. "I have a grandson in the Air Corp."

"That's swell," Red said; he's tough and can take anything. "Suppose I sit down and talk it over?"

One of the other grandmothers took her teeth out of a glass of cold water and snarled, "Beat it, character!"

We went into another beer parlor. The barkeep was friendly. "Any dames around?" we asked.

He nodded. "Some real beauties—so they say."

"Where are they?" Razz asked.

"I don't know," the bartender said. "I been looking for them myself. I've only been here 10 years."

Ducharme stood up. "This is disgusting," he said. "I'm going to wolf it alone."

We said okay and he went out. Razz and I had a few more beers and scouted the town again. A cute-looking girl waiting for a streetcar stopped us with "What time is it, soldiers?"

"Eight P.M., honey," we said eagerly.

"Good Gawd—as late as that! My mommy will bawl me out for coming home so late."

"Good-bye, honey," we said. We walked around

some more; then I said: "Let's drop in at the USO and knock off a couple of letters."

"You drop in," Razz said. "See you in camp."

The USO was nice and quiet, and I wrote two letters and danced with a gal who can rent herself out as an ice cube any day. I went back to camp. Ducharme and Razz were asleep: you could tell from their heavy snoring that they had hit the hay some time ago. It was almost midnight.

The next morning as we came in from roll call, Ducharme yawned and said, "What a night! Five minutes after I left you guys I walked into Lana Turner's twin sister. Had an apartment of her own. I was up all night." Red winked. "Hope I can duck the dog today and grab some shut-eye. I'm all in."

I asked, "Just after you left us, huh?"

Red nodded. "Just about five minutes."

"I didn't do so bad either," said Razz. "Just after I left you, some blonde came by in a car and gave me a lift. She was lonesome as hell. We rode around for a while and then went up to her hotel room and killed a bottle. She was stacked—and like a stove."

"I must 'a been asleep when you got in," I said.

Razz thought for a moment. "Must have been about 4 in the morning when she drove me back to camp. You have any luck?"

"Yeah," I said. "Couple of minutes after I left you I walked down to that boathouse by the river, and a babe was swimming in the moonlight. A redhead —looked like the champ of all the pin-up girls. We got to talking and first thing you know, I stripped to my shorts and we swam out to her yacht. Big boat. She has all kinds of dough, two Packard roadsters and a trunk full of C cards. Husband died and left her a wad. We had some time—just the two of us. Going out there again tonight."

Razz looked at me. "Sounds good. When did all this happen?"

"About five minutes after I left you," I said, staring him right in the eye.

"But this is absurd! I don't even know the man!"
—A/S Gerry Turner.

MAIL CALL

DEEP IN THE HEART

DEAR YANK:

Recently I was a dinner guest of the president of the Texas Christian Federation of Women's Clubs in Brownwood, Tex. The hostess told me she had tried to get her club to invite soldiers to members' homes, and I thought GIs would like to see the reply she got from one of the members. Unfortunately it is representative of what the "better class" of moguls really think. Here's the letter:

Dear Mrs. President. When you propose that we ask soldiers to our homes we feel as though you have failed us in the most critical situation which has ever arisen to face us. To ask the women of Texas to place their daughters on the altar of sacrifice to the evil that will come from the program which you presented is asking too much. I know our boys are lonely, but unless they have manhood enough to deny themselves some things for a few short months I do not believe they are courageous enough to sustain our democratic government.

Let us just look at the situation. If the social contacts at the camps were the end of those meetings quite another outlook could be seen, but you know those boys will go out on the week ends and contact our girls again. This time they will not be chaperoned, and for the virtue of how many girls who have thus lost their purity will we be held accountable? We just can't do this. Do not let us sell our daughters in such a racket. Maybe a few would meet life companions, but think of the sorrow and misery and sin we would be leading the numberless ones into! Men and women of the convention were hurt by your proposal. The decision almost wholly was that we mothers and fathers will not stand for this. We feel that the class of boys whom the girls would meet under your plan are the ones who deliberately want to meet strange girls and they are not the best class of selectees. Many are filled with uncontrolled passion and lust, and many of them are married. I am willing to sacrifice my time, my money and all my material profits for my country, but I cannot give my daughter in such a useless cause.

Well, I just thought you'd like to know what to expect when this melee is over.

Camp Bowie, Tex.   —PFC. JAMES L. SCOTT

DEAR YANK:

I have never wanted to be quoted publicly before, and this is the first time I have ever written to any publication, but this is also the first time I have ever been so burned up. As a native Texan, and mighty proud of it, I found the letter submitted by a Camp Bowie (Tex.) soldier, which had been written by a member of the Texas Christian Federation of Women's Clubs in Brownwood, Tex., the most disgusting piece of writing I have ever had the misfortune to read. It is certainly the least representative of any I have ever read about Texas women. . . . Brother, she is no real Texan.

On Maneuvers   —LT. H. H. MONTGOMERY

DEAR YANK:

. . . . She very plainly shows that she herself does not have any knowledge of the term "our democratic government," of which she speaks. . . . This woman has certainly made a bad impression of herself, her club and the state of Texas as a whole. . . .

Panama   —PVT. ELWOOD J. HALE

DEAR YANK:

. . . Any girl who would have relations with a fellow under the conditions proposed by the woman in Texas is not the type coming up to my level and caliber. That, I believe, speaks for the entire personnel of the armed services of our country.

Antigua   —PFC. WILLIAM D. TAYLOR

DEAR YANK:

. . . And that remark about Deep in the Heart. We're proud of who wrote it, as we want our gals as we left them and we don't want them on the altar of sacrifice. We are glad the mothers of Texas are holding on to their daughters and that they hold their respect.

Attu   —SGT. DELMOS DANIELS

DEAR YANK:

"I am willing to sacrifice my time, my money, and all my material profits for my country, but I cannot give my daughter. . . ." This is from that letter quoted in YANK. To it I add a poem:

THE ULTIMATE SACRIFICE

My daughter is precious; she's finer than gold,
But hardly constructed for soldiers to hold.
    A soldier's the sort
    For rapine and slaughter,
    Not fit to escort
    A patriot's daughter.
I'll sacrifice time, but dear me! I falter
When requested to lay my poor girl on the altar.

I know that the men must be awfully lonely;
I'd like to assist them if possible, only
    The boys may be tempted
    To ask for a date;
    No girl is exempted
    When staying out late
From possible harm by inordinate passion
And a plunge into ruin in the most expedite fashion.

Beware of the soldier who comes to your house;
It's a hundred to one he's a wolf or a louse.
    You will certainly find,
    If you scratch a GI,
    A lecherous mind
    And a wandering eye.
The soldier who enters your home's of a surety
An imminent threat to your daughter's security.

Camp Shelby, Miss.   —S/SGT. GRANT A. SANDERS

DEAR YANK:

. . . . The remark about selling daughters to American soldiers is one of the most stupid remarks any normal person has ever made. . . .

India   —S/SGT. JOHN GRIDER °

° *Also signed by Pvt. Peter Manquacine.*

DEAR YANK:

. . . I have never known of a Christian person with such a nasty and inconsiderate attitude toward the men and boys that are serving their country in these trying times. Any girl that has to have a chaperon along on a date to remain pure and clean is not the type of girl that a soldier would like to be seen in public with. . . .

Hawaii —PVT. DORSEY WIGGINS °

° *Also signed by Sgt. Lester, T-5s Howell, Rouse and Wilkinson and Pfc. Lemmens.*

DEAR YANK:

YANK acted in good faith in publishing Pfc. James Scott's letter in regard to the feelings of the mothers of Brownwood—it was James Scott who acted in ill faith in submitting a letter without explaining the circumstances surrounding the letter. . . . [It] was written over three years ago by a woman who lived approximately 150 miles southwest of Brownwood and who, at that time, had probably not met a single one of our new brand of GIs. It was written to a woman who lived in Austin, Tex. A copy of that letter was sent to a Brownwood woman because it was outrageously dramatic enough to be funny. . . .

—MUZELLE STANLEY
Brownwood, Tex. City Recreation Supervisor

MERCY FOR JAPS

DEAR YANK:

As God is my witness I am sorry to read of the way two American soldiers treated the enemy on Makin Island; they shot some Japanese when they might have been able to take them alive. I don't believe in killing unless it has to be done. I am a servant of God, so when I get into battle I hope by His help to take as many Japs alive as I can. If I am compelled to destroy lives in battle I shall do so, but when U. S. troops throw grenades into an enemy position and Japs run out unarmed we should make an effort to take them alive. I know that if I were in a dugout and forced to run out I would want mercy.

Camp Davis, N. C. —PVT. RALPH H. LUCKEY

DEAR YANK:

We just read the letter written by that servant of God, Pvt. Luckey, and wish to state that he has the wrong slant. . . . After being in combat and seeing medics being killed trying to help our wounded makes you want to kill the bastards. . . . Fair play is fine among sportsmen but we are fighting back stabbers! . . .

Hawaii Jap Killers °

° *Signed by Pvt. P. Stupar.*

DEAR YANK:

. . . NO MERCY FOR MURDERERS!

On Maneuvers —PVT. SAM BONANNO

DEAR YANK:

Brother, Pvt. Luckey better live up to his last name if he goes into combat with the idea of taking Jap prisoners alive!

Port of Embarkation —SGT. CARL BETHEA °

° *Also signed by 13 others.*

DEAR YANK:

We are all Navy men who are suffering from combat fatigue. Many of us have been strafed by Jap Zeros while floating helplessly in the sea and have seen what the soldiers and marines have gone through in this fight. If Pvt. Luckey heeds his own call for mercy for Japs, his soul will belong to God but his body will belong to the Japs. . . .

—VETS OF WORLD WAR II
Norfolk Naval Hosp., Portsmouth, Va.

DEAR YANK:

. . . If I had another chance I certainly would do the the same thing those Yanks on Makin did. Shoot 'em and shoot 'em dead. I know what I'm talking about. I have been there.

Camp Blanding, Fla. —T/SGT. J. N. OLSEN

DEAR YANK:

. . . Please notify the FBI, G-2, anything—but have that guy locked up!

Fort Custer, Mich. —CPL. S. SCHWARTZ

DEAR YANK:

Has Pvt. Luckey ever seen his friends and buddies shot down by the Japs? Has he ever carried our dead out of the jungle for burial? I have—and more, during the eight months I spent on Guadalcanal. Pvt. Luckey will have no dead Japs on his conscience when they kill him.

—PVT. C. E. CARTER
Harmon Gen. Hosp., Longview, Tex.

DEAR YANK:

. . . Luckey is out of this world and should be confined in a small room heavily padded on four sides.

Bermuda —S/SGT. ARTHUR J. KAPLAN

DEAR YANK:

Me and my buddies sure were mad as hell when we read Pvt. Ralph Luckey's letter. He sure shot off his mouth about our treatment of the Japs. The trouble is that he has had it nice and soft so far. . . .

Trinidad —PFC. EDWARD STAFFIN

DEAR YANK:

. . . We don't know whether to feel sorry for this guy or just laugh the thing off. . . .

—M/SGT. W. F. HARDGROVE °
NC Hosp., Mitchel Field, N. Y. (South Pacific)

° *Signed also by M/Sgt. R. M. Stephens (SWP); T/Sgts. L. C. Sheehan (Britain) and N. Sedorick (Britain); S/Sgts. P. F. Teraberry (Italy, Africa), R. I. Vogel (Italy, Africa), L. V. Behout (CBI), J. M. Haresign (Italy) and H. R. Garrison (New Guinea); Sgts. W. J. Polera, P. Nadzak (CBI) and J. Seginah (Britain), and Cpl. M. J. Bursie (New Guinea).*

DEAR YANK:

. . . Wake up, Luckey. The Jap doesn't care if God is his witness or not.

—PFC. CHARLES J. NICHOLS
Worthington Gen. Hosp., Tuscaloosa, Ala.

DEAR YANK:

It's evening. We're sitting about two feet from our foxhole thinking about a letter written by Pvt. Ralph H. Luckey from Camp Davis, N. C. in a recent issue of YANK. Do you mind if we ask him a question? Pvt.

Luckey, you're now living in an Army camp, just as we did. Making friends, just as we did. Friends who, in time, will be much closer, dearer, to you than you would believe possible.

We bunked together, ate together, laughed and played together, worked and dated together. Recently we fought together. During the battle, Blackie was wounded and taken prisoner. When we advanced several hours later, we found Blackie. His cheeks were punctured by sharp sticks—pulled tight by a wire tourniquet, the sticks acting as a bit does for a horse's mouth. There were slits made by a knife along the center of his legs and on his side—just as if an artist had taken pride in an act of torture well done.

We continued to move on. Do you think that we also continued to remember the niceties of civilized warfare?
Central Pacific   —S/SGT. B. W. MILEWSKI

This is the last of a series of GI comments in reply to Pvt. Luckey's letter. YANK has received a great number of letters on the subject, but only two readers supported the point of view advocated by Pvt. Luckey.

THANKS

DEAR YANK:

I would like to express my thanks to some unknown GI who looked after my mother when she wasn't feeling well on a train trip from Illinois to California this past December. Perhaps I can return the favor some day, soldier.
The Aleutians   —PFC. B. FELDMAN

A COLONEL SPEAKS

DEAR YANK:

Allow me, a low-serial-number Regular Army colonel, to add to the gripe of Pvt. David W. Wallace [who complained that "practically every café fit to patronize in Cairo, Egypt, is out of bounds to American enlisted men."—Ed.] It griped me, too, when in Cairo, to see privately owned, operated-for-profit night clubs open to all the public *except* GIs. Not only that, but with military police at the door to keep out the "untouchables."

Well, Wallace, let me describe what you were missing. Club No. 1 on my list: Infested with greasy looking Levantines of indeterminate origin accompanied by their high-priced "companions." Tom Collins quite expensive, made up of lukewarm Orange Crush and poor gin. . . . A helluva big check after a not very thrilling evening. Club No. 2: Fairly nice crowd except for one fat civilian surrounded by some hard-looking tarts on the make. He was trying rather unsuccessfully to get some young officers over to his table. Floor show lousy —belly dancers couldn't get even a trial on a Minsky circuit. Food fair, but "extras" very expensive. Officers there looked as if they wouldn't mind rubbing shoulders with other ranks.

No, soldier, you didn't miss much.

Just the same, I didn't like the signs "Military Personnel—Officers Only" one bit. One American GI is worth a helluva lot more than the best of the civilians I saw at those night clubs I attended. And from what I saw of our enlisted men in Cairo they would, by their neatness, general gentlemanly conduct and military

bearing, be an asset to any of the privately owned open-to-the-public clubs I've ever seen anywhere.

I hope the situation in Cairo changes under new management.
Italy   —An Officer and American Soldier

MONOTONY

DEAR YANK:

Monotony, monotony, all is monotony. The heat, the insects, the work, the complete absence of towns, women, liquor. Every too often the incredible routine inspection for diseases which couldn't possibly be there, under the circumstances. The irregular mail, which has become regular in its irregularity. The pay ritual; the eagle screams and so does the local GI, who has no choice but to send the money home—a prudent but singularly unsatisfying action. On a more personal basis, the monotony of prefixing the name with those three little —awfully little—letters: pfc.

All this monotony, and more, existed before. Then came the brilliant idea of subscribing to YANK. It all seemed so simple at the time. "Just send us your money order for two bucks," you said, "and before you know it YANK will be coming around regularly to cheer your spirit and brighten your days." So I did it. I sent the money order for two bucks. And what happened? I found that I had added a new monotony to the existing ones. With dreary, weary regularity I found myself writing letters to YANK on a regular basis, always dealing with the same topic: Where is the magazine? With equally monotonous regularity did I get no answer. Fellers, enough is enough. The heat, the insects, the lack of diversion—all these things you can do nothing about. But this one-sided correspondence. . . . Write to me, huh? Better yet, if you can possibly see your way clear, send me the damn magazine!
New Hebrides   —PFC. H. MOLDAUER

So *that's* where that two bucks came from.

PRAISE FOR MEDICS

DEAR YANK:

We have been and still are in combat and have decided to spend a little time in order to let you know about some real fighting men. They are the first-aid men in the Medics. They are doing a wonderful job here in the front lines. We infantrymen here take our hats off to them and would like to see them get a little more credit and praise.
Italy   —PVT. JOE MC GUIRE °

° *Also signed by Pfc. E. Charon.*

DEMOCRACY?

DEAR YANK:

Here is a question that each Negro soldier is asking. What is the Negro soldier fighting for? On whose team are we playing? Myself and eight other soldiers were on our way from Camp Claiborne, La., to the hospital here at Fort Huachuca. We had to lay over until the next day for our train. On the next day we could not purchase a cup of coffee at any of the lunchrooms around there. As you know, Old Man Jim Crow rules. The only place where we could be served was at the lunchroom at the railroad station but, of course, we had to go into the kitchen. But that's not all; 11:30 A.M. about two dozen German prisoners of war, with two American guards, came to the station. They entered the lunchroom, sat at the tables, had their meals served, talked, smoked, in fact had quite a swell time. I stood on the outside looking on, and I could not help but ask myself these questions: Are these men sworn enemies of this country? Are they not taught to hate and destroy . . . all democratic governments? Are we not American soldiers, sworn to fight for and die if need be for this our country? Then why are they treated better than we are? Why are we pushed around like cattle? If we are fighting for the same thing, if we are to die for our country, then why does the Government allow such things to go on? Some of the boys are saying that you will not print this letter. I'm saying that you will. . . .

Fort Huachuca, Ariz. —CPL. RUPERT TRIMMINGHAM

DEAR YANK:

I am writing to you in regard to the incident told in a letter to you by Cpl. Trimmingham (Negro) describing the way he was forced to eat in the kitchen of a station restaurant while a group of German prisoners were fed with the rest of the white civilians in the restaurant. Gentlemen, I am a Southern rebel, but this incident makes me none the more proud of my Southern heritage! Frankly, I think that this incident is a disgrace to a democratic nation such as ours is supposed to be. Are we fighting for such a thing as this? Certainly not. If this incident is democracy, I don't want any part of it! . . . I wonder what the "Aryan supermen" think when they get a first-hand glimpse of our racial discrimination. Are we not waging a war, in part, for this fundamental of democracy? In closing, let me say that a lot of us, especially in the South, should cast the beam out of our own eyes before we try to do so in others, across the seas.

—CPL. HENRY S. WOOTTON JR. *

Fairfield-Suisun AAF, Calif.

* *Also signed by S/Sgt. A. S. Tepper and Pfc. Jose Rosenzweig.*

DEAR YANK:

You are to be complimented on having the courage to print Cpl. Trimmingham's letter in an April issue of YANK. It simply proves that your policy is maturing editorially. He [Cpl. Trimmingham] probes an old wound when he exposes the problem of our colored soldiers throughout the South. It seems incredible that German prisoners of war should be afforded the amenities while our own men—in uniform and changing stations—are denied similar attention because of color and the vicious attitude of certain portions of our country. What sort of a deal is this? It is, I think, high time that this festering sore was cut out by intelligent social surgeons once and for all. I can well understand and sympathize with the corporal's implied but unwritten question: why, then are we in uniform. Has it occurred to anyone that those Boche prisoners of war must be still laughing at us?

Bermuda —S/SGT. ARTHUR J. KAPLAN

DEAR YANK:

. . . I'm not a Negro, but I've been around and know

what the score is. I want to thank the YANK . . . and congratulate Cpl. Rupert Trimmingham.

Port of Embarkation —PVT. GUSTAVE SANTIAGO

DEAR YANK:

Just read Cpl. Rupert Trimmingham's letter titled "Democracy?" in an April edition of YANK. We are white soldiers in the Burma jungles, and there are many Negro outfits working with us. They are doing more than their part to win this war. We are proud of the colored men here. When we are away from camp working in the jungles, we can go to any colored camp and be treated like one of their own. I think it is a disgrace that, while we are away from home doing our part to help win the war, some people back home are knocking down everything that we are fighting for.

We are among many Allied Nations' soldiers that are fighting here, and they marvel at how the American Army, which is composed of so many nationalities and different races, gets along so well. We are ashamed to read that the German soldier, who is the sworn enemy of our country, is treated better than the soldier of our country, because of race.

Cpl. Trimmingham asked: What is a Negro fighting for? If this sort of thing continues, we the white soldiers will begin to wonder: What are *we* fighting for?

Burma —PVT. JOSEPH POSCUCCI (Italian) *

* *Also signed by Cpl. Edward A. Kreutler (French), Pfc. Maurice E. Wenson (Swedish) and Pvt. James F. Malloy (Irish).*

DEAR YANK:

Allow me to thank you for publishing my letter. Although there was some doubt about its being published, yet somehow I felt that YANK was too great a paper not to. . . . Each day brings three, four or five letters to me in answer to my letter. I just returned from my furlough and found 25 letters awaiting me. To date I've received 287 letters, and, strange as it may seem, 183 are from white men and women in the armed service. Another strange feature about these letters is that the most of these people are from the Deep South. They are all proud of the fact that they are of the South but ashamed to learn that there are so many of their own people who by their actions and manner toward the Negro are playing Hitler's game. Nevertheless, it gives me new hope to realize that there are doubtless thousands of whites who are willing to fight this Frankenstein that so many white people are keeping alive. All that the Negro is asking for is to be given half a chance and he will soon demonstrate his worth to his country. Should these white people who realize that the Negro is a man who is loyal—one who would gladly give his life for this our wonderful country—would stand up, join with us and help us to prove to their white friends that we are worthy, I'm sure that we would bury race hate and unfair treatment. Thanks again.

Fort Huachuca, Ariz. —CPL. RUPERT TRIMMINGHAM

Since YANK printed Cpl. Trimmingham's letter we have received a great number of comments from GIs, almost all of whom were outraged by the treatment given the corporal. His letter has been taken from YANK and widely quoted. The incident has been dramatized on the air and was the basis for a moving short story published recently in the *New Yorker* magazine.

PIN-UPS

DEAR YANK:

We boys do not approve of your very indecent portrayal of the spicy looking female in a recent edition of our much-loved and eagerly read YANK. It seems the intelligent-looking Irene Manning would never pose for such a suggestive-looking picture. We may seem old-fashioned, but sending YANK home to wives and sweethearts with such a seductive-looking picture, we feel compelled to make an apology for this issue.

Is this the much publicized "Pin-Up Girl" that the Yankee soldiers so crave? We have our doubts! Miss Manning is well dressed, but the pose—phew! (Hays office please take note.)

Believe it or not, our average age is 23.

Britain   —SGT. E. W. O'HARA *

* Also signed by Cpl. P. Pistocco Jr. and D. E. Clark.

DEAR YANK:

I don't know who started this idea of pin-ups, but they say that it is supposed to help keep up the morale of the servicemen, or something like that. Here is my idea of the help it is. In the first place, I would say that 24 out of 25 of the men in the service are either married or have a girl at home whom they respect and intend to marry as soon as this war is over. . . . How many of you GIs would like to go home and find the room of your wife or girl friend covered with pictures of a guy stepping out of a bathtub, draped only in a skimpy little towel, or see the walls covered with the pictures of a shorts advertisement or such pictures? None of you would. Then why keep a lot of junk hanging around and kid yourself about keeping up morale? . . .

I would much rather wake up in the morning and see a picture of a P-51 or 39 hanging above my bed or over the picture of my wife, whom I think is the best-looking girl in the world, than of some dame who has been kidded into or highly paid for posing for these pictures.

Myrtle Beach AAF, S. C.   —PFC. JOSEPH H. SALING

DEAR YANK:

Sgt. E. W. O'Hara, in a recent letter about pin-ups in YANK, speaks of "suggestiveness" in the "seductive-looking" picture of Miss Irene Manning. For the life of me, I can't see anything suggestive about it. Shouldn't you say that the suggestiveness and the suggestive look come from an "unclean" mind, not from the picture? . . .

Panama   —S/SGT. CLIFF CROUCH *

* Also signed by S/Sgt. Raymond Cox.

DEAR YANK:

. . . Don't slam our pin-ups. If I had a wife I would make sure her picture was up, but Irene Manning will do until that big day.

Fleet Post Office   —SIC. R. C. WALTERS

DEAR YANK:

. . . Maybe if some of those panty-waists had to be stuck out some place where there were no white women and few native women for a year and a half, as we were, they would appreciate even a picture of our gals back home. The good sergeant [and the other two signers of his letter] alibi that perhaps they are old-fashioned and go so far as to apologize for the mag [when

sending it home]. . . . They must be dead from the neck up—and down. They can take their apology and jam it and cram it. And Pfc. Joseph H. Saling isn't he just too too? We suggest that when the next issue of YANK hits the PX these little boys refrain from buying it, as it is too rugged a mag for them to be reading. Perhaps later, when they grow up. We nasty old Engineers still appreciate YANK *with* its pin-ups.

Alaska   —T-5 CHET STRAIGHT *

* Also signed by T-5s F. A. Wallbaum and Cooper Dunn and Pfcs. Robert Ross, Lloyd W. Finley and Elom Calden.

DEAR YANK:

. . . I can't understand why you would even publish such a letter. In my opinion Sgt. O'Hara owes Miss Manning an apology for his rude description of her picture. I have that picture over my locker and like it very much. I suggest Sgt. O'Hara go out and learn the facts of life from someone who has been around. Also, the boys in my platoon agree with me that he should be examined for Sec. 8. Keep the pin-up pictures coming. We like them.

Camp McCain, Miss.   —CPL. JOHN R. CREICH

DEAR YANK:

Why we GIs over here in the Pacific have to read your tripe and drivel about the Wacs beats me. Who in the hell cares about these dimpled GIs who are supposed to be soldiers? All I have ever heard of them doing is peeling spuds, clerking in the office, driving a truck or tractor or puttering around in a photo lab. Yet all the stories written about our dears tell how overworked they are. I correspond regularly with a close relative of mine who is a Wac, and all she writes about is the dances, picnics, swimming parties and bars she has attended. Are these janes in the Army for the same reasons we are, or just to see how many dates they can get? We would like them a hell of a lot better, and respect them more, if they did their part in some defense plant or at home, where they belong. So please let up on the cock and bull and feminine propaganda. It's sickening to read about some doll who has made the supreme sacrifice of giving up her lace-trimmed undies for ODs.

New Hebrides   —SGT. BOB BOWIE

DEAR YANK:

I was disgusted when I opened the pages of a recent YANK and saw some silly female in GI clothes. I detest the Wacs very thoroughly and I hope I never meet one. That is also the opinion of all my buddies.

New Zealand   —PVT. WILLIAM J. ROBINSON

WACS HIT BACK

DEAR YANK:

After reading the letters of Sgt. Bob Bowie and Pvt. William Robinson [in a February issue] I think it is about time the Wacs had their say. Their stubborn, prejudiced attitude makes many of us wonder if it is really worth it all. . . . There are many heartbreaking stories behind many of our enlistees, stories that have not been published and will never be known, and there is a wealth of patriotism and sincere motives to be found in these girls.

Fort Crook, Nebr.   —PVT. CAROL J. SWAN

DEAR YANK:

. . . After reading Sgt. Bowie's disgusting opinion of the Wacs I must say that I think he's one hell of an American.

Indiantown Gap, Pa. —PVT. HELEN LONDON

DEAR YANK:

Hell hath no fury like a Wac criticized. . . . Many of these frilly females Sgt. Bowie blows his top about are a lot closer to action than a smug soldier who apparently has enough time to sit at his desk in the New Hebrides and write letters critical of the Wacs.

Fort Sheridan, Ill. —PFC. MILDRED MC GLAMERY

DEAR YANK:

. . . We have *not* given up lace-trimmed undies; most of us still wear civilian underwear. And, incidentally, I'll bet two months' pay that Sgt. Bowie was drafted. At least we all know we did not have to be forced to serve our country. We volunteered.

Selman Field, La. —WAC PRIVATE

DEAR YANK:

. . . As for sacrificing lace-trimmed undies for ODs, most of us didn't have any like that to sacrifice, as the majority of the Wacs were working girls.

Boston, Mass. —CPL. SOPHIE WOITEL °

° *Also signed by Pvt. Sybil Watson.*

DEAR YANK:

. . . To doff lace-trimmed panties and don ODs takes far more courage than it does to shoot a Jap through the heart.

Great Falls AAB, Mont. —1ST/SGT. EDITH F. KROUSE

DEAR YANK:

. . . Thanks for the bouquets, boys. Go right on sticking the knife in our backs. . . . When it's all over we'll go back to our lace-trimmed undies and to the kind of men who used their anger on something besides the Wacs.

ASTP, Madison, Wis. —T-4 JANE NUGENT

DEAR YANK:

. . . Thorns to Pvt. Robinson and to Sgt. Bowie. Without the roses.

Freeman Field, Ind. —CPL. FRANCES CLOUGH °

° *Also signed by Cpls. Adelaid J. Swett, Nora F. Fields and Beatrice Schweitzer and Sgt. Adelaide Bishop.*

DEAR YANK:

About five months ago—while winding up 3½ years in the Pacific—I wrote to your magazine an article about how much I detested the Wacs. But now I realize what a first-class heel I was. . . . My narrow-minded opinion has changed entirely, and I am very proud of those gallant American women. . . What this country needs is more of those wonderful girls. . . . Please print this, as I got quite a few letters from Wacs after they read my last article, and every one of them wrote such nice letters and wished my buddies and me the best of luck. I felt more ashamed than I have ever been before.

—PVT. WM. J. ROBINSON

Letterman General Hospital, Calif.

"MORE SHOOTIN' "

DEAR YANK:

A recent article described an incident in which a new replacement asked a fellow GI how to load his M1; this during the heat of battle with the enemy 10 yards away. Is it any wonder? I've been knocking around this Army for 24 months—14 months overseas—and have yet to learn how to load an M1 and jive it. I've never been taught to handle anything but the '03, but when action was imminent in the Aleutians I was handed an M1, a rifle I knew little about.

Ever since my induction I've been rushed through training so damned fast that I'm still wondering what the Army is all about. Six-week training took me to POE. Now that I'm in the States we're being rushed through training again. Hell! What this Army needs in training is "more shootin' and less salutin'" and more time to do it in.

Camp Shelby, Miss. —PVT. JOHN GRAHAM

FOR OFFICERS ONLY

DEAR YANK:

The *Sad Sack* cartoon called "Officers Only" in a December issue sure hit this town at the opportune moment. Military authorities here have decreed that "establishments featuring dancing, dining and drinking must either entertain commissioned officers or enlisted personnel exclusively or provide separate facilities for the two sections of the Army forces." This means that a GI cannot have dinner in a public dining room with his brother, uncle, father or friend, if they are officers.

I wonder if this is democracy? Take a look at your *Message Center* column and see the number of GIs who are trying to contact friends who are officers. If a GI and a friend who happens to be an officer are lucky enough to hit the same town at the same time, why can't they have a drink and dinner together?

—T/SGT. ALBERT L. WHEELER

Second Air Force, Colorado Springs, Colo.

DEAR YANK:

Reading T/Sgt. A. L. Wheeler's letter [in a January issue of YANK] where he told about the segregation of officers and enlisted men in Colorado Springs, Colo., made me disgusted. In these days when we Americans are fighting to maintain our democratic way of living, military authorities in Colorado Springs "decree" (I've seen that word in reference to totalitarian governments in Europe) that public establishments must entertain either commissioned officers or enlisted men only. I wonder if the foxholes in Italy and the bomb shelters in the Pacific maintain the same high standard of segregation.

AAB, Harding Field, La. —M/SGT. EDWARD G. RODDY

DEAR YANK:

Let's discuss this "democracy" stuff. Is the United States Army a democracy? Do you elect your leaders? Do you have the power to censure them? Do you have freedom of speech concerning things military? Are you tried by a jury of other soldiers? Of course not! Can you imagine an army where such things would be possible? Then let's not ask "Isn't this a democracy?"

because you can't run an army that way. Your country is a democracy but your Army is not, and neither is any other army.

I am a company commander. I like some of my men exceedingly well. I would get the greatest pleasure in having a few drinks with them. But I have found, in 10 years in the regular service, that it is not possible to be a leader, a father, a disciplinarian, an example in things soldierly, unless I keep a certain distance, thus maintaining a sort of awe, a myth of superiority, let us say.

Those leaders, whom enlisted men would always have followed through thick and thin, all conform to pretty much of a pattern—friendly, able, fair to all, kind, decent of mind and speech. But there's something else—a little secret of theirs. This is the secret: they never become *intimate* with their men. An enlisted man's respect and admiration for officers would have soon vanished had the officers become familiar enough to call them "Joe." Their myth would have burst like a bubble. The hero would have lost his heroism. He would disillusion the enlisted man by descending to their level. Your good officers are not the ones who will go partying with the enlisted men. It can't be. I wish it could. Some of my boys are the best in the world.

POE   —Infantry Lieutenant, Regular Army

DEAR YANK:

The "Infantry Lieutenant, Regular Army" need not have stated he was a Regular Army man, with 10 years' service; one could easily have deduced that by merely reading his letter. We'd like to know where he gets the idea that officers are supposed to maintain a "sort of awe, a myth of superiority," as he so egotistically states it. Maybe in the old Army he managed to get by that way, but the new Army is composed of lots of men who don't go for that sort of Army. These men are capable of thinking for themselves because they've been doing it a long time before they entered the service—so the lieutenant's "bubble of a myth" has been busted as of the date of their entrance.

Most amusing was his statement that becoming intimate with the men would be "dethroning the hero and disillusioning the men by descending to their level." What a bigot! . . .

The Aleutians   —CPL. EARL BRANDT *

    * Also signed by 23 others.

DEAR YANK:

. . . . There seems to be some argument about the segregation of officers and enlisted men. . . . We have officers over here that I, and I'm sure most of my buddies, would gladly go to hell for. I've lain in the same foxhole with a brigadier general and two lieutenant colonels. They were just as scared as I was, and they weren't bitching because there were EM in the same hole. These officers ate out of a mess kit and sweated out the same chow line I did. We respected them because they were men as well as officers. I expect to go home in a few weeks or months. I am afraid I am going to run into difficulties with some of those pretty shave tails, but I guess I'll just grin and bear it.

Guadalcanal   —CPL. CHARLES E. FREAD *

    * Also signed by Sgt. A. E. Gardner.

DEAR YANK:

. . . . The officers who haven't been in combat are usually the ones who throw their rank around, while the officers who have been through hell with their men are content to sweat out the line with the boys. I knew a major who was loved and respected by every man in his unit; it certainly wasn't because he pulled his rank. . . .

Italy   —T/SGT. WILLIAM BARNES (Ranger)

DEAR YANK:

The "Infantry Lieutenant, Regular Army" speaks of democracy. . . . I was at the Anzio beachhead and am now in a base hospital. I'm sure the men on the Cassino and Anzio fronts would lose their respect and admiration for their officers if they had not called them "Joe." For the *good* officers are the ones who go partying with the men. . . . When your officers call you "Joe," you know that even though you are a private that word "Joe" means a buddy. . . .

Italy   —PVT. JACK K. CHANCY *

    * Also signed by Pvts. Joe Busciglio and Terry Marico.

DEAR YANK:

. . . . I have just got back from two and a half years' service in the South Pacific, and during that time I was on nearly every island there. . . . I know officers who didn't do anything but peddle newspapers or Coca-Colas before they got in the Army. I know one man in a Seabee outfit who was a WPA foreman before he got in, and if he had to live off the Government before he got in the service, well, I guess that's as good a place as any for him. . . .

Harmon Gen. Hospital, Tex.   —CPL. HASTEN J. PEEK

DEAR YANK:

I would like to answer the lieutenant who said he was a company commander in the Infantry. He stated that if the officers would go on parties with the enlisted men and also live with them, the enlisted men would soon lose respect for the officers. I would like to ask this lieutenant if he has lost respect for his father? He lived with him, ate with him and sat beside him in the shows. . . . I think that a company commander who is unable to associate with his men, and still keep their friendship and respect, should not be a company commander. . . . I would like to tell the lieutenant that I have visited the Russian Army camp, and in their day room I found as many officers as soldiers playing pool together. I work with them every day, and I have seen captains working in the grease pits beside the enlisted men. What do you think of the Russian Army?

Iran   —T-4 JOHN T. EWING JR.

USO SOLDIERS

DEAR YANK:

I am going on to my fourth year overseas now and have three campaigns to my credit. I fully sympathize with those boys in the States who don't like to be called USO soldiers. The majority of the so-called foreign-service men that give this name to the soldiers in the States were or never will be within a thousand miles of a Jap or a German. I wish to apologize on behalf of the Infantry in this area for the wrong done to our comrades in arms back in the States. There are a hell of a lot more USO soldiers over here than there are back in the States. . . .

New Caledonia   —SGT. HERBERT G. HUNT

DEAR YANK:

. . . After all a guy back in the States is waiting to be called for overseas duty the same as we were. Why take it out on a fellow because he is still in the States? . . .

New Guinea —CPL. P. R. LUCARONI

DEAR YANK:

. . . We are a couple of GIs who want to get into the fight. We came over with a light ack-ack outfit which we thought was going places, but we turned out to be a bunch of service-club commandos. . . .

India —PVT. E. A. HIGGINS °

° *Also signed by Pvts. Kovalick, McHenry, William Campbell and Walters.*

AILMENT

DEAR YANK:

One morning I missed our duty formation and I thought I would cover up by going on sick call. Well, the doctor asked me what was bothering me, so I told him my stomach hurt, thinking I'd just get some pills and that would be all. But no, some guys had been sick from some bad meat they got in the rations, so the first thing I knew I was in the station hospital, marked "Meat Poisoning." Well, the doctor there saw I wasn't poisoned, so he started examining me and poking me in the gut with his finger. "Does that hurt?" he said. Well, he pushed so hard he just about put a hole through to my back, so I said "Yes." "Well, you got ulcers," he said, and the next thing I knew I was here in the general hospital. Well, they X-rayed me and stomach-pumped me, and they couldn't find anything wrong, so they sent me to see a brain doctor. Well, he asked me all kinds of fool questions and then he said to me: "You got nervous stomach." The next thing I knew they sent me to see a board of officers and they said: "You're no good in the Army. We're gonna send you home."

So YANK, here I am waiting to go home, and I never felt better in my life. I got started to thinking how everybody would call me 4-F and how I'd miss the Army and YANK. I don't want to go home. Tell me YANK, what can I do?

—PVT. JOSEPH GRANT

Ashford General Hospital, W. Va.

CIVILIANS

DEAR YANK:

It has come to our somewhat startled attention that the home front is shamelessly relaxing on the war effort. In a recent issue of a picture magazine there appeared revolting photos of an utterly "forget the war" spectacle at Miami, Fla., where literally thousands of vacationists pack the sunny city in search of race tracks, cool drinks, spicy shows and radiant sunshine, mindless of we who merely exist in our humble tents. Lonely wives who wish to visit their soldier-husbands are unable to because these pleasure-seekers occupy all available places of abode. War Bond booths close early (or do not open at all) because the race tracks are far more enticing

and, to those who are lucky, they pay ready cash. I wonder what a proud father would say if he had just put $18.75 on the nose of a horse and then received word from the War Department that "we regret to inform you that your son was killed in action"? . . .

Funny how people just don't think any more. . . .

Britain —PFC. THOMAS E. MEEK °

° *Also signed by Sgts. Ronald R. Coleman and Leroy C. Barth, Cpls. Richard H. Little and Salvatore H. Manganaro, and Pfc. William Clubough.*

DEAR YANK:

Lt. Tom Harmon has been quoted as telling a Detroit audience that he was ashamed of them and what they needed was a first-class bombing raid. Such a statement, especially coming from a man as high in public regard as Lt. Harmon, makes us burn. Prior to coming overseas, we had ample opportunity to observe civilians and gain a pretty fair idea of their feelings and attitudes. Civilians are accused of "not knowing there is a war on," but is there a family, a civilian, in the States who isn't worried about the fate of a friend or loved one overseas? What opportunity do they have for proving sincerity outside of doing their job, taking volunteer defense tasks and putting every cent they can spare into bonds? Maybe the people we know are exceptional, but we doubt it. They, and we believe the great mass of civilians, are doing these unspectacular things. A few are complaining, patronizing the black market, etc., and the whole people are maligned for it. How many soldiers are shameless goldbricks? Back to Lt. Harmon—why are we over here if not to prevent our homes from ever feeling a "first-class bombing raid"?

New Caledonia —PFC. DONALD R. HARKNESS °

° *Also signed by Pfc. Sam Bibler.*

RETURNING VETERANS

DEAR YANK:

Some of us have noticed with disgust the conduct of some of the sick and wounded soldiers returning from overseas. They think they should be petted and pampered and fussed over. The practice is more so among men who have never heard a gun fire. These screwballs want everyone to jump at their request. They spill their guts in the wards to all nurses and medical men that will lend an ear to their bull, despite the instructions they receive upon arrival in the U. S. to keep their mouths shut. We give you credit, boys, but how about buttoning your traps up and acting like real soldiers when you get off that boat, instead of acting like a bunch of maniacs. You guys might just as well know now as further on down the line that if you think people should kneel before you and bow "Allah, Allah," then you are nuts. This letter isn't meant for all returning boys, just those punks who are acting like damn fools and yelling 4-F to every civilian in sight when they get off the boat.

—M/SGT. H. COPPLE

Oliver General Hospital, Augusta, Ga.

FREE SPEECH

DEAR YANK:

I'm writing to the fellows who write the gripes and groans in *Mail Call* and I want them to know that as long as that column stays and the boys keep writing you about it, there will always be an America. My hat comes off to you fellows in India, Italy, the Aleutians, the South and Central Pacific and every place else I'm not. I read the papers about the war, as for the past three years I haven't been fortunate enough to get into it (or out of it for that matter), but they don't tell me and the rest of us four-effers what you guys really feel as individuals. I say to all you guys, go ahead and bitch and gripe, and to all you other guys, go ahead and smack 'em down for it. You birds don't know it but you're telling the world how you feel when you tell YANK. . . . In this way maybe the big shots can read what you're thinking, and when the war is through the people will know what your thoughts are and base their arguments on them instead of trying to figure out what they think your thoughts are.

Fort Jackson, S. C. —PVT. JOSEPH J. STRIZZI

LIBERATION OF ATHENS

BY SGT. JOE McCARTHY

ATHENS, GREECE—Liberation is getting to be old familiar stuff in Europe these days, but the feeling that swept this great city when it found itself free of Germans was something extra special, in a class by itself.

That was because the Greek people, as enemies of Hitler's fascism and as loyal members of the United Nations during the four years when such loyalty brought nothing but suffering, were also in a class by themselves. This country fought the war the hard way. It stood up against the Germans back in 1940 and early 1941, when Britain was unable to help and Russia and the U. S. were still sitting it out on the sidelines. Standing up against Germany wasn't considered the fashionable thing to do in Europe in those days.

When the Germans turned the full force of their then magnificent *Panzer* divisions toward Greece and finally overwhelmed the country, the Greeks still refused to make any kind of deal. There were no Petains or Lavals here. Rather than work for the Germans, the Greeks preferred SS torture chambers, firing squads and starvation.

Athens therefore had more than the usual reasons to cheer when the last dead-panned German soldier marched out of the city between lines of singing and marching men, women and children who waved Greek, British and American flags in his face. And the welcome the Greeks gave the British troops entering Athens during the next few days was bigger and louder than the American Legion conventions and the receptions for Lindbergh in 1927 all put together.

I arrived in Athens on a Saturday night, two days after the last Germans departed and two days before Lt. Gen R. M. Scobie led the main British invasion force in by sea from Alexandria and Taranto. I drove into the city by jeep along the shore road from Megara with a detachment of Red Devils, the veteran British paratroopers who had fought in the line at Cassino and other major operations. We found the road blown up by the retreating Germans in four or five places, but Greek men and women—working all day on their own with picks and shovels—mended it.

In every country village along the road, church bells were ringing and people pressed forward to our jeep, shaking our hands, giving the thumbs-up salute and offering us bread, cakes and fresh fruits even though food is scarce here. One woman handed a large bundle to one of our men and was lost in the crowd before he could give it back to her. He opened it later and found a large hand-knitted blanket, two clean sheets and a pillowcase.

When we reached downtown Athens, it was impossible to drive the jeep on until Greek Partisan soldiers opened a path for us through the mobs of people. We finally managed to reach the Grande Bretagne Hotel. When we climbed out of the jeep, the crowd swallowed us up, and the next thing I knew I was being squeezed, shaken, thumped, kissed and then picked up and carried down the street on somebody's shoulders. Luckily I heard a boy near me speaking English. I leaned down, shouting in his ear to make myself heard above the roaring crowd, and asked him to get me off the shoulders of these people and into the hotel across the street.

"Are you American?" he shouted back.

"Yes," I hollered.

"I am 17 years old and an American citizen," he shouted. "I want more than anything else to get into the American Army. How can I do this?"

"*Viva Americano!*" the crowd roared.

"Tell these people to let me down," I yelled at the boy, "and get me into the hotel across the street and I'll tell you all about it."

He finally managed, with fluent Greek persuasion, to squeeze me to the door of the hotel, but not before I had been kissed on the cheeks by three men, two women and two girls. After one of the girls had finished kissing me, she said very formally, in perfect English: "I hope you don't misunderstand this welcome. We Greeks are very enthusiastic people." In the hotel lobby the boy who had saved me from the crowd explained that his name was John Hatzis and that he was born in Boston, where his father used to work for the Boston and Albany Railroad.

When I told him that I, too, came from Boston, he was all excited. He said he came to Athens when he was 10 to spend a few years, and the war prevented his return to the States. His case is not unusual. We found the country full of Greek-Americans with sisters, brothers or wives in Memphis, St. Louis, New York or San Francisco. In fact, there seem to be more Greek-Americans here than Italian-Americans in Italy.

John told us the celebration in the streets had been going on steadily for three days, ever since the first Germans started to leave. We watched the people from the windows of the hotel, burning red flares and firing skyrockets evidently saved for this long-awaited occasion. All the Greek political organizations were out in force, with placards, flags and songs. The Greeks are great ones for chanting slogans while they march. There was a big representation of the Kappa Kappa Epsilon, the Greek Communist group, weaving along the street in a procession like a snake dance and roaring in perfect harmony like a college fraternity: "Kap-pa Kap-pa Ep-see-lon." It sounded like the campus at Ann Arbor, Mich., the night before the Minnesota game.

We had expected to find Athens without electricity or water, but the whole city was brightly lighted and water flowed from every faucet with more force and quantity than you could find in Rome or Naples. This, however, wasn't because of luck or German kind-heartedness. Just before they left, the Germans sent an expert demolition outfit to destroy the huge power plant in Piraeus, which supplies Athens and other cities and towns in this section with electricity. But the night shift at the power plant, with the help of a few Partisans, fought them off and saved the plant, killing nine Germans, wounding 25 and taking several prisoners.

The Germans also attempted to destroy the great dam at Marathon, an action that would have left Athens without water this winter. A force of ELAS soldiers turned them back. The Nazis did blow up the docks in Piraeus, however, leaving millions of dollars worth of damage.

The people in Athens need clothing and food badly, but they're not starving as they were in 1941 and 1942. When you ask why the food situation improved this year, they all give the same answer: the International Red Cross.

"Without the Red Cross food, we would have all been dead," they say. "That was our only source of food. The children especially owe their lives to the Red Cross. We fed our babies on nothing but their canned and powdered milk. The Germans slaughtered all our cows for beef."

The Greeks don't like to talk about the winters of 1941 and 1942, before the Red Cross began to deliver food in large quantities. "Everywhere you went you saw people actually collapsing and dying on the streets of hunger," one man told me. "I remember one time I saw the body of a young girl stretched across the sidewalk. A German soldier came walking by and stepped right over her. He didn't have the decency to walk around the body. Things like that you can't forget."

Greeks say with a sad smile that the Red Cross food-distribution centers managed by Swiss and Swedes were the only "white markets" in Athens. Practically everything in the city was bought and sold in the black market, sponsored originally by German profiteers. The Nazis ruined the financial structure of Greece. The inflation here is terrific.

Before the war the Greek *drachma* was worth about 160 to the American dollar. As I write, the *drachma* is worth almost 100 billion to the dollar and its value is still dropping. One cigarette costs 80 billion *drachmas*. One egg costs 8 billion *drachmas* and in some places one bottle of beer costs 4 billion *drachmas*. Paper money is so plentiful and worthless the barbers are using 500-*drachma* notes to wipe the lather from their razors. The par value of money in Athens drops so quickly that employers have to pay their help three times weekly. Wages are paid partly in bread and partly in *drachmas*. The employees spend their *drachmas* as soon as they get their hands on them for fear the value may take another drop within the next hour.

The inflation makes people distrust any kind of paper money no matter what country it's from, but most people will accept British 10-shilling notes and U. S. $1 bills. Nobody, however, wants $10 or $20 bills because you can't get them changed. If you go to a broker on the Athens Stock Exchange and ask him to change an American $10 bill, he won't give you more than $4.50.

The Greek Government of Prime Minister George Papandreou, which returned here from Italy a few days after the invasion, is taking immediate steps to stabilize the *drachma* but admits the job will be tough.

The Government will also have its hands full making peace among the local political parties. The two parties struggling for power are the EDES, an extremely nationalistic "Greece First" movement, and the EAM, a left-wing workers' organization that isn't as communistic as most people outside Greece think it is.

The EAM consists of several antifascist labor and Partisan groups. Kappa Kappa Epsilon, the Greek Communist Party, is only one of those EAM groups right now. Like the FFI in France, the EAM is riding on the crest of a popularity wave because its army, the ELAS, fought so well against the Germans during the occupation. The EDES has plenty of support, too, because it is so bitterly anti-Bulgarian. The average Greek hates Bulgaria even more than he hates Germany.

Greeks take their politics seriously. The day after we arrived in Athens the EDES attempted to parade through the town, and the procession happened to meet a large EAM group that had apparently been parading since the Germans left. One word led to another, and guns were pulled. A wild fight broke out, and before the police could break it up eight people were killed and many were wounded. The fight brought the holiday mood in Athens to an abrupt end, and the whole city that night was tense.

The next day the EAM people surrounded the downtown headquarters of the EDES and refused to let anybody leave or enter the building. The Greeks say that this intense party rivalry was deliberately encouraged by the Germans.

Few European countries have suffered more cold-blooded cruelty from the Germans than Greece in the past 3½ years. On my second day here I went to the SS headquarters building—the place where, as one Greek officer described it, "they took you when they knocked on your door in the night." SS headquarters was a big four-story building on one of the nicest streets in town. The entrance had been partly demolished by a grenade thrown by a Partisan during the last days of the German occupation, and we had to climb over the wreckage in the hallway.

The SS agents apparently left in a hurry, but they tried to take everything with them. The rooms were bare of furniture, but papers and documents were scattered over the floor.

In one room I bent down and looked at some letters and photographs that must have been dumped out of a trunk in somebody's attic. Most of them were souvenirs of a wedding—pictures of a bride and groom, letters and wires of congratulations, gift cards and other intimate mementos carefully saved and cherished by some woman for years. They concerned nobody except the man and the woman who owned them, and here they were, scattered on the floor of the Nazi Storm-Troop headquarters, dirtied and torn. I looked again at the pictures and the name and noticed that the couple was Jewish.

I went upstairs and looked at the small cells where the Nazis made their victims sweat it out awaiting the third degree or a flogging or the firing squad. The cells were tiny cubicles without ventilation except for a small opening in the door, the size of a saucer. They weren't big enough to allow a man of medium height to stand up inside.

In one cell I saw some handwriting in pencil on the plaster wall: "Today I am to be shot. Long live Greece!" Then a name and date.

On the floor above the cells there was another room with nothing in it but a hook on the wall about 7½ feet from the floor. The SS men hung prisoners by the wrist from this hook, stripped off their clothes and flogged them with a lead-tipped lash. The marks of the lash cut into the walls below the hook. The floor and walls were smeared with bloodstains. It looked as though the Nazis had the habit of slapping their bleeding victims around the room a little bit just for the hell of it after they'd finished the floggings.

On the same floor in another room I saw the radio they used to turn up loud so the screams wouldn't disturb the neighbors.

In the back of the SS building there is a big yard surrounded by high walls. The Greek police told me that SS men used to force their prisoners to run around this yard carrying heavy rocks in their arms until they fell from exhaustion.

The police officers also told me one about the SS men I had never heard. Before they fled Athens, they killed many Greek collaborationist stool pigeons who had worked faithfully for them during the last three years. They didn't want to leave behind anybody who knew too much about their work in Greece, possibly out of fear that the collaborators might testify against them in war-criminal trials some day soon.

In Athens alone during the occupation, the Germans killed in cold blood more than 15,000 Greeks. According to the International Red Cross, the Nazis allowed 450,000 Greeks to die of starvation, most of them in the winter of 1941. The Greek Government says another 45,000 were massacred in northern Greece by the Bulgarians.

Perhaps the most respected man in Athens is Archbishop Damaskinos, head of the Greek Orthodox Church, who risked his life to stand firmly for the rights of his people against the Germans all during the occupation.

Shortly before the Germans left Athens they announced they were going to kill 50 hostages in reprisal for sabotage. Archbishop Damaskinos and 49 of his bishops and priests went to the place of the scheduled execution and offered to take the place of the condemned men. The Germans, realizing that the archbishop had too much prestige to be trifled with, reluctantly called off the executions.

After a German soldier was wounded in Piritidopiion, a suburb of Athens, 150 men, women and children were dragged out into the streets of the district to be shot. Then their houses were burned. Archbishop Damaskinos immediately made a strong protest to the German commander in chief in Athens, Gen. Felmy. The general replied coldly by letter that the archbishop was "spreading British propaganda" and said that mass killings like this were the most efficient means of preventing sabotage.

Another time, in Athens, the Germans shot 14 people for some vague reason, taking them at random from streetcars and busses that happened to be passing near the place of execution. They buried the bodies without identifying them. The archbishop went to the burying place himself, although the Germans threatened to shoot him, and had the bodies dug up. The people whose relatives were missing all assembled in the cemetery and identified the dead from neckties, coats, hats and other articles of clothing found on the bodies.

The archbishop tells other stories, like the one about the country town where all the men were machine-gunned in the village square and all the women and children were locked in the schoolhouse, which was set afire. One German, unable to stand the sight, finally ran back to the door and let a few of the victims out.

Archbishop Damaskinos is a striking man, 6 feet 4, with a tremendous beard. He's only 54, but the strain of the last three years has left its mark on him, and he looks like 70. When he speaks of the Germans he becomes bitter.

"Their cruelty has marred the soul of Greece," he says. "They have built up such a barrier of blood and murder between our people and theirs that it seems impossible that friendly relations between the two countries can ever be restored."

That night I had dinner with a young Greek who had lived in America and had worked for the British Intelligence in Athens for the last two years. He had been imprisoned by the Germans and had narrowly escaped the firing squad. We were having a quiet conversation about pleasant things. I was telling him about food in New York and what the college football season was going to be like this year.

He mentioned how excited the Greeks were at the prospect of seeing American movies again for the first time since 1940. The movie houses in Athens are advertising such coming attractions as "The Life of Abraham Lincoln" and "The Road Back"—pictures they had received just before the Germans came and had been saving carefully ever since. Then when he started to tell me how newsdealers were now selling old copies of the *National Geographic* magazine and the *Reader's Digest,* I interrupted him.

"Listen," I said, "suppose you had to do it all over again. Do you think it would be worth it?"

The smile left his face. "What do you mean?" he said.

I could tell from the way he looked at me what the answer was going to be, and I wished I hadn't mentioned it. "Well," I said, "let's say the Germans come back next year, and you people find yourselves in the same spot you were in 1941. Do you think you could face three more years of hunger and killings? Or would you give up and say what the hell is the use and try to make a bargain with the Germans?"

I never saw a man get really mad so quickly. He looked as though I had said something dirty about his mother. For a minute I thought he was going to stand up and take a punch at me.

Finally he began to get himself under control. He didn't say anything for a while. Then he doubled up his fist and gave the table one sharp blow.

"Make a bargain with the Germans?" he said. "My God, it would be treason to our dead."

I think he will feel the same way 20 or even 50 years from now. I wonder if we will.

"Ammunition hell! This is mimeograph paper!"

—Sgt. Basil Hartwell.

GI ARTIST IN BETHLEHEM

A favorite sightseeing trip for soldiers in the Middle East is the journey to the town of Bethlehem where Christ was born. CPL. RICHARD T. GAIGE drew these sketches of Bethlehem's Church of the Nativity which stands on the site of the manger.

COURTYARD. The courtyard is crowded with postcard salesmen who yell at visiting GIs, "Hey, Yankee, wanna buy?" This shrine is said to be the oldest Christian church in use but it has been altered since it was built by Emperor Constantine in 330. The door, called the Eye of the Needle, is tiny. It was designed to keep pagans from driving their horses into the church.

GROTTO. Cpl. Gaige made this sketch of the Grotto of the Nativity when a group of South African, Cape and Bantu Negro British soldiers were visiting the shrine. Their white chaplain spoke from the altar in English which was translated into Afrikaans. But the African soldiers recited the Lord's Prayer in English. Walls and ceiling are covered with lamps and religious paintings.

BASILICA. The Basilica of the Church of the Nativity is built like a citadel over the traditional site of the manger. In the main aisle, a wooden floor protects the remains of the fifth-century mosaics which are shown to visiting GIs through trap doors. Greek Orthodox and Armenian sects, and Roman Catholics worship here.

COURTYARD

BASILICA

GROTTO

HOSPITAL SHIP

By Sgt. MACK MORRISS

An East Coast Port—The *USHS Acadia,* her hull a startling white with huge red crosses blazing amidships, tied up at the pier where a band and a fleet of ambulances awaited her.

The band played a march, and aboard ship the wounded said yeah, they knew there'd be a goddam band, but why didn't they swing it. The band played maybe a couple of more military pieces and then jived into something that was stronger on the reeds than on the brass.

And the wounded from Italy hobbled to portholes or swung up stairways to the open decks, leaned on the rail and beat time to the music with whatever limbs they had left. From all over the port side of the ship the battle casualties made like hep cats and watched as the *Acadia* discharged the first of her cargo, the commissioned cases who were able to walk.

They moved across the gangplank and stepped into waiting GI busses. Trained Negro litter bearers handled their luggage. Then came the psych cases, each one escorted by two men. Then the walking enlisted men, most of them with only a few personal belongings in little Red Cross ditty bags but some with barracks bags which they surrendered to the Negro boys. At the end of the gangplank two Negro soldiers grabbed every man under the arms and helped him negotiate the low step down to solid ground, that last step he took to get back to the States. One of the casualties bent over and put both palms flat on the concrete pier, yelped in mock amazement and danced rather uncertainly into his bus. He was the only one. The rest of the boys from Salerno and the Volturno and beyond hardly changed expression. Some of them seemed to relax tensed lips to let out the breath they'd been holding. But that was all. No dramatics.

The litter patients came last. The Negro handlers, who deserve the reputation they have as experts in the work, moved them into the ambulances in a smooth effortless stream. In five hours the *Acadia* was emptied.

The whole business of getting back home was just about as simple as that. The swing music was as inappropriate, perhaps, as the marches for the men who couldn't walk—and none could walk very far—and there was a profound incongruity about it: but war is full of incongruities, and the wounded wanted the jive even if they did come ashore with

dead pans. They were pretty solemn about it, those with an arm or a leg gone or the few who were blind, but there were no tears. Nobody bawled, no matter how much he felt like it if he felt like it at all.

Earlier, several hours before the 800-patient hospital ship had docked, there wasn't a dead pan aboard. On B deck, Ward 31 was getting ready to disembark. Since every ward in every hospital has its comic, 31 had its paratrooper from the West Virginia hills. He and the Chief, an Oklahoma Indian, kept the bulkheads ringing with their patter.

There was an excess energy, pent up after days at sea, and the wounded sought safety valves for its release. The Chief calmly put his GI cane across his knee, threatened profanely to break it, thought better of the idea and instead banged it merrily on the deck. The paratrooper, his face and arm scarred and an eye missing because of a hand grenade some now-deceased German used in a hand-to-hand fight at Salerno, looked out the porthole to see a launch chugging alongside. He erupted.

"The U. S. Navy—in dangerous waters. Look at 'em! Goddam! Let me off this boat. I wanna get at them USO soldiers," he howled, switching services. "Oh, let me at 'em!"

He registered a burlesque ferocity and, crouching into a fighter's posture, strode up and down the narrow passage between the tiers of bunks. It will take a while for him and the others to get over that feeling which he expressed as comedy but which he actually felt as a kind of tragedy. It is an emotion most returning soldiers have, for a while, regarding servicemen who of necessity are still on duty in the States.

A grave guy from Iowa stood on his one good foot and grinned at the paratrooper.

"Lookit him," spouted the 'trooper, still going strong. "Goddam Infantry soldier. Went out, him and his outfit did, to fight the whole Jerry army. We had to come floatin' down to get him out of it. Goddam Infantry."

The sober infantryman defended himself briefly: "We was trapped."

A Japanese-American captain limped through the ward. The paratrooper followed him with his one eye. "Goddam good fighters, them fellers. We used to send out patrols and the Jap boys would bring 'em back in. Our jump suits were too much like the

Jerries'. Them Jap boys was takin' no chances. It was sort of rough on us. Rugged but right, though."

"Rugged, but right," echoed the happy Chief. Then he started needling some kid about having been overseas 19 months and coming home now to a wife with a 2-month-old baby. The heckled soldier swore comically, boasted that for a guy like him it was easy and invited the Chief to go to hell; it was his kid all right.

Meanwhile the paratrooper threw his arms around a middle-aged nurse and asked for a date to get blind drunk ashore. The nurse tactfully refused and the 'trooper said well, he still loved her anyway. Among other nice things about the *Acadia* were 43 nurses who had a high average of good looks.

Two men, each with a foot encased in plaster casts that left only their toes uncovered, suddenly tumbled off a bunk and started whirling between the tiers. One was a Seabee, the other a soldier. They were trying to pull the hairs off each other's toes imprisoned in the casts. The ward looked on half-interested. The Seabee won.

A blind sergeant, his hands on the shoulders of another soldier, walked majestically toward his bunk. The ward fought its tendency to hush. Somebody reached out and tickled the blind guy under the arm. He grinned and felt for his bed. The two playful foot casualties came at him from either side and started tickling. The sergeant roared and lashed out in an arc around him, laughing. He had lost his eyes when a clip of cartridges exploded in his face, detonated by a hit on the chamber of his M1.

It was an hour before docking time. From the opposite ward came the smell of coffee and luncheon meat.

"When do we eat, goddam it?" yelled the wounded in 31.

THE COLONEL AND THE PAPER BOY

By Cpl. RICHARD EELLS

OUR colonel was sweet. He organized our post exchange and he organized our camp paper. More than that, he pictured himself as possessing extraordinary parental relationships. He told us he was our mother because he fed us and kept the mess hall going. He told us he was our father because he gave us money. He said he had never been defeated in anything. He said he would do anything to avoid defeat. He said that was the way to be a good soldier. Our colonel came from Vermont—just like maple sugar.

Our post exchange made the colonel very proud. It was the only store of its kind in the South, he claimed, that was out of debt. One month it made a dividend of $20. That was the month the pinball machine was installed. The colonel wanted something diverting.

For the most part, the pinball machine was used by officers because the enlisted men were too busy with their duties. During the evenings the same lack of pinball time existed, since there were obviously more animate and pleasurable diversions than shooting a toy gun.

The colonel spent a considerable part of each day playing with his new little pleasure machine.

The paper boy also played with it. The paper boy was 12 years old, was trying to finish grammar school and was a dead shot. The colonel was obviously over 12 years old, had finished grammar school and rumor had it he was a dead shot, too.

The object of this particular game was to shoot down the enemy. The highest possible score was 75,000.

The colonel never played the pinball machine without the assistance of his adjutant.

"'At's a baby. Look at that shot! That gives me a final score of 35,000."

"Right, colonel," replied his adjutant. "Let's see now, that places you first, myself second, the PX officer third, the supply officer fourth and the intelligence officer last. It certainly is a swell game."

"Bet it is," agreed the colonel, walking over to the counter of the PX. "Our pinball machine at the officers' mess is child's play. This is different. This is just like being out there and givin' 'em hell."

"Right, colonel," repeated the adjutant.

"You know, this gives me an idea. Let's have these scores typed up and posted here on the machine. Nothing like a little competition, you know; good for morale."

"Right, colonel."

When the paper boy played the pleasure device he had to stand on his toes to sight the gun, but he didn't mind. After his first try he rolled up a score of 45,000. And with the nonchalance of Louis XIV he wrote his name and score above that of the colonel's and walked out.

The next day the colonel was hot and red and not at all sweet. He was playing the pinball machine grim as death. His adjutant stood next to him, pale, intense and with a handful of nickels. "Well, you did it. Knew you could, colonel."

"Yep, by God, 47,000," was the gratified reply.

The colonel and his adjutant left and in a few minutes the paper boy entered.

"Hey, Jimmy," said the soldier behind the counter, "the Ol' Man just beat your score. But it took him two solid hours to do it."

"That so?"

"Yeah, the ol' boy had phone calls from all over the country, but he let them all wait. Had to beat that lucky paper boy, he said."

"Hey, this ain't luck, this's skill. I wasn't even tryin' yesterday. Watch me now."

Jimmy dug a nickel out of his dungarees and started to fire. First try he got 55,000.

"See that?" Again he wrote his name and score above the colonel's.

It took the colonel three days of concentrated playing to top the paper boy's score. But finally after spending the average private's monthly pay he wrote down 56,000. This time he had a notice posted which read:

> "The weekly high score on this machine will be mentioned in our camp paper."

This was Saturday.

Sunday the paper boy had five nickels. He played for about half an hour and finally rolled up a score of 70,000. A few minutes later everyone in camp knew about it. A soldier in the orderly room typed the new score: paper boy, 70,000; colonel, 56,000; adjutant, 40,000; supply officer, 35,000; intelligence officer, 5,000.

The next week was terrific. Monday the colonel sweated over the pinball machine all day. Tuesday was the same. Wednesday he looked flatulent. Thursday the turgid condition became audible. Friday this sign appeared on the bulletin board:

> "The use of the pinball machine is henceforth restricted to the use of military personnel only."

Saturday the colonel's name appeared in the camp paper as the winner of the week.

"That's the new submarine crew."—Leo Salkin, Pho M 3c, San Diego, Calif.

THE ROTATION OF SGT. REGAN

By Sgt. RAY DUNCAN

ALASKA—"Don't stand so near the road, corporal," said Sgt. Regan. "Them prime movers don't give a damn what they hit."

Later he said: "You oughta wear a muffler under that field jacket, corporal. This wind goes right through a guy. Here, take mine."

The sergeant's big face was wrinkled with anxiety. In the Aleutian Islands you make friends quickly, but there's no affection as swift or as deep as a soldier's regard for his replacement. Before any man can be rotated back to the States his replacement must arrive and take over.

"A rugged deal," sighed the corporal, "really a rugged deal." He took off his glasses to wipe away the fog, and his blue eyes looked watery without them. Little clouds of fog danced along the spongy ground past the legs of the men.

"Even worse than I expected," continued the corporal, gazing down the muddy slope to the bay and the big humps of barren ground beyond.

"Oh, you'll like it here," said Sgt. Regan quickly. "Time goes fast here. It don't seem like 26 months since I came to this island."

"That's the third time you said that." The corporal turned up the collar of his jacket. It was a stiff new field jacket, issued two weeks before at the port of embarkation. The sergeant was wearing a ragged and shapeless garment.

"Hey, Regan!" somebody yelled, "you can turn your equipment in any time now!"

"Wantcha shake hands with my ree-placement," grinned Regan. "This here's the supply sergeant, corporal, good guy to know." He laughed at his joke and put his big hand in the middle of the corporal's slender back, like a mother presenting her only child to company. "Well," said the supply sergeant, "so you finally got here. Regan's really been sweatin' you in!"

The corporal smiled. "Rugged deal," he said. He'd been through all this before. Regan had walked him through every hut on the island, saying: "Wantcha shake hands with my ree-placement!" And everyone said: "So you're the replacement!" as if they couldn't tell from the new field jacket and from the way Regan beamed and hovered around.

Everyone in the mess hall turned around when Regan suddenly yelled: "Hey! Where is he? Where did he go?"

"It's all right," somebody said, "he just went to get a second cup of coffee."

"Why didn't you tell me you needed coffee?" Regan said sharply when the corporal came back. "Don't never run off like that again without tellin' me!"

After chow the two hit their sacks together. Regan had made sure that the corporal got a bunk beside his own.

"I didn't ast you to shake hands with Miller over there," whispered the sergeant. "On purpose I didn't, 'cause he lost his ree-placement last week."

"Lost him?"

"Yeah. Miller's been here 27 months now, an' last week his ree-placement finally come up from the States. So Miller was showin' him how to check shipments on the dock. The ree-placement fell into the ice-cold water an' broke both legs an' caught pneumonia. Hell of a tough break for Miller," sighed the sergeant. "His own damn fault though—should've kept his eye on the boy."

"Rugged deal," said the corporal. As they were walking back to the headquarters hut he said: "Say, what kind of flowers are those up there?" He pointed up the slope, where a few blue blossoms were visible through the fog.

"Ain't no flowers on this island," said Regan.

"I'd like to go up there an' pick some."

"Fergit it," said the sergeant sharply. He took hold of the corporal's thin arm. "You stay off them slopes, they're dangerous."

"Hey, Regan," somebody yelled, "your orders are

bein' cut! The boat's due here this afternoon. You can go aboard tonight!"

"Yeah?" whooped Regan. "Wantcha shake hands with my ree-placement. This calls for a goddam celebration! I hear there's cokes in the PX today."

Regan set his coke down and went over to the juke box to play "I'll Be Home for Christmas." When he turned around the corporal had disappeared.

"I know," Regan yelled while they were searching behind the PX counters. "I know! Them flowers —he went out to pick them goddam flowers!"

Regan and a dozen friends fanned out and started moving up the slope in the fog. The sergeant couldn't hold himself down to a walk. He kept bouncing up and down on the spongy tundra. For a moment the fog broke, and they saw a boat moving into the dock below. "I gotta leave," groaned Regan, "I gotta check out." And he hurried off.

"And one more thing," said Regan's CO, "bring your replacement in here before you go. I want to talk to both of you together. You can pick up your orders when you bring him in."

"Yessir," said Regan, "he's around somewhere."

Which was true. The corporal couldn't have left the island, because no boats or planes had gone. But he could have fallen over a cliff, or sunk into the muskeg, or frozen to death by this time. Regan wondered wildly if someone could have kidnaped him to use for *their* replacement. Regan was running now and groaning out loud. It might take the Army months to get another man up here.

"Hey, Regan!" somebody yelled after him, "you're gettin' mighty careless with that replacement of yours. What's the idea of leavin' him all alone over there in the library hut?"

Regan made the corporal help him turn in his bedding, and then gave him some baggage to carry down to the dock.

"You had me worried to death," he said for the sixth time. "Thought you might've been killed or froze!"

"Rugged deal," said the corporal. They were standing by the dock's edge near the gangplank, and the sergeant's friends were crowded around them in the dark.

"Say, corporal," said Regan, "does everybody in the States say 'rugged deal' all the time?" He had a sudden urge to shove the corporal, in his new field jacket, off the dock into the icy water. Better not, thought the sergeant; they could still pull me off this boat and back to duty. And that, thought Sgt. Regan as he backed up the gangplank toward the States—that would be a very rugged deal.

A GI INVADES THE FASHION FRONT

By Cpl. HYMAN GOLDBERG

"ALL the emphasis was placed on sex," said the newspaper story. "Skirts were two or three inches above the knee, hips were closely swathed to show every curve, busts were overdraped or overexposed —beauty was completely shorn away."

That's what a fashion expert said about what had happened to women's fashions after the last war. After I took a cold shower I went out to see if the same thing was happening to women's fashions this time.

My survey lasted several days, and now that it's over and I am back from a nearby rehabilitation center where they give the Keeley Cure, I am able to report that there seem to be two schools of thought among the fashion designers.

These opposing schools are represented by Russeks, the New York store on Fifth Avenue that specializes in fur coats, and by Bergdorf Goodman, the ultrafashionable Fifth Avenue store where, as they say, "the mood is proud and positive and confident, discarding understatement." Those pretty words were interpreted by one of the leading fashion writers of the country as meaning: "What the women are going to wear for the boys who come home will accentuate nudity." She explained that there will be great big open spaces in strategic places in the dresses and that black straps in those open spaces will make them seem even more open.

Russeks was holding what the spokesman for the store called a "Pink Champagne Party of Design Studio Furs" when I went up there. A pretty lady with a boyish bob called over a waiter and twisted my arm until I consented to drink a glass of the bubbly needled grape juice. Then she gave me a seat among all the magazine and newspaper fashion writers who were guzzling the stuff with apparent pleasure.

Some time later I discovered they had some stuff imported from Scotland, and after I had cleared my palate with a bit of caviar, I switched. Before the show actually started a man got up in front of the merry throng and gave a brief lecture on what he thought of the new season's styles.

"I," he said modestly, "am an authority on fashions; I live fashions, I dream fashions." He was wearing a blue suit which he told me later was made of the lightest English flannel, a shirt with blue-and-white stripes and a bow tie also with blue-and-white stripes but with stripes running horizontally, not vertically, as on the shirt. Me for that stuff.

After he had established himself as an expert to his and our satisfaction, he went on to tell about the things he was afraid would happen to women's fashions after the war is over. "After the last war," he said, "women's skirts climbed to a point four or five inches above the knee." I applauded happily but was shushed by my neighbors—a couple of magazine girls who hadn't heard yet about the uptown trend towards nudity.

The fashion show finally began, and the lady with the boyish bob, whom I will call Miss Castle, because that's her name, acted as the master, or rather, mistress of ceremonies. Two blondes, a redhead and two brunettes came out of a little doorway at one end of the big mirror-lined room, waved their hips and incidentally showed the clothes they were wearing. At first I had a little trouble, probably because of the pink champagne, because somehow I could see right through the clothes the girls were wearing. After a while, however, I adjusted myself to my environment.

What they are proud of at Russeks, I gathered, are their shoulders. It seems they have a designer, by name of Ralph Marano, who thinks more of a woman's shoulders than anything else. Marano is missing a great deal, but that is neither here nor there. Some of the coats this fall and winter season will keep a woman warm all over. Some of them, which are shorter, won't.

The coats I saw are all made of high-class animals, like mink (in the wild and bottle-fed state), leopards and Persian lambs. A little way off Fifth Avenue, I am told, it is possible to get less costly furs, such as alley cat and Shetland ponies.

One number that looked very good was called by Miss Castle a "dramatic Somali leopard wrap coat with the Marano saddle shoulder." Don't ask me why it's called a saddle shoulder; there were no stirrups on it. Miss Castle said that the nice thing about this little number is that it's the "easiest way to wear a fur coat. You just throw it over your shoulders and off you go." She depressed all us fashion writers, however, by remarking that Somali leopard is hard to get nowadays "because of all that fighting that went on in Somaliland."

I asked a nearby expert how much a thing like that would cost and she whispered back: "Not more than a couple of thousand dollars." I am told that you can't borrow money under the GI Bill of Rights to buy fur coats.

Miss Castle described one of the hats worn by one of the long-legged models as a "dark purple, passionate hat made of glycerine feathers." To me it looked like the hat was made of that candy cotton they sell at the circus.

At one point it sounded to me as if Miss Castle had described one of the coats as having "a pointed brassiere." That didn't seem possible, so I asked someone sitting next to me who obviously knew about such things. She sneered at me. It turned out that what Miss Castle had actually said was "the coat has a pointed revere," and the expert explained that a revere is like the lapel on a man's coat.

One of the blond models came out wearing a coat made of something called "nutria," and Miss Castle described her coat as "every woman's coat, because it hides all unnatural protuberances." The model frowned, opened her coat and looked herself over. I think it would be a crime against nature for a girl like her to wear such a coat.

Another coat was described as a white broadtail lamb. We were warned that this coat is not suitable for skiing. "Every time some girls see a white coat, they want to go skiing in it," said Miss Castle. She said the only skiing possible in such a coat could be done at a night club.

It was with great reluctance that I tore myself away from my colleagues of the fashion press, such as the Countess Willaumez and the Countess de Mun, whom I last saw gaily guzzling a glass of pink champagne. But duty called, and I made a forced march up to Fifth Avenue and 58th Street, to Bergdorf Goodman's modest little nine-story shop, where another fashion show was going on.

At Bergdorf Goodman, the clothes, as the store's spokesman says, "carry no suggestion of a truant queen playing dairymaid; they are clearly designed for the lady who gracefully lives up to the importance of her place in the world." They also go in for "fervent fitting" and "severely superb Oxford gray with strict stripes." One suit, according to the store spokesman, is "molded softly, as if by a deft thumb stroke from beneath." The haughty model who wore it looked as if she had been wearing the suit when the job with the thumb was done.

I was given a fancy pink booklet that was supposed to explain what the 20 or so models were wearing. According to Bergdorf Goodman, women should wear one dress in the morning, another in the late afternoon and still another dress for dinner. And any woman who doesn't, she's a dope.

Here are some of the simple things Bergdorf Goodman would like women to wear: for the morning, a black crepe with black silk braid on sleeves and at high throat; for the late afternoon, a black wool dress laced up the front; for the evening, a black "velvet sheath, outlined in jet at its shallow decolletage." That's where the kicker is, in that "decolletage" jive. That means it's cut away, all the way down the front.

It didn't seem possible that the model who was wearing that little number could really hold herself together unless she had miraculous muscular control. I must have expressed my amazement, because a lady fashion writer sitting next to me leaned over and whispered a few facts of life that were new to me and which I will pass on because maybe things were different when you left home.

All that glitters, she told me, is not gold, and appearances are deceiving. It seems they sell those things, or anyway reasonable facsimiles of those things, in the stores, for women who have been overlooked by nature. And unless you know the lady real well, you can't be sure.

To such a pass, men, has the world come.

"Single."—Pvt. Thomas Flannery.

"Bring any late comics with you, men?"—Cpl. E. Maxwell, AAF, Carlsbad, N. M.

MESS HALL IN ALASKA

By Sgt. A. N. MALOFF

ALASKA—He stood out by the side of the runway and waited, as he always did. When the weather permitted, the planes would take off in the morning and come back in the afternoon. Or they would take off in the afternoon and come back in the evening. He would always stand by the side of the runway and wait for them to return. Sometimes he would stand a long time, and they would never come back.

He was the only one who came out to watch any more, and the others never understood it. "Joe Buza," they said, "he's nutty. He's plane-nutty." He used to tell them he had to know how many tables to set up in his mess hall, but they laughed at him. He didn't know himself exactly why he wanted to watch, but he was always there. Every day there was a flight he would walk over to Operations and ask when the men were coming back. If it was Kiska, it meant he had to prepare an early lunch; if it was Attu, he would have the KPs set up a few tables in the middle of the afternoon. Then he would walk out to the runway and watch.

He dug his face deeper into his mackinaw, trying to shield the tip of his nose with his collar. He moved around a little to keep from standing still and shoved his back into the wind. The sound of footsteps behind him made him turn around. It was one of the cameramen from the photographic unit at the hangar line.

"You sweating it out, too?"

"Yeah," Joe said. "Will they be coming in soon?"

The man nodded. "In a minute, I guess. There's just one. A fighter. We took a gun out of the nose and put a camera in. Something about one of the boys spotting some Jap ships."

They heard the engine before they saw the plane. It must have been hidden in the fog. Then it circled slowly, dropped its wheels, gently lowered itself onto the ground and taxied down the runway. It pulled up at the end of the field, turned around and moved back to the center again where the mechanics were waiting for it.

The pilot lifted himself out of the cockpit and jumped down. He turned to the cameraman and grinned in satisfaction. "This is it, boy. Just what the doctor ordered. Develop them right away and bring them over. The colonel will want them right away." The pilot started unstrapping his parachute. "Right away," he said again.

Joe walked back to the mess hall. He never used to worry about feeding the men, but it was different now. He didn't like to set up the tables with all the food and watch some of them stay that way—clean and untouched. Some days some of the planes didn't come back, which meant some of the men would never eat again. Those were the days he hated, and he always made the KPs elbow the floor and told the cooks to make hamburgers or a stew so the unused meat wouldn't go to waste.

He kicked open the door to the kitchen and entered. The cooks had already started to prepare supper and the KPs were standing around, smoking and waiting to see whether they could get a couple of hours off. He sat down on a box and picked up the menu for tomorrow. One of the men came over to him. "Sarge," he said, "we set up the mess hall for supper already. Is it okay for us to take off for a couple of hours?" Joe bent his head toward the dining room and looked it over. "Okay, Sherwood. Be back by 4. Don't make me send for you."

He half expected the telephone call that came in the evening. Lt. Johnson of the Operations Room. There was a big flight the next day, starting early. Could he have an early breakfast ready for about 30 or 35 men, early, say about 0430? "Sure, lieutenant, anything. Anything at all. Hot cakes and cereal and—— Yeah, okay, lieutenant. Anything I can do——"

Something was up, something pretty big. He could see that by the way the men ate their chow the next morning, concentrating on every bite they put in their mouths. Maybe it was what that fighter brought in yesterday; he didn't know. There was too much quiet in his mess hall, and the men passed the coffee too promptly. It bothered him. Then they got up and left. Joe liked it that the tables were dirty and the food bowls were mostly empty. That was the way it should be. No waste, and everyone in his place.

At Operations, after the rest of the squadron had eaten breakfast, they told him he could expect the planes back in time for dinner if everything went all right. You couldn't be sure because you never knew how much flak and fighter opposition the men would meet. But dinner looked like a safe bet, maybe even a little earlier.

The clerk at the desk smiled. "Buza, I can't figure you out," he said. "You're like an old maid half the time. Always afraid you'll be missing something. Why don't you relax?"

"It's not that," Joe answered. "It's the tables. I got to get them ready, don't I?"

By the time he reached the mess hall again, the men were just finishing the cleaning. There wasn't so much to do after breakfast—clean off the tables and sweep the floor. Someone would bring out the silverware and the cups, enough for each man; then they would wait until just before the men came to put out the food and coffee. Joe walked over to the pantry and pulled out a pack of paper napkins. He saved them for special occasions, like Christmas dinner or maybe a squadron party sometime, but today was special—more special than other days, because 14 of the big boys took off today, and that was more than usual. He put the napkins under the silverware and made sure the forks were at the left. He lit a cigarette and took a long pull. In another hour or so he would walk out to the field to watch them come in. Another hour at least.

The wail of a siren jerked him to his feet. It took a second before he recognized it; then he ran to the window. A field ambulance tore down the company street, skirted the corner on two wheels and raced for the runway. Everyone seemed to be running. Men streamed out of the hangars and pulled up sharply at the edge of the flying field. A jeep shot out of the headquarters enclosure and dashed toward the fire house. The red light at the head of the control tower started blinking furiously, then

remained on. A plane sitting at the end of the field spun around and pulled itself out of the way.

Joe shoved through the crowd. Then he saw it, limping in out of the fog. He saw it circle slowly and lose altitude. The wings leaned over to one side. The wheels edged into position and the plane started to level off. The engine whined in an unsteady cry and the body quivered with the effort. Painfully the nose tilted downward and as painfully the plane slipped onto the runway, bounced nervously into the air for a few feet, dropped onto the ground and rolled to a stop. It just lay there.

Joe pushed forward with the others. They watched the crew come out of the plane, bunched together as if for protection. The captain punched a finger through the black hole where a .50-caliber had struck. His face was blank and half-believing, tired beyond weariness. The crew stood around him, waiting for him to do something. Then the words poured out as if he couldn't stop them, as if he could tell his story only once and then forget it.

"They caught us. They were waiting for us and they caught us. We were like rats, caught, and we didn't know what hit us. In the fog and in the clouds, that's where they were. Forty, 50, something like that, and they hit us with everything. We didn't have a chance. They bombed us from above and then they passed over us with their machine guns. It happened quick, like I'm telling it. You could see how our men exploded with the ships. Only some exploded. Some burned. We got away. I don't know how. They hit us with everything they had."

He stopped and pulled his lips tight over his teeth. The crowd made room for him, and he passed through it. His crew followed after him, still not talking.

Joe Buza stayed there after everyone had gone. One out of 14! No one was coming back now, but he stayed there and waited. He pecked at the ground with the toe of his shoe. He didn't want to go back just yet, because the others would be eating and he didn't want to see them. Maybe another would return. He propped a cigarette between his lips before he remembered he couldn't smoke there. Overhead the sky was empty and the fog was thick.

But for the KPs clearing away the plates, the dining room was empty. Everyone had eaten. Tables were covered with patches of bread and half-used platters of butter. On the floor was a little pool of water where someone had spilled a cup. He pushed the water with his foot so it would dry quickly.

In the back were the unused tables where the combat crews were supposed to eat. They would have to be cleaned off now, just like the others. Just as if the men had eaten there, even though they hadn't. The floor was clean of crumbs and all the bread was still neatly piled. Joe toppled a pile so it wouldn't look so neat. Tomorrow the men would have hamburgers for dinner because he couldn't waste the meat. He picked up the meat dish.

A KP had been standing behind him. "Sarge," he said, "I think this butter ought to be put away. It's been standing pretty long." Joe looked at him for a minute before he understood. There was a lost mission in his voice. "Soldier, it's not your job to think here," he said. "It's your job to scrub this floor till it's clean enough to kiss." He moved into the kitchen and stopped suddenly. Muttering to himself, he turned, walked to the garbage can and dumped the meat.

GUADALCANAL GOES GARRISON

BY SGT. BARRETT McGURN

GUADALCANAL—The two years since the Marines splashed ashore here in America's first offensive of the second World War have brought a lot of changes. The sad truth, chums, is that Guadalcanal has gone garrison.

According to one story going the rounds, seven enlisted men in a bomber crew were turned in to their orderly room after a raid on Rabaul. One crew member was charged with having a light beard as the ship laid its lethal eggs, and others were picked up for wearing baseball caps and sweat shirts. Whether the yarn is true (and one fellow insists he was one of the seven), there is no doubt Guadalcanal is going strictly GI.

Where men once lived in comfortable foxhole sloppiness, barracks cots are now primped above rows of shoes shined like shaving mirrors. Saluting, once banned because it was a dead giveaway to snipers, is now compulsory at many 'Canal camps. You have reveille, retreat, manual of arms, close-order drill and inspections. On this damp rock inspections are particularly painful because a rifle cleaned Friday night is likely to be rusty Saturday morning unless it is coated overnight with oil so heavy you'll get gigged if you don't find time to clean it off.

Those popular Guadalcanal mixed-uniform styles —fatigue hat with sun-tan suit, or fatigue pants with sun-tan shirt—are now forbidden. And at Service Command Headquarters Company, the voice of the first sergeant may be heard of an evening driving the company out to police up the area—in the dark, of course.

Henderson Field, the Jap-built airport where some of the earliest Jap-American fighting took place, might remind you now of the Penn Station in Pittsburgh when you see Red Cross girls serving free coffee and doughnuts from their trailer to the boys. There are now nearly 200 white women here —the Red Cross girls, Army and Navy nurses and New Zealanders. Stunned delight greeted the first of them a few months ago, but now there are grumbles from such characters as the truck drivers, who have to wear shorts when they give themselves and their trucks a simultaneous bath in the Malimbu River.

Many a GI arriving from the States still has a vague idea that he will soon be engaged in brisk hand-to-hand bayonet duels with the Japs. Instead, he learns that not a Jap has been seen for more than a year, although occasional rumors come through that a few are still up in the hills.

Rather than a primitive jungle beach, the GI newcomer finds a bustling civilization of a sort. Two piers for oceangoing ships run out from the black volcanic sand, and offshore lie so many ships that Guadalcanal now rates as one of the great American seaports.

On land the GI finds more than 200 miles of roads, some of them much busier than Main Street on Saturday night back home—so busy, in fact, that one chaplain never travels except between 1,200 and 1,300 hours and 1,700 and 1,800 hours. At these times the roads empty magically while the drivers chow up. Overhead the GI sees some of the 4,500 miles of telephone wire that are strung on poles on the 'Canal. And if he looks around he'll find other unwarlike facilities.

At a spot where patrols once encountered Japs, there is now a pleasant sun-bathed farm, which will soon cover 2,500 acres (nearly four square miles) and increase its daily production of a ton of fresh vegetables to 15 tons. The 'Canal also has a lumber camp that turns out more than seven miles of board a day.

As late as January 1943, Jap artillery pieces hidden in the hills shelled one area. Now there is a gravel quarry here, with two 40-ton gasoline shovels keeping 100 trucks busy every day running to airfield and road-repair projects.

Where the battle of Tenaru raged some three months after the first landings by the Marines there now stand two laundries that wash up to 20 tons of clothes daily.

There is an ice-cream plant that turns out 200 quarts a day—vanilla, chocolate and strawberry. Each Army outfit gets its turn, provided it picks up its allotment. Across the road from the plant is a rubber grove where the Marines maintained an important bivouac area during the fighting.

Running these States-like projects are GIs, many of whom have never seen a Jap. "This is the last thing I ever thought I'd be doing on Guadalcanal" is a frequent comment. True to Army tradition, some like it this way, some don't.

Pfc. James W. (Slim) Litton of Shreveport, La., foreman of one of two parts of the vegetable farm, feels half-and-half about his job. He is stormed with applications from other ex-farmers who would like to trade rifles for rakes, and he is aware that the only GI element in the soldier-farmers' lives is their mess hall. There are no Army calls. When the ground is dry, the 60 EM get up with the sun and plow until dusk, just as they would as civilians. When it rains they work on their equipment, which, by the way, is so excellent that, according to Slim, "a poor man couldn't look at it" in the States.

It does his farmer's heart good for Slim to see the miracles of the Guadalcanal earth, which must be among the most fertile in the world. The farmers picked 3,500 watermelons off two acres; one of the melons weighed 60 pounds. Corn grows fast. There is a standard joke that you must jump back when you plant it or the stalk will hit you in the eye. Two months after planting you may have 18,000 ears per acre ready for the chow line. The farm's crops are valued at several million dollars, thanks to the GIs, the fuzzy-headed natives who help them and the civilian experts from the Foreign Economic Administration who give them technical advice.

Still Slim has a gripe. "I felt better in the Infantry," he says. "More exercise. If we wasn't climbing a hill, we was fixing to climb one."

The 40 lumberjacks here have the same sort of professional amazement for the marvels of Guadalcanal. But they reserve the right to register a minor gripe or two.

Two-man teams—like the Californians, Pfc. Walter Shipman of Silverado and Pvt. Henry Alexander of Wilmington—chop down 8 to 12 jungle giants a day, trees averaging 150 feet in height. Just as

Slim's domain might be part of the Pennsylvania farmland, so the island's jungle lumber camp resembles the Oregon woods, with the cry of "Timber!" echoing through the forest. The yell is not a gag, for an instant after it is heard there is a crack, a hesitant crinkling far overhead and then a final shuddering crash as the tree collapses like a KO'd heavyweight.

Winding through the jungle with its wearying tangle of "wait a minute" vines, you find Shipman and Alexander already at work lopping branches from their victim and brushing red ants from their glistening sweat-drenched backs.

The GI lumberjacks admire the 'Canal timber for its hardness and quality. There is a lot of mahogany, teak and rosewood, and some rubber. Some trees are so hard that axes bounce right off, Alexander says. "I don't know what they are," he says. "Some of this wood I never saw in my life before." But no matter how tough the tree, Alexander and Shipman usually get it down in about half an hour, even when the trunk is four feet thick. The wood here is of such good quality that, according to a latrine rumor, the wood in one crude little 'Canal bridge would be worth $1,000,000 to furniture manufacturers.

S/Sgt. Lad Belehrad of Yonkers, N. Y., the "timber cruiser" whose job is hunting for good lumbering sites in the jungle, says he and some of the others are so impressed that they're considering remaining on the 'Canal after the war. In five months, he says, a man could make enough to take it easy for the rest of the year.

But the lumberjacks gripe about the stifling 'Canal jungle, one of the hottest places on earth to swing an axe or push a saw. There is also so much shrapnel imbedded in the trees that teeth are often ripped out of saws. Among the many jungle mysteries is a strange tree whose inky black sap raises a blister on the skin that lands GI lumbermen in the hospital.

At the gravel pit T-4 John Childs of Jefferson, Tex., member of a Negro Engineer regiment, has been running a shovel for eight months. He has no kicks at all. Ever since he was a little kid and hung around the trucks his father worked on, Childs has loved heavy equipment.

In population Guadalcanal is now the equal of many leading American cities. That means, there are odd jobs here no GI ever dreamed of when he got that letter from the draft board.

At the spot where Carlson's Raiders left the perimeter and made their bloody sortie into Jap territory in the hills above Henderson, there stands a station hospital PX where Pfc. Orval Hjermstad works full time as a soda jerk. "I'll never do this when I go back," says Hjermstad, a mechanic in civilian life from Wallace, S. Dak. "Too much work. I twisted out 1,882 nickel cokes in one day." But he prefers soda-jerking to his experiences with the Infantry on Munda.

Four GIs on the 'Canal do nothing but repair musical instruments. Live music is popular here, but few places on earth are harder on music-making devices. Cases mold, wood instruments come unglued, ants destroy gut strings, and the wire strings that are generally substituted rust in three days to three weeks even when vaselined. Most wood instruments have to be wired and bracketed together, which is just too bad for the tone. Electric-light bulbs are kept burning day and night inside pianos to keep the felt dry, but retuning is necessary once a week. One morning a drummer found a rat had eaten through one head of his drum and out the other.

The repair work on musical instruments goes on only a few yards from where the Japs had one of their main gasoline burial pits. Their plan was to protect the fuel from bombs and bullets. The idea worked so well that the fuel was ready for our use when we captured the area.

Pianos aren't the only things that are kept dry with electric-light bulbs. Unit armories keep .45s dry that way, and Finance had to do the same thing with the piles of cash in its safe; even dollar bills were mildewing. Incidentally, Finance has other troubles with its bills. Crap games are rough on money. Each month Finance has to ship $50,000 worth of paper money back to Washington to be destroyed.

The 'Canal has a full-time boxing promoter, Sgt. John Williams, former Chicago Golden Gloves welterweight champ, whose Saturday-night fights, staged near the place where the Japs had one of their big Lunga supply depots, draw up to 14,000 yowling patrons.

Williams finds that a lot of well-known Stateside fighters, now GIs, don't like to fight in these latitudes because the heat is so exhausting. Bouts have to be held to three 1½-minute rounds. Just the same he has put together a good stable; Coxswain Bob Foxworth of Sandusky, Ohio, AAU light-heavy champ last year; Cpl. Leroy Evans, 220-pounder who was Max Baer's sparring partner and who is hard to match; Marines Moe and Harvey Weiss, twins from the Bronx, N. Y., Cpl. Petie Mateo, who fought Small Montana unsuccessfully for the world bantamweight title, and Garvey Young, Marine,

who beat Freddie Cochrane, welterweight champ, in a nontitle fight.

Pfc. Needom Langley of Spring Hope, N. C., one of the 'Canal's full-time chauffeurs, figures he has clocked 15,000 miles up and down the island in his eight months here, even though most of the driving is along a 20-mile stretch from Kukum to Koli. Guadalcanal is 100 miles long, most of it still primitive bush with some natives wearing grass skirts—items that are only tourist bait on many another South Sea isle.

Guadalcanal has a full-time paper-storage clerk, Cpl. Byron D. Gilmore of La Crescenta, Calif. In his warehouse he has 35 million sheets in one tarpaulin-covered pile 17 feet high. In another pile are 10 million sheets of bond paper.

One of the former Jap hospitals used to stand near this warehouse, and for a long time QM's stock of shoes and uniforms was stored there. The building has been destroyed. "Tojo's Ice House," down the road, is also out of commission, but for many months it supplied sweltering American troops with several dozen two-foot cakes of ice a day. A Jap generator still helps light a large part of Henderson Field.

Bridge rebuilding is also in the island's catalogue of unusual GI occupations. Flash floods, pouring down from the mountains—some of which are a mile and a half high—will raise a stream 12 feet in 12 hours and knock out the piles under bridges by hurling big trees against them. Some bridges have had to be replaced three times in a year. A new system of pontoon bridges is eliminating much of the piling, however, and the bridges are lasting longer.

Even art has arrived here. T-4 William Simpson, a sculptor in civilian life, was transferred from his mule pack-howitzer outfit after he created a model for a monument to the Guadalcanal dead. Washington officials are considering the model, a seated symbolic figure, and if it is approved, Simpson will direct the project. It will be 30 feet high. Meanwhile Simpson has been assigned to the Lunga Art Academy, a woodshed operated by Special Service where GIs may pick up art materials free or do their sketching and painting in privacy and quiet.

Guadalcanal is so quiet now that its very peace is the main complaint. "You might say we liked Guadalcanal a lot better when the bombs were dropping," said a lieutenant.

A captain agreed. "When the Japs were here," he said, "there wasn't any coke or ice, but it was a lot more interesting. In January a year ago, when three or four days passed without a raid, the men would say: 'I hope there'll be a raid tonight—a little excitement.' Now this retreat every night; it's chicken."

"The hardest part of the war," observed a major, "is just sitting around doing nothing."

Many of the Guadalcanal troops do rear-echelon work, servicing combat men farther north, and some truck and duck drivers put in 12 hours on many days. But there is almost always time to kill.

Some of the men are using it to study. There are correspondence courses in bookkeeping, accounting, physics, math, Diesel engines, mechanics and refrigeration. And there are face-to-face classes in shorthand, grammar and geography.

But the favorite time killers are the movies. The 'Canal has 150 theaters, many of them just coconut logs or oil drums in front of an outdoor screen. Audiences have been known to sit through an inch of rainfall to see a grade-C picture. What the theaters lack in roofs and soft seats, they make up in fancy names—the Coconut Bowl, Roxy, Oceanview, Lunga Palace.

The Lunga, with 2,800 bench seats, boasts a silver backdrop cut from a 900-pound barrage balloon that a destroyer towed in from the sea. It took 14 bathers three mornings to scrub off the sea and beach stains. Another 'Canal movie, on the site of the Matanikau River battle, has a 25-foot screen, one of the highest on the island.

GIs have introduced so many diversions that sometimes the Guadalcanal scene resembles a summer resort in the States. At Kukum, you'll see outboard motorboats and sailing skiffs and an occasional aquaplaner. GIs in diving masks study the beautiful colors of underwater coral. On Sundays, fishing parties in an outboard motorboat, made from floats of wrecked planes, travel up a river that was once a savage battle site. On the roads you may see a runabout made from salvaged plane wheels and a washing-machine motor, capable of more speed than the MPs allow.

Some GIs have trained the mute green parrots of the island to sit on their shoulders. Others, like T-4 Lewis G. Fife of Ogden, Utah, grow flowers around their pyramidal tents—for beauty and to keep the dust down. (The giant zinnias are so robust here that you can transplant them in full bloom from the gardens of outfits that are moving out.) Still other GIs make rings, P-38 models, bracelets and necklaces out of Jap propellers, bullets, shells and other odds and ends.

It's a changed Guadalcanal.

AFTER THE BATTLE AT KWAJALEIN

By Sgt. MERLE MILLER

KWAJALEIN ISLAND IN THE MARSHALLS—Although there is still some occasional rifle fire and the smoke still curls from the ruined concrete pillboxes, the veterans of the Army's 7th Division are now sitting under the trees or lying on the ground with V-Mail blanks, writing their first letters home.

Most of the letters are short and simple. The men cannot say that they are on Kwajalein, cannot give details of the action they fought here, cannot name friends who were injured, cannot give the date and cannot say where they came from and where they are going. They can't say much of anything except "I'm still alive and well." But that is enough.

The officers are wearing their insignia again. There are heated arguments about whether the 1st Platoon of Company A killed more Japs than the 3d Platoon of Company L. Hardly anyone knows for sure just how many Japs he did kill.

"When it gets past 10, you lose count and lose interest," says Pfc. James Carrigan of San Saba, Tex., a BAR man who accounted for 12.

Down on the beach about one man in 15 has suc-ceeded in finding his own barracks bag in the disorganized piles there. Those who have located their own toilet articles are sharing their razors and soap with a dozen other GIs. Some of the soldiers are bathing in the surf, wearing shoes to protect their feet from the sharp, jagged coral.

Everywhere burial details are removing the remains of the last dead Japs. A few minutes ago an unarmed private in a Graves Registration unit adjusted his gas mask and went into a small pillbox near the center of the island, an area that was supposed to have been completely cleared of Japs during the morning of the second day of the battle.

A split second later, the private ran yelling from the pillbox. He thought he had seen ghosts. Following him were two emaciated but very much alive Japs in shorts, their hands in the air. They are now changing into fatigues with PW painted on the back.

This morning hundreds of tropical white birds, driven away by the battle, have returned to the island and are resting again on the tops of what they still recognize as trees. A Special Service officer is looking for the best place to hang the screen for the outdoor movies that will begin in a few days. A site for a Post Exchange will be selected tomorrow.

Already a half dozen bulldozers are rolling the runways of the half-completed airstrip so hurriedly abandoned by the Japs. The engineers are surveying the site, discussing the best places to build hangars. The remaining skeletons of the Jap revetments are sadly out of line, they say.

A Negro port battalion is unloading food, ammunition and supplies from newly arrived cargo ships. The men are putting up their shelter halves in the few cleared spaces and AA crews are finding permanent positions for their guns.

Jeeps, half-tracks and tractors are moving along the battle-torn main highway, passing medium and light tanks which are returning from the front area.

The few enemy bicycles here are too small and too mangled to ride. But T-5 Robert Fuller, a coast artilleryman from Kansas City, Kans., started tinkering with the engine of a shrapnel-scarred truck with a left-hand drive. A few minutes later he was taking passengers all over the island.

Everywhere the foundations of blockhouses and the charred remains of barracks and storehouses are being searched for souvenirs. There are enough Jap rifles for everybody and once in a while a rare hara-kiri knife with a silver blade and a handle that some say might be gold.

No one who has acquired a complete Imperial Marine or Jap Navy uniform would consider selling it, but a pistol, carried only by the enemy officers, can be had for a month's overseas pay of a private.

Anybody can pick up right now the Jap post cards that make those of the French variety seem mild by comparison. There are also a few sets of travel prints of Australia, New Zealand, Pearl Harbor and San Francisco with Japanese captions under the photographs. The experts, of course, point out that these are the high points of a planned Nipponese tour of the Pacific, which somehow never came off.

Near what used to be a Jap food dump, there are piles of boxes of small, soggy crackers and a pasty stuff in cans that nobody will sample. Also there are 150 cases of beer, guarded by four MPs with guns.

No one cares about the beer, anyway. It isn't very good, much weaker than the PX stuff, and warm. There is no ice on this island. Besides, there are plenty of bottles of *sake* around here.

Hot coffee and hot chow are available for the first time in the company's CPs. Vienna sausages, beans, meat and vegetable hash are being cooked over dozens of fires in shell craters.

There is a rumor that bacon and eggs will be served tomorrow. No one puts much stock in it.

Tonight it will be possible to sleep, but not many of us will. The sickening odor of the dead Japs still fills the air, and there may still be a live one around who is unwilling to surrender.

No one can do much sleeping 24 hours after a battle anyway.

"Don't ask me what to do, we didn't have destroyers in that pond at Fort Bragg!"—*Sgt. Frank Brandt.*

WHY I LEFT GRAND CENTRAL PALACE

By Pvt. KNOX BURGER

I AM the guy people point at and say: "He was stationed at the Grand Central Palace Induction Center in New York"—they lower their voices—"an hour's train ride from home, and he asked for a transfer to Kansas." Then they tap their heads sympathetically and stare after me as if I were their long lost two-headed uncle from Topeka.

At 480 Lexington Avenue we had two bars and a model agency in the same building with us.

It was nice being able to step off the post and onto a sidewalk, but the fine edge of excitement was blunted a little by that damp rag you had in your hand. This was used for washing the glass doors in front of the place, in sight of half a million passersby, all highly amused at seeing The Soldier at Work. And usually four or five friends and acquaintances managed to turn up in the crowd. "Well, well, well," they'd say, eyeing my Grand Central pallor, which just about matched my faded coveralls. Then they'd follow up with a number of clever references to the 46th Street Front, the Lexington Avenue Local Commandos et al.

But a good man could get ahead at the Palace, if he played his relatives right. All you had to do was be a nephew of somebody in the front office above the rank of captain and, presto, Pfc—like that! For the unfortunate few who, through some weird freak of birth, failed to fall into this category, it took a little more time. We had a separate T/O. The T-5 in charge couldn't flex his wrist for the hash marks.

It was nice, going home every week end, too. Soldier returning from the wars. The reverential greetings from the little kids (that's all there are left, brother) hanging around the station platform. "Still a private, eh?" they would ask deferentially as I descended the steps of the "six-twenty-four."

"No," I would mutter confidentially. "In reality I'm one of these boy colonels. Left my eagles on my other blouse."

Their innocent eyes would dilate with respect. "They must have a hell of a lot of colonels down there," one would lisp, "because my old man was down for his physical the other day, and he says he saw you down on your hands and knees scraping up chewing gum."

Well, as a matter of fact, they did have us dislodging gum that the selectees, not wanting to foul the trash barrels, had thoughtfully deposited on the floor. Three of us scraped some four bushels of the stuff, in various stages of pliability off one floor in three days, setting a new inter-Allied record. It was the second floor, so naturally we were designated G-2 from that point on by the boys assigned to the other floors. You naturally get that sort of professional jealousy everywhere.

And I'd have enough money to buy the place, psychiatrists and all, if I had a dollar for every selectee who's stopped and whispered: "Hey, Mac—some place to be stationed, eh? How'd you go about getting it?" It might not be such a bad idea to buy it, paint it white like an elephant and turn it back to its rightful owners. Only thing is, insiders say that the Army's contract with the real-estate people has a clause, inserted after our squad won the gumathon, which states that when the building reverts to its civilian status, I go with it. Now I'm not one to balk at being rehabilitated, but there's no sense in letting your cup overflow.

So when you point at me, you're pointing at a man who knows when he's had enough.

Kansas, I never saw you before, but I love you.

WHEN WE GET OUR NEW T.O. . . .

By Sgt. RAY DUNCAN

"TABLE of organization," said the adjutant to me, as if that explained everything. Good old table of organization. I've been batting my head against one of those things ever since I started tucking in my necktie.

In order to find what fiend dreamed it up, I reached for the History of the United States Army.

The table of organization is as old as the armed forces. They had it in George Washington's time.

And in those days things were even worse. Each of the 13 colonies had a different T.O. for its fighters. Imagine the headaches that Washington had when he called his staff in for a little pep talk, back in the 1770's:

WASHINGTON: Remove your powdered wigs, gentlemen, and make yourselves at home. I've called you together to explain about ratings. There won't be any for a while, until we get our new table of organization.

GEN. JONES: Speaking of ratings, sir, why are those Minute Men simply loaded with brass and stripes, while the Militia never gets a rating? Those Minute Men are just a bunch of glamor boys——

GEN. SMITH: I resent that! Who held Concord Bridge? Who fired the shot heard round the world? Where was the Militia when——

WASHINGTON: Gentlemen, please!

GEN. WHITE: Sir, what about that sergeancy for my public-relations man? He's a smart boy—that was his idea at Bunker Hill, saying, "Don't fire until you see the whites of their eyes!"

GEN. STANDISH: Now wait a minute! If we're going to start throwing sergeancies around, let's not forget the corporal who's painting the murals in the Officers' Tavern on the post. He also happens to be doing an oil portrait of my wife, and she won't let me rest till he's promoted.

WASHINGTON: We'd like to, awfully, but we're governed by the table of organization.

[*Just then Ethan Allen, still muddy from the battle of Ticonderoga, bursts into the room.*]

ETHAN ALLEN: We've just taken Ticonderoga, sir, me and my Green Mountain Boys. I ask nothing for myself, but all the Green Mountain Boys should get tech sergeancies out of this. Of course the leader of a group of tech sergeants should have a lot more rank than I've got——

WASHINGTON: Quite right, and we're working on something for you. At present, however, the table of organization——

[*An exhausted messenger staggers into the room and reports to Gen. Washington.*]

MESSENGER: Sir, I've just come from Valley Forge The men are cold and hungry and exhausted, but they don't mind that so much. What gripes them is the fact that for six weeks now there haven't been any promotions.

WASHINGTON: Unfortunately they're already over their quota of ratings, as provided by the table of organization.

MESSENGER: One more thing, sir, I ran all this way without stopping. I'm considered the best runner in the whole Signal Corps. How about a stripe on the first of the month? I ran through snow and cold——

WASHINGTON: Yes, I just came from Valley Forge, I know how cold it is. Unfortunately, all ratings are frozen——

[*Someone titters, which makes Washington frown angrily. The messenger goes. Gen. Benedict rises and clears his throat.*]

GEN. BENEDICT: Sir, as you know I've just returned from an expedition into Canada. My men have seen foreign service! They're entitled to the ratings, rather than these USO Commandos who did all their fighting at home in New York and New Jersey. All my men should advance one grade. And the officers, too—except, of course, myself.

WASHINGTON: Why, general, I wouldn't think of advancing the others without promoting you, too.

GEN. BENEDICT: That's very nice of you, sir.

WASHINGTON: However, until we get our new table of organization, there simply isn't a thing we can do. That will be all, gentlemen.

[*All mumble angrily as they go, leaving only Washington and his aide, Col. Hawkins.*]

WASHINGTON: What a session that was! These generals can't get it through their heads that a table of organization is a table of organization!

COL. HAWKINS: By the way, sir, Capt. Childers was here yesterday, and he asked me to remind you of your promise. He said you'd understand.

WASHINGTON: Oh, yes! Capt. Childers. Very nice fellow. There's a man in his outfit I promised to promote to staff sergeant. I forget his name—he's the one who rode around the streets yelling, "The British are coming!"

COL. HAWKINS [*after thumbing his files*]: Oh yes, here it is. Revere, Paul, no middle initial. Hmmmm. I'm very sorry, sir, but there are no ratings available in his outfit's table of organization——

WASHINGTON [*angrily*]: Hawkins, please don't bother me with those clerical details! That Revere did a fine piece of work, and he deserves recognition for it. Capt. Childers was most anxious! Take care of it on the first of the month. I'm leaving immediately for Valley Forge.

COL. HAWKINS: Yessir. Before you go, sir, I was wondering how my chances are for a promotion this month——

WASHINGTON [*as he goes out the door*]: I'd like to very much, old man, but it's simply impossible. Can't do a thing under the present table of organization.

"He sort of corresponds to our Chaplains."—*Sgt. Charles Pearson.*

"Supplies, supplies, always supplies! Don't you ever bring in any women?"—*Cpl. Ernest Maxwell.*

"I think the MI will do for that shot."—*Sgt. Roger Cowan.*

"Don't be silly, darling; they'll adore you!"—*Pfc. Joe Kramer.*

"—And what else did they teach you in the engineers back at Fort Belvoir?"—*Sgt. Douglas Borgstedt.*

"Something smells terribly good. I wonder what it could be."—*Pvt. Thomas Flannery.*

HOUSES OF ITALY

By Sgt. NEWTON H. FULBRIGHT

WITH THE FIFTH ARMY IN ITALY—The house on the east bank of the Rapido River was a very fine house for a CP. Like all Italian houses, it was built entirely of stone; there was no wood in its construction at all. It was two-storied, and there were many rooms. A room on the ground floor of a strong two-story house, on the side that is as far from Jerry as you can get, always makes a fine company or battalion CP.

There were barrels of *vino* in this house. The men drank the *vino* and slept in the beds and cooked in the large, smoky, messy fireplace, and lived as well as can be expected on the Italian front.

Looking back over the whole Italian campaign, especially the "40 days and 40 nights" on the Rapido River and the high cold hills above Cassino and the celebrated Abbey, I feel that the big, dingy and terribly dirty old houses of Italy have had an epic meaning in the lives of us all.

After I was captured by the Germans at Altavilla, I learned from them how to appreciate a good house. And there is something about a house—aside from its massive stone walls, tile roof and thick braced concrete floors above your head—that is spiritual, emotionally embracing and warm.

Sitting on a bed roll with two or three massive *vino* barrels in an opposite corner, I have enjoyed with our men a particular joviality and comradeship, a sort of high security, while German shells thundered a few short yards away.

"The Tedeschi is a madman," someone may say. "Listen at that—like a mad ol' man coming in the house an' kicking the dogs off the porch an' smashing cooking pots and glass bottles all over the kitchen."

We made a costly attempt to cross the Rapido on Jan. 21. After that we stayed in our houses, and the Jerry stayed in his on the smoothly sloping west side of the river. Occasionally someone at an OP would call down to us in Company M and report that the Jerry had been spotted in a house across the river. Then our mortars out in the yard would get busy. Sgt. Quentin D. Barrington of Hubbard, Tex., or Sgt. Hubert (Cowboy Slim) Simons of Rosenthaul, Tex., would drop a dozen or two HE Heavies through the roof, and the OP would report the Jerry running away and diving into dugouts.

That would make the Jerry sling a few back at us. We would receive a barrage of Screaming

Mimis, or a tank would open up across the river and throw a few fast ones at one of our houses.

"I don't like this," Cpl. Harlan Copeland of Waco, Tex., a member of Cowboy Slim's mortar section, would protest. "Tear down one of the Tedeschi houses and he comes right back and wants to tear one of yours down! Somebody's gonna get hurt if this keeps up."

I remember, in particular, the excitement we had one afternoon.

I had just returned from our 1st Battalion area, up the river toward Cassino, and was standing in the road near our house, looking at a pile of mortar ammunition. The ammunition had come up during the night. Someone who didn't know what he was doing had piled it against a strawstack. A shell could set the strawstack on fire and blow up the whole dump.

I had turned away and taken a few steps when a heavy German shell—the "north of Rome" kind—crashed with a great shattering of earth and flame a few yards in front of me in the yard of the house where Cowboy Slim had his mortars. Instinctively I ducked and turned back toward the strawstack, but at that moment another shell struck it. I jumped up; there were some slit trenches in the field to the left, but just then a shell landed there, too.

"To hell with it!" I yelled, running as fast as I could. I headed for the house, about 70 yards away, where our company CP was located. As I crossed the road a shell crashed into the roof of a shed attached to Cowboy Slim's house. Something as big as a stove cap sailed by my head.

Inside the CP 1st Lt. Robert Hand, company executive officer from Seattle, Wash., stood with a wad of chicken feathers in his hand. Everyone laughed as I came dashing in.

"Barrington and I were preparing supper," said the lieutenant, holding up the chicken feathers, "when they caught us outside."

I looked back, and the strawstack was blazing like a bonfire at a college football rally.

It took a few minutes before the first shell in the mortar ammunition dump went off. Shells burst sporadically after that, sending blazing brands and sparks flying through the air. When the big explosion came about 30 minutes later, it flattened me against the wall.

I stood up, spitting dirt and dust. The others

were looking at me anxiously out of blinking, dust-rimmed eyes. I went out in the yard and looked up at the roof of the house. Nothing but a railway gun dropping one in the upper story could have made such a noise. But the house seemed to be as sound as ever. A charred brand, still smoking, was driven into the wall. A shelter half a few feet away, covering a small pile of ammunition, was on fire.

One of the men ran up and yanked the shelter half off the ammunition. I looked toward the road where the blazing strawstack had been. In its place I saw a crater wide enough to hold a heavy truck. A shed that had stood near the stack was now only a pile of scattered stones.

Telephones began ringing, battalion from regiment, regiment from division. What had happened?

We made a check and reported back: 400 rounds of HE Heavies blown up and one man with a tooth knocked out.

Cpl. Copeland was the casualty. As he dove for safety through a hole in the side of the house, he made the mistake of turning to look back. The next man crashed through, struck Copeland in the mouth with his helmet, and out went the tooth.

An hour later an old grandmother, two other women, two little girls and two little boys came up the road to fill their bottles from the *vino* barrels. The grandmother, whom we called "Mama," saw the chicken feathers first thing and made a dive for the CP.

"Tedeschi!" I shouted. "Tedeschi—boom-boom!"

"Tedeschi, hell!" the old woman shouted back, shaking her head and waving her arms. Her meaning was unmistakable. "The damn Americanos! Americanos!" We rocked with laughter.

And I shall always remember another house, the one we had high up on Mount Cairo with a deep, narrow canyon separating us from the Germans in their houses a few yards higher up the steep, terraced hillside.

This was a three-story house, constructed entirely from flinty mountain stone; the walls were nearly three feet thick, and the floors above were of heavy concrete, supported by iron beams. The forward company CP was located in a tight little room on the ground floor, with a fireplace and one high, narrow window.

It looked out over an abrupt cliff; the tiny blasted roofs of the village of Cairo lay far below, and beyond this, smoky from shells and the belching muzzles of many British and American heavy guns, was the picturelike valley of the Rapido. The yard was encircled by a thick stone wall, waist high. There was a well of clear, clean water at one corner of the house. There were many rooms inside, safe rooms, and at the edge of the yard was another strawstack where the men could get clean straw for their beds.

I had found this place one morning after we had moved into the area in the night to relieve an American battalion that had been holding here for some time. Company K, with possibly 25 men in

As he dove through a hole in the side of the house, he made the mistake of turning to look back.
Cpl. Jack Ruge.

three houses across the canyon, was trying to hold terrain formerly defended by a complete battalion. The nine machine gunners of our 1st Platoon were with them. I entered the house with the idea of bringing up our 2d Platoon to help them out. And this was such a strong house, sitting so ideally on a protruding hump of rock 50 yards above the canyon, that I immediately fell in love with it.

Inside I found an old Italian lying in bed—a virtual bag of bones in a tangle of dirty, ragged quilts and blankets.

In a thin voice he wailed: "I dunno—I'm no good for anything. I'm a sick old man."

"You speak English?" I asked.

"I work in Jersey, New York—in New Haven many years," he said.

Later in the afternoon—assisted by Pfc. Henry Hohensee, a Ganado (Tex.) boy known as the Dutchman and as Eighth Corps, who has a Purple Heart and three Oak Leaf Clusters to his credit—I succeeded in opening up and wiring in the forward CP. Cpl. R. L. Scott of Blue Ridge, Tex., returned to bring up the 10 men who then composed our 2d Platoon.

That night the Dutchman built a roaring fire in the fireplace, and we hung a blanket over the window. The men gathered around and had a roaring bull session until midnight. Two men stood guard in the upper story; the machine guns were trained on the Jerry across the draw.

Early in the evening Cpl. Scott helped the Dutchman brew up a canteen cup of bouillon for the old man in the next room. "They say it's good, else they wouldn't put it in the K rations," said the Dutchman.

The following day was quiet. The Jerry threw rounds intermittently in the draw where the battalion before us had lost 60 men. But he would never get any of us that way—we had learned long ago to keep out of draws.

In the afternoon we heard that the battalion had been suddenly ordered to withdraw to the valley again. The order, as finally acted on by Company K, called for us to withdraw from the houses immediately after dark. We were to proceed by way of a donkey trail that intersected the Terelle road several hundred feet down the almost-vertical face of the mountain.

Company K began the withdrawal shortly after dark, but as the men filed up the draw toward our house, the Germans opened a phony attack against the French, on the ridge above Terelle, over against the right horizon.

The withdrawal was held up at our house; after we left there would be no one in this sector at all. But a phony attack is nothing but sound and fury, with little or no displacement of troops; as the Jerry on the hillside above remained inactive, Company K continued its withdrawal by way of the trail.

Our 2d Platoon had been designated to withdraw with their weapons by way of the Terelle road. They had scarcely left the house to begin the climb up the terraced slope behind us when German shells began falling all over the place. We ducked inside as three crashed in the yard. Shell fragments leaping across the yawning canyon struck fire from the rocks like a whole battalion of attacking Jerries. The Dutchman and I were alone in the house. Our telephones had been ripped out, so we were isolated. Some 30 minutes later, when the Jerry artillery shifted toward the Terelle road, we ducked out the back door and scurried down the donkey trail to safety.

As we caught up with Company K, which was taking a break where the trail entered the main road, someone drove up in a jeep with an order for them to return to their positions at once.

"We'll blow for a moment," I said to the Dutchman as the company prepared to move out. I threw my roll down and sat on it. Since one cold wet night in November, I've carried a standard roll of six blankets inside two shelter halves. It's plenty heavy but it's always convenient once we reach a stopping place.

We reached the top of the hill ahead of Company K, only to find that the counterattack had played out. A few artillery shells were still falling on the hill, but we were going down again as scheduled.

"Eighth Corps," I said, "to hell with the road!" We were too tired to follow the road anyway. We just slid vertically down the mountain. We knew that the road, winding about in the perambulating style of all mountain roads, would pick us up again. A rain had started to fall, and we sat at the side of the road until the battalion went by, then slid down to the next turn.

At one of the turns we met Cpl. Scott, sloshing along with a wet roll slung over his shoulder. Just as we were doing, he was thinking of the wonderfully warm house we had just left, the roaring fire singing in the fireplace and the gallon can of coffee simmering on the coals. "Dutch," he said, "the old man will die. Nobody to take care of him."

Toward morning the Dutchman and I crawled into the one good room of a blasted house on the slope above the village of Cairo and went to sleep.

MY OLD OUTFIT

By Sgt. MACK MORRISS

They started out together at Fort Jackson back in the States and fought their way across Europe until the faces were no longer familiar and you could count the old men on the fingers of one hand.

MAASTRICHT, HOLLAND—We walked at five-yard intervals on either side of the concrete highway and watched without much interest the Typhoons and P-47s that were strafing something off to the left.

The planes went into long dives and pulled out in tight circles to come back and strafe again. The sound of their machine guns reached us long after they had pulled out of the dives. We glanced occasionally at the ready-made German foxholes, dug by impressed civilians and lining the road every 10 yards. They were chest deep and round, with dirt piled neatly beside them; but every one was smooth on the inside so we knew that Jerry had never used them.

We plodded along past wrecked vehicles and modern homes with well-kept yards, and glanced at the terrain off to our left where the war was. Dutch kids by the side of the road, wearing bright orange bows in their hair or on their jackets, reached for our hands.

"Good-bye," they said. They say that either way, whether you're going or coming, as a greeting or as a farewell.

Hutch was walking behind me.

Hutch is Mack Pierce, a mortar sergeant in F Company. He used to be in A Company, where he was a line sergeant, then an artificer and finally mess sergeant. He was a mess sergeant for 18 months, and then he went over the hill and got busted. He transferred to F Company after that, and they finally gave him three stripes again, but he didn't care. He never did care much for things like that.

This was our anniversary—Hutch's and mine. We had been in the Army four years. We were members of the Tennessee National Guard, inducted Sept. 16, 1940, among the oldest of the "New Army." Today we were moving up to an assembly area where our outfit—the 30th (Old Hickory) Division—would get set for an attack.

It was a bright day, as days go here. The 2d Battalion was two parallel OD lines moving across the brow of a hill up ahead and swinging around the shaded curve behind us. They were leaving Maastricht, a fair-sized town taken two days before. Now

—after France and Belgium and Holland—they were headed for Germany.

I was with Hutch down in F Company because Hutch is the only line soldier left out of the old bunch from the highlands of east Tennessee who came into the Army as Company A. There were about 150 of us then. Now there are only four in the regiment. There's Hutch, down in the 2d Battalion. Then there's Porky Colman, a mess sergeant now; Charlie Grindstaff, still cooking; and Herman O. Parker, still driving a truck. They're all that's left of old A Company.

We started out in the Army at Fort Jackson, S. C., when they were singing the song "I'll Never Smile Again." Lord, we were sentimental about that song. I remember Hilton was just married and was leaving his new wife. Crockett slugged the juke box in the drug store at Columbia; Tommy Dorsey's arrangement came out soft and smooth, and Hilton cried. We were all privates then, going into the Army for a year.

Since then, Hilton's kid brother had become a tail gunner in a Fort and had gone down over France. Hilton got out of the Army and his wife had a baby on the same day. Hilton stayed out of the Army for two years. Now he's in the Navy somewhere. Crockett went from a basic private up to first sergeant and then to OCS. Now he's a first lieutenant in an infantry outfit over here.

Hutch Pierce and I walked up the road. Somebody—a replacement—sang briefly and then stopped. The infantry doesn't sing much, especially moving up. Not after St. Lo and Mortain, they don't sing much. The replacement chanted: "Or you might grow up to be a mule. Now, a mule is an animal with long funny ears."

Hutch and I talked along the way. When we got a break we lit K-ration cigarettes and tried to reconstruct A Company.

It was a picturesque outfit. Those originals were close-knit, clannish and independent as only hill people can be. It was a company with a heart and a soul. Its code was "Independence." Its motto, in our own language, was "take nothin' offen nobody." That was a philosophy that needed tempering. It works better in combat than in garrison. We had our troubles.

I had seen Col. Crumley in London. He's had a desk job there now since his lungs finally took him out of the field into the hospital. He was a first lieutenant when we went to Jackson, then company commander and then battalion commander. We talked about the old company before it broke up. Crumley was hard, but he loved the company. He was a better soldier than any of us, but he was proud of us—a man who lived by our philosophy and tempered it, too. We learned to take a lot, as the infantry does.

It has been three years since Crumley was with us as a company officer, but Hutch said: "When you're out here you appreciate a man like him."

We tried, Hutch and I, to tell each other what little we knew of the men who came in with us. The outfit had deteriorated slowly in the natural process of transfers and discharges, like an eroded hillside gradually falling away.

Harry Nave, the company clerk, went into the Air Forces as a cadet and got killed in training. Lardo Boring went into the Air Forces, too, and the last we heard, he had pulled his missions and was back home. Lardo used to be in the machine-gun section.

Earl Marshall went into the Paratroops, and so did Bill Longmire. Elmer Simerly was in the Airborne Infantry. Bill Potter went to OCS and the last we knew he was in New Guinea. Red Mason was a lieutenant over there somewhere. Ralph Snavely was one of the first to transfer out. He went down to the Southwest Pacific, too. Lucian Garrison went to Italy and got wounded, and so did Capt. Ritts. Ed Mottern was in Iceland for a long time but he's probably over here now.

Hutch had seen Pony Miller on the beach back in June. Pony is a first now, and an executive officer. Hutch said he'd heard that Howard Fair went in with the 1st Division on D-Day. Charles Hurt got his jaw broken on maneuvers just before A Company came overseas, so he stayed in the States.

Doc Sharp was transferred; he's down in the Islands with a jungle-training unit, still letting the cards fall the same as always. Jack Ellis came over with another regiment in the division, but he got wounded and we lost track of him. Fred Davis was a captain in the TDS the last we knew.

A Company came to England with only 12 of the old National Guard bunch still left and just a few of our first and second batches of selectees. Now there's only one line soldier left from the first group of selectees we trained—a boy named J. C. Wright. Wright was wounded some time back, but he rejoined the company later as an acting platoon sergeant. Then they got a new lieutenant, and he and J. C. had an argument. J. C. is platoon guide now.

The outfit came to France on D-plus-9. Three weeks went by before they hit it rough. Then, on July 7, the regiment spearheaded the way across the Vire River and fought down through the hedgerows toward St. Lo.

It was a war foreign to the sage fields and pine thickets of South Carolina. It was a war from one piled-up mass of earth and shrubbery to another, with the Artillery blasting savagely and the infantry moving up 50 yards behind it. Those hedges are old, and the decay has built up at their base to form solid walls. Each one of them was a wall of fire, and the open fields between were plains of fire. The flanking hedges on either side belonged to him who could cover them.

Two of the boys from the hills stopped there. One of them was Bill Whitson, black-haired, with a face so dark that his teeth seemed whiter than they really were. He was built like a god—broad and tall. He lived like a happy devil, untamed and untameable. Whit never took anything very seriously. He moved with the corded grace of a panther, lethal and full of power. He could make the sling of his '03 rifle crack like gunfire when the leather hit the hardness of his hand.

Whit raised his head out of a foxhole and a piece of shrapnel caught him flush in the temple. He died somewhere northeast of St. Lo. Bull Bowers got hit there, too, the same day.

Bull is a big boy, almost pudgy, with round cheeks that are a perpetual cherry red. His name is James, but he's always been called Bull because when his voice changed it came out low, deep and throaty, so that whatever Bull said he said it in a rumble with a drawl.

Bull is easygoing. He never pushes anybody unless somebody pushes him. His make-up is not the make-up of a tough platoon sergeant. Bull's a platoon sergeant who swore softly rather often, but never with very much conviction.

So when they pulled Bull out of the foxhole, after the shrapnel had gone into him, he looked at his legs and then said to nobody in particular, without a great deal of violence and in a slow rumble: "Them gawdam sons o' bitches."

Bull was evacuated. Two days later Dale May left the outfit because of sickness. He had stomach trouble—ulcers or something.

Dale got to be a sergeant right after we came into the Army because he was one of the few men in the outfit with service in the Regulars. He had pulled a hitch at Schofield Barracks, and he told us stories about the Old Army—of afternoons off, tailor-made khaki blouses, white gloves and chrome bayonets, and how he was pulling KP when his discharge papers came through and he could go back to the mainland.

Dale was a tech sergeant when he left A Company. The boys in the kitchen hear he's in a Quartermaster outfit now.

The regiment's objective was the high ground to the west overlooking St. Lo. They took it, so they were a protective screen for the outfits that went into St. Lo itself. Then A Company moved south toward Tessy-sur-Vire.

On July 28, the regiment hit trouble. The next day the 1st Battalion went in to attack near a place called Le Mesnil Opac. There were hedgerows again, and a long slope exposed to observation and heavy fire. One of the men wounded in the action was Pfc. James R. Baines.

We always called him Beans. He had been a tech sergeant but had got busted. When he made platoon sergeant he told one of the boys who got another rocker with him: "Well, they made everybody else, now they made us." That was back in the States. Nobody cared much for stripes back there any more than they do over here now. Too many people on your back, too much worry, too much bother. Beans got hit by shrapnel and was evacuated. The next night Clyde Angel was killed.

Clyde was blond and fair. He talked with the nasal twang of east Tennessee. He was a mess sergeant and before that he had been a cook in the company, just as his brother Monk had been a cook for us before him. There were two other cooks, men who had come to the company later, who were killed with Clyde.

The kitchens were dispersed and everybody was dug in. Charlie Grindstaff said Clyde had the best shelter in the area. He and the other two dug a deep one and covered it with logs and dirt. Then Jerry came over, dropping big-stuff bombs that straddled the shelter. The concussion killed all three of them in the hole. A Company's kitchen was blown to hell. Now Porky uses the battalion h.q. blackout tent for a cook tent.

The next night the regiment made its objective beyond Tessy-sur-Vire and later moved on to relieve elements of the 1st Division near St. Barthelmy. St. Barthelmy is close by Mortain, not far from the base of the Cherbourg peninsula. It was between Mortain and Avranches by the sea that our armor had roared southwest into Brittany after the breakthrough at St. Lo. At St. Barthelmy A Company gave everything it had. It was there that the regiment was hit—hard.

The SS had counterattacked with tanks, and the German artillery was trying to cut through to split our forces in Normandy and Brittany. The Germans hit savagely. They ran over A Company and C Company. The regiment fought like animals with everything that would fire and then fought hand-to-hand with the German infantry that poured in behind the tanks.

Jerry almost made it. The fight went on for four days while the division struggled and gave ground but never broke. Then, on the fifth day, the power was gone and we went back into St. Barthelmy. The SS spearhead was blunted and then broken off. But Bud Hale was gone, and Ed Markland.

Bud was the top kick. He was a little guy with delicate hands and a skin that stretched tight across the cheekbones. His eyes were the eyes of all his family. At home the Hales have eyes that are all alike. Frances, Virginia, Luke, Sara, Bud, Mary, Nell and Sonny—they all have eyes that are their medium of expression. Bud played football at home the year we won the state championship and before. He was the kind of boy who drew people to him. Over here one of the new boys in the kitchen put it right: "We had to take the chow up to the line, and when I could see Bud I felt like the whole company was there."

After the SS ran over the company, Bud was listed as missing in action. So was Markland.

Ed and I were mortar corporals together for a long time, and our anniversary today would have been a great day for him. The division commander came around this morning presenting medals to a few officers and men in the regiment. The general order for the award of the Silver Star included T/Sgt. George Edward Markland "for gallantry in action in France."

The day after Angel was killed Ed's outfit had been held up by fire from a dug-in position. Ed crawled up ahead, "consistently exposed himself to murderous enemy mortar and artillery fire." We adjusted our own artillery on the strongpoint and the attack went on. Ed wasn't here to get in on the little ceremony by the road this morning, but he may catch the later one. A Company doesn't refer to Bud and Ed as MIA but as captured. Jerry got a lot of prisoners that day. Ernest Oaks was hit there, too.

When the SS overran our antitank positions and knocked out four of the guns, Oaks had to be evacuated. He had been in A Company for a long time —part of the triumvirate of Potter, Oaks and Russell. When we came into the Army none of them was 20. They were wild. They laughed and did insane things. Russell—we called him "Reb" although all of us are Southerners—was wide-eyed during our training on the machine gun. The nomenclature delighted him. One day the section sergeant had us naming the parts of the piece and he picked up a tiny pin and asked Reb to identify it.

Reb gazed thoughtfully at the pin.

"That," he said, "is the forward cam lever for the plunger guide on the barrel extension with the swivel pawl."

St. Barthelmy-Mortain was the division's great trial. It was infantry against armor, and the division fought for survival. Col. Frankland, the 1st Battalion's commander, saved his own CP by killing the crew of a German tank with his .45. Parts of five German *Panzer* outfits hit the division, striking along the main highways and the back roads. The division was committed to the last man. The artillery was overrun and fought as infantry. The engineers and cavalry were on the line. Thirty Jerry tanks were destroyed. The engineers got a Mark IV with a bazooka. An AT commander stopped another with a bazooka and killed the crew with a carbine as they tried to get out.

In the fog of the morning of Aug. 7, the regiment and division survived. Our artillery, TDs, rocket-firing planes and armor were thrown in to add strength to a line that was thin. A Company survived.

One battalion of a sister regiment was isolated for three days, cut off on a cliff and blasted mercilessly. When the Germans came forward under a white flag to talk surrender, the battalion said: "Go to hell."

Our 2d Battalion—Hutch's outfit—helped get them out.

Hutch has had the experiences of a line soldier. A machine-gun bullet burned the back of his neck. The blast of Screaming Minnies cartwheeled him off his feet. A little piece of shrapnel cut across the top of his foot, but he didn't bother to have it treated.

Hutch laughed and said: "The damndest thing I've seen in combat happened that day. We went up after the battalion that was lost. There was a goat up there. He was a sorry-looking goat, sort of a dirty gray.

"Well, we were getting artillery, and every time a shell would come in this goat would dive for a foxhole. Then he would raise his head up and if he didn't hear anything he would come out. There were plenty of foxholes and he knew what they were for. He'd do it every time."

We laughed at the picture of a bewhiskered goat in a foxhole. One infantryman said: "Yeah. The reason he beat me into one was because he had four legs and me just two."

A Company had two of our originals left in the line after St. Barthelmy. Now both of them are gone —perhaps to come back to the outfit, perhaps not to come back to it at all.

Both went back with fatigue, with nerves that had stood all they could stand for a while.

One of them left just a few days ago, after a river crossing that stirred up a fight. It was a fight like a dozen others the company has had. But it was one too many for him.

The other one who went back is a twin. He and his brother are identical. There were some of us who had soldiered with them every day and still couldn't tell them apart. They're squat and tow-headed and when they laugh their faces crease into a fan of wrinkles from the outside corners of their eyes. They grinned almost always, but when they got mad their lips quivered and they trembled all over, and we were surprised that they did. Not long before the company left the States, one of them was transferred and the other stayed on alone. But part of him was gone.

Yesterday, in a courtyard, Parker and I lay sprawled on the trailer of his jeep and watched as the infantry went past on the outside lane. It was a patrol coming in. "Hit anything?" somebody asked. A voice answered: "Nuh." The patrol went by silently.

"Was that some of us?" I asked Parker.

"Doggone," said Herman, "I don't know. I don't know anybody in the company any more."

LULLABY

By Sgt. CHARLES E. BUTLER (*Britain*)

For a photograph with the caption: "Here are three American soldiers who were killed in battle on the beach at Buna, New Guinea. This photograph, emphasizing the grim facts of war, was released to give the American public a more realistic picture of the war."

Was it evening, with a slow wind falling
Upon the gray and broken stillness in the leaves,
The birds calling in terror, and the sky
Broken with wings, and on the drifting shore
The slow tide curling inward, curving and rippling,
Fold upon foam-edged fold, folding at last
Upon you in the sand? Was it evening then,
And quiet, falling to sleep in the silence,
You, with your cheek soft on the ultimate pillow
And your outstretched hand reaching no more for the
    gun,
Or love, or the things of life, sleeping there, sleeping?

You have come a long way to lie on the sand,
Forgetful of the motion of
The slow, incessant waves
Curving and falling, the white foam lifting
The white sand drifting
Over your face, your outflung hand,
Drifting and creeping
Slow and incessant and cool . . . .
You have come a long way, a world away, to sleep.

The page will remember a little while;
You are a warning now; a message,
Sleeping like children on the rippled shore,
Forgetful now for ever of the slow
Whispers of the curling water
Sifting the sand around you with its long
Reiterant falling and lifting whispering music . . .
You are a message now, forgetful, sleeping;
The idiot print of Time on the wave-washed shore . . .

Sleep now, forgetful of the drifting sand,
The strange cries of birds in the green forest;
Sleep, cold on the sand, immortal on the fading page,
Emphatic, grim, forgetful . . . Sleep, sleep . . .
Silence will shield the shrieking of the birds,
The wild, quick beating of their wings against the tree
    fronds;
The storm will pass . . . Silence will cover it;
Sleep . . .

INTERVIEW WITH TITO OF YUGOSLAVIA

By Sgt. WALTER BERNSTEIN

PARTISAN HEADQUARTERS, SOMEWHERE IN YUGOSLAVIA [By Cable]—Marshal Josip Broz—Tito of Yugoslavia —is a man of high intelligence and sensitivity, dedicated with his people to the job of freeing his country and establishing a federal democratic Yugoslavia.

I can report this after walking from the Adriatic Coast deep into liberated territory to interview Tito. I was the first correspondent to visit him in his Partisan headquarters.

To get here I had to hike day and night for what seemed like months, most of the time over mountains and part of the time through German-occupied territory. It was a tribute to Partisan strength and organization that we finally arrived more or less intact.

The interview took place at night in the house that Tito shares with other members of his staff. The location of the house is naturally secret. It is heavily guarded by tough Partisan soldiers who shoot first and ask you to halt afterward. I was taken there by a young Partisan lieutenant.

The night was very black, and I had no idea where we were going. Once we crossed a stream on a slippery log. Several times we were stopped by guards who appeared silently in the darkness.

In the distance we could hear the roar of a waterfall. The sound grew louder as we approached and finally we could see it, the water churning white and phosphorescent in the night. Tito's house was next to the waterfall, under an overhanging mountain that protected it from air raids.

We walked up to the house. There were more guards at the entrance, young men with tommy guns over their shoulders and captured German pistols in their belts. The lieutenant conferred briefly with them and one of the soldiers went in the house. The rest of us waited outside. It was cold near the waterfall, and the spray fell all around us like thin rain. Finally the soldier came out of the house and led us around to the side.

We stepped up onto the porch and stopped in front of the door. The lieutenant knocked, opened the door and stuck his head inside. Then he pushed open the door and stepped back, and I walked in. Tito was seated at a desk facing the door, and he stood up when I entered. I didn't know whether to salute, but he held out his hand and I shook it instead. He showed me to a chair next to his desk.

A huge dog that looked like a wolf was sleeping by the chair. He stirred when I sat down, but Tito said a few words in Croatian and the dog lay still again. Then Tito sat down.

He has one of the most impressive faces I have ever seen. It is Slavic, with high, wide cheekbones. It is a strong face, but not hard. Its most striking quality is one that you do not expect from a leader in such a bloody war, and that is kindness. It is a very kind face, almost gentle. Tito's eyes are set deep and wide apart, and it is difficult to tell their color. The skin underneath is soft and a little pouchy from fatigue. His forehead is high—what people like to call an intellectual forehead—and his hair is abundant and combed straight back. It is brown, with flecks of gray brushed in.

Tito's face is the face of a man who knows himself and the world around him. It could be the face of an artist or of a big businessman who directs a huge industry. And, in a sense, this man is both of these.

He was wearing a gray uniform of heavy wool, simply cut and of excellent material. On each collar he wore three gold quarter-wreaths on a red rectangle, and on the cuff of each sleeve he had a gold half-wreath enclosing a star.

The room was also simple, small and square, with a patterned red rug on the floor. The walls were covered with a kind of wrapping paper, heavily seamed and reinforced with strips of some white material that looked like parachute silk. One wall was covered with a large map of Yugoslavia. In the corner of the room there was a pot-bellied stove, its pipe running out through the wall. There was little furniture: a small table in a corner, four straight-backed chairs, a large flat desk facing the door and behind the desk a day bed with a dull-green flowered cover. At the head of the bed there were two small tables, each with a radio on it. Even here you could hear the dull roar of the waterfall.

A young girl came in immediately after I had entered and sat down on the other side of the desk. Her name was Olga, and she was an interpreter. Tito speaks fluent German and Russian but no English. The girl spoke English well with a pleasant accent.

Tito would look at her when he talked and then turn to me when he had finished. He talked softly and unhurriedly but without hesitation. As he talked he would finger some of the objects on his desk: a GI flashlight, a copy of "Essential English," a case of British cigarettes. He smoked steadily, putting the cigarettes in a holder shaped like a little pipe. Tito's movements were like his voice—deliberate and sure.

He gave the instant impression of being a leader. I had heard Allied officers refer to Tito as a "big man," and I could see what they meant. He talked of little things; he was tired and didn't feel like discussing large problems; but even so, the qualities of strength and decision came through. But it seemed a strength with compassion, and a decision built out of theory and experience. He seemed that rare kind of man who could achieve a complete fusion of thought and action. Looking at him and listening to him, I could understand the miracle of organization that the Partisans have created—the formation first of a complete army and now of a state with all its components, out of absolutely nothing and against the most savage terror and treachery.

This was the man who had organized a whole people, bewildered and sold out, into a new and powerful state. Knowing nothing about him, we had called him the "Mystery Man of the Balkans," but the only mystery seemed to be why we knew nothing about him, why we had not been informed about this man earlier.

Tito did not talk of his life, but it was evident in everything he said. He was born in a village near Zagreb in Croatia. His father was a peasant, very poor, and Tito became a metal worker. He was drafted into the Austro-Hungarian army in the first World War and captured by the Russians. After the October Revolution in Russia, he asked permission to join the new Red Army and fought with it for the remainder of the Russian civil war. Then he returned to Zagreb, where he became a leader of the workers.

But the Yugoslavia government imprisoned him, and Tito spent four years in jail. He left the country after his release and passed some years traveling around Europe. He was in Paris when the Spanish War broke out. Contrary to published reports, he did not go to Spain himself but he organized the large Yugoslav delegation that fought there against the Fascists. When the Germans attacked Yugoslavia, Tito was already in Belgrade, preparing to organize resistance.

Tito is married and has two sons. His wife is in Slovenia, working with the Slovenian Committee of National Liberation. His 20-year-old son is a sergeant in the Red Army and has been decorated as a Hero of the Soviet Union. He received the award in the battle of Moscow, where he lost one of his hands. He is now in officers' school in Russia. The other son, 5 years old, is in Yugoslavia.

Tito holds four positions in the new Yugoslav state. He is a member of the executive committee, called AVNOJ, which is the Partisans' congress. He is head of the National Committee of Liberation, which is their cabinet and he is minister of war and commander in chief of the National Army of Liberation and Partisan Detachments in Yugoslavia. (The National Army of Liberation is Tito's regular army. The Partisan Detachments are his organized civilian guerrilla fighters.)

He is deeply loved by the people of Yugoslavia, not only because he has led them well but also because he has fought and suffered with them. There are many stories of Tito's bravery. During the first German offensive, he led 12 men in a counterattack against an Italian company. He was himself wounded in the left arm during the terrible fifth German offensive, when it seemed that the entire Partisan army would be destroyed. He is probably one of the finest strategists of this war, mainly because his strategy is based on sound politics as well as good military tactics. He still goes to the front, especially during German offensives.

Tito's cosmopolitan quality becomes more apparent the longer you are with him. He is no simple peasant leader but a man of the world. Actually Tito is an extremely sophisticated man in the highest sense of the word. There are also moments when he gives the impression that he could have been a fine actor; he carries himself well and wears his uniform with a flair. When he was hiding from the Gestapo in Belgrade or Zagreb, he posed as a wealthy businessman. And he always got away with it.

Tito talked about America. He has a feeling for the U. S. that is characteristic of many Yugoslavs. It stems not only from blood ties with the thousands of Slavs who emigrated to America but also from their innate love of democracy and their conception of the U. S. as a great democratic country. Tito talked about how he had wanted to go to America when he was young but was too poor to make the trip.

He talked of the republican tradition in America and what an inspiration it has been to Yugoslavia. He deplored the idea, prevalent in the U. S., that there is civil war in Yugoslavia and emphasized the unity of the people against the Germans and against the native fascists.

He talked about the Partisan army, proudly and

with conviction. He pointed out that they have no discipline problem, that they have succeeded in welding the different racial and religious elements in Yugoslavia into a harmonious whole, and that this unity would continue after the war. He said the major problems of his army are physical: food and tanks and antitank guns and an air force of its own, however small.

Here Tito emphasized that his army had been receiving direct and valuable help from the Allied air forces, but he pointed out that there are many qualified Yugoslav pilots anxious to fly for the Partisans who are just sitting around in Allied territory.

But the food problem is the most pressing. The Partisans can continue to lift arms and ammunition from the Germans but the army cannot function at its highest efficiency on a half-loaf of bread a day. If they could get enough food to feed the army, the civilian population could somehow manage to feed itself, he said. As it is, the civilians have to give to the army and no one gets enough.

He talked briefly about the hardships of the people, speaking without sentimentality and with great pride in what they have done. He spoke particularly about the young girls in the army, marching day and night over mountains and then going straight into battle. He regards this as something not desirable in itself; it is only necessary because other Yugoslavs ran away or refused to fight when the Germans invaded the country.

I asked Tito about the treatment of prisoners. He said it was only recently that the Germans agreed to recognize his forces as an army. Before that they called them bandits and executed all they caught. Now the Germans have been compelled by the size and successes of the Partisans to treat them as they treat other Allied armies. One of the main reasons for this, of course, is that the Partisans have been capturing too many Germans.

Tito leaned forward and emphasized here that there has never been an order issued by his headquarters to kill prisoners, but it is a fact that his army does not take many. By this time the soldiers are a trifle bitter toward the Germans, especially because they have had the habit of killing all the Partisan wounded they could find. Those prisoners that the Partisans do take are usually held for exchange.

This just goes for the Germans. As far as the native fascists—the Ustachi or Croatian fascists—they are considered by the Partisans as beyond any rehabilitation and are usually shot. There are about 100,000, and they occasionally are too bestial even for the Germans, I was told.

Captured Chetniks (Serbian troops of Gen. Draja Mikhailovitch) are first offered the chance to join the Partisans. If they refuse they are sent back to their homes with instructions to stay there and behave themselves. The Partisans regard many of these Chetniks as simply poor, ignorant peasants who were drafted by Mikhailovitch and told they were fighting for the Allies. Most of them, I was told, are glad to escape from service under Mikhailovitch and from collaboration with the Germans, but some do return to their units after being released. One Chetnik was captured 11 different times. I asked why they didn't finally shoot him. "Don't be ridiculous," I was told. "We got 11 rifles from that man."

I asked Tito about the quality of the fascist opposition. He said the Germans were unpredictable, sometimes good, sometimes not so good. It depended largely on how much superiority they thought they had. They don't like to fight at night, and night fighting is right down the Partisan alley. Tito said the Ustachi were good fighters because they know they will be killed if they are caught. The Bulgarians were also good, he said; there is a Bulgarian corps fighting against the Partisans in eastern Yugoslavia, and they are fierce fighters. The Chetniks are not so hot, Tito added—there are only about 15,000 of them at this point, and they are dwindling rapidly. Unless bolstered by a strong supporting force of Germans or Ustachi, he said, they do not have much stomach for fighting.

We talked about an hour, and then it was time to go. Olga, the girl interpreter, looked tired; everyone I met at headquarters looked tired, which seemed natural under the circumstances. I stood up to go, and Tito rose to shake hands again. He said he hoped the American people would finally learn the truth about Yugoslavia. We stood for a moment without talking, and then he said, half to himself:

"Our people will continue to fight against the invader, no matter who he is, whether German or Chetnik or Ustachi."

We shook hands, and I turned to go. I opened the door, and the young lieutenant moved into the room, holding the door open. It was very dark outside. The noise of the waterfall was suddenly loud, and the cool wet spray drifted lightly into the room. Marshal Tito was still standing behind his desk as I went out. He is not a tall man but he filled the room. Then the door closed.

SURPRISE PARTY AT ENIWETOK

By Sgt. MERLE MILLER

ENIWETOK ISLAND, ENIWETOK ATOLL, THE MARSHALLS [By Cable]—Almost everything about the battle for this island had a fantastic and unexpected quality.

The operation began in the usual fashion with an uninterrupted barrage of 16-, 8- and 5-inch shells laid down by U. S. battleships, cruisers and destroyers. From our troopships only a few hundred yards offshore, all of Eniwetok seemed on fire. Red, yellow and black smoke blanketed the island, while a dull gray smoke clung to the shattered trees and bushes. At dawn our destroyers moved closer, almost hugging the beach.

Then Navy Avengers raked the area with a dive-bombing and strafing attack, barely clearing the tops of some of the trees. This aerial bombardment began soon after morning chow, which included fresh eggs because this was the day of battle. By the time our assault boats had gathered in the rendezvous area, coconuts and huge palm fronds were floating out from the beach.

Suddenly the bombardment ceased; for a single, incredible minute there was silence. That silence seemed to underline the question all of us were asking ourselves: where were the Japs?

At no time had the enemy answered the Navy's surface and air bombardments. None of our observers had sighted a single Jap on the island—or any other living thing. Some of the men of the 106th Infantry wondered out loud whether Eniwetok was another Kiska, whether the Japs had fled without a fight.

There was nothing to make the infantrymen change their minds as the first two assault waves piled out of amphibious tractors and threw themselves over the steep fire trench that ran along the entire beach, then stood upright and moved inland. There was still no sign of Japs.

As troops under Lt. Col. Harold I. (Hi) Mizony of Spokane, Wash., moved north, and troops under Lt. Col. Winslow Cornett of White Plains, N. Y., moved south, the guns of the destroyer force shifted their fire ahead of the troops to clear the way north and south.

By this time the fourth wave had hit the beach. Sgt. John A. Bushemi of Gary, Ind., YANK staff photographer, who later was fatally wounded by a shell from a Jap knee mortar, landed in this wave, together with Harold Smith, Chicago *Tribune* correspondent; CPO D. A. Dean of Dallas, Tex., master at arms of our transport; 1st Lt. Gerhard Roth of Portland, Oreg., and Sgt. Charles Rosecrans of Honolulu, Central Pacific G-2 photographers, and this correspondent.

There was still no resistance. The only sounds were the sounds of our BAR and rifle fire, spraying every tree that might contain a sniper and every exposed shell crater.

Sgt. Mat Toper of New York, N. Y., lay flat on his back on the fire trench and lit the first of 20 cigars he'd managed to keep dry through the landing operation. Pfc. Albert Lee, a Chinese-American tank gunner from Los Angeles, Calif., grinned and said: "This is the easiest one yet." Lee had made three previous assault landings.

Our rear elements, preceded by tanks, were moving up to the front. At 1010 a cooling rain began to fall, and in a few minutes you couldn't see more than a few feet ahead.

It was then that the Japs decided to let us know they were present and ready to fight. The high-pitched ring of Jap rifle fire sounded on all sides, our first warning that there were nearly as many Japs behind as in front of our own lines. Knee-mortar shells, from positions on both ends of the island, began to sprinkle the landing beach, just short of the incoming boats. A few shells hit the troops south of the beach party, killing six men and wounding eight.

As 1st Lt. John Hetherington of Mt. Vernon, N. Y., transportation officer, headed back for the beach in search of his motor sergeant, Sgt. Robert Flynn of Albany, N. Y., he saw some engineers blasting away at what looked like a small pile of mangrove leaves, evidently knocked down from a tree by one of the Navy blasts.

Just ahead were some communications men, cleaning their rifles and sharing a D-ration chocolate bar. As the engineers moved out, Lt. Hetherington saw a Jap rise up from under the leaves, knife in one hand, grenade in the other. The lieutenant fired his carbine once and squeezed the trigger for a second shot. The carbine jammed, but that didn't matter; his first shot had plugged the Jap in the head. Under the palm fronds and dried leaves, Hetherington found a neatly dug square hole, four feet deep. Inside were three other dead Japs.

He saw hundreds of similar holes later on; we all did. Some were spider trenches, connected by carefully covered underground passages, a few with corrugated tin under the fronds and mangrove leaves. Many of the trenches had been built for a single Jap, others for two or three or four men. None of the holes was large enough to accommodate more than six Japs, and almost all of them were so well hidden that it was possible to step over and beyond the holes without seeing them. The Japs had allowed platoon after platoon of American troops to pass through before they opened up.

Sgt. Chris Hagen of Fairmont, Minn., a squad leader, and eight riflemen became separated from their platoon in the landing. Just as they walked over the fire trench, in the area through which almost the whole battalion had passed without encountering resistance, scattered Jap rifle fire came from their rear, barely clearing their heads. They dropped to the ground.

"Underground," shouted Hagen. "The sons of bitches are underground." His squad began throwing grenades into every pile of fronds. Three Japs darted out of one hole and ran for the beach. Hagen fired once and hit the first one before he'd gone 15 yards. He hit the other two a few yards farther on. In the next 20 minutes, Hagen killed 12 Japs by pitching grenades into a dozen holes. Pfc. Joseph Tucker, a rifleman from Live Oak, Fla., accounted for at least nine more, and the entire outfit cleaned out about 50 in some 20 unconnected holes, all dug underground in an area that was not more than 40 yards square.

As Lt. Col. Mizony, rounding out 22 years in the Army, moved up with 18 of his enlisted men, including battalion CP personnel, Capt. Carl Stoltz of Binghamton, N. Y., commander of a heavy-weapons company, yelled: "Look out, Hi!" The colonel hit the ground, and Stoltz, a former Binghamton cop, got the underground sniper with a carbine. He found four others in a tin- and palm-covered trench on the beach. As he started to walk over it, the captain stopped, looked down and noticed a movement inside. He killed two Japs with the carbine and the other two with grenades. Capt. Stoltz and Sgt. Hagen will be recommended for Silver Stars.

In almost the same area, Pfc. Sam Camerda of Akron, Ohio, and Pfc. William (Mac) Wemyrs of Tennessee, headquarters intelligence men, found three more Japs—two in one hole and one in another. S/Sgt. Delbert (Pop) Markham, former shipyard worker from California, came across a blanket-covered body a few yards inland. He pushed the blanket aside, and a Jap hand, holding an unexploded grenade, twitched. When Markham finished, the hand was still.

Meanwhile the company commanded by Capt. Charles Hallden of Brooklyn, N. Y., was being harassed from the rear and facing heavy and light machine-gun fire a few yards ahead. As they crossed the island in a rapid advance, they came upon two coconut-log pillboxes reinforced with sand, the kind that had been common in the Gilberts and at Kwajalein but were few and far between here. They cleaned out each box with flame throwers, red flares and demolition charges, followed by grenades and BAR fire.

When the company reached a native village and the smoking ruins of some Jap concrete installations, a young native stuck his head up from a hole and shouted "friend." The advance halted while the native guided 1st Sgt. Louis Pawlinga of Utica, N. Y., and a search party to other holes, where they found 33 natives—four men, 12 women and 17 children—only three injured. They were taken to the beachhead.

Just before noon the troops circled south, although there were some Japs still alive on the western side of the island. As 1st Lt. George Johnson of Sikeston, Mo., moved up with his company, the leader of the second squad, Sgt. Earl Bodiford of Pocahontas, Tenn., fired at a covered foxhole. The muzzle of a rifle moved in the shadows. Bodiford raced forward, grabbed the gun from a dazed Jap and hurled it as far as he could. He killed the Jap and moved on.

By early afternoon we had run up against concentrated underground defenses and were held up by knee-mortar fire. Shells were falling on every side, in and around the CP and ahead and just behind the front lines. Lt. Col. Cornett ordered the line held and called for reinforcements.

The sun was shining again and the atmosphere was overwhelmingly hot and muggy. Black flies covered everything—guns, clothes, faces and hands. Knee-mortar fire was falling throughout the area, no spot was safe from snipers and there was Jap heavy machine-gun fire up ahead. Lt. Col. Mizony called for some Navy Avengers.

Johnny Bushemi, Chief Dean, Lt. Roth and Sgt. Rosecrans, the photographers; Smith, the correspondent, and I crouched behind a medium tank to smoke our first cigarettes in several hours and tell one another what had happened since we'd become separated that morning. Just before the Avengers swooped in at 1445, Capt. Waldo Drake, USN, Pacific Fleet PRO, and Hal O'Flaherty of the Chicago *Daily News* joined us. When the short, concentrated aerial strafing was completed, five of us—Johnny, Capt. Drake, Smith, O'Flaherty and I—started forward to take a look at the damage.

Johnny was winding his movie camera a few yards behind the rest of us when we stopped to examine a bullet-riddled chest filled with Marshallese books. We were just beyond the fire trench on the lagoon side of the beach, perhaps 75 yards behind the front lines. That area had been under sporadic knee-mortar fire throughout the morning, but for at least two hours none of the 60-mm grenades had fallen there.

I stayed behind for a minute to pick up a Marshallese Bible, and Smith, O'Flaherty and Capt. Drake, followed by Johnny, had gone not more than 20 paces up the line from the trench when the first shell landed in our midst. I ducked into an exposed hole, just below the chest of books, and the others threw themselves on the open ground. Shells burst all around us, chasing Lt. Roth, Sgt. Rosecrans and Chief Dean as they raced for the beach and pinning the rest of us in a diminishing circle of fire.

Each explosion kicked up dirt and sand as it landed; we thought each shell would be our last. No one knows how many bursts there were in all—probably five or six—but after two or three interminable minutes the explosions stopped. Johnny was bleeding profusely.

Capt. Drake had a gash above his right eye and Smith had been nicked in the right arm by shrapnel. The three of us ran 300 yards down the beach to get the medics. Capt. Drake, blood pouring from his wound, refused treatment until we had started back with a litter for Johnny.

By the time we reached the shallow crater where O'Flaherty was waiting with Bushemi, Johnny had already lost a tremendous amount of blood from shrapnel wounds in his left cheek and neck and in his left leg. But he was still conscious, and as we returned through the sniper-infested area inland from the lagoon beach, he asked for his two cameras. He carried both of them until we reached the advanced aid station in a demolished coconut-log emplacement. There he was given more sulfanilamide and two plasma applications.

Johnny was conscious, joking with all of us and asking how badly Capt. Drake was hurt, until after he had reached our transport. He died at 1750, a little less than three hours after he was wounded, while Navy surgeons were tying the arteries in his neck. His last words were: "Be sure to get those pictures back to the office."

Meanwhile elements of the 22d Marines had taken an advanced position on the northern end of Eniwetok, working toward the seaward side. Pvt. James Syrell of Oswego, N. Y., saw five Japs emerge from the ground not more than five feet away, each carrying a pistol. He threw grenades and got all five. The day before, on Engebi Island in the northern tip of Eniwetok Atoll (captured in six hours, five minutes), Syrell accounted for some 30 others.

During the night the advance continued on Eniwetok, the marines pushing seaward on the eastern end and the soldiers continuing northward. They moved barely 15 yards at a time, tanks leading the way, flanked on each side by infantrymen—BAR men spraying every foot and riflemen throwing grenades into each mound.

There was no organized counterattack, and only two attempts at resistance by more than small handfuls of Japs. At about 2000, an hour after the advance began, a dozen Japs tried to swim through the lagoon to reach the rear. Spotted by a destroyer searchlight, they were wiped out when they reached the beach.

The second attempt came at 0100, when 40 Japs leaped from their holes about 30 yards from the marine lines and raced forward. Brandishing sabers, hurling grenades and screaming "Banzai! The f- - -ing marines will die!", they leaped into the marine foxholes. There was hand-to-hand combat, jiujitsu, knifing and bayonetting. In less than 20 minutes, 40 Japs and 20 marines were killed on a line not more than 30 yards long.

Then the entire battalion was ordered back 300 yards to mop up the southern, lagoon side of the island for the second time. They found almost as many live Japs hiding under their feet this time as during the first advance.

At 0900 Capt. Hallden saw a Jap manning a knee-mortar position behind a well-concealed coconut-log emplacement. The captain fired his carbine and the Jap wilted. This mortarman was believed responsible for Johnny's death.

Every few minutes supplies were moved in over the beachhead. The Engineers were already surveying behind the lines for our installations.

Dead Japs were being piled up on the beach, but many still remained where they had fought and died—underground. At almost any spot on the island there were still some Japs alive, and occasionally rifle fire broke out around the aid station. Several times mop-up squads came back to clean out all the holes they could find. Then, after they had left, the fire would break out again in another spot. A few Japs, not many, were taken prisoner. There had been a steady stream of American casualties flowing back to the aid stations the first day, but our casualties were lighter now.

By late afternoon of the third day, Eniwetok was secured.

PT BOAT MISSION

By Sgt. DAVE RICHARDSON

ON A PT BOAT IN SOUTHWEST PACIFIC WATERS—
Tiny red lights drifted past us in the water between
our PT boat and the smoldering hulk of the enemy
barge. "Those are dead Japs," said Harry Long
MM2c of Stroud, Okla. "They probably jumped out
to swim for shore but got it from our machine guns.
The red lights on their life jackets are supposed to
guide rescue boats."

It was almost dawn and we were nearing the end
of an all-night mission that cost the enemy two
large barges, one small supply landing craft and a
large number of dead Japs. Riding with us on the
mission was the "Old Man," Lt. Cmdr. John D.
Bulkeley, who commanded the PTs at Bataan and
brought Gen. MacArthur out of the Philippines on
his way to Australia.

I had met Cmdr. Bulkeley that afternoon at a
PT base, hidden away from Jap planes and submarines up one of the hundreds of rivers that wind
among New Guinea's towering mountains. The base
was alive with activity. Motor torpedo boats, their
camouflaged outlines blending with overhanging
jungle foliage, bobbed in the dispersal areas. Ma-
chinists' mates, stripped to the waist under the
scorching sun, were gassing up the boats and tun-
ing their powerful super-marine engines. Gunners
cleaned their weapons and loaded more ammunition aboard.

In the midst of this activity stood a stocky, round-
faced man in his early 30s, shirtless like the sailors
with whom he was talking quietly. This was Cmdr.
Bulkeley. In his jungle hut hung an officer's blouse
bearing four rows of ribbons, including the Congressional Medal of Honor, but out here in the sun
the only tip-off on his rank was the way the men
addressed him.

A sailor approached Bulkeley with a wide grin.
"Commander," he said, "I got hold of another
tommy gun for our boat today."

"Fine, fella," the commander replied. "Get all the
guns you can. But don't take 'em away from the
jungle fighters. They need them more than we do."

Two soldiers edged over to Bulkeley and asked
if it would be okay for them to go on the night's
mission. "Sure," said the commander, "glad to have
you. What can you shoot best—Browning or tommy
gun?" The soldiers, stationed at a nearby bivouac
area, were looking for the chance to knock off a few
Japs.

A couple of sailors who work around the PT base
also asked permission to go out on the mission,
even though they would have to put in a full shift
next day, either in the radio shack, kitchen, ordnance hut, torpedo tent or on construction.

"Wanta come along with us tonight?" the commander asked me. "Sure," I said.

Every PT bristles with machine guns, cannons
and torpedoes, but extra firepower is always welcome. Only about half the men on each crew are
needed to man the fixed weapons. The rest grab
tommy guns, BARs, Garands, Springfields, pistols
or grenades when the action starts.

Word had passed around that Cmdr. Bulkeley,
who holds a staff job at the base, would be going
along on the night's patrol, one of his regular
weekly check-ups on the tactics and efficiency of
the crews. Like Bulkeley, several of the skippers are
Annapolis men. They are kiddingly called "trade-
school graduates" by the other officers and sailors,
most of them Naval Reserves who volunteered for
PT training at the Motor Torpedo Boat Squadron
Training Center in Melville, R. I.

The skippers selected for the night's mission were
briefed, and then officers and crews filed in for
early chow at 4 P.M. It was obvious that the PT
base is a paradise compared with Army living
standards in New Guinea. Our meal was served in
a mess hall on metal plates instead of mess kits.
The bread was fresh, baked that same day by a
sailor at the base. The meat, butter, cold drinks and
even cokes, the men told me, were stored in big
refrigerators.

After chow we headed for the boats, passing
screened wooden and thatch huts used for living
quarters and offices. There wasn't a single typewriter around. "We leave red tape and paper work
to the flagship down the coast," Bulkeley said. "This
is a combat base."

As a vivid orange sunset painted the sky ahead,
our two PTs roared out of the jungle hide-out's
winding river and skimmed along the smooth waters
of the Solomons Sea toward the scene of our night's
patrol. Cmdr. Bulkeley took his favorite position in
a movie director's canvas armchair atop the narrow
deck. Binoculars and a pistol were slung over his
khakis.

Puffing contentedly on a cigar, the commander
explained the task assigned to the PTs. "We work

hand in hand with the Fifth Air Force in blockading the coast against Jap reinforcements and shipping," he said. "The bombers patrol the waters in the daytime and we take over at night. In this way we're weakening Jap resistance in New Guinea so the Infantry and Artillery will have an easier job."

In less than a year, the PT fleet operating in this area has sunk more than 150 Jap vessels, without the loss of a single motor torpedo boat through enemy action and with casualties so few they can be counted on the fingers of one hand.

PTs have much in common with the bombers that share their vigil, Bulkeley said. A PT crew is just about the same size as a Liberator or Flying Fortress crew. Living and fighting in the close quarters of a PT have made the lives of the officers and men just as informal as those of a bomber crew. Like bombers, PTs have distinctive names and pictures on their cockpits—*Miss Malaria, Ball of Fire, Jolly Roger* and *Cock of the Walk*. And like Air Force men, the PT crews paint miniature Jap vessels on their cabins as a record of each victory.

Just before dusk turned to darkness, we made out a blob of land ahead of us. It was Jap-held territory. The gunners tried a few practice bursts. Our skipper, Lt. (jg) Herbert P. Knight of Wichita, Kans., ordered the engineer to cut the motors to idling speed so we could move up as noiselessly as possible. For several hours we patrolled the coast line, following a plotted course, our binoculars searching the dark foggy night for Jap craft.

Then a light drizzle began and we donned rainsuits. A little later the rain was succeeded by a mist blanketing the glassy sea. Small groups of us took turns going below to the tiny galley for hot coffee and sandwiches.

I took a look around inside the boat and was surprised at the size of the cabins. An outside view of the PT had given an impression of smallness, but inside there were bunks with mattresses for each officer and man, lavatories, spacious lockers for clothes, a navigation room and even a guest room. Books, magazines and pin-up girls were scattered through the cabins.

At 4:30 A.M., when I was back up on deck, Louis Schaff QM3c of Pekin, Ill., shouted from his bow gun:

"Barge two points off the port bow."

The skipper, Lt. Knight, spun the wheel hard to port and opened the throttle. He yelled down through the open hatch to the radio room. Edward Masters RM3c of Brooklyn, N. Y., messaged the other PT to follow us into the attack. All hands clambered to the guns as Lt. (jg) John Dromey of Boston, Mass., second in command, barked orders. Several hundred feet ahead of us, the other PT spun around to follow us toward our target.

"It's a Jap all right," said Lt. Knight. Our engines leaped to life and we hurtled toward the dark shape on the water. "Okay, boys," the skipper yelled, "let 'em have it."

The misty black night blazed with the light of tracer bullets and our PT boat throbbed under the recoil as a bedlam of gunfire answered Lt. Knight's command. Tracers poured into the enemy vessel, a small supply landing craft. It seemed to fold up amidship in a pall of smoke, then suddenly sank with a gush.

"There's another one, a big baby, over to starboard," shrilled Raymond Connors S1c, a Jersey City (N. J.) youngster manning one of the machine guns. Lt. Knight spun the wheel again, and the PT boat left a phosphorescent wake of foam as we closed in on our second victim.

This time we couldn't count on the advantage of surprise; our attack on the first barge had betrayed our presence. But speed, maneuverability and firepower were in our favor. The Jap craft loomed up ahead—a 70-foot barge heavily loaded with men and supplies. Tree branches camouflaged the vessel; evidently it hugged the shore by day to avoid detection by our bombers.

The barge had swung from its southerly course and headed north at our approach. Now tracer bullets spewed forth. I remembered what John Burg MM1c of Decatur, Ill., had said: "One hit in the right place might blow our thin mahogany hull to smithereens. We can't afford to get hit anywhere." But the tracers passed harmlessly over our heads.

"Pour it on," ordered Lt. Knight, and every member of our crew let the barge have it except officers, radioman and engine-room man, who had their hands full already. Behind us, as we knifed past the Jap, the second PT sent its tracers into the barge's hull. But still it floated. We started circling to make another run.

Suddenly Eddie Ryscik SC3 of Port Chester, N. Y., the cook, piped up: "Damned if there isn't a third one dead ahead. And just as big." We veered to starboard and passed within yards of the barge. Two of our machine guns were jammed now, but the rest of the guns spouted white tracers of lead at the hull. This new vessel was the same kind as the last one, and apparently just as unsinkable. The other PT tagged along behind us and fired away, but as we turned, we saw that both Jap barges were still afloat and headed for the shore.

Then we noticed that they had stopped moving. Evidently their engines were hit. We made another run, followed by the other PT. This time there was no return fire from the first big barge, but the second one came to life and shot cannon and machine-gun bullets our way. We made two more runs, silencing the second barge but still not sinking either of them.

"These are gonna be tough," said the skipper. "Our bullets are glancing off the sides. The things must be armor-plated. Shoot lower this time. Hit 'em below the water line."

On this run we idled our engines and slid by both barges so close we could look into them. Just as we passed each of the barges we attacked again, then spurted ahead to get out of the way.

Finally, on the fifth run, our boat slowed down and idled past the second big barge, only a few feet from it. We tossed hand grenades and fired point-blank into its bottom. As we left, it seemed to break in two, nosed into the water and sank.

Now both PTs stood by and sailors boarded the battered and smoldering hulk of the Jap barge still afloat. Suddenly one of the sailors whipped up his .45 and fired. "One of the Japs was still alive," he yelled over to us. "He tried to grab a rifle."

Cmdr. Bulkeley, who had boarded the barge with the sailors, was tugging at a Jap gun. One of the crew members took out two of the bolts that fastened the gun to the deck, but still it wouldn't come loose.

Abruptly I realized that dawn had come. We could see into the barge quite clearly. Dead Japs with full packs were heaped in the stern. In the bow were large boxes of food and drums of gasoline. The barge had armor-plated sides and Diesel engines. We counted four machine guns and a 20-mm cannon on the gunwales and bow.

A small fire in the bow crackled under the roof of fresh branches and edged toward the gasoline drums. This and the coming of daylight cut short the examination of the barge. Cmdr. Bulkeley abandoned his efforts to get the Jap gun loose and scrambled aboard the PT, dripping with sweat. The crew followed. "Make one more run and sink this one," the commander ordered. "Then let's beat it for home."

The other PT fired into the bottom of the barge and scurried out of the way. Listing and splintering, the Jap boat sank in a gurgle of water. After a last look around, the PTs opened up and made tracks for home at top speed.

"Those big barges were the toughest babies to sink I've ever seen," said Cmdr. Bulkeley. "We sank Jap freighters off Luzon (in the Philippines) faster than that."

We noticed uneasily that we were in full view of the Jap-held coast line only half a mile away. It was 5:45 A.M. now—no time to be prowling in Jap waters, because shore observation posts might send for planes. The gunners reloaded and scanned the skies.

Half an hour later we heard a shout overhead. Tom McHale F1c of Providence, R. I., had spotted a tiny speck in the sky from his stern-gun position. But the plane was 20,000 feet up and miles behind us, evidently on a routine dawn reconnaissance. It disappeared a few moments later in a cloud bank, and the gunners relaxed again.

Most of the crew went below when the PTs entered friendly waters. We drank warm coffee to shake off the morning chill, then stretched out on bunks for a little shut-eye. It was time for the Fifth Air Force to take over the day shift.

"You're sure lucky I found you today. Tomorrow I'm going in the army!"—*Sgt. Irwin Caplan.*

"What the hell do you mean you're glad we're not playing for keeps?"—*Cpl. Art Gates.*

On the following pages
are some of the best
photographs made by
Yank staff photographers.

Yanks wade ashore on Makin Atoll.—Sgt. JOHN BUSHEMI

A soldier of the Shamrock Battalion moves up on Makin. —Sgt. JOHN BUSHEMI

Feeding ammunition to a P-40 in
North Africa.—Sgt. GEORGE AARONS

Gun captain of an LST in the Pacific.
—Sgt. JOHN BUSHEMI

GI with a BAR moves over a ridge on Attu.—Sgt. GEORG MEYERS

A soldier of the emperor lies dead on Attu.—Sgt. GEORG MEYERS

In liberated Rome a Yank holds an Italian baby.—Sgt. GEORGE AARONS

U. S. cruiser framed in a U. S. gunsight off Buka.—Sgt. DILLON FERRIS

Marines wade through surf to strike Cape Gloucester.—Sgt. RICHARD HANLEY

Yanks and a Sherman tank in France.—Sgt. REGINALD KENNY

Building an airfield in China.—Sgt. LOU STOUMEN

Bathing time for Burmese nurses.—Sgt. ROBERT GHIO

Nazi prisoners at Anzio observe an LST.—Sgt. GEORGE AARONS

A fresh-caught Jap is interviewed at Hollandia.—Sgt. RICHARD HANLEY

In Syria, Free French execute convicted Nazi spies.—Sgt. GEORGE AARONS

272

The Army unloads supplies as it moves
into New Guinea.—Sgt. RICHARD HANLEY

B-25s on a raid in Africa.
—Sgt. GEORGE AARONS

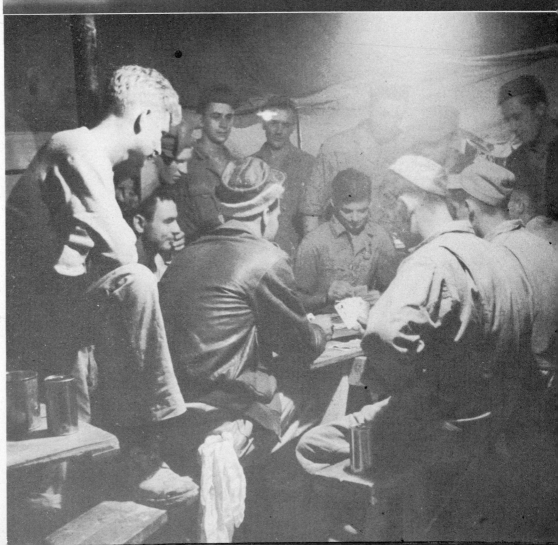

U. S. flyers in Africa relax.
—Sgt. GEORGE AARONS

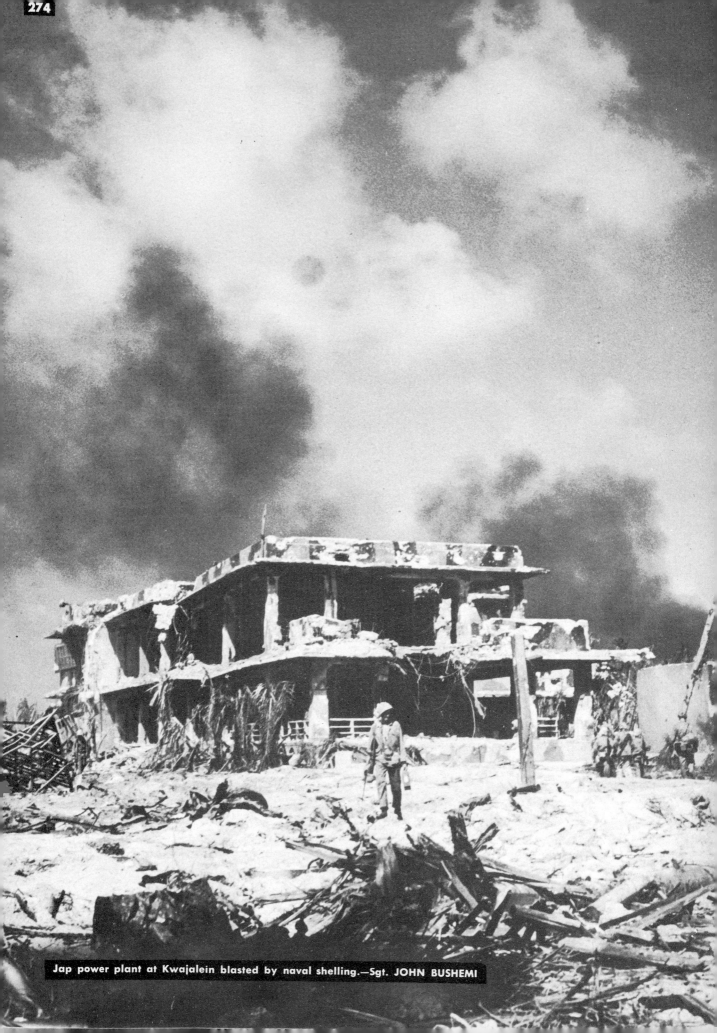

Jap power plant at Kwajalein blasted by naval shelling.—Sgt. JOHN BUSHEMI

Bugle lesson in the Fijis.
—Sgt. JOHN BUSHEMI

A mule train winds along the hills below Rome.—Sgt. GEORGE AARONS

A GI baker in Africa carries his wares
messward.   —Sgt. GEORGE AARONS

A Yank in Italy piles up a load of
dead Nazi mines.—Sgt. JOHN FRANO

American troops and half-tracks move into Tunisian town.

Outside Cerami, Sicily, camouflaged howitzers fire at Germans.—Sgt. PETE PARIS

From the bow of an LST, Yanks wave a greeting to France.—Sgt. REGINALD KENNY

A light machine gunner peers through the New Guinea jungle.—Sgt. JOHN BUSHEMI

Infantrymen in New Georgia wait for action at their post.—Sgt. JOHN BUSHEMI

Pass at the pyramids.
—Sgt. GEORGE AARONS

Desert dust in Africa.
—Sgt. STEVEN DERRY

Tight fit in a Pacific transport.—Sgt. RICHARD HANLEY

Approaching Japanese positions in New Georgia.—Sgt. JOHN BUSHEMI

This wave has just hit the beach at Eniwetok in the Marshalls.—Sgt. JOHN BUSHEMI

"The Hump," air supply line to China, from 16,000 feet.—Sgt. ROBERT GHIO

Italian kids play with a captured Nazi self-propelled howitzer.—Sgt. GEORGE AARONS

Mountain climbing lesson in Italy.—Sgt. GEORGE AARONS

An artillery observation post in Sicily attracts a fan. —Sgt. PETE PARIS

A GI mule skinner in Hawaii with one of his big-eared charges. —Sgt. JOHN BUSHEMI

Italian partisans take cover with a Yank patrol in the Nemi valley. —Sgt. GEORGE AARONS

An American MP stands guard in Algiers' Casbah. —Sgt. JOHN FRANO

GIs, silhouetted on a ridge, pass ammunition on Attu.—Sgt. GEORG MEYERS

On Adreanof Island in the Aleutians, the wind made tent life tough.—Sgt. GEORG MEYERS

A soldier helps his wounded friend. Admiralty Islands.—Sgt. BILL ALCINE

German prisoners in France
await removal to prison camp.
—Cpl. JOE CUNNINGHAM

Civilians give Lt. Gen. Mark
Clark a warm welcome to
Rome.—Sgt. GEORGE AARONS

Thirty yards from the Japs in New Guinea, these GIs hold fire.—Sgt. DAVE RICHARDSON

Cassino's ruins are half
obscured by battle
smoke.
—Sgt. GEORGE AARONS

Processing a Nazi prisoner in Sicily.—Sgt. PETE PARIS

Eniwetok natives take cover from Jap fire.
—Sgt. JOHN BUSHEMI

Near an Anzio hospital tent a nurse digs in.
—Sgt. GEORGE AARONS

Yanks stalk Jap
snipers on Makin.
—Sgt. JOHN BUSHEMI

Fifth Army men wait
for the ship that will
take them to battle.
—Sgt. GEORGE AARON

First aid near front lines in New Guinea.
gt. DAVE RICHARDSON

Six combat-wise sergeants stroll down an Italian street.
—Sgt. JOHN FRANO

A tired mess sergeant in North Africa feeds himself for a change.—Sgt. GEORGE AARONS